JEREMIAH

VOLUME 21

THE ANCHOR BIBLE is a fresh approach to the world's greatest classic. Its object is to make the Bible accessible to the modern reader; its method is to arrive at the meaning of biblical literature through exact translation and extended exposition, and to reconstruct the ancient setting of the biblical story, as well as the circumstances of its transcription and the characteristics of its transcribers.

THE ANCHOR BIBLE is a project of international and interfaith scope: Protestant, Catholic, and Jewish scholars from many countries contribute individual volumes. The project is not sponsored by any ecclesiastical organization and is not intended to reflect any particular theological doctrine. Prepared under our joint supervision, THE ANCHOR BIBLE is an effort to make available all the significant historical and linguistic knowledge which bears on the interpretation of the biblical record.

THE ANCHOR BIBLE is aimed at the general reader with no special formal training in biblical studies; yet, it is written with the most exacting standards of scholarship, reflecting the highest technical accomplishment.

This project marks the beginning of a new era of co-operation among scholars in biblical research, thus forming a common body of knowledge to be shared by all.

William Foxwell Albright
David Noel Freedman
GENERAL EDITORS

THE ANCHOR BIBLE

JEREMIAH

A NEW TRANSLATION
WITH INTRODUCTION AND COMMENTARY
BY
JOHN BRIGHT

Doubleday & Company, Inc.
Garden City, New York

ISBN: 0-385-00823-6
Library of Congress Catalog Card Number 65–13603
Copyright © 1965 by Doubleday & Company, Inc.
Second Edition
Fifteenth Printing
1980

PREFACE

In line with the purpose of the Anchor Bible Series, this book does not propose to be a commentary on the Book of Jeremiah. Rather, it aims to present the text of that book in a fresh translation in such a way that it can be read with understanding and appreciation—even, it is hoped, by those who may have had no prior acquaintanceship with it, or with the Bible generally. All parts of the present book are designed to serve that end. The introductory chapters seek to tell just enough of the historical setting of Jeremiah's career, his life and message, and the structure and composition of his book, to enable the reader to proceed intelligently to the text itself. The COMMENTS that accompany the various sections of the text have a similar aim: to examine the passage under discussion, place it in its setting and thereby, I trust, enhance the reader's enjoyment of it. The notes on the text make no pretense of providing a complete commentary, but have the aim simply of justifying the translation where this appeared to be necessary, and of explaining such points as seemed to require clarification if the reader was not to be left confused. The book is, in short, focused throughout upon Jeremiah's own words. It has, I think I may honestly say, the single aim of allowing the prophet to speak (if that is not too patronizing a way of putting it) over the gap of years and the barrier of language with as much clarity as possible. The prophetic word is an ancient word but one, I am persuaded, that retains its relevance. If what I have written should enable any to hear it, or hear it more clearly, I shall be more than satisfied.

I suppose that few authors can boast of having written a book without assistance from others. Certainly I cannot. I should like, therefore, to take this opportunity to express my gratitude to those who have helped me along the way. First of all, I must thank Professor W. F. Albright, to whose scholarship and unfailing encouragement I owe so much. He has called my attention to certain articles which I should otherwise have missed, and has made several suggestions for the improvement of the introductory chapters. Especially do I owe thanks to Professor David N. Freedman, who read the entire manuscript in its first draft and made countless valuable suggestions, most of which—and far more than I could expressly acknowledge—have been incorporated in the completed work. His labors went far beyond the call of his duty as an editor, and this book is infinitely the better as a result. Let it be said clearly, however, that acknowledgment of indebtedness in no way shifts the blame for any shortcomings the reader may detect to other shoulders than my own. I also owe particular thanks to Mrs. F. S. Clark, who did all the typing both of the preliminary and the final draft of the manuscript and, in spite of the many strange words that it contains—and, I may add, in spite of what may for want of a better word be called my penmanship—did it superbly. The task of correction amounted to almost nothing. Finally, I must thank my wife for her help in checking and correcting all of the copy, and for putting up with my abominable disposition and my chronic unavailability all the while the book was in preparation.

John Bright

CONTENTS

II. INCIDENTS FROM THE LIFE OF JEREMIAH

III. THE BOOK OF CONSOLATION

IV. ORACLES AGAINST FOREIGN NATIONS

APPENDIX

PRINCIPAL ABBREVIATIONS

1. Publications

AJSL	American Journal of Semitic Languages and Literature
ANET	Ancient Near Eastern Texts Relating to the Old Testament*
BA	Biblical Archaeologist
BASOR	Bulletin of the American Schools of Oriental Research
BDB	F. Brown, S. R. Driver, and C. A. Briggs, eds., *A Hebrew and English Lexicon of the Old Testament**
BH	*Biblia Hebraica**
BJRL	Bulletin of the John Rylands Library
BL	H. Bauer and P. Leander, *Historische Grammatik der hebräischen Sprache**
CBQ	Catholic Biblical Quarterly
Ehrl.	A. B. Ehrlich, *Randglossen zur hebräischen Bibel**
GK	*Gesenius' Hebrew Grammar,* ed. E. Kautzsch*
HTR	Harvard Theological Review
HUCA	Hebrew Union College Annual
ICC	International Critical Commentary
IEJ	Israel Exploration Journal
JAOS	Journal of the American Oriental Society
JBL	Journal of Biblical Literature
JNES	Journal of Near Eastern Studies
JQR	Jewish Quarterly Review
JSS	Journal of Semitic Studies
KB	L. Koehler and W. Baumgartner, *Lexicon in Veteris Testamenti Libros**
VT	Vetus Testamentum
ZAW	Zeitschrift für die alttestamentliche Wissenschaft

* For complete reference, see Selected Bibliography.

2. VERSIONS

AJV	The American Jewish Version of 1917
Aq.	Ancient Greek translation of the Old Testament by Aquila
ARV	The American Revised (or American Standard) Version of 1901
EVV	English versions generally
KJ	The Authorized Version of 1611, or the King James Bible
LXX	The Septuagint
MT	Masoretic Text
RSV	The Revised Standard Version, 1953
Symm.	Ancient Greek translation of the Old Testament by Symmachus
Syr.	Syriac version, the Peshitta
Tar.	Aramaic translations or paraphrases
Theod.	Ancient Greek translation of the Old Testament by Theodotion
Vrs.	Ancient versions generally
Vulg.	The Vulgate

3. OTHER ABBREVIATIONS

Akk.	Akkadian
Ar.	Arabic
Bab.	Babylonian
Ger.	German
Gr.	Greek
Heb.	Hebrew
Lat.	Latin
OT	Old Testament

INTRODUCTION

THE PROPHETS OF ISRAEL:
SOME PRELIMINARY REMARKS

Jeremiah of Anathoth, whose life and sayings this book will seek to present, was one of the prophets of Israel. That statement, though it may at first glance seem to be no more than a common-place, is actually the essential statement to be made about the man. Jeremiah was a prophet. One could, to be sure, add to it a great many other statements about Jeremiah, for he was both one of the great figures of Israel's history and a person whom one can readily admire. He was a man of great spiritual insight and depth, a man of driving eloquence who was possessed of unusual poetic gifts; he was, moreover, in the profoundest sense of the word a brave man, a passionate and exceedingly human man who captures our sympathies as few figures from ancient times do. And one could say a great deal more. But such statements, true though they may be, would add little to our understanding of Jeremiah. If we would understand Jeremiah, it is not as a great and gifted man that we must approach him, but as what he was first and last—a prophet.

Now the prophets of Israel were a unique phenomenon, with-out real parallel in the ancient world—or anywhere else, for that matter. And it is just because of their uniqueness, because they do not lend themselves to comparison with any class or group with which we are familiar, that they are so frequently misunderstood, or so imperfectly understood that their true place in the history of Israel's religion is missed. We must, therefore, begin by asking who the prophets of Israel were. Many of us, no doubt because that is what the word "prophet" has come to mean in popular parlance, are inclined to think of them as foretellers of the future, men who with uncanny accuracy predicted coming events. And certainly there is truth in this. The prophets repeatedly announced the com-ing of events both in the near and the more distant future; and it was doubtless in no small part because so many of their more important predictions actually came to pass that their words were so piously preserved. Yet to think of them merely as inspired predictors of the future is, to say the least, to view them one-sidedly and do them grave injustice. Again, because the prophets attacked abuses in the social order, and because most of them were at loggerheads with the ruling elements and with many of the major institutions of the society of their day, we are tempted to think of them as rebels against the existing order, champions of the oppressed classes, radical social reformers. Now the prophets certainly did attack social abuses; they championed the cause of the poor, and they called down the divine judgment upon those responsible for their mistreatment. Yet to depict them as revolutionaries or social reformers is both an egregious modernization and little better than caricature. Then, too, there are those who, moved by the ethical teachings of the prophets, impressed by the majesty of their conception of God, and feeling that it was surely they who imparted these insights to Israel, have been inclined to regard them as great religious teachers, thinkers, spiritual pioneers, who through the truths they proclaimed lifted Israel above the level of a purely cultic and national religion to the heights of ethical monotheism. But, again, although the prophets certainly did impart great truths of lasting relevance, to understand them as religious teachers is to misunderstand them fundamentally. So we must again ask: Who were these men? What did they believe themselves to be?

The word "prophet" (Heb. *nābī'*) probably means—though this is disputed—"one who has been called" (i.e., by the Deity). But in attempting to say what the prophets were, we are hampered by the fact that the term seems to be applied to widely differing types of people. It is applied to an Amos, and to that group from which Amos explicitly dissociated himself (Amos vii 14); to a Jeremiah, and to those who were his bitterest opponents. It is applied to men who danced in ecstatic frenzy till they fell down senseless, and to men who, so far as we know, said all that they had to say in cold possession of their faculties. It is applied to seers who for a fee would tell a man where his lost donkeys were (I Sam ix 7 f., 20), and to men who spoke of greater things and got no fee—save persecution. The truth seems to be that the term "prophet" came to be used as a designation for various originally separate functions. Certainly it could be applied to the greatest spirits that Israel ever produced, and to men—some of them surely well-intentioned, others just as surely frauds—who, to say the least, reflected no credit on their office. In view of this ambiguity, it would be well at the outset to say a few words (a complete discussion is out of the question here) regarding the nature and the history of the prophetic movement in Israel.

1

So far as we know from our sources, prophets first made their appearance in Israel somewhat prior to the establishment of the monarchy—thus some four hundred years before Jeremiah was born. The stories that tell of the Philistine wars and of the elevation of Saul to the kingship give us some idea of their activity. Here we see bands of prophets, in frenzied excitement, "prophesying" to the accompaniment of music (I Sam x 5–13). Saul, we are told, fell among them and, feeling the spirit of Yahweh rush upon him, began to "prophesy" in their midst. On another occasion (I Sam xix 18–24) we are told that Saul, seized by the spirit in their company, stripped off his clothes and wallowed on the ground all day and all night, "prophesying." Prophets of this sort clearly represented an ecstatic, "pentecostal" strain in Israel's religion, psychologically akin to similar manifestations in various other religions, including Christianity. They seem to have been intensely patriotic men who in their dervish-like frenzy fired their compatriots to fight Yahweh's holy war against the Philistine oppressors.

We hear of ecstatic prophets again in the mid-ninth century, at which time they seem to have been especially active. This was when Ahab and Jezebel attempted to give the cult of the Tyrian Baal official status in Israel and when, at the same time, the nation was locked in mortal struggle with the Aramean kingdom of Damascus. Those stories in the Books of Kings (I Kings xvii–II Kings x) that tell of the doings of Elijah, Elisha, and other prophets are especially revealing. Here we see groups called "the sons of the prophets" (bᵉnē hannᵉbī'īm) living a communal life in the neighborhood of some holy place (II Kings ii; iv 38–41), supported by the gifts of the devout (II Kings iv 42–44). At their head was a "master," who in some of these stories (cf. II Kings vi 1–7) is none other than Elisha himself. Apparently they could be distinguished by their dress (II Kings i 8; cf. Zech xiii 4), and perhaps by some distinctive marking or tonsure (I Kings xx 41; II Kings ii 23). Elevated to ecstasy by music and dance, they would give their oracles singly (II Kings iii 15) or in groups (I Kings xxii 1–28); for their services it was customary to give them a fee (II Kings v 20–27). Although their behavior caused many to regard them as crazy (II Kings ix 11), they were nevertheless ardent patriots, as they had always been. They followed the army in the field (II Kings iii 11–19), they encouraged the king to strike against Israel's foes (I Kings xx 13 f.) and, in the tradition of holy war, expected him to show them no mercy (I Kings xx 35–43). At the same time, being stout nationalists and fanatically zealous for Yahweh, they found Jezebel and her foreign abominations odious. They opposed her, in some cases quite literally, to the death (I Kings xviii 4).

Ecstatic prophecy, then, played an important role in Israel's history. But although it was, as we see it in the Bible, a phenomenon that was thoroughly Israelite in spirit, it was not one peculiar to Israel, for parallels to it may be found among neighboring peoples, specifically the Canaanites. Various examples could be adduced[1]; but perhaps it will suffice to remind the reader of the four hundred and fifty prophets of Baal whom Elijah confronted on Mount Carmel and who, calling on their god in frenzy, gashed themselves with knives till they were covered with blood (I Kings xviii 17–29). Although we have no real evidence that Israelite ecstatics practiced self-mutilation, (except perhaps Zech xiii 6), it is clear that the phenomenon of prophetic ecstasy was not confined to Israel. Nor are we led by it to the essential nature of prophecy in Israel, the distinguishing mark of which was not, or did not remain, ecstasy.

But Israel had from very early times known another type of prophet: a prophet who was in no proper sense an ecstatic and who did not function as a member of a prophetic band, but who came as a lone individual bringing a message from his God—a message, it may be added, that the recipients often had no wish to hear. It is probable that this type of prophecy, too, had antecedents outside Israel. The eighteenth-century B.C. Mari texts from Upper Mesopotamia show us examples of men who came, unbidden and unexpected, to deliver a message from the god[2]; and it is sig-

---

[1] For example, the eleventh-century tale of Wen-Amun (cf. ANET, pp. 25–29), which tells among other things how an Egyptian official encountered an ecstatic prophet in the Canaanite city of Byblos.

[2] Cf. M. Noth, "History and the Word of God in the Old Testament," BJRL 32 (1950), 144–206.

nificant that the population of Mari at this period was of the same stock as Israel's own ancestors. Nevertheless, regardless of its antecedents, the phenomenon of prophecy as it developed in Israel was unique, without a real parallel anywhere.

As an early example of this latter type of prophet one thinks of Samuel. Samuel is a difficult figure to evaluate, chiefly because the sources portray him in such a variety of ways[3]: now as a warrior hero like the Judges before him (I Sam vii 3–14); now as a judge in a narrower sense, a "minor judge" (I Sam vii 15–17); now as a seer who for a fee gave oracles on matters of private concern (I Sam ix 5–10, 20), now as one who discharged priestly functions (I Sam ix 13; x 8, etc.). But above all Samuel is depicted as a prophet, one who brought a message that he had received from Yahweh. One recalls how—in some of the sources, against his own will—he announced the divine designation of Saul as king; and one also recalls how, when Saul had shown himself disobedient, Samuel came at the command of his God and publicly revoked that designation (I Sam xv). Samuel's motives are ambiguous and cannot concern us here. But it is probable that, nurtured in the traditions and institutions of Israel's primitive tribal order, he feared the monarchy and desired above all things that the new order be kept subordinate to the old. It is to be noted that, although apparently not himself an ecstatic, he co-operated with the ecstatic prophets and seems to have shared their patriotic aims (I Sam x 1–16; xix 18–24).

Prophets of the type just described appear again and again in biblical records relating to the tenth and ninth centuries. The monarchy having been established, they do not appear as a group to have been hostile to the institution. But they reserved the right to criticize it, its rulers and policies, in the light of an older tradition and, when they felt it to be in error, to seek to correct it—by direct political action if need be. One thinks of Nathan, who was a member of David's court, yet who (II Sam xii 1–14) did not hesitate to come to his king in Yahweh's name and denounce him to his face for his crime against his retainer Uriah—a clear violation of covenant law. Or one thinks of Gad, another of David's court prophets, who when David had taken his census (II Sam xxiv)—a prepar-

---

[3] See the evaluation of Samuel by W. F. Albright, *Samuel and the Beginnings of the Prophetic Movement* [the Goldenson Lecture for 1961] (Cincinnati, Ohio: Hebrew Union College Press).

atory step toward systematic taxation and conscription, both inno-
vations, and abhorrent to men nurtured in the old tradition—
came to the king at Yahweh's command to offer him his choice of
punishment. Or again, one is reminded of Ahijah of Shiloh who,
outraged at Solomon's highhanded policies and religious laxity, met
Jeroboam by the road (I Kings xi 26–40) and, in Yahweh's name
announcing the disruption of Solomon's kingdom, designated him
king over northern Israel. Prophetic activity of this sort—designating kings and, because opposed to the establishment of a dynasty,
designating other kings to succeed them—is a characteristic feature of the history of northern Israel in the years that followed.
But the outstanding representative of early Israelite prophecy is
surely Elijah. One recalls how when Ahab had done Naboth to
death in order to have his vineyard (I Kings xxi), Elijah confronted
him and passed death sentence upon him in the name of Yahweh.
But above all one thinks of Elijah's bitter opposition to the
policies of Ahab and Jezebel, how in effect he declared holy war
upon them and labored unceasingly for the extirpation of Baalism
from Israel. He, through his successor Elisha and the prophetic
bands with whom the latter consorted, set off the revolution that
drowned Ahab's house in blood.

With Elijah and the struggle against Ahab's house the earlier
prophetic movement reached the climax of its activity. But even as
it did so it underwent a crisis, as the result of which it seems in the
years that followed progressively to have lost its way. No doubt
this was in part occasioned by Jezebel's persecution, which fell
with especial fury on the prophets. Although many of them—perhaps most of them—stood firm, some of them, being only human,
gave way. Surrendering to the state, they placed themselves at its
disposal and contented themselves thereafter with saying only what
the king wished to hear. This meant that prophets who still opposed the state and its policies were obliged to oppose their fellow
prophets as well. We have a graphic illustration of this in I Kings
xxii 1–28. Here we see four hundred prophets, elevated to ecstasy,
with unanimous voice assuring Ahab that Yahweh would give him
victory over the Arameans, while one lone prophet, Micaiah ben
Imlah, said just the opposite, declaring that the other prophets were
possessed by a lying spirit from on high. It is to be noted that
Micaiah, although he knew full well what it would cost him, stoutly
refused (vs. 14) to speak any word in Yahweh's name save the

one that Yahweh had given him. This is the earliest illustration that we have of something that later seems to have been distressingly common: prophetic word flatly contradicting prophetic word, and prophet pitted against prophet. One can imagine the confusion of the hearers! This schism within the ranks of the prophets, begun—so we have supposed—under the lash of persecution, was probably still further widened as a result of the successful purge of Ahab's house, which the prophets themselves had helped to instigate. It is not unlikely that many of them, feeling that their aims had been achieved and satisfied that Yahweh's will had been done, rested their attack upon the now (in their view) reformed state and began thereafter to place their patriotic zeal at its disposal. Far from criticizing it further and blind to its shortcomings, by the nationalistic oracles that they uttered they gave it the blessing of Yahweh.

In any event, whatever the contributing causes may have been, there is evidence that by the mid-eighth century the prophetic orders had in large measure abdicated their original function. The mid-eighth century saw Israel and Judah in a period of great prosperity and military strength—though one that was soon to be ended by the westward advance of Assyria. It also saw the northern state, at least, in an advanced state of social and moral decay. Unethical practices, the heartless oppression of the weak, highhanded infractions of covenant law, were common (Amos). The rich, through means both legal and illegal, took every advantage of the poor and robbed them of their property, and the state did nothing to prevent it; indeed, the leaders of the state were deeply implicated. At the same time, the national religion had been corrupted by the infiltration of pagan practices (Hosea), particularly the practice of the fertility cult with its immoral rites, to such a degree that, in some of its manifestations at least, it was scarcely recognizable as Yahwism. Yet to all this the prophets as a group seem to have uttered no effective protest. No doubt there were sincere men among them. But if we may trust such allusions to them as we find in the prophetic books of the Bible (and there is no reason why we may not), we must conclude that as a group they had become mere professionals, hangers-on at court and shrine, many of them time-servers interested chiefly in their fees (e.g., Mic iii 5, 11), who felt no impulse to criticize the state and the society of which they were a part.

2

But it was, providentially, just at this time—in the middle and
latter part of the eighth century, thus one hundred years before
Jeremiah's day—that the prophetic movement entered a new phase.
The first of the "classical" prophets, those prophets whose words
are preserved for us in the prophetic books of the Bible, stepped
upon the stage of history: first Amos and then Hosea in northern
Israel, followed shortly by Isaiah and Micah in Judah.

The classical prophets were both a new thing in Israel and the
continuation of an ancient tradition. That they were something new
is obvious. Certainly they were not representatives of the prophetic
orders as these had existed up to their time. On the contrary, dis-
gusted with the venality of these prophets and convinced that their
pleasing oracles were not Yahweh's word, they were at pains to
dissociate themselves from them completely (cf. Amos vii 14;
Mic iii 5, 11). Moreover, they differed from their predecessors in
a variety of ways. Though they underwent profound psychic experiences, and though on occasion they acted out their prophecies
mimetically as their predecessors had done, they were not ecstatics[4];
rather, in full possession of their faculties, they delivered their
prophecies in the form of polished poetic oracles, usually of the
highest literary quality. Though we know that some of them gathered disciples about them (e.g., Isa viii 16), and suspect that all
of them did, they did not give group oracles, but prophesied quite
alone. And, though they frequently delivered their messages at the
shrines, and frequently employed cultic terminology, and though
some of them were drawn from the ranks of the clergy (perhaps
in some cases even from the ranks of the cultic prophets), they
emphatically did not speak as paid personnel of the cult. Finally—
and in this they differed from the entire prophetic tradition that

---

[4] Whether the classical prophets should be described as ecstatics or not
depends largely on one's definition of ecstasy. In spite of the excellent discussion of Johannes Lindblom, *Prophecy in Ancient Israel* (Oxford: Blackwell,
1962), Chs. I–III, I should prefer not to use the word in this connection.
Though they underwent various supernormal experiences, the classical
prophets apparently did not (at least as a rule) *deliver* their messages while
in a state of ecstasy, as the *nebī'īm* frequently did. I feel, therefore, that
to speak of them as ecstatics invites confusion.

had preceded them—though they often took issue with the policy
of the state and sought by all the powers at their command to correct it, they never, so far as we know, indulged in revolutionary
activity. Their word was a word from their God, and they were
willing to leave its implementation to him.

Yet, in spite of these differences, the classical prophets carried
forward the tradition of their predecessors. This is not merely that
they were called by the same title (*nābī'*) and cast their message
in the same oracular form as a message from Yahweh. It is, rather,
that in many of their distinctive viewpoints they were at one with
their predecessors, that the major points of their attack lay precisely
in those areas that had been of essential concern in the older
prophetic tradition. Now one cannot, of course, generalize beyond
a certain point regarding the message of the great prophets. The
prophets differed from one another in background, in temper and
personality, in station in life; and the details of their messages
differed. But certain features are more or less common to them all.
All of the great eighth-century prophets attacked the sins of society,
the crimes of brother against brother; they attacked the worship
of gods other than Yahweh, and the importation of foreign features
into the cult of Yahweh; and they attacked the elaborate but often
empty ritual by which men hoped to satisfy the divine demands. In
its essential features this attack was certainly not new. One has
but to think of the censure administered by a Nathan or an Elijah
to their respective kings because of their crimes against their subjects, or of the entire ninth-century prophetic struggle to rid Israel
of the Tyrian Baal, in order to realize that it was not.

Nevertheless, it must be said that the classical prophets, though
standing in an old tradition, carried out their criticism of society
with a moral insight and a radical consistency never known before.
Theirs was a time that called for some new word from Israel's God.
That new word they brought; yet it was in its essence not new, but
a very old word radically re-interpreted and adapted to the new
situation. The message of the classical prophets was rooted in the
traditions of Israel's distant past, in the recollection of Yahweh's
gracious deeds toward his people and the covenant that he had
made with them in the wilderness, and in awareness of the stringent
stipulations attached to that covenant: to worship no god save Yahweh and scrupulously to obey his covenant law in every dealing
with the brother. A keen sense of the primitive and essential nature

of Israel's faith informed all that the prophets had to say. As they evaluated the society of their day in the light of it, there issued a message of judgment, for Israel, as they saw it, had violated Yahweh's covenant and laid itself open to his wrath. All the eighth-century prophets gave warning of judgment to come, a judgment which Yahweh would himself execute in the context of historical events, and—though often feeling the futility of it—they summoned their people to repent. At the same time, all of them—though some of them, such as Amos, had little to say about it—because they held fast to the confidence that Yahweh's promises and purposes were sure (this, too, an essential feature of Israel's primitive faith), looked beyond the disaster that was coming to a better future.

But here we must guard ourselves from misunderstanding the prophets. We are not to think of them merely as spiritually sensitive men, alive both to their religious heritage and to the corruption of the society in which they lived, who felt moved to make, and who had the gifts to make, an effective protest. A modern might be inclined to evaluate them so; but it would be entirely to misunderstand the evaluation that they placed on themselves. The prophets came, every one of them, to their work with a profound sense of divine vocation: they had been *called*. Some of them tell us explicitly of their experiences in this regard. Isaiah, for example (Isa vi), describes how in a vision he found himself in the heavenly court, in the very presence of the thrice-holy God himself, and how he was there commissioned to carry the divine message to his people. Ezekiel had various strange visions, in one of which (Ezek ii 8–iii 3) he devoured a scroll upon which God's word for his people was written. And Jeremiah, as we shall see (Jer i), felt the divine hand on his lips and knew that the divine word had been placed in his mouth. Although other prophets do not similarly confide in us, there is reason to believe that all of them came to their work through some definite experience of call. They *knew* that they had been commissioned by Yahweh to be his messengers. The word they spoke was Yahweh's word, not their own. This is why they prefaced it with a "this is what Yahweh has said" and had the temerity to phrase it in the first person as if Yahweh himself was the speaker, and their mouth his mouth. Nor did they merely feel permitted to do this; they were *compelled* to do it. Yahweh's hand had been laid upon them and, regardless of their own inclinations, they had no choice but to say what he had told them to say. That this could evoke serious inner tension is obvious; Jeremiah himself is the best witness to that fact.

But how, one might ask, could the prophets and their hearers be sure—and how can we be sure—that the word that they spoke was actually a word from God? That is a reasonable question, and one that poses itself inevitably. Nor is it one that might occur only to a scientifically trained modern who perhaps cannot convince himself that God really speaks so to men—or exists in any personal way, for that matter—and who is inclined to believe that the prophetic word is adequately explainable out of the prophet's own psychology. Ancient Israelites, who had no doubt that Yahweh spoke through his prophets, were forced in their own way to ask the question too. The very fact that the prophetic word was not an abstract teaching, an explication of timeless truth, but a specific directive for a specific situation, posed the question. It posed the question because what came as Yahweh's word for one situation was not always the same as the word for another situation. Thus, for example, an Isaiah could assure his king (e.g., Isa xxxvii 33–35) that Yahweh would never allow Jerusalem to be taken, while a Jeremiah had to assure the kings of his day that that was just what Yahweh was going to do. Worse than this, it not infrequently happened that in a single given situation one prophet would declare that such-and-such was Yahweh's word, while another prophet would simultaneously declare it to be the exact opposite. How could the hearer tell which prophet really had the word, or if either did?

That was an acute question in ancient Israel, and one that Jeremiah himself faced more than once, as we shall see. Nor was it ever really answered. On one occasion when Jeremiah had the question thrown squarely in his face (see chs. xxvii; xxviii) he could— aside from the moral certainty that he was right (and even he at times had doubts about that), and the observation that those who contradicted him did not sound like the great prophets of the past (one supposes that he was thinking of Amos, Hosea, and the other eighth-century men)—offer no answer save to say (xxviii 8 f.) that history would have to tell! In short, there was *no* proof of the truth of a prophet's word: the word would have to bring its own vindication.

And there we shall have to leave the matter. One simply cannot prove the truth of the essential claim of the prophets that they spoke a word from God, and any attempt to do so is a waste of time. Faith will affirm that they did. Those of contrary opinion will offer other explanations. But for the purposes of this book one point must be stressed, and stressed again: it is only as men who believed, who *knew,* that the word that they spoke was the word of their God that the prophets are to be understood at all. If we will not take this conviction of theirs seriously, we cannot begin to understand them—indeed, will only succeed in misunderstanding them. To that, one can only add that their words have in the truest sense been vindicated by history. By this one does not mean merely that a great number of their predictions demonstrably came to pass, but rather that their words have stood the test of time. Though specific words addressed to specific situations of the ancient past, they have about them an eternal quality; they are enduring words. To this day men still read them—even men who are strangers to the household of faith—and find in them worthwhile instruction, courage, and inspiration to a better quality of living. And still to this day they nurture the faith of those thousands who hear in them, no less than did ancient Israel, the word of their God.

THE BACKGROUND OF JEREMIAH'S CAREER:
THE LAST DAYS OF THE KINGDOM OF JUDAH

Before one can hope to read the words of Israel's prophets with understanding and appreciation, it is necessary first of all to gain at least a general knowledge of the times in which they lived and the situation to which they addressed themselves. In view of what has already been said the reasons for this are obvious. The very nature of the prophetic office as the prophets themselves understood it demands of us a concern with history. Had the prophets been religious teachers, philosophers, or thinkers who propounded timeless truths concerning God, man, and the proper conduct of life, it might be possible to abstract their words from history and appreciate them for their intrinsic worth and their literary quality without troubling too much about the circumstances that called them forth. But the prophets, it cannot be said too often, were nothing of the sort. On the contrary, they saw themselves as messengers of their God, commissioned to convey to the people the word that their God had given them. This conviction of theirs, whatever we may think of it, must be taken with utmost seriousness if we are to understand them. Because of their function their word was always a specific word: a specific directive to a specific people, caught up in the never-to-be-repeated events of a specific and never-to-be-repeated time in their history. Moreover, it was essentially a word that interpreted events, the events through which the people were passing or were about to pass, in the light of the divine demands and promises. And this is why it is only against the background of their times that the sayings of the prophets come alive—indeed, in many instances, make sense at all.

This statement, true of all the prophets, is peculiarly true of Jeremiah. This is not to say that Jeremiah was any more concerned to address the concrete situation that confronted him than were the others. Perhaps it is simply that, thanks to the wealth of biographical and historical detail which his book contains, his words

and deeds can be related to precise dates and known events to a
degree that is possible in the case of no other prophet. But, whatever the reason may be, it is certainly true that the words of no
other prophet (with the possible exception of Isaiah's) more viv-
idly reflect the march of political events than do his. Jeremiah's
life was lived in a time of upheaval in the ancient world. It was
one that brought to the little kingdom of Judah sudden and violent
swings of the pendulum of fortune, brief moments of hope, but
for the most part crisis after crisis and, in the end, unmitigated
disaster. It was Jeremiah's lot to witness the death of his country.
Beginning his career as the tottering Assyrian empire relaxed its
grip on its former holdings, in forty short years Jeremiah saw his
country pass through a period of independence, saw it fall victim
to the imperial ambitions first of Egypt, then of Babylon, before
finally watching it destroy itself in a futile attempt to get free of
the latter. Every act, every scene, of this tragic drama is reflected
in his book. Out of the agony of his people, and his own personal
agony, there came that somber note, that note of pathos and anguish,
so characteristic of his message. Without knowing something of
these tragic times, one cannot know Jeremiah.

Thanks to information given us in the book, we can date Jeremiah's career with precision. It began (i 2) in the year 627 and
lasted until some time after the destruction of Jerusalem by the
Babylonians in 587. This, then, is the period that we must attempt,
with what brevity and clarity can be managed, to sketch.[1] Fortunately, it is quite well known. Our major biblical historical sources
—the narrative of Kings (II Kings xxi–xxv), supplemented by the
account of the Chronicler (II Chron xxxiii–xxxvi)—are, it is true,
rather meager and leave many gaps. But much additional information is yielded by the Book of Jeremiah itself—which is an invaluable source of historical knowledge—and also, though to a much
lesser degree, by the books of the other prophets who were active
during Jeremiah's lifetime (Zephaniah, Nahum, Habakkuk, and
Ezekiel), as well as by archaeological discoveries which will be
mentioned in the course of our discussion. Moreover, certain cuneiform records, particularly the Babylonian Chronicle, portions of

---

[1] I have in this chapter purposely kept footnotes to a minimum. Those who
wish a somewhat fuller treatment than is possible here, together with citation
of relevant literature, are referred to my book, *A History of Israel* (Philadelphia: Westminster Press, 1959; London: SCM Press, 1960).

which have but recently been published,[2] illumine the political history of the entire period and supplement the information gained from the Bible in the most remarkable way.

1

Jeremiah, as we have said, began his career as a prophet in the year 627. Since he was little more than a lad at the time (cf. i 6), he must have been born around 645 or shortly before—thus toward the end of the long reign of Manasseh (687–642). At that time the little kingdom of Judah was a vassal state of the Assyrian empire, and had been for very nearly a hundred years. Let us, then, begin by taking a brief look backward to see how this came about, and what it entailed, in order to set the stage and gain perspective.

When the empire built by David fell apart at the death of his son Solomon (ca. 922), there remained in its place the two rival states of Israel and Judah, the former in the north with its capital ultimately at Samaria, the latter in the south with its capital at Jerusalem. Of these, Israel was by far the larger and wealthier, but both were, by modern standards at least, incredibly tiny. (The two together were no larger than Wales, or one of our smaller states, such as Vermont.) These two lived side by side, now at war with one another, now in peaceful alliance, for almost exactly two hundred years. Though they had fought with their neighbors repeatedly, and had on occasion been invaded and humiliated, and though their fortunes had not been unaffected by the currents of larger world affairs, they had, down to the middle of the eighth century, retained their status as independent kingdoms. The world situation was such as to permit this. One must realize that Israel's entire history since her occupation of Palestine had until this time been spun out in a great power vacuum; it was one of those interludes in which no world empire existed—neither in the Nile Valley,

2 See Wiseman (for complete reference, see Selected Bibliography). This book includes a reprint of a portion of the Chronicle published in 1923. There is also a considerable periodical literature on this subject, selections from which I have cited, *A History of Israel*, p. 302. The study "The Babylonian Chronicle" of D. N. Freedman (BA 19 [1956], 50–60), which will be found particularly helpful, is now reprinted in *The Biblical Archaeologist Reader*, eds. G. E. Wright and D. N. Freedman (New York: Doubleday Anchor Books, 1961), pp. 113–27.

nor in Mesopotamia, nor elsewhere. Assyria, it is true, had in the ninth century begun to show signs of resurgent power, and had on more than one occasion sent her armies across the Euphrates into the west, taking tribute from the petty states there (including Israel). But this had not been permanent conquest. Assyria had been too troubled by internal dissensions, too greatly threatened by powerful neighbors, to make her conquests stick; as a result, her history had been a succession of advances and retreats. It was such a period of retreat that had allowed Israel and Judah, in the first half of the eighth century, to regain a measure of strength and prosperity unknown to either since Solomon. This, incidentally, was the situation to which the first of the classical prophets, Amos, addressed himself.

But soon after the eighth century had passed its midpoint, there took place a sudden and decisive change. Tiglath-pileser III (745–727) ascended the Assyrian throne and inaugurated a new phase in that country's history. Assyria's period of empire had begun; from now on she would come to conquer, occupy, and rule. As Tiglath-pileser's forces advanced into the west, subduing one by one the little kingdoms there, a coalition was formed to resist him, the leaders of which were Rezin, king of the Aramean state of Damascus, and Pekah ben Remaliah (737–732), who had usurped the throne in Israel. These kings tried to get Judah to join them. But Judah, apparently preferring to pursue an independent course, refused; whereupon the confederates took steps to whip her into line. In 735/4, soon after Ahaz—the grandfather of Manasseh, during whose reign Jeremiah was born—had succeeded to the throne in Jerusalem, coalition troops invaded Judah and closed in on the capital city, their intention being to depose Ahaz and replace him with a creature of their own choosing. Ahaz, feeling his position to be hopeless and terrified at what seemed to be in store for him, saw no course save to appeal to Tiglath-pileser for aid. And this he did (against the earnest warnings of Isaiah, it may be added), sending an enormous tribute to the Great King and acknowledging his overlordship. With that, Judah became a dependency of the Assyrian empire, and had remained so ever since.

This is not to say that manful attempts were not made to extricate the nation from this position. It was a humiliating position, and not one that a proud people would be likely to accept willingly and without a fight. It is true that Ahaz' policy saved Judah from the coalition—which Tiglath-pileser utterly crushed (in 733/2), ravaging Damascus and large portions of Israel, and incorporating the territory thus conquered as provinces of the empire. It also enabled Judah to escape the fate that overtook Israel in 722/1 when, because of renewed rebellion, Tiglath-pileser's successors, Shalmaneser V (727–722) and Sargon II (722–705), invaded what was left of her territory, destroyed her capital city, Samaria, and ended her existence as a nation. Yet the price of the safety thus bought was high, and the results scarcely happy. Judah was no longer a free country, but a pawn of a foreign power, obliged to accede to its wishes in all matters of state and to render to it a tribute which, we may be sure, was not inconsiderable. Ahaz' action in placing his country in this position was surely resented, and must have seemed to many (as it did to Isaiah) both craven cowardice and a sinful want of faith in Yahweh. All this, plus the enforced recognition of Assyria's gods in the temple in Jerusalem (vassals in the ancient world were normally expected at least to "tip their hats" to their overlord's gods), and the distressing religious and moral laxity attendant upon it, conspired to produce a ground swell of discontent. Not a few were ready to go to any extreme in order to force a change.

Ahaz' son Hezekiah (715–687) seems to have shared these sentiments, for he reversed his father's policy at every point, bending his efforts increasingly toward independence, while at the same time undertaking sweeping religious reforms. The details cannot concern us here. Matters came to a head when Sennacherib (705–681) took the throne of Assyria. It was then that Hezekiah, encouraged by unrest in various parts of the empire and relying upon aid promised by Egypt, at that time ruled by the vigorous Twenty-fifth (Ethiopian) Dynasty, formally declared his independence and joined a considerable coalition of states in open rebellion. But this led only to disaster (again, as Isaiah warned). In 701, Sennacherib fell upon the coalition and broke it, invaded Judah, reduced her fortified cities and slaughtered or deported their population, and finally, having blockaded Hezekiah in Jerusalem and forced his surrender, laid the land under ruinous taxation. Though Jerusalem was spared destruction, and though Hezekiah retained his throne—and may even have dared to revolt a second time[3]—his

___

[3] I have elsewhere (*A History of Israel*, pp. 282–87) argued for the plausibility of a second revolt, in the course of which the dramatic deliverance of Jerusalem described in II Kings xviii 17–xix 37 and Isa xxxvi–xxxvii took place. But the point is not of material concern here.

efforts to regain independence were completely unsuccessful. It couldn't be done! So it was that when Hezekiah died, his son and successor Manasseh gave up the effort, declared himself a loyal vassal of Assyria, and so remained (as far as we know from the Book of Kings and from Assyrian records) throughout his long reign (687–642).

Humanly speaking, one can hardly see how Manasseh could have done otherwise. The odds were simply too great! What, after all, could this tiny splinter of a country, poor in manpower and material resources, flanked to the north and west by Assyrian dependencies, its capital but ten miles from the frontier of the province of Samaria, hope to do against such a colossus? Moreover, it was during the years of Manasseh's reign that Assyria's empire reached its greatest physical expansion. The climax of this came with the conquest of Egypt by Sennacherib's successors, Esarhaddon (681–669) and Asshurbanapal (669–627). The Egyptians, who had felt themselves threatened—as indeed they were—by Assyria's advance to their very frontier, had made it their standing policy at every opportunity to foment unrest among the vassal states of Palestine and Phoenicia, hoping thereby to loosen Assyria's hold on that area. Scarcely a one of the almost innumerable revolts that had troubled the western part of Assyria's empire through the preceding generations was without Egyptian backing. It was, therefore, inevitable that the Assyrians, who were well aware of this, would one day move to suppress the nuisance at its source. And this they succeeded in doing. In a series of campaigns, begun by Esarhaddon and culminating with the capture and sack of the ancient capital of Thebes by Asshurbanapal in 663, Egypt was invaded, conquered, and its political independence ended. With the sole power that could even promise to underwrite revolt against Assyria removed, it is scarcely surprising that Manasseh remained docile.

Nevertheless, Manasseh's policy—essentially a repudiation of that of his father, and a return to that of his grandfather Ahaz, who had brought the country into subjection to Assyria in the first place—had disastrous consequences, as the account in II Kings xxi (cf. vss. 2–7) is at pains to point out. This was especially true where religious matters were concerned. Since vassals were expected to give at least nominal recognition to their overlord's gods, it is scarcely surprising that altars to Assyrian astral deities were erected within the temple confines. In view of his position, Manasseh perhaps had little choice in this. It is clear, however, that in his case compliance went beyond the merely perfunctory and constituted a repudiation of all that his father Hezekiah had tried to do. That king's reform measures were cancelled, local shrines were restored, pagan practices of all sorts were given free rein, the fertility cult with its ritual of sacred prostitution being tolerated even within the temple itself (cf. II Kings xxiii 4–7; Zeph i 4 f.). In addition, there was a general aping of foreign fashions and ways (Zeph i 8), together with an enormous interest in the occult arts, which were currently enjoying an unprecedented popularity in Assyria as well. Most sinister of all, the barbarous rite of human sacrifice, an abomination to all true Yahwists, began on occasion to be practiced in Jerusalem, the king himself apparently taking the lead (II Kings xxi 6).

It was, in short, a time of thoroughgoing religious decay, and one that posed an immense, and in some ways a novel, threat to the integrity of Israel's faith. It is, to be sure, unlikely that any widespread and conscious abandonment of the national religion had taken place. It was, rather, that the essential distinction between Yahwism and paganism had become so blurred in the minds of so many people that they were able to practice pagan rites alongside the cult of Yahweh, and perhaps even dedicate those rites to Yahweh, without any awareness that they were guilty of apostasy in doing so. Yet it meant that Yahwism was dangerously close to becoming a polytheism. It must be remembered that popular belief had regarded the heavenly bodies as members of Yahweh's heavenly assembly, that host of angelic beings who did his bidding; introduction of the cults of astral deities would naturally encourage people to think of these beings as gods, and to worship them as such. One short step, and Yahweh would have become the head of a pantheon, and Israel's faith would have lost its distinctive character. Moreover, since the very toleration of such rites betokened a forgetting of Yahweh's covenant, the inevitable result was a widespread disregard of covenant law with attendant incidents of violence and injustice (Zeph i 9; iii 1–7). The gravity of the situation can scarcely be exaggerated. Yet those who ventured to protest— and there must have been those who did—were dealt with severely (II Kings xxi 16). The author of Kings can say no good word of Manasseh, but instead brands him as the worst king Judah ever had, whose sin was alone enough to explain the destruction of the nation (II Kings xxi 9–15; xxiv 3 f.). Jeremiah, who was born while these conditions obtained, was clearly horrified by them, as we shall see.

2

But, even as it must have seemed that Judah was fated to lie helpless under the Assyrian heel for all time to come, a change of fortune was being prepared for her which would, far sooner no doubt than any in Jerusalem would have dared to predict, make her once more a free country. The period of Assyria's greatest expansion was also the beginning of her decline and fall. The first cracks, indeed, in the empire's massive structure might have been detected by a careful observer about the time (as we have supposed) that Jeremiah was born.

The truth is that Assyria was overextended. Unceasing wars had begun to exhaust her strength, and she was experiencing increasing difficulty in imposing her will on subject peoples, almost none of whom had anything but hate for her, and this at the very time when she found herself threatened from beyond her frontiers as perhaps never before in her history. This last threat lay in various Indo-Aryan peoples to the north and east. Chief among these were the Medes, a people who had been settled in western Iran since the ninth century, and against whom Assyrian kings had repeatedly campaigned, but who now could no longer be controlled and were rapidly becoming a potential menace. In addition, hordes of barbarian Cimmerians and Scythians, who had in the late eighth century begun to pour down from beyond the Caucasus, were by now established along Assyria's northern frontier: Cimmerians and Scythians in northwestern Iran, Cimmerians over large parts of eastern Asia Minor. Esarhaddon, who understood the threat that these peoples posed, had sought to protect himself—much as the Romans were later to do on the northern marches of their empire —by allying with the Scythians against the Cimmerians and Medes. Asshurbanapal fought the Cimmerians in Asia Minor but, though he was victorious on every occasion and successfully defended his borders, the menace was by no means removed.

Within the empire, too, there was much unrest, as a result of which Asshurbanapal found himself, approximately midway in his reign, in serious trouble. Egypt, so recently invaded and conquered, could not, as it turned out, be held. Psammetichus I (664–610), a native prince who was to be the founder of Egypt's Twenty-sixth (Saite) Dynasty, although still at the time a nominal vassal of Assyria, began gradually expanding his power until he had united most of Egypt under his rule. Then, presumably as soon as he felt strong enough, he withheld tribute and seceded from the empire. Asshurbanapal apparently could do nothing to prevent it.

In Babylonia, meanwhile, where Asshurbanapal's brother Shamash-shum-ukin ruled as deputy king, unrest was chronic, as it had been for generations. In 652 this exploded into a general rebellion that nearly tore Assyria asunder. The leader was Shamash-shum-ukin himself, who had the support of the Chaldean population of the area and was aided by the kingdom of Elam to the east, as well as by various peoples of the Iranian highlands. Disaffection seems to have spread into Palestine and Syria, no doubt at the instigation of Psammetichus, and perhaps of other enemies of Assyria as well. It is not inconceivable that Manasseh, who was probably no more loyal to Assyria than he had to be, was either actively involved or so affected as to fall under grave suspicion; this is, at least, a plausible explanation of the notice in II Chron xxxiii 11–13 to the effect that he was on one occasion hauled before the Assyrian king in chains, but then shown clemency and restored to his throne. It was at about this time, too, that Arab tribes of the Syrian desert, taking advantage of Assyria's preoccupation elsewhere, poured into Edom, Moab, and other lands of eastern Palestine and Syria, spreading destruction everywhere. This was a catastrophe from which Moab, at least, seems never fully to have recovered.[4]

Asshurbanapal, it is true, was able to master the situation, though only after a bitter struggle which left the empire badly shaken. In 648, after a two-year siege, his forces stormed Babylon and ended the rebellion there, Shamash-shum-ukin having taken his own life. A few years later (ca. 640), he marched against Elam, took Susa, and brought the Elamite state to an end. Meanwhile, he took bitter vengeance on the Arab tribes and reasserted his authority in Palestine, resettling people deported from Babylonia and Elam in Samaria and elsewhere (Ezra iv 9 f.). Reconquest of Egypt, however, was by this time out of the question, and it is unlikely that Asshur-

[4] This may be the setting of at least some of the poems of Jer xlviii (and of Isa xv–xvi); see COMMENT on Sec. 40.

banapal even considered attempting it; and this was a setback, for it meant that the Egyptians, no longer seriously threatened, were free to resume their historic role of intervention in the affairs of western Asia. Yet, in spite of this, thanks to Asshurbanapal's energetic efforts, the empire had been held essentially intact, and so it remained as long as that king lived. In his later years, though of these little is known, it appears that Asshurbanapal, having subdued all who had opposed him, found time for works of peace, among other things assembling one of the great libraries of the ancient world, in which he caused copies of the myths and epics of Babylon (the Babylonian creation and flood stories first came to light here) to be preserved.

Asshurbanapal lived, as we now know, until 627.[5] In Judah, meanwhile, his vassal Manasseh had died and been succeeded by his son Amon (642–640), who apparently continued his father's policy. This unfortunate king, however, was soon assassinated (II Kings xxi 19–26) by certain of his palace family, presumably high officials. It is probable that the authors of this plot represented elements committed to independence at any price, who had hoped by their action to force a change in the national policy. Apparently, however, the general feeling was that the time was not ripe for such a step, for we are told that an assembly of leading citizens had the assassins summarily executed, and Amon's young son Josiah made king in his stead. This Josiah, who was but eight years old when he was placed on the throne, was just coming of age when Asshurbanapal died and Assyria's collapse began. Under him, Judah became at last a free country.

Asshurbanapal's death was the beginning of Assyria's end. This took place, as was just indicated, in 627—the very year in which Jeremiah began his career as a prophet. Two years previously (629) Asshurbanapal's son Sin-shar-ishkun had come to the throne as his

[5] Reconstruction of the events at this point differs slightly from that found in my earlier work (*A History of Israel*, pp. 293–96), where Asshurbanapal's death is placed ca. 633 or soon thereafter. Recently published texts, which came to my attention after the above-mentioned pages were written, show that Asshurbanapal died in 627, his son Sin-shar-ishkun having been associated with him on the throne for two years prior to that time. Cf. C. J. Gadd, "The Harran Inscriptions of Nabonidus," *Anatolian Studies* 8 (1958), 35–92. On the chronology, cf. R. Borger, "Mesopotamien in den Jahren 629–621 v. Chr.," *Wiener Zeitschrift für die Kunde des Morgenlandes* 55 (1959), 62–76 (but see n.[6]).

father's co-regent and successor designate. But when the old king died a certain general, who had wished another son, Asshur-etil-ilani, to have the throne,[6] launched a general revolt which plunged the country into civil war. The details of this struggle are wholly obscure, though it must have lasted about four years (627–624?) before Sin-shar-ishkun finally triumphed. It sealed Assyria's doom, for it left her helpless before her foes. In view of recent studies, it is probable that an unsuccessful Median assault upon Nineveh described by Herodotus (I, 102), in the course of which their king Phraortes lost his life, took place at about this time.[7] If so, we must suppose that the Scythian irruption into western Asia of which Herodotus also tells (I, 104–6), occurred, if it occurred at all (and some such irruption is by no means improbable), during the reign of Phraortes' son and successor Cyaxares, rather than earlier. But at our present state of knowledge we cannot move beyond the realm of conjecture on this point. In any event, we have no evidence that such an invasion took place at the beginning of Jeremiah's career, as a number of scholars have supposed.[8] What is certain is that Babylon took advantage of the turmoil to make herself free. This we know from the Babylonian Chronicle. The leader of this uprising was the Chaldean prince Nabopolassar (626–605), who became the founder of the neo-Babylonian empire. In October 626, after various preliminary engagements, Nabopolassar dealt the Assyrians a decisive defeat outside Babylon and, in the following month, took the throne there. Try as they did, the Assyrians could not dislodge him. In a very few years (the Babylonian Chronicle

---

[6] Borger ("Mesopotamien . . .") believes that Sin-shar-ishkun and Asshur-etil-ilani were one and the same person, the latter name being his throne name. But the interpretation adopted is at least as likely (so Professor W. F. Albright in a private communication).

[7] Cf. R. Labat, "Kaštariti, Phraorte et les debuts de l'histoire mède" (*Journal Asiatique* 249 [1961], 1–12). Labat, among other things, argues on the basis of certain manuscripts in which the work of Herodotus is preserved that Herodotus intended to include the years of Scythian domination of which he speaks within the reign of Cyaxares, and that Phraortes was killed ca. 625, or soon after (623?).

[8] We shall return to this subject in the next chapter. We know that a people called the Umman Manda participated in the destruction of Nineveh in 612, and the capture of Harran in 610 (see below). It is quite probable that these were Scythians. It is by no means impossible that they may at one time have ranged through Syria and Palestine, as Herodotus states. But, if so, this must have taken place somewhat later in Josiah's reign, rather than as Jeremiah began to prophesy.

for the years 622–617 is missing) we find Assyria with her back to the wall, fighting for her life against the combined onslaughts of Babylonians and Medes. In the course of all this, her empire in the west went by default.

The precise steps by which Judah regained her independence can only be conjectured. We may suppose that during Josiah's childhood and youth affairs of state were in the hands of advisers who pursued a discreet course vis-à-vis Assyria. The notice in II Chron xxxiv 3a that in the eighth year of his reign Josiah "began to seek the God of David his father" may indicate that even this early (633/2) the decision had been made to reorientate the national policy as soon as that should appear expedient. In Josiah's twelfth regnal year (629/8), which would be just after Sin-shar-ishkun had taken the throne in Assyria, the new policy was apparently put into effect: the Assyrian gods were repudiated (itself tacitly a declaration of independence) and sweeping reform measures instituted (II Chron xxxiv 3b–7). At about this time, too, Josiah moved to take possession of the provinces into which the Assyrians had divided the territory of the erstwhile northern state. How he accomplished this, and when, is uncertain[9]; but since these provinces had been abandoned by Assyria, they could not have offered much resistance, even had they wished. Josiah may even have done this while still nominally a vassal of Assyria, that country being by this time both unable to prevent it and willing to go to any lengths to keep Judah from allying itself with Egypt—as some in Judah apparently wished to do (cf. Jer ii 18, etc.). In any event, it could not have been long after Jeremiah began to preach that Assyria, torn as she was with civil strife, ceased to exercise even nominal control in Palestine. His country at last free, Josiah could carry out his reform measures unhindered.

3

Josiah's reform was far the most thoroughgoing in Judah's history, and an event of extreme significance. In the minds of the Bible writers, indeed, it so far overshadowed all of Josiah's other royal

[9] Josiah at least for a time also gained control of portions of the coastal plain, as is indicated by a Hebrew ostracon found at Yabneh-yam; cf. J. Naveh, IEJ 10 (1960), 129–39; F. M. Cross, Jr., BASOR 165 (1962), 34–46.

acts that they tell us virtually nothing else about him. Since this is so, and since Jeremiah's attitude toward it constitutes one of the major problems of his book, it is important that we consider it in some detail.

We know of this reform from the parallel accounts in II Kings xxii–xxiii and II Chron xxxiv–xxxv. Since these accounts differ somewhat, we cannot be sure of the various steps by which it was carried out. According to Kings (II Kings xxii 3; xxiii 23) the entire reform took place in Josiah's eighteenth regnal year (622) and was based on "the book of the law," a copy of which had been found in the temple in the course of repairs to that structure. But not only is it unlikely that so many drastic measures could have been carried out successfully in the course of a single year; the very fact that the temple was being repaired when the lawbook was found indicates that reform was already in progress, for the repairing and purification of the temple was itself a reform measure. The Chronicler, on the other hand (II Chron xxxiv 3–8), tells us that the reform was carried out in several steps, and that it had been going on for some years before the lawbook was found. Though he too schematizes his material, placing virtually the whole of the reform in Josiah's twelfth year and leaving almost nothing to be done in the eighteenth, his picture of a reform accomplished progressively over a period of years is assuredly correct. We may suppose that the decision to make changes in the national policy had been taken as early as Josiah's eighth year (633/2), and that by his twelfth year (629/8)—coincident, as we have seen, with a change of rulers in Assyria—the independence-reform movement having gathered momentum, a purge of foreign cults of all sorts was begun, which reached into northern Israel also as Josiah took over that area. Then in the eighteenth year (622), Assyrian control having ended, the finding of the lawbook, which evoked in Josiah the profoundest consternation, gave the reform new impetus and drove it to yet more radical conclusions. Reform and independence thus went forward in step with one another.

In any event, what the reform sought to achieve is quite clear. It was, primarily, a consistent purge of all non-Yahwistic cults and practices (cf. II Kings xxiii 4–14, 24). Such as were of Assyrian origin, being galling reminders of the nation's humiliation and anathema to all patriotic people, were doubtless the first to go. But pagan cults of all sorts, some of them introduced by Manasseh, young Jeremiah himself. We shall see later how he thundered against the idolatry with which the land was filled and, predicting its dire consequences, pleaded with the nation to repent. We shall also see how passionately he longed for the return of the exiles of northern Israel and the reunion of Israel with Judah in the worship of Yahweh. Zephaniah also prophesied at this time. A man of the stamp of Isaiah, Zephaniah assailed the religious and moral decay which Manasseh had allowed to flourish as a prideful rebellion against Yahweh which had invited his wrath (e.g., Zeph i 4–6, 8 f., 12; iii 1–4, 11). Announcing that the day of Yahweh's judgment was at hand (e.g., i 2 f., 7, 14–18), he declared that the nation had no hope save in repentance (ii 1–3), for which it had now been offered one last chance (iii 6 f.). Preaching of this sort undoubtedly aroused sympathy for the political and religious policy that Josiah pursued.

The finding of the Deuteronomic law brought all these inchoate feelings to a focus and gave them direction. Though probably re-edited in the generation preceding the reform, this was no new law, still less a document piously concocted for the occasion, but rather a homiletical collection of ancient laws that stemmed ultimately from the legal tradition of Israel's earliest period. Apparently of northern Israelite origin, it had been brought to Jerusalem presumably after the fall of Samaria, where, at sometime between the reigns of Hezekiah and Josiah, it had been reformulated and made into an instrument of reform. Since this is so, its laws could not themselves have been for the most part so very novel. What was novel was the description that Deuteronomy gives of the Mosaic covenant and its stringent demands, demands which the official religion had all too largely failed to stress, or externalized. Particularly disturbing must have been the desperate urgency with which this lawbook over and over again insists that the nation must worship Yahweh alone and obey his covenant law, or face destruction. We cannot doubt that this came to the godly Josiah and his advisers as the very voice of Israel's God: conform to this law or perish! Small wonder that Josiah (II Kings xxii 11) rent his garments in dismay! It must have seemed to him that if this was in fact Yahweh's law, the nation was living in a fool's paradise in assuming that Yahweh was irrevocably committed to its defense. In bringing the people into covenant to obey the law, it was undoubtedly his conviction that he had chosen the course, and the only course, that could save the nation from ruin.

How the reform actually worked out it is difficult to say, since we know almost nothing of the latter years of Josiah's reign (between 622 and his death in 609). Certainly there was no foreign power that could interfere with Josiah's freedom to pursue whatever course he chose. Assyria was by this time *in extremis*. As was noted above, the Babylonian leader Nabopolassar had, in 626, driven the Assyrians from his country and made himself king there. By 616 Nabopolassar was on the offensive, having marched far up the Euphrates and administered the Assyrians a serious defeat. At this moment, surprisingly, Assyria found an ally in Egypt. Presumably Psammetichus, aware that Assyria was no longer a threat, wanted to preserve that country as a buffer against a potentially more dangerous Medo-Babylonian axis. No doubt, too, he hoped as the price of his aid to gain a free hand in Egypt's ancient sphere of influence in Palestine and Syria. In any event, his troops reached Mesopotamia in 616 in time to help the Assyrians check Nabopolassar's advance. But then the Medes began to play a decisive part. After various maneuvers, the Median king Cyaxares stormed the ancient Assyrian capital of Asshur in 614. Nabopolassar, arriving too late to participate, concluded a formal treaty with him. Then, two years later (612) and after still further maneuvers, the allies closed in on Nineveh itself and, after a three-month siege, took it and razed it to the ground; the Assyrian king Sin-shar-ishkun apparently perished in the debacle. Remnants of the Assyrian army, it is true, retired westward to Harran where, with their backs to the Egyptians, they endeavored to keep resistance alive. But in vain. In 610 the Babylonians aided by the Umman Manda (probably the Scythians) took Harran also, and the wreckage of the Assyrian forces fell back across the Euphrates into the arms of the Egyptians.[10] Assyria was done for.

Since we are told nothing of Josiah's actions during this period, we do not know what steps he may have taken to ensure the continued enforcement of his various measures. But since he seems

[10] A. Malamat (IEJ 1 [1950/51], 154–59) has argued that the Scythian invasion of the west mentioned by Herodotus (I, 104–6), which carried them south to the frontier of Egypt, took place just after this assault on Harran. If such an invasion occurred (as is not unlikely), ca. 610—or the years immediately preceding—would be a plausible time for it. But at present we lack evidence to say more.

to have been sincerely zealous for the reform, and since no foreign
power was in a position to coerce his policies in any way, we may
be sure that as long as he lived the reform was officially maintained. But to evaluate its results is another matter. By what standards does one do this? The author of Kings, who based his judgment
of the various rulers on their official policies, paints a glowing picture of Josiah, hailing him (II Kings xxiii 25) as the very best
king Judah ever had. But this simply means what has already
been suggested: that this writer found Josiah's policy in accord
with the divine will, and that Josiah never retreated from it. It does
not allow us to suppose that the reform revolutionized the national
character and ushered in an era of righteousness: no reform ever
did. We may be sure that before, during, and after Josiah's reign
there were good men and bad men in Israel, godly men and profane,
moral men and fornicators, law-abiding men and swindlers. Nor
have we any means of measuring what effects the reform may have
had—though assuredly it had its effects—on private morality and
the spiritual temper of the people generally. The truth probably is
that it produced many good results, along with others that were not
so good, but that it failed to evoke the thoroughgoing repentance,
the enduring change in the national character, which some had felt
to be necessary.

That the reform had beneficial results can hardly be doubted. To
be sure, it aroused opposition and created problems, as any such
sweeping measure must. In particular, the priests of abolished Yah-
wistic shrines were understandably not eager to surrender their
ancient prerogatives and meekly integrate themselves with the
priesthood of Jerusalem, and many of them refused to do so (II
Kings xxiii 9). It is likely, indeed, that the Jerusalem clergy, to
whom the reform had given a virtual monopoly, did not welcome
those who complied save in a status of inferiority. In addition, the
closing of the local shrines must inevitably have led, or so one
would imagine, to a dangerous secularization of life in large parts
of the country, since it meant that few people in outlying areas,
Jerusalem being too far away, could participate in cultic occasions
regularly. How Josiah proposed to deal with this problem, or if he
saw it as a problem, we do not know. Yet, in spite of all this, the
reform assuredly brought great benefits to the nation. The abolition
of pagan cults with their nameless rites could not have failed to be
a blessing to the country, morally and spiritually. Moreover, the

state having been committed to the observance of covenant law, and Josiah himself being a just man (cf. Jer xxii 15 f.), we may suppose that public morality and the administration of justice underwent, at least temporarily, a significant improvement. To be sure, we can measure none of these things. But it is safe to assume, in view of the numerous analogies which history offers, that official policy was not without its good effects upon the corporate life of the people.

At the same time, it is clear that the reform produced no profound change in the national character, but rather tended, as reforms usually do, to stop short with external measures. One gains the impression, indeed, that its chief result was a heightening of religious activity and, withal, a blind complacency regarding the nation's future that was dangerous in the extreme. Now one might with justice observe that no officially sponsored measure can be expected to change the character of a nation. Nevertheless those who had wanted such a change found themselves bitterly disappointed with the outcome. This was certainly true of Jeremiah, whose evaluation of the reform will concern us in a later chapter. There is evidence that he had, even before Josiah's death, become deeply disillusioned with the whole thing. More than once he complained that no real repentance had come of it, but only an ever more elaborate cultus (e.g., vi 16–21), and that the wealthy and powerful, confident that the presence of Yahweh's temple was the nation's sufficient defense, were using the cultus as a cloak for the most egregious violations of covenant law (vii 1–15; cf. v 20–31). It seemed to him that the very possession of the lawbook had helped to create a climate in which the prophetic word could no longer be heard and that, because of this, the nation remained obdurate in its sins (viii 4–9). In this he was probably right. The reform, for all the stringent moral demands of the Deuteronomic law, probably did contribute to the general complacency. Since the law had, after all, seemed to make the national safety dependent upon reform, the popular mind naturally supposed that by making that reform the divine demands had been met—for so their clergy assured them (vi 13 f.; viii 10 f.). The national confidence in the permanence of temple, dynasty, and state, as guaranteed by Yahweh's promises, was therefore fortified. It was a confidence that was ill-prepared to withstand the impending tragedy.

4

It was in the year 609 that tragedy first struck. This year witnessed both Josiah's death and the end of Judah's independence. The story of the years just preceding has already been related: how the Medes and the Babylonians had allied to bring Assyria to the ground, in 612 destroying Nineveh, and in 610 ejecting the refugee Assyrian government from Harran. But Assyria's crash was not to bring peace to Judah. There was the corpse of an empire to be divided, and about it the vultures gathered: the Medes, the Babylonians, and the Egyptians. The first of these busied themselves extending their control through the areas east and north of the mountains, in Iran, in Armenia and into Asia Minor, and do not concern our story directly. But the Babylonians, already in control of the whole of the Mesopotamian plain, and the Egyptians, who desired to further their own interests in Asia, both had their eye on erstwhile Assyrian holdings west of the Euphrates. And between the upper and nether millstones of their rival ambitions Judah was caught and crushed.

In 609 Necho II (610–594), who had succeeded his father Psammetichus on the throne of Egypt, marched with a large force northward to Carchemish on the Euphrates to assist the Assyrians in a last effort to retake Harran. At Megiddo, now within the territory of reunited Israel, Josiah tried to stop him. Whether Josiah acted as an ally of Babylon, or independently, is unknown; but he could hardly have wished an Egypto-Assyrian victory, the result of which would have been to place his country at the mercy of Egypt's ambitions. Be that as it may, it was a futile and suicidal action. Josiah was killed and brought dead in his chariot to Jerusalem amid great lamentation (II Kings xxiii 29 f.; II Chron xxxv 20–25). His son Jehoahaz was made king in his place.

Meanwhile Necho proceeded on to the Euphrates. Although the assault on Harran failed completely (we do not know whether Josiah's action delayed the pharaoh long enough to affect the outcome or not), Necho was left for the moment in control of Palestine and Syria. So he set out to consolidate his position. Naturally, he accorded Judah rough treatment. Having summoned Jehoahaz, who had reigned but three months, to his headquarters at Riblah in central Syria, he deposed him and deported him to Egypt (II Kings xxiii 31–35), and then placed Jehoiakim, another of Josiah's sons, on the throne as his vassal and laid the land under heavy tribute. Jehoiakim was obliged to raise this by means of a head tax levied on all landholding citizens. Whether the pharaoh at this time reduced Judah's territory to its pre-Josianic dimensions or not is unknown; but it is probable that he did. Judah's independence was thus ended.

For a few years after the campaign of 609 Necho was able to hold his gains. The Babylonians were not yet ready to challenge him. In 608/7 and 607/6 Nabopolassar and his son Nebuchadnezzar were occupied with campaigns in the northern mountains, presumably to secure their flank in that quarter in the face of the Egyptian army marshaled west of the Euphrates. During this time, save for raids in force across the river by both sides, the Babylonians seeking a bridgehead north of Carchemish from which to attack Egyptian forces based on that city, the Egyptians counterattacking to prevent it, the front remained quiet; no decisive blow was struck. And through these years Jehoiakim remained the pharaoh's vassal.

As regards events in Judah we have little tangible information. But, even aside from loss of independence and the burden of Egyptian taxation, one senses that all was not well. Neither in ability nor in character was Jehoiakim the equal of his father, as Jeremiah, who despised him, was at pains on occasion to say publicly. Early in his reign he showed his disregard for his subjects' welfare when, apparently dissatisfied with his father's palace, he set out to build a new and finer one and, presumably because his depleted treasury lacked the necessary funds, used forced labor to do it (Jer xxii 13–19). This action, which seems to us, as it did to Jeremiah, that of a petty and irresponsible man, appears to have been quite typical of him. As one would expect, Jehoiakim did not exert himself to keep the reform intact. The reform had always had its opponents, and these had doubtless increased in number. The tragic events of 609, indeed, must have seemed to many sufficient proof that the Deuteronomic theology which undergirded the reform was untrue, for compliance with the law's demands had not forestalled disaster as promised. In any event, though there was scarcely a return to the excesses of Manasseh's reign, and possibly no official revocation of the reform, popular pagan practices crept back (Jer vii 16–18; xi 9–13; Ezek viii), and public morality deteriorated. Those who dared to rebuke this drift met harassment and persecution, and in some cases death (Jer xxvi 20–23).

So matters continued until 605 when, at a stroke, the delicate balance of world power was upset and Judah was brought face to face with a new and more fearful emergency. In the late spring or early summer of that year Nebuchadnezzar launched his all-out attack. Leaping upon the Egyptian forces at Carchemish, he sent them in headlong rout (cf. Jer xlvi 2–12) and then, pursuing them southward, dealt them a second and yet more crushing defeat near Hamath in central Syria. Nothing stood in the way of a Babylonian sweep southward into Palestine. In August 605, however, news of Nabopolassar's death obliged Nebuchadnezzar to halt his advance and hasten home; in September 605 he took the throne in Babylon, although the first official year of his reign began with the following New Year (April 604).[11] But the Babylonian army soon resumed its advance and at least by the end of 604 was in the Philistine plain, where it took and ravaged Ashkelon (cf. Jer xlvii 2–7)[12]; leading elements of that city's population were deported to Babylon.[13] Consternation reigned in Judah, as contemporary prophetic utterances (cf. Hab i 5–11; Jer v 15–17; vi 22–26, etc.) show. Possibly as the Babylonians overran Philistia, certainly soon after, Jehoiakim transferred his allegiance to Nebuchadnezzar and became his vassal (II Kings xxiv 1). Judah's fortunes had come full circle; she was once more within the orbit of a Mesopotamian power.

But Jehoiakim had taken this step only from necessity, and apparently with the intention of rectifying the situation at the earliest

[11] The reader will note a discrepancy of one year between dates in Kings and in certain passages in Jeremiah (cf. II Kings xxiv 12; xxv 8 and Jeremiah lii 28 f.). This may be because the latter reckoned Nebuchadnezzar's reign from his first official year, while the former counted from 605, when he first appeared in the west and was recognized as *de facto* ruler there. See the article of Freedman cited in n.2.

[12] An Aramaic letter found in Egypt may well contain the futile plea of its king to the pharaoh for aid. My article discussing it (BA 12 [1949], 46–52) now appears in *The Biblical Archaeologist Reader* (see n.2), pp. 98–105. A date in 604 now seems best. For further literature on the subject, cf. Wiseman, p. 28. On reference to this event in a newly edited fragment of the poet Alcaeus, see J. D. Quinn, BASOR 164 (1961), 19 f.

[13] Ashkelonian princes, seamen, etc., are listed among captives in Babylon in a text dating from 592. Presumably they were taken at this time. For the text, cf. E. F. Weidner, *Mélanges syriens offerts à M. René Dussaud*, Vol. II (Paris: Paul Geuthner, 1939), pp. 923–35.

opportunity. Three years later (in 601) he thought he saw his chance. Late in that year, as the Babylonian Chronicle tells us, Nebuchadnezzar moved against Egypt and was met by Necho in a pitched battle near the frontier. The details of this engagement are unknown but, since Nebuchadnezzar returned home afterward and spent the following year reorganizing his army, it was certainly no Babylonian victory. Presumably encouraged by this, Jehoiakim rebelled (II Kings xxiv 1). It was a fatal mistake. Though Nebuchadnezzar was unable to bring his main army to bear at once, he immediately ordered such Babylonian contingents as were available in the area, together with auxiliary troops from the Aramean lands, Moab and Ammon (II Kings xxiv 2), to move against Judah and do what damage they could; apparently, in outlying areas, this was considerable (cf. Jer xxxv 11). Finally, in December 598, the Babylonian army marched. In that very month Jehoiakim died; since he was responsible for the nation's predicament and *persona non grata* with the Babylonians, it is quite likely that he was assassinated in the hope of gaining milder treatment thereby (cf. Jer xxii 18 f.; xxxvi 30). His son Jehoiachin, an eighteen-year-old boy, was placed on the throne (II Kings xxiv 8), and within three months Jerusalem surrendered. Nebuchadnezzar, apparently somewhat appeased, behaved with relative leniency. Contenting himself with deporting the king, the queen mother, the court officials, military leaders, and skilled artisans to Babylon, and seizing a considerable booty, he allowed the little state to continue in existence, placing the king's uncle Zedekiah, another of Josiah's sons, on the throne as his vassal (II Kings xxiv 10–17). Judah had been granted a brief respite.

5

The events of 598/7 had demonstrated beyond question the overwhelming superiority of Babylonian arms, and one would think that the experience would have taught Judah's rulers the folly of rebellion and constrained them, however reluctantly and tentatively, to accept the inevitable. But clearly the lesson had not been learned. Zedekiah's reign (597–587) saw nothing but continual agitation until the nation, as if possessed with the wish to destroy

itself, finally succeeded in doing just that. Within ten years the
end had come.

Wise leadership was lacking. The deportation of 597, though not
in itself large,[14] had cost the country its ablest and most experienced leaders; the nobles who were left to guide its policies seem
all to have been ultranationalists of the most reckless sort. Zedekiah,
although he appears to have been well-intentioned (cf. Jer xxxvii
17–21; xxxviii 7–28), was a weakling unable to control them,
and fearful of popular opinion as well (Jer xxxviii 5, 19). It must
be said, in fairness, that Zedekiah was very young (he was only
twenty-one at his accession; II Kings xxiv 18), and that his
position was ambiguous in that his nephew Jehoiachin was still
regarded as the legitimate king. It is true that Zedekiah is called
"king" in all of our sources; but his position seems actually to have
been that of a regent. Texts discovered in Babylon mention
Jehoiachin as a pensioner of the court there, and refer to him as the
"king of Judah,"[15] while jar handles found in Palestine bearing
the inscription, "Eliakim, steward of Jehoiachin," show that the
crown property was still his. Jews in Babylon even reckoned dates
from the year of his exile—which was also the first (and only)
official year of his reign (Ezek i 2, etc.). Many in Judah felt similarly and longed for his speedy return (Jer xxviif.). Indeed, a theological madness was abroad, the belief that Yahweh would soon
intervene to break the power of Babylon and bring the exiled king
home. All this produced a ferment which Zedekiah, his authority
undercut as it was by the ambiguity of his position, could not control.

An explosion was narrowly averted in Zedekiah's fourth year
(594/3). During the previous year (cf. the Babylonian Chronicle)
there had been an uprising in Babylon in which (judging from Jer
xxix) some of the deported Jews, incited to disorderly acts by the
wild promises of their prophets, seem to have been involved. We
cannot say how far this unrest among the Jews carried, but certain

[14] II Kings xxiv 14, 16 give 10,000 and 8000 respectively, which are probably
rough estimates. Jer lii 58 gives the precise figure of 3023, which may count
only adult males. Or the figure may be taken from a Babylonian list giving
the number of prisoners actually delivered, i.e., those who survived the
march.

[15] See W. F. Albright, "King Joiachin in Exile" (BA 5 [1942], 49–55),
now reprinted in *The Biblical Archaeologist Reader*, pp. 106–12. For the text
in question see the work cited in n.[13], above.

of their prophets were executed by Nebuchadnezzar, undoubtedly because of their seditious utterances. Although this rebellion was rather quickly suppressed, it apparently stirred hopes throughout the west that Babylon was cracking, for in 594/3 we find ambassadors of Edom, Moab, Ammon, Tyre, and Sidon (Jer xxvii 3) foregathered in Jerusalem to discuss plans for revolt. There too, prophets were inciting the people, telling them that Yahweh had broken the yoke of Babylon and would, within two years (Jer xxviii 2–4), bring Jehoiachin and the other exiles triumphantly back to their homeland. Jeremiah's vigorous opposition to talk of this sort will concern us in a later chapter. Suffice it to say that he denounced it as a lie and urged the people to remain submissive to Babylon. And the projected rebellion was in fact abandoned, though whether because Egyptian backing could not be secured, or because the conspirators could not agree among themselves, or because of other reasons, we do not know. Zedekiah sent envoys to Babylon (Jer xxix 3), and may even have gone himself (Jer li 59), to assure Nebuchadnezzar of his loyalty.

This amounted, however, only to a temporary postponement. Five years later (by 589), borne along on a wave of patriotic fervor and supported by confidence of divine assistance, Judah was in open rebellion. We do not know by what steps the nation was committed to this course. The Bible tells us nothing, and the Babylonian Chronicle breaks off with 594 and does not resume until 557. There was certainly an understanding with Egypt, whose pharaohs, Psammetichus II (594–589) and his son Hophra (589–570), were once more actively intervening in the affairs of western Asia. Nevertheless, revolt does not seem to have been widespread. So far as we know, only Tyre, to which Nebuchadnezzar subsequently laid siege, and Ammon (cf. Jer xl 13–xli 15; Ezek xxi 18–32 [vss. 23–37H][16]) were involved; other neighboring states were apparently lukewarm or hostile to the idea, with Edom even coming in finally on the side of the Babylonians (cf. Obad vss. 8–14; Lam iv 21 f.; Ps cxxxvii 7). Zedekiah himself, judging by his repeated consultations with Jeremiah (Jer xxi 1–7; xxxvii 3–10, 17; xxxviii 14–23), was far from assured in his own mind, but unable to withstand the enthusiasm of his nobles.

The Babylonians reacted swiftly. Probably by the autumn of

[16] Whenever a citation of verse is followed by the initial H or E, it refers to a variant numbering as between the Hebrew and English texts.

589 their army had arrived in Palestine and begun operations. The Babylonian strategy was to drive Judah's forces—such as they could not destroy in the field—back upon their fortified cities, which they then reduced one by one, meanwhile holding Jerusalem under an ever-tighter blockade. The details of the action cannot be traced. We only know (II Kings xxv 1; Jer lii 4) that by January 588 Jerusalem was under siege, and that (cf. Jer xxxiv 6 f.) operations against outlying strong points went forward until, finally, only Lachish (Tell ed-Duweir, in southwest Judah, at the edge of the coastal plain) and Azekah (Tell ez-Zakarīyah, in the foothills some eleven miles to the northeast) still held out. This phase of the operations is graphically illustrated by the Lachish Ostraca (a group of twenty-one letters written on pieces of broken pottery found in the ruins of Lachish in 1935 and 1938).[17] In one of these letters (IV), an officer in charge of what may have been an observation post informs the garrison commander at Lachish that he is watching for his fire signals, since he can no longer see those of Azekah. We may assume from this that Azekah, too, had by this time fallen. As reverses such as this followed one upon another, morale in Judah sank, and many even of the country's leaders were overwhelmed by a spirit of defeatism. This too is illustrated from the Lachish Letters, in one of which (VI) it is complained that some of the princes "weaken the hands [i.e., the morale] of the people"— the very thing of which Jeremiah was accused (Jer xxxviii 4)!

But then, probably in the summer of 588, the beleaguered land was given new hope. News came that the Egyptians were advancing to the rescue. Perhaps the Egyptians moved in response to a direct appeal by Zedekiah, for still another of the Lachish Letters (III) tells us that the commander of Judah's army had gone to Egypt at about this time. The Egyptian advance, at any rate, brought a brief respite, for the Babylonians were forced to lift their blockade of Jerusalem and move to meet this new threat (cf. Jer xxxvii 5). A wave of relief swept over the city, and hopes soared, as passages in Jeremiah indicate (cf. xxxiv 8–11; xxxvii 3–10). But not for long. Nebuchadnezzar's forces made short work of the Egyptians, and soon—within a few weeks, one imagines—were back at Jerusalem and had resumed the siege in earnest.

Though Jerusalem continued to resist with incredible stubborn-

[17] Cf. ANET, pp. 321–22 for a translation of some of them, with further bibliography. Most of them date to 589/8.

ness for approximately a year longer, its case was hopeless. Zedekiah wished to surrender (Jer xxxviii 14–23), but feared to do so. In July 587 (Jer lii 5 f.), just as the city's food supply was exhausted, the Babylonians breached the walls and poured in. Zedekiah with some of his soldiers fled in the night toward the Jordan (II Kings xxv 3 ff.; Jer lii 7 ff.), no doubt hoping to reach temporary safety in Ammon. But Babylonian troops overtook him near Jericho and brought him as a prisoner to Nebuchadnezzar's headquarters at Riblah in central Syria. Nebuchadnezzar showed him no mercy. Having forced him to witness the execution of his own sons, he caused him to be blinded and taken in chains to Babylon, where he died. A month later (II Kings xxv 8 ff.; Jer lii 12 ff.) Nebuzaradan, commander of the royal bodyguard, arrived in Jerusalem and, acting on Nebuchadnezzar's orders, put the city to the torch and leveled its walls. Various ecclesiastical, military, and civil officials, together with certain of the citizenry, were hauled before Nebuchadnezzar at Riblah and executed, while others of the population were rounded up and deported to Babylon.[18] The state of Judah had ended.

The land was a shambles. As archaeological evidence testifies, all, or virtually all, of the fortified towns of Judah's heartland had been razed to the ground, most of them not to be rebuilt for generations to come. Only in the Negeb, which had probably been separated from Judah in 597, and in the district north of Jerusalem, did towns escape destruction. The population that remained was sparse indeed. Aside from those deported to Babylon, thousands must have died in battle or of starvation and disease; a considerable number— surely more than we know of—had been executed, while others had fled for their lives. Those left in the land were chiefly poor peasants (II Kings xxv 12; Jer lii 16) whom Nebuchadnezzar considered incapable of stirring up trouble. Nebuchadnezzar first tried the experiment of organizing the ruined land within the provincial system of the empire. As its governor he appointed one Gedaliah, a man of noble family whose father Ahikam had been one of Josiah's ministers and a leader in the reform (he once saved Jeremiah's life; Jer xxvi 24), and who had himself (as a seal bearing his name found at Lachish indicates) apparently been chief minister in

---

[18] The exact figure of 832 persons (Jer lii 29) seems to include only those taken from the urban population of Jerusalem. On this figure, see the remarks in n.14.

Zedekiah's cabinet. In all likelihood because Jerusalem was no longer inhabitable, the new governor placed the seat of his administration at Mizpah (probably Tell en-Naṣbeh, about eight miles north of the city).

But this experiment soon failed (Jer xl–xliv; cf. II Kings xxv 22 ff.). Though Gedaliah sought to conciliate the people, and labored to restore the land to some semblance of normalcy, diehards regarded him as a collaborationist. How long his period of office lasted we do not know, since our biblical sources do not state the year in which it ended. The account in Jeremiah leaves the impression that it lasted but a few months—though it may have been a year or two, or even longer.[19] In any event, a plot to kill him was hatched by one Ishmael, a member of the royal house, with the backing of the king of Ammon, whither Ishmael had fled and where unrest still continued. Though Gedaliah had been warned of this, he was apparently too high-minded to believe it. As a reward for his trustfulness, he was treacherously struck down by Ishmael and his fellow conspirators, together with such of his friends as were with him at the time and a small party of Babylonian troops that happened to be in Mizpah; a senseless massacre of innocent individuals then followed. In spite of energetic pursuit by Gedaliah's men, Ishmael made good his escape to Ammon. Gedaliah's people, quite naturally fearing Nebuchadnezzar's vengeance, resolved to flee to Egypt; and this they did in spite of Jeremiah's strenuous protests, taking that prophet with them. In 582 (Jer lii 30) Nebuchadnezzar ordered a third deportation from Judah, and this may represent a belated reprisal for these disorders. It is probable that at this time the province of Judah was abolished and the bulk of its territory incorporated into the neighboring province of Samaria. But of the details we have no information.

Here the story, so far as it concerns us, ends. At this point darkness descends upon the land of Judah, a darkness that does not lift until more than forty years later when, the Babylonian empire having been destroyed by Cyrus the Persian, exiled Jews were allowed to return to their homeland and resume their life as a people there.

---

[19] For further discussion see COMMENT on Sec. 34.

THE BOOK OF JEREMIAH: ITS STRUCTURE, COMPOSITION, AND MAJOR CRITICAL PROBLEMS

Before attempting to sketch the career and message of Jeremiah against the background of the events described in the preceding chapter, it is necessary first of all to say a few words regarding the Book of Jeremiah itself.[1] This would have to be done in any case, since for the appreciation of any book some understanding of its composition, arrangement, the type of literature it contains, and the like, is essential. And because of the fact that, our entire knowledge of Jeremiah being derived from his book, the reconstruction that one offers of the prophet's life and message will inevitably depend upon one's understanding of the book and the critical problems attaching to it, it is particularly desirable that these matters be given some attention at this point.

Now a chapter such as this presents both its writer and its readers with a problem, and it would be well to face up to it frankly at the outset. It is a problem to which, so far as I know, no satisfactory solution has been found—or, perhaps, can be found. The problem, in a word, is that while such a chapter is necessary if the reader is to be introduced to the life and words of the prophet, no really satisfactory place for it seems to exist. It is an essential preliminary to the intelligent perusal of the book, yet the very reading of it necessarily requires some familiarity with the book if the argument is to be followed. A vicious circle, certainly, and one that has, I am sure, troubled everyone who has ever attempted an introduction to a book of the Bible. (One recent commentator on Jeremiah[2] has even placed his chapter on the subject at the very end of his volume —which, if it cannot be said to solve the problem, at least indicates a clear awareness of it!) The present chapter contains, as such

[1] This chapter follows in part the outline of my article, "The Book of Jeremiah: Its Structure, Its Problems, and Their Significance for the Interpreter," *Interpretation* 9 (1955), 259–78.

[2] Weiser (see Selected Bibliography for complete reference).

chapters usually do, a great many references to passages in the text of the book. Indeed, there are far more of these than I could wish, and I fear that the reader will grow tired of looking them up. Yet I know of no help for this if the chapter is not to be lengthened unduly by liberal quotations. The reader who is not familiar with the Book of Jeremiah might do well to undertake an initial reading of the discussion that follows (the same could be said of the next chapter, too) merely with the aim of gaining a general impression, and then perhaps return to it, should he desire to do so, after having confronted the book at first hand.

1

It cannot be denied that the Book of Jeremiah makes, at least on first trial, extremely difficult reading. The same could be said, for that matter, of most of the prophetic books. Nor is this entirely because these books so often allude to persons, situations, and events of which the reader can hardly be expected to know, or because they presuppose viewpoints, develop concepts, and use terminology unfamiliar to him. These are, to be sure, real difficulties. But they are, after all, difficulties that inhere in the attempt to understand any ancient literature, and are only to be expected. What makes these books particularly, and one might say needlessly, difficult is the very manner of their arrangement—or, to be more accurate, their apparent lack of arrangement. The reader who meets them for the first time is likely to be quite at a loss. All seems confusion. There is no narrative for him to follow, nor can he trace any logical progression running through them and binding their parts together into a coherent whole. No sooner has he grasped a line of thought, and prided himself that he is following it tolerably well, than it breaks off and something quite different is being discussed. The impression he gains is one of extreme disarray; one can scarcely blame him for concluding that he is reading a hopeless hodgepodge thrown together without any discernible principle of arrangement at all.

This is, to be sure, dismaying. Yet, if it is an observation that has caused many a reader to give up in despair, it is nevertheless a sound one, and the beginning of understanding. The prophetic books are indeed not books (i.e., literary productions from the pen of an author or authors) as we understand the term. Nor are they books in the sense that most of the New Testament writings (e.g., the Gospels or the Pauline epistles)—or, for that matter, various of the writings of the Old Testament (e.g., the historical books Joshua through II Kings)—are books. They are, rather, collections of prophetic sayings and other material which have a long and complex history of transmission behind them. The more carefully one studies them, the more apparent this becomes.

The careful reader will, it is true, detect in the Jeremiah book (and in other prophetic books as well) certain obvious grand divisions which bear the earmarks of having at one time had separate existence one from another. In other words, one gains the impression that the Jeremiah book is a collection of shorter "books," plus miscellaneous material. The conclusion of one such book is to be seen in xxv 1–13a (through "all that is written in this book").[3] This is even more apparent in the Septuagint text (the Septuagint, or LXX, is the Greek translation of the Old Testament made in Egypt in the course of the last three centuries B.C.) which, having omitted all reference to Babylon in the preceding verses, concludes vs. 13 at this point and then, omitting vs. 14 entirely, inserts between vss. 13 and 15 the whole of chapters xlvi–li (in a different order).[4] But if xxv 1–13a forms the conclusion of a book, the original scope of that book is indicated by vss. 1–3, where the date of 605 is given, and where it is declared that Jeremiah had at that time preached without interruption for twenty-three years, ever since his call in 627 (cf. i 2). In view of this fact, and in view of verbal and thematic similarities between this passage and chapter i (especially vss. 15–19), it is hard to resist the conclusion that chapter i (in its present form) and xxv 1–13a are companion pieces, the beginning and ending of a Jeremiah book that originally included words of his uttered between his call and the fourth year of Jehoiakim (605). That this time-span coincides with that covered by the scroll which Jeremiah dictated in 605 (cf. ch. xxxvi) has not escaped attention, some scholars even believing that we

---

[3] Let it be repeated that, in order to follow the discussion here, the reader should refer to the translated text. He will observe that the material is there presented according to the grand divisions described in this and the ensuing paragraphs.

[4] See further the COMMENT on ch. xxv (Sec. 20). In LXX the last words of vs. 13 ("which Jeremiah prophesied against all the nations") appear as the heading of vss. 15–38, which are placed after chs. xlvi–li.

have in xxv 1–13a the conclusion of that scroll.[5] It is true that chapters i–xxiv as they now stand contain a great deal of material that is later than 605. But this is best explained on the supposition that this book, circulating as a separate Jeremiah book—to some, no doubt, the only Jeremiah book known—in the course of time had other and later Jeremiah material inserted into it.

Chapters xlvi–li, which consist of oracles directed against foreign nations, comprise another separate "book," the heading of which appears (in the Hebrew text, or Masoretic text [MT] as it is called) in xlvi 1. Similar blocks of material are to be found in other prophetic books.[6] The relationship of these sayings to Jeremiah does not concern us here; some of them are undoubtedly his, others apparently anonymous. But that they had a separate history of transmission is evident, and is witnessed to by the fact noted above that they appear in the LXX at a different place and in a different order from that found in the Hebrew Bible (MT) and our English versions.

A third "book" is introduced in xxx 1–3. This book includes all of chapters xxx–xxxi, and perhaps xxxii–xxxiii as well, and contains practically the whole of Jeremiah's message of hope (it is sometimes referred to as "The Book of Consolation"). As one can readily see, xxx–xxxi hang together about, and develop, the theme struck in xxx 3 ("For look! The days are coming—Yahweh's word —when I will reverse the fortunes of my people . . . and restore them to the land that I gave to their fathers—"); xxxii, the basis of which is a biographical incident, has the same theme, as does xxxiii. The entire section stands as a separate block of material in the midst of a series of chapters mostly biographical in character (xxvi–xxix; xxxiv–xlv).

We have, then, what appear to be three separate Jeremiah "books": i 1–xxv 13a; xxx–xxxi (xxxii–xxxiii); and xlvi–li. Between the first of these and the second, and between the second and the third, there lie, as we have indicated, a series of biographical narratives. These have been blocked together, and arranged chronologically, in the translation that follows. The conclusion of the Jeremiah book (ch. lii), like that of the first part of the Book of Isaiah (cf. Isa xxxvi–xxxix), takes the form of a historical appen-

[5] Or its preface, as some think. For discussion, see the COMMENT *ad loc.*
[6] For example, Isa xiii–xxiii (for the most part); Ezek xxv–xxxii; all of Nahum and Obadiah; Zeph ii 4–15.

dix. This tells of the fall of Jerusalem—the crucial event of Jeremiah's lifetime—and repeats for the most part material found in II Kings xxiv–xxv.

But to point out these various separate "books" does little to alleviate the reader's difficulty. For it is plain that even these are not books as we understand the term. On the contrary, each of them shares the character of the Jeremiah book as a whole: they give the impression of being loose collections without any plan of arrangement consistently carried through. Certainly—and this must be stressed—no part of the Jeremiah book is arranged in chronological order, and any conclusions based upon the assumption that such is the case are false conclusions. For example, one has only to check the dates given at the beginning of the various biographical incidents in chapters xxvi–xxix; xxxiv–xlv, or note the order in which these chapters are given in the translation, in order to see that their arrangement in the book has nothing whatever to do with chronology. As for chapters xxx–xxxi, these provide us, as we shall see, with some of Jeremiah's earliest utterances, side by side with material from 587 and after. Chapters i–xxv do, it is true, begin with Jeremiah's call in 627 and conclude with the "book" of the year 605, thus conveying the impression that their material falls between these dates. And such may originally have been the case. But that these chapters now contain later material is obvious (e.g., xxi 1–10; xxii 24–xxiii 8; xxiv). And, even leaving such material aside, the arrangement is not otherwise consistently chronological; one cannot assume, here any more than elsewhere, that early position in the book argues per se for early date, late position for later date.

If any principle of arrangement can be observed, it would seem on the surface to be a topical one. Thus chapters i–xxv contain words of censure, warning, and judgment, chapters xxx–xxxiii a message of hope, chapters xlvi–li oracles directed against foreign nations, the rest biography. And yet, even though the principle of arrangement followed seems in general to be a topical one, it must be said that it is not consistently carried out. Thus, for example, chapters i–xxv, mostly of warning and judgment, do contain oracles of hope (e.g., iii 11–18; xvi 14–15; xxiii 1–8); and chapters xxx–xxxiii, mostly of hope, are nevertheless not without words of doom (xxxii 28–35). Moreover, even where a topical arrangement is most obviously intended (as in xxx–xxxiii; xlvi–li), one finds no trace of inner coherence, or of a clearly developing progress of thought. The impression of disorder with which one begins is only strengthened.

Matters are further complicated by the presence in the Jeremiah book of various types of material. This is something that may be observed in other prophetic books as well, but nowhere is it more marked than here. Most noticeably, as a glance at the translated text will show, the Book of Jeremiah is partly in prose, partly in poetry, these being present in almost equal proportions. Moreover, not all of the poetry is of the same type, nor is all the prose. For example, the reader observes that Jeremiah now speaks for himself in the first person, now speaks in the name of God in the same person, now is spoken of in the third person. True, it is not so simple as that; but the reader who sees as much is by way of becoming a Form Critic.

As is universally agreed, there are three major types of material in the Jeremiah book: poetic sayings, biographical prose, and prose discourses. The presence of these types was noted long ago by B. Duhm[7] who believed that the Jeremiah book came into being through the editing together of the prophetic writings of Jeremiah and the biographical narratives of Baruch, with expansions by Deuteronomistic redactors (i.e., Exilic and post-Exilic protagonists of the theology of Deuteronomy and of Josiah's reform who, in the view of Duhm and others, edited the Jeremiah book). Duhm's criteria were further developed and applied by various scholars, particularly S. Mowinckel[8] who, with greater stress on the role of oral tradition, designated the three types A, B, and C respectively. We shall return in a moment to describe these types in greater detail, for they are an important key to the understanding of the book. They do not, however, furnish any key to its arrangement, but rather add to its chaotic appearance, for the book is certainly not arranged according to its literary types. On the contrary, these are found commingled through its various parts in what can only be called a grand disarray.

Confusing as all this is, it nevertheless provides us with our cue for the understanding of the composition of the Jeremiah book, which

[7] Duhm (see Selected Bibliography for complete reference), pp. XI–XX.
[8] S. Mowinckel, *Zur Komposition des Buches Jeremia* (Oslo [Kristiana]: J. Dybwad, 1914). More recently cf. Mowinckel, *Prophecy and Tradition* (Oslo: J. Dybwad, 1946); also Rudolph (see Selected Bibliography for complete reference), pp. XIII–XVII.

was nothing if not a long and complex process: it is the merit of recent research that it has fully recognized that fact. Our notions of what books are and how they are written are scarcely applicable here at all. We are accustomed to speak of the canonical prophets as the "writing prophets" to distinguish them from earlier prophets, such as Elijah or Elisha, whose collected sayings have not been preserved. This causes us to picture the prophet at his desk producing the book that bears his name, much as a modern author would. But the process was nothing of the kind. It is evident from what has been said that neither the Jeremiah book, nor prophetic books generally, were produced in that way at all; they could not possibly have been written by a single hand, or even collected by a single hand, in the order in which we now have them. To understand the books of the prophets as books in the modern sense is to misunderstand them. They are, rather, collections of collections—anthologies if you wish—which were brought together by many hands over a considerable period of time.

This does not, of course, mean that the prophets could not or did not write, or that the composition of their books was not also a literary process. It is likely that most of the prophets could write. As for Jeremiah, the fact that on occasion he dictated his words may mean that he did not write with facility, or it may not: Paul, who was anything but illiterate, seems habitually to have dictated (I Cor xvi 21; Col iv 18; II Thess iii 17). In any event, it is certain that the first steps in the composition of the Jeremiah book were accomplished by the prophet himself. One thinks particularly of the scroll that he prepared in 605 for public reading in the temple (ch. xxxvi). Now it is futile, one thinks, to speculate regarding the precise contents of this scroll; commentators who do so are indulging in guesswork. All that one can say with assurance is that it contained a selection of the prophet's words uttered between 627 and 605, or a digest of them,[9] and that in comparison to the length of the present book it was relatively brief (but perhaps the equivalent of a number of chapters)—for it was read aloud thrice in a single day (xxxvi 10, 15, 21) with appropriate intervals between. The

[9] Most scholars would seek the contents of the scroll among the poetic oracles of Jeremiah (Type A). Some, however, would find it in the prose discourses (Type C): cf. O. Eissfeldt, *Einleitung in das Alte Testament* (Tübingen: J. C. B. Mohr, 2d ed., 1956), pp. 424–26; Oesterley and Robinson, *Introduction to the Books of the Old Testament* (New York: Macmillan, 1934), p. 306. The question is not to be settled dogmatically.

scroll, as we know, was destroyed by Jehoiakim, but was subsequently recreated by Jeremiah with the addition of further sayings (xxxvi 32). But, again, we do not know which sayings these were, nor can we be sure whether they were added when the scroll was rewritten, or gradually over a period of time, or both. Be that as it may, in this scroll, and in other evidences of writing on Jeremiah's part (such as the letter described in ch. xxix) we may see the first steps in the composition of the Jeremiah book.

Nevertheless, the completed book stood only at the end of a long and intricate process. Nor was this process one that involved literary activity alone, as many older scholars were inclined to believe—say the editing together of a book of Jeremiah's sayings and a book of Baruch's memoirs, with expansions and additions by later redactors.[10] On the contrary, full place must be allowed for the oral transmission of the material. After all, we must remember that although writing was known throughout Israel's entire history, books were few, writing materials scarce, and the rate of illiteracy undoubtedly quite high; vast bodies of literature, especially in the earlier periods, were handed down primarily by word of mouth. As for the prophets, they did not formally publish their oracles—they preached them. We may assume that their words were heard, remembered, passed on from mouth to mouth, and often not written down until after a longer or shorter lapse of time. Oral tradition certainly played its part in the transmission of their sayings and in the collection of the material found in their books.

To be sure, we must not overplay this feature as some have done, as though the bulk of the literature of the Bible was transmitted orally until post-Exilic times.[11] This is, on the face of it, incredible. The written tradition began early and existed side by side with the oral.[12] In the case of Jeremiah, we know that the written tradition

[10] For example, Duhm; more recently, R. H. Pfeiffer, *Introduction to the Old Testament* (New York: Harper & Bros., 1941), pp. 504–11.

[11] This is the view of various Scandinavian scholars, following principles laid down by H. S. Nyberg, *Studien zum Hoseabuche* (*Uppsala Universitets Årsskrift*, 1935). One thinks especially of I. Engnell, but also, in varying degrees of H. Birkeland, S. Mowinckel, E. Nielsen, and others. For an evaluation, see G. W. Anderson, HTR 43 (1950), 239–56 or, more briefly, C. R. North, *The Old Testament and Modern Study*, ed. H. H. Rowley (Oxford: Clarendon Press, 1951), pp. 76–81.

[12] See especially G. Widengren, *Literary and Psychological Aspects of the Hebrew Prophets* (*Uppsala Universitets Årsskrift*, 1948); and recently, A. H. J. Gunneweg, *Mündliche und schriftliche Tradition der vorexilischen Prophetenbücher* (Göttingen: Vandenhoeck and Ruprecht, 1959).

had begun by the year 605, and almost certainly earlier, since there is no reason to assume that Jeremiah dictated his scroll by a sheer feat of memory. Moreover, we ought not to lay one-sided stress on the role played by "schools" of the prophets' disciples in the oral transmission of their sayings for, after all, though we may assume that the prophets gained disciples, we know little or nothing about them. At any rate, where the prophetic books are concerned, it is not a question of literary activity *or* oral tradition, but of both. We must assume that the two interacted, the oral tradition sifting, shaping, grouping, and supplementing the material, the written tradition serving as a control on the vagaries of the oral. Out of this interaction, and after a long and complex process, the prophetic books as we know them came into being. The very complexity of the process accounts for their seeming disarray.

2

The Jeremiah book as we have it came into being through the gradual coalescing of various streams of Jeremiah tradition. The basic components of the book are the three types of material which have been noted above, and which are for convenience designated, following Mowinckel, as A, B, and C. Though there is room for disagreement in the allocating of material among them, the three together make up the bulk of the book's contents and are an important key to its understanding. Some further description of them is, therefore, in order. The ideal procedure would be to quote examples of each of these types in full (and of the various subtypes that are possible) in order that the reader might follow the discussion without the necessity of turning to some other part of the book. But to do this would take pages. The few examples that are given in the ensuing paragraphs are intended merely to suggest to the reader in a general way what the various types are. He is urged, here especially, to follow through by looking up in the translated text at least a sampling of the passages that will be referred to, in order to fill out the picture.

Type A consists primarily of the prophetic oracles of Jeremiah. The bulk of the material in the pre-Exilic prophetic books is of this type, and to it the greater part of the poetry in the Jeremiah book belongs. Here we have brief addresses (or fragments of same) cast in metrical form,[13] in which the prophet publicly proclaimed the word of Yahweh. These normally follow formalized—though by no means rigidly formalized—patterns. They are characterized by the fact that in them the prophet, employing the first person singular of direct address, speaks as the mouthpiece of Yahweh: the "I" is Yahweh, not the prophet. Examples of this type of address may be culled at random from almost any part of the book (save the biographical narratives). A few must suffice here to illustrate the point, and even these will not be quoted in full. In ii 2b–3 an oracle begins as follows:

> This is what Yahweh has said:
> I remember your youthful devotion,
>   Your bridal love,
> How you followed me through the desert,
>   The untilled land.
> Israel was Yahweh's own portion,
>   His harvest's first yield.
> All eating of it are held guilty;
>   Punishment overtakes them—Yahweh's word.

In ii 4 f. another oracle begins:

> Hear the word of Yahweh, O house of Jacob,
>   All you clans of Israel's stock!
> This is what Yahweh has said:
> "What was it your fathers found wrong in me
>   That they departed from me so far
> And, following 'Lord Delusion,'
>   Deluded became?"

Or, to take one further example, in iv 5 f. a saying begins as follows:

> Proclaim it in Judah!
> Spread the news in Jerusalem! Say,

[13] It is, in my opinion, more methodical to restrict the designation A to poetic sayings, and to include under it all poetic sayings transmitted as Jeremiah's, regardless of the fact that some of them are later and anonymous. At the same time, I should classify under Type C all discourses couched in the distinctive style of the Jeremiah prose, by no means implying in doing so (see below) that genuine sayings of Jeremiah may not have been uttered in prose. In other words, neither category involves a prior judgment regarding the genuineness of the material assigned to it. For a somewhat different allocation of the material, see Rudolph.

"Sound a blast on the horn through the land!
Shout aloud, and say,
'Band together! Let us get
To the fortified towns!'
Hoist toward Zion the signal!
Get to safety! Do not wait!
For I'm bringing calamity out of the north,
A shatt'ring disaster."

In each of these cases it is clear that Yahweh is conceived of as speaking through the prophet's mouth. Prophetic oracles of this sort are normally introduced by certain characteristic formulae, for example (as in the ones just quoted), "This is what Yahweh has said," or the imperative. Other typical introductory formulae will be noted in the course of the COMMENTS. One cannot, to be sure, apply such criteria mechanically in delineating the various oracles, for often only fragments of oracles have been preserved, while, equally often, a number of oracles, or fragments of oracles, have been linked together either in the course of oral transmission, or editorially, to form a more or less continuous discourse (ch. ii is a good example). In such cases it is not always easy to decide where one unit leaves off and another begins. Nevertheless, in reading this type of material, one must always begin by isolating the various shorter units, for no original connection between an oracle and what precedes it and follows it may be assumed.

As a subhead under A (perhaps better as a separate type) we should list another class of material which is virtually peculiar to the Jeremiah book: the "confessions." Although it is true that other prophets frequently speak in the first person and tell of their experiences, there is no real parallel to these little self-revelations in which Jeremiah lays bare before us his most intimate feelings.[14]

14 H. Graf Reventlow, *Liturgie und prophetisches Ich bei Jeremia* (Gütersloher Verlagshaus Gerd Mohn, 1963) appeared while the manuscript of this book was in the hands of the publisher. I regret that it is impossible to give Reventlow's views extended discussion. I can only say that I am not convinced by his cultic-ritual interpretation of these and other passages in the book (e.g., the account of Jeremiah's call in ch. i), and continue to regard them as authentic reflections of actual experiences in the prophet's life. Cf. G. Fohrer's remarks concerning this trend in criticism (essentially a misapplication of form-critical method) in JBL 80 (1961), 309–12, with which I am in fundamental agreement. Note should also be taken here of the more restricted study of E. Gerstenberger, "Jeremiah's Complaints: Observations on Jer. 15:10–21" (JBL 82 [1963], 393–408), which has likewise recently

Within this classification one should properly place not only those matchless passages telling of the prophet's inner struggle which are usually labeled his "confessions" (xi 18–xii 6; xv 10f., 15–21; xvii 14–18; xviii 18–23; xx 7–13, 14–18), but also those numerous other passages where Jeremiah, speaking in the first person, gives vent to his anguish or tells of his thoughts (e.g., iv 19–21; v 3–5; viii 18–23 [ix 1E]). Characteristic of such passages is the fact that in them Jeremiah speaks in his own name: the "I" is not Yahweh, as in the oracles, but the prophet himself. Note, for example, the beginning of one of the confessions (xx 7):

> You seduced me, Yahweh, and I let you;
>> You seized and overcame me.
> I've become a daylong joke,
>> They all make fun of me.

Or, note the confession that begins in xx 14:

> Cursed be the day
>> Whereon I was born!
> The day my mother bore me,
>> Be it ever unblessed!

Obviously, in these passages Jeremiah is speaking for himself, not for his God. The same is true of such a passage as iv 19–21, which begins:

> O my bowels, my bowels! I writhe!
>> O walls of my heart!
> My heart is in storm within me,
>> I cannot be still.
> You have heard, O my soul, the trumpet blast,
>> The battle shout.

It is quite possible that most pieces of this sort were never spoken publicly, but were heard only by the prophet's inmost circle of friends. Although they have been transmitted in connection with other material—in some cases (e.g., in ch. iv) interwoven with oracular sayings in such a way that we have side by side the prophet's

appeared, and which would, by a different line of argument, equally forbid us to find biographical material in the confessions. I must express my disagreement both with the method followed in this study and with the conclusions reached.

preaching of doom and his personal agony when that doom came—
our first task is again to isolate the individual unit. Original connection between such pieces and their present context cannot be
assumed.

Type B is biography. Here again, no other prophetic book has
quite the like, although similar excerpts are to be found elsewhere
(e.g., Amos vii 10–17). The bulk of chapters xxvi–xxix; xxxiv–xlv
falls into this class, as do other passages elsewhere in the book. It
is unnecessary to give illustrations here; the reader may turn at random to II, Incidents from the Life of Jeremiah (Secs. 21–35). This
material typically provides us with a narrative account, often with a
wealth of circumstantial detail, in which Jeremiah is referred to in
the third person. Normally each section is introduced with precise
chronological data (e.g., xxvi 1; xxviii 1; xxxvi 1), though this is
not always the case (e.g., xix 14–xx 6). Sometimes the Biographer
has done no more than provide the setting and framework for a
prose discourse of Jeremiah (e.g., xxxiv 1–7); indeed, most of his
accounts embody longer or shorter addresses by the prophet. Occasionally, underlying the Biographer's narrative, one may detect an
autobiographical account (e.g., xxxii 6–16; xxxv) which leads one
to believe that the Biographer now and then drew upon, or recorded,
reminiscences of the prophet himself.[15] We should not, it is true,
speak of a "Jeremiah Biography," for what we have here is no
connected biography of the prophet, but rather a series of vignettes
(out of chronological order, too) describing certain crucial incidents
in his life. Yet, for want of a better word, we may call the creator
of this material the "Biographer." Though it cannot be proved that
he was Baruch, it is entirely likely that he was.[16] At any rate, he
could hardly have been one who was not a contemporary, even an
eyewitness, of the events which he recorded.

Type C, as will appear in a moment, gives rise to the major
critical problem of the book. Here we have prose discourses, cast
in a monotonous, wordy, yet highly rhetorical style, closely akin to

[15] This seems to me the best explanation of these passages; the discourses
of xxxv 12 ff. of course fall into Type C.

[16] The fact that he refers to Baruch in the third person need not argue to
the contrary. One wonders if ch. xlv could have had another source. Note, too,
that the biographical accounts cover the period from 609 (ch. xxvi) to the
end of Jeremiah's career; Baruch is known to have been Jeremiah's intimate
from 605 (chs. xxxvi, xlv) until after 587 (xliii 3). In any event, one cannot
agree with H. G. May (JBL 61 [1942], 139–55) that the Biographer lived
several generations later.

that of Deuteronomy. Characteristically this material is presented in an "autobiographical" framework, in which God addresses Jeremiah and tells him what he is to say or do (e.g., vii 2, 16, 27 f.; xvi 1–13; xviii 1–12; xix 1–13); sometimes this even takes the form of an actual dialogue (xi 1–17). At other times, however, this characteristic style of address is dropped, and the material is cast merely as prose oracles (e.g., xvi 14–18; xxxi 27–34, 38–40; xxxiii). This type of material is found scattered throughout the book. Blocks of it are mingled with the poetry of chapters i–xxv and xxx–xxxi, while not a little entered the book in connection with the work of the Biographer (e.g., xxvii; xxix 16–20; xxxii 17–44; xxxiv 12–22; xxxv 12–17, etc.). In vii 2–15 and in xxvi 2–6 we have a case where the same discourse entered the book at two places, at the second through the agency of the Biographer and in abridged form, at the first independently and, apparently, in full.

To illustrate all the above points is out of the question. One typical example must suffice. The prose discourse in xi 1–17 begins as follows (on the text, see the notes that accompany the translation):

> The word that came to Jeremiah from Yahweh: "Speak to the men of Judah and the citizens of Jerusalem and say to them, 'This is what Yahweh, the God of Israel, has said: Cursed be the man who does not comply with the terms of this covenant, the terms which I laid upon your fathers when I brought them out of the land of Egypt, out of the iron furnace, namely: Obey my voice and do exactly as I command you. Then you will be my people, and I will be your God; and this will allow me to carry out the oath that I swore to your fathers to give them a land flowing with milk and honey, as I have in fact done.'" Then I answered, "Amen, Yahweh!"
>
> Then Yahweh said to me, "Proclaim all these things in the cities of Judah and in the streets of Jerusalem, and say, 'Hear the terms of this covenant and fulfill them! For I solemnly warned your fathers when I brought them up from the land of Egypt. . . .'"

It is unnecessary to quote further. What has been given will suffice to allow the reader a preliminary impression of the characteristic style of these passages, and also to illustrate the typical way in which so many of them are articulated in the form of a conversation between God and the prophet.

Each of these types of material (A, B, and C) had its own history of transmission. The poetic oracles, as has been said, represent a selection of Jeremiah's public preaching. Though most of these oracles cannot be dated with precision, we have them from all periods of Jeremiah's ministry from the beginning onward, the heaviest incidence coming perhaps in the reign of Jehoiakim, and the lightest—for reasons that can only be surmised—in the period between the first deportation in 597 and the end of the prophet's life. These oracles were delivered orally, and were doubtless transmitted orally for a time before being reduced to writing. But there is no reason to assume that this period of oral transmission was necessarily and in every case a long one. Indeed, we know that the prophet dictated certain of his sayings to Baruch in 605. Since we need not assume that he was illiterate, he may well have written down others himself, and it is not beyond belief that he may even on occasion have done this before delivery.[17] As for the "confessions," it is probable that most of these were never uttered publicly, and that a purely oral transmission even within the prophet's circle of friends was very brief, although we may suppose—as we may in the case of the oracles also—that, even after they had been written down, they continued to be repeated orally and, in the process, sifted, supplemented, and grouped with other material.

Aside from the generous quota of textual and exegetical difficulties with which they present us, the poetic sayings in the Jeremiah book give rise to relatively few critical problems. All the "confessions" and the overwhelming majority of the oracles may confidently be held to have come from Jeremiah himself and to represent as close an approximation as is possible of the prophet's *ipsissima verba*. There are some sayings, to be sure, which are of anonymous origin, some of them from a slightly later time than Jeremiah's own. This is only to be expected—and is something, it should be added, that in no way prejudices the worth of the material in question. As sayings of Jeremiah were transmitted among those who were in agreement with his words, it is only natural that some of them should have been expanded and adapted to later

[17] Cf. G. B. Gray, *The Book of Isaiah*, ICC (Edinburgh: T. and T. Clark, 1912), liv, quoted with approval by Widengren, *Literary* . . . , p. 92.

situations; and it is equally natural that, as collections of the prophet's words began to be made, various anonymous sayings that were treasured in the circle of his followers should have been drawn into these collections along with the genuine utterances of the prophet. Yet, instances of this sort, considering the size of the book, are remarkably few. Some of the oracles against foreign nations in chapters xlvi–li are of unknown origin; in xxx–xxxi Jeremiah's words have in places been expanded and applied to the situation of the exiles in Babylon; of the poetry of i–xxv, the poem in x 1–16 is of somewhat later date. Otherwise, disputed portions amount only to a verse or two here and there.[18]

The biographical prose occasions even fewer difficulties. These accounts bear on their face the stamp of authenticity and must have been set down by one, whether Baruch or another, who was a contemporary and an intimate of the prophet. As noted above, "biography" is a misnomer, since we do not have here a real biography of the prophet, but a series of disconnected narratives which tell of certain critical incidents in his life, and which have entered the book in an order that is not chronological. It is probable that these were produced separately, and at first circulated separately. It is, moreover, entirely likely that the Biographer's work was in written form from the beginning—although, of course, the writing itself was doubtless based upon the oral accounts of eyewitnesses as well as the Biographer's own memory; and although, even after having been written down, the stories continued to be related orally and may, in the process, have been verbally expanded and, on occasion, linked with other material.

In the case of the prose discourses (Type C), however, the problem is much more complex. These, as already indicated, are cast in a monotonous, rather inflated style, loaded with stereotyped expressions, which has its closest parallel in the Deuteronomic literature (Deuteronomy, and the framework of the historical books Joshua through II Kings). Material of this sort is found in all parts of the Jeremiah book and comprises, all told, perhaps somewhat more than a quarter of its bulk. The opinion has been widely held that these discourses represent the work of Exilic, or even post-Exilic, "Deuteronomists" (i.e., a school of disciples committed to the aims and ideals of those men who produced the Deuteronomic

---

[18] Critical issues of this sort will be discussed in the COMMENTS *ad locc.*

literature) whose aim it was to present the teachings of Jeremiah
in such a way that the prophet would appear to have been one
who both shared their views and who had, moreover, provided in
advance an explanation of the nation's tragedy in terms of Deuteronomic theology.[19] Not a few scholars have held that this material
badly misrepresents, if it does not completely distort, the mind of
the prophet, and question if one can lay any weight on it in seeking
to reconstruct his message; some have even discarded it altogether,
at least as far as its historical value is concerned.[20] The problem is
a serious one, all the more so because some of the noblest passages
in the book (the "Temple Sermon" in vii 1–15, and the New Covenant passage in xxxi 31–34, to mention only two) are couched in
this rather pedestrian "Deuteronomistic" style.

A thorough discussion of this problem would be out of place in
a book of this sort. I have elsewhere expressed my own views on
the subject at some length.[21] Suffice it here to say that the style of
these discourses, though indeed closely akin to that of the Deuteronomic literature, is a style in its own right with peculiarities
and distinctive expressions of its own; it is by no means glibly to be
classified as "Deuteronomistic." It is, moreover, not a late style, but
a characteristic rhetorical prose of the seventh/sixth centuries. With
this last, internal evidence agrees, for such relevant allusions as
these prose pieces contain suggest that this material was given fixed
form not much after the middle of the Exilic period—thus within
a few decades at most after Jeremiah's death. Though it may well
have undergone some verbal expansion after that time at the hands
of editors and scribes, there is really no reason to place any of it
(or anything in the book, for that matter) after the Exile. These

[19] For a presentation of this view in English, see conveniently J. P. Hyatt,
"Jeremiah and Deuteronomy" (JNES 1 [1942], 156–73)—also other articles
by the same author, as well as his treatment of Jeremiah in *The Interpreter's
Bible*, V, 777–1142 (subsequently, "Hyatt"; for complete reference, see Selected Bibliography). See also H. G. May, JBL 61 (1942), 139–55, who places
this material in the post-Exilic age. For a full listing of relevant literature
and a balanced discussion of the problem, see H. H. Rowley, "The Prophet
Jeremiah and the Book of Deuteronomy" (*Studies in Old Testament Prophecy*, ed. H. H. Rowley [Edinburgh: T. and T. Clark, 1950]), pp. 157–74.
[20] So, long ago, Duhm; cf. pp. xvii f.: "They [the Deuteronomists] have no
interest whatever in the properly historical; they write theology, not history."
So also H. G. May (see n.[19]) and other contemporary scholars; the position
of Hyatt, although similar, is much more moderate.
[21] J. Bright, "The Date of the Prose Sermons of Jeremiah," JBL 70 (1951),
15–35. More recently, see W. L. Holladay, JBL 79 (1960), 351–67.

points ought to be kept firmly in mind in evaluating this material. They should, at least, guard us from too hastily drawing negative conclusions with regard to it. At any rate, one wonders if it is not, to put it mildly, unlikely that any major distortion of Jeremiah's career and message could have been perpetrated at a time when hundreds of people who knew him well still lived.

At the same time, it must be admitted that these discourses scarcely provide us—certainly not as a rule—with Jeremiah's *ipsissima verba*. Though the prose tradition of Jeremiah doubtless had its origin in his preaching, it does not record that preaching verbatim, but rather as it was remembered, understood, and repeated in the circle of his followers. We may suppose that, when Jeremiah preached, his hearers—and these may well have included, and almost certainly did include, men who were in sympathy with the Deuteronomic reform and the theology that undergirded it—often recalled the gist of what he had said without remembering his exact words, and that, as they passed on what they had heard, there grew up a tradition of Jeremiah's preaching based on his words, but not preserving them exactly. Though some of this material seems to have been reduced to writing fairly early (the Biographer, as noted above, on occasion embodied such discourses in his work), it is probable that in general it received fixed form somewhat later than did the poetry and that, even after this had occurred, it continued to be expanded and shaped in transmission. This last may be argued from an observation of the Septuagint (LXX), which characteristically preserves the text of these discourses in a form markedly shorter than that found in the Hebrew Bible (MT). Although the textual traditions behind LXX and MT in all likelihood diverged from a common archetype in the course of scribal rather than oral transmission, the very differences between them, far more marked here than in other parts of the book, would seem to indicate that even after the text of these discourses had been fixed, variant and expanded forms of it continued to circulate.

One must, therefore, allow for the possibility that in the course of this process not merely a verbal expansion of the prophet's words, but also a development and adaptation of his thought, the application of it to new situations, and even on occasion some misunderstanding of it, may have taken place. Nevertheless, let it be repeated, the prose tradition of Jeremiah is in itself no late tradition, but one that developed on the basis of his words and apparently sought to present his message as his followers understood it. In some places, indeed—the "Temple Sermon" in vii 1–15, to cite but one example —the thought is demonstrably consonant with that of the prophet's authentic utterances, and one feels intuitively that a summary of the words actually used by him has been preserved rather exactly; in other places one gains the opposite impression. We are not, however, permitted to operate on this material by the methods of literary criticism, as if by peeling off "non-genuine" accretions we could arrive at the "genuine" words of the prophet. To attempt such a thing is a wholly subjective procedure. Viewed as literature, the prose discourses are a unity and are to be treated as such; they afford no stylistic canon for separating "genuine" from "nongenuine" words. On the other hand, to form a priori notions of what the prophet could and could not say, and then to attempt a separation on that basis, is indefensible and no more than a projection of the critic's own predilections. The only proper course is to accept the prose discourses for the separate Jeremiah tradition that they are, examine each of them for itself, comparing the picture of Jeremiah there given with that afforded by the unquestioned poetic and biographical sections, and then draw such conclusions as seem to be indicated. My own conviction is that, in spite of undeniable verbal differences, the contrast between the Jeremiah of the poetry and the Jeremiah of the prose (and, one might add, between Jeremiah and the "Deuteronomists") has been, by many scholars at least, badly exaggerated.

3

The above types of material, then, represent separate streams of Jeremiah tradition, each with its own more or less complex history of transmission. As these streams converged the Jeremiah book came into being. But the details of the process of grouping, collecting, and editing which finally issued in the completed book are for the most part unknown to us, and can only be surmised.

We may suppose that the first step was taken as separate oracles, confessions, prose discourses, and biographical incidents began to be drawn together in the course of transmission—whether orally or in writing, or both, whether by the prophet's own hand or another's —into short traditionary complexes and these, in turn, into longer editorial units. The basis upon which such groupings were made seems for the most part to have been that of common theme, common occasion, or even catchword. Examples of shorter traditionary complexes may be culled at random from almost every part of the book. Thus in chapter ii various relatively brief oracles, all of them indicting the national sin—most of them coming from the earliest period of Jeremiah's ministry (cf. vs. 18; Assyria is still a world power), but given their present form after the death of Josiah in 609 (cf. vs. 16)—have been drawn together into what almost has the appearance of a single long poem. Again, in iii 1–iv 4 a poetic unit (iii 1–5, 19–25; iv 1–2, 3–4) and a prose complex (iii 6–18), both stressing the nation's "adultery" (i.e., apostasy) and pleading for repentance, have been woven together into a thematic unit. In like manner, in xxi 11–xxiii 8 oracles both in prose and in poetry, which date to various periods between 609 and sometime after 587, have been brought together because of their common theme: "the royal house of Judah" (xxi 11). And, in xxiii 9–40 there is a similar complex of sayings with the theme: "the prophets" (vs. 9). These, and many others, will be described further in the COMMENTS that accompany the text.

Longer units of material, apparently editorial in nature, are likewise to be found everywhere. For example, in chapters i–vi—the components of which are miscellaneous and date, one may believe, all the way from the beginning of Jeremiah's career until at least after 597—one may note a general coherence of arrangement which can hardly be accidental. Thus, in chapter i the prophet is given his call, in which he is made an "overseer" (vs. 10) over the nations, and allowed some inkling of the doom that he must proclaim because of the sinfulness of the people. In chapter ii that sin is indicted at length, as it is in iii 1–iv 2, where an eloquent plea for repentance is added. Then, with iv 3–4 serving as a transition, the threat of judgment is introduced: "lest my wrath break out like fire and burn so that none can quench it." This last supplies the theme for the whole of iv 5–vi 26, which consists of a series of separate sayings and complexes of sayings, all telling of the impending doom. The unit then concludes (vi 27–30) with the sorrowful verdict of the prophet—here the "assayer" of his people—probably uttered after the calamity of 597, to the effect that this "refining" process had brought about no purification of the national character.

Another excellent example may be found in chapters xviii–xx. Here we have pieces representative of all the major types of material in the Jeremiah book drawn together into a unit with an editorial heading (xviii 1). The basis of this unit consists of two prose discourses (xviii 1–12; xix 1–13), which were probably brought together because of the catchword common to both ("potter," "potter's vessel": xviii 2 ff.; xix 1, 10 f.), as well as by the common theme of the national apostasy. To the second of these discourses there is appended a biographical incident (xix 14–xx 6), doubtless because Jeremiah's action in smashing the pot, and his words in that connection, were correctly remembered as the occasion for his being put in the stocks. To the biographical incident, in turn, a block of confessional material has been appended (xx 7–18), perhaps because of the catchword māgōr-missābīb ("terror all around") which occurs in both (vss. 3, 10), perhaps also because it was persecution of this sort that caused the prophet to give vent to his frustration and despair. After the first prose discourse, and before the second, we find a poetic oracle (xviii 13–17), doubtless drawn in because its theme (the national apostasy) is that of both discourses and, in particular, develops the thought of vs. 12 (but note also the catchword "hissing, whistling": xviii 16; xix 8); and a further confessional piece, which is remarkably similar in tone to that of xx 7–13 (cf. xviii 18 and xx 10; xviii 21 ff. and xx 11 f.).

In the course of such a process as the one just described, it is not surprising that the same material should on occasion have entered the book at more than one place. This accounts for the extraordinary number of doublets in the Jeremiah book.[22] When we encounter them, it is usually beside the point to ask in which place such duplicated material is original, and in which secondary.[23] The problem before us is not one of literary criticism. Rather, we have to do with sayings that were uttered separately, and in the first instance transmitted separately, whether orally or in writing, or both; as complexes of material took shape, it would be quite easy for the same saying to be drawn into two or more such complexes, and thus appear in the completed book in more than one

[22] These doublets will be indicated in the COMMENTS. For a convenient listing, see S. R. Driver, *Introduction to the Literature of the Old Testament* (New York: Charles Scribner's Sons, 1913), p. 277. This book is now reprinted in paperback form (Cleveland: Meridian Books).

[23] It is interesting that LXX normally deletes such material on its second occurrence.

context.[24] Whatever the reasons, doublets are numerous. We have poetic sayings repeated in similar, or quite different, connections (e.g., vi 12–15 and viii 10–12; vi 22–24 and 1 41–43; xxiii 19–20 and xxx 23–24, etc.); and we have the same phenomenon in the case of prose sayings (e.g., xvi 14–15 and xxiii 7–8). We also have instances of the same material entering the book both in poetic form and in the form of prose discourse (cf. ii 28 and xi 12–13; xxiii 5–6 and xxxiii 14–16; xxxi 35–37 and xxxiii 19–22); and also as a prose discourse and as a part of a biographical narrative (cf. vii 2–15 and xxvi 2–6).

How much of the grouping of material described above took place in the course of oral transmission, and how much through editorial activity, it is impossible to say. But we must constantly remind ourselves that the writing down of Jeremiah's sayings began early and at the hand—or, more accurately, the lips—of the prophet himself, specifically in the scroll which he dictated to Baruch in the year 605 (ch. xxxvi). This scroll, which originally contained a selection of his preaching through the first twenty-three years of his ministry, no doubt constituted in its recreated form the basis of the material which we now find in chapters i–xxv. We have, therefore, to reckon with the likelihood that many of the above-mentioned complexes and editorial units represent combinations made by the prophet himself. It is true, as has already been indicated, that chapters i–xxv in their present form contain much material that comes from the period after 605, as well as a great deal from before that date that would scarcely have been included in the scroll (not only was the scroll relatively brief, but many of Jeremiah's sayings—and one thinks especially of his confessions—would certainly have been left out as unsuitable for the purposes for which the scroll was intended). We should, however, take our cue from the statement in xxxvi 32: the recreated scroll contained many sayings not found in the original one. This doubtless refers primarily to additions made at the time of rewriting, but it is entirely possible that still further—and later—sayings were inserted as time went on. It was, we may suppose, somewhat in this way that

---

[24] Aside from this, one should probably allow the prophet the right to repeat himself on various occasions—as what modern preacher does not? It may be added that a similar situation obtains in the case of the teachings of Jesus in the Gospels, where it frequently happens that a given saying will appear in more than one of them, but in different contexts; yet in this case the span of oral transmission covers only a very few years.

the collection of material found in chapters i–xxv, which is the basic Jeremiah collection, gradually took shape.

Meanwhile, a great deal of Jeremiah material, of all types (save confessions) and dating both from before and after 605, never found its way into the framework of chapters i–xxv, but continued to circulate separately or in independent collections, orally, in writing, or both. One thinks of the collection of oracles of a hopeful nature, both in poetry and in prose, now found in chapters xxx–xxxi, and of the biographical account and the prose discourses which follow in chapters xxxii–xxxiii, and which have the same theme; of the row of separate biographical accounts and appended discourses which now occur in such pell-mell order in chapters xxvi–xxix; xxxiv–xlv; of the oracles against foreign nations, for the most part in poetry but concluding with a brief biographical incident (li 59–64), which appear in the Hebrew Bible (and the English versions) as chapters xlvi–li, but which in the Septuagint are placed after xxv 13a, and in a different order.

How, and when, all this was added to the basic Jeremiah collection, and why it was added in the order that it was, are matters of well-nigh pure speculation. But it was certainly not done all at once by any one hand. (Would not, in that case, at least the biographical accounts have been placed in chronological order?) If we may indulge our fancy, we may imagine that the biographical chapters xxxvi and xlv were first attached to the (now expanded) scroll, since both have to do with the occasion of its writing and would form a fitting conclusion to it. We may further imagine that chapters xxvi and xxxv were then inserted before chapter xxxvi, since both relate to the reign of Jehoiakim. Then we may guess that chapters xxvii–xxix (which belong together) were put after chapter xxvi because of the erroneous heading in xxvii 1 (LXX omits), which seems to give these events the same date as those of chapter xxvi, although in fact they belong to the fourth year of Zedekiah (xxviii 1). Then, since the letter of chapter xxix deals with the hope that Jeremiah extended to the exiles, it is not surprising that III, The Book of Consolation (chs. xxx–xxxi [Sec. 36]), with additional biographical and other prose material of the same theme (chs. xxxii–xxxiii [Sec. 37]), should have been inserted at this point. The fact that this last is dated to Zedekiah's reign (xxxii 1; xxxiii 1) may explain why chapter xxxiv, also of Zedekiah's reign, was placed where it is. It then only remained for the long biographical section, chapters xxxvii–xliv, to be inserted after chapter xxxvi and before chapter xlv, leaving the latter to the end as Baruch's "signature," as it were. With that, save for the addition of the oracles against foreign nations (chs. xlvi–li), and the historical account of chapter lii, the Jeremiah book as we know it was complete.

All this, however, is within the realm of conjecture, and none of it is to be insisted upon dogmatically. The process was complex and, moreover, did not everywhere follow the same lines. The oracles against foreign nations—which, as noted more than once, stand as chapters xlvi–li in MT, but in LXX are inserted after xxv 13a in a different order—are again the best illustration. It is plausible to suppose that these oracles circulated separately until sometime after the textual traditions lying behind LXX and MT had diverged, and then were drawn by independent processes into both. As late as approximately the second century B.C., though the text had long achieved fixed form, and the Jeremiah book been accorded canonical status, no single standard form of the book (and no single standard text) as yet existed.

4

The one thing, then, that stands out in what has been said thus far is the utter complexity of the process by which the Jeremiah book was formed. If this has been stressed perhaps to the point of tedium, it is because it directly affects the interpretation of the book, and one's appreciation of it, and has, moreover, the greatest bearing upon the critical problems with which one must deal before one can attempt to reconstruct the life and message of Jeremiah.

As far as the reader's enjoyment of the book is concerned, this should be obvious. Every book must be read for what it is, for what a book is controls one's understanding and appreciation of it. That is a truism. For example, if one studies a play, a novel, or a philosophical treatise, one may assume that it has a unity of structure, a logical progression which carries the argument steadily forward, or a coherence of plot so executed that each part of the story grows out of what precedes and leads into what follows. On the other hand, if one reads an anthology of poems, or a collection of short stories or essays, one expects neither chronological progression nor logical connection between the parts; one does not assume that the first poem or story lies chronologically before, or logically leads into, the second—and so on. To interpret an anthology as if such were the case would be to misinterpret. It would be to find ideas that were never in the author's mind—would be, in fact, to confuse the mind of the author with the mind of the editor of the anthology. Such a volume has a certain unity, to be sure, in that each of its parts stems from the mind of the same author, but it does not have a structural unity. Or, to put it better, such unity of structure as it may have was imparted to it not by the author, but by the editor.

The Book of Jeremiah, like most of the prophetic books, is a kind of anthology—or, to be more accurate, an anthology of anthologies—and is to be read as such. Logical or chronological progression must not be demanded or expected. The reader must not take offense at rough transitions, inconsequence of arrangement, or the fact that passages now and again sit ill in their context or are, for no apparent reason, repeated elsewhere. Above all, he must resist the temptation to regard such passages as secondary intrusions on that account, as some critics have been inclined to do. Moreover, he must bear in mind constantly that no assured deductions regarding the date of a saying can be made from its place in the book, nor must he suppose that by establishing the date of a given passage anything has necessarily been said concerning the date of passages immediately adjacent.

The reader would do well to content himself, at least at first, with a leisurely perusal of the individual poems, discourses, and narratives—or, at most, the short thematic units—allowing a general impression of the prophet and his work to form itself gradually from these *disjecta membra* as he goes along. Since, dismayingly enough, individual units in the prophetic books for the most part follow one another without obvious indication of the transitions between them (Can one imagine a volume of Shakespeare in which the various sonnets and lyrics are printed continuously with no space left between?), the reader has as his first task that of setting these units apart. This is not always an easy thing to do, and in the COMMENTS that accompany the text the attempt has been made to offer some help in this regard. Even so, the Jeremiah book, though most rewarding reading, is not, as mentioned before, easy reading. One is, perhaps, well advised to read slowly, a little at a time, savoring as one reads, rather than attempting to gulp the whole book at one or two sittings.

But what has been said concerning the nature of the book also bears directly upon the problems that must be faced in the attempt to reconstruct Jeremiah's career and message. Since this last will be the subject of the next chapter, it might be well, in order to avoid encumbering the discussion there, to say a few preliminary words at this point. To reconstruct the career of Jeremiah is difficult. For the period after 609, to be sure, we have the dated narratives of the Biographer; arranged in chronological order (as it has seemed wise to present them in the text that follows), these provide us with a reliable outline of the latter part of the prophet's life. For the rest, however, both for filling in the details of Jeremiah's preaching during the years after 609, and for our entire knowledge of his activity prior to that date, we have to rely on his undated sayings. And therein lies the problem. One's interpretation of these sayings, and therewith the understanding of Jeremiah's career that one derives from them, will depend in large degree upon the date that one assigns to them. Yet few of them can be dated with more than approximate precision, in many the internal evidence upon which dating depends is ambiguous, and many cannot be assigned any definite date at all. It is because the evidence can be so variously interpreted that reconstructions of Jeremiah's life have differed so widely. But, whatever one's conclusions may be in detail, it is here especially that the composite nature of the book, together with the fact that it is not—at least with any consistency—arranged chronologically, must be kept steadily in mind. One must remember that early position in the book does not necessarily argue for early date, or late position for late date; nor are adjacent sayings necessarily of the same date. Each individual saying must be dated, if it is possible to date it at all, for itself alone.

The crux of the problem concerns the early ministry of Jeremiah —i.e., the period before 609, for which there is no biographical narrative at all. Various questions impose themselves upon which opinions divide. Do the poems telling of the "Foe from the North" (especially in chs. iv–vi) have as their background a Scythian invasion in the early years of Jeremiah's ministry, or not? What was Jeremiah's attitude toward the Josianic reform? Was there a long silence on his part after that reform had been accomplished? Was Jeremiah even active at the time, or did he begin his ministry only late in Josiah's reign or at the beginning of Jehoiakim's? All these questions directly involve the interpretation of various undated sayings. Since some position must be taken with regard to them, I shall provisionally state my own at this point, leaving supporting reasons —specifically those that concern the dating of the various sayings —to be further set forth in the pages that follow.

As regards the "Foe from the North," the opinion was widely held among older commentators that these were the Scythians who, it was believed, ranged southward through Palestine just as Jeremiah began to prophesy; the poems in question were commonly designated as "Scythian poems."[25] This hypothesis, to be sure, was supported only by the statement of Herodotus (I, 104–6) that after the death of the Median king Phraortes in his unsuccessful assault upon Nineveh, the Scythians dominated all western Asia for twenty-eight years, even carrying their depredations as far as the frontiers of Egypt, where the Pharaoh Psammetichus bought them off; it was supposed that their irruption into Palestine must have taken place at the beginning of Jeremiah's career. But contemporary evidence of such an irruption is lacking, and it must be said that a Scythian domination of western Asia coincident with the latter part of Asshurbanapal's long reign is difficult to credit. One wonders to what degree scholars were pressed to this interpretation by the belief that since the relevant poems are for the most part found in the early chapters of Jeremiah's book, they must be related to the early years of his activity. In any event, among recent commentators, though a number of them continue to relate chapters i–vi in the main to Josiah's reign, the Scythian interpretation of the "Foe from the North" has tended to fall from favor.[26] And, at least as the Scythian interpretation has conventionally been stated, this is as well. Scythians (if these are the Umman Manda of the Babylonian Chronicle) begin to play a role in contemporary texts at a somewhat later date (in connection with the events of 612–610), and it is possible that even Herodotus intended to place their activity in Cyaxares' reign.[27] If there was a

[25] This interpretation was popularized by Duhm and widely adopted. It will be found, among English works, in Peake, Smith, Skinner (for complete references, see Selected Bibliography), etc.

[26] Most recent commentators drop them, e.g., Rudolph, Weiser, Steinmann, Leslie (for complete references, see Selected Bibliography).

[27] See the article of Labat cited in previous chapter, n.[7] (*Journal Asiatique* 249 [1961], 1–12).

Scythian thrust into the west, it is probably best understood as coming later in Josiah's reign, coincident with Assyria's final collapse.[28] But even though such an invasion now appears as a distinct possibility, at the present state of our knowledge, caution is indicated. Moreover, not a few of the poems of the "Foe from the North" (e.g., v 15–17) seem far more appropriate to the Babylonians than they do to wild Scythians.

I should, therefore, be inclined to agree with those scholars who place the bulk of chapters iv–vi between the later years of Josiah and a time well on in the reign of Jehoiakim, when the Babylonian menace had begun to be a reality. Some of the poems in question may well reflect the terror inspired by Scythians and Medes as these peoples were launching their final assault upon Assyria (whether or not the Scythians later ranged into the west and threatened Judah directly, may be left open) in the latter part of Josiah's reign. To say all this, however, by no means implies that Jeremiah may not have had a premonition of invasion and doom at a much earlier period. Much of the language of these poems is rather conventionalized and suggestive of the imagery associated with the day of Yahweh's judgment; some of them may well have been composed early in Jeremiah's career when as yet no definite foe threatened, only ultimately to find their realization in the coming of the Babylonians.[29]

Regarding Jeremiah's attitude toward the Josianic reform there has always been the widest disagreement among scholars, some holding that he actively—even enthusiastically—supported it, others holding that he was in principle bitterly hostile to it, still others believing that, while generally favoring its aims, he took no active part in it. This chaotic divergence of opinion is in a way understandable enough, since the data in the book bearing directly on the point is both ambiguous and meager. On the other hand, it has been rather generally agreed that, the reform having been made, Jeremiah entered a period of silence which lasted through most of the rest of Josiah's reign. This last opinion is based on the belief that few if any of the prophet's sayings are to be dated in the

[28] See the article of Malamat cited in previous chapter n.[10] (IEJ 1 [1950/51], 154–59).

[29] See, e.g., Welch (for complete reference, see Selected Bibliography), pp. 97–131. It is to be noted that earlier prophets, such as Amos (and see, much earlier still, the poem in Deut xxxii), announced the coming judgment without naming any specific foe.

decade immediately following 622. This supposed hiatus in Jeremiah's ministry is explained by some on the theory that, being satisfied with the reform, he had for the moment no occasion to speak; by others on the assumption that, embarrassed because his earlier threats of doom had not materialized, he was impelled to keep silence until a new "Foe from the North," the Babylonians, appeared on the scene.

In view of the paucity and ambiguity of the data, it is unlikely that there will ever be complete agreement regarding Jeremiah's attitude toward the reform. Nevertheless, I believe, and will later attempt to show, that there is sufficient evidence for asserting that he was initially in sympathy with its aims and even stronger evidence that he subsequently found himself bitterly dissatisfied with the outcome. But I feel that the theory of a long silence on Jeremiah's part after the completion of the reform needs seriously to be questioned. It is, on the surface of it, difficult to believe that one so perceptive as Jeremiah would not have seen the shallowness of the reform until many years had passed, and equally difficult to believe that, having seen it, one so outspoken would have remained silent. And, as a matter of fact, although the sayings that can with complete confidence be placed in this period are not numerous, it is my belief that there are nevertheless some that fit best precisely here. In other words, it is unlikely that any significant interruption of Jeremiah's activity ever took place.

This brings us to those scholars who believe that Jeremiah did not even begin to prophesy until near the end of Josiah's reign, or the beginning of Jehoiakim's (i.e., ca. 612 or 609).[30] Their reasons for taking this position are various, and need not be discussed in detail here. To speak in general, however, they believe that not only the poems regarding the "Foe from the North," but all other genuine sayings of Jeremiah in i–vi and elsewhere commonly associated with the pre-reformation period are best explained against the background of the emerging Babylonian menace. Since, as noted above, most scholars place no oracles in the period immediately after the reform in any case, this means that, as far as the poetic sayings of Jeremiah are concerned, his ministry prior

[30] As examples, see: F. Horst, "Die Anfänge des Propheten Jeremia," ZAW 41 (1923), 94–153; H. G. May, "The Chronology of Jeremiah's Oracles," JNES 4 (1945), 217–27; J. P. Hyatt, "Jeremiah and Deuteronomy," JNES 1 (1942), 156–73; J. P. Hyatt, "The Foe from the North in Jeremiah," JBL 59 (1940), 499–513.

to 609 or 612 becomes a total blank. Does this not indicate that it had not yet begun? To be sure, it is explicitly stated that Jeremiah began his ministry in the thirteenth year of Josiah (627); but such statements are all to be found in the prose tradition (i 2; xxv 3; cf. iii 6), which these scholars agree in mistrusting. The point, too, is sometimes made[31] that since the poems of the "Foe from the North" refer to the Babylonians, and since it seems to be indicated in i 13 ff. that that foe was imminent at the time of Jeremiah's call, it follows that the call must have taken place, not in 627, but at a later time, after the Babylonians had begun to threaten.

It is impossible to do more than take a position on this question here. For my own part, I am unable to share these scholars' skeptical attitude toward the prose tradition,[32] and am, therefore, unwilling to discard the explicit chronology of the book at this point, short of compelling, objective evidence. It is, after all, rather difficult to believe that the prose tradition, little or nothing in which seems to come from much after the middle of the Exilic period—thus within living memory of the events—could have falsified Jeremiah's career to this extent. Moreover, as will be indicated in the pages that follow, not a few of Jeremiah's poetic sayings are best understood if placed precisely during the period of Josiah's reforming activity; some, it is believed, can only be understood so. And, let it be repeated, the period immediately after the reform is in all likelihood by no means a blank. There is, in other words, abundant evidence from the poetry of the book that Jeremiah was active both before and after 622. As for the assertion that i 13 ff. links the "Foe from the North" with Jeremiah's call, and thus places that call after the Babylonians had become a threat, one can only say that such is not the case. Leaving aside possibility of a Scythian invasion late in Josiah's reign, to say nothing of the fact that Jeremiah may have been oppressed by a premonition of doom years before any tangible foe threatened (this was true of Amos, for example), the composite nature of chapter i must be recognized. As will be pointed out in the COMMENT, there is no evidence whatever—and some to the contrary—that the call (vss. 4–10) and the two visions (vss. 11 f. and 13 ff.) occurred at even approximately

[31] For example, H. G. May, JNES 4 (1945), 225; J. P. Hyatt, JBL 59 (1940), 499.
[32] I have stated my reasons elsewhere; see the article cited in n.[21].

the same time. Or, to repeat: adjacent position by no means proves identity of date.

For these and other reasons, one feels abundantly justified in adhering to the traditional chronology, i.e., that Jeremiah began his career in the thirteenth year of Josiah's reign (627). That is to say, the early chapters of the book (i–vi) are neither to be retained en bloc in Josiah's reign, nor removed en bloc to a later date, for they contain material which dates all the way from the beginning of Jeremiah's ministry until well on into the reign of Jehoiakim. Each smallest unit must be examined and dated for itself. The same is true of other parts of the book as well, and must control our reconstruction of Jeremiah's career and message. With these preliminary remarks in mind, that is the subject to which we must now turn.

THE LIFE AND MESSAGE OF JEREMIAH

To undertake a description of the life, the character, and the message of a man such as Jeremiah within the confines of a single chapter is no easy task. It is probable that no one has ever attempted it (and every commentator on Jeremiah has) without a feeling of inadequacy. Nor is this so merely because of the mass of data that must be sifted and the numerous critical problems that must be dealt with within limited space, but because of the stature and the complexity of the man himself. To do full justice to this most human and most appealing—some would say, the greatest— of all the prophets and, above all, to put into words what the prophetic office meant to him, the compulsion that it laid upon him and the tensions to which it subjected him—this would require a large volume. And, even then, much would remain unsaid. The ensuing pages, therefore, make no claim to be exhaustive. They have, rather, the modest aim of presenting a summary sketch of the prophet's career, in the hope that the reader may be assisted thereby to form from the bits and pieces of the book—the isolated sayings and the disconnected incidents which it contains—a coherent impression of the man and his work. It is understood that the picture outlined here is to be filled out from the text of the book itself, and the COMMENTS that accompany it.

Now one cannot, let it be repeated, write a biography of Jeremiah —and this in spite of the fact that we know far more of his life than we do of that of any other prophet. The facts at our disposal are too meager. The nature of the problem has already been alluded to in the preceding chapter. It is true that the biographical narratives which the book contains provide us, when arranged in chronological order, with an invaluable outline of Jeremiah's career after the year 609. But no more than an outline! The biographical narratives describe only a series of isolated incidents and do not form a continuous account. And, since none of this material relates

to the years before 609, it affords us no help in the reconstruction
of Jeremiah's early career, to say nothing of his life before he received his call to the prophetic office. We are, therefore, both for
filling in the details of the years after 609 and for our entire knowledge of the prophet's activity prior to that date, forced to rely on
what can be inferred from his undated sayings. Since—again as indicated in the preceding chapter—few of these can be dated with
more than approximate precision, numerous areas of uncertainty
and possible disagreement remain, especially as regards points of
detail. Nevertheless, a general reconstruction of the prophet's career
is possible and may be attempted with some confidence. In the
pages that follow the policy will be to proceed as far as possible
according to chronological order, tacitly assigning to passages the
dates that seem most likely and basing the discussion upon them,
but for the most part leaving the supporting reasons for such dating to be adduced in the COMMENTS. Scripture references, unless
otherwise indicated, will refer to the book of Jeremiah.

1

Concerning Jeremiah's home and family background we know
nothing save the bare facts that are given us in the superscription
of his book (i 1 f.). We are told that he began his career as a
prophet in the thirteenth year of Josiah's reign (627). Since he
was still a very young man at the time (i 6), perhaps scarcely
of age, he must have been born (so we have surmised) around
645 or shortly before—thus near the end of the long reign of the
notorious Manasseh. His birthplace was Anathoth, a town in the
old tribal territory of Benjamin some three miles northeast of Jerusalem, the site of which is probably Râs el-Kharrûbeh near the
present-day village of 'Anata, which preserves the ancient name.
Among its inhabitants were men of priestly lineage (Anathoth is
mentioned in a list of Levitic cities which probably dates to the
tenth century: Josh xxi 18), and Jeremiah himself was of a priestly
family, the son of one Hilkiah. This Hilkiah is not to be confused
with the man of the same name who functioned as high priest
during Josiah's reign (II Kings xxii 4 ff.): there is nothing in the
book that would lead one to suppose that Jeremiah was the high
priest's son, and much to the contrary. There is, on the other hand,

much merit in the suggestion, repeatedly made, that Jeremiah's family was descended from Abiathar who, having served as David's priest, was subsequently deposed by Solomon in favor of his rival Zadok and banished to his home in Anathoth because of his complicity in Adonijah's attempt to usurp the throne (I Kings ii 26 f.). Since it is unlikely that so small a village as Anathoth contained several unrelated priestly families, the supposition is by no means unreasonable. If this is correct, it means that Jeremiah could claim as proud a lineage as any man in Israel, for he could, through Abiathar, boast of descent from none other than the house of Eli (cf. I Sam xiv 3; xxii 20; I Kings ii 27), the priests who had been custodians of the Ark at Shiloh in the days of the old tribal league, and beyond that—so tradition would have it—from the family of Moses himself. Such an ancestry would do much to explain Jeremiah's profound feeling for Israel's ancient traditions, his recollection of the shrine of Shiloh and its fate (vii 14; xxvi 6), his deep and sympathetic concern for the people of northern Israel, to say nothing of his close spiritual kinship to northern Israel's great prophet, Hosea.

Of Jeremiah's childhood and youth we know nothing. He must have been almost of an age with the young King Josiah, who came to the throne as an eight-year-old boy in 640; he thus grew to maturity, as did his king, in the last decade of Asshurbanapal's reign, as Assyria's long period of world domination was drawing to a close. Regarding his early training, and the factors that prepared him psychologically and spiritually for the prophetic office, we can do little more than guess. It is safe, however, to assume an upbringing in a home of conservative piety where Israel's ancient traditions, and the words of her prophets, were known and recited. It is certain, at any rate, that while still a boy Jeremiah had become familiar with the sayings of Hosea and had been profoundly impressed by them, for his early preaching in particular, both in language and in thought, reveals with unmistakable clarity the influence of that great prophet. Whether or not Jeremiah had received any specific training as a priest we cannot say. But he had probably acquired certain definite attitudes regarding what the duties and responsibilities of the priesthood were ideally supposed to be. Since priests and Levites were traditionally not merely cultic functionaries, but also custodians of the law whose business it was to instruct the people in their moral and religious obligations, it may be that a high view of the priesthood, formed from boyhood experience, contributed to Jeremiah's extreme bitterness against the clergy of his day. Beyond all this, we may suppose that this sensitive lad had indulged in long hours of meditation upon the nature of Yahweh's covenant and its demands, as well as upon the explosive international situation, of which, living as he did but a few miles from the capital, he could scarcely have been unaware. He had undoubtedly been shocked and revolted by the paganism with which the land had been filled since Manasseh's reign, and which, in the light of his (presumably) conservative upbringing, could only have appeared to him as a mortal sin against Israel's God. The conviction had doubtless begun to form itself in his mind that nothing short of a complete about-face could save the nation from judgment. True, we know none of these things. But when the call of the divine word came to him, as shortly it did, we are not to suppose that it fell as seed upon unplowed ground.

Like Isaiah and Ezekiel—and, one suspects, all the others of the goodly fellowship of the prophets—Jeremiah took up his work at the behest of a definite experience of call (i 4–10). This came to him in the year 627, the very year in which the great Asshurbanapal died in Nineveh and Assyria's final collapse began. The circumstances of this call—whether it took place in the course of some cultic occasion as did Isaiah's, or privately—are unknown to us. But it brought to Jeremiah the inescapable awareness that his life had been claimed by Yahweh, indeed that he had been predestined for the prophetic office even before he had been born. Yet, Jeremiah did not receive the call with eagerness, but rather sought to escape it, protesting that he was too young. Young he was. But one wonders if this was his real reason, or if he did not even then see all too clearly the awful cost of the prophetic office and if he did not, in spite of the assurance of divine aid (i 17–19), simply shrink from what he knew was in store for him. The truth is that Jeremiah did not want to be a prophet; nor did he, so far as one can see, ever completely reconcile himself to his calling. His contempt for those unthinking men who, not realizing the gravity of what they did, rushed eagerly to seize the prophetic office, was and remained unbounded (cf. xxiii 16–22). Nevertheless, the divine compulsion was laid upon him, overruling his objections. He felt on his lips the touch of Yahweh's hand, and knowing that Yahweh's word had been placed in his mouth, he had no course but to speak it. And this he did, unremittingly, as long as he lived.

Jeremiah began his ministry with the awful conviction that his country was under judgment. Although the two visions of i 11–16, one of them telling of the terrible foe that would come from the north, may have come to him somewhat later, it seems clear that Jeremiah was from the beginning haunted by that premonition of doom which was later to become well-nigh his entire burden. It was no doubt primarily because of this that Jeremiah never married. It is true that the passage (in prose) in which he tells how Yahweh had forbidden him to marry (xvi 1–4) was very probably uttered later. Yet since young men of the day customarily married quite early in life, one would expect Jeremiah under normal circumstances to have done the same. The fact that he did not may be taken as indication that he had been oppressed by some intimation of disaster, some compulsion against taking such a step, ever since his youth. In any event, he was never to know the joys of home and family. How much this may have added to the almost pathetic loneliness of his life we can only guess.

The situation that obtained as Jeremiah began to preach has already been sketched (see the earlier chapter "The Background of Jeremiah's Career . . ."). Suffice it to say here that Judah was by this time in fact, if not in name, a free country and that Josiah's efforts at reform were already under way. But the finding of the lawbook which was to give that reform direction was five years in the future; the evil legacy of Manasseh's reign, of paganism and immorality, still encumbered the land from end to end. Against this paganism the young Jeremiah thundered—as did Zephaniah, who was active at the time. We have samples of Jeremiah's early preaching in chapter ii (though the chapter was given its present form in Jehoiakim's reign), in iii 1–iv 4, and elsewhere in the book. This shows him profoundly shocked at the prevailing apostasy, savagely attacking it, and warning of its dire consequences. It seemed to him that his people's entire history since their entry into Palestine had been one long tale of gross ingratitude and forgetfulness of the divine grace, which was senseless, inexcusable, without parallel among the nations of the world (ii 4–13) and, moreover, contrary to nature (cf. v 20–25; xviii 13–17). Judah, he declared, has run after strange gods with the unrestrained passion of a camel in heat (ii 23–25). Unfaithfulness to Yahweh has perverted the national character, stained it with a stain that nothing can wash (ii 20–22), and placed the nation in a predicament from which neither its hand-made gods (ii 26–28) nor all its political cleverness (ii 18 f.) can save it. Borrowing the language of Hosea, Jeremiah likened Judah to an adulterous wife who has repeatedly betrayed her husband and forfeited all claim upon him, yet who fatuously continues to count on his indulgent forgiveness (iii 1–5).

The vehemence of Jeremiah's assault upon the national sin can scarcely be exaggerated. Yet that was not the whole of his message, for he was not without compassion and hope. Like Hosea, the young Jeremiah coupled with bitter censure a moving and impassioned plea for repentance (iii 19–iv 2) and held out the assurance that, should this be sincerely forthcoming, the nation might once again find its place as Yahweh's people and receive the promises which had been given to Abraham (cf. iv 2 and Gen xviii 18, etc.). Moreover—and presumably as Josiah was extending his control into northern Israel—Jeremiah voiced the lively hope that the lost sons of Ephraim would soon be restored to their land (xxxi 2–6, 15–22; iii 12 f.) and would join with Judah in the worship of Yahweh on Mount Zion (xxxi 6). Whether Jeremiah so intended it or not, preaching of this sort undoubtedly helped to prepare the climate for the measures which Josiah was attempting to put into effect.

Jeremiah's precise attitude toward the reform, which reached its climax in 622, five years after he had begun to preach, is, as was pointed out in the preceding chapter, disputed. That he took an active part in its implementation is, to be sure, most unlikely. Certainly it cannot be argued from xi 6 that he became a peripatetic evangelist in its interests, for this passage, as will be pointed out below, is not to be interpreted in this way. Moreover, the reform, since it was put into effect by royal initiative, and through the solemn covenant of Judah's elders (II Kings xxiii 1–3), scarcely required such evangelizing activity to ensure its adoption. At the same time, it is almost unthinkable that Jeremiah could have opposed Josiah's effort to rid the land of the very paganism against which he had preached with such vehemence, or that king's attempt to revive the theology of the ancient Mosaic covenant in which the young prophet had himself presumably been nurtured. In any event, it is quite wrong to argue from the fact that Josiah did not consult Jeremiah with regard to the newly found lawbook, but rather an otherwise unknown prophetess (II Kings xxii 14–20), that Jeremiah was out of sympathy with the reform, for he was at the time still young, relatively unknown, and without official standing in the court. Nor should one appeal to such a passage as viii 8 f. as proof that Jeremiah regarded the Deuteronomic law itself as a fraud, for these rather cryptic verses (see the COMMENTS *ad locc.*) probably do not intend to make any such assertion.

All things considered, the most plausible supposition is that Jeremiah, though taking no direct part in the reform, and though not necessarily approving of all of its features, was initially in favor of its essential aims. The very fact that he received his call shortly after Josiah had begun the implementation of his policy might suggest that the young prophet had felt the excitement which that policy presumably evoked. He could scarcely have been unaware of what the king sought to do, or indifferent to it; and nothing in his early utterances at least would lead one to suppose that he was opposed to it. We know, indeed, that Jeremiah later expressed almost unbounded admiration for Josiah (xxii 15 f.); and this he would scarcely have done had he regarded that king's major official action as an error, if not a sin. And, although the hope that he expressed for the restoration of northern Israel was by no means politically motivated, it nevertheless betrays at least a measure of sympathy with—certainly no hostility toward—Josiah's policy. Finally, there is the fact that in later years it was precisely the men of the reform and their sons who more than once stood up for Jeremiah and saved his life. One thinks of Ahikam ben Shaphan (xxvi 24), Gemariah ben Shaphan and Elnathan ben Achbor (ch. xxxvi), as well as others who will be mentioned below or in the course of the COMMENTS. One cannot explain these names away as mere coincidence (cf. II Kings xxii 12), as some have sought to do. The behavior of these men does not, to be sure, tell us anything directly regarding Jeremiah's attitude toward the reform; but it does tell us something of the reformers' attitude toward Jeremiah! Far from regarding him as a foe, they were at least to some degree in agreement with what he said.

But whatever Jeremiah may have thought of the reform in the first place, he was scarcely very long in becoming aware of its inadequacies. The view is widely held, it is true, that there was a long silence on Jeremiah's part after the reform had been completed, which lasted through most of the rest of Josiah's reign (until 609 or shortly before). This has been referred to in the preceding chapter. The point is difficult to settle, since we have no evidence save Jeremiah's undated sayings, very few of which can be fixed in time beyond dispute. Moreover, the fact that we know almost nothing of internal affairs in Judah during Josiah's later years—the years that saw the final destruction of Assyria at the hands of the Medo-Babylonian coalition—makes it doubly difficult to prove that this or that saying was, or was not, uttered during this interval. It may well be that for a short while after 622 Jeremiah, in sympathy with what the reform sought to do and impressed with its positive achievements, was able to rest his attack. But, if so, this can hardly have been for long; a silence of a decade's duration is unlikely in the extreme.

In support of this position we may appeal not only to intrinsic probability, but to certain lines of tangible evidence. The prose tradition of Jeremiah (xxv 3; cf. xxxvi 2) certainly remembers no period of silence on Jeremiah's part, but depicts him as unremittingly active in proclaiming the divine word from the day of his call onward. And, if one hesitates to lay weight on this, we have the evidence of Jeremiah's famous "temple sermon" (vii 2–15), an unquestionably authentic utterance which is precisely dated (xxvi 1) in the very beginning of Jehoiakim's reign (i.e., autumn of 609, or winter of 609/8). From this address it is clear that, whatever the immediate effects of the reform may have been, no lasting amelioration of the national character had resulted. Oppression, injustice, unethical behavior, the worship of false gods (vss. 6, 9)—in short, flagrant violations of covenant law—were everywhere rampant, all the while the people, confident that zealous prosecution of the cultus was all that was required of them, found security in the mere physical presence of Yahweh's temple in their midst (vss. 4, 10 f.). It is evident from this that the Deuteronomic theology, with its stress upon the stringent moral demands of the Mosaic covenant, had been widely misunderstood or ignored. But such a state of affairs could scarcely have developed in the few short months since Josiah had met his death. On the contrary, one must assume that the reform either had never profoundly affected the conduct of daily affairs, or had badly eroded even during that good king's reign. Indeed, Jeremiah himself said as much, for in another passage (ii 16) he explained the disaster of 609, the disaster that cost Josiah his life and the nation its independence, precisely as the result of persistent apostasy. If iii 6–11 is to be dated after the reform (as well it may be), we have Jeremiah's flat statement (vs. 10) that the reform had been made insincerely.

We should not, to be sure, conclude from all this either that the reform was a failure, or that Jeremiah became so embittered with its results that he turned against it and regretted that it had ever been made. That would be far too hasty a judgment. After all, in purging the land of pagan practices and committing the nation to the observance of covenant law, the reform had accomplished what it set out to do and may, from that point of view, be accounted a success. Since Josiah was sincerely committed to his policy and never reversed it, and was himself a man of personal probity (xxii 15 f.), we may assume that the reform was officially maintained as long as he lived, and that the moral tone of the nation underwent a significant if impossible-to-measure improvement. It is really unthinkable that Jeremiah disapproved of all this, or that he wished for a return to pre-reformation conditions. Indeed, when Josiah's son Jehoiakim to all intents and purposes allowed the reform to lapse, and its ideals to go by the board, Jeremiah was bitterly censorious.

Nevertheless, Jeremiah did not evaluate the spiritual temper of his people merely in terms of official policy—as did the author of Kings, who found Josiah's reign wholly good, Jehoiakim's wholly bad. It is unlikely that Jeremiah was ever completely satisfied with the situation even when the reform was at its height. What he had desired and demanded was sincere and heartfelt repentance, an inner change in the national character, a wholesale turning on the part of the people to loyal obedience to Yahweh—and this the reform did not produce. Of course, it is in a way unfair to complain that it did not, for no officially sponsored measure can be expected to have such results. Whether Jeremiah had in his youthful enthusiasm hoped for too much of the reform, only to be disappointed, or whether he had been skeptical of its possibilities all along, is a question that cannot be answered. The point is, however, that he had always felt that the only hope of the nation lay in an inner turning to Yahweh in word and deed; since the reform, whatever he may have expected of it in the first place, had not—we would add, could not have—produced that, he could not have regarded it as sufficient. On the contrary, he sensed intuitively—for there are not, and never have been, statistics on the subject—that no real repentance, no significant change in the spiritual temper of the people, had taken place. Indeed, he sensed that the reform, in that it led people to suppose that Yahweh's demands had been adequately complied with, had set up a false feeling of security that blocked the path to repentance. He could not, therefore, remain satisfied with it.

That Jeremiah ultimately arrived at this evaluation of the situation is certain. Since he was at once an exceedingly perceptive and outspoken person, it is difficult to believe that he did not arrive at it rather promptly, and even more difficult to believe that, once having done so, he was content to hold his peace. And there are, in fact, a number of sayings in the book that fit, if not demonstrably, at least most plausibly in the period immediately following 622. These make Jeremiah's attitude abundantly clear, and show that he was neither blind to the state of affairs nor long silent about it. On the contrary, he declared (vi 16–21) that the people had shown themselves both obdurate to the demands of the law and deaf to its warnings, and that the reform had resulted only in an ever more elaborate cultus without any real return to the ancient paths; the demands of Yahweh's covenant having been lost behind cultic externals (cf. vii 21 ff.), the crimes of society continued unabated (v 26–29) and the clergy, having come to terms with them, uttered no rebuke (vs. 30 f.). Of genuine repentance Jeremiah could see no sign. Rather, it seemed to him (viii 4–7) that the people, obdurate in backsliding and without the sense of wild creatures who at least instinctively obey the laws that govern their existence, were plunging on to their ruin like a horse charging headlong into battle; though boasting of Yahweh's law, their very pride in its possession had deafened their ears to the hearing of Yahweh's word (viii 8 f.), which had become to them a hateful thing to which they were unwilling to listen (vi 10). Jeremiah came to a most pessimistic evaluation of society. He felt that it was rotten to the core: high or low, not a man was to be found who acted with probity, and in awareness of Yahweh's requirements (v 1–9). Yet to this people, whose crimes against the covenant stipulations were notorious, the clergy was unctuously offering the divine peace (vi 13–15; viii 10–12), assuring them that no trouble would ever come near them (v 12 f.). And this, said Jeremiah, is a bald-faced lie!

In short, Jeremiah saw that the reform had by no means satisfied Yahweh's demands or brought the nation into conformity with his will: some deeper repentance, some inward and heartfelt assumption of the covenant obligations, would have to be forthcoming if the nation was to escape the judgment (iv 3–4; cf. iv 14; Deut x 16). Far from being carried away by the excitement of Assyria's fall (cf. Nahum), Jeremiah felt himself ever more heavily weighted down by that premonition of doom with which he had begun his ministry. It may have been—though we cannot tell—at about this time that Jeremiah underwent the two visionary experiences which are described in i 11–16, and which further clarified for him the word that he had to speak. In the first of these, the sight of an almond rod (*šāqēd*) brought to his mind the word *šōqēd* (watching) and the assurance that Yahweh was watching over his word of judgment to bring it to pass: though delayed, it would surely come. In the other, he saw a boiling pot tipped from the north and about to spill; and this told him of the foe that would come from the north as the agent of Yahweh's judgment. It may have been just as the Babylonians, together with the Medes and the Umman Manda, overwhelmed Assyria that the conviction came to him that here *was* that foe. Though most of the poems describing the "Foe from the North" (mostly in chs. iv–vi) were probably composed slightly later, some of them may well have been uttered in Josiah's reign.

2

The year 609 was a fateful one, both in the history of Judah and in the life of Jeremiah. That was the year, it will be recalled, which witnessed the tragic death of Josiah in his attempt to halt the forces of Pharaoh Necho on their march to the Euphrates, and the end of Judah's brief independence when, a few months later, the pharaoh deposed Josiah's son Jehoahaz and elevated to the throne the latter's brother Jehoiakim—another of Josiah's sons—to rule as his vassal. This last was by no means the least of misfortunes, for all that we know of Jehoiakim shows him to have been a person who was utterly unfit to rule. Wanting in political wisdom, as he was later to demonstrate conclusively, he was also a petty tyrant, willful, selfish, and contemptuous of the prophetic word, who would neither heed advice nor brook rebuke (cf. xxvi 20–23; xxxvi). If it is true, as II Kings xxiii 31, 36 seems to indicate (cf. I Chron iii 15), that he was actually older than his brother Jehoahaz, it may be that the people, well aware of his character, had on his father's death intentionally passed him by. This, however, is uncertain (it would require us to suppose that Josiah was only fourteen when Jehoiakim was born: cf. II Kings xxii 1; xxiii 36) and is not to be insisted upon. In any event, Johoiakim early revealed his true colors. Apparently soon after he had taken the throne, having decided, it would seem, that his father's palace was not good enough for him, he set out to build a new and finer one. Presumably because his treasury, depleted by Egyptian exactions (II Kings xxiii 33, 35), lacked the necessary funds, he impressed labor for the purpose. This provoked Jeremiah to one of the most scathing utterances that he ever delivered (xxii 13–19). Asking this spoiled young man if he thought that having a fine house with luxurious appointments made a man a king, and advising him to consider his own father if he wished to know the true marks of royalty, he predicted that Jehoiakim would one day be given a donkey's funeral—dumped on the garbage heap outside the city gates with no one to lament his passing. One scarcely wonders that relations between Jehoiakim and Jeremiah remained somewhat less than cordial!

Under Jehoiakim the reform, already wearing thin, may be said to have lapsed. The king, we may suppose, had little feeling for it, while not a few of the people, no doubt chiefly in outlying areas where Josiah's ban upon local shrines had left something of a spiritual vacuum, had never reconciled themselves to it. Moreover, the tragic events of 609 had almost certainly done much to destroy popular confidence in the theology upon which the reform had been based, for, after all, compliance with the demands of that theology had not forestalled disaster, as promised. Whatever the reasons, the ideals of the reform seem not to have been maintained. Although there was scarcely a return to the officially sponsored paganism of Manasseh's day, non-Yahwistic cults and practices once again made their appearance (vii 6, 9, 16–20). And, as the "Temple Sermon" (vii 2–15) makes clear, instances of social injustice had become deplorably common, while personal morality and ethics—if Jeremiah is to be believed—stood at a shockingly low level (cf. ix 1–8[2–9E]; v 1–9). Yet, at the same time, the confidence persisted, a confidence based in the official theology of the nation, that Yahweh was committed by his immutable promises to the defense of the Davidic line, and of the temple which he had chosen as the earthly seat of his rule (vii 4). It was a confidence which by this time had hardened into dogma. And upon this dogma, parroted by the clergy and reinforced by the words of prophets (v 12; xiv 13, etc.), the people rested secure. Any attempt to question it would be deeply resented, indeed regarded as both treason and blasphemy—for was it not tantamount to accusing Yahweh of faithlessness to his covenant with David?

The situation being what it was, it is not surprising that Jeremiah's life entered a tragic phase. His message increasingly became one of stern warning of disaster to come; and, since this ran counter both to popular belief and official theology, and was offensive not only to the nation's leaders but to the populace generally, it earned for him opposition, hatred, harassment, and even physical abuse. This began to fall upon him at the very beginning of Jehoiakim's reign, and continued ever thereafter. The situation was, in Jeremiah's view, simply intolerable. Standing in the court of the temple (vii 2–15), he assailed the notion that the physical presence of the temple brought protection and declared that the malpractices which the people had thought to cover up with their busy religiosity had turned it into "a robbers' hide-out"—a cave to which bandits fled for safety—and would, unless corrected, cause Yahweh to destroy it as he had long ago destroyed his house at Shiloh. This was, as we have said, in Jehoiakim's accession year. And we know (ch. xxvi) that it very nearly cost Jeremiah his life. Had not certain princes, notably Ahikam ben Shaphan (vs. 24)—one of the leaders in Josiah's reform and perhaps a son of that king's secretary of state (II Kings xxii 12)—taken his part, he would assuredly have been put to death—as others, less fortunate than he, were (vss. 20–23).

This experience, though it must have shaken Jeremiah, did not silence him. On the contrary, he continued his denunciations, not sparing the king, as we have seen. Indeed, he pronounced sentence upon the Davidic monarchy itself (xxi 11–xxii 9), because, commissioned by Yahweh to secure justice according to the demands of covenant law, it had failed of its duty and forfeited its right to exist. The abandonment of the reform covenant was to him no less than a conspiracy against the divine King which had placed the nation under judgment (xi 9–13), a judgment from which all of its cultic activity could not save it (xi 14–17; xvii 1–4). Though deeply moved by Josiah's death and touched by the sad fate of

Jehoahaz (xxii 10–12), he refused to concede that the tragedy of 609 was a contradiction of Deuteronomic theology, declaring rather that it was a positive illustration of the truth of that theology, for it had come as punishment for forsaking Yahweh (ii 16). At the same time, Jeremiah never regarded that punishment as more than provisionary. On the contrary, the conviction deepened with him— probably between 609 and 605 as the Babylonians and the Egyptians sparred for position along the Euphrates River—that the Babylonians were Yahweh's appointed agents of judgment, who would shortly fall upon the unrepentant nation and destroy it without pity. It was probably during this interval that Jeremiah uttered many of those poems telling of the awful "Foe from the North," which we find in chapters iv–vi. The nation, he declared, was doomed, without any hope save in repentance from the heart (iv 14); priests and prophets who say differently lied (iv 9 f.; v 10–14, etc.).

As a result of such talk Jeremiah soon found himself *contra mundum*. His life became a history of persecution. We have just noted how, at the very beginning of Jehoiakim's reign, he almost lost his life because of his "Temple Sermon." His foes, seeing from this incident that they could not secure his death by legal means, thereafter sought in whatever way they could to silence him. On one occasion (xix 1–xx 6), after he had gone outside the city and, in the presence of certain of the priests and elders, smashed a clay pot, declaring as he did so that just so would Jerusalem be smashed beyond repair, he was seized by a temple officer—when he had the temerity to return to the temple and repeat the gist of what he had said there—and clapped in the stocks overnight. It appears (xxxvi 5) that for some time he was forbidden to enter the temple at all. Beyond this, though we cannot reconstruct the details, he was subjected to incessant harassment. He was jeered at, cursed, ostracized (xv 10 f., 17; xvii 15; xx 7) and repeatedly plotted against (xviii 18; xx 10). On one occasion, we cannot tell when, the citizens of his own town of Anathoth resolved to kill him if he persisted in speaking as he had (xi 18–23); and in this plot members of his own family, concealing their cowardly designs with friendly words, were implicated (xii 6).

Few indeed are the men who could endure such treatment with equanimity, and Jeremiah was certainly not among them. On the contrary, his spirit almost broke under it. He gave way to fits of angry recrimination, depression, and even suicidal despair. This we see clearly from his "confessions" which, though none of them can be dated exactly, were in all probability uttered during Jehoiakim's reign. Here we see him lashing out at those who abused him in the most violent language, calling on his God to espouse his cause and judge them without mercy (xi 20; xii 3; xv 15; xvii 18; xviii 18–23; xx 12). Jeremiah hated his calling and the loneliness that it had brought him, and longed to quit it (ix 1[2E]; xv 10 f., 17 f.); more than once he was tempted to do so (xx 9). He reminded his God that he had never desired the prophetic office in the first place (xvii 14–18), and he spat his contempt at those facile prophets who, because they lacked all conception of the nature of the divine demands, eagerly rushed to proclaim their word (xxiii 16–22). In language that was little short of blasphemy he charged that his God had "seduced" him, had taken unfair advantage of him in persuading him to be a prophet, and then had left him to suffer the consequences (xv 15–18; xx 7). He even declared that his God—the very God whom he had once called "the fount of living water" (ii 13)—had been to him in his hour of need no better than a dry brook (xv 18). Jeremiah was, in short, torn between the compulsion of his calling, which drove him in one direction, and his own desires and self-interest, which impelled him in another. The day came—and it is scarcely surprising that it did, for such tension is really beyond the powers of the human spirit to endure—when Jeremiah found himself at the point of surrender; cursing the day of his birth, and the agony that life had brought him, he cried out for the peace of death (xx 14–18).

That, of course, is not the whole of it. Were it so, we might put Jeremiah down as a weakling, a quitter, a small-spirited man whose faith was not great enough to endure the testing that was imposed upon it. And nothing could be farther from the truth. For all of Jeremiah's despair, for all his complaining and railing against his lot, he could not bring himself to quit the prophetic office, and did not do so. He was compelled to speak the word that had been given him. As he himself put it (xx 9), the word was like a fire shut up in his bones which, try as he might, he could not hold in. Indeed—and let us not forget it—we should know nothing of this turmoil and tension, nothing of Jeremiah's feelings at all, if he had not in his "confessions" confided in us. We may safely assume that his enemies, and the public generally, did not know of his weakness, but must on the contrary, since neither reason nor threats could sway him, have thought him a person inflexibly, not to say mulishly, stubborn. In truth, Jeremiah, though inwardly hurt and in despair, remained to outward appearance a veritable "wall of bronze" (i 18; xv 20), a man of unflinching courage who never, so far as we know, tempered the word that his God had given him by the omission of so much as a syllable. In his weakness he was strong (cf. Heb xi 34); or, better, he was driven by his calling to exhibit a strength that was not by nature his. More than this, Jeremiah seems himself to have understood that his complaints and recriminations were unworthy of him, and would have to be put aside if he wished to continue in the prophetic office from which he could not, and would not, retreat. There is evidence (xv 19–21) that he struggled to purge himself of this weakness in his character—and not without success, for, in spite of the curses that he hurled at those who abused him, he seems never to have ceased to intercede for his people in prayer (xv 10 f.; xviii 20; cf. vii 16; xi 14; xiv 11).

As we have seen, Jeremiah had become increasingly convinced that the Babylonians were to be Yahweh's agents of judgment upon his people. When Nebuchadnezzar crushed the Egyptian forces at Carchemish in 605 (cf. xlvi 2–12) the conviction became certainty. No doubt some of the poems telling of the "Foe from the North," mentioned above, were uttered as the Babylonians swept southward toward Palestine. In that same year Jeremiah made a last effort to bring his country to its senses (ch. xxxvi). Calling his friend and secretary Baruch, he dictated to him a selection or digest of his preaching through the preceding twenty-three years and, since he himself was forbidden to enter the temple (vs. 5), he ordered Baruch to take the scroll just composed and read it there at the earliest opportunity. It was perhaps more than a year later, in December 604 (vs. 9), that a favorable opportunity presented itself. By this time, as indicated above, the Babylonian army had rolled into the Philistine plain and was completing the reduction of the city of Ashkelon; a day of national fasting was proclaimed in Jerusalem, and Baruch, taking advantage of the crowds that thronged the temple for the occasion, read the scroll publicly then. When certain of the king's cabinet, among them Gemariah ben Shaphan and Elnathan ben Achbor, both apparently sons of protagonists of Josiah's reform (II Kings xxii 12), heard of this, they sent for Baruch and requested that he read the scroll again. Baruch did so. The princes, tremendously impressed by what they had heard, felt duty bound to bring it to the king's attention; and this they did, after urging Baruch to get Jeremiah and go into hiding. The king demanded to hear the scroll. But not with any intention of heeding it! Rather, he expressed his contempt for it by snatching it from the reader's hands whenever the latter had completed three or four columns, hacking off with a penknife the portion just heard, and throwing it into the fire—and so on till the scroll was consumed. He would undoubtedly have had Jeremiah executed had he been able to lay his hands on him (vs. 26). As we have seen above, Jeremiah subsequently (vs. 32) recreated the scroll, with additions; and this doubtless formed the nucleus about which the Jeremiah book as we know it began to be collected.

After this experience Jeremiah seems no longer to have felt any hope of correcting the state—though he did not give up the effort (xiii 15–17). It seemed to him that his people were as constitutionally incapable of repentance as a leopard is of changing his spots (xiii 23), indeed they were beyond prayer (vii 16; xi 14; xiv 11)—though the very fact that the injunction not to pray is so often repeated leads one to suspect that Jeremiah never ceased to pray. When Jehoiakim's folly in rebelling against Nebuchadnezzar (in 601 or 600) had at last brought the nation to the brink of disaster, little was left for Jeremiah save to preach its funeral oration: Yahweh has been obliged to hate the people whom he had loved so dearly, and give them into the hands of their foes (xii 7–13). Graphically, with pathos unparalleled, Jeremiah told of the coming disaster, and the sad fate that awaited his people (e.g., viii 13–17; ix 16–21[17–22E]; x 17 f.; xxii 20–23): the awful Day of Yahweh was at hand, and a ruin so total that it might appear that the earth had been "uncreated" and primeval chaos reigned again (iv 23–26). Yet, when the tragedy struck (in 598/7), Jeremiah, his heart nearly broken, lamented the suffering of his people as only a Jeremiah could (e.g., iv 19–21; viii 18–23 [ix 1E]; x 19–21). Movingly, pityingly, he told of the sad fate of the young king Jehoiachin, innocent victim of his father's folly (xiii 18 f.; xxii 24–30). Yet never once did he yield in his insistence that all this had come as Yahweh's righteous judgment on the nation for its sin (xiii 20–27).

3

In the events of 598/7, the surrender of Jerusalem to the Babylonians and the deportation of its king and leading citizens, Jeremiah's dire predictions found their vindication. Yet, shattering
though this disaster was, it did not amount to the total destruction
which Jeremiah apparently had expected. On the contrary, as we
have seen above (in the chapter "The Background of Jeremiah's
Career . . ."), Nebuchadnezzar, apparently somewhat mollified by
the city's prompt capitulation, allowed the state to remain in existence with a member of the Davidic house—Zedekiah, the uncle
of the deported Jehoiachin and another of Josiah's sons—as its ruler.
With that, the last tragic act of the drama began, and Jeremiah, increasingly alienated from the men who guided his country's destiny,
plumbed new depths of suffering.

The state of mind in Judah after the deportation of 597 is in
many ways difficult to understand. To be sure, it is not in the least
surprising that influential elements in the country should have
wished to continue the struggle for independence. Love of freedom
is a universal and laudable quality, and one that requires neither
explanation nor justification; ancient Israelites seem to have been
generously equipped with it. Moreover, ever since the days of the
Assyrian conquests, the standing policy of those who desired resistance had been to wait for a favorable opportunity, form a coalition, and seek assistance from Egypt—which assistance Egypt was
usually happy to promise, it being in line with her interests to do so.
Although this was a policy that had seldom worked, it was tried
again and again, no doubt because no effective alternative presented itself. It is, therefore, not surprising that Judah's leaders
should have toyed with it. What is surprising is that they did so at
this time and, apparently, with every hope of success. Although
Nebuchadnezzar had behaved with relative leniency, he had demon-
strated beyond doubt both the overwhelming superiority of Babylonian arms and the fact that he was himself not a man to be
trifled with. One would think that this would have been evident to
all, and that the nation would have bowed to the inevitable, at
least for a time. But nothing of the sort! On the contrary, Judah's
leaders, though no doubt brave enough men and sincerely patriotic,

seemed totally unable to assess the realities of the situation. As if bent on seeing how far Nebuchadnezzar could be pushed, they indulged in continual agitation and scheming until, finally, having committed the nation to open rebellion, they brought down upon it that king's merciless wrath.

Mere patriotism, the natural desire of a proud people to reverse an intolerable situation, will not suffice to explain such conduct, nor will the probability that, the nation's best leadership having been deported to Babylon, most of Zedekiah's ministers were politically naïve. To whatever degree such factors may have entered in, the foolhardy policy to which the nation was committed had its deepest roots in theology, specifically in the confidence that although Yahweh might chasten his people, he would never allow his holy city and chosen dynasty to be destroyed; and this, in turn, seems to have given rise to the conviction that, since Yahweh's chastening judgment had already fallen, the future was bright with promise. Such notions were fathered, of course, by the official national dogma which we see expressed in the Royal Psalms (e.g., Pss. ii, xx, xxi, lxxii, lxxxix, cxxxii, etc.; cf. II Sam vii 8–17). But one wonders if there had not been a tendency to generalize from the promises uttered by Isaiah when Sennacherib invaded the land (cf. Isa xxxvii 21–35 and similar passages) to the point that these were interpreted to mean that Yahweh was at all times unconditionally committed to the defense of Jerusalem. One wonders, too, if those prophets who opposed Jeremiah in this regard did not consider themselves as Isaiah's disciples. Whatever the reasons, there were those, as will presently appear, who believed that the deported Jehoiachin and the other exiles would soon return to Jerusalem in triumph, bringing the looted temple treasures with them. At the same time, the feeling seems to have existed among those left in Jerusalem that they were the righteous ones, the pure "remnant" who had survived the judgment, to whom the land and the promises now rightfully belonged (cf. ch. xxiv; Ezek xi 15; xxxiii 24). It was probably among these that dynastic hopes began to be attached to Zedekiah (xxiii 5 f.).

To such sentiments Jeremiah gave no quarter. Rejecting the notion that the deportation of 597 had drawn off the wicked and spared the righteous, he likened the people who were left to ore so impure that it could not possibly be refined (vi 27–30). Indeed, he went so far as to say (ch. xxiv) that the best fruit of the nation, those with whom its future rested, had been plucked away, leaving only worthless culls—figs too rotten to eat. The hope of a speedy fulfillment of the promises to David he rejected utterly. Though he did not deny that those promises had validity, the wordplay of xxiii 5–6 is more than a hint that he did not expect them to be fulfilled in Zedekiah. And, in spite of his profound sympathy for the deported Jehoiachin, he declared flatly that neither he nor any of his sons would ever sit on the throne of Judah again (xxii 24–30). It is true that not long after this, Jeremiah did promise the exiles in Babylon that they would one day return to their homeland; but this, he said, would not be soon.

Nevertheless, within four years of the first deportation ardent patriotism, supported by notions such as those just described, very nearly pushed the nation into an open break. It will be recalled that in 594/3, very probably encouraged by disturbances in Babylon during the preceding year, various of Nebuchadnezzar's vassals in the west began to toy with the idea of rebellion; ambassadors of the kings of Edom, Moab, Ammon, and Tyre and Sidon met in Jerusalem (xxvii 3), no doubt at Zedekiah's invitation, to discuss plans. Meanwhile, nationalistic prophets were whipping up a popular frenzy by declaring that Yahweh had broken the yoke of Babylon, and would within two years (xxviii 2–4) bring Jehoiachin, the other exiles, and all the booty taken by Nebuchadnezzar, back to Jerusalem. Jeremiah flatly contradicted such talk. Wearing an ox-yoke on his neck, he appeared before the conspirators and bade them tell their respective kings to wear the yoke of Nebuchadnezzar if they wished to escape destruction (xxvii 2–11). He gave the same message to his own king (xxvii 12–15), and also repeated it publicly in the temple (xxvii 16–22). It was presumably at this time, too, that he sent a letter to the exiles in Babylon (xxix 1–14, 21–23), telling them to disregard the wild promises of their prophets, conduct themselves in a peaceable manner, and settle down for a long stay; although he comforted them with the assurance that they would one day return to their homeland, he explicitly declared that this lay far in the future. In saying such things, be it noted, Jeremiah by no means spoke as a pacifist, or one who was pro-Babylonian in sentiment (according to li 59–64 he pronounced a doom-oracle on Babylon in this very year), but rather out of the overwhelming conviction that Yahweh, creator and Lord of all things, had in his infinite wisdom chosen to give the earth into the

hand of Nebuchadnezzar: to resist Nebuchadnezzar was, therefore, to resist Yahweh (xxvii 5–8).

Words such as these of course brought Jeremiah into collision
with those prophets who had been saying just the opposite. One of
them, Hananiah, publicly contradicted him (ch. xxviii), and, in
effect, gave him the lie—though it was Jeremiah who had the last
word. A certain prophet among the exiles in Babylon, Shemaiah,
was so infuriated by Jeremiah's letter that he wrote (xxix 24–32)
to one of the high-ranking temple priests demanding that he have
Jeremiah disciplined and silenced. It was a time when prophetic
word was hurled in the teeth of prophetic word, and Israel's God
was invoked in support of diametrically opposite courses of action.
Could one blame the bystanders at such scenes, many of whom may
sincerely have wanted to know what the divine will was, if they
found themselves somewhat confused? How could one tell which
prophet was speaking the truth? Unfortunately, there was no way
save, as Jeremiah himself admitted (xxviii 9), to wait and see
whose word came to pass—which was scarcely helpful to men
who had to face immediate decisions! Nevertheless, Jeremiah *knew*
that his word came from Yahweh, and he was compelled to stand
up for it against those who contradicted him (although, as xxviii 6
indicates, he could cheerfully have wished that their hopeful predictions were true). It was probably at about this time that his quar-
rel with the professional prophets, which had been chronic throughout his ministry, reached new heights of intensity. Perhaps some
of the sayings in xxiii 9–40 (e.g., vss. 16–22, 23–32), though none
can be dated precisely, belong here. Few words that Jeremiah
ever uttered are more scathing. Heatedly accusing these prophets
of purveying nothing but their own wishful thinking, he declared
that they had never been commissioned by Yahweh to speak his
word at all, but rather were upstarts and liars who misled the people
with their dreams and fraudulent oracles. With no group was Yahweh's prophet more bitterly, more irreconcilably at odds than with
the prophets!

As it turned out, the proposed rebellion came to nothing—though
we have no way of saying to what degree, if at all, this outcome
was influenced by Jeremiah's words. Nor do we know anything of
Jeremiah's activity—or, indeed, of internal affairs in Judah generally—during the next five years. When next we meet him, Judah
was being overrun by the Babylonian army, and the last desperate

hour had begun. The events have already been sketched; let us fix them once more in our minds. Encouraged by promises of Egyptian aid, the decision to revolt had been made, presumably in 589. The Babylonians reacted swiftly. Probably by the autumn of the same year their army had invaded the land; by January 588 (lii 4) they had placed Jerusalem under blockade and were proceeding with the reduction of outlying strong points. These they took one by one, until later in the year only Lachish and Azekah (xxxiv 6 f.) —and finally Lachish alone—remained of all of Judah's fortified towns. Temporary relief came, probably in the summer of 588, when the approach of an Egyptian army (xxxvii 5) forced the Babylonians to lift their blockade of Jerusalem and move to meet this new threat. But the respite was temporary; the Egyptians were quickly driven back, and the siege was resumed. It lasted for approximately another year, until July 587 (lii 5 f.), when the city fell. Thanks to the Biographer, we have a rich and circumstantial account of Jeremiah's activity and fortunes during these tragic months.

It is clear that Zedekiah had acted under pressure from his nobles, whom he had not the strength to resist, and was far from certain that he had chosen the right course. He desperately wanted reassurance. More than once he sent to Jeremiah asking for a word from Yahweh, and hoping to receive such a reply as Isaiah had given to Hezekiah when Sennacherib was threatening Jerusalem (e.g., Isa xxxvii 33–35), namely, that Yahweh would defend the city for his own sake and for the sake of his promises to David and, miraculously intervening, would force Nebuchadnezzar to withdraw (cf. xxi 2). The first such occasion (xxi 1–7) was soon after the Babylonian attack had begun, and before the actual blockade of the city had become effective. But Jeremiah gave Zedekiah no encouragement. On the contrary, he assured him that Yahweh himself was fighting for the Babylonians, and that such of Judah's forces as were still in the field would soon be driven back into the city, and the city put under siege and taken. Throughout the whole of this trying time Jeremiah's advice to Zedekiah was consistently that he surrender (e.g., xxxiv 1–7). Even when the siege was temporarily lifted, Jeremiah replied to a further inquiry from Zedekiah (xxxvii 3–10) that it would certainly be resumed, and that even if the Babylonian army consisted entirely of casualties, these would get up from their beds and take the city. And when, during this same interval, certain of the people in violation of their solemn oath took back into bondage slaves whom they had previously released, Jeremiah, expressing himself in some of the most stinging language that ever escaped his lips (xxxiv 8–22), declared that for this crime the city's doom was sealed. Jeremiah even went so far as to advise the people to desert if they wished to save their lives (xxi 8–10). As the situation grew more desperate, many of them did so (xxxviii 19; xxxix 9).

Judah's policy had indeed brought it to the brink of disaster; as events were soon to show, Jeremiah's gloomy predictions were entirely correct. Nevertheless, they were scarcely helpful to the war effort, and not the sort of thing for which those in authority were likely to thank him. On the contrary, they came to regard Jeremiah as a defeatist, if not a traitor. Yet these men, however ill-advised they may have been, were not necessarily villains but were—at least, the best of them—men sincerely dedicated to what they believed to be their country's best interests. How one's country is best to be served is a question upon which men may at any time legitimately disagree, and it is not surprising that in Judah's last hours her citizens were not of one mind on the point. Those in the saddle at the moment were of the party that favored alignment with Egypt, and a bold stroke for independence. They undoubtedly included men who, fully aware of the risks, quite simply preferred to die rather than submit to Babylon any longer. One can only admire their courage. In the opposite camp were those who for prudential or other reasons felt that the nation had no course but to remain in the Babylonian orbit, at least for the moment. Among them were cowards no doubt, but also assuredly men of unimpeachable patriotism whose only thought was to save their country. Which group was acting in accordance with the divine will? How could one tell, when prophets were giving oracles in the name of Yahweh in support of each? Both were convinced that they were in the right. No middle ground remained between them: in the view of the party in power, one was either committed to resistance—or a traitor.

Jeremiah actually did not belong in either category. He advised submission to Babylon; but to mark him down as a Babylonian sympathizer, or a collaborationist, would be to do him a grave injustice. Though his words undoubtedly had the effect of undermining morale, they were not motivated by pro-Babylonian sentiments, as many of Judah's leaders seem, no doubt quite sincerely, to have believed (xxxviii 2–4; cf. xxxii 3–5). He did not desire a Babylonian victory, and to predict it was something that gave him no pleasure at all. Be it noted that, after the city had fallen, when the Babylonians, who themselves believed him to be on their side, promised him preferred treatment if he would come with them to Babylon (xl 1–6), Jeremiah without hesitation refused. A strange traitor this, who would accept no reward for his treason, indeed pointedly spurned it! On the other hand, to suppose that Jeremiah spoke as he did because of pacifistic leanings, or from personal cowardice, would be, if possible, even more unfair. To call him a pacifist would be both to modernize him and to forget that, far from asserting that Yahweh had no part in the struggle, he repeatedly declared (e.g., xxi 5) that Yahweh was actively engaged in it—on the Babylonian side! As for cowardice, one has only to remember that though Jeremiah advised all and sundry to desert, he did not himself take his own advice. Had he been a coward, he would have said nothing and simply have slipped out to the Babylonians at the first opportunity. And, finally, we cannot understand Jeremiah merely as a man who, realizing that resistance is suicidal, counsels surrender as a means of saving at least something from the wreckage. He did indeed realize that resistance was suicidal; but his counsel was not politically motivated, or dictated by mere prudence, but was based in the word of Yahweh that had come to him. He was convinced that the Babylonians were the instrument of Yahweh's judgment upon the nation for its breach of covenant; he therefore had no course but to warn it that in resisting the Babylonians, it resisted the will of its God and courted inevitable destruction.

Nevertheless, although one may with justice call this patriotism on a deeper level, it is understandable that Judah's leaders did not see it so. To them, Jeremiah was an enemy of the country whose presence could not be tolerated. So they set about to destroy him. We learn of this in chapters xxxvii–xxxviii where, as some believe (see the remarks below), two parallel accounts of Jeremiah's arrest and imprisonment (xxxvii 11–21 and xxxviii 1–28a) have been preserved side by side. The story, briefly, is as follows: When the Babylonians had lifted the siege of Jerusalem because of the approach of the Egyptian army, Jeremiah attempted to leave the city in order to go to his home in Anathoth on a matter of family business—very probably the matter of land purchase of which we learn in xxxii 6–15, and of which we shall speak later. But when he got to the city gate he was arrested by the officer of the guard on suspicion of desertion and, in spite of his protestations of innocence, hauled before a panel of princes who, after a summary hearing, had him beaten and thrown into a dungeon (actually a waterless cistern with deep mud at its bottom), and there left to die. He almost certainly would have died had not an Ethiopian eunuch in the service of the palace, one Ebed-melek, learned of his plight and begged the king—who, too great a weakling to withstand his nobles (xxxviii 5), had apparently washed his hands of the matter, and was unaware of what had been done—for permission to get him out. Zedekiah, clearly more than half convinced that Jeremiah had been telling the truth, readily acceded. Whereupon Jeremiah was pulled up from the cistern and transferred to the court of the guard, where he remained in confinement as long as the city held out. During this interval, Zedekiah secretly interviewed Jeremiah, once more asking for a word from Yahweh. Jeremiah's advice to him was, as previously, that he surrender; but this advice Zedekiah was afraid to follow.

After the city had fallen the Babylonians allowed Jeremiah to remain with Gedaliah—a son, it will be recalled, of the Ahikam who had once saved Jeremiah's life (xxvi 24) and (probably) a grandson of Josiah's secretary of state—whom they had appointed governor of the ruined land. The story of Gedaliah's brief tenure of office has already been sketched (see earlier chapter "The Background of Jeremiah's Career . . ."), and need not be repeated here. There are two accounts telling how Jeremiah came into the new governor's company (see the comments below). According to one (xxxix 3, 14), Jeremiah was released directly from the court of the guard and entrusted to Gedaliah for safe keeping. According to the other (xxxix 11 f.; xl 1–6), he was found somewhat later by Nebuzaradan, commander of Nebuchadnezzar's bodyguard, among a mass of prisoners being assembled at Ramah for deportation, and given the choice of going to Babylon or staying with Gedaliah; Jeremiah elected to stay. Whatever the details, Jeremiah found himself in the company of the new governor, and there, presumably, he remained until that unfortunate individual was assassinated (chs. xl–xli). Of his activity during this interval we know nothing, though it is tempting to suppose that some of his words

of hope addressed to Judah (in chs. xxx–xxxi) were, in their original form, uttered at this time. When Gedaliah was murdered and
his followers, fearing Babylonian reprisals, considered flight to
Egypt, they turned to Jeremiah for guidance from Yahweh (xlii
1–xliii 7). Jeremiah declared emphatically that it was Yahweh's
will that they stay in the land. But his words were disregarded,
and the company set out for Egypt, taking the old prophet with
them against his will.

The refugees found asylum at Tahpanhes (Daphne), the present-
day Tell Defneh, just within the Egyptian frontier. There the last
words that we have from Jeremiah's lips were uttered (xliii 8–13;
xliv), words condemning his people for their obdurate apostasy and
want of faith, and announcing that Yahweh's judgment would overtake them even in this far land to which they had fled. And there
our story ends; we hear of Jeremiah no more. Presumably, since
he was by this time well along in his sixties, he did not long survive.

4

One who reads the Book of Jeremiah for the first time, reviews
the prophet's life and ponders his message, is likely to come away
somewhat depressed. He will, to be sure, have encountered poetry
of surpassing beauty, flashes of light and hope, of tenderness and
triumphant faith; he will doubtless have come to admire the devotion, the moral earnestness, and the stubborn courage of the man,
and will have been moved by the intensely human qualities which
he reveals to us in the midst of suffering. Yet the preponderant
impression that one gains of Jeremiah is likely to be a gloomy one:
of an intolerant man scathing in censure, of an embittered man
filled with recrimination, frustration, anguish, and black despair.
That Jeremiah should have been styled "the weeping prophet" is—
though this is little better than a caricature—at least understandable.
He was, let it be admitted, as the world evaluates such things, a
failure—a heroic failure, to be sure, but a failure nevertheless. His
words were never at any time heeded; he could not, for all his
efforts, deter his people from the suicidal course that he knew they
were following. Nor was he a man who was able to achieve serenity,
some triumphant inner peace, in the midst of the frustrations that

beset him. Jeremiah did not arrive at sainthood. Nevertheless, we must be careful not to patronize Jeremiah in our evaluation of him, for few men cast a longer shadow over his people's history than did he; perhaps more than any other one person he enabled them to survive the disaster which had overtaken them. In a true, though limited, sense Jeremiah was a savior of Israel.

One must realize that the fall of Jerusalem, and the Exile that ensued, constituted not merely a political catastrophe, but a spiritual emergency of the first order. This was so primarily because the national religion as it was popularly conceived had always said that such a thing could never happen: Yahweh would not allow it! The official religion of the kingdom of Judah was based in Yahweh's eternal covenant with David (cf. II Sam vii 4–17; xxiii 1–7, etc.). It was believed that Yahweh had chosen Zion and its temple as his earthly abode, and had promised to the Davidic dynasty an everlasting rule. Although it was understood that the king, being but Yahweh's vicegerent, might through his sins bring punishment upon himself and his people, it was not doubted that the dynasty itself was eternal and would in the end triumph over all its foes. This theology, regularly reaffirmed in the cult (see the Royal Psalms mentioned above, e.g., Pss ii, xx, xxi, lxxii, lxxxix, cxxxii), was the seedbed from which grew the expectation of an ideal Davidide—the Messiah—under whose just and beneficent rule all the divine promises to the nation would be made actual (cf. Isa ix 2–7; xi 1–9; Mic v 2–4, etc.). Such a belief undeniably imparted to the state of Judah a remarkable stability (it was ruled by the Davidic dynasty through its entire history); nor was it necessarily in disharmony with Israel's primitive faith, in which Yahweh's unconditional promise to his people was a prominent feature (cf. the covenant with Abraham in Gen xv, etc.). Yet it brought with it the danger that in the popular mind the aims of God and of state would be identified, and helped to foster the conceit that God was unconditionally committed to the defense of nation and dynasty; the stern stipulations of the primitive Mosaic covenant tended to sink into the background.

By Jeremiah's day, no doubt in good part as a result of Jerusalem's remarkable deliverance from Sennacherib's army a century before—and in fulfillment of Isaiah's words—belief in the inviolability of Zion had hardened into a dogma. The notion that the city could fall, and the dynasty end, was simply not entertained. Though

Josiah's reform had attempted to call the nation behind this some-what facile theology to an older notion of covenant, and to reacti-vate that covenant's stringent demands, this had, as we have seen, not gone deep enough fundamentally to change inherited ways of thinking and had, moreover, largely been cancelled by the disillu-sionment of Josiah's tragic death and the unfortunate events that followed. Down to the end, the nation reposed its confidence in the physical presence of Yahweh's house in its midst, and in his promise to David of a line that would never end. Secure in this confidence, it marched blindly to disaster.

This meant, of course, that when disaster struck, the official re-ligion was powerless to explain it. And this meant, in turn, that in the minds of many people, disillusioned and confused, Yahweh's very status as God was thrown into question. Not a few were moved to question his justice (xxxi 29; Ezek xviii 2, 25; Lam v 7), while others, no doubt reasoning that the Babylonian victory had demon-strated the superiority of Babylon's gods, were tempted (so, at least, one may suppose from the sweeping polemic against them in Isa xl–xlviii, uttered slightly later) to offer them worship. And still others, accepting the tragedy as the judgment of Yahweh, were trapped in hopeless despair, fearing that Yahweh had cast off his people forever (Ezek xxxiii 10; xxxvii 11; Isa lxiii 19). The very survival of Israel's faith, and the survival of Israel as a people, was threatened. And, humanly speaking, one can say that Israel would not have survived had she not been able to find some ade-quate explanation of the tragedy in terms of her faith, specifically in terms of Yahweh's sovereign power, justice, and faithfulness to his promises. One shudders to think what the result would have been had the only voices of religion raised in her midst been those of priest and professional prophet proclaiming the inviolability of Zion and the eternity of the Davidic line. Had that been all her religion could say, Israel would assuredly have never won through but, sucked down into the maelstrom of history, would have ceased to exist as a recognizable entity, like the other little peoples of west-ern Asia destroyed by the might of Assyria and Babylon. That this did not occur was due in no small measure to men such as Jeremiah—and others of like mind, such as Ezekiel and the au-thor(s) of the Deuteronomic history (Deuteronomy–II Kings)—who gave the tragedy explanation in terms of Israel's faith, and pointed the way beyond it.

Precisely in that Jeremiah's was a message of judgment, it was a saving message. By ruthlessly demolishing false hope, by ceaselessly asserting that the tragedy was Yahweh's doing, his righteous judgment on the nation for its sin, Jeremiah as it were drew the national disaster within the framework of faith, and thus prevented it from destroying faith. While many were being swept from their moorings, and others were plumbing the depths of despair, those who had heard and received the prophetic word were given something to cling to. The tragedy could not be for them the death of God, for even in the tragedy he was in sovereign control, and unimpeachably just. Such men would be driven—through despair and beyond it—to a searching of their own hearts, to penitence, and a new commitment.

In other ways, too, the preaching of Jeremiah—and that of Ezekiel—enabled the people to survive the dark days that lay ahead. No doubt without fully knowing that they did so, these prophets prepared the way for that new community of Israel which would one day rise out of the wreckage of the old, a community based upon individual decision and loyalty in a way that the old had not been. Now it is seriously misleading to speak of Jeremiah and Ezekiel as the discoverers of individual religion, as handbooks so often do. Israel's faith, for all of its strong feeling for the corporate nature of society, had never at any time been unaware of the rights and responsibilities of the individual under Yahweh's covenant law. Nor did earlier prophets such as Amos or Micah, when they condemned the sins of the people, address mere faceless masses, but rather, seeing before them specific cases of oppression and wrong, hurled their denunciations at those specific individuals who had by their crimes brought the nation under judgment. And their message was not merely an attack on the national sin, but a summons to all who would hear to decide for Yahweh's word— often enough against the temper and the policy of the nation. In this, Jeremiah and Ezekiel were at one with their predecessors. Moreover, neither of them proclaimed an individual—as over against a corporate—religion, for both were concerned primarily with the destiny of the Israelite people, and both looked forward to the formation, beyond the catastrophe, precisely of a new *community*. Neither knew anything of religious individualism in the modern sense, nor would they have sanctioned it if they had.

Nevertheless, the fact remains that, unlike their predecessors,

Jeremiah and Ezekiel had perforce to confront the problem, not of the future of the nation (it had no future), but of Israel's survival as a people beyond the nation's destruction. As for Jeremiah, his expectations for the future will concern us in a moment. It is true that he nowhere precisely defines the external organization of the new community which he was confident would emerge beyond the catastrophe (a future Davidic king, and thus a restored Davidic state, plays virtually no role in his thinking—except for the brief saying in xxiii 5–6 and its prose parallel in xxxiii 14–18, really none at all); presumably it was not given to him to see that far. But that he expected Israel to survive—as the community of Yahweh's people, and forever—is certain. The point to be made here, however, is that in whatever way Jeremiah (or Ezekiel) may have conceived of the future community, this could not be, and would not be, a mere revival of the old: history would see to that. The old national-cultic community to which every citizen automatically belonged was ended; it would never be recreated again. Her statehood destroyed, her people scattered through the world, Israel would never again be coterminous with any political unit or geographical area. If she was to survive as a recognizable entity at all, this would of necessity be in the form of a community based far more in the loyalty and personal commitment of individuals than the old community had ever been. Such a community did in fact emerge, in the Exile and after. And the very fact that Jeremiah—and Ezekiel—stressed, perhaps to a unique degree, the inward and personal nature of man's relationship to God surely prepared for its formation.

That Jeremiah's own relationship to his God was intensely private and inward was no doubt due in good part to his unusually sensitive and introspective nature, as well as to the loneliness which the faithful discharge of his office enforced upon him. No doubt, too, the very fact that the national cult became to him increasingly an abomination in which he could not participate drove him to encounter his God—who himself found the empty temple ritual loathsome—in the privacy of his inmost soul. And it was perhaps in part because he had learned from bitter experience how shallow an officially sponsored reform could be that he came to understand that the divine demands could be met only by a repentance and obedience that sprang from the heart. In any event, no prophet stressed more strongly than he the native corruption of the heart—that is, of the mind and will (e.g., xvii 9 f.)—or more earnestly insisted upon the need of inward cleansing, a radical inner change (iv 3 f., 14, etc.). This, plus the fact that he not only censured the corrupt cultus, but declared that its sacrificial ritual had never been more than peripheral to Yahweh's demands (vi 16–21; vii 21–23)—even declared (vii 2–15) that Yahweh could do very well without his house!—surely prepared for the day when Israel's faith would have to go on without temple and without external cult at all—a thing which the ancient mind would not have regarded as possible. And when the blow had fallen and Jews found themselves far from their homes, it was Jeremiah who was the first to assure them (xxix 10–14; cf. Ezek xi 16; Deut iv 27–31) that even in the land of their exile they could meet Yahweh—without temple and without cult—if they sought him with all their heart. Men who heard such words and received them were not left without hope.

With that we come to what is perhaps the most remarkable thing of all: that this same Jeremiah, who so pitilessly demolished false hope, held out to his people a positive hope for the future. The precise nature and extent of that hope is, to be sure, a subject of debate. Poetic oracles of a hopeful nature uttered during and after the crisis of 587 are relatively few and, in part, marked by a style not otherwise characteristic of the Jeremiah poetry; not a few scholars have denied the genuineness of all, or most, of such passages, while others, believing that they stem from an earlier period of Jeremiah's ministry, impose upon them a different interpretation. On the other hand, prose sayings of similar tenor, though relatively more numerous and explicit enough, are involved in the general problem of the prose discourses mentioned in the preceding chapter, and are regarded by not a few scholars as the work of later editors. The problem is not one to be brushed aside lightly. Further discussion of it will be found in the COMMENTS below—especially those relating to chapters xxx–xxxiii, where the bulk of the sayings in question have been collected (a general position with regard to the prose discourses has already been taken).

Nevertheless, real though the problem is, that Jeremiah did not leave his beaten people comfortless may be regarded as certain. Let it be remembered that he had since his call (i 10) seen it as his commission not merely "to uproot and tear down," but also "to build and to plant." That is to say, he had always understood—and in spite of the word of judgment that was to be his burden—

that his ministry was to serve a constructive purpose. Let it be re-membered also that in his youth he had offered hope to the remnant of northern Israel (iii 12 f.; xxxi 2–6, 15–22), describing in moving language the fatherly compassion of Yahweh which, over the miles and the years, still followed this segment of his people. Moreover, the judgment with which Jeremiah through the years had threatened the people of Judah was always, in principle at least, a conditional one: it was a judgment that sincere repentance could avert. Though Jeremiah ultimately reached the point where he no longer expected such repentance to be forthcoming, there is not the slightest evidence that he ever abandoned the belief that if it should be, Yahweh would mercifully pardon. Indeed, he expressly assured certain groups whose loyalty to their God had been outstanding (the Rechabites, ch. xxxv) that they would survive the destruction of the nation and continue forever to exist as a definable com-munity. Finally, one recalls that when the first exile took place in 597, Jeremiah clearly regarded this as an interim—though not, to be sure, a short one—as his letter to the deportees in Babylon indicates (xxix 10–14).

Nor may we suppose that Jeremiah subsequently abandoned hope —say, as the final collapse drew near. The incident of xxxii 1–15 clearly indicates that he did not. Here we are told that Jeremiah, while confined in the court of the guard during Jerusalem's last siege, purchased from his cousin a plot of land in Anathoth. The transaction was consummated according to proper legal procedure, and the deed signed by witnesses and placed "on file"; and this was done in order to signify (vs. 15) that Israel had yet a future— and that in her own land. It is true (vs. 16–17a, 24 f.) that Jeremiah himself scarcely dared to believe this, but felt keenly that he had been made to do a foolish thing. But the compulsion of Yahweh's word again overpowered him. Knowing his God as a God who would never abandon his people, he who could see no hope acted in hope nevertheless. It was undoubtedly this confidence in the land's future in accordance with the divine promises that ex-plains both Jeremiah's refusal to go to Babylon (xl 1–6) and his bitter opposition when flight to Egypt was proposed (xlii 7–22).

In view of all these things, the question really is not *if* Jeremiah held hope for the future; the only question concerns the form in which that hope was cast. And here one thinks particularly of the famous "New Covenant" passage in xxxi 31–34, one of the truly great passages in all of prophetic literature. In view of the position taken with regard to the prose discourses of the book, and in view of what is otherwise known of Jeremiah's preaching, there is no reason to doubt that this passage is in its substance, if not necessarily in every word, his. It is thoroughly characteristic of him; it is hope phrased as a Jeremiah *would* phrase it. It is not a hope based in the promises to David as that of the official theology had been, or one that anticipated some future reconstitution of the monarchy and its institutions: the covenant with David with its immutable promises is not mentioned at all. Rather it is the expectation of a new act of divine grace through which Yahweh would restore the primitive Mosaic covenant, yet in a far profounder way. As once he had called his people from bondage in Egypt and given them his covenant in the wilderness, so now in this present bondage he would renew that covenant with them and, forgiving all their sins, would inscribe its law upon their hearts, thus giving them power to obey it, and so truly to be his people. Thus the very Exodus theology which, in Jeremiah's preaching (classically in ii 4–8), had doomed the nation was made the foundation of its hope. The awful chasm between the demands of Yahweh's covenant law, by which the nation stood condemned, and the sure promises of Yahweh, which faith could not surrender, was bridged from the side of the divine grace. So it was that Jeremiah could come to the end of his ministry, his eyes fixed not on the smoking ruins of Jerusalem or on Israel's sorrowful state, but on the starry heavens above where dwelt Israel's God, a God whose purposes were immutable, and who would never while the earth endured cast off his people (xxxi 35–37).

Jeremiah died, as he had lived, a failure as the world judges such things. Yet it was thanks not least to his words, and his life, that his people were enabled to *live*—toward God's future.

ON THE TEXT AND ITS TRANSLATION

I trust that the preceding chapters, though they make no pretense to completeness, will have provided the reader with enough of an introduction to the Jeremiah book, its historical setting and message, to enable him to proceed to the reading of it with a measure of understanding and appreciation. That, after all, is the purpose for which this entire book has been written. But before releasing the reader, as it were, to the enjoyment of the prophet's own words, and at the risk of interposing too many of my own between him and them, one further subject requires comment. The Book of Jeremiah is entirely in ancient Hebrew, the present book entirely in English. In other words, Jeremiah is here made to speak a language not his own: his words have been translated. Since this is so, the reader is owed some explanation regarding the problems of translation as these relate to the Jeremiah book, and the way in which I have attempted to deal with them in the pages that follow. In particular, approximately half of the book being in poetry, a brief introduction to Hebrew meter is called for, in order that the reader may know what to expect of it, and be prepared to form his own impression of my efforts at an English rendition.

1

To translate anything from one language into another is, as anyone who has ever attempted it knows, a ticklish business. At least this is so, or is especially so, when what is being translated may claim to be classed as literature. The translator faces a twofold task, and he cannot for so much as a sentence forget it if he hopes to succeed in discharging his obligation. He must catch the precise meaning of the words in their original language, and then bring that meaning into the recipient, or translation, language with equal precision; and he must do this in such a way that the literary quality of the original is preserved and, as far as possible, its idiom re-created. In other words, he must see to it that what was *communicated* to readers of the original language—of intellectual under-standing, of spiritual perception, of aesthetic appreciation, or what not—is also communicated to readers of the recipient language. And that, regrettably, is another way of saying that his task is impossible. The thing simply cannot be done to perfection, and for obvious reasons. On the one hand, few translators are so *equally* conversant with both languages of their concern—especially where the original language is an ancient one—that they can always be sure that they have in fact captured the precise meaning. On the other hand, no two languages (least of all English and Hebrew!) are sufficiently alike in structure and vocabulary to allow the literary quality and the idiom of the one to be recaptured in the other without loss. Translations of course have to be made, and have been made since ancient times. Some have been models of accuracy, some indeed classics of literature. But it is safe to say that no trans-lation has ever been made, or ever will be, that can claim to be 100 per cent successful.

This, of course, goes far to explain why there can never be a once-for-all translation of the Bible into English, or even one that will be universally acceptable at a given time and place. Not only can no translation be perfect, but, because of its two-sided nature, the task of translation may be conceived of in more than one way. Consequently there is a legitimate place at one and the same time for various translations of widely different aim and character. Most of us, indeed, like to make use of several. Fundamentally, two types of translation are possible: a "word-for-word" translation, or what may be called a "sense-for-sense" translation. Each of these has its legitimate place, its advantages, and its limitations. The trans-lator will favor one or the other, depending upon which side of his twofold task he feels impelled to lay the greater stress. In practice, however, since neither option can be followed to the total exclusion of the other without disastrous results, translations usually represent something of a compromise between them.

In translating "word-for-word" the aim is that each word, each idiom, each turn of phrase in the original text be reproduced as literally as possible in the recipient language (hereafter to be referred to as English, since that is what it is in our case). Such a

procedure undeniably lifts the translation above subjective interpretations on the part of the translator. It results, at best, in a
rendition that is verbally accurate, behind which the knowledge-
able student can often enough discern the words of the original
without even consulting the text. It is not surprising that versions
of the Bible intended for general use in synagogue or church have
been inclined to follow this procedure: it is, for the purpose, the safe
and right procedure. Nevertheless, it has its limitations. What makes
sense in one language does not, if rendered literally, necessarily
make sense in another. Languages are so different in structure,
vocabulary, and idiom that a "word-for-word" translation may issue in something so pedestrian and wooden, not to say quaint, as
scarcely to be English. It is of course true that through the translated Bible, and thanks especially to the enormous popularity of
the King James version, numerous Hebraisms have entered the
English language and enriched it, some of them, indeed, becoming
so completely domesticated that we no longer recognize them as
foreign. But as many others have retained their strangeness; some
are virtually incomprehensible to all save the most inveterate readers
of the Bible. A literal rendition may, therefore, in spite of its verbal
accuracy, have the effect precisely of obscuring the sense—to say
nothing of the literary quality—of the original, and thus of blocking
communication.

In making a "sense-for-sense" translation, on the contrary, the
procedure is to examine the meaning of the original, sentence by
sentence, clause by clause, phrase by phrase, and then to seek to
reproduce the idiom of the whole in the appropriate English idiom.
This undoubtedly enables the translator, if he is equal to his task,
to do greater justice to the literary quality of the original (if he is
overzealous, it may tempt him to improve upon it!), and also to
phrase its message in words that will be readily understood by the
contemporary reader. Most of the "modern-speech" translations of
the Bible have, in varying degrees, followed this course—and what
a worthy service the best of them have performed! At the same time,
there are obvious dangers here. A "sense-for-sense" translation, if
it makes for greater clarity, also allows for—indeed necessitates—a
greater degree of subjective interpretation on the part of the translator; and this might well in itself obscure the meaning and, while
communicating, communicate the wrong thing. Carried to extremes,
the result might be a mere paraphrase, which contents itself with

getting the general sense but which, because too slovenly to concern itself with details, fails to do even that and is, therefore, not really a translation.

The translation offered in these pages seeks, as others before it have done, a middle position. It is not a "word-for-word" translation; yet it is based on a careful study of the words and, indeed, tries to follow the wording of the original in so far as this is consistent with English idiom, and thus with clear communication. It is a "sense-for-sense" translation in that it seeks to bring the meaning of the Hebrew into acceptable English, and thus to avoid the woodenness which a literal reproduction of words not infrequently imposes; yet it has striven diligently—with what success the reader in command of Hebrew must judge—at all points to remain true to the precise force of the original. Paraphrase has been resorted to only in cases of dire necessity and, where this has been done (indeed, wherever the Hebrew original and the English words used to translate it significantly diverge), it has been indicated in the NOTES. My aim has been to produce a translation both reasonably readable and accurate.

The translation is based on the Hebrew text—or Masoretic Text (MT), as it is called, after those scribes who gave it its present and normative form. Emendations have been indulged in only where the Hebrew is manifestly corrupt and/or where the ancient versions seem clearly to offer a preferable reading. Such emendations are invariably indicated in the textual footnotes. Fortunately, the Hebrew text of Jeremiah is quite well preserved. That is to say, at least, that considering the extreme length of the book there are relatively few passages where the text is so seriously damaged that it cannot be translated at all. Nevertheless, although the Hebrew text is in general greatly to be preferred to that of any ancient version, and certainly ought not to be recklessly emended, it is not sacrosanct. In numerous instances it offers, demonstrably or apparently, an erroneous or inferior reading. The translator must, therefore, allow full weight to the witness of the versions.

Far the most valuable of all the ancient versions is, of course, the Septuagint (LXX)—i.e., the Greek translation of the Old Testament made in Egypt in the course of the last three centuries B.C. (the translation of Jeremiah must have been made at least by the second century, and its Hebrew exemplar must have been in ex-

istence at least a century earlier). Although the quality of LXX—
and therefore its usefulness to the translator—varies from book to
book, and also within books, in the case of Jeremiah its importance
is extremely great.[1] In no book do LXX and MT diverge more
widely. The divergence does not, however, consist in an extraordinary number of contradictory readings (of which more are to be
found in certain other books than in Jeremiah), but rather in differences in arrangement and in omissions on the part of LXX.
The striking example of a different arrangement concerns the oracles
against foreign nations and has already been mentioned in the
chapter "The Book of Jeremiah . . .". These, it will be recalled,
appear in MT as chapters xlvi–li, but in LXX are found between
xxv 13 and 15 (LXX omits vs. 14), and in an entirely different
order. One wonders if these oracles were not absent from the
original collection of the Jeremiah book, and if at some time after
the textual traditions that lie behind MT and LXX had diverged
they were not separately imported into both. This problem, however,
has to do more with the collection and arrangement of the book
than with the text itself, and need not further detain us here.

The omissions of LXX present us with a more delicate problem.
The text of Jeremiah in the LXX translation is approximately one
eighth shorter than that of MT. (According to one scholar's com-
putation[2] LXX lacks some twenty-seven hundred words that are
represented in MT, while adding no more than about one hundred
that are not represented there.) These omissions range in length
from a word or two, or a phrase, up to entire sections (e.g., xxxiii
14–26). In some cases they may have been made intentionally (e.g.,
LXX habitually omits doublets on their second occurrence), in
others perhaps accidentally through scribal error (e.g., was it because of homoioteleuton—i.e., the scribe's eye leaping over material
between two sentences with similar endings—that LXX omits xxxix
4–13?). But the majority of omissions cannot be explained in
either of these ways. Nor can it be assumed that the translators of
LXX were responsible for them—although it is by no means ex-
cluded that they may on occasion have abridged the text in non-

[1] For a brief and readable orientation to the whole subject, the reader would
do well to consult H. M. Orlinsky, "The Septuagint—Its Use in Textual Criticism," BA 9 (1946), 22–34. See also the work of F. M. Cross, Jr., referred
to in n.[3], below.

[2] Cf. Giesebrecht, p. XXV (see Selected Bibliography for complete reference).

essential ways in order to secure a smoother translation, or for other reasons.

It now seems clear from discoveries at Qumran, where manuscript fragments representing both the longer and the shorter form of the text have been found, that the MT and LXX of Jeremiah are based on different recensions of the Hebrew text of that book.[3] At what period the textual tradition from which LXX derived diverged from that behind MT we do not know. Nor is it possible to recreate the history of either. (Perhaps much more can be said once the Qumran discoveries have all been published, and sifted by experts.) But, judging by the variations between them, both LXX and MT may be assumed to have had relatively long histories of scribal transmission behind them. Where they diverge, it is often impossible to decide which of them is to be preferred. Did the tradition behind MT add, or did that behind LXX subtract? Possibly both processes were at work. Particularly in the prose portions MT seems to have a decided tendency toward the conflation of variant readings, as over against LXX which tends to preserve only one. And in certain cases of wider divergence (see, e.g., the COMMENT on ch. xxvii) it is difficult to resist the conclusion that the shorter text of LXX is the more original. But in other cases one is not certain. In order to settle the question it would be necessary first of all by sound text-critical method to re-establish the parent text which presumably lay behind both traditions, and from which both diverged. But that is a task which, in the present state of knowledge (certainly of my own), seems not yet to be possible, and one which in any case lies well outside the purpose of this book. The translation, therefore, will follow the longer form of the text found in MT, which is, after all, the form with which most readers are familiar from their English Bibles. Significant omissions by LXX will be noted *ad locc.*, but to indicate them all would be tedious and pointless.

[3] Cf. F. M. Cross, Jr., *The Ancient Library of Qumran* (New York: Doubleday & Co., 1958, rev. ed. Anchor Books, 1961), Ch. IV. See especially p. 187 where a manuscript fragment in Hebrew (4QJer[b]) exhibiting in Jer x the shorter text and transposed order of LXX is described (cf. the COMMENT on x 1–16 [Sec. 10], below). Another fragment is said to have the longer form of MT. Still other fragments of Jeremiah (from chs. xlii–xlix) have now been published (2Q13). Their text seems to be basically that of MT, but with a few readings that agree with LXX and other Vrs. (and a few independent readings). Cf. M. Baillet, J. T. Milik, and R. de Vaux, *Discoveries in the Judean Desert, III: Les "Petites Grottes" de Qumran* (Oxford: Clarendon Press, 1962), pp. 62–69.

2

The fact that the Jeremiah book is partly in prose, partly in poetry, means that the translator is faced with two entirely different sets of problems—although both fall within the general problem of translation described at the outset. It also means that the reader is faced with a double problem of appreciation, since manifestly prose and poetry cannot be read and enjoyed in the same way. It would, therefore, be well at this point to make a few introductory remarks concerning the prose and the poetry of the book, and concerning the nature of Hebrew poetry itself, in order that the reader may see what has been attempted in the translation and, it is hoped, find increased pleasure in his reading.

1. As regards the prose, little need be said beyond a statement of the principle that has guided its translation. It must be admitted that the prose of Jeremiah—particularly that of the prose discourses earlier described in the chapter "The Book of Jeremiah . . ."—is not, at least to our taste, the best of which the ancient Hebrew was capable. It is a rather inflated style. It lacks the terse stylistic economy of the classic prose of the "Golden Age" (tenth century) —such as we find, for example, in the stories of Saul and David in the books of Samuel—and is, if not without a certain rhetorical eloquence, repetitious and wordy and, moreover, loaded with stereotyped expressions. It tends to long sentences, which at times seem to wind on interminably without regard for punctuation as we understand it. In a word, it is not a style that can be translated literally into English (and this beyond the mere fact that no language can be translated verbatim into another) without creating a rather unfavorable impression. This statement, to be sure, is not altogether true of certain of the narrative accounts of Jeremiah's "Biographer"; but it is emphatically true of the prose discourses.

Now the translator does not have the right, I think, to "prettify" the style of his exemplar, or otherwise to improve upon it. To do that would not be to *translate*. The translator must strive to reproduce what is before him, including its quality of style—whether good, bad, or indifferent. At the same time, in the case of the prose of Jeremiah, may one not ask if a faithfully conscientious reproduction of its pedestrian and somewhat undisciplined style would not, in itself, be to misrepresent its literary quality to English-speaking readers? In other words, may we not assume that this material, if not the best of classical Hebrew prose, is nonetheless a literate prose? Or, to put it still otherwise, does the fact that the prose of Jeremiah strikes us as stylistically inferior necessarily mean that Jeremiah's contemporaries regarded it as bad Hebrew? I see no reason to believe that they did. The prose of Jeremiah seems, indeed, to have been—like that of the Deuteronomic literature (Deuteronomy–II Kings)—a rhetorical prose characteristic of the seventh and sixth centuries B.C. It is, granted, not the best Hebrew style to be found in the Bible; but I believe that we can assume that it was regarded as at least an acceptable style, and one, moreover, not without a certain eloquence of its own.

And this sets the translator's task. He must, I think, without attempting to disguise the monotonous and wordy style of this prose, and certainly without permitting himself to depart from its meaning, seek to make of it an English prose as stylistically acceptable as the Hebrew presumably was. And this I have tried to do— though how well I have succeeded I do not myself know. I have not attempted to make excellent English prose of it (as if I were capable of that!), but I have allowed myself, while following the Hebrew text faithfully and not resorting to paraphrase, to bring its syntax into conformity with acceptable English in so far as this could be done without twisting the meaning of the original. If the reader finds the result somewhat less than brilliant, that is doubtless in part the fault of the translator; but it is partly owing to the literary quality of the original, which no attempt has been made to conceal. Let the reader who finds it pedestrian and uninspiring as literature, look behind it to the message it carries. And that is anything but pedestrian and uninspiring!

2. Now to the poetry. Here it is necessary, without launching into an extended and technical discussion,[4] first of all to say a few

---

[4] The reader who wishes to pursue the subject further may be referred to the old, standard work of G. B. Gray, *The Forms of Hebrew Poetry* (London: Hodder & Stoughton, 1915); or the more recent work of T. H. Robinson, *The Poetry of the Old Testament* (London: Duckworth, 1947). For a briefer discussion, cf. W. O. E. Oesterley, *The Psalms*, Vol. I (London: SPCK, 1939), Ch. IV. In recent years, various studies of Hebrew poetry in the light especially of the Old Canaanite poetry of Ugarit (Ras Shamra) have led to many significant advances, but the literature on the subject is scattered through the files of learned journals and is, for the most part, highly technical in character. Perhaps the article of W. F. Albright, "The Old Testament and Canaanite Language and Literature" (CBQ 7 [1945], 5–31), will give the reader as good an introduction to these new developments as is available.

words concerning the nature of Hebrew poetry in general, and then to give the reader some idea of the way in which the translation of it has been handled in the pages that follow.

In order to appreciate Hebrew poetry, one must begin by banishing from one's mind most of one's inherited notions of what poetry ought to be. For one thing, although it is quite fond of employing assonance (i.e., recurrence of similar sounds), Hebrew poetry has no rhyme. It is true that recurrence of identical sounds (pronominal suffixes or verbal endings) at the end of verse-members on occasion yields an effect that approximates rhyme (Jer i 5 is an example); but even if one chooses to call this device rhyme (and I doubt that one should), it is far too uncommon to be considered characteristic. Moreover, Hebrew poetry does not exhibit— at least in the view most commonly held (though this is disputed, as we shall see in a moment)—that regular recurrence of accented and unaccented syllables which, to us, constitutes meter: its verse does not move steadily on in tetrameters or pentameters, whether iambic, trochaic, anapaestic, or dactylic. It was because features such as these—the distinctive marks of poetry to the Western mind —are lacking in Hebrew verse, and because Hebrew prose is itself frequently so musical, that for many centuries no essential difference between the two seems to have been observed. (As the reader knows, in older English versions of the Bible prose and poetry are printed alike.) It was, in fact, only in the eighteenth century, with the pioneering work of Bishop Robert Lowth, *De Sacra Poesi Hebraeorum* (1753), that Hebrew poetry first began to be recognized for what it is. Though subsequent research has naturally gone far beyond them, Lowth's preliminary observations were, nevertheless, fundamentally sound.

The characteristic marks of Hebrew poetry are essentially two: parallelism of members, as Lowth was the first to see; and the (more or less) regular recurrence of accented syllables within the individual members. We shall say more of each of these in a moment. But, first of all, it is only fair to warn the reader that we are entering disputed territory here. The whole subject of Hebrew meter is beset with unsolved problems, upon which there is the widest disagreement among scholars. Perhaps it is inevitable that it should be so. Meter, after all, is determined primarily by the accenting and pronunciation of words; and we really do not know how words were pronounced in pre-Exilic Judah, still less how they may have been stressed in poetic delivery. As a result of these uncertainties two different theories of Hebrew meter have their advocates today. The classical theory, and still the most widely held, is the so-called accentual system (or Ley-Sievers system, after the scholars most influential in its development). In this theory, accented syllables alone are regarded as determinative; it is believed that in the various lines of a poem these will recur in a more or less regular pattern, but that the unaccented syllables between them may vary in number (though scarcely more than three) as necessity dictates. Opposed to this is the so-called alternating system. Advocates of this system[5] hold that both accented and unaccented syllables are determinative, and believe that in each line these follow one another in regular alternation (one for one)—to use our terminology, in the form of iambs or trochees. Strong arguments can be advanced for either position, but it would be out of place to debate the issue here. In view of the uncertainties that surround the whole subject, one should certainly preserve an open mind about it. In these pages, however, both because it seems to work better in the case of the Jeremiah poetry, and for want of contrary conviction on my part, the more commonly held accentual system has been adhered to.

With this in mind, let us return to the distinctive marks of Hebrew poetry. Each line of Hebrew verse consists of two—or, as is not infrequently the case, three—parts, or verse-members. To avoid confusion, we shall refer to the individual verse-member, the shortest unit within the line, as a colon[6]: thus a line of two members is a bicolon, a line of three members a tricolon. In Hebrew verse the syntactical unit (sentence, clause, phrase) characteristically coincides—though this is not always the case—with the metrical unit

---

[5] Recently S. Mowinckel and F. Horst in particular. Cf. Mowinckel, "Zum Problem der hebräischen Metrik," *Festschrift für Alfred Bertholet* (Tübingen: J. C. B. Mohr, 1950), pp. 379–94; Mowinckel, *The Psalms in Israel's Worship*, Eng. tr., D. R. Ap-Thomas (New York: Abingdon, 1962), Vol. II, pp. 159–75, 261–66; Horst, "Die Kennzeichen der hebräischen Poesie," *Theologische Rundschau*, NF 21 (1953), 97–121. See also Professor Horst's commentary on Job in the *Biblischer Kommentar* series (now sadly interrupted by the author's death), for a splendid example of the application of this theory in practice. Mowinckel in his latest work (*The Psalms in Israel's Worship*, Vol. II, pp. 162, 173) concedes that "popular poetry and improvised prophetic speech" may have a less regular meter than "professional poetry" (Psalms, Proverbs, Job).

[6] The terminology employed in this connection has, unfortunately, not been standardized. Sometimes the shortest verse-member is called a stich, sometimes a hemistich, sometimes—loosely—a line. We shall, for consistency's sake, follow the practice of W. F. Albright and others in referring to it as a colon, and the longer unit of two or three cola as a line.

(colon). Within a line the cola normally stand in some kind of parallelism with one another as regards their thought—though frequently the entire line will be paralleled by the next line. (Or, the situation may be even more complicated in that, say, in the case of four cola, the first may be paralleled by the last, the second by the third—and so on.)

This parallelism of thought may be of various kinds, the most striking of which were noted by Bishop Lowth long ago. It may be synonymous (i.e., the second colon will in some way repeat and reinforce the thought of the first); for example, Ps xxiv 3:

> "Who shall ascend the mount of Yahweh?
> Who shall stand in his holy place?"

Or it may be antithetical (i.e., in two cola the same thought will be expressed first positively, then negatively); for example, Prov x 1:

> "A wise son delights [his] father,
> But a foolish son is a grief to his mother."

Frequently, however, the parallelism is merely formal ("synthetic" was Lowth's word), with the second colon carrying forward the thought of the first; for example, Ps ii 6:

> "But I have installed my king
> On Zion, my holy mount."

Here there is no real parallelism of thought at all, although in cases of this kind it frequently happens that the two formally parallel cola of one line will be balanced in thought by the two cola of the next. Since Lowth's day, of course, various other types of thought-parallelism have been suggested; but we shall not attempt to review them all here.

Since, as has just been indicated, parallelism is frequently no more than formal, many have found it more profitable to class possible types according to form.[7] So viewed, parallelism may be complete or incomplete. In the former case, each word in one colon will be balanced by a corresponding word in the other. One might schematize this: a b c / a b c. So, for example, Ps lxxxiii 15[14E] (words joined with hyphens are single words in Hebrew):

> "As - the - fire   ignites   the-forest,
> As - the - flame   sets-ablaze   the-hills,"

---

[7] G. B. Gray (see the work cited in n.[4]) was apparently the first to do this.

In the case of incomplete parallelism, two possibilities occur: words in the first colon that do not find their parallel in the second may be compensated for by the addition of other words, or they may not. As an example of the latter we may cite Ps lxxii 2, where it is said of the king:

> "May-he-judge   thy-people   with-righteousness,
>   Thy-poor   with-justice"

Here one word in the first colon finds no parallel in the second; and this is not compensated for by the addition of any other word. We might schematize it thus: a b c / b c. Needless to say, other variations are possible (e.g., a b c / a b, etc.). It should be noted, however, that in many such cases—and this is true of the example just cited—the syllable count in each of the two cola is the same, so that the second colon, though apparently shorter, may have taken as long to recite as the first.

As a simple example of incomplete parallelism with compensation Ps xc 8 may be cited:

> "Thou‑hast‑set   our-iniquities   before-thee,
> Our-secret-sins   in-the-light-of   thy-face."

Here the verb of the first colon is not paralleled in the second; but in its stead an additional word is added at the end in compensation. This might be schematized thus: a b c / b c d. Where such compensation takes place, possible combinations are almost unlimited. Sometimes the result is a strikingly "stairlike," or climactic effect, as for example in Ps xxix 1 f., where the arrangement might be schematized thus: a b c d / a b e f / a b e g:

> "Ascribe to Yahweh, you heavenly beings,
> Ascribe to Yahweh   glory and strength;
> Ascribe to Yahweh   the glory of   his name."

This arrangement, incidentally, is paralleled in Canaanite (Ugaritic) literature, from which Psalm xxix seems originally to have been adapted.

To illustrate all the above points adequately, and others that might be made, would require far more space than is available here. But perhaps a few further examples chosen at random from the poetry of Jeremiah will serve to make the matter sufficiently clear for the reader's enjoyment. In i 5 we read (literally):

"Before   I-formed-you in-the-womb   I-chose-you;
Before   you-came   from-the-womb I-consecrated you;
A-prophet   to-the-nations   I-appointed you."

The verse is a tricolon. In the first two cola the parallelism is synonymous and formally complete: each word in one is balanced by a corresponding word in the other (incidentally, two different Hebrew words are rendered by the English "womb"). The scheme is a b c d / a b c d. The third colon, however, stands in merely formal parallelism to the preceding two and carries forward their thought; only its verb is paralleled in them, while other words are drawn in as compensation. Again, in ii 2 we read:

"I-remember   the-devotion-of   your-youth,
the-love-of   your-bridal-days."

We shall say more of the meter of this passage (the beginning of which is literally: "I remember of you the devotion of your youth") presently. But it offers us a parallelism which is synonymous in thought, but formally incomplete and uncompensated (a b c / b c). The same is true of ii 20, where we read:

"Long-ago   you-snapped   your-yoke,
Shook-off   your-lines."

In ii 6, on the other hand, we have cola in synonymous parallelism with a striking stairlike arrangement, which might be diagramed thus:

"They never said, 'Where is Yahweh,
     Who brought us up from Egypt's land,
     Who guided us through the desert,
         Land of steppe and ravine,
         Land of drought and darkness,
         Land   through which nobody passes,
            Where no human being dwells?' "

Again, in ii 18 we find two lines, each a bicolon. Within the lines the parallelism between the cola is purely formal, the real parallelism being between the two lines themselves. This parallelism is both synonymous and formally complete:

"Now what good is it going to Egypt / to drink Nile water?
Or what good is it going to Assyria / to drink Euphrates water?"

Further examples of synonymous parallelism in various formal arrangements could be multiplied at will.

Antithetic parallelism is considerably less frequent, but the reader will now and then come across examples of it. Thus, in xii 2b, after a series of bicola in which the parallelism is synonymous, we read:

> "Near   art-thou   in-their-mouth,
> But-far   from-their-heart"
>   (literally "kidneys").

Here the parallelism is antithetic. The second colon, moreover, is shorter by one word than the first—though, since the word "from-their-kidneys" (*mikkilyōtēhem*) is a long one, it may have the same number of accents (the syllable count is the same in each colon, viz. seven). In ii 11 we find a parallelism which is antithetical and formally complete, and which lies, moreover, not between the cola within the lines, but between the lines themselves:

> "Has ever a nation changed gods / (though these are not gods)?
> But my people have changed their 'Glory' / for the useless one."

In ii 32 we have two lines of two cola each. In the first line the cola are in synonymous parallelism (a b c / b c); in the second the parallelism is purely formal, but the whole line stands in antithetic parallelism to the first:

> "Will a maid forget her jewels / or a bride her sash?
> But my people—they've forgot' me / days beyond count."

We have space for no more examples. Those that have been given are chosen at random and but scratch the surface of the wealth of possible combinations in which parallelism can be expressed. But perhaps they will suffice to prepare the reader for an appreciation of this phenomenon so characteristic of Hebrew poetry.

As was indicated above, in the accentual system which is followed here, meter is reckoned on the basis of the accented syllables within the cola of a line, the unaccented syllables being variable. Accented syllables in a given colon may be as few as two, or as many as four—though some scholars are inclined to divide most "fours" into two cola of two beats each. Thus, if a line has two cola (i.e., is a bicolon), each with three accented syllables, its meter is spoken of as 3/3; if the first colon has three accented syllables, and the second two, it is spoken of as 3/2—and so on. In Hebrew verse the 3/3 and the 3/2 meters are by far the most common; but lines with all possible combinations of two, three, and four beats will be found (2/2, 4/4, 2/3, 4/3, etc.). In the case of tricola, the combination may be 3/3/3, 3/2/2, 2/2/3, 4/4/3—and so on and on. But at this point the reader should be warned not to expect of Hebrew poetry a rigid regularity of meter. As far as Jeremiah is concerned at least, it is unusual for the meter to continue exactly the same through the length of an entire poem. This is no doubt in part because the prophet felt no compulsion to employ a rigidly regular meter, in part perhaps because at many places in the book material of originally separate origin seems to have been brought together secondarily into the form of longer, apparently continuous, poems. But we must not forget, too, that frequently we cannot be altogether sure what the meter is because we do not know how the poet intended the words to be stressed and pronounced in oral recitation.

Once again, a few illustrations may help to clarify the point (the Hebrew is given in transliteration with the accents indicated).[8] For example, in i 5 one reads:

$$b^e\acute{t}erem \qquad {}'ess\bar{a}r^ek\bar{a} \qquad babb\acute{e}ten \qquad y^eda{}'t\acute{\imath}k\bar{a}$$

$$\bar{u}b^e\acute{t}erem \qquad t\bar{e}\bar{s}^{e}{}' \qquad m\bar{e}r\acute{e}hem \qquad hiqda\check{s}t\acute{\imath}k\bar{a}$$

$$n\bar{a}b\acute{\imath}{}' \qquad lagg\bar{o}y\acute{\imath}m \qquad n^etatt\acute{\imath}k\bar{a}$$

The verse is a tricolon. The first two cola have four accented syllables each, the third has three; the meter, therefore, is 4/4/3. As a further example, let us take ii 2f.:

[8] A few remarks here may assist the reader in pronunciation. The consonants may for the most part be pronounced as they would be in English. For the present purpose, h, t, and $\acute{s}$ may be given the value simply of h, t, and s; s may best be pronounced as ts, while $\check{s}$ is sh; q may be pronounced as k; ' and ' may both be treated as silent consonants. Actually there are subtle distinctions in all of these cases, but they need not be gone into here. The vowels, too, may for convenience be given the value that they would normally have in English: a as in "hat," e as in "bed," i as in "pit," o as in "pot," u as in "pull"; $\bar{a}$ as in "father," $\bar{e}$ as in "they," $\bar{\imath}$ as in "machine," $\bar{o}$ as in "hole," $\bar{u}$ as in "flute." Vowels written above the line ($^e,{}^a,{}^o$) are to be treated as extremely short, i.e., something like the final vowel sound in "little" or "battle," or the first vowel in "begin," as it is normally pronounced (not "bēgin," but rather something like "buhgin" or "bĭgin"—really "bgin").

zākártī   lāk   ḥésed   neʿūráyik / ʾaḥᵃbát   kelūlōtáyik

lektēk   ʾaḥᵃráy   bammidbár / beʿéreṣ   lō'   zerūʿáh

qódeš   yiśrāʾél   leyahwéh / rēʾšít   tebūʾátôh

kól   ʾōkeláw   yeʾšámū / rāʿáh   tābó'   ᵃlēhém

                                            neʿum yahweh

Here we have four lines, all probably best taken as bicola (though some would regard the first as a tricolon: zākártī lák / ḥésed neʿūráyik / ʾaḥᵃbát kelūlōtáyik). In the first three of these the meter is 3/2 (if the first line is taken as a tricolon its meter is 2/2/2, or possibly 2/2/3), while in the last it shifts to 2/3, or more probably 3/3, depending on whether or not the poet wished an accent to be placed on the first word of the line. The last line ends with neʿum yahweh ("Yahweh's word," or "oracle of Yahweh"), a characteristic formula of conclusion; but this stands outside the meter.

One final example must suffice. Let us take ii 6 f., which reads:

(6) welṓ'   ʾāmerū́   ʾayyḗh   yahwéh

     hammaʿᵃléh   ʾōtā́nū   mēʾéreṣ   miṣráyim

hammōlī́k   ʾōtā́nū   bammidbár

beʿéreṣ   ʿᵃrābáh   wešūḥáh

beʿéreṣ   ṣiyyáh   weṣalmā́wet

beʿéreṣ   lō'   ʿābár   bāh   ʾíš

     welṓ   yāšab   ʾādám   šám

(7) wāʾābí'   ʾetkém   ʾel   ʾéreṣ   hakkarmél

le'ekól   piryáh   weṭūbáh

wattābṓ'ū   watteṭammeʾū́   ʾet   ʾarṣí

     wenaḥᵃlātí   śamtém   letōʿēbáh

As it stands, the meter seems to be: 4/4, 3/3/3, 3/3, 4/3, 3/3. If, however, we suppose that the sign of the direct object (ʾet- or ʾot-) was not written in pre-Exilic Hebrew poetry (it certainly was not in early poetry), and if we further omit the article before karmel, it would be possible to take the first colon of vs. 7

also as a "three" (wā'ābī'ᵃkem 'el 'éreṣ karmél, or the like). It is possible, too, that the 4/4 at the beginning of vs. 6 is similarly to be taken as a 3/3 (omitting the *nota accusativa* in the second colon, and not accenting the first word of the first colon), in which event the passage has a regular meter throughout.

I trust that the foregoing remarks, though sketchy, will serve to introduce the reader to the characteristic features of Hebrew poetry, and thus enable him to proceed to the translation that follows with enhanced pleasure. In that translation I have tried, so far as it lay within my ability, to recapture the poetic quality of the original. I will not pretend that I have succeeded. On the contrary, I find myself at more than one place distinctly dissatisfied with what I have done. Yet, to a degree, this cannot be helped. Nothing can be translated without loss, and in the case of poetry this is doubly, triply, so. Not only must one reproduce the precise meaning of the original, as one must in any translation; one must do this in such a way that the poetic structure, and the beauty, of the original is not obscured, but faithfully conveyed to the reader. To succeed in that, the translator would himself have to be a poet, perhaps a poet equal in stature to the author whose work he is translating, and even then he would not succeed completely. Poetry simply cannot be translated without great loss; any attempt to translate it is, therefore, inevitably to some degree a failure.

Nevertheless, to recapture the poetic quality of the original is just what the translator must seek to do. I suspect (I say I suspect; I do not know it, for I have never attempted to translate any other poetry) that Hebrew poetry is at once harder and much easier to translate than, say, the poetry of some modern Western language. Several factors would seem to make it easier. Since it has no rhyme, the translator is under no obligation to seek any—indeed, must avoid doing so. Since there is (at least in the system followed here) no regular alternation of accented and unaccented syllables, it is not incumbent upon him to shape his lines into iambic pentameters or the like; and, needless to say, this allows him far greater freedom in the selection of words. On the other hand, Hebrew poetry presents difficulties of its own. The translator must attempt to produce lines that resemble those of the original and, above all, have something of its "feel"; they must be lines of approximately the same length as the original lines, and lines in which the rhythm of the original—its sharp, recurring accentual beat—is in a measure recreated. This would not in any case be an easy thing to do; and the task is rendered more difficult by the very nature of the Hebrew language. Hebrew requires far fewer separate words than does English. For example, it attaches the conjunction to the following word; it expresses pronominal subject and object with the verb as a single word (e.g., "that I may see him" appears as one word in Hebrew); it attaches prepositions, possessive pronouns, and also the definite article to the noun ("and in the/his house" is one word). This does not, of course, mean that these short attached words were not regarded as words in their own right, or that the resulting combinations are in fact single words; rather, it is simply that the Hebrew had a prejudice against writing monoliteral words separately. From a semantic point of view these combined forms contain as many words as are required in English to say the same thing. Nevertheless, the fact remains that Hebrew does write fewer separate words than English. And this means that a faithful English translation of a Hebrew text will inevitably be more "wordy" than the original and will, moreover, tend to carry more accented syllables. Add to this the fact that the best of Hebrew poetry (and Jeremiah's clearly falls in this class) employs an exceedingly lean style, one marked by an extreme economy of words, and the translator repeatedly finds himself put to it to catch the brevity and the accentual rhythm of the lines without resorting to an English so terse as to be cryptic. And beyond all this, it may be added, Jeremiah's poetry (like that of the other prophets) abounds in instances of assonance and of wordplay which cannot be captured in English at all, but must be tamely indicated in a footnote.

Nevertheless, in the ensuing pages it has been my aim to the best of my ability to imitate the structure and rhythm of the original. I have striven as far as possible to produce lines of approximately the same length as those of the original, and with the same number of accented syllables. Needless to say, I have again and again failed in this. Whether because of the insuperable differences in language structure just outlined, or because a word of the right force and length does not exist in English (or because I was simply not clever enough to find it), the thing now and then could not be done, and the English line would come out a beat longer (occasionally a beat shorter) than the original. I have tried to avoid this, and I believe that I have seldom transgressed by more than a beat,

one way or the other. I can think of no case where there is a line
longer than four, or shorter than two, accentual beats—the maxi-
mum and the minimum, respectively, for the Hebrew colon.

Perhaps a few examples would serve to illustrate what has been
attempted. Here, then, are English translations of i 5; ii 2 f. and
ii 6 f.—the passages given in transliteration above. Accents are
placed where they would normally fall in oral recitation. First, i 5,
a tricolon in which the meter is 4/4/3:

> "Before I had formed you in the womb I chose you;
>
> > Before you were born I set you apart,
> >
> > > And appointed you prophet to the nations."

As for ii 2 f. it consists of four bicola, the first three of which are
3/2, the last 3/3 or 2/3 (on the problem of the meter, see above):

> "I remember your youthful devotion,
>
> > Your bridal love,
>
> How you followed me through the desert,
>
> > The untilled land.
>
> Israel was Yahweh's own portion,
>
> > His harvest's first yield.
>
> All eating of it are held guilty;
>
> > Punishment overtakes them—Yahweh's word."

In ii 6 f. we have a series of bicola (with one tricolon), the number
of accentual beats in each colon being 3 or 4 (on the meter, again
see above):

> "They never said, 'Where is Yahweh,   (4; perhaps 3)
>
> > Who brought us up from Egypt's land,   (4; perhaps 3)
>
> Who guided us through the desert,   (3)
>
> > Land of steppe and ravine,   (3)
> >
> > > Land of drought and of danger,   (3)
> > >
> > Land through which nobody passes,   (3)

Where no húman béing dwélls?'   (3)

To a lánd like a gárden I broúght you,   (4; perhaps 3)

To éat of its boúntiful frúit.   (3)

But you éntered and foúled my lánd,   (3)

And máde my héritage loáthsome."   (3)

These are only random samples, but they are typical of what has been attempted throughout the poetic sections of the book. Perhaps if the reader would pronounce the translation aloud, at a somewhat measured pace, letting the stress fall *strongly* where it naturally would in oral delivery, he would gain a fair impression of the meter of the original.

3

And now, finally, a few remarks of a miscellaneous nature. The aim of the translation has been, as noted above, to present the text of Jeremiah in vernacular English while, at the same time, remaining scrupulously faithful to the meaning of the original. In line with the first part of this aim, "thees" and "thous" have been generally dispensed with. Exception has been made, however (and the same policy is followed in RSV), in cases of direct address to the Deity. I am aware, of course, that the Hebrew has no such special, honorific form of address: in Hebrew one addresses his God, his king, his friend, and his slave with the same second-person form. Nor do I, for one, feel that any significant point of doctrine has been compromised if the Deity is addressed in the (to us) familiar form, "you." Yet, there are many, I know, who find such a practice distasteful, and I must say that to me it has a certain "chummy" sound that I greatly dislike. Perhaps this is no more than ingrained habit, like removing one's hat in church (or putting it on in the synagogue); but it *is* ingrained—as are most points of manners. For this reason the archaic second person has been retained in address to the Deity (and its retention made, I must say, for some metrical difficulties which I would gladly have escaped!). The few exceptions that will be noted occur—and quite properly, I believe—at places in the "confessions" where Jeremiah addresses his God in a decidedly familiar, if not irreverent, manner.

The name Yahweh, the personal name of Israel's God, has been used wherever it occurs in the original. No doubt it will have an unfamiliar sound to some readers, and will jar upon the sensibilities of others. Nevertheless, since it *is* a proper name, there is much to be said for retaining it; its use may serve to remind us of the extremely personal way in which the ancient Hebrew thought of his God. Nor does there appear to be any satisfactory alternative. "God" is too general a term and is, moreover, needed to translate the Hebrew, *'elōhīm;* "the LORD" (so KJ and RSV) is again not a personal name, and is too easily confused with "the Lord" (Heb. *'adōnāy*). "Jehovah," on the other hand, though it conveys the force of the personal name and is established to a degree in usage, is a word that arose through a misapprehension, and should not be perpetuated (the scribes, not wishing the divine name to be pronounced, combined the vowels of *'adōnāy* with the consonants *yhwh* to indicate that one should pronounce *'adōnāy;* in later Christian circles the combined form—*yehōwāh*—was taken as the pronunciation). Finally, to use the bare consonants, YHWH, would probably be to confuse the majority of readers and would, moreover, give no indication of the pronunciation—which is important in metrical contexts. For these reasons "Yahweh" has been used. In light of these remarks, I trust that none will take offense.

Except for a few minor transpositions which will be explained at the proper place in the COMMENTS, the translation follows with one major exception the order found in the Hebrew and English Bibles. That exception concerns the dated (biographical) passages of the book, most of which are in chapters xxvi–xxix, xxxiv–xlv, though some are found elsewhere. It was felt that the reader would get a clearer grasp of Jeremiah's life if these passages were brought together and placed in an order according to chronology. They will be found in the translation after chapter xxv. The order of the translation is, then, as follows: chapters i–xxv (except the dated passages); the dated passages from throughout the book, in chronological order; chapters xxx–xxxiii (the "Book of Consolation"); chapters xlvi–li (oracles against foreign nations); chapter lii (historical appendix). It is hoped that this slight and, I think, justifiable rearrangement will add to the reader's pleasure and profit. No attempt has been made to place the other material of the book in chronological order, since this would involve too great a degree of subjectivism and would lead to results of which no one could be confident.

In the NOTES that accompany the text the reader will encounter a number of abbreviations other than those referring to books and periodicals: these also have been included under the listing "Principal Abbreviations." Since some may be unfamiliar, a brief word of explanation is in order. Most such abbreviations refer to various versions of the Bible. EVV denotes English versions generally. Particular versions most frequently referred to are the King James version (KJ), the American Revised (or American Standard) Version of 1901 (ARV), the version prepared by the Jewish Publication Society of America (1917) usually referred to as the American Jewish Version (AJV), and the Revised Standard Version (RSV). "Vrs." denotes ancient versions generally. Those most frequently referred to include the Greek Version, or Septuagint (LXX), the Syriac (Syr.), the Latin Vulgate (Vulg.), and the Aramaic translations or paraphrases known as the Targums (Tar.). Aquila (Aq.), Symmachus (Symm.), and Theodotion (Theod.) are other Greek translations made in the second century A.D. MT, of course, refers to the standard Hebrew, or Masoretic, text of the Bible. At numerous places in MT it is indicated by means of vowel pointing and/or marginal notations that consonants which would normally be read in one way are to be read in another. In such cases the consonantal text is called the Ktib ("what is written"), while the notation indicating a different reading is called the Qre ("to be read").[9] To discuss all these terms adequately would re-

---

[9] The reader is no doubt aware that the Hebrew alphabet includes only consonants, the pointing used to indicate vowels having been added much later. This makes at times for considerable ambiguity, since the same consonants, vocalized differently, will have different meanings; e.g., *dābār* ("word"), *dᵉbar* ("word of"), *dibbēr* ("he spoke"), and *dabbēr* ("speak!" or "to speak") all have the same consonantal spelling (*dbr*). If the reader will bear this fact in mind, many of the textual notes in the pages that follow will perhaps seem more reasonable to him than they otherwise might. Frequently, when spelled out in full, the reading of MT and that of a suggested emendation will seem to have little resemblance to one another, although the consonantal text presupposed for each may be the same. Thus, for example, at vii 3 MT reads, "then I will let you dwell" (*wa'ᵃšakkᵉnāh 'etkem*), while in the NOTES the reading, "that I may dwell with you" (*wᵉ'eškᵉnāh 'ittᵉkem*) is suggested; the two do not appear very similar, but they actually have the same consonants (*w'šknh 'tkm*). Again, at xxiii 17 MT reads "[saying] to those who despise me, 'Yahweh has said,'" (*limᵉna'ᵃṣay dibbēr yhwh*), while LXX reads, "[saying] to the despisers of Yahweh's word" (*limᵉna'ᵃṣē dᵉbar yhwh*); again the consonants are the same (*lmn'ṣy dbr yhwh*).

quire far more space than is available here. The reader who desires further information should consult one of the standard handbooks on the subject.[10]

[10] One might recommend B. J. Roberts, *The Old Testament Text and Versions* (University of Wales Press, 1951), or, somewhat briefer, E. Würthwein, *The Text of the Old Testament,* Eng. tr. P. R. Ackroyd, (New York: Macmillan, 1957).

SELECTED BIBLIOGRAPHY

Note: The following list does not aim at completeness. It includes commentaries and other works most frequently cited in this book. Whenever in the ensuing pages an author is cited without mention of title, the book listed below is intended.

Bauer, H., and Leander, P. (abbr. BL), *Historische Grammatik der hebräischen Sprache*. Halle: M. Niemeyer, 1922.

Brown, F., Driver, S. R., and Briggs, C. A. (abbr. BDB), eds., *A Hebrew and English Lexicon of the Old Testament*. Boston: Houghton, Mifflin, 1906; Oxford: Clarendon Press, 1907, repr. 1953, 1957.

Driver, S. R., *The Book of the Prophet Jeremiah*. London: Hodder & Stoughton, 1906.

Duhm, B., *Das Buch Jeremia* (Kürzer Hand-Commentar zum Alten Testament). Tübingen and Leipzig: J. C. B. Mohr, 1901.

Ehrlich, A. B. (abbr. Ehrl.), *Randglossen zur hebräischen Bibel*, IV. Leipzig: J. C. Hinrichs'sche Buchhandlung, 1912.

Giesebrecht, F., *Das Buch Jeremia* (Handkommentar zum Alten Testament). Göttingen: Vandenhoeck & Ruprecht, 2d ed., 1907.

Hyatt, J. P., *Jeremiah* (The Interpreter's Bible, V). New York: Abingdon Press, 1956.

Kautzsch, E., ed., *Gesenius' Hebrew Grammar* (abbr. GK). The 2d Eng. ed. rev. by A. E. Cowley from the 28th Ger. ed. (1909). Oxford: Clarendon Press, 1910, repr. 1946 and after.

Kittel, R., ed., *Biblia Hebraica* (abbr. BH). Stuttgart: Privilegierte Württembergische Bibelanstalt, 3d ed., 1937 and after.

Koehler, L., and Baumgartner, W. (abbr. KB), *Lexicon in Veteris Testamenti Libros*. Leiden: E. J. Brill, 1951; Grand Rapids, Michigan: Wm. B. Eerdmans, 1953.

Leslie, E. A., *Jeremiah*. New York: Abingdon Press, 1954.

Nötscher, F., *Das Buch Jeremias* (Die Heilige Schrift des Alten Testaments). Bonn: Peter Hanstein Verlagsbuchhandlung, 1934.

Peake, A. S., *Jeremiah* (The Century Bible, 2 vols.). Edinburgh: T. and T. Clark, 1910–12.

Pritchard, J. B., ed., *Ancient Near Eastern Texts Relating to the Old Testament* (abbr. ANET). Princeton University Press, 1950.

Rahlfs, A., ed., *Septuaginta*. Stuttgart: Privilegierte Württembergische Bibelanstalt, 1935.

Rudolph, W., *Jeremia* (Handbuch zum Alten Testament, I, 12). Tübingen: J. C. B. Mohr, 1947, 2d ed., 1958.

Skinner, J., *Prophecy and Religion*. Cambridge University Press, 1922.

Smith, G. A., *Jeremiah*. New York: Harper & Bros., 4th ed., 1929.

Steinmann, J., *Le prophète Jérémie*. Paris: Editions du Cerf, 1952.

Volz, P., *Der Prophet Jeremia* (Kommentar zum Alten Testament). Leipzig and Erlangen: A. Deichertsche Verlagsbuchhandlung, 1922.

Weiser, A., *Das Buch des Propheten Jeremia* (Das Alte Testament Deutsch). Göttingen: Vandenhoeck & Ruprecht, 1955.

Welch, A. C., *Jeremiah, His Time and His Work*. Oxford University Press, 1928, repr. Oxford: Blackwell, 1951.

Wiseman, D. J., *Chronicles of Chaldean Kings (626–556 B.C.) in the British Museum*. London: The British Museum, 1956.

Ziegler, J., *Ieremias* (Septuaginta—Auctoritate Societas Litterarum Göttingensis). Göttingen: Vandenhoeck & Ruprecht, 1957.

I. THE DIVINE JUDGMENT UPON JUDAH AND JERUSALEM

1. JEREMIAH'S CALL AND COMMISSION
(i 1–19)

Superscription of the Book

I 1 The sayings of Jeremiah ben Hilkiah, of the priestly family that lived in Anathoth in the land of Benjamin, 2 to whom the word of Yahweh came in the days of Josiah ben Amon, king of Judah, in the thirteenth year of his reign 3 —and also in the days of Jehoiakim ben Josiah, king of Judah, and down to the end of the eleventh year of Zedekiah ben Josiah, king of Judah, that is, to the deportation of Jerusalem's population in the fifth month of that year.

Jeremiah's Call

4　The word of Yahweh came to me, thus:
5　"Before I had formed you in the womb I chose you;
　　Before you were born I set you apart,
　　And appointed you prophet to the nations."
6 Then I said, "Ah, my Lord Yahweh! Look! I don't know how to speak. I'm only a boy!" 7 But Yahweh answered,
　　"Never say, 'I am only a boy';
　　For you'll go on what errands I send you,
　　And you'll say what I tell you to say.
8　Don't be afraid of them!
　　For I'm with you to come to your rescue—Yahweh's word."
9 Then Yahweh stretched out his hand and touched my mouth. And Yahweh said to me:
　　"There! I have put my words in your mouth.
10　See! I have made you an overseer this day
　　Over nations and kingdoms,

To uproot and tear down,
To destroy and to raze,
To build and to plant."

Two Further Visions

11 And the word of Yahweh came to me, thus: "What do you see, Jeremiah?" I said, "An almond rod is what I see." 12 Then Yahweh answered, "You see very well! For I am watching over my word to perform it."

13 The word of Yahweh came to me a second time: "What do you see?" And I said, "What I see is a bubbling pot, and it is tipped from the north." 14 Then Yahweh said to me:
"From the north will disaster be loosed
Upon all who dwell in the land.
15   For see! I am calling
    All the kings of the north—Yahweh's word—
And they will come and will each set his throne
    Right in front of Jerusalem's gates,
Against all her surrounding walls,
    Against each of Judah's towns.
16   So I'll utter my sentence upon them
    For their tale of wrong in forsaking me,
In sending up offerings to other gods,
    And bowing down to their own handiwork."

The Divine Charge, and Promise

17   "As for you—gird up your loins!
    Stand up and say to them
        Whatever I tell you to say.
Don't lose your nerve because of them,
    Lest I shatter your nerve right before them.
18   And I—see! I have made you today

a-a Hebrew has "all the clans of the kingdoms of the north," which combines variant readings; omit "clans" with LXX (xxv 9 omits "kingdoms"). On "kings" see NOTE.

> A fortified city,
>   An iron pillar,
> A wall of bronze
> Against all the land:
> Against Judah's kings and princes,
>   Its priests and landed gentry.
> 19   Attack you they will; overcome you they can't,
>   For I'm with you to come to your rescue—*b*Yahweh's
>   word."*b*

b–b Transposed from the middle to the end of the colon; so LXX.

NOTES

i 1. On Jeremiah's home and family background, see the chapter "The Life and Message of Jeremiah" in the Introduction.

2. *the thirteenth year* (of Josiah): 627. For a sketch of Jeremiah's career, see referent chapter, previous NOTE.

3. *the eleventh year of Zedekiah . . . the fifth month.* July/August 587 (cf. lii 12 ff.). Jeremiah was actually active (cf. chs. xl–xliv) for some time after this date.

7. *on what errands I send you.* Literally "upon whatever I send you." The sense could also be (the prepositions *'al* and *'el* being frequently interchanged in the Jeremiah book), "to whomsoever I send you," or even, "wherever I send you."

11–12. Hebrew contains a wordplay that cannot be translated: *almond* (*šāqēd*) and *watching* (*šōqēd*). Apparently, as Jeremiah looked at an almond rod (a stick, not a flowering branch), the word "watching" leaped to his mind by association; and this came to him as Yahweh's assurance that he was watching over his word to bring it to pass.

13. *bubbling.* Literally "blown upon," i.e., draft is applied to the fire beneath the pot, bringing it to a boil.

and it is tipped from the north. Literally "and its face (surface?) is from the face (side, direction) of the north." G. R. Driver (JQR 28 [1937], 97) suggests *ūpānūy* ("and it is turned," i.e., tipped) for *ūpānāw* ("and its face"), which is attractive, but probably unnecessary. The picture in the prophet's mind is ambiguous and disputed; but it seems to be one of a cooking pot, or wash pot, boiling over a fire, and tipping so that its contents ("face," i.e., surface) are about to spill in a southerly direction. Whether it was a literal pot bubbling over a literal fire that the prophet saw (as is likely enough), or one visible only to his mind's eye, cannot be said.

15. *All the kings of the north.* The word usually translated "kingdoms" (*maml⁽ᵉ⁾kōt*) probably has the meaning "kings" here (cf. the next colon), as occasionally in Phoenician, and elsewhere in the Bible; cf. W. F. Albright, JBL 63 (1944), 218, n. 70; W. F. Albright, HUCA 23 (1950/51), 34; also Z. S. Harris, *A Grammar of the Phoenician Language* (New Haven: American Oriental Society, 1936), p. 118.

16. *sending up offerings.* Not necessarily "burning incense" (so most EVV), though this meaning is frequently required. The verb (*qṭr*) is also used of burning offerings of the fat of animals (I Sam ii 16; Ps lxvi 15), or of meal (Amos iv 5).

18. *landed gentry.* Literally "the people of the land"; here, however, not the populace generally but, as frequently, a technical term for the important landholders.

COMMENT

Aside from vss. 1–3, which are editorial and provide the superscription of the book (its "title page," one might say), the chapter is a thematic unit describing those experiences through which Jeremiah received his call to the prophetic office and had that call confirmed and further clarified. The material unquestionably derives from the prophet's own reminiscences, and may have been originally brought together by him, perhaps as an introduction to the scroll which he dictated in the year 605 (see ch. xxxvi). Since it provides authentication of his right to speak the word of Yahweh, it would have served that purpose admirably. Subsequently, the chapter was made the introduction of the Jeremiah collection found in chapters i–xxv (the conclusion of which, in xxv 1–13a, seems to have been composed as a companion piece to it), and now serves to introduce the book as a whole.

But, in spite of its unity of theme, the chapter is not an original unit. Not only does it tell not of one experience, but of several; it combines words that were originally spoken on separate occasions, and transmitted separately. The call itself is described in vss. 4–10, and takes the form of a dialogue between Jeremiah and Yahweh; it should be compared with similar accounts elsewhere, such as the call of Isaiah (Isa vi) or of Ezekiel (Ezek i–iii). Its salient features are: Jeremiah's awareness that he had been predestined for the prophetic office since before his birth; the overruling of his objections and the promise of divine aid; and the placing of the divine word in his mouth. This last is extremely important. The prophet understood himself quite literally as the mouthpiece of Yahweh, the messenger who reported what he had heard Yahweh say in the heavenly council (cf., e.g., xxiii 16–22; also the recurring formula with which oracles are introduced: "This is what Yahweh has said."). According to vs. 2, the call took place in the thirteenth regnal year of Josiah (627). It is probable, indeed (Rudolph, p. 3), that before the present superscription was added, the datum given in vs. 2 (perhaps, "The word of Yahweh that came to me in the thirteenth year of Josiah," or the like) served to introduce the account of the call. Note that vs. 2 mentions only this date in the reign of Josiah; note, too, that vs. 3 seems to dangle, almost as if an afterthought.

The two visions described in vss. 11–12, 13–16 took place somewhat later—though no doubt relatively early in Jeremiah's ministry. The first of them, the point of which hangs on a wordplay (see NOTE on 11–12, above), brought to Jeremiah the assurance that Yahweh was "watching over his word to perform it." This suggests that Jeremiah had already been active for some time, and had begun to be troubled about the fulfillment of the word (of judgment) that he was proclaiming. In the second vision, which presumably came somewhat later still, the sight of a boiling pot, tilted from the north and about to spill its contents in the opposite direction (see further, NOTE on 13), brought to Jeremiah his first intimation of the "Foe from the North," who was to be the agent of Yahweh's judgment. But the identity of this foe, later clearly the Babylonians, is here left vague: it is no more than the certainty of coming disaster. Like the account of the call, these visions are in dialogue form (for the same pattern see, e.g., Amos vii 1–9; viii 1–3), and conclude with a word from Yahweh explaining their meaning. In the case of the second vision, this last seems to have been somewhat expanded above its original form, and the meter is in places obscured (some regard vss. 14 ff. as prose; cf. RSV); but a parallelism is observable, and a metrical form seems to have been intended.

The account of these visions did not originally continue vss. 4–10. The fact that the second of them is introduced (vs. 13) with "The word of Yahweh came to me a second time" indicates that the two visions were originally transmitted together, but separately from the account of the call (had all three stood together, one would expect "second time" in vs. 11, and "third time" in vs. 13). Verses 17–19, on the contrary, in which Jeremiah is told to take up his calling without fear, reach back to the account of the call and carry forward its thought. One wonders—though one cannot be sure—if these verses did not originally continue and conclude vss. 4–10, only to be separated in the present arrangement of the material. In any event, they serve to bring the chapter to a splendid conclusion.

2. THE INDICTMENT OF THE NATION'S SIN
(ii 1–3; 14–19; 4–13; 20–37)

Unfaithfulness to Yahweh and Its Dire Consequences

II ¹ᵃThe word of Yahweh came to me, as follows: ² "Go, cry
in the ears of Jerusalem, and say, This is what Yahweh has saidᵃ:
> I remember your youthful devotion,
> > Your bridal love,
> How you followed me through the desert,
> > The untilled land.
3 Israel was Yahweh's own portion,
> > His harvest's first yield.
> All eating of it are held guilty;
> > Punishment overtakes them—Yahweh's word.

14 "Is Israel a bondman?
> > A house-born slave, perhaps?
> Then why has he been like a prey
15 > > Over which the lions roar
> > > With clamorous din?
> They have left his land a shambles,
> > His cities in ruins and abandoned.

16 "The men of Memphis and Daphne,
> > They too ᵇhave cracked your skull.ᵇ

17 "Wasn't this what brought it upon you—
> > Your forsaking Yahweh your God? ᶜ[   ]ᶜ
18 And now, what good is it going to Egypt
> > To drink Nile water?

ᵃ⁻ᵃ LXX has only "And he said, 'Thus says the Lord.'"
ᵇ⁻ᵇ Reading yᵉrōʿūk for MT yirʿūk ("they graze") with various commentators.
Others prefer yᵉʿārūk ("they lay bare," i.e., shave).
ᶜ⁻ᶜ Hebrew adds "At the time of the one leading you in the way," which
may be a corrupt dittography of the first words of vs. 18; LXX omits.

What good is it going to Assyria
    To drink Euphrates water?
19 Your sin will get you a flogging,
    Your defections will bring you to book.
So consider and see how bitterly evil it is
    To have left Yahweh your God
    a[   ]*a*
—Word of the Lord Yahweh of Hosts."

Unparalleled Forgetfulness of the Divine Grace:
Yahweh's Case against His People

4 Hear the word of Yahweh, O house of Jacob,
    All you clans of Israel's stock!
5 This is what Yahweh has said:
"What was it your fathers found wrong in me
    That they departed from me so far
And, following 'Lord Delusion,'
    Deluded became?
6 They never said, 'Where is Yahweh,
    Who brought us up from Egypt's land,
Who guided us through the desert,
    Land of steppe and ravine,
        Land of drought and of danger,
Land through which nobody passes,
    Where no human being dwells?'
7 To a land like a garden I brought you,
    To eat of its bountiful fruit.
But you entered and fouled my land,
    And made my heritage loathsome.
8 The priests never asked, 'Where is Yahweh?'
    Those skilled in the law did not know me;
The rulers were rebels against me;
    And the prophets—by Baal they prophesied,
        And followed 'the useless ones.'

a–a The colon "and my [?] (*paḥdātī*) was not to you" is corrupt and can
only be translated by conjectural emendation.

9 "So—still I must state my case against you—Yahweh's
      word—
    To your children's children I'll state it.
10 For cross to the western isles, and look!
      Send out to Kedar and closely observe!
      And see—was there ever the like?
11 Has ever a nation changed gods
      (Though these, to be sure, are not gods)?
    But my people! They've traded my Presence
    For—'Lord Useless!'
12 Be appalled, O heavens, at this!
      ᵉShudder and shudder again!ᵉ—Yahweh's word.
13 For it's a twofold wrong that my people have done:
    Me they've forsaken,
        The fountain of living water,
    To hew themselves cisterns,
        Cisterns that crack
          And cannot hold water."

Lust for Foreign Gods: The Sin that Cannot Be Hid

20 "Long ago you snapped your yoke,
        Shook off your lines,
          And said, 'I will not serve!'
    Nay, on every high hill,
        Under every green tree,
          There you sprawled, a-whoring.
21 A Sorek vine I planted you,
        Of wholly reliable stock.
    But what a ᶠfoul-smelling thing you've become,
        A strange, wild vine!ᶠ
22 Though you scrub yourself with lye,
        And use as much soap as you wish,

ᵉ⁻ᵉ I have read *harbēh* for *ḥārᵉbū* with LXX, since this involves a minimum
of emendation. See NOTE.
ᶠ⁻ᶠ Reading *lᵉsōriyyāh gepen* with Duhm and others; MT *lī sūrē haggepen*
divides the words erroneously.

Still the stain of your guilt is before me—
   Word of the Lord Yahweh.

23   "How can you say, 'I'm not defiled,
     Have never followed the Baals'?
   Look at your behavior in the Valley!
     Understand what you've done!
   You're a swift she-camel
     Crisscrossing her tracks

24   *[   ]*
   Snuffing the wind in her heat.
     Who, in her rut, can restrain her?
   Males need not trouble to chase her;
     In her month they will find her.

25   Spare your feet, so nearly bare,
     And your throat, so parched and dry!
   But you said, 'It's no use! No!
     For I love strange gods,
       And after them will I go.'

26   "As a thief is dismayed when caught,
     So dismayed are *ʰIsrael's peopleʰ*;
   They, their kings and princes,
     Their priests and prophets,

27   Who say to a tree, 'My father are you!'
     And to a stone, 'It was you who did bear me!'
   Ah, but they've shown me their back,
     And not their face.
   Yet when trouble comes they cry,
     'Arise, and save us!'

28   But where are your gods which you made for yourself?
     Let them rise, if they can, and save you

ᵍ⁻ᵍ Hebrew has "a wild ass [or: 'a heifer'] schooled to the desert," which
disturbs the figure and does not fit grammatically; perhaps it is a gloss or
variant reading. With a slight change (*pōreṣāh lammidbār* for *pere' limmūd
midbār*) one might read "breaking loose into the desert"; cf. L. Köhler, ZAW
29 (1909), 35 f.
ʰ⁻ʰ LXX "sons of Israel"; MT "house of Israel."

In your time of distress.
For as numerous as your cities
Are your gods, O Judah."

A *Fate Richly Deserved*

29 "Why complain to me?
     You have all rebelled against me—Yahweh's word.
30 In vain have I smitten your sons,
     They took no correction.
     Your sword has devoured your prophets
     Like a ravening lion.
31 ⁱ[   ]ⁱ
     Have I been like a desert to Israel,
     Or a land of dark despair?
     Why, then, say my people, 'We are free!
     We will come to thee no more'?
32 Will a maid forget her jewels,
     Or a bride her sash?
     But my people! They've forgot me
     Days beyond count.

33 "How well you set your course
     To seek for 'love!'
     And so to deeds of sin
     You've schooled your ways.
34 Yes, there on the skirts of your robe
     Is the lifeblood of ʲinnocent men.ʲ
     No burglars these, whom you caught red-handed,
     ᵏ[   ]ᵏ
35 Yet you say, 'I am guiltless!
     His wrath has indeed passed me by!'
     Ah me! but I'll bring you to judgment

ⁱ–ⁱ Hebrew has "O generation—you! See the word of Yahweh," which seems
to be a marginal comment by a later reader. LXX is different.
ʲ–ʲ Heb. "poor, innocent [men]," probably combines variants; "poor" is omitted
with LXX.
ᵏ–ᵏ Heb. "But upon [or: "because of"] all these." The colon cannot be translated.

For saying, 'I've done no sin!'
36   How slight a thing you think it
     To alter your course!
   But Egypt too will disappoint you,
     Just as Assyria did.
37   Thence too will you come away,
     Your hands on your head,
   For Yahweh has spurned those you've trusted,
     No success will you gain thanks to them."

Notes

ii 2. *devotion.* Heb. *ḥesed* has a wide range of connotations. Usually God's gracious favor toward his people, or the favor of men to men, it does not properly describe a quality that men exhibit toward God. Here, however, its use is conditioned by the figure of marriage employed to describe the covenant relationship between Yahweh and Israel. This figure goes back to Hosea (cf. Hos i–iii, etc.). In the days of wilderness-wandering Israel was Yahweh's bride, devotedly loyal to him.

3. *Yahweh's own portion.* Literally "holiness (i.e., a thing set apart, consecrated) to Yahweh." The first fruits were holy to Yahweh and could not be put to profane use (e.g., Exod xxiii 19; Num xviii 12 f.). Just so, Israel belonged to Yahweh and could not be harmed with impunity.

14–15. Verses follow vs. 3 (see COMMENT for explanation). If Israel is Yahweh's own, why is he like a prey torn by lions? Reference is presumably to the nation's long oppression by Assyria.

15. *With clamorous din.* Literally "they gave forth their voice," i.e., roared loudly.

in ruins. Or "burned" (so Qre).

16. *The men of Memphis and Daphne.* The Egyptians. Memphis (Heb. *nōf*), the ancient capital, was near Cairo; Daphne (Heb. *taḥpanḥēs*), today Tell Defneh, was in northeast Egypt (cf. xliv 1). The verse was added after 609 as a further illustration of Judah's woes.

18. Refers to overtures of a political nature, no doubt advocated by rival parties in Judah. Assyria and Egypt hold the balance of world power, a situation that did not obtain after the very beginning of Jeremiah's career.

5. *'Lord Delusion,' deluded.* This attempts to catch the Heb. wordplay: "They followed the *hebel* and became *hebel*"; *hahebel* ("wind, emptiness, vacuity") is apparently a pun on *habba'al* ("the lord"), i.e., Baal, the god of fertility.

6. *danger.* Heb. *ṣalmāwet* is literally "black darkness," but it frequently connotes distress or extreme danger (e.g., Pss xxiii 4; xliv 20[19E]). LXX has "barren" (*galmūdāh*).

8. *Those skilled in the law.* Literally "the handlers of the law," i.e., priests and Levites whose duty it was to interpret the law.

The rulers. Literally "shepherds" (i.e., of their people). The term was current in the ancient Orient and occurs frequently in the Bible (e.g., vi 3; xxiii 4).

'the useless ones.' Literally "things that do not profit" (*lō' yō'îlū*), again apparently a pun on Baal (cf. vs. 5), or "the Baals" (cf. vs. 23).

9. *state my case.* My legal complaint (*rîb*). The picture of Yahweh making a *rîb* against his people occurs repeatedly in the prophetic books.

10. *the western isles.* Literally "the isles (shores) of the Kittites." Derived from the Phoenician colony of Kition on Cyprus, the name denotes the inhabitants of Cyprus as a whole, then, by extension, those of the islands and coastlands farther to the west.

Kedar. Arabian tribe of the desert to the east of Palestine (cf. xlix 28 ff.).

11. *my Presence.* So following a scribal correction (literally "my glory"); MT "its (their) glory." Reference is to the effulgence of the divine presence, the *kᵉbōd Yahweh,* conceived of as enthroned in the temple.

For—'Lord Useless.' Heb. *bᵉlō' yō'îl* ("for what does not profit"), again a pun on Baal.

12. *Shudder and shudder again.* The wording is G. A. Smith's. Heb. "shudder and be very dry (?)" is impossible. See textual noteᵉ⁻ᵉ. Save for the fact that there is no textual evidence for it, one is tempted to read "shudder greatly, O earth" (so BH), which would provide a better parallel with the preceding colon. Various scholars suggest that *ḥārīm bō* be read for *ḥārᵉbū,* which is likewise attractive, though it gives a poorer parallel with "heavens." Summons to the heavens and the earth and to the mountains and the hills to witness is characteristic of Yahweh's *rîb* (e.g., Mic vi 1 f.).

20. Reference is to the fertility cult, whose rites included sacred prostitution and the ritual self-dedication of young women to the god of fertility (e.g., Hos iv 11–14).

21. *Sorek vine.* A red grape of excellent quality (cf. Isa v 2).

23. *in the Valley.* The valley of Ben-hinnom, just south of Jerusalem,

where heathen rites were practiced prior to Josiah's reform (cf. vii 31; II Kings xxiii 10, etc.).

Crisscrossing her tracks. I.e., restively pacing to and fro in heat.

24. *Males . . . chase her.* Literally "All who seek her need not weary themselves."

25. The first two cola are literally "Withhold your foot from bare-footedness, and your throat from thirst," i.e., do not run till your shoes wear out, and you faint with thirst, chasing false gods.

27. *tree . . . stone.* Again the gods of fertility, to whom the people ascribe their very existence.

29. *complain.* The word is again *rīb* (cf. vs. 9). The people think they have a *rīb* against Yahweh; he replies by resuming his *rīb* against them.

30. *Your sword . . . prophets.* Manasseh probably executed prophets (cf. II Kings xxi 16); Jehoiakim certainly did (xxvi 20–23).

31. *We are free.* The meaning of the verb is uncertain, and the translation a guess; LXX has "We will not be ruled over."

33. *'love.'* Presumably the gods of fertility and their immoral rites.

34. *No burglars these. . . .* Literally "You did not catch them breaking in." No guilt attached to killing a burglar caught breaking and entering, as the law specifically states (Exod xxii 1 f.[2 f.E]).

36. On the situation presupposed, see COMMENT below.

COMMENT

This chapter provides us with what is perhaps the classic example of Jeremiah's attack upon the sins of his people. Moreover, since the bulk of its material apparently stems from the earliest period of the prophet's ministry, it affords us a splendid impression of his preaching prior to the completion of Josiah's reform (in 622). There is a striking unity of theme. The entire chapter is dominated by the charge of flagrant and inexcusable apostasy, delivered with stinging eloquence and with the use of a series of vivid and rapidly changing figures, while through the whole of it there runs a note of solemn warning, of pleading, indeed of argument, as Yahweh through his prophet states his *rīb* (his complaint, legal case) against his people (e.g., vss. 9 ff.).

Its thematic unity, together with the skillful manner in which the material has been arranged, gives the chapter a remarkable coherence. One might almost gain the impression that it consists of a single long poem, or address. But this is not so. The argument, though lucid enough, does not progress steadily forward as one would expect in a continuous composition, but rather leaps to and fro. Moreover, the careful reader will observe sudden changes in the person of address (more evident in Hebrew than in English), as well as certain historical allusions which indicate that all the material could not possibly have been composed at the same time. It is therefore clear that we have to do not with a single continuous composition but, as is usually the case in the prophetic books, with a collection of originally separate poems, or fragments of poems, drawn together because of their common theme.

To isolate the individual poems is not easy. Some are incomplete; and some that apparently are complete seem to be composed of originally disparate fragments. Moreover, the usual introductory formulae are, for the most part, lacking. Nevertheless, certain divisions are clear. To begin with, vss. 4–13 quickly separate themselves from their context. These verses belong together and have their own introduction; they interrupt the line of thought begun in vss. 2–3, which line of thought is then resumed in vs. 14 and continued to vs. 19, where it finds its conclusion. Moreover, in vss. 4–13 the person of address (the "you, your") is second masculine plural, whereas in vss. 2–3 and 14–19 it is second feminine singular. We have here, then, two separate poems; in order that they may be read as such, the material has been slightly rearranged above.

In vss. 4–13 a forgetfulness of Yahweh's past favor is alleged which reaches back to the beginning of Israel's life in the Promised Land, and which has issued (vss. 11 ff.) in an apostasy so complete as to amount to a change of gods. This seems clearly to reflect pre-reformation conditions, before the abuses introduced by Manasseh had been put aside. The poem in vss. 2–3 and 14–19 first recalls Israel's devotion to Yahweh in the desert and her protected position as his people (vss. 2–3), and then puts the question (vss. 14 f.): If Israel is Yahweh's own possession, how is her present sad condition (for a century a vassal state of Assyria, often invaded and brutally mistreated) to be explained? Answer: apostasy has brought her to this pass (vss. 17–19), and no amount of political cleverness can save her from it. Since vs. 18 clearly depicts Assyria as still a world power, the poem must originally have been composed at the very beginning of Jeremiah's ministry. But, since vs. 16 just as clearly alludes to Judah's humiliation at the

hands of the Egyptians in 609, the poem was given its present form
—footnoted down to date, as it were—in the early years of Jehoiakim's reign.

The rest of the chapter falls into two major divisions. In vss.
20–28 we have a piece probably consisting of three originally
separate parts (vss. 20–22, 23–25, 26–28). Here the nation's
apostasy is characterized in a variety of figures (an ox that breaks
its yoke, a vine that bears strange fruit, a stain that will not wash
off, the lust of a camel in heat), and the disillusionment that it will
surely bring is predicted. Clear indices of date are lacking; but the
section fits well in the pre-reformation period. Finally, in vss. 29–37
there is a further unit of two parts (vss. 29–32, 33–36), which
were probably of separate origin (the person of address again
shifts). Here, in a highly argumentative tone, it is declared that
the people have no complaint against Yahweh, but are without
excuse and deserving of his wrath. Indices of date are again ambiguous; but the piece fits well in Jeremiah's earliest period. If, as
some believe, vss. 36 f. refer to Judah's position after 609, this
poem, too, may have been edited in Jehoiakim's reign. But, since a
willing alliance rather than a vassal's submission seems to be in
question, these verses (like vs. 18) may well allude to some unknown political maneuver in Josiah's reign.

The chapter thus contains a collection of Jeremiah's sayings that
deal with a single theme, the bulk of which come from early in his
ministry, but which were given their present form in Jehoiakim's
reign. This last may well have been done by Jeremiah himself, no
doubt in connection with the scroll of 605. The chapter is now
editorially linked with chapter i by a brief introduction (vss. 1–2a;
LXX omits) which begins with the words used to introduce the
three visions there (i 4, 11, 13). Chapter ii thus serves, in its
present position, to carry forward the thought of chapter i: Jeremiah, who had been called and commissioned by Yahweh and told
to be ready to speak whatever word Yahweh gives him, now receives that word and speaks it—boldly.

3. A PLEA FOR REPENTANCE
(iii 1–5; 19–25; iv 1–4; iii 6–18)

The "Adulterous Wife": the Need for True Repentance

III 1 *^a*The word of Yahweh came to me,*^a* as follows:
"If a man should divorce his wife,
   And she should leave him
And become the wife of another,
   Can he take her back again?
That would bring great pollution, would it not,
   Upon that land?
Yet you, who have whored with hosts of lovers—
   You would return to me?—Yahweh's word.

2   Look up to the high, bare hills, and see!
   Where have you not been tumbled?
By the roads you sat waiting for them
   Like an Arab in the desert.
You've polluted the land
   With your whorish depravity.

3   So the showers were withheld,
   And the spring rains never came.
But yours the harlot's shameless brow,
   You refused to be abashed.

4   Right then, did you not, you began to cry, 'My Father!
   You were my friend in my youth!

5   Will he nurse a grudge forever,
   Retain his anger always?'
So*^b* you said! But you did—
   Evil to your utmost!

^{a–a} Restored conjecturally, after ii 1. Hebrew has only "saying" ["as follows"];
LXX, Syr. omit even "saying."
^b Reading *hēnnāh* ("these things") with Volz, etc. MT has *hinnēh* ("behold").

19   "Then I said to myself,
     'How gladly would I treat you as a son,
   And give you a land that is lovely,
     Domain of all nations' most fair!'
   But I said, 'You must call me My Father—
     And from foll'wing me never turn back.'

20   ^cAh, like a woman playing false^c with her lover,
     So have you been false to me, house of Israel!—
         Yahweh's word."

21   A cry is heard on the heights,
     The weeping entreaties of Israel's folk.
   Ah, they've perverted their ways,
     They've forgotten Yahweh their God!

22   "Turn back, backsliding sons,
     I would cure your backslidings!"

   "Behold we come to thee,
     For thou art Yahweh our God.

23   ^dTruly the hills are a swindle,^d
     The hubbub on the heights.
   Truly in Yahweh our God
     Is Israel's help.

24   But the Shame, it has devoured
     All our fathers e'er acquired from our youth;
   Their flocks and herds,
     Their sons and daughters.

25   Our shame, be it our bed;
     Our disgrace, be it our cover!
   For against Yahweh our God we've sinned,
     We and our fathers,
       From our youth until this day.
   And we have not obeyed the voice of Yahweh our God."

---

^{c–c} Reading *'ak kib^egōd* with LXX; MT *'āk̲ēn bāg^edāh* ("surely a woman has played false . . .") does not suit the context.

^{d–d} So LXX, Syr., Vulg. Hebrew "Truly in vain [is] from the hills" is impossible (unless a word has been lost). But probably "from" represents enclitic *mem*, in which case Hebrew reads just as does LXX.

IV

1 "If you return, O Israel—Yahweh's word—
       To *me* return,
    If you put your vile things aside,
       Nor stray from my presence,
2   Then might you swear, 'As Yahweh lives,'
       Truthfully, justly, and rightly;
    And the nations by him would bless themselves,
       And in him exult."

3 Yes, this is what Yahweh has said to the men of Judah and
to ᵉthe citizens ofᵉ Jerusalem:
    "Plow up your unplowed ground!
       Do not sow among thorns!
4   ᶠTo your Godᶠ circumcise you;
       Remove your heart's foreskin,
          O men of Judah, O Jerusalem's citizens;
    Lest my wrath break out like fire,
       And burn so that none can quench it,
          So wicked have been your deeds."

The Two Bad Sisters:
Hope for Northern Israel and Appended Sayings

III 6 In the days of King Josiah Yahweh said to me, "You
saw, did you not, what that apostate, Israel, did—how she
went up onto every high hill and under every spreading tree,
and there played the harlot? 7 And I thought that after having done all this she would come back to me. But she did
not. And that faithless one, her sister Judah, saw this. 8 ᵍShe
saw,ᵍ too, that it was precisely because Israel, that apostate,
had committed adultery that I turned her out and gave her
a bill of divorce. Nevertheless, faithless sisterʰ Judah was not
afraid, but went herself and played the harlot too. 9 Indeed,

ᵉ⁻ᵉ Added with five manuscripts and most Vrs.
ᶠ⁻ᶠ So LXX and other Vrs. Hebrew "to Yahweh" is less smooth, since he is
the speaker.
ᵍ⁻ᵍ So with LXX manuscripts, Syr. Hebrew "I saw" does not suit the context.
ʰ Heb. "her sister." LXX omits the word here and in vs. 10.

because immorality mattered so little to her, she polluted the land, committing adultery with stones and trees. 10 Nor in all this did sister Judah, that faithless one, return to me with her whole heart, but only pretended to do so—Yahweh's word."

11 Then Yahweh said to me, "That apostate, Israel, can come nearer to justifying herself than can faithless Judah. 12 Go, proclaim these words toward the north, and say:

'Come back, backslidden Israel—Yahweh's word—
I'll not receive you in anger,
For I am gracious—Yahweh's word—
I do not nurse grudges forever.
13   Only own to your guilt
That, defying Yahweh your God,
You have lavished your favors on "strangers"
Beneath every leafy tree,
And have paid no heed to my voice—Yahweh's word.

14 Turn back, backsliding sons—Yahweh's word—for I am your Lord. And I will take you, one from a city and two from a district, and bring you to Zion. 15 And I will give you rulers after my own heart, who will rule you wisely and well.'"

16 [Then, when you have multiplied and grown numerous in the land] "In those days—Yahweh's word—they will no longer say, 'The Ark of the Covenant of Yahweh!' It will not enter their minds; they will neither remember it nor miss it, nor will another one ever be made.

17 "At that time Jerusalem will be called Yahweh's throne; and all the nations will gather to it,ⁱ and will no longer follow their own stubbornly wicked inclinations.

18 "In those days the house of Judah will join the house of Israel, that together they may come from the north country to the land that I gave ʲtheir fathersʲ for an inheritance."

ⁱ Hebrew adds "to the name of Yahweh, to Jerusalem," which is probably a gloss; LXX omits.
ʲ–ʲ So LXX and other Vrs. Hebrew "your fathers" may represent an adaptation to the form of address of vss. 14–15 (cf. vs. 16a). Or, perhaps the phrase "upon ['al] the land that I gave your fathers" originally concluded vs. 15.

NOTES

iii 1. *Can he take her back again.* LXX "Can she return to him . . .";
but Heb. "can he return to her . . ." approximates the language of
Deut xxiv 1–4, which is the law cited here. The sense is: if under the
circumstances just described reunion is legally impossible, what right has
Judah, who has "whored" with many false gods, to return to Yahweh?

that land. LXX, "that woman." But Hebrew again approximates the
language of Deut xxiv 1–4; cf. also vs. 2.

2. The verse alludes to the immoral rites of the fertility cult. Indeed,
Judah is so avid for "lovers" that she waits for them, like a band of
Arabs waiting to waylay a caravan.

3. *shameless.* Added to bring out the meaning.

4. *Right then . . . you began to cry.* Literally "Did you not from
now (i.e., beginning just now when drought came) cry to me . . ."; i.e.,
Judah, who had long forgotten her God, began to cry to him for help
when trouble came.

5. *you did— Evil to your utmost.* Literally "you did evil things, for
you were able"; fine words are not backed by deeds. The verse leads into
vs. 19.

19. Yahweh would gladly establish his people in possession of the
land promised to their fathers. But they must not only call him "Father"
(as they do: vs. 4); they must match their words with deeds (as they
do not: vss. 5, 20 f.).

Domain of all nations' most fair. Literally "Heritage of the beauty of
the beauties (i.e., most beautiful heritage) of the nations," and probably
not, ". . . of the hosts of the nations" (KJ, ARV); *ṣibe'ōt* is taken as
construct plural of *ṣebī'* (cf. BL, 72 p'; GK, 93 x) rather than of *ṣābā'*.

21. *heights.* The high places where the cult of fertility was practiced
(cf. vs. 2). The people call on Yahweh in their need (vss. 4 f.), but continue to propitiate Baal.

22. *Turn back . . . backslidings.* There is a play on the root *šūb*
which the translation seeks to catch: *šūbū bānīm šōbābīm / 'erpāh
mešūbōtēkem.* The words seem to be drawn from Hos xiv 1, 4 (vss.
2, 5H).

24. *the Shame.* Baal. "Shame" (*bōšet*) frequently occurs in the Bible
as an intentional alteration of "Baal"; here it is used for the sake of
the wordplay with "shame" in vs. 25.

25. The last line is not metrical. The verse may have been somewhat
expanded with liturgical expressions.

iv 1. *vile things*. Idols. The last two cola are divided after LXX and other Vrs. Heb. "If you put your vile things from my sight / And stray no more," has much the same sense, but is less smooth metrically.

2. *swear, 'As Yahweh lives.'* To take oath by Yahweh is to claim him as God.

by him . . . in him. Yahweh (though one would expect "by . . . in me"). Perhaps there is an allusion to the promise to Abraham (cf. Gen xviii 18 and similar passages): if the people truly repent, Yahweh can make good his promises to their fathers (cf. the thought of vs. 19).

3. *Plow up your unplowed ground.* Prepare yourselves inwardly for a new manner of living. The phrase either quotes Hos x 12, or adapts a current saying.

4. On the circumcision of the heart, cf. Deut x 16.

iii 6. *that apostate, Israel.* Literally "apostasy-Israel" (so also vss. 8, 11, 12); i.e., she is apostasy personified. The verse refers to the fertility cult (cf. ii 20; iii 2, 21).

7. *that faithless one.* A substantive; it suggests that Judah is faithlessness personified (so also vs. 10).

9. *because immorality mattered so little to her.* Literally "through the lightness (i.e., lightheartedness, carelessness: the word must be derived from *qll*) of her whoring."

she polluted the land. Taking the verb as Hiphil with various Vrs. (cf. vs. 2). Hebrew has the Qal: "she was polluted with the land."

stones and trees. Again the fertility cult (cf. ii 27).

12. *backslidden.* Literally "apostasy" as in vs. 6. I have attempted to catch the wordplay: *šūbāh mᵉšūbāh yiśrā'ēl.*

13. *You have lavished your favors on "strangers."* Literally "You have scattered your ways to strangers" (i.e., foreign gods). The idiom is peculiar, but emendation is probably unnecessary.

paid no heed. The verb should be second person feminine singular, as throughout vs. 12b–13 (and so LXX, Vulg.). The Heb. plural may represent singular with enclitic *mem*.

14. *Turn back, backsliding sons.* The wordplay is that of vs. 22 (see above).

I am your Lord. "I am your *ba'al*," which can mean "your lord" (owner) or "your husband"; here the former is appropriate. Again there is a play on "Baal." Yahweh, not Baal, is the true *ba'al* (lord) of Israel.

district. Heb. *mišpāḥāh.* Properly a subdivision of a tribe (or clan), the word can denote a geographical or political subunit (a district), and so apparently here (parallel word is "city").

15. *rulers . . . rule.* Literally "shepherds . . . shepherd"; see NOTE on ii 8.

16. The words in brackets supply an editorial transition between vss. 14–15 and what follows (note the change in person).

Comment

As most commentators agree, this section is composed of two
originally independent units, and in the interests of clarity these have
been separated in the translation. There is, first, a rather long poetic
piece which begins in iii 1–5, is resumed in iii 19–25, and concluded in iv 1–4; and there is a complex of material mostly in prose
(iii 6–18) which has been inserted in the midst of this poem, interrupting the connection between vss. 5 and 19. This—to us rather
awkward—arrangement was undoubtedly chosen because of the
marked similarities in theme and phraseology which the two units
exhibit. Both are dominated by the charge of apostasy, and in both
this is characterized as "adultery"—a figure that goes back to
Hosea. Moreover, the key word in both is the Heb. *šūb,* a word
which can mean either "turn away" (apostatize) or "turn back"
(repent); and this word is played upon in a variety of ways (cf.
iii 1, 7, 10, 12, 14, 19, 22; iv 1). In its present form, the section
serves to carry forward the thought of chapter ii, both by reinforc-
ing the charge of unfaithfulness, and by adding to it a passionate
plea for repentance together with the assurance of Yahweh's forgiveness and mercy.

The poetic material in iii 1–5, 19–25; iv 1–4 forms a continuous
unit. It begins (iii 1–5) by likening Judah to an adulterous wife
who has forfeited all legal claim upon her husband, yet who fatuously continues to count on his indulgent forgiveness. This thought
is resumed in vss. 19–22a. Here Yahweh, as if puzzled as to how
he can make good his promises to so faithless a people, expostulates
with them and pleads for sincere repentance. Then, in vss. 22b–25
(perhaps somewhat expanded in transmission), Jeremiah places in
the mouth of the people a liturgy of penitence in which they make
abject, heartbroken confession of their sin. To this Yahweh responds
(iv 1–2): if their repentance is sincere, they can truly be his people again, and he can make good the promises made to their fathers. The piece concludes with a formally separate oracle of solemn warning (iv 3–4): let repentance be from the heart—or face
Yahweh's unquenchable wrath. In the present arrangement of the
book, this furnishes a transition into the section that follows (see
iv 5–31).

The poem just described is unquestionably a sample of Jeremiah's preaching prior to 622. Similarities to Hosea, characteristic of the young Jeremiah, are striking. Not only is the dominant theme (the adulterous wife) borrowed from that great prophet of northern Israel; there are verbal similarities—perhaps even quotations—as well (see NOTES on iii 22; iv 3). It is, moreover, reform preaching. The whole passage is, one might say, very "Deuteronomic" in its concern, even taking its start from a point of law which, though assuredly more ancient, is stated in the Deuteronomic Code (see NOTES on iii 1). In addition, the tone of the passage suggests an early date. A sin is charged and admitted (iii 24 f.) which reaches back through all the generations of the past; there is no hint of a reform that has failed or, indeed, of any reform. At the same time, catastrophe does not seem to be imminent. Rather the divine wrath is held before the people as no more than an undefined threat (iv 3–4), a possibility lying in the future which, at this stage, is both contingent and avoidable. Features such as these tended, understandably enough, to sink into the background in Jeremiah's later preaching.

The material in iii 6–18 has had a somewhat more complicated history. This section begins with a prose monologue addressed to Jeremiah by Yahweh (vss. 6–12a) in which the two adulterous (i.e., apostate) sisters, Israel and Judah, are compared—to the immense disadvantage of the latter. This is a further development of Hosea's theme of the adulterous wife, and one played upon to the fullest by Ezekiel (Ezek xvi, xxiii). There is no reason, however, to assume dependence on Ezekiel or to question the essential genuineness of the passage. Its diction, as I have pointed out elsewhere (JBL 70 [1951], 35), is not dependent on Ezekiel's, but has its closest affinities with that of Jeremiah's own poetry, and Hosea's. The monologue just described leads into a poetic passage (vss. 12b–13) in which the prophet summons northern Israel to return to Yahweh, and assures her of his mercy. There is no reason to doubt that the passage thus far dates to the reign of Josiah, as vs. 6 explicitly states. The appeal to Israel is closely paralleled in xxxi 2–6 and xxxi 15–22, both of which belong to this period, and fits well in the context of Josiah's expansionist activity in the territory of the defunct northern state. If vs. 10 brands Josiah's reform as a failure, as some think, the passage dates after 622; but, since this may be a reference to earlier efforts at reform (such as Hezekiah's) which came to nothing, it is perhaps unwise to insist upon it.

The section as a whole, however, did not receive its present form in Josiah's reign. Verses 14–15 (probably prose) may, to be sure, continue the foregoing: though these verses are usually regarded as a later addition addressed to exiled Judah, it is quite as likely that they were spoken to northern Israel and are, thus, a prose parallel to vss. 12b–13 (note that in xxxi 6 northern Israel is summoned to worship Yahweh on Mount Zion). Verses 16–18, on the other hand, do seem to presuppose the exile of Judah and the loss of the ark (presumably in the destruction of the temple although M. Haran [IEJ, 13 (1963), 46–58] has plausibly argued that it had already been removed by Manasseh), and were in all likelihood added after 587. They are probably of anonymous origin, although the ideas expressed (particularly in vs. 16) are in no way inconsonant with Jeremiah's thought. In any event, they serve (and the situation is not dissimilar in chs. xxx–xxxi, as we shall see) to apply the hope which Jeremiah had once extended to northern Israel to the situation of the exiles in Babylon.

4. THE COMING JUDGMENT
(iv 5–31)

Alarm! Invasion Is Coming!

IV
5   Proclaim it in Judah!
       Spread the news in Jerusalem! Say,
  "Sound a blast on the horn through the land!
       Shout aloud, and say,
  'Band together! Let us get
       To the fortified towns!'
6   Hoist toward Zion the signal!
       Get to safety! Do not wait!
  For I'm bringing calamity out of the north,
       A shatt'ring disaster.
7   The lion has roused from his thicket,
       The mauler of nations has marched,
         Has left his base,
  To make your land a shambles,
       With your cities in ruins and abandoned.
8   For this with sackcloth gird you,
       Wail and howl!
  For Yahweh's hot anger
       Has not passed us by."

9   "In that day—Yahweh's word—
       The king will lose his courage,
       The princes too,
  The priests will be stunned,
       And the prophets dumfounded."
10   Then I said, "Ah, Lord Yahweh,
       Indeed thou hast badly deceived

This people, and Jerusalem,
Telling them, 'All shall be well'—
And now the sword is laid to the throat!"

The Stormwind of Judgment

11 At that time it will be said to this people and to
                          Jerusalem:
    "A wind scorching hot from the bare desert heights
        Straight on toward My Daughter-My People;
    Not to winnow, not to sift,
12   A wind too strong for that,
            It comes at my behest.
    Now it's I myself who utter
        Sentence upon them."

13 Look! Like a cloud rack he mounts,
        Like the stormwind his chariots,
    Swifter than eagles his horses—
        Woe to us! We are ruined!
14 Wash your heart of guile, Jerusalem,
        If you wish to be saved.
    How long will your baneful designs
        Find lodgment within you?
15 For hark! A runner from Dan!
        One bringing bad tidings from Ephraim's hills!
16 "Report it *[   ]*!
        Spread the news 'round Jerusalem!
    Enemies*b* come from a land far away,
        Raising the shout against Judah's towns.
17 Like watchmen at a field

---

a-a Heb. "to the nations. Behold." cannot be correct, but proposed emendations
are all conjectural. To read (D. N. Freedman) *laggōy* (with enclitic *mem*)
hazzeh involves little change and makes excellent sense ("Report it to this
nation").
b Heb. "watchers" (*nōṣᵉrīm*), which one might understand as "besiegers"
(so RSV) save that the verb does not elsewhere have this force. The reading
"enemies" (*ṣārīm*), adopted by many scholars, involves the dropping of but
one letter. Perhaps "watchers" is a misplaced variant of "watchmen" in vs.
17.

They have ringed her round about,
For 'twas me she defied—Yahweh's word."

18 "Your ways and your deeds
Have brought all this upon you.
It's this sin of yours that's bitter,
That has stabbed you to the heart."

Jeremiah's Anguished Cry: Yahweh's Complaint

19 O my bowels, my bowels! I writhe!
O walls of my heart!
My heart is in storm within me,
I cannot be still.
°You have heard,° O my soul, the trumpet blast,
The battle shout.

20 Disaster comes hard on disaster,
All the land is laid waste.
Laid waste of a sudden my tents,
In an instant my curtains.

21 How long must I see the standard,
Hear the blast of the horn?

22 "Ah, but my people are fools!
Me they know not.
Stupid sons are they,
Senseless—they.
Clever are they to do wrong,
To do right—they don't know how!"

The Awful Day of Judgment: a Vision and an Oracle

23 I saw the earth—lo, chaos primeval!
The heavens—their light was gone.

24 I saw the mountains—and lo, they were quaking,
And all the hills rocked to and fro.

°–° So Qre; and Ktib is probably not first person, but the archaic form of the
second feminine singular, of which there are a number of examples in
Jeremiah (vs. 30; ii 20, etc.).

25   I looked—and behold, no human was there,
      And the birds of the skies had all flown.

26   I looked—and behold, the tilled land was desert,
      Its cities all lying in ruins—
   Before Yahweh,
      Before his fierce anger.

27   Ah, this is what Yahweh has said:
   "A waste shall the whole land be
      (though I'll make no full end).

28   For this let the earth lament,
      And the heavens above don mourning;
   For I've spoken *and not relented,*
      I've purposed and will not turn back."

Daughter Zion's Death Agony

29   At the cry, "Horsemen and archers!"
      All the land takes to flight.
   They scuttle *for the caves,
      Crouch* in the thickets,
         Scramble up the cliffs.
   Every city is deserted,
      Not a person left in them.

30   *And you—what mean you*
      Dressing in scarlet,
   Binding on bangles of gold,
      Smearing your eyes with paint?
   In vain do you primp!
      They loathe you who accost you,
      It's your life that they seek.

31   Ah, a cry I have heard like a woman's in labor,

d–d Placed before "I've purposed" with LXX.
e–e So LXX; Heb. "all the city" has intruded from the last colon.
f–f Added with LXX.
g–g Again with LXX (cf. "in them"); Heb. "all the city."
h–h So LXX. Hebrew adds a word which does not fit the context: "And you
(fem.) despoiled one (masc.) what mean you (fem.)."

A screaming[i] like hers who is bearing her first.
It's the cry of Daughter Zion, gasping,
    Hands outstretched,
  "Ah me! I am dying.
  The murd'rers—they've killed me!"

[i] So following LXX and supposing a noun *ṣeraḥ (Ehrl., etc.) in place of MT ṣārāh ("anguish"). [An asterisk designates a word presumed to exist, but which is nowhere instanced in any text—Tr.]

NOTES

iv 7. *The mauler of nations.* So, happily, G. A. Smith; literally "despoiler, destroyer."

8. *For Yahweh's hot anger / Has not passed us by.* Contrast ii 35.

10. *Then I said.* Most commentators read, "And they shall say." But this emendation is poorly supported (only LXX^A and Arabic) and unnecessary. Jeremiah protests that the words of the false prophets, which purportedly came from Yahweh, and which he has allowed them to speak, have misled the people. Cf. I Kings xxii 19–23, where Yahweh sends a "lying spirit" to lure Ahab to his doom.

the throat. This force of the word (*nepeš*) is well attested in Ugaritic, and is not infrequently demanded in the Bible (e.g., Isa v 14).

11. *My Daughter-My People.* I really do not know how to translate Heb. *bat 'ammī* in a way that is not awkward. The term is a poetic, and endearing, personification of the people, and is a favorite one with Jeremiah. EVV "the daughter of my people" is misleading: "daughter" and "people" are in apposition.

12. *A wind too strong for that.* Literally ". . . these things." One could delete *mē'ēlleh* as a dittography of *mālē'* and read "A wind full gale." The sense, however, is not altered: the judgment comes like the sirocco blowing from the desert; it is too strong a wind for winnowing grain, as it carries away wheat and chaff together (i.e., the judgment does not separate good from bad, but engulfs both alike).

15. *Dan.* At the northern limit of Palestine, near the headwaters of the Jordan.

Ephraim's hills. The territory lying just a few miles north of Jerusalem.

19. *I cannot be still.* Hiphil of *ḥrš* is usually intransitive; but one can read, "I cannot still it" (i.e., my heart).

23. *chaos primeval.* Heb. *tōhū wābōhū.* The words are those used in Gen i 2 to describe the formless void that existed before creation. Indeed, in this poem, which is one of the most powerful descriptions

of the Day of Yahweh in all prophetic literature, one might say that
the story of Genesis i has been reversed: men, beasts, and growing things
are gone, the dry land itself totters, the heavens cease to give their
light, and primeval chaos returns. It is as if the earth had been "uncreated"; it is, if one cares to put it so, a ruin of "atomic" proportions.

27. *though I'll make no full end.* Most scholars either delete the
colon or, by omitting or altering the negative, read, "I will make a full
end. . . ." This does seem to fit better here. Perhaps we have an alteration or insertion on the basis of v 18, which is editorial. But perhaps
the colon means what it says: the land will indeed be a waste, but it
will not be the "full end" described in vss. 23–26.

30. *Smearing your eyes.* Literally "tearing" (i.e., widening). The
practice is still common in the East to paint about the eyes to make
them seem larger and more lustrous. Jerusalem is here depicted as a
streetwalker who decks herself out to attract clients (i.e., allies); these,
however, loathe her and accost her only to kill her.

31. *screaming.* Or "groaning." See textual note[f].

Ah me . . . killed me. A paraphrase; literally "Woe is me! For my
soul (life) faints before murderers."

COMMENT

The remainder of chapter iv, and all of chapters v and vi, belong
together. In the present arrangement of the book, they constitute a
long editorial unit made up of a series of originally separate sayings, and complexes of sayings, all of which in one way or another deal with the terrible disaster that is about to befall the nation. The entire section thus develops the theme sounded in iv 3–4.
There, it will be recalled, following a long and impassioned plea for
repentance, solemn warning is given that a complete and inner
change must take place, amounting to a circumcision of the heart.

> "Lest my wrath break out like fire,
> And burn so that none can quench it."

It is this note that supplies the major theme of the chapters that
follow (iv 5–vi 30): Such repentance has not been forthcoming
—so the Day of Judgment comes!

Since the section is a very long one, it has seemed more suitable
to deal with it chapter by chapter. The remainder of chapter iv has,
for convenience, been broken down as follows: (1) Vss. 5–10:

these verses contain a poem (vss. 5–8) telling of the coming of the "Foe from the North," to which has been appended (vs. 9) a brief oracle describing the dismay which this will evoke, and (vs. 10) a complaint uttered by Jeremiah—presumably as disaster drew near—that Yahweh had misled his people in allowing them to believe that such a thing could not happen. (2) Vss. 11–18: this piece begins with an oracle (vss. 11–12) announcing the catastrophe as Yahweh's judgment. Then follows a further poem (vss. 13–17) describing the approach of the foe, which is interrupted (vs. 14) by a last plea for repentance, and followed (vs. 18) by a brief comment resuming the theme of vs. 10 and explaining that calamity has been brought on by sin. (3) Vss. 19–22: Here there is a poem in "confessional" style (vss. 19–21) in which Jeremiah cries out in anguish as he sees his country being destroyed and, attached to it, a brief oracle (vs. 22) in which Yahweh laments the stupidity of his people which has been the cause of it all. (4) Vss. 23–28: a vision (vss. 23–26) in which Jeremiah gazes in horror at the judgment that is coming; and a brief oracle (vss. 28–29) declaring that Yahweh has ordained it and will not relent. (5) Vss. 29–31: a poem once more describing the approach of the foe and the plight of Jerusalem, here likened to a courtesan done to death by her lovers.

None of this material can be dated with precision. The poems are, to be sure, so graphic that one might suppose that they were composed while invasion was actually in progress. But, though some of them may have been, this is by no means necessarily true of them all. The prophet had long been haunted by a premonition of disaster, and his imagination was exceedingly vivid. Moreover, he probably worked, albeit in a most original way, with symbolism and phraseology developed long before his time to describe the Day of Yahweh. The poems that tell of the coming of the foe may have been composed at any time between the latter years of Josiah (or even earlier) and the actual approach of Nebuchadnezzar's army in 605/4; and some of them may be as late as the eve of the Babylonian invasion in 598/7. The "confessional" bits, on the other hand (especially vss. 19–21), were probably wrung from Jeremiah as invasion struck. The section thus combines in masterful fashion predictions of judgment uttered by the prophet over a period of years, and expressions of his own personal agony when it came to pass.

5. THE COMING JUDGMENT (*continued*)
(v 1–31)

The People that Cannot Be Pardoned

V

1   "Range through Jerusalem's streets,
    Look and observe!
  Search her markets and see
    If a man you can find—
  If any there be who does justly,
    Strives after truth,
  That I may forgive her—
    *ª*Word of Yahweh.*ª*

2   Though they swear, 'By the life of Yahweh,'
    They do *ᵇ*nothing but*ᵇ* perjure themselves."

3   Thine eyes, O Yahweh,
    Do they not look for truth?
  Thou didst smite them—no pain did they feel,
    Didst smash them—they would not accept correction.
  Their heads were harder than rock,
    They would not repent.

4   Then I thought, "These are only the poor!
    They act like fools,
  Since they know not the way of Yahweh,
    Nor the claims of their God.

5   I will get me to men of high station,
    And speak with them;
  They, surely, would know the way of Yahweh,
    The claims of their God."

ª⁻ª Added with LXX; Yahweh is the speaker.
ᵇ⁻ᵇ Reading *'ākēn* ("surely") with various manuscripts, Syr. MT has *lākēn* ("therefore").

But they! To a man they had broken the yoke,
    Cast off the lines.
6 And so—a lion from the forest will slay them,
    A wolf of the desert will rend them,
Near their cities a leopard is lurking,
    Who dares to come out will be torn;
For many have been their crimes,
    Countless their backslidings.

7 "Why should I forgive you?
    Your people have left me
    And sworn by no-gods.
Though *I gave them their fill,* they whored;
    At the harlot's house *they tarried.*
8 Stallions, sleek and lusty, they,
    Whinnying each for his neighbor's wife.
9 Will I fail to punish this?
    —Word of Yahweh—
On a nation such as this
    Will I not avenge myself?"

False Security: the Terrible Foe

10 Go up through her vine rows—destroy!
        Yet make no full end.
    Strip away her branches;
        They are not Yahweh's.
11 "Ah, they've played me utterly false,
        Israel and Judah alike—Yahweh's word."
12 They've belied Yahweh,
        And said, "Not he!
    Misfortune will not overtake us,
        Nor famine nor sword will we see."
13 The prophets—they're full of wind!

c–c See NOTE.
d–d Reading *yitgōrārū* with LXX. MT has *yitgōdādū*, which elsewhere means
"to gash one's self" (cf. xvi 6; xli 5). EVV "they trooped" presupposes a
meaning derived from the noun *gᵉdūd* not otherwise attested.

The word is not in them.

14 Therefore, this is what Yahweh, God of Hosts, has said:
"Because they[e] have uttered this word,
ʳThus will it be done to themʳ:
See! I am making my words
In your mouth a fire,
And this people a pile of wood
That it may consume them.

15 "Look! I am bringing against you
A nation from far, O house of Israel—Yahweh's word.
A nation enduring it is,
A nation that's ancient,
A nation whose language you know not,
Nor can you make out what they say.
16 An open grave their quiver,
All of them fighters!
17 They'll eat up your harvest and food,
Your sons and daughters as well;
They'll eat up your flocks and your herds,
Your vines and fig trees too;
They'll demolish your fortified towns
In which you trust—with the sword!"

18 "Yet even in those days—Yahweh's word—I will not make a full end of you. 19 And when they[g] say, 'Why did Yahweh our God do all this to us?' you shall answer them, 'Just as you forsook me and served alien gods in your own land, so must you serve foreigners in a land that is not yours.'"

Rebellion, Injustice, Complacency

20 In the house of Jacob declare this,
In Judah proclaim it:

e Heb. "you." The emendation is conjectural, but required by the context.
ʳ–ʳ In MT the colon stands at the end of vs. 13, where it fits poorly; LXXᴬ omits. Perhaps it has fallen out of vs. 14 (cf. Duhm, Rudolph, etc.).
g Heb. "you" does not suit the context, and is probably influenced by the preceding verse.

21 "Hear this now,
        You people stupid and senseless,
    Who have eyes, indeed, but see not,
        Ears, but cannot hear.
22 You do not fear *me*?—Yahweh's word—
        Or tremble before me?
    Who have set the sand as Sea's frontier,
        An eternal decree which it may not transgress;
    *h*Toss it may, but it cannot prevail,*h*
        Its billows may roar, but they cannot get through.
23 But this people! Theirs has been
        A heart contumacious and rebel;
            They have turned and have gone,
24 Never saying to themselves,
        'We should fear Yahweh our God,
    Who gives the rains in season,
        The showers of autumn and spring,
    And the weeks appointed for harvest,
        Secures for us.'
25 Your misdeeds have blocked these things,
        Your sins have kept the blessings from you.

26 "Yes, among my people are scoundrels,
        Who watch [?] like fowlers [   ].
    They set their traps;
        It's men they catch.
27 Like a basket that's full of birds,
        So their houses are filled with loot;
    And so they've grown great and rich,
28   They are fat, *i*they are sleek.*i*
    Nay more, they wink at evil;
        They plead not the case,
    The orphan's case, to win it;
        Nor judge they claims of the poor.

---

h–h So with LXX and other Vrs. Hebrew has plural verbs, but without subject, unless it be "its billows" in the next colon, which is awkward. Some
think that the subject ("its waters" or the like) has been lost.
i–i See NOTE.

29   Will I fail to punish this?
       —Word of Yahweh—
       On a nation such as this
       Will I not avenge myself?"

30   An appalling, a shocking thing
       Has occurred in the land:
31   The prophets—they prophesy falsely,
       And the priests—they lord it beside them;
       And my people—they love it that way.
       But what will you do when it ends?

NOTES

v 1. Cf. Gen xviii 22–33 for a similar thought (God would spare Sodom if ten righteous men could be found in it). See xv 1–4 for an even more pessimistic evaluation.

2. Cf. iv 2. To swear by Yahweh is to claim him as God and, in the light of their behavior, this is perjury. It is uncertain whether Yahweh or Jeremiah is the speaker.

3. *Their heads were harder*. Literally "They made their faces harder . . . ." Some (e.g., Giesebrecht) think the calamity referred to is that of 609, but one cannot be sure (cf. ii 30).

4, 5. *claims*. Heb. *mišpāṭ* is not to be translated "law" (so most EVV), but refers to the ordinances by which God rules and to which his people must conform; cf. viii 7.

6. Either Yahweh or Jeremiah may be taken as the speaker. The figure introduced at the end of vs. 5 (cf. ii 20) is carried forward: the people are like oxen who have escaped their master's yoke—and his protection.

7. *I gave them their fill*. Some manuscripts read, "I took their oath" (š instead of ś), and a few scholars (e.g., Weiser) prefer this. Reference would then be to the covenant between Yahweh and Israel, made at Sinai and repeatedly renewed in solemn ceremony (perhaps specifically to the covenant engaged in under Josiah: II Kings xxiii 1–3).

they whored. Literally "committed adultery." Reference seems to be to both apostasy ("no-gods") and (vs. 8) the literal immorality which resulted.

9. *punish this*. Literally "these," which could be taken as "these things" or "these people."

10. *Yet make no full end*. Cf. iv 27. Here again, many believe that

the negative (or the colon) is not original. This may be so. But if "strip away her branches" likens the judgment to a thorough pruning, a "full end" has not been made.

12. *Not he.* I.e., "he will do no such thing." The people, and specifically the prophets, misrepresent Yahweh in denying that he will bring disaster; cf. Zeph i 12.

13. *they're full of wind.* Literally "they will become wind," i.e., will be shown to be the windbags that they are. There is a play on the word *rūᵃḥ,* which can mean either "wind" or the divine "spirit" with which the prophets claimed to be filled. Verse 13 is usually taken as the continuation of vs. 12: the people say that prophets, like Jeremiah, who predict disaster are "full of wind." But the words of vs. 12b are what *false* prophets were saying (cf. xiv 13 f.), and vs. 13 is Jeremiah's own indignant rejoinder. Verse 14 continues the thought: the true prophetic word in Jeremiah's mouth is a destroying fire.

16. *An open grave their quiver.* I.e., their arrows are deadly. The figure is strange (LXX omits), but suggested emendations ("their mouth," etc.: cf. Ps v 10[9E]) are conjectural.

22. Cf. Ps civ 5–9; Job xxxviii 8–11. God in creation set bounds to the watery chaos and established the dry land. In the mythology of various ancient peoples this was a physical conflict between the god and the chaos monster.

23. *have turned and have gone.* I.e., broken through Yahweh's restrictions, as the sea cannot. Some, feeling that "gone" is rather weak, transpose two letters and read "and prevailed" (i.e., have revolted successfully); cf. the same verb in vs. 22.

26. *Who watch [?] like fowlers [   ].* Hebrew of this colon is most uncertain.

27. *loot.* Literally "deceit," i.e., ill-gotten gains.

28. *they are sleek.* The meaning of the verb (*'āśᵉtū*) is uncertain. The text is possibly corrupt; LXX omits the colon. Perhaps it originally read *šāmᵉnū 'ābū kāśū* ("they are fat, thick, and sleek"); cf. Deut xxxii 15.

they wink at evil. Literally "they pass over deeds of evil." EVV understand this as knowing no bounds in wickedness; but this is questionable, and many scholars emend (LXX omits "deeds of evil"). Perhaps it is best to take the verb in the sense of "overlook," "excuse," as in Amos vii 8; viii 2; Mic vii 18; Prov xix 11, and supply the preposition *lᵉ* or *'al* before "deeds" (or perhaps this did not need to be expressed in poetry). Overlooking evil is just what they do in not espousing the cause of the helpless.

to win it. Literally "that they (i.e., the orphans) may have success," or "that they may make it (the orphans' case) succeed." The sense is the same in either case.

the poor. LXX "the widow," which is equally good.

31. *prophesy falsely.* I.e., as in vs. 12; or "by the Lie" (i.e., Baal). Either sense is possible.

lord it beside them. The sense is ambiguous: literally "rule (the verb need not be emended) at their hands" . . . which can mean "at their side," or "at their (i.e., the prophets') direction," or "on their (i.e., the priests' own) authority."

when it ends. I.e., presumably, when the predicted crash comes, and the lies which the clergy have uttered (cf. vs. 12) are exposed for what they are.

Comment

The poems in chapter v follow upon those of iv 5–31 without break (see above) and further develop the theme of the judgment that is about to come upon the nation. The material has for convenience been divided into three units, or complexes, each of which is in turn made up of shorter poems, or fragments of poems, no doubt originally uttered on separate occasions. It must be admitted, however, that these components flow one into another so smoothly, and without indication of transition, that it is frequently difficult to determine their precise dimensions.

In vss. 1–9 we have a piece cast in the form of a dialogue between Jeremiah and Yahweh. Its theme is: Can this people be forgiven? Yahweh is the first speaker (vs. 1): find a single righteous man in Jerusalem and forgiveness is possible. But (vs. 2) none can be found: they claim Yahweh as their God, but their deeds belie their words. Beginning in vs. 3 (or possibly in vs. 2) Jeremiah is the speaker. He says, in effect, that his own experience bears out this verdict: he has not found a man, high or low, who has the slightest understanding of Yahweh's character and demands; the nation (vs. 6) therefore, is ripe for judgment (vs. 6 may be taken either as Jeremiah's own sorrowful conclusion, or as Yahweh's rejoinder). Then follows an oracle addressed to the people which (vs. 7) resumes the theme of vs. 1 ("Why should I forgive you?"), and concludes (vs. 9) with a stereotyped formula (cf. vs. 29; ix 8 [ix 9E]) announcing that judgment is sure. The piece cannot be dated with precision, although the fact that disaster, though certain, does not seem to be imminent, and is still theoretically avoidable, would argue against placing it too late. Perhaps a date in Josiah's reign, or at the very beginning of Jehoiakim's, would be as good a guess as any.

Verses 10–19 form a complex which at its beginning (vs. 10) and in its editorial conclusion (vs. 18) sounds the theme "—not . . . a full end." The material, however, is highly composite. Indeed, vss. 10–14, which announce the terrible judgment that is coming because of the people's faithlessness to Yahweh and their blind refusal to believe that he would take action against them, seem to be made up of originally separate fragments. Both the speaker and the person addressed shift, and the progress of thought is not easy to follow; perhaps the order of the material has in places been disturbed. Then (vss. 15–17) there is an originally separate poem telling of the irresistible advance of the invader who will be the agent of divine judgment. Since this invader is described in terms that seem clearly to indicate the Babylonians (cf. vs. 15: "a nation from afar . . . ancient"), this poem was probably composed during the first part of Jehoiakim's reign. The prose conclusion in vss. 18–19 is editorial, and presumably of Exilic date.

In vss. 20–31, after a characteristic formula of introduction (vs. 20), there is a poem (vss. 21–25) dilating upon the unnatural folly of the people in rebelling against their God and not remembering his mercies; and this leads without break into an originally separate poem (vss. 26–29) assailing them for the crimes whereby they make mockery of Yahweh's covenant law. This last poem concludes with the formula used in vs. 9. Appended to it is a brief fragment expressing shock at the highhanded behavior of the clergy and the people's acquiescence in it. The material of this complex seems to be relatively early. The judgment is presented as a moral certainty, but is not further defined; in vss. 21–25, indeed, the only tangible evidence of divine displeasure is a drought, as in iii 3 (which is pre-622). The abuses described in vss. 26–31 are similar to those denounced in the "Temple Sermon," which (see below, vii 2–15) was uttered just after Jehoiakim took the throne; these verses may, therefore, have been composed at about the same time, or even during the latter part of Josiah's reign.

6. THE COMING JUDGMENT (*concluded*)
(vi 1–30)

Jerusalem Besieged: a Warning

VI

1   Get to safety, you of Benjamin,
      Out of Jerusalem!
  In Tekoa blow the trumpet!
      On Bet-hakkerem light the beacon!
  For evil peers down from the north,
      A shatt'ring disaster.

2   Daughter Zion, *are you like
      A meadow most delightful,*

3   To which the shepherds come
      With their flocks?
  They've pitched their tents all 'round her,
      They graze each one his part.

4   "Ready the battle against her!
      Up! We'll attack at noonday!
  Too bad! The daylight is waning,
      The shadows of evening grow long.

5   Then up! We'll attack in the darkness,
      And lay her strongholds in ruins!"

6   For this is what Yahweh of Hosts has said:
  "Cut down her trees! Cast up
      Against Jerusalem a mound!
  Ah, the city of falsehood,
      Naught but oppression within!

7   As a well keeps fresh its water,

---

a–a The text is uncertain. See NOTE.
b–b So LXX. Heb. *hī' hā'îr hopqad* is ungrammatical; the translation, "This
is the city to be punished" (cf. EVV), is forced.

So keeps she her wickedness fresh.
'Outrage! Robbery!'—the cry within her;
    Ever before me are sickness and wounds.
8 Be warned, Jerusalem,
    Lest I turn from you in disgust;
Lest I make you a desolate waste,
    A land uninhabited."

"Filled with the Wrath of Yahweh"

9   This is what Yahweh of Hosts has said:
"ᵉGlean it! Gleanᵉ like a vine
    The remnant of Israel.
Pass your hand as a vintager would
    Over the tendrils."

10   To whom can I speak,
    Give a warning they would hear?
Ah see! Their ears are "uncircumcised,"
    They cannot give heed.
Ah see! The word of Yahweh is to them
    A reproach that pleases them not.
11   So I'm filled with the wrath of Yahweh,
    Weary of holding it.

"Pour it out on the tots in the streets,
    On the bands of youths as well;
For both husband and wife will be taken,
    Graybeard and patriarch too.
12   Their homes will be handed to others,
    Their fields and wives as well,
When I lash out and strike
    Those who dwell in the land—Yahweh's word.
13   From the least on up to the greatest,
    Every one's greedy for gain;

ᵉ⁻ᵉ Reading *'ōlēl 'ōlēl* (infinitive and imperative) with Duhm and others (cf. 9b and LXX), for MT *'ōlēl yᵉ'ōlᵉlū* ("they shall glean thoroughly").

From prophet on up to priest,
Every one practices fraud.
14 Yet they treat my people's fracture
With nostrums, and cry,
'It is well! It is well!'
But it is not well!
15 *Were they shamed* by their loathsome behavior?
No! They neither felt shame
Nor knew how *to blush.*
And so—they will fall with the fallen,
'At the time of their doom' they'll go down—Yahweh
has spoken."

Elaborate Ritual No Substitute for Obedience

16 This is what Yahweh has said:
"Stand at the crossroads, and look;
Ask for the ancient paths,
Where the good way lies. That take,
And find for yourselves repose.
But they said, 'We'll not take it!'
17 So I stationed over them* watchmen:
'Give heed to the trump of alarm!'
But they said, 'We'll not heed it!'
18 Therefore hear, O nations!
*[   ]
[   ]*
19   Hear, O earth!
Watch! I will bring disaster
Upon this people,
The fruit of their schemes;

---

d–d Pointing the verb *hᵃbōšū;* but one could retain MT and translate, "They ought to have been ashamed."
e–e Pointing *hikkālēm* as in viii 12; MT here has *haklīm.*
f–f MT "at the time (when) I have punished them"; but read *pᵉquddātām* for *pᵉqadtīm,* as in viii 12.
g Hebrew has "over you," which is awkward in the context.
h–h The latter part of the verse (Heb. "and know, O congregation, what is in them") is corrupt; but emendations are unconvincing, and the cola are left untranslated.

For they've paid no heed to my words,
And my law they have spurned.

20 What want I with incense imported from Sheba,
Sweet cane from a faraway land?
Your holocausts find no favor,
Your offerings please me not.

21 And so, this is what Yahweh has said:
'Watch! I will place before this people
Obstructions to send them sprawling;
Fathers and sons together,
Neighbor and friend will perish.'"

Again: the Terrible Invader from the North

22 This is what Yahweh has said:
"Look! A people coming
From the land of the north,
A great nation stirring
From the earth's farthest bounds.

23 Armed with bow and blade,
Cruel are they and ruthless.
On they come with a roaring like the sea,
Mounted on chargers,
Drawn up in battle array—
Against you, Daughter Zion!"

24 We have heard the report,
Our hands hang limp;
Anguish has gripped us,
Pangs as of childbirth.

25 Go not forth to the field,
Or walk by the road,
For the sword of the foe
Is—terror everywhere!

26 Ah My Daughter-My People, gird sackcloth on,
Wallow in ashes!
Mourn as you would for an only son,

Lamentation most bitter.
For soon, very soon,
Ruin[i] is upon us.

Jeremiah, "Assayer" of His People

27 "I have made you my people's assayer,[j]
To observe and assay their conduct."
28 They are all [k]the most stubborn of rebels,[k]
Peddlers of slander,[l]
Corrupt to the very last man.
29 The bellows blow fiercely,
But the lead [m]comes whole from the fire.[m]
It's useless to go on refining,
The wicked are not removed.
30 Refuse silver men will call them,
Because Yahweh's refused them.

[i] Literally "the destroyer" (*haššōdēd*); LXX, however, reads *haššōd*.
[j] See NOTE.
[k–k] Heb. *sārē sōrerīm;* LXX omits *sārē*, and it may be a dittography; in which case read "they are all of them rebels."
[l] See NOTE.
[m–m] MT is corrupt. Read *mē'ēš tam* (or *tittōm*) with various scholars. For another proposal, see now M. J. Dahood, *Biblica* 44 (1963), 298.

NOTES

vi 1. *In Tekoa blow.* Heb. *biteqōa' tiqe'ū.* The assonance cannot be caught in translation; the name of Tekoa (south of Bethlehem) was no doubt chosen for the sake of it.

Bet-hakkerem. Probably 'Ain Kârem, west of Jerusalem.

light the beacon. Again an assonance: *śe'ū maś'ēt.* The latter word denotes a fire (or smoke) signal in the Lachish Letters (IV:10); cf. Judg xx 38, 40.

2. *are you like / A meadow most delightful.* The text is uncertain. RSV, "the comely and delicately bred I will destroy" (other EVV similarly) is scarcely correct: the verb (*dāmītī*) can mean either "be like" or "be silent," while the word translated "comely" (*nāwāh*) normally means a "pasture." Read the sentence as a question, *halenāwāh me'unnāgāh*, following Volz and others. The verb is taken (cf. KB) as second feminine

singular. (The archaic form is frequent in Jer.) Possibly, however, point as Piel (*dimmītī*) and translate, "Have I likened. . . ."

3. *shepherds . . . flocks*. Enemy kings and their troops (cf. ii 8); they speak in vss. 4 f.

his part. Literally "his hand"; cf. II Sam xix 44; II Kings xi 7, etc., for this meaning.

4. *Ready*. Literally "sanctify." The expression derives from the ancient institution of Holy War, and refers to the ritual preparation of warriors for battle. But it is frequently used in an attenuated sense (e.g., Mic iii 5), and so perhaps here.

7. *Outrage! Robbery*. The words *ḥāmās wāšōd* ("violence and spoil") seem to be the characteristic cry of one set upon by robbers (Rather like, "Help, police!"?).

10. *uncircumcised*. I.e., incapable of receiving the divine word; cf. iv 4; Acts vii 51.

12. *lash out and strike*. Literally "stretch out my hand"; cf. xv 6; Isa v 25, etc.

13. *From prophet on up to priest*. The preceding bicolon suggests this translation. But whether or not one can suppose a hierarchy with prophets at the bottom and priests at the top is uncertain. The sense is inclusive: all the clergy including these.

14. *With nostrums*. Literally "lightly, superficially."

16. *at the crossroads*. Literally "by the roads." The sense could be: stop where you are. Emendation is unnecessary.

17. *I stationed over them watchmen*. "Watchmen" are prophets who warn of danger (e.g., Ezek iii 16–21). The verb suggests repeated action, i.e., "I set again and again. . . ."

19. *my law*. Or, "my teaching." But in this context reference is probably to the Deuteronomic law (cf. COMMENT below); and note viii 8 f. where *written* law (presumably that of Deuteronomy) and Yahweh's prophetic "word" are in parallelism.

20. *Sheba*. Country in southwest Arabia, center of the trade in incense and spice.

holocausts. Whole burnt offerings (*'ōlāh*), in which the entire animal was consumed on the altar. The wording of the colon follows Skinner.

offerings. Animal sacrifice (*zebaḥ*) in which only choice portions were offered on the altar, the rest being consumed by the worshipers.

23. *blade*. Heb. *kīdōn* is usually supposed to be a javelin. But the Scroll of the War of the Sons of Light against the Sons of Darkness (one of those found at Qumran) makes it clear that, at that time at least, it was a sword 68.7 cm. long, comparable to the Roman *gladius*. Cf. Y. Yadin, *The Scroll of the War of the Sons of Light against the Sons of Darkness* (Oxford University Press, 1962), pp. 124–31 for full discussion.

26. *My Daughter-My People*. Cf. iv 11 and NOTE there.

only son. This is the proper meaning of Heb. *yāḥīd* (cf. Gen xxii 2; Judg xi 34, etc.); but the word carries the overtone of "beloved," and so LXX.

27. *assayer*. Hebrew adds, "a fortress" (*mibṣār*). This may be a gloss on *bāḥōn* ("assayer") confused with *baḥan* ("tower"). Perhaps, if vocalized *mᵉbaṣṣēr*, the word may (cf. KB) mean "one who searches through," i.e., "a tester" (and so RSV). If so, it may be a correct gloss; or it may be taken with "bronze and iron" (see NOTE on vs. 28) as an additional colon to follow this one: ". . . my people's assayer / a tester of bronze and iron." But possibly all three words were drawn in secondarily from i 18.

28. *Peddlers of slander*. Hebrew adds "bronze and iron," which is out of place (see NOTE on vs. 27).

29. *comes whole from the fire*. In ancient times lead was placed with silver ore in a crucible; when this was superheated, the lead oxidized and served as a flux to carry off the alloys. Here the ore is so impure that the process fails: the alloys are not removed.

The wicked. The figure is dropped; the wicked are the dross that cannot be drawn off.

COMMENT

The theme of impending judgment, which has dominated chapters iv and v, is still to the fore in chapter vi. The chapter, like the preceding ones, is composed of originally independent pieces, and these can be set apart with relative ease. They are:

1. Verses 1–8. This piece consists of an exceedingly vivid poem describing the coming of the "Foe from the North" to lay siege to Jerusalem (1–5), which leads into an oracle from Yahweh (6–8) announcing this as his judgment upon that city for its sins. No precise date can be assigned. But the fact (8) that disaster can still be avoided if the people will only take warning may indicate that this is one of the earlier of the poems of this type.

2. Verses 9–15. This piece, like v 1–9, takes the form of a dialogue between the prophet and Yahweh. It begins (9) with Yahweh's command to glean Israel as a grape-gatherer would glean a vine. In vss. 10–11a Jeremiah, whose lot it is to proclaim this word, speaks. He protests that no one will listen to such a word and that he has, therefore, held it in until he is, as it were, about to explode. To this Yahweh replies (11b–12) commanding Jeremiah

to hold it back no more, but to pour it out upon the people, young and old alike, since the coming judgment will engulf them all. Then follows a further movement (13–15) assailing the general corruption of the people, particularly of the clergy who, greedy for gain, lull the nation into a false sense of security. Verses 12–15 are repeated with slight variations at viii 10–12; but they fit the present context splendidly and may well be in their original position here. The piece cannot be dated with precision, although vs. 14 clearly reflects the post-reformation complacency when priest and people alike imagined that the nation had by its action gained peace with its God and assurance of his continued protection.

3. Verses 16–21. This appears to be an example of Jeremiah's preaching after—and not necessarily long after—Josiah's reform. The piece, which is oracular in style, declares in effect that the people have refused both of the alternatives posed by the Deuteronomic theology: they have not obeyed its summons to return to the ancient ways (i.e., the Mosaic covenant as depicted in Deuteronomy), nor have they heeded its warnings (16–17). They have, in fact (19–21), spurned Yahweh's law and thought to satisfy his demands by an ever more elaborate cultus. And Yahweh will not have it! A date in the latter part of Josiah's reign suits admirably.

4. Verses 22–26. This is another—and vivid—poem describing the approach of the "Foe from the North," part of which reappears in another context in l 41–43. It is not impossible that this poem was originally composed in the course of a barbarian threat late in Josiah's reign (see the remarks on the Scythian problem in the Introduction, the chapter entitled "The Book of Jeremiah . . ."), and that it later found a new and more terrible fulfillment as the Babylonians advanced through Syria and Palestine in 605/4.

5. The chapter, and the editorial unit of which it is a part (see above), concludes (27–30) with a further dialogue between Jeremiah and Yahweh. This dialogue resumes the thought of i 10: Jeremiah, who was there appointed "overseer" of the nations, is here (27) addressed as the "assayer" of his people, whose duty it is to examine their conduct. The assayer then gives his verdict (28–30): the people are hopelessly impure metal, slag indeed, and cannot possibly be refined. The piece seems to play upon a favorite theme of Isaiah (e.g., Isa i 24–26), namely, the description of the coming judgment as a refining process designed to bring forth a purified remnant of the people. But now the judgment has fallen,

and the refining process has failed: purification of the national character is impossible. One wonders if these verses were not composed
after the deportation of 597 (ch. xxiv, which dates to that period,
expresses a similar thought); but it must be admitted that some
earlier calamity (such as that of 609) could be in view.

7. THE "TEMPLE SERMON"
AND APPENDED SAYINGS
(vii 1–34; viii 1–3)

The "Temple Sermon"

VII 1 The word that came to Jeremiah from Yahweh: 2 "Stand in the gate of Yahweh's house and there proclaim this word. Say, 'Hear the word of Yahweh, all you of Judah who enter by these gates to worship Yahweh! 3 This is what Yahweh of Hosts, the God of Israel, has said:

" 'Reform the whole pattern of your conduct, *a*so that I may dwell with you*a* in this place. 4 Do not put your trust in that lie: "This is Yahweh's temple, Yahweh's temple, Yahweh's temple!" 5 No! Only if you really reform your whole pattern of conduct—if you really behave justly one toward another, 6 no longer oppress the alien, the orphan, and the widow [nor shed innocent blood in this place], nor follow other gods to your own hurt— 7 only then *b*can I dwell with you*b* in this place, in the land that I gave to your fathers of old for all time to come.

8 " 'Look! You are putting your trust in a worthless lie! 9 What? You think you can steal, murder, commit adultery, perjure yourselves, burn sacrifices to Baal, and follow other gods of whom you know nothing, 10 and then come and stand before me in this house, which bears my name, and say, "We are safe!"—just so you can go right on doing all these abominations? 11 A robber's hide-out—is that what this house, which bears my name, has become in your opinion? But look! I too can see—Yahweh's word. 12 Yes, go, if you will, to my place that used to be in Shiloh, where I first established my resi-

a–a The reading follows Aq., Vulg. and differs from MT only in vocalization. See NOTE on vs. 3.
b–b So Vulg.; see NOTE on vs. 3.

dence, and see what I did to it because of the wickedness of my people Israel. 13 And now, because you have done all these things—Yahweh's word—and did not listen, though I spoke to you earnestly and persistently, nor answer when I called you, 14 I will treat the house which now bears my name, and in which you place your trust, the place which I provided for you and your fathers before you, just as I treated Shiloh. 15 And I will cast you out of my sight, just as I cast out all those kinsmen of yours, Ephraim's entire progeny.'"

The Cult of the Queen of Heaven

16 "As for you, you are not to pray for this people; do not offer in their behalf any entreaty or prayer, or make intercession with me, for I will not listen to you. 17 Don't you see what they are doing in the cities of Judah and in the streets of Jerusalem?— 18 how the children gather wood, and their fathers kindle the fire, while the women knead dough to make cakes for the Queen of Heaven, and how they pour out libations to other gods in order to spite me. 19 Am I the one they are spiting?—Yahweh's word. Is it not rather themselves, to their own confusion?" 20 Therefore, this is what Lord Yahweh has said: "See! My hot anger is about to be poured out on this place, on man and beast, on the trees of the field and the produce of the ground; and it will burn and never be quenched."

Yahweh Demands Obedience, Not Sacrifice

21 This is what Yahweh of Hosts, the God of Israel, has said: "Put your burnt offerings with your other sacrifices, and eat the meat! 22 For when I brought your fathers out of the land of Egypt, I said nothing to them, nor gave them any command, regarding burnt offerings and sacrifices. 23 But this one commandment I did give them: 'Obey my voice, and I will be your God, and you shall be my people. Conduct yourselves in all things just as I command you, that it may go

well with you.' 24 But they neither obeyed nor paid any attention, but ᶜfollowed their own stubbornly wicked inclinationsᶜ
and got worse instead of better. 25 From the day your fathers
came out of the land of Egypt until the present, I ᵈsent to
themᵈ all my servants the prophets, ᵉagain and again,ᵉ with
urgency and persistence; 26 yet they neither heeded me nor
paid any attention, but with willful obstinacy did worse than
their fathers.

27 "And you will say all these things to them, but they will
not listen to you. You will call them, but they will not answer. 28 So you will say to them, 'This is the nation that
would not obey the voice of Yahweh its God, nor accept
correction;

> Truth is dead,
> Gone from their mouth.'"

The "Valley of Slaughter"

29   Cut off your locks and cast them from you;
> On the heights take up a dirge,
> For Yahweh has rejected, abandoned
> The brood of his wrath.

30 "For the people of Judah have done what is highly displeasing to me—Yahweh's word. They have placed their detestable cult objects in the house that bears my name, in order to
defile it. 31 They have built the ᶠhigh placeᶠ of Tophet in the
valley of Ben-hinnom in order to burn their sons and daughters in the fire—a thing that I never commanded, nor did it
even enter my mind.

32 "Therefore, believe me, days are coming—Yahweh's word—
when they will no longer speak of Tophet, or of the valley
of Ben-hinnom, but of the valley of Slaughter; for they will

ᶜ⁻ᶜ Hebrew apparently offers variant readings: "They walked in the counsels
of/in the stubbornness of their wicked heart." Omit the first with LXX.
ᵈ⁻ᵈ So for smoothness with LXX manuscripts, Syr.; Heb. ". . . to you."
ᵉ⁻ᵉ Hebrew has "by day" (yōm), which cannot be right. Perhaps read yōm
yōm (Syr.), "daily," i.e., regularly. But some think yōm is a dittography.
ᶠ⁻ᶠ So LXX. See NOTE.

bury in Tophet till there is no room left. 33 Then the corpses of this people will be left to feed the carrion birds and the wild beasts, for there will be no one to frighten them away. 34 And I will banish from the cities of Judah and from Jerusalem's streets sounds of mirth and gladness, the voice of bridegroom and bride; for the land will be a desolate waste."

Astral Worship and Its Awful Punishment

VIII 1 "When that time comes—Yahweh's word—they will exhume the bones of the kings of Judah, and the bones of its nobles, together with those of the priests and the prophets and the citizens of Jerusalem; 2 and they will spread them out before the sun and the moon and all the heavenly host, whom they have loved and worshiped and followed, whom they have consulted, and to whom they have done obeisance. They will never be gathered or buried, but will be like so much dung to fertilize the soil. 3 And to all the survivors that are left of all this evil family in all the various places*g* to which I shall have driven them, death will seem preferable to life—word of Yahweh of Hosts."

g Hebrew erroneously repeats "that are left" after this word; omit with LXX, Syr.

NOTES

vii 1–2. LXX has only, "Hear the word of the Lord, all (you of) Judah," which doubtless reflects more exactly the actual spoken form of the address.

3. *dwell with you in this place.* MT "and I will let you dwell" understands "this place" as referring to the land. But the temple is here the center of interest, and in vs. 12 the "place" is Yahweh's house. The "place" that Yahweh chooses, to "cause his name to dwell" there (cf. vs. 12), is, in Deuteronomic usage, regularly the temple (e.g., I Kings viii 29 f., 35; Deut xii 11; xiv 23). See also the very similar expression in I Kings vi 12 f.

4. *This is.* Hebrew has plural, which doubtless refers to the whole complex of buildings. The word "temple" denotes a palace or royal

residence. It was believed that as Yahweh had promised to David's dynasty an eternal rule, he had also chosen Zion as his (earthly) dwelling place forever (e.g., Ps cxxxii); the very presence of the temple, where the Divine King sat enthroned, was felt to assure the nation's protection.

6. The clause in brackets is a prohibition in the midst of a series of conditional clauses, and may be an expansion. It could be retained by reading *lō'* for *'al*.

7. *dwell with you.* MT again has "let you dwell."

9. Note that the crimes listed are violations of the eighth, sixth, seventh, ninth, first and second commandments, i.e., constitute an almost total breach of the covenant stipulations.

10. *which bears my name.* Literally "upon which my name is called," i.e., which is my personal property (so also in vss. 11, 14, 30).

11. *A robber's hide-out.* Literally ". . . cave." The figure grows out of the two preceding verses. The people addressed commit all sorts of crimes, and then flee to the temple for safety (thinking through participation in its cult to escape the consequences of what they have done) just as bandits lie low until pursuit dies down, and then go out to commit fresh depredations.

But look! I too can see. The words are ambiguous and could be understood: "Look! I am not blind"; or "Well, I too so regard it" (and will treat it accordingly); or, "I too have seen" (all these things).

12. *Shiloh, where I first established my residence.* Literally ". . . where I made my name to dwell at the first." Shiloh (Seilûn), in the territory of Ephraim, was the site of the shrine that housed the Ark in the days of the Judges. The Bible (aside from Ps lxxviii 60 f.) does not tell of its destruction, but archaeological evidence indicates that the Philistines destroyed it after the battle described in I Sam iv (after 1050 B.C.).

16. Cf. xi 14; xiv 11. The very fact that this injunction not to pray is so often repeated causes one to wonder if Jeremiah, while realizing the futility of it, ever ceased to pray for his people.

18. *Queen of Heaven.* At this period probably the Assyrian-Babylonian goddess Ishtar, who is called by this title; but perhaps her cult had been identified with that of some Canaanite goddess. M. J. Dahood (*Revista Biblica* 8 [1960], 166–68) argues that the goddess is Shapash.

21. *Put your burnt offerings with your other sacrifices.* "Other" is added to bring out the sense. Burnt offerings were entirely consumed on the altar, while parts of other sacrifices were eaten by the worshipers (cf. on vi 20). The point seems to be that God does not care which way sacrifice is performed. This thought is developed in the next two verses: in the days of the Exodus God gave his people no instructions regarding sacrifice, but rather commanded them to obey him and be his people. The force of this passage, and others like it (e.g., Amos

v 21–25; Hos vi 6; Mic vi 1–8; Isa i 10–17), has been much disputed. It is unlikely, however, that it is to be taken either as a categorical rejection of the sacrificial system as such, or as a statement that there was no sacrifice in the wilderness. The point lies in the balance between vss. 22 and 23. The words "Obey my voice, and I will be your God, and you shall be my people" are the formula of covenant (cf. Deut xxvi 16–19): God's essential demands (e.g., as found in the Decalogue) did not concern ritual matters, but the keeping of the Covenant stipulations.

24. *got worse instead of better.* Literally "They were [or with some manuscripts, EVV, "they went"] backward and not forward."

29. *The brood of his wrath.* Literally "the generation of his wrath" (i.e., with which he is angry).

31. *high place.* Hebrew has plural, but only one high place seems to be in question, that of Tophet. This was located in the valley just south of Jerusalem, and was the scene of pagan rites, including human sacrifice, in Manasseh's reign (II Kings xxiii 10). The last clause of the verse suggests that people were actually offering their children to Yahweh, (they thought) under the impression that he desired it (cf. Mic vi 7). Had they misunderstood the command to dedicate all first-born to Yahweh (Exod xiii 2)?

32. *till there is no room left.* Heb. *mē'ēn māqōm.* Many understand this as "because there is no room elsewhere." But the expression need not have this force (cf. *mē'ēn yōšēb:* iv 7; xxvi 9, etc.); and Tophet does not receive an overflow of corpses, but is one great grave, so full that many bodies cannot be buried at all (vs. 33).

viii 2. *the heavenly host.* I.e., the stars. The language of the verse is derisive; the astral deities whom they have so loved look down on their bones with cold unconcern.

to fertilize the soil. Literally "on the surface of the ground."

COMMENT

The section consists of a series of originally separate prose sayings (with one brief snatch of poetry) which have been worked together in such a way that the whole gives the impression of being a single connected discourse. This has been achieved, as elsewhere in the Jeremiah prose, by articulating the various shorter units within a framework in which Yahweh addresses the prophet directly and tells him what he is to say (cf. vii 1–2a, 16–19, 27–28). There is, moreover, a unity of theme in that all parts of the section have to do with cultic abuses, whether the practice of pagan rites, or the misuse of the official cult of the temple itself.

After the characteristic heading (vii 1), the section begins with Yahweh's command to Jeremiah (vs. 2a) to stand in the temple gate and speak (LXX, incidentally, omits vss. 1–2a). Then follows (vii 2b–15) the famous "Temple Sermon" in which Jeremiah begs the people not to believe that the mere presence of the temple will protect them, and warns them that Yahweh will destroy both temple and nation if they do not radically amend their conduct. That the "Temple Sermon" ends with vss. 14 f. is clear from chapter xxvi, where we have the same address in briefer form (xxvi 2–6), for there we are told (xxvi 7 f.) that as soon as Jeremiah had threatened the destruction of the temple he was set upon by the crowd and nearly put to death. In vii 16–19 Yahweh again addresses Jeremiah, telling him not to pray for the people and calling his attention to their worship of the Queen of Heaven; this leads (vs. 20) into a brief oracle announcing their doom. Then follows (vss. 21–26) a further oracle attacking the people for their attempt to satisfy Yahweh's demands through the cult alone while disobeying his covenant stipulations, at the end of which (vss. 27–28) Yahweh again addresses Jeremiah and tells him what to say. The section then ends with two further sayings (vii 29–34; viii 1–3) directed at various pagan practices, and announcing the awful judgment that is coming.

The material seems in the main to relate to Jehoiakim's reign. The "Temple Sermon," indeed, as we know from xxvi 1, was delivered shortly after that king took the throne (in the autumn of 609, or the winter of 609/8). The attack on empty sacrifice (vii 21–26) could well have been uttered at about the same time, or even in the latter part of Josiah's reign (it is very similar in spirit to vi 16–21). The other sayings likewise fit the period after 609 when, as we have seen, pagan rites began once more to make their appearance. But some of them (especially vii 29–34) may refer to the sins of Manasseh's reign, which seem to have been regarded at least by Jeremiah's disciples (xv 3–4), as they were by the author(s) of Kings (II Kings xxi 10–15; xxii 14–20; xxiii 26; xxiv 3 f.), as the direct cause of the nation's doom, a doom which Josiah's efforts only succeeded in postponing.

The prose discourses of Jeremiah (see Introduction, "The Book of Jeremiah . . ."), as their stereotyped style indicates, do not provide us—at least, not consistently—with the prophet's *ipsissima verba,* but rather preserve the gist of what he said as that was remembered and repeated by his followers. We have, therefore, in evaluating them to reckon with verbal expansion, and even with the possibility of some adaptation, of the prophet's thought. But there is no reason to question the essential authenticity of this material, which is, for the most part, fully in his spirit. It is certainly not late material. Indeed, the very fact that, so far as we know, no such mass desecration of the dead as that described in viii 1–3 (or in vii 32 f.) ever took place, might argue that this section at least was in fixed form prior to 587.

8. AN INCORRIGIBLE PEOPLE
AND THEIR TRAGIC RUIN
(viii 4–23)

Headlong to Ruin, Blindly Complacent

VIII

4   [And you shall say to them: This is what Yahweh has
said]
Does one fall down, and not get up?
Or miss the way, and not turn back?

5   Why, then, has *this people slid back*[a]
In backsliding perpetual?
They cling to deceit,
Refuse to turn back.

6   Though I listened attentively,
No such word did they say.
Not a man regretted his wickedness,
Saying, "What have I done?"
Each of them plunges ahead
Like a horse charging headlong to battle.

7   Why, the stork in the skies
Knows her seasons;
The dove, the swift, and the thrush
Observe their time of migration.
But my people! They know not
How Yahweh rules.

8   How can you say, "Why, we are the wise,
For we have the law of Yahweh"?
Now do but see—the deception it's wrought,
The deceiving pen of the scribes!

a–a Reading *šōbab hāʿām hazzeh*. MT combines this with a variant reading,
šōbᵉbāh yᵉrūšālēm ("Why has Jerusalem slid back?"), which LXX omits.

 9   Shamed are the wise,
         Stunned and trapped;
     Why, look! They have spurned the word of Yahweh,
         So what manner of wisdom have they?

10   "And so—I will give their wives to others,
         Their fields to new owners;
     For from least on up to greatest
         Every one's greedy for gain;
     From prophet on up to priest
         Every one practices fraud.
11   Yet My Daughter-My People's fracture they treat
         With nostrums, and cry,
     'It is well! It is well!'
         But it is not well!
12   Were they shamed by their loathsome behavior?
         No! They neither felt shame
             Nor knew how to blush.
     And so, they will fall with the fallen,
         On the day of their doom they'll go down—Yahweh
                 has spoken."

Terror and Black Despair

13   *b*"Ah, but I'll harvest them!"*b*—Yahweh's word—
         Not a grape on the vine,
     Nor a fig on the tree;
         All withered the leaves."
             c[   ]*c*

14   Why sit we still?
         Band together! Let us get
     To the fortified towns,
         And there meet our doom.

---

b–b Revocalize MT *'āsōp 'ₐsīpēm* either as *'e'ₑsōp 'ₐsīpām* ("I will gather their harvest," cf. LXX), or *'āsōp 'ōsₑpēm* ("I will thoroughly harvest them"), or possibly *'ₑsōp 'ₐsīpām* ("Gather their harvest!").
c–c The colon (literally "And I gave them they shall pass over them") is corrupt and untranslatable; LXX omits.

For Yahweh our God has doomed us,
　　Given us poison to drink,
　　　For we sinned *d*against him.*d*
15 We hoped for peace—
　　No good came;
　　For a time of healing—
　　Instead, sheer terror!
16 From Dan we can hear
　　The snorting of his horses
　　At the sound of the neighing of his steeds
　　The whole land quakes.
They have come to devour the whole of the land,
　　The towns and their dwellers.

17 "Ah see! I am sending among you
　　Poisonous snakes,
　　That cannot be charmed away;
　　And they will bite you—fatally!*e*—Yahweh's word"

Jeremiah's Passionate Grief

18 *f*Grief has overcome me,*f*
　　My heart is sick.
19 There! Hark! The cry of My Daughter-My People
　　Far and wide through the land:
"Is Yahweh not in Zion?
　　Is her King no longer there?
[Why have they provoked me with their idols and futile foreign
　　gods?]
20 The harvest is past,
　　The summer is ended,
　　　But for us—no rescue still!"

d-d So for smoothness with LXX; Heb. "against Yahweh."
e Transfer (Rudolph) the meaningless *mablīgīṭī* from the beginning of vs. 18,
and read for it *mibbᵉlī gᵉhōt* ("without recovery"); cf. LXX (LXX also omits
"Yahweh's word").
f-f The first word of the colon (see textual note*e*) belongs with vs. 17; it
then reads *ʿālay* (i.e., *ʾālāh*) *yāgōn ʿālay*.

21   For My Daughter-My People's breaking I'm broken.
       I mourn; dismay has seized me.
22   Is there no balm in Gilead?
       Or no physician there?
       Why, then, has there been no healing
       For the wound of My Daughter-My People?
23*g*   O that my head were water,
       And my eyes a fountain of tears,
       That day and night I might weep
       For the slain of My Daughter-My People!

g ix 1 in English text.

NOTES

viii 4. The words in brackets are an editorial link with the preceding section (LXX omits "You shall say to them"); what follows are Jeremiah's own reflections (cf. vss. 6, 7, 9).

miss the way . . . turn back. There is a play on the verb *šūb;* literally "Does one turn (i.e., away) and not turn (i.e., back)?"

5. *this people slid back.* The play on *šūb* continues through this verse: "slid back" (*šōbab*)—"backsliding" (*mešūbāh*)—"to turn back" (*lāšūb*).

6. *No such word.* Literally "not so" (*lō' kēn*). Most scholars take this as, "they spoke not aright" (i.e., the truth). But the point here is that Jeremiah, though he has listened closely, has heard no such words of penitence as those that follow.

plunges ahead. Literally "has turned (*šūb* again!) in his course" (singular, with Qre).

7. *thrush.* The precise species of bird is uncertain; see the lexicons.

How Yahweh rules. Heb. *mišpaṭ yhwh,* Yahweh's "order," "ordinance," "rule," or the like. Wild birds instinctively know the order of nature established by Yahweh that rules their existence, but Israel does not know the divine rule (*mišpāṭ*) that governs her.

8–9. The second half of vs. 8 is literally "Truly, behold, it is to *šeqer* ('falsely' or, 'a delusion': cf. iii 23) it has wrought, the *šeqer* ('false, deceitful') pen of the scribes." The force of vss. 8–9, chiefly because of this rather ambiguous sentence, is much disputed. The point, however (Rudolph), lies in the contrast of "the law of Yahweh" with the "word of Yahweh": possession of the law has made the spiritual leaders deaf to the word. The law referred to is a written law, no doubt primarily Deuteronomy, but perhaps other bodies of written law as well. But it is

"Ah, but I'll smelt and assay them!
   What else can I do in view of [ᵈtheir wickedness (?)ᵈ]?
7 Their tongue is a deadly arrow,
     ᵉDeceit the words of their mouthᵉ;
   One greets his neighbor amicably,
     While inwardly laying an ambush.
8 Will I fail to punish this?
     —Word of Yahweh—
   On a nation such as this
     Will I not avenge myself?"

Jerusalem's Ruin—with a Prose Explanation

9 For the mountains ᶠI take upᶠ a wailing,
     For the steppeland pastures a dirge;
   For they're wastes through which nobody passes,
     Nor hear they the lowing of herds;
   Both the birds of the air and the beasts
     Have fled, have gone.

10 "I'll make Jerusalem rubble,
     A jackals' lair,
   And Judah's towns an awesome waste
     Where no one dwells."

11 Who is he that is wise enough to explain this? Who is he
to whom Yahweh's own mouth has spoken, that he may declare
its meaning?
     Why is the country done for,
       Laid waste like a desert where nobody travels?
12 And Yahweh said,ᵍ "Because they forsook my law which I
laid before them, and did not listen to my voice or conduct
themselves in accordance with it, 13 but instead, obeying their

ᵈ⁻ᵈ This reading (rā'ātām), followed by various commentators, is a guess.
Hebrew has bat 'ammī ("because of My Daughter-My People"), which cannot be right. LXX read rā'at ("because of the wickedness of") bat 'ammī.
The probability is that something (perhaps several words) has fallen out.
ᵉ⁻ᵉ See NOTE.
ᶠ⁻ᶠ See NOTE.
ᵍ LXX adds "to me," which may be preferable.

own stubborn inclinations, followed the Baals of which their
fathers taught them." 14 And so, this is what Yahweh of Hosts,
the God of Israel, said:

> "Ah, but I'll feed them[h] with wormwood,
>> Give them poison to drink!

15 I will scatter them among nations of which neither they nor
their fathers knew, and I will send the sword after them until
I have annihilated them."

A Dirge over Jerusalem

16 [i][This is what Yahweh of Hosts has said: Consider and—][i]
> Call for the keeners to come,
>> For the skilled women send;
17   Let them come all a-hurrying
>> And take up over us a lament,
> Till our eyes overflow with tears,
>> And our lashes stream with crying.
18   Ah, the loud wailing
>> That is heard from Zion!
> "How ruined are we,
>> How covered with shame!
> For we must leave the land,
>> [j]Be hurled from our homes."[j]

19   Ah listen, you women, to Yahweh's word,
>> Let your ears receive the word of his mouth.
> Teach a lament to your daughters,
>> Each one to her friend a dirge.
20   For Death has come up through our windows.
>> Has entered our castles,
> Cutting down the child in the street,
>> And the youth in the squares.

[h] Hebrew adds, redundantly, "this people"; LXX omits.
[i–i] See NOTE.
[j–j] Heb. "They have cast down our homes" (hišlīkū miškᵉnōtēnū) is awkward. LXX read hišlaknū . . . : "we must cast aside (i.e., abandon) our homes"; but perhaps even better, point as Hophal: hošlaknū mimmiškᵉnōtēnū.

21   *k*[   ]*k*
      Till the corpses of men lie strewn
          Like dung across the fields,
      Like sheaves behind the reaper,
          Which nobody gathers.

The Coming Exile: Lament and Intercession

X

17   Pick up your pack from the ground,
          You who dwell under siege!
18   For thus Yahweh has spoken:
          "Ah, out I will sling
      Those who dwell in the land,
          Now, right now,
      Nay will press hard upon them
          *l*And squeeze them dry."*l*

19   Ah me, for my hurt,
          My incurable wound!
      I who had thought this to be
          A grief I could bear!
20   Ruined is my tent,
          My cords all snapped!
      My children have left me
          And are no more.
      None now to spread my tent,
          To raise my curtains!
21   Ah, the shepherds were stupid
          They sought not Yahweh;

k–k Hebrew has here, "Speak! Thus the oracle of Yahweh," which is an obvious intrusion; LXX omits. The word *dabbēr* ("speak"), originally pointed as *deber* ("pestilence"), is doubtless a gloss on "Death" in vs. 20.
l–l Hebrew ("so that they may find") is scarcely correct, the verb having no object. Various emendations are proposed. Read (cf. G. R. Driver, JQR 28 [1937], 107) *yimmāṣū* (from *māṣāh*) for *yimṣeʾū* (from *māṣāʾ*): "so that they may be squeezed out, drained." The word is used of Gideon's squeezing the fleece (Judg vi 38).

So nothing went well,
And their flock is all scattered.

22   Hark, a report! Look, there it comes!—
Commotion immense from the northern land,
To make of the cities of Judah
A waste, a jackals' lair.

23   I know, O Yahweh,
That no mortal can order his way,
Nor is it in living man
His steps to direct.

24   Correct us,[m] Yahweh, but within reason,
Not in thy wrath, lest thou bring us[m] to naught.

25   Thy fury pour out on the nations
That know thee not,
And upon the realms
That invoke not thy name.
For [n]they've feasted on Jacob[n]—consumed him,
And his pasture laid waste.

[m] So LXX, Lat.; Hebrew has ". . . me," which may be intended in a corporate sense, as often in the Psalms.
[n–n] After these words Hebrew repeats "They have feasted on [devoured] him"; repetition omitted with LXX and Ps lxxix 7 (vs. 25 repeats Ps lxxix 6 f.).

NOTES

ix 1. Verse numbers in ix follow those of the Hebrew Bible; in EVV (except AJV) viii 23 appears as ix 1, and the material of this section as ix 2–22.

2. The text of the first bicolon is corrupt (Heb. "They bend their tongue. Their bow is falsehood. And not for truth are they strong in the land"). The translation generally follows LXX, redividing the cola, supplying or understanding "like" before "bow," reading the last verb singular, and omitting "for" before "truth" (but this may be merely the "emphatic *lamed*"; cf. F. Nötscher, VT 3 [1953], 380).

And know not Yahweh. Jeremiah is the speaker. If MT is retained, vss. 1–5 must be regarded as a dialogue. See textual note[b–b].

3. *as crafty as Jacob.* Heb. '*āqōb ya'qōb* is literally "will indeed act

craftily, overreach"; but the pun on Jacob's name is unmistakable (cf. Hos xii 3–5[2–4E]).

4. *Perverted, too weak to change.* "They act pervertedly, they weary themselves (i.e., wear themselves out trying) to turn." Hebrew in this colon and the next is corrupt ("To act pervertedly they weary themselves. Your sitting is in the midst of deceit. Through deceit they refuse . . ."). Redivide consonants following LXX: *heʿewū nilʿʾū šūb / tōk beṭōk mirmāh bemirmāh.*

5. *to know Yahweh.* The situation is as at the end of vs. 2; see NOTE there.

7. *Deceit the words of their mouth.* So LXX; with a redivision of clauses Hebrew reads "Deceit he has spoken with his mouth." The shift from third masculine plural suffix ("their tongue") to third masculine singular suffixes and verbs, while not unusual, is disconcerting; one is tempted to read "his tongue" (dittography) in the preceding colon (but cf. vss. 6 and 8). The verse may be out of context.

9. *I take up a wailing.* LXX, Lat., Syr. have "Take up"; but MT is preferable, since Jeremiah is the speaker (vss. 9 and 10 are separate fragments). MT also has "a weeping and a wailing," which seem to be variants; LXX has only one.

11. *to explain.* Or "to understand"; but in view of the context it is better to take the verb (*weyābēn*) as Hiphil (Rudolph).

16. The words in brackets do not belong in this context. The oracular introduction is out of place since, in what follows, Yahweh is not the speaker. "Consider and" both overloads the first colon and fits awkwardly; LXX omits. The words either begin an oracle, or fragment, now lost, or are an editorial link to the foregoing.

skilled women. Professional mourners; so also the "keeners" (feminine).

20. *Death.* Heb. *māwet* (or *mōt*)—the Canaanite god of infertility, death, and the underworld was *Mōt.* It is as if the god of death has entered their homes and stalked through their streets.

x 17. The force of the first colon is uncertain. Some render, "Gather your bundle! Out of the land!" But in either case the sense is: prepare for departure.

21. *shepherds . . . flock.* Judah's rulers and their people.

23. *in living man.* Literally "in man who walks." Delete "and" before the next word (Rudolph); Hebrew has "who walks and to direct. . . ."

COMMENT

The material of chapter ix follows upon that of viii 4–23 without break and, for the most part, develops the same major themes. In vss. 1–8 there is a traditional unit somewhat similar to v 1–9 and v 20–29, and concluding with the same stereotyped formula. Its theme, like that of viii 4–12 and the two pieces just mentioned, is the incurable depravity of the people. Verses 1–5 (see NOTES on vss. 2, 5) are a soliloquy of Jeremiah in which he voices his despair at the dishonesty and mendacity of his countrymen and expresses his wish to be quit of them. This leads (vss. 6–8) into an oracle from Yahweh announcing their judgment (vs. 6, incidentally, takes up the figure of the assaying and refining of metal, noted in vi 27–30). This piece, like those mentioned above, seems to come from a relatively early period in Jeremiah's ministry (perhaps at the very beginning of Jehoiakim's reign, or even earlier) before disaster was imminent.

Following this are two brief fragments: a lament (vs. 9), and an oracle announcing Jerusalem's destruction (vs. 10). This last is in turn followed by a prose commentary (vss. 11–15), apparently of Exilic date, which deals with the burning question: Why has Yahweh allowed his country to be destroyed? The answer given, though doubtless not in Jeremiah's own words, is thoroughly in keeping with his thought: Because of its stubborn apostasy and disobedience. In vss. 16–21 the note of bitter lament is resumed. These verses are a dirge (probably two originally separate poems) over the ruin of Jerusalem, perhaps uttered on the very eve of the siege and deportation of 598/7.

The concluding verses of chapter x (vss. 17–25) continue the thought of chapters viii–ix and may originally, before the insertion of the material in ix 22–x 16 (see next section), have stood immediately after ix 1–21 (note the catchword "gather, pick up" in ix 21 and x 17). This section (vss. 17–25) begins (vss. 17–18) with a brief oracle, no doubt uttered as the Babylonians closed in upon Jerusalem in 598/7, telling the people to get ready for deportation. Then follows (vss. 19–21) a soliloquy in which Jeremiah, speaking for the nation, laments the ruin that has come and the stupidity of the rulers that has brought it to pass. This leads (vs.

21) into a brief ejaculation announcing the approach of the foe. The section then concludes (vss. 23–25) with a prayer of Jeremiah begging Yahweh for mercy. Verse 25 repeats Ps lxxix 6 f.; since this psalm is of Exilic date, it is probable (unless one assumes that the psalmist quoted Jeremiah) that the verse is a later addition.

10. MISCELLANEOUS SAYINGS
(ix 22–25; x 1–4a; 9; 4b–8; 10–16)

Man's Proper Boast

IX

22   This is what Yahweh has said:
  "Let the wise not boast of his wisdom,
    Let the strong not boast of his strength,
    Let the rich not boast of his riches.

23   But who would boast, let him boast in this:
    That he has the wisdom to know me—
  That I, Yahweh, do gracious deeds,
    Justice and right in the earth;
  For in such I delight—Yahweh's word."

Circumcised—Yet Uncircumcised

24 "Look! The days are coming—Yahweh's word—when I will punish all those who are circumcised physically: 25 Egypt, Judah, Edom, Ammon, Moab, and all those with shaved temples who live in the desert; for all the nations are uncircumcised —and all the house of Israel is uncircumcised in heart."

Yahweh and the Idols: a Poem of Later Date

X   1 Hear the word which Yahweh has spoken concerning you, O house of Israel! 2 This is what Yahweh has said:
  "Learn not the nations' customs,
    Nor fear celestial omens,
      Even though the nations fear them.

3   *a*What the peoples believe in*a*—pure delusion!

a–a The sense is uncertain; see NOTE.

It's but wood chopped out of the forest,
Graved by the artisan's hand,
4a　　And decked with silver and gold—

9b　　Hammered silver
Imported from Tarshish,
And gold from Uphaz—
Violet and purple their clothing,
The work of skilled men are they all,

4b　Fastened with hammer and nails
To keep them from wobbling.
5　Like scarecrows are they in a cucumber patch—can't talk!
Have to be carried—can't walk!
Fear them not—they can do no harm,
Still less is it in them to help."

6　There is none like thee, O Yahweh;
Great art thou,
And great is thy name in might.
7　Who would not fear thee,
Thou King of the nations?
Yea, that is thy due.
Among all the nations' wise ones,
And in all their domains,
There is none like thee.
8　One and all they are stupid and foolish,
　　　c[　　　]c

10　But Yahweh is truly God,
The living God is he,

---

b On the position of the verse, see COMMENT. After "Uphaz," Hebrew reads, "the work of the artisan and the goldsmith's hands," which seems to be a variant of the last colon of the verse (LXX combines the two).
c–c Hebrew is unintelligible: "The instruction of 'nothings' [the idols] is wood." No convincing solution has been proposed. In the context, the sense would seem to be that the wise men of the nations know only what their idols tell them, which is worthless. But the colon (perhaps the whole verse) may well be a variant of vs. 3a (note the words *hebel*, *hū'*, and *'ēṣ*, which occur in both).

   The King everlasting.
  Quakes at his wrath the earth,
   Nor can nations endure his fury.

11 *d*

12 Who made the earth by his power,
   Established the world by his wisdom,
   By his skill stretched out the heavens.

13 At the sound of *e*[his thunderous voice (?)]
   [ ]*e*
  A roaring of waters in heaven.
   He brings up the clouds from the farthest horizons,
   The rainstorm with lightning provides,
   And sends forth the wind from his storehouse.

14 All mortals stand stupid and witless,
   Every smith is ashamed of his idol;
   For a fraud are his images,*f* lifeless things;

15 Nonentities they, a ridiculous joke.
   At the time of their doom they will perish.

16 Not like these is the Portion of Jacob.
   Nay, framer of all is he,
  And Israel his very own tribe—
   Yahweh of Hosts his name.

d The verse is a gloss in Aramaic. It reads: "Thus shall you say to them, 'The gods who made neither the heavens nor the earth shall vanish from the earth and from under these heavens.' "
e–e Text is damaged. Hebrew has "at the sound of his giving forth . . ."; the verb has no object. LXX omits altogether; but the words are present also in li 16 (li 15–19 repeat vss. 12–16), where LXX seems to read them. Something—possibly several words—has fallen out.
f Hebrew reads singular, but the context requires plural.

Notes

ix 22. In most EVV the verses that follow are ix 23–25 (see Note on ix 1).

23. *in such.* I.e., in such things as those just listed; but possibly "such people," as the wise one described in this verse.

24–25. The oracle is directed at a group of nations and peoples, including Judah, all of which practiced circumcision. Very possibly (Ru-

dolph) they were members of an anti-Babylonian coalition otherwise unknown to us, formed under Egyptian leadership (Egypt is named first).
Perhaps the confederates made propaganda of the fact that they all
practiced circumcision, whereas the Babylonians did not. The point seems
to be that Yahweh rejects their boast: in his view all Gentiles are "uncircumcised" (i.e., not members of his covenant people), and the people
of Judah are no better, for they are not circumcised in heart (i.e., inwardly
and spiritually).

24. *circumcised physically.* Literally "circumcised as to the foreskin."

25. *those with shaved temples . . . in the desert.* Arab tribes (cf.
xxv 23; xlix 32). Nebuchadnezzar was obliged to fight these people,
as we know from xlix 28–33; the Babylonian Chronicle mentions one
such campaign in 599/8.

x 2. *customs.* Literally "way," in this context their religious practices.

3. *What the peoples believe in.* Literally "the statutes (*ḥuqqōt*) of the
peoples," i.e., perhaps, their "religion, religious customs" (cf. Lev xviii
3). But the word (plural) is strange here; the context speaks of an idol
(singular). The text is in disorder, but no convincing solution presents
itself. Some read *ḥittat* ("the 'fear' of the peoples," i.e., the idol); but
perhaps read *mūsar*, "the (religious) teaching, instruction" (the word
occurs in vs. 8b, which looks very much like a variant of this line;
see textual note*e–e*.

Graved by the artisan's hand. Literally "the work of the artisan's hand
with a *ma'aṣād*," which is probably not here an ax (EVV), but a
graving tool of some sort.

9. *Uphaz.* Location unknown; but the reading "Ophir" (various Vrs.)
is not to be preferred.

4b. *keep them from wobbling.* The verb must be taken as plural; cf.
the suffix of the preceding verb, and the verbs in vs. 5.

13. The first colon describes Yahweh's voice as the thunder that
accompanies the storm. But the text is damaged. See textual note*e–e*.
The latter half of the verse is almost identical with Ps cxxxv 7.

16. *the Portion of Jacob.* I.e., Yahweh (cf. Pss xvi 5; lxxiii 26; cxix
57, etc.). The term stresses the intimate relationship between Yahweh
and his people. As Yahweh has chosen Israel as "his very own tribe,"
so Israel has Yahweh as her "Portion"; she need not fear—and must
not worship—any other God.

COMMENT

The material of ix 22[23E]–x 16 is miscellaneous in character and interrupts the connection between ix 21 and x 17 (see above). Chapter ix concludes with two brief sayings, one in poetry (vss. 22–23), the other in prose (vss. 24–25). The first of these describes that quality which God most desires in man, and in which a man may legitimately take pride. Although one cannot prove that it comes from Jeremiah, there is no objective reason to deny it to him. The second saying, which pronounces judgment on various circumcised peoples, including Judah, is cryptic and difficult to interpret (see the NOTES above); but, although one cannot be sure of its date, or the circumstances that provoked it, it too reflects Jeremiah's spirit authentically enough (cf, vs. 25 and iv 4; vi 10, etc.).

In x 1–16 there is a poem which, though of great power and depth, is all but universally conceded to come from another hand than Jeremiah's. Striking similarities to various passages in the latter part of Isaiah (e.g., Isa xl 18–20; xli 7; xliv 9–20; xlvi 5–7) suggest an Exilic date. The poem begins as an oracle from Yahweh (vss. 1–5) urging the people not to adopt the religion of the heathen or worship their gods—which are, after all, but chunks of wood and metal. This leads (in vs. 6) into a hymn extolling Yahweh as the sole and incomparable God who is ruler of all creation. But although the meaning is in general clear enough, the text shows evidence of dislocation, and the progress of thought is not always easy to follow. Verse 9, in particular (perhaps vs. 8 as well), seems obviously out of place in its present position, while vss. 6–7, in which Yahweh is addressed directly, likewise sit somewhat awkwardly in the context.

The poem has clearly undergone a complex history of transmission, and it is unlikely that it lies before us in its original form. Verse 11, to begin with, is an obvious gloss: it is a sentence in prose which both interrupts the thought and is written in Aramaic, not Hebrew. Verses 12–16 reappear in another context at li 15–19, and may well at one time have been transmitted separately. But it is in vss. 1–10 that disturbance is most in evidence. Here LXX differs from MT considerably, omitting vss. 6–8 and 10 altogether and placing vs. 9 after the first colon of vs. 5 (which it reads differently). This has the merit of allowing vs. 9 to stand at least approximately in its proper context, and also of removing whatever awkwardness may arise from the change of address in vss. 6–7. But it does not solve all the problems, for vs. 9 still fits poorly where LXX has it, and without vss. 6–8, 10 the transition from vs. 5 to vs. 12 is exceedingly abrupt. Nevertheless, LXX finds support in a fragment found at Qumran (4QJer^b) which, in three successive—though damaged—lines, preserves parts of vss. 4, 9, and 11, in that order, apparently omitting vss. 6–8, 10 (cf. F. M. Cross, Jr., *The Ancient Library of Qumran*, Anchor edition, p. 187).

One cannot be sure at the present state of knowledge which form of the text is the more original (the longer form followed by MT is also witnessed at Qumran), although one is inclined to believe that the shorter form is in general preferable. Since any attempt at detailed reconstruction remains somewhat subjective, the translation above follows the order of MT, save only that vs. 9 is inserted (with Rudolph and others) after the first colon of vs. 4. Admittedly this is a conjectural procedure. But the verse seems to have fallen from its original position (see, further, the NOTES above) and then, perhaps after having been recopied in the margin, seems to have been brought back into the text at different places in the various textual traditions. And read with vs. 4, it yields an excellent sense.

11. THE BROKEN COVENANT,
AND OTHER SAYINGS
(xi 1–17; xii 1–6; xi 18–23; xii 7–17)

Jeremiah and the Covenant

XI 1 The word that came to Jeremiah from Yahweh: 2ª "Speakᵇ
to the men of Judah and the citizens of Jerusalem 3 and say to
them, 'This is what Yahweh, the God of Israel, has said: Cursed
be the man who does not comply with the terms of this covenant, 4 the terms which I laid upon your fathers when I brought
them out of the land of Egypt, out of the iron furnace, namely:
Obey my voice and do exactly as I command you. Then you will
be my people, and I will be your God; 5 and this will allow
me to carry out the oath that I swore to your fathers to give
them a land flowing with milk and honey, as I have in fact
done.'" Then I answered, "Amen, Yahweh!"

6 Then Yahweh said to me, "Proclaim all these things in the
cities of Judah and in the streets of Jerusalem, and say, 'Hear
the terms of this covenant and fulfill them! 7 For I solemnly
warned your fathers when I brought them up from the land of
Egypt, and until this day have continued without ceasing to
warn them: Obey my voice! 8 Yet they neither obeyed nor paid
any attention, but instead followed one and all their own stubbornly wicked inclinations, till I brought down upon them all
the terms of this covenant which, in spite of my command to
them, they had not fulfilled.'"

9 Then Yahweh said to me, "A conspiracy exists among the
men of Judah and among the citizens of Jerusalem. 10 They

ª Hebrew begins the verse, "Hear [plural] the words of this covenant." But
the plural does not fit between vss. 1 and 3, in which Jeremiah personally is
addressed. Perhaps the words are a marginal comment drawn from vs. 6.
ᵇ Read singular (*dabbēr*) with LXX and other Vrs. Hebrew again has plural,
probably under the influence of the preceding clause. (Note: *wedibbartām*
in BH is a typographical error for *wedibbartem;* cf. Rudolph, p. 66).

have gone back to the sins of their ancestors, who refused to
listen to what I said, and have themselves followed other gods
in order to worship them. Israel and Judah alike have broken
my covenant which I made with their fathers." 11 Therefore,
this is what Yahweh has said, "Believe me, I am going to bring
a disaster upon them, which they will not be able to escape; and
when they cry to me, I will not listen to them. 12 Then the
townsmen of Judah and the citizens of Jerusalem will go and
cry to the gods to whom they have been sending up sacrifices;
but these will not be of the least help to them in their time of
distress. 13 Truly, as many as are your cities, so many are your
gods, O Judah! And as many as Jerusalem's streets, so many are
the altars that you have erected° to burn offerings to Baal.

14 "As for you, do not pray for this people! Do not offer in
their behalf any entreaty or prayer, for I am not going to listen
when they cry to me ᵈin their time ofᵈ distress.

15   ᵉWhat does my beloved in my house
          Working out clever schemes?
     Can vows and holy meats
          Turn disaster from you?
          Will you by these escape?
16   Leafy olive tree, lovely to behold—
          So did Yahweh name you.
     But with mighty thunder clap
          He sets alight its foliage—
          Shattered are its branches.ᵉ

---

c Hebrew adds "altars to the Shame" (Baal), which is either a gloss or a variant of "to burn offerings to Baal." LXX omits.
d–d Read *bᵉēt* with manuscripts, Vrs.; MT *bᵉʿad* ("on behalf of") is a dittography from the preceding clause.
e–e The text is exceedingly corrupt, and any reconstruction conjectural. The
one offered here is based on suggestions of various scholars; cf. especially
BH, Rudolph, J. P. Hyatt (JBL 60 [1941], 57–60). 15ab: read *meh līdīdī*
(or, better, *līdīdātī*) *bᵉbētī* / *ʿāśᵉtāh mᵉzimmōt* (or, *mᵉzimmāh*). 15c: read
hanᵉdārīm ("can vows . . .") with LXX; Heb. *hārabbīm* ("the many") is
impossible. Others, however, suggest *haḥᵃlābīm* ("can fat . . .") or *habᵉrīʾīm*
("can fat animals . . .") 15d: read *yaʿᵃbīrū* (MT, Qal) *mēʿālayik* (*kī* dittography) *rāʾātēk*. 15e might better be left untranslated: Heb. *ʾāz taʿᵃlōzī*
("then you might exult") is scarcely right; the reading follows LXX, which

17 Yahweh of Hosts, who planted you, has pronounced evil
against you, because of the wickedness which both Israel and
Judah have done in provoking me by sending up offerings to
Baal."

A Plot against Jeremiah's Life

XII

1   Just art thou, O Yahweh;
        I cannot dispute with thee.
            Yet there are cases of which I would ask thee.
     Why do the fortunes of wicked men prosper,
        And swindlers invariably thrive?
2   Thou hast planted them—aye, they take root;
        They grow—and aye, bear fruit.
     Near art thou in their mouths,
        But far from their hearts.
3   But thou, O Yahweh, dost know me, dost see me,
        Dost examine my thoughts toward thyself.
     Drag them off like sheep to the shambles,
        Mark them out for the day of slaughter!
4   Since they've said, "He'll not see ᶠwhere we end."ᶠ

5   "If you've tired from running a footrace,
        How will you race against horses?
     And if not on your guard in country that's safe,
        How will you do in the thicket of Jordan?
6   For even your brothers, your very own kin,
        Even they have betrayed you,
            Even they are in full cry behind you.

---

at least makes tolerable sense and (*'im 'al zō't tā'ūzī* [?]) presupposes approximately the same consonants as MT. 16a: Hebrew preserves variant readings, "fair of fruit/of form"; omit the first with LXX. 16d Heb. "he sets
fire to her" (*'alehā*). The context requires masculine; read (*be*) *'alēhū* (". . . to
its leaves"). The figure is of a tree struck by lightning.
ᶠ⁻ᶠ "Our end" (*'aʰᵃrītēnū*); LXX has "[God will not see] our ways" (*'orḥō-
tēnū*), which may be preferable.

Do not trust them,
Even though they address you as friends."

XI

18 So Yahweh let me know, and I knew it;
Only then *saw I* through their foul deeds.
19 For I'd been like an innocent lamb
Led to the slaughter,
Not knowing that it was against me
They had hatched their plots:
"Let's destroy the tree *in full sap,*
Cut him off from the land of the living,
That his name be remembered no more."
20 O Yahweh of Hosts, who judgest aright,
Thou assayer of motives and thoughts,
Let me see thy vengeance upon them,
For to thee I've committed my case.

21 And so, this is what Yahweh has said concerning the men of Anathoth who seek *your life,* and who say, "Do not prophesy in the name of Yahweh, or we will kill you."— 22 *So this is what Yahweh of Hosts has said*: "Believe me, I am going to punish them! Their youths will die by the sword, their sons and daughters by famine, 23 and no remnant of them will be left. For I will bring calamity on the men of Anathoth, the year of their doom."

g–g So LXX; Heb. "thou didst show me" would fit only if "O Yahweh" is supplied. Does MT conflate *rā'îtî* and *hir'anī* ("he showed me")?
h–h Heb. *belaḥmō* ("with its bread"), which EVV take to mean "with its fruit." Commentators have long read *belēḥō* ("in its sap"). But probably no emendation is needed; enclitic *mem* between noun and suffix (**bilēḥimō*, or the like) has probably been misunderstood by the scribes (suggested by M. J. Dahood; cf. *Gregorianum* 43 [1962], p. 66).
i–i LXX "my life."
j–j Many delete these words with LXX. But they are probably original, vs. 21 being an explanatory expansion which makes them redundant.

"I Have Forsaken My House"

XII

7   "I've forsaken my house,
     Abandoned my heritage,
  Given my dearest beloved
     To the hand of her foes.

8   She's been to me, my heritage,
     Like a lion in the wood;
  She has roared defiance at me,
     Therefore—I hate her.

9   Does my heritage remind me of a speckled bird of prey,
     Attacked by birds of prey from every side?
  Go then, assemble the ravenous beasts,
     Bring them to dine.

10   Many the shepherds who've looted my vineyard,
     Trampled my field;
  They've made my delightful field
     A desolate waste.

11   They've left it a waste;
     Wasted it mourns before me.
  All the land is laid waste,
     But no one gives it a thought."

12   Over all the steppeland heights
     Brigands have come.
  Ah, the sword of Yahweh, it devours![k]
     No flesh has peace.

13   They planted wheat—thorns they reaped;
     All their toil was for naught.
  Dismayed are they at their crop,
     At Yahweh's hot anger.

[k] Hebrew adds here "from one end of the land to the other," which is not metrical and may be an expansion (cf. xxv 33).

Yahweh's Conditional Promise to Israel's Neighbors

14 This is what Yahweh has said: "As regards all my wicked neighbors who have harmed the possession that I gave to my people Israel as an inheritance— Ah, but I am going to pluck them from their lands, and will, moreover, pluck the house of Judah from their midst. 15 Then, having uprooted them, I will once more have compassion on them and restore them, each to his heritage and each to his land. 16 Then, if they will really learn the religious practices of my people, and will swear by my name, 'As Yahweh lives,' just as once they taught my people to swear by Baal, they will be allowed to develop among my people. 17 But if any of them will not listen, then I will utterly uproot that nation and destroy it—Yahweh's word."

NOTES

xi 4. *and do.* Heb. "and do them," i.e., the stipulations of the covenant just mentioned. LXX omits "them," which is smoother; perhaps it has crept in from vs. 6.

5. *and this will allow me.* Literally "in order that I may."

7–8. LXX omits save for the last two words ("they had not fulfilled"; in Heb. *weˡō̄' 'ā́śū*). The destruction of the nation is presupposed (vs. 8); see the COMMENT.

8. *the terms of this covenant.* Literally "the words of. . . ." These include its stipulations and conditions (so in vss. 3, 6), and also the attendant promises and threats. Here, of course, the punishment arising from non-fulfillment of the stipulations is in mind.

which, in spite of . . . not fulfilled. Literally "which I commanded (them) to do, but they did not."

13. The verse is a prose parallel to ii 28. See textual note*.
14. Cf. this verse with vii 16; xiv 11.

xii 1. *I cannot dispute with thee.* A paraphrase to bring out the force: "In the right art thou, O Yahweh, whenever I would argue with thee." Or: "In the right wouldst thou be . . . if I were to argue . . ." (which Jeremiah refuses to do). Jeremiah will not in principle question the justice of God, who is ever "in the right, just" (*ṣaddı̄q*); no legal complaint (*rı̄b*) can be brought against him. Yet (next colon) there are specific cases of right (*mišpāṭīm*) that Jeremiah wishes to discuss. For a different interpretation, see W. L. Holladay, *Interpretation* 17 (1963), pp. 280–82.

2. *their hearts*. Literally "their kidneys"—conceived of as the seat of the affections.

3. *examine my thoughts*. Literally "assay my heart"—the seat of thought and will. Cf. vi 27 where Jeremiah is to "assay" his people; here God "assays" Jeremiah. Some think this verse belongs with xi 20 (or is a variant of it). This may be correct; but Jeremiah may well have had personal animus against these people.

4. *where we end*. See textual note *f–f*. This is the last line of the verse; it fits poorly with the rest and may originally have followed vs. 3, or (see preceding NOTE) perhaps vs. 2. The first part of vs. 4 reads: "How long must the land mourn / And all the grass of the field (LXX) be withered? / For the wickedness of those who dwell in it / Both beasts and birds have vanished." These are doubtless words of Jeremiah, but apparently from another context.

5. *not on your guard*. Heb. *bōṭēᵃḥ*, "are unsuspecting, feel secure," as in Judg xviii 10; Isa xxxii 9 f. and, especially Amos vi 1. Emendation is unnecessary. As one who cannot keep up in a footrace cannot hope to compete with horses, so one who has not formed the habit of being on guard at all times, even where there seems to be no need for it, is not likely to survive in a jungle inhabited by lions; cf. xlix 19; l 44.

xi 20. *assayer of motives and thoughts*. Literally ". . . of kidneys and heart"; cf. NOTES on xii 2, 3.

thy vengeance upon them. "Thy *nᵉqāmāh* from them." Perhaps the sense is "deliverance from them," rather than vengeance (from a suggestion by G. E. Mendenhall).

I've committed. Heb. "I have revealed" (*gillītī*); but perhaps better, vocalize *gallōtī*, "rolled upon," i.e., "entrusted" (cf. Pss xxii 9[8E]; xxxvii 5).

xii 9. *speckled bird of prey*. The word "speckled" can mean "hyena" (cf. KB; and so LXX, which misunderstands the verse). Some prefer this and, deleting "bird of prey" on its first occurrence, see the picture of a hyena attacked by predatory birds.

11. It is impossible to recapture the assonance in translation; "waste" (vs. 10)—"they've left it a waste"—"wasted"—"is laid waste"—"no one gives": *šᵉmāmāh—šāmūhā* (so point) *lišᵉmāmāh—šᵉmēmāh—nāšammāh —'ēn 'īš šām*.

13. *their crop*. The context requires this; Heb. "your. . . ."

14. *my wicked neighbors*. The syntax here is awkward and it is not clear

where the direct discourse begins. But emendations do little to relieve the difficulty.

have harmed. "touched," which could be in the sense of "were contiguous to," or of "did injury to."

16. *religious practices.* Literally "ways" (LXX singular); here, as in x 2, etc., in the sense of "religion."

will be allowed to develop. Literally "will be built up," i.e., will prosper (Mal iii 15), produce progeny (xxxi 4; Gen xvi 2; xxx 3).

COMMENT

Chapters xi and xii (and perhaps xiii also), although their material is rather heterogeneous in character, seem to form an editorial unit. The basis of this unit is a complex of prose sayings (xi 1–17) very similar in structure to vii 1–viii 3, the various parts being articulated within a framework in autobiographical style (cf. vss. 2 f., 5b, 6, 9, 14) in such a way as to form a continuous discourse which is, in fact, a conversation between Yahweh and the prophet. The theme of this complex is Jeremiah's preaching with regard to the covenant. Attached to it (xi 18–xii 6)—perhaps to indicate that preaching of this sort caused Jeremiah to be persecuted, perhaps because of catchword or theme (cf. xi 18 f. and "conspiracy" in vs. 9; also the motif "tree" in vss. 16 and 19)—is Jeremiah's own account of how his relatives and fellow townsmen in Anathoth plotted to kill him. Unfortunately, we cannot say when this occurred, or what specific provocation may have led to it. Following this piece is a poem (xii 7–13) describing Yahweh's sorrowful rejection of his people, probably composed while Judah was being overrun by marauding bands just prior to the Babylonian attack in 598/7 (cf. vss. 9 f., 12, and xxxv 11; II Kings xxiv 2). Finally, there is a brief prose saying (xii 14–17) telling of Yahweh's purpose for Israel's neighbors. Since this passage lacks the distinctive clichés of the Jeremiah prose (Type C), it is difficult to evaluate. But, although it plays on certain key Jeremianic words (cf. the verbs "pluck up ["uproot"], build up, destroy," and i 10), it also expresses ideas not otherwise attested in Jeremiah's sayings, and may be of anonymous—though not necessarily late—origin.

The meaning of xi 1–17 has been much discussed. The style of the passage is as "Deuteronomic" as any in the book (see the remarks on Type C: Introduction, "The Book of Jeremiah . . ."), but there is no reason to doubt that it reflects Jeremiah's actual sentiments and activity. It represents him first as urging obedience to "this covenant," then as bitterly censuring the people for their breach of it. Does "this covenant" refer to that made under Josiah, or simply to the ancient Mosaic covenant? Now, to be sure, one ought not to draw too sharp a distinction here, since Josiah's covenant was viewed as a ratification and reactivation of the Mosaic covenant as described in Deuteronomy. But in all probability it is Josiah's covenant that is referred to here. The expression "this covenant" suggests a recent and specific covenant, rather than the ancient and well-known covenant made at Sinai. Moreover, the expression itself is peculiarly Deuteronomic (Deut v 3; xxix 9, 14 [vss. 8, 13H]) and is used of the Josianic covenant in II Kings xxiii 3. But, then, does vs. 6 force us, as some think, to picture Jeremiah as an itinerant evangelist who went up and down the country preparing the way for Josiah's reform? It does not seem likely. For one thing, the expression "in the cities of Judah and in the streets of Jerusalem" is a stereotype in Jeremiah, and does not imply visits to all parts of the country. Moreover, the very term, "this covenant," suggests that Deuteronomy is known and that "this covenant" (Josiah's on the basis of Deuteronomy) has been made. The passage, therefore, does not cast light on Jeremiah's activity prior to the reform, but represents him *after* that reform as urging the people to fulfill the terms of the covenant, and lashing out at them for their failure to do so. The passage seems in the main to relate to Jehoiakim's reign, when the reform was lapsing. In its present form, however, it is of Exilic date, as vss. 7–8 indicate; but these verses seem to be an expansion (LXX omits all save the last two words).

The text of xi 18–xii 6 also presents problems. As it now stands, this passage begins very abruptly (the pronouns in xi 18 have no antecedent), and ends (xii 6) with Jeremiah being apprised of the plot against him—which is just what he knew at the beginning! Manifestly xii 6 precedes xi 18 in time. The simplest solution (so Peake, following Cornill) is to assume that the material has been placed in reverse order and that xii 1–6 should be read before xi 18–23. This order is followed in the translation, and it yields an excellent sense. Jeremiah begins (xii 1 f.) by questioning Yahweh concerning the prosperity of the wicked. He is told, in effect (xii 5), that if this upsets him, he will soon have much more to upset him, for (xii 6) his own family is plotting to kill him. This leads smoothly into xi 18–23, where Jeremiah, now aware of what is happening, cries out to Yahweh to take his part. To be sure, dislocation of the text seems to be somewhat more complicated than this (see NOTES); but extensive rearrangement of the material seems unnecessary.

12. THE LINEN WAISTCLOTH,
AND ATTACHED SAYINGS
(xiii 1–27)

The Linen Waistcloth: an Acted Parable

XIII 1 Yahweh spoke to me thus: "Go, buy yourself a linen waistcloth and put it about your middle. Do not soak it in water." 2 So I bought a waistcloth as Yahweh directed me, and I put it on. 3 Then the word of Yahweh came to me a second time, 4 "Take the waistcloth which you have bought, and which you have on, and go at once to 'the Euphrates,' and there hide it in a cleft in the rock." 5 So I went and hid it at "the Euphrates," as Yahweh had directed me. 6 Then, after a considerable lapse of time, Yahweh said to me, "Now go back to 'the Euphrates' and get the waistcloth which I told you to hide there." 7 So I went to "the Euphrates," and dug, and got the waistcloth from the place where I had hidden it. And, naturally, the waistcloth was ruined, unfit for use.

8 Then the word of Yahweh came to me, as follows, 9 "This is what Yahweh has said: Just so will I ruin the pride of Judah, and the great pride of Jerusalem— 10 this wicked people who refuse to listen to what I say, and who, following their own stubborn inclinations, have gone after other gods in order to worship them and do obeisance to them—till it resembles this utterly worthless waistcloth. 11 For just as a waistcloth clings to a man's middle, so I made the entire house of Israel and the entire house of Judah cling to me—Yahweh's word—that they might be my people, and a source of renown and praise and glory to me. But they would not listen."

The Parable of the Wine Jars

12 *a*"You will repeat to them this saying,*a* 'Every jug should
be filled with wine.' *b*They will reply,*b* 'Ah, don't we know it!
Indeed every jug should be filled with wine!' 13 Then you will
say to them, 'This is what Yahweh has said: Believe me, I am
going to fill all the inhabitants of this land—the kings who sit
on David's throne, the priests, the prophets, and all the citizens
of Jerusalem—with drunkenness; 14 and I will smash them one
against another, old and young alike. No pity, no mercy, no
compassion will deter me from destroying them.'"

A Last Warning

15   Hear and give heed! Be not proud!
          For Yahweh has spoken.
16   Give glory to Yahweh your God
          Before he brings darkness,
      Before you stumble and slip
          On the darkening heights,
      And the light you had hoped for he turns into gloom,
          Changes to blackness.
17   But if listen you will not,
          In secret my soul will weep
              Because of your pride;
      And, bitterly sobbing,
          My eyes with tears will stream;
              For captive is Yahweh's flock.

To the Royal Family

18   Say*c* to the king and queen-mother,
          "Come down from your throne;

a–a LXX, "You will say to this people," seems to be a variant, and may be
preferable. After these words Hebrew adds, "This is what Yahweh, the God
of Israel, has said"; omit with LXX, since the oracle begins only in the next
verse.
b–b Perhaps better with LXX, "and if they reply" ('*im* lost by haplography).
c The verb should be plural with LXX; Hebrew has singular.

For *from your head*^d has fallen
　Your beautiful crown."
19 In the Negeb the towns are blockaded;
　None can break through.
All Judah has been deported,
　Wholly deported.

A Punishment Richly Deserved

20 "Lift up your eyes, Jerusalem!^e
　See how they come from the North!
Where is the flock that was given you,
　Your beautiful flock?
21 What will you say when ^f[　　]
　　[　　]
Whom you yourself had taught
　　[　　]^f
Will pangs not seize upon you
　Like a woman's in labor?
22 And if you should say to yourself,
　'Why does all this befall me?'
It's for your great guilt
　That your limbs are exposed,
　　Your body ravished.

23 "Can the Negro change his skin,
　Or the leopard his spots?
Then you might also do good,
　Who are trained to do ill.
24 Like flying chaff I'll drive them
　On the desert wind.

25 "This is your lot, your measured share,
　From me—it's Yahweh's word—

d-d Heb. *mar'ᵃšōtēkem* is unusual, and most scholars alter to read *mērā'-šēkem* (cf. LXX and other Vrs.); but M. J. Dahood (CBQ 23 [1961], 462) points as *mērā'šōtēkem* and sees a form of the plural of "head" (*rašt*) attested in Ugaritic. Emendation may, therefore, be unnecessary.
e Supplied with LXX. See NOTE.
f-f See NOTE.

Because you forgot me
And trusted the Lie.
26 It was I myself who snatched
Your skirt up over your face,
Exposing your shame.
27 Your whoring! Your rutting!
Your wanton affairs!
On the hills, in the fields
I have seen your indecencies.
Ah, woe to you, Jerusalem!
Will you never be clean?"

NOTES

xiii 1. *waistcloth*. The usual undergarment (*'ēzōr*); not a breechclout, but a short skirt worn wrapped about the hips, and reaching about half-way down the thighs. The translation "girdle" (so older EVV) is inaccurate; this was a sort of waistband worn outside the skirt.

7. *dug*. Though one could translate "searched," there is no reason to object to "dug"; in hiding the waistcloth, Jeremiah doubtless covered it with dirt—or silt had covered it in the meantime.

10. *till it resembles*. "That it may be like" (or possibly, "and let it be like"). The subject of the verb is the "pride" of Judah (vs. 9); the intervening words are a parenthesis.

11. *a source of renown*. Literally "a name."

12. *Every jug should be filled with wine*. Or ". . . is/will be filled . . . ," or "let . . . be filled. . . ." This may have been a popular proverb (everything to its intended use, or the like). But the scene here seems to be (as in Isa xxviii 7 ff.) a drunken feast. The revelers use the proverb as a witticism; they are the jugs, and they mean to be filled with wine. Jeremiah's point is: Yahweh will fill them—with drunkenness (i.e., will rob them of ability to act), and will smash them like the jugs they joke about.

16. *Before he brings darkness*. Or, "before it grows dark"; but cf. the last lines of the verse.

18. *Come down from your throne*. "Be seated, low down," i.e., take a lowly seat; cf. Isa xlvii 1.

20. *Jerusalem*. See textual note[e]. Whether original or not, this is the correct subject. The imperatives "lift up" and "see" are feminine singular

(Ktib, LXX). The suffix "your" (with "eyes") is also to be read singular with LXX.

21. The first part of the verse cannot be translated with any assurance. Literally: "What will you say when he (LXX "they") set over you (or, "punish you"; or, "summon against you"), and you yourself had taught them, over you (or, "against you") friends for a chief (head)." See the commentaries for further discussion.

22. *your limbs*. Literally "your skirts"; apparently a euphemism, and so understood by LXX. "Your body" is literally "your heels" which is also a euphemism.

24. *drive them*. One is tempted to read "drive you," as do various scholars (and RSV). But the verse may be original in some other context.

25. *the Lie*. Probably here, as elsewhere, a term for pagan gods, specifically Baal.

27. *Your whoring*. Properly, "your adulteries"; but it is doubtful that the technical distinction is to be insisted upon here. "Your rutting" is literally "your neighings," i.e., animal passion, as in v 8. The verse refers to practice of the cults of the pagan gods, and the immoral rites associated with them.

Will you never be clean. Literally "You will not be clean. After how long yet?"

COMMENT

Chapter xiii contains a number of originally unrelated sayings, the first two of which are in prose, the rest in poetry. The chapter opens with the perplexing account of the acted parable of the linen waist-cloth (vss. 1–11), which consists of a narrative in autobiographical style followed by an oracle from Yahweh explaining the significance of the action. Attached to this (vss. 12–14), probably because it too involves a parable, is a brief saying which takes its start from a popular witticism having to do with wine jars (see NOTE on vs. 12).

The remainder of the chapter is in poetry, and consists of several short pieces (vss. 15–17, 18–19, 20–27—the last itself composite) similar in theme to the poems in the preceding chapters. Most of them were apparently composed not long before the first deportation, in 597; one of them, indeed (vss. 18–19), addressed to Jehoiachin and the Queen Mother (cf. II Kings xxiv 8, 12), clearly was uttered just prior to Jerusalem's surrender in that year.

The interpretation of the incident of the waistcloth has been much debated. Did Jeremiah actually perform these actions, or did they take place in a vision or in the prophet's imagination? In all likelihood, the former. The action, like the smashing of the clay pot in chapter xix, or the wearing of the ox-yoke in chapters xxvii–xxviii (but unlike the visions in ch. i, where no action was involved), was symbolic and intended to convey a message. To do so, it would have to be witnessed—or, at least, known to have been performed —as an imaginary or visionary action could not be. We may suppose, then, that Jeremiah actually hid the waistcloth. But did he really make two journeys to the Euphrates River, each of them a round trip of some 700 miles? It puts a strain on credulity to suppose so (and besides, who in Judah then would have witnessed the symbolism?). When all is said, there is much in favor of the suggestion, adopted by various scholars, that Jeremiah actually went to Parah, a short distance northeast of Anathoth (cf. Josh xviii 23), where there is an abundant supply of water (today 'Ain Farah). Since Parah and Euphrates ($p^e r\bar{a}t$) were very similar in sound, the former could have stood symbolically for the latter. Indeed "to Parah" (so in xiii 1–7, save in vs. 5) and "to the Euphrates" would be spelled identically (*prth*), thus causing later readers to suppose that Jeremiah went twice to the Euphrates (Aq. actually reads *eis pharan*).

But what is the meaning of the parable? Jeremiah clearly acts the part of Yahweh while, equally clearly, the waistcloth represents Israel. But what is the significance of the soaking in Euphrates water that ruins the waistcloth? Some argue that this refers to political entanglements with Mesopotamian powers, which have corrupted the character of the nation. This, however, does violence to the sense of vs. 9, where it is clearly indicated that the soaking is symbolic of the Exile through which Yahweh will punish the great pride of his disobedient people (cf. Weiser). But the sense of the passage is not that Judah will be taken into exile "a good piece of cloth," and brought back ruined. Nothing is said of bringing the waistcloth back (i.e., of the return); all that is said is that the nation's pride will be destroyed in the Exile. But would this not, as some think, contradict Jeremiah's predictions of an ultimate return (e.g., xxix 10–14)? Not any more than scores of passages in which he predicted the destruction of the nation with no word of hope for the future. One cannot, after all, expect that any prophet should express his entire theology in each of his utterances.

13. IN TIME OF DROUGHT
AND NATIONAL EMERGENCY
(xiv 1–22; xv 1–4)

The Great Drought: Supplication and Divine Response

XIV 1 The word of Yahweh that came to Jeremiah regarding the drought:

2   Judah mourns,
     Her cities pine,
    Lie prostrate in grief,
     While Jerusalem's cry goes up.

3   The*a* nobles, they sent
     Their menials for water;
    To the cisterns they came,
     No water they found;
    They return with their vessels unfilled;
     Dismayed and bewildered.
      They cover their heads.

4   *b*[Tilling the soil has stopped (?)]*b*
     For there's been no rain in the land,
    Dismayed are the farmers,
     They cover their heads.

5   Why, even the doe in the field
     Calves and abandons her young,
      Since grass there is none;

6   While the wild asses stand on the hills,
     Panting for air like jackals,
    Their eyes all glazed
     For want of fodder.

7   "Even though our misdeeds do accuse us,
     Act, O Yahweh, for the sake of thy name!

a Heb. "their . . . ," LXX "its . . ."; the difference is immaterial.
b-b This follows LXX. See NOTE.

Ah, many have been our defections,
　　Against thee have we sinned.

8　　°O Yahweh,° who art Israel's hope,
　　And its savior in time of distress,
Why art thou like one in the land as an alien,
　　Like a traveler who stops but a night?

9　　Why art thou like a man who is caught by surprise,
　　Like a soldier who fails in the pinch?
Nay thou, O Yahweh, art amongst us,
　　We are called by thy name, are thine;
　　　Ah, leave us not!"

10　　This is what Yahweh has said to this people:
"Just so they have loved to wander,
　　Never checking their steps.
So Yahweh does not accept them,
　　But now will remember their guilt,
　　　And punish their sins."

Sword and Famine: Jeremiah's Vain Attempt to Excuse His People

11 And Yahweh said to me, "Do not pray for the welfare of this people. 12 When they fast, I will not listen to their entreaties, and when they offer burnt offerings and cereal offerings, I will not accept them; on the contrary, I will make an end of them—by the sword, by famine and disease."

13 Then I said, "Ah, look, my Lord Yahweh! The prophets have been saying to them, 'You shall not see the sword, nor experience famine, for I will give you enduring peace in this place.'" 14 But Yahweh replied, "What the prophets have been preaching in my name is a lie! I did not send them, or commission them, or speak to them. The prophecies that they have been giving you are fraudulent visions, worthless divinations, and their own wishful thinking." 15 Therefore, this is what Yahweh has said: "As regards the prophets who prophesy in my

°–° Added with LXX and various manuscripts; cf. also xvii 13.

name and, although I did not send them, keep saying, 'Sword and famine will never come to this land'—those prophets will themselves meet their end by sword and famine. 16 And the people to whom they have been prophesying will be hurled out into the streets of Jerusalem, victims of famine and sword, with no one to bury them—them, or their wives, or their sons and daughters. I will pour out their doom upon them.

17 "And you shall speak to them this word:
'Let my eyes with tears overflow,
By night and by day, never ceasing;
For My Daughter-My People*d* is shattered and broken,
Wounded most sore.
18 Go I forth to the fields,
Then see—those slain by the sword!
Do I enter the town,
Then see—the pangs of starvation!
Ah, prophet and priest alike
e[Have roamed to a land that they know not (?)].'"*e*

Supplication Resumed

19 "Hast thou utterly cast aside Judah?
Inwardly loathest thou Zion?
Why, then, hast thou stricken us
Past all cure?
We hoped for peace—
No good came;
For a season of healing—
Instead, sheer terror!
20 We acknowledge, Yahweh, our misdeeds,
And our fathers' guilt.
Ah, we've sinned against thee!
21 Spurn us not, for thine own name's sake!
Demean not thy glorious throne!

d Hebrew adds "Virgin" before this appellation. Omit with LXX; the colon seems overloaded.
e–e So following LXX. See NOTE.

Remember, and break not,
    Thy covenant with us!
22 Of the nations' vain idols can any bring rain?
    Can the heavens themselves give showers?
    Art thou not the One, O Yahweh?
      Our God, and on thee do we wait.
      For it's thou who hast made all these things."

Yahweh's Final Answer

XV 1 Then Yahweh said to me, "Even were Moses and Samuel to stand before me, I would still have no sympathy for this people. Send them from my presence, and let them go! 2 And if they should ask you, 'Where shall we go?' say to them, 'This is what Yahweh has said:

Those marked for the plague—to the plague,
    Those marked for the sword—to the sword,
    Those marked for starvation—to starvation,
    Those marked for captivity—to captivity.

3 I'll commission against them four kinds of things—Yahweh's word: the sword to slay, the dogs to drag off, and the carrion birds and the wild beasts to devour and destroy. 4 And I'll make them a sight that will horrify all the kingdoms of the earth—because of Manasseh ben Hezekiah, king of Judah, and what he did in Jerusalem.' "

NOTES

xiv 1. The verse is an editorial heading to the entire section; what follows is not an oracle from Yahweh. The unusual formula (literally "What was the word of Yahweh to Jeremiah") recurs in xlvi 1; xlvii 1; xlix 34.

2. *Her cities.* Literally "her gates" (*pars pro toto*), as frequently in Deuteronomy (and cf. xv 7).

3. *They cover their heads.* A gesture of dismay and grief (cf. II Sam xv 30). But the final bicolon of the verse may be a doublet of vs. 4b; LXX omits it.

4. *Tilling the soil has stopped.* This follows LXX (*ᵃbōdat hā'ᵃdāmāh*

ḥādᵉlāh [or *tammāh*] or the like), though one has little confidence in the reading. Heb. "Because of the ground (which) is dismayed" (*ba'ᵃbūr hā'ᵃdāmāh ḥattāh*) cannot be right. By reading *ba'ᵃbūrāh* (*h* lost by haplography) one could translate, "Because of it [i.e., the drought] the soil is dismayed," which would fit fairly well, save that the verb is elsewhere used of persons. The corruption is probably deep-seated. Perhaps (cf. Volz, Nötscher) transfer "farmers" to this colon, and read, "On account of the soil the farmers are dismayed"; and then read vs. 4b as the last cola of vs. 3 (which LXX omits).

7. *for the sake of thy name.* I.e., thy reputation, honor (e.g., Josh vii 9; Isa xlviii 9–11); but, since to the Hebrew the "name" often suggests the essential character of the person, the sense may be: "as the (covenant) God that thou art," "as befits thy character."

8. *O Yahweh.* See textual note^{e–e}. The verse addresses Yahweh as Israel's God and asks why, in this time of need, he seems to show no more interest in the land than would a resident alien or a chance traveler.

9. *Like a soldier who fails in the pinch.* Literally "Like a mighty man who cannot save," i.e., a warrior who, for all his prowess, cannot help when most needed.

We are called by thy name, are thine. A double translation to bring out the sense; literally "we are called by thy name," which means (cf. vii 10, etc.) "we belong to thee."

10. Verse 10b either quotes Hos viii 13 (cf. Hos ix 9) or, more probably, is a liturgical formula.

12. *cereal offerings.* I.e., offerings of grain, flour, or cakes (see the regulations in Lev ii). But possibly the *minḥāh* here refers to sacrificial gifts in general, rather than specifically to the cereal offering.

15. *As regards the prophets.* We begin the direct discourse here for smoothness' sake; but the syntax is somewhat awkward to our taste (cf. xii 14).

16. *their doom.* Or "their wickedness"; *rā'āh* can mean either moral evil or disaster.

17. The first line is an editorial transition in the style of the prose passage preceding, linking it to the poem that follows—which is not an oracle.

18. *Have roamed to a land that they know not.* So following LXX (reading *lō'* for *wᵉlō*). But the meaning is so uncertain that any translation is conjectural. The verb (*saḥᵃrū*) means "to roam, travel about (in pursuit of livelihood)," then "to do business, trade"; cf. Gen xxxiv 21; xlii 34 (the participle means "merchant"; Gen xxiii 16; xxxvii 28). One is tempted to read (BH following Condamin) *nisḥᵃbū* (cf. xv 3): "have been dragged to a land that they know not"; but the conjecture

is without support. Some, following MT but reading *'et* for *'el,* translate,
"roam the land and know nothing." Assurance is impossible. On the
verb *shr* see now E. A. Speiser, BASOR 164 (1962), 23–28, and the
remarks of W. F. Albright, *ibid.,* 28.

19. Verse 19b repeats viii 15.

20. *our fathers' guilt.* Not merely the fact that their fathers had sinned,
but the corporate guilt of the nation accumulated through the generations.

21. *thy glorious throne.* Yahweh was conceived as enthroned in the
temple, and this was felt to guarantee the nation's safety (cf. vii 2–15).
If he allows his people to suffer, would that not cast reflections on his
power?

22. In the last two cola one could translate "in thee do we hope,"
and "it is thou who hast done [or "doest"] all these things."

xv 1. *Moses and Samuel.* Two of the towering figures of Israel's
history, both were remembered as men who had interceded with God
for the people (e.g., Exod xxxii 11–14, 30–32; Num xiv 13–19; I Sam
vii 8 f.; xii 19–23).

4. The last part of the verse is similar in sentiment to various passages
in Kings (II Kings xxi 10–15; xxiii 26; xxiv 3) and may represent an
adaptation of Jeremiah's thought among his followers.

COMMENT

In chapters xiv through xvii, which seem to form an editorial section, the material is for the most part as heterogeneous as any in
the book. Opening this section, however, there is a rather long composition (xiv 1–xv 4), partly in poetry, partly in prose, which has
the appearance of being a coherent and skillfully executed literary
unit. Its theme, announced in the heading (xiv 1), is the great
drought.

The passage begins (xiv 2–6) with a graphic description of the
drought and the suffering that it has caused. One can see that it is a
national emergency. Then (vss. 7–9) there follows what one might
call a liturgy of penitence and petition, as the people cry out to Yahweh for mercy, confessing their sins and their utter dependence
upon him. Whether Jeremiah actually heard such a liturgy recited
in the temple on some national fast day, or whether he himself composed it and placed it in the mouth of the people, cannot be said
(Hos vi 1–3 is a similar piece); but its sentiments are exalted, and
it breathes a heartfelt emotion and apparent sincerity. Neverthe-

less, an oracle from Yahweh (vs. 10) announces that, because of the people's chronic unfaithfulness, their prayers will not be answered. Then follows (vss. 11–16) a prose section in autobiographical style in which Jeremiah tells how he had himself been forbidden to pray for this people and how, when he had tried to excuse them by pointing out that their prophets had misled them, Yahweh had refused to accept his excuses, announcing instead the awful fate that would overtake prophets and people alike. This leads, through an editorial transition, into a brief poem of lament (vss. 17–18). In vss. 19–22 the liturgy is resumed, but with heightened intensity and urgency, as the people renew their confession of sin and cast themselves upon Yahweh's mercy, begging him to remember his covenant with them. To this Yahweh then gives his second and final answer (xv 1–4): their supplications are rejected; not even those famed intercessors, Moses and Samuel, could save this people: let them go to their doom!

It is best to read the passage as the literary unit that it is. Jeremiah, indeed, may well have been the one who so composed it, since all of its parts—save a few editorial touches (see NOTES) —may be held to go back to him. Nevertheless, the unit is a secondary one; that is to say, it is made up of shorter pieces originally uttered on different occasions. One is not, to be sure, driven to this conclusion merely by the fact that the passage combines prose and poetry, for Jeremiah could very well have composed a piece employing both (cf. ch. i). But the poetry itself does not all refer to the same date. In the bulk of it the situation is that of drought, without any hint of enemy invasion (cf. xiv 2–6). In vss. 17–18, on the other hand, the situation (and it is not to be taken as predictive!) is precisely that of the ravages of war. The theme "drought" in fact applies only to xiv 2–9, 10, 19–22, while in the rest the theme is "sword, famine, and disease" (xiv 12, 13, 15 f., 18; xv 2 f.). The probability is that a piece originally composed in time of drought has here been expanded and adapted (and perhaps by Jeremiah himself) to a later situation.

The original poem (i.e., the one relating to the drought) seems to have included xiv 2–10, 19–22. But this poem requires some conclusion and, since xv 1–4 does not seem to provide it, one must assume that it has been lost or displaced. One is tempted to ask if the isolated oracle in xvii 1–4, relics of which may also be seen in xv 13–14 (see NOTES there), may not originally have served this purpose. At least this oracle, which seems to relate to some occasion of ritual atonement (Volz, Rudolph), would form an excellent answer to the liturgy of xiv 19–22. But, since this is in the realm of speculation, it is best not to insist upon it.

14. ORACLES AND CONFESSIONS
IN POETRY AND PROSE
(xv 5–21; xvi 1–21)

Jerusalem's Terrible Fate

XV

5 "Who will have pity upon you, Jerusalem?
  Who will condole with you?
Who will go out of his way
  To ask how you are?
6 It was *you* who deserted *me*—Yahweh's word—
  And kept getting worse.
So I lashed out against you and smashed you,
  Tired of relenting.
7 With the pitchfork I tossed them
  In the outlying towns,
Did bereave, did destroy my people,
  Since they did not change their ways.
8 Their widows I made to outnumber
  The sand by the sea;
ᵃOn the mother of young men I broughtᵃ
  A destroyer at noonday,
Let fall upon her suddenly
  Anguish and terror.
9 She who bore seven collapses,
  She gasps for breath;
Her sun has gone down in broad day;
  Dismayed is she and distraught.
Yet—their remnant I'll give to the sword
  In the face of their foes—Yahweh's word."

ᵃ⁻ᵃ Heb. "I brought to them, upon the mother of the youth" is hardly right. Many emendations are offered, the simplest being to omit "to them" with LXX, which at least yields a tolerable sense.

Jeremiah's Inner Struggle

10   Ah me, my mother, that you bore me
        To accuse and indict the whole land!
     Neither lent I, nor loan received,
        *b*Yet all of them curse me.*b*

11   But I swear, O Yahweh, for their good I have served
                         thee,
        And with thee for the foe interceded
     In the time of his trouble and woe.
        Ah, but thou knowest!*c*

12–14 *d*[   ]*d*

15   Remember me, Yahweh! Take note of me!
        Avenge me of those that harass me!
     Do not through thy patience destroy me!
        Consider! For thy sake I suffer abuse.

16   There were thy words, and I ate them;
        *e*And it was my joy,*e* my heart's delight,
     That I bore thy name, was thine.
        O Yahweh, thou God of Hosts.

17   Not for me to sit with the crowd,
        Laughing and merry.
     Gripped by thy hand I did sit all alone,
        For with rage thou didst fill me.

18   Why, O why, is my pain without end,
        My wound ever worse, defying all cure?
     Ah, truly you are a dry wadi to me,
        Whose waters have failed.

---

b–b Add *kī* (lost by haplography) and redivide consonants to read *kullᵉhem qilᵉlūnī* (cf. BH).

c The text of the verse is disturbed. See NOTE.

d–d On the omission of these verses, see NOTE.

e–e Heb. "And thy word [so Qre, manuscripts, Vrs.; Ktib plural] was. . . ." Omit "thy word(s)" as a dittography or mistaken gloss from the preceding colon (Duhm, Giesebrecht). LXX (cf. NOTE on vs. 16), dividing the clauses differently, reads, "Consume them, and let thy word be my joy," but this is scarcely preferable.

19   At that, Yahweh answered me as follows:
"If you repent, I'll restore you
    To serve me once more.
If you mix not the cheap and the precious,
    As my mouth you shall be.
Let *them* come over to you;
    Don't *you* go over to them.
20   Then before this people I'll make you
    An impregnable wall of bronze.
Attack you they will—
    Overcome you they can't;
For with you am I
    To help you and save you—Yahweh's word.
21   From the grasp of the wicked I'll snatch you,
    From the clutch of the ruthless release you."

Jeremiah Is Forbidden a Normal Life— with Attached Sayings

XVI 1 The word of Yahweh came to me as follows: 2 "You are not to marry and have sons and daughters in this place. 3 For this is what Yahweh has said concerning the children who are born here in this land, and concerning the mothers who bear them and the fathers who beget them: 4 They will die horrible deaths! Unlamented and unburied, they will be like so much manure to fertilize the soil. Meeting their end by sword and starvation, their corpses will be left to feed the carrion birds and the wild beasts."

5 Yahweh said further: "Do not enter any house where there is mourning. Take no part in their lament, and do not condole with them; for I have withdrawn my peace from this people— Yahweh's word—my gracious favor and compassion. 6 Both great and small will die in this land. Unburied and unlamented, no one will gash himself or shave his head for them; 7 no one will ᶠbreak bread with the bereavedᶠ to comfort him for the dead,

1–1 Heb. "break for them on account of mourning." Read *leḥem* (so LXX) for *lāhem*, and point *'ābēl* instead of *'ēbel*.

nor will any one *pour for him*[g] the cup of consolation, not even
for his father or his mother. 8 And as for a house where there is
feasting, you are not to go there either, and sit with them eating
and drinking. 9 For this is what Yahweh of Hosts, the God of
Israel, has said: See! I am going to banish from this place—
before your eyes, and in your days—sounds of mirth and gladness, the voice of bridegroom and bride.

10 "And when you tell this people all this, and they say to you,
'Why has Yahweh threatened us with such terrible misfortune?
What is our crime? What sin is it that we have committed
against Yahweh our God?'— 11 then answer them, 'It is because
your fathers forsook me—Yahweh's word. They followed other
gods, worshiping them and doing obeisance to them, and forsook
me and did not keep my law. 12 And you, for your part, have
done even worse than they did. Yes, look at you—each following
his own stubbornly wicked inclinations and refusing to listen to
me! 13 So I will hurl you óff this land into a land which neither
you nor your fathers have known, and there you can serve other
gods all the time, since I certainly will show you no favor.'"

14-15 [   ]

16 "Watch! I am going to send for many fishermen—Yahweh's
word—who will fish them out. And, after that, I will send for
many hunters, who will hunt them out of every mountain and
hill, and from the clefts in the rocks. 17 For I have my eye on
all their doings; they are not concealed from me, nor is their
iniquity hid from my sight. 18 'I will repay' their sinful iniquity
double, because they have polluted my land with the carcasses
of their detestable idols, and filled my property with their abominations."

19   Yahweh, my strength, my stronghold,
          My refuge in time of distress,
        To thee shall nations come
          From the ends of the earth, and say,

g-g So LXX; MT ". . . for them" does not suit the context.
h-h On omission of these verses, see NOTE.
i-i Heb. "I will first repay." Omit "first" with LXX; it is probably a gloss to
make it clear that this will precede the restoration described in vss. 14–15.

"Naught but lies have our fathers possessed,
  Mere nothings, of no use at all.
20 Can a mortal make gods for himself?
    Nay, such are not gods!"
21 "So look! I am going to teach them,
    Right now am going to teach them,
  My power and might;
    And they'll know that my name is Yahweh."

NOTES

xv 6. *kept getting worse.* Literally "kept going backward," i.e., back-sliding (cf. vii 24).

7. *With the pitchfork I tossed them.* The figure is that of winnowing grain by tossing it into the wind, which blows the chaff away.

the outlying towns. Literally "the gates of the land," *pars pro toto* as in xiv 2.

9. *She gasps for breath.* Taking *napšāh* as the subject and under-standing it as "her throat," as in Ugaritic and occasionally in the Bible (cf. iv 10): "her throat gasps." One could translate, "She gasps out her *nepeš*," and take it as "she faints." But she does not "give up the ghost" (KJ, ARV)'; see the next lines.

10. *To accuse and indict the whole land.* Literally "a man of legal strife (*rīb*) and legal contention (*mādōn:* the root denotes a process at law) to the whole land." Jeremiah is like one who is perpetually at law with his people.

11. The reading, which is somewhat conjectural, is based on sugges-tions of various scholars (cf. BH, Rudolph). 11a: Read *'āmēn* with LXX for *'āmar;* literally "So be it, Yahweh, if I did not . . ." Jeremiah responds to curses by what amounts to an oath: let the curses come true if he has not acted with integrity (which he swears that he has). Also point *šērattīkā* instead of *šērītīkā* (?), which is unintelligible. "For their good" (literally "for good") could have the sense of "well," "with good intent." 11b: transpose "the foe" from the end of the verse and (cf. LXX) read *'el* or *lᵉ* before it in place of *'et.* "The foe" (collective) apparently refers to Jeremiah's own enemies. 11c: Supply "his" (collec-tive) following LXX. 11d: the colon begins vs. 15 in Hebrew, where LXX omits it. Since (see next NOTE) vss. 12–14 are an intrusion, vs. 15 follows vs. 11 directly.

12–14. The verses seem to be a damaged variant of xvii 1–4 (q.v.). Vss. 13–14 are certainly a variant of xvii 3–4. Vs. 12 is cryptic ("Can one break iron, iron from the north, and bronze?") and textually uncertain; perhaps Rudolph is correct in regarding it as a corruption of xvii 1.

15. *Avenge me of.* Perhaps more literally, "Avenge thyself for me on (of). . . ." But perhaps (cf. xi 20 and NOTE there) the verb *nqm* has rather the sense of, "Deliver me from. . . ."

Do not through thy patience destroy me. Literally ". . . take me away," i.e., through being so lenient with my persecutors that they have time to destroy me.

16. *There were thy words.* Literally "Thy words were found" (cf. the same verb in ii 34; v 26); cf. Ezekiel's vision (Ezek ii 8–iii 3) in which he ate a scroll containing Yahweh's words. LXX reads, "by the despisers of [transposition of letters] thy words," and attaches to vs. 15.

I bore thy name, was thine. Cf. xiv 9 and NOTE there (also vii 10 f., etc.).

17. The first line is literally "I did not sit in the company of the merrymakers and [did not] rejoice." The words "and rejoice" seem to form a separate colon which is, however, too short. Perhaps words have been lost. LXX again reads differently.

18. *a dry wadi.* Literally "a deceitful (brook)," a stream that goes dry in summer and cannot be depended upon for water. Remember that Jeremiah had once (ii 13) called Yahweh "the fountain of living water"!

19. *If you repent, I'll restore you.* Still another play on *šūb* (cf. ch. iii, *passim*, etc.): "If you turn [from such talk as the above], I will turn you [i.e., restore you to the prophetic office]." The play continues in the last bicolon: "come over" and "go over" are both forms of *šūb*.

To serve me once more. Literally "before me you'll stand," i.e., as an attendant or slave in the service of his lord; cf. I Kings i 2; x 8; xii 8, etc.

If you mix not the cheap and the precious. "If you bring forth [i.e., separate] the precious from the worthless"; or, "if you bring forth [i.e., utter] what is precious, without the worthless." Talking as he has, Jeremiah cannot be Yahweh's mouthpiece; cf. "as my mouth you will be" and i 9–10.

20. A virtual repetition of the call; cf. i 8, 18–19.

xvi 5. *mourning.* The word (*marzēaḥ*) seems here to denote a mourning feast, as in Aramaic—a wake, one might say.

6. *gash himself . . . shave his head.* These were mourning customs (cf. xli 5; Amos viii 10; Mic i 16; Isa xxii 12); they are forbidden, presumably because of pagan associations, in Lev xxi 5; Deut xiv 1, etc.; but they do not seem here to be disapproved of per se.

7. *cup of consolation.* A custom not elsewhere alluded to in the Bible.

8. *house where there is feasting.* One wonders if *bēt mišteh* may

not be a technical term for a banquet hall or tavern. But since the balancing word in vs. 5, *bēt marzē^aḥ*, is scarcely a funeral parlor, one cannot be certain; cf. Eccles vii 2.

13. *all the time.* Literally "day and night." LXX omits, and reads, ". . . other gods who will show you no mercy."

14–15. These verses are repeated at xxiii 7–8, and will be treated there.

18. *double.* Cf. the thought of double punishment with Isa xl 2. There is no evidence of literary dependence on Second Isaiah here; but both passages show that the feeling was abroad in the Exilic period that punishment had been in excess of deserts. Second Isaiah, in particular, wrestled profoundly with that problem.

carcasses. The idols, being lifeless, are like so many corpses defiling the land; cf. Lev xxvi 30.

COMMENT

Beginning at xv 5, and continuing through chapter xvii, the material is miscellaneous in character, and one is often put to it to say what principles may have governed its collection in the order in which we find it. As for the remainder of chapter xv, the first component is a poem, cast in the form of a word from Yahweh, describing the terrible fate of Jerusalem (vss. 5–9). This poem, which probably reflects the situation of 598/7, was no doubt transmitted in connection with the preceding section because of thematic similarities to xv 1–4; xiv 17–18, etc. Following upon this—perhaps because of the catchword "mother" (vs. 10; cf. vss. 8–9), perhaps because of the theme of intercession (vs. 11) which occurs also in the preceding chapter (xiv 11–16)—is one of Jeremiah's "confessions." Its text is much disturbed, and in vss. 12–14 material from another context has intruded. These verses, which interrupt the connection between vss. 11 and 15, seem to be a damaged variant of xvii 1–4 (see, further, NOTE on vss. 12–14) and will be treated at that place. In vss. 10–11, 15–18 Jeremiah, protesting that he has been faithful in the discharge of his office, cries out in anguish at the hatred and the loneliness that this has brought him, and even complains that Yahweh has failed him in his hour of need. Answering this outburst, and concluding the chapter (vss. 19–21), is a "private oracle" addressed to Jeremiah telling him, in effect, that he must purge himself of such sentiments if he wishes to continue in the prophetic office, and renewing to him the promise of divine aid if he will obey.

We do not know precisely when Jeremiah underwent this experience, though it was probably during Jehoiakim's reign. Nor can we assume that it marked a turning point in his life in the sense that he was constrained by it to put his complaints and recriminations from him once and for all. It is far from certain that Jeremiah ever experienced such a decisive turning point. Indeed, one may wonder if, to the end of his life, he ever escaped his inner struggle and found complete peace of mind in the discharge of his calling. Nevertheless, vss. 19–21 (cf. the words of vs. 20 with i 8, 18–19) clearly have the sound of a second call. They show us that Jeremiah, for all his angry outbursts, knew perfectly well that such talk was unworthy of his calling, and might well cost him his prophetic office if persisted in. They also show us that, although it is probable that he never achieved complete inner peace, or completely reconciled himself to his lot, he came finally to understand that he simply had no future save to continue as the prophet of Yahweh that he had been called to be in his youth.

Chapter xvi contains a complex of prose material with a snatch of poetry at the end. The basis of this complex (vss. 1–13) is a passage in autobiographical style in which Jeremiah tells how he had been forbidden to marry, or even to participate in the normal joys and sorrows of his people, as a sign of the terrible fate that was about to overtake them. The passage was doubtless placed where it is because, like xv 10–18, it stresses the loneliness of Jeremiah's life, and also because of the theme "sword and famine" (vs. 4) which is so prominent in xiv 11–18; xv 1–4. In spite of its pedestrian style (underlying which, nevertheless, one in places suspects a poetic original) its material is unquestionably authentic. The very fact that Jeremiah did not marry requires us to suppose that he felt some such compulsion, for bachelorhood was almost unheard of in ancient Israelite society. He must, moreover, have had this feeling since the very beginning of his career, else he would have married while still a youth, as young men of his day normally did.

Attached to the above passage are three brief sayings: an oracle predicting Israel's restoration to her land (vss. 14–15), a further oracle of doom (vss. 16–18), and a poetic fragment looking to the conversion of the heathen (vss. 19–21). The first of these

is out of place where it is, and was apparently drawn in to soften
the harshness of the message of judgment. It is repeated in xxiii
7–8, where it is in context, and will be treated there. The poetic
piece is frequently denied to Jeremiah on the grounds that it shows
dependence upon the thought of later prophets, such as Second
Isaiah and Ezekiel. But, though this may be correct, one should
be cautious (cf. Weiser). The passage swarms with Jeremianic expressions, and the idea of the turning of the nations to Yahweh
rests on very old tradition (cf. various pre-Exilic Psalms), was
certainly current in "Deuteronomic" circles of Jeremiah's day (e.g.,
I Kings viii 41–43), and is not without echoes in the words of
Jeremiah himself (e.g., iv 1–2).

15. MISCELLANY
(xvii 1–27)

Guilt That Cannot Be Erased

XVII

1 "Etched is Judah's sin
    With iron pen,
  With diamond point engraved
    On the plaque of their heart,
      And the horns of *their altars.*^a

2 *b*While their children remember their altars and their Asherim, by leafy trees, on lofty hills 3 the mountains in the open country.*b*

  *c*Your wealth and all your stores
    For spoil I will give,
  As the price of all your sins
    Throughout your domain.
4   You'll be forced to let go the holding,
    The one that I gave you;
  And I'll make you to serve your foes
    In a land that you know not.
  For a fire is lit in my nostrils
    Which forever shall flame."*c*

Trust in Man, and Trust in God

5   [This is what Yahweh has said]:
  Cursed be the man who in man puts his trust,

---

a–a So with many manuscripts, Vrs.; MT has "your altars." The word *mizbeḥōtām*, which occurs in the next line and is the correct form, may actually belong here as a variant reading.
b–b See NOTE.
c–c The text is disturbed, but can be restored, though in places conjecturally, with the aid of xv 13–14, which these verses repeat with variations. See NOTE.

And makes mortal flesh his support,
    While his heart turns aside from Yahweh.
6 Like the desert scrub is he,
    Without hope of anything good;
For he dwells in a waste most arid,
    A salt, uninhabited land.

7 Blessed is the man who trusts in Yahweh,
    Whose mainstay is Yahweh.
8 For he is like a tree that is planted near water,
    That sends out its roots toward the stream,
That fears[a] not the coming of heat,
    For verdant its leaves remain;
In seasons of drought untroubled,
    It fails not to yield its fruit.

God Knows the Heart of Man, and Rewards Justly

9 The heart is of all things most crafty,
    And desperately sick.
      Who understands it?
10 "I, Yahweh, explore the heart,
    Assay the emotions,
To reward each man for his conduct,
    As his actions deserve."

Riches Unjustly Gained: a Proverb

11 Like a partridge hatching eggs that it laid not,
    So is he who gets riches unjustly.
Midway in his life they will leave him;
    In the end he'll be seen for a fool.

Yahweh Enthroned in the Temple, the Hope of Israel

12 A majestic throne
    Set on high from the first
      Is the place of our shrine.

[a] So (yīrā') with Ktib, LXX; Qre has "sees" (yir'eh).

13   Yahweh, thou hope of Israel,
        They'll be shamed, all who leave thee;
     They'll be writ in the earth who forsake thee,
        For they've left the fountain of living water.

Jeremiah Cries to Yahweh for Help

14   Heal me, Yahweh!—then healed I shall be.
        Save me!—then I shall be saved.
        For thou art my praise.
15   Look at them saying to me,
        "Where is the word of Yahweh?
        Let it but happen!"
16   *But I never pressed thee to send disaster,*
        Nor wished I the day of woe.
     Ah, *thou* dost know what my lips have said;
        Open it lies before thee.
17   Be not the cause of my ruin,
        Thou, my refuge in time of distress!
18   Let them that hound me be shamed—not *me!*
        Let it be their courage that snaps—not *mine!*
     Bring thou upon them the day of disaster!
        Break them, and break them again!

On Keeping the Sabbath

19 Yahweh spoke to me thus: "Go, stand in the People's Gate,
by which Judah's kings go in and out, and in all the other gates
of Jerusalem, 20 and say to them, 'Hear the word of Yahweh,
you kings of Judah, and all you people of Judah and citizens
of Jerusalem who enter these gates! 21 This is what Yahweh has

---

e–e Reading for *wᵉsūray* (so Qre) *wᵉsūrē mēʾaḥᵃrekā* (or *mēʾimmᵉkā*, or the like): "those who turn aside from thee." See NOTE.
f–f Hebrew has, "As for me, I did not press from being a shepherd (*mērōʿeh*) after thee," from which only a forced meaning can be derived. Most scholars read *lᵉrāʾāh* "[asking] for evil" (Aq., Symm. *mērāʾāh;* Syr. *bᵉrāʾāh*). But possibly (Skinner) the consonants (*ʾṣt*)*y m rʿ h* conceal the words *yōm rāʾāh*, "the day of evil" (cf. vs. 18, and *yōm ʾānūš* in the next colon), and we should read *lōʾ ʾaṣtī* (*lᵉ*) *yōm rāʾāh* (and omit "after thee"?).

said: Take care, as you value your lives, not to bear any burden on the Sabbath day, or bring it through the gates of Jerusalem. 22 Do not carry a burden from your houses on the Sabbath day, or do work of any sort, but keep the Sabbath day holy, as I commanded your fathers— 23 who, nevertheless, did not obey or pay any attention but, with deliberate stubbornness, refused either to listen or accept instruction.

24 " 'And now, if you will really listen to what I say—Yahweh's word—and bring no burden through the gates of this city on the Sabbath day, but keep the Sabbath day holy by doing no work on it, 25 then there shall pass through the gates of this city kings who sit on David's throne, and ride in chariots and on horses— they and their princes, together with the people of Judah and the citizens of Jerusalem—and this city will abide forever. 26 And people will come from the towns of Judah, from the environs of Jerusalem and the land of Benjamin, from the Shephelah, the hill country and the Negeb, bringing burnt offerings and sacrifices, cereal offerings and incense [together with those bringing thank offerings] to the house of Yahweh. 27 But if you will not listen to me—that is, by keeping the Sabbath day holy, and not bearing any burden or coming with it through the gates of Jerusalem on the Sabbath day—then I will set fire to those gates, and the fire will consume Jerusalem's palaces, and will never be quenched.' "

Notes

xvii 1. *iron pen*. More accurately, "iron stylus."

their altars. See textual note*ᵃ⁻ᵃ*. The scene seems to be an occasion of atonement when the blood of the sin offering (see the regulations in Lev iv–v) was smeared on the "horns" of the altar (protuberances at its four corners); but the sin is as it were engraved there, and will not come off. One wonders if vss. 1–4 may not have been the original conclusion of the poem and liturgy in time of drought in xiv 1–10, 19–22 (see COMMENT on Sec. 13).

2. Verse 2 and the first words of vs. 3 are textually uncertain and can be rendered metrically only with forcing. Moreover, the transition to vss. 3–4 is rough (note the change in person of address) and words

may have been lost. Perhaps one should omit "their altars" as belonging in the preceding line (or perhaps read "their *maṣṣēbōt*"
[sacred pillars] in place of it). Some Vrs. read "beneath every leafy
tree." The reading, "the mountains in the open country," follows Theod.
(*har*ᵉ*rē* for MT *h*ᵃ*rārī*, "my mountain"). The sense seems to be
that while the people propitiate Yahweh (for rain?), they continue to
propitiate the gods of fertility too. The "Asherim" were objects of wood
representing the goddess Asherah.

3–4. The text is restored with the aid of xv 13–14. 3a: Add "and,"
with numerous manuscripts, Vrs., and xv 13 (which omits "all"). 3c:
Read "As the price" with xv 13 (where Hebrew has the negative, "not
for price"; but LXX omits it); Hebrew here has "your high places,"
which cannot be right. Again, "of all your sins" follows xv 13 (omitting
"and"); Hebrew here has "of sin." 4a: "You will let drop your hand"
(reading *yād*ᵉ*kā* for *ūb*ᵉ*kā*); xv 14 lacks this colon. 4e: "a fire is lit"
follows xv 14; Hebrew here has, "You (plural) have kindled a fire,"
which would fit save that the person of address is singular elsewhere
in vss. 3–4.

5. The words in brackets are an editorial transition (LXX omits); what
follows is not an oracle.

10. *Assay the emotions.* Literally ". . . the kidneys"—conceived of
as the seat of the emotions (the "heart" was the seat of thought and
will); cf. xi 20; xii 2, etc.

11. The proverb seems to be based on a popular belief that the
partridge (the precise species of bird is uncertain) appropriates and
hatches (this is the probable meaning of the verb *dgr*: cf. Isa xxxiv 15)
the eggs of other birds; naturally, the young will soon leave their false
mother. And so it is with a man who gets wealth by taking it from others.

12. *Set on high from the first.* Literally "a height from the first,"
perhaps "a primeval height" (cf. the mountain of the gods). But perhaps
(so LXX) point *mūrām* ("exalted") instead of *mārōm*.

13. *writ in the earth who forsake thee.* See textual note*ᵉ⁻ᵉ*. The sense
is usually taken to be that names of apostates will be inscribed in the
dust (and soon erased and forgotten). But some (recently M. J. Dahood,
Biblica 40 [1959], 164–66, on the basis of Ugaritic evidence) take "earth"
to denote the underworld; i.e., they will be listed for death.

fountain of living water. Cf. ii 13. Hebrew adds at end, "[i.e.] Yahweh"
—a correct gloss.

16. *what my lips have said.* "The output of my lips." Dividing the cola
differently, one could read: "Ah, thou dost know! What my lips have said
has been before thee."

19. *the People's Gate.* The gate is not otherwise known, and the text
may be corrupt. But it is unwise to emend to "the Benjamin Gate"
(so RSV); for this is to choose an easier reading. The Benjamin Gate

was well known (cf. xxxvii 13; xxxviii 7) and would hardly have been misunderstood.

23. *with deliberate stubbornness, refused.* Literally "stiffened their neck not to. . . ."

25. *kings who sit.* Heb. "kings and princes who sit," is factually in-accurate, since only the king occupied the throne; omit "and princes" as a dittography from the next clause.

will abide forever. Or, "will be inhabited . . . ," which comes to the same thing.

26. The clause in brackets is rather awkward and possibly an expansion.

27. *those gates.* Literally "its (i.e., Jerusalem's) gates," just mentioned.

COMMENT

The material of this chapter is heterogeneous in the extreme. One might almost imagine that it represents, if one might put it so, the contents of Jeremiah's "miscellaneous file," or perhaps of some cupboard in the editor's home where odds and ends of things had been stored.

The first part of the chapter is in poetry, and contains: an oracle (vss. 1–4), textually much damaged (and omitted by LXX), a splinter of which has already been observed intruding at xv 12–14; a bit of wisdom poetry (vss. 5–8) contrasting the righteous and the wicked, very similar in thought to Ps i; a fragment (vss. 9–10) concerning the deceitfulness of the human heart, which Yahweh alone can understand; a proverb (vs. 11) having to do with the man who gets riches unjustly; a further fragment (vss. 12–13) hailing the temple as the place of Yahweh's throne; and, finally (vss. 14–18), another of Jeremiah's "confessions," in which he cries to Yahweh to save him from his persecutors. None of these pieces can be dated. But the oracle in vss. 1–4, the fragment in vss. 9–10, and the confession (vss. 14–18) bear on their face the stamp of Jeremiah's mind and may confidently be ascribed to him. As for the other pieces, with the possible exception of vss. 12–13—which stand somewhat in contrast to Jeremiah's attitude toward the temple as expressed, say, in vii 2–15 (but cf. those—recently Weiser—who link these verses to the confession that follows, and defend their genuineness)—one can only say that positive reasons for denying them to Jeremiah do not exist.

In the latter part of the chapter (vss. 19–27) there is a prose discourse urging the keeping of the Sabbath and, indeed, making this the condition of the nation's existence. This rather one-sided emphasis upon the Sabbath is strange coming from Jeremiah, who elsewhere so often and so sharply rebukes the notion that Yahweh's favor can be gained, and the nation's well-being secured, through diligent prosecution of the cult. It is, therefore, entirely likely that we have in this passage an instance of the further development— possibly the misunderstanding—of Jeremiah's thought in the circles of those who perpetuated his words. Nevertheless, contrary to the opinion of some, the passage is not, either in style or content, necessarily very late. Moreover (cf. Rudolph), there is every likelihood that it does develop actual words of Jeremiah on the subject. Jeremiah must certainly have held the Sabbath in respect and, though the least legalistic of men, must have regarded the breaking of it as serious (even Amos, whose attitude toward the cult was, if possible, more intransigent than Jeremiah's, did: Amos viii 4–6). Sabbath was, after all, an integral part of covenant law (the Decalogue!), over the breach of which Jeremiah repeatedly showed the profoundest concern (e.g., vii 8–10). To him, indeed, obedience to the covenant stipulations was precisely the condition upon which the national existence depended. It is most unlikely that, in urging such obedience, he would have made an exception of the Sabbath, especially when the breakers of it were doubtless motivated primarily by their own greed (as in Amos viii 4–6). The probability is, therefore, that although this discourse develops Jeremiah's thought in a one-sided way, it is nevertheless based upon his expressed sentiments.

16. JEREMIAH AT THE POTTER'S HOUSE
—WITH ATTACHED SAYINGS
(xviii 1–23)

Jeremiah at the Potter's House

XVIII 1 The word that came to Jeremiah from Yahweh: 2 "Go down at once to the potter's house, and there I will tell you what I have to say." 3 So I went down to the potter's house, and there was the potter busy at work at his wheel. 4 And whenever a vessel that he was working on would turn out poorly, *as clay sometimes will in the potter's hands,* he would reshape it into another vessel of whatever sort *seemed best to him.*

5 Then the word of Yahweh came to me: 6 "Can I not do to you just as this potter does, O house of Israel?—Yahweh's word. See! Like clay in a potter's hand, so are you in my hand, O house of Israel. 7 Thus I might at one moment announce my intention to uproot, break down, and destroy a certain nation or kingdom; 8 but should that nation which I have threatened repent of its wickedness, I would think better of the evil that I had intended to do to it. 9 Again, I might at another moment announce my intention to build up and to plant a certain nation or kingdom; 10 but should it then do what is displeasing to me, and not obey my voice, I would think better of the good things that I had said I would do for it.

11 "Now then, say to the men of Judah and the citizens of Jerusalem, 'This is what Yahweh has said: Look! I am shaping evil against you, laying plans against you. Turn, then, every one of you from his wicked behavior and reform the whole

a–a Reading *kaḥōmer* for *baḥōmer* with some manuscripts. Hebrew ("when the vessel that he was making with the clay was spoiled in the potter's hand") is awkward and probably conflates more than one reading. But perhaps, with LXX, read simply "in his hands" for the whole clause.
b–b So with LXX and other Vrs. It is at least smoother than Hebrew which, to our taste, redundantly reads ". . . to the potter."

pattern of your conduct.' 12 But they will reply, 'It's no use! No, we will follow our own plans, and will act each of us as his own stubbornly wicked inclinations direct.'"

Israel's Unnatural Conduct and Its Consequences

13 [Therefore] this is what Yahweh has said:
"Ask, pray, of the nations,
  Who ever heard of the like?
It's an utterly shocking thing
  That Virgin Israel has done.
14 ᶜDo flints depart from the fields,
  Or the snow from Lebanon?
Do flowing streams run dry,
  Or bubbling springs?ᶜ
15 But my people have forgot me,
  To the Fraud they burn offerings;
ᵈAnd they've stumbled from their way,ᵈ
  The ancient trails,
To journey on bypaths,
  An ungraded road,
16 So making their land a horror,
  A hissing forever,
At which all who pass, appalled,
  Will shake their heads.
17 Like a wind from the east I will drive them
  Before the foe.
My back, not my face, ᵉI will show themᵉ
  On their day of disaster."

ᶜ⁻ᶜ As it stands in MT the verse cannot be translated. Numerous reconstructions of the text are suggested; the one offered here is that of W. F. Albright (HUCA, 23 [1950/1], p. 23 f.). Read ṣōr ("flint, pebble") for miṣṣūr ("from the rock"); yinnāšᵉtū ("are dried up") for yinnātᵉšū ("are plucked up")— transposition of letters; zābīm ("flowing") for zārīm ("foreign"); mᵉqōrīm ("springs") for qārīm ("cold")—haplography. See NOTE.

ᵈ⁻ᵈ Hebrew reads, "they have caused them to stumble in their ways"; but "they" has no antecedent. Read wayyikšᵉlū for wayyakšīlūm (cf. LXX and other Vrs.); the m may be taken as enclitic (cf. M. J. Dahood, ZAW 74 [1962], pp. 207–9).

ᵉ⁻ᵉ Point verb as Hiphil with Vrs.; MT has Qal ("I will look at them").

Jeremiah Reacts to a Plot against His Life

18 They said, "Come! Let us lay plans against Jeremiah. For priestly instruction, and the counsel of wise men, and the prophetic word, will never cease. Come, let us bring charges against him, and let us pay no heed to anything that he says."

19   Give heed, O Yahweh, to me!
       ᶠHear me state my case!ᶠ
20   Is evil fair payment for good,
       That they've dug a pit to kill me?
    Think how I stood before thee
       To speak for their welfare,
         And turn thy fury from them.
21   So—hand over their sons to starvation!
       Spill them out to the power of the sword!
    Let their wives be childless and widowed!
       Let their men be victims of plague,
         And their youths cut down by the sword in battle!
22   Let a cry be heard from their homes
       When, sudden, thou bringest marauders upon them!
    For they've dug a pit to take me,
       And traps have set for my feet.
23   But thou, Yahweh, dost know
       All their plotting against me to kill me.
    Forgive not their crimes,
       Nor blot out their sin from thy sight!
    But let them be hurled down before thee—
       Deal with them whilst thou art angry!

ᶠ–ᶠ "Listen to the voice of my *rīb*" (reading *rībī* with LXX and other Vrs. for *yᵉrībay:* ". . . of my adversaries"). Both readings are possible, but the one chosen yields a slightly better parallelism.

NOTES

xviii 3. *at his wheel*. Literally "at the two stones." The apparatus consisted of two stone wheels on a vertical axle, the lower of which was spun by the feet, while the upper carried the clay which the potter shaped as the wheel revolved; cf. Ecclesiasticus xxxviii 29–30.

4. *And whenever*. The tense of the verbs is iterative. Jeremiah apparently saw this happen more than once as he watched.

7. Cf. the infinitives here and in vs. 9 with those in i 10.

8. *which I have threatened*. The clause modifies "that nation," but it is out of place in Hebrew (". . . that nation repent of its wickedness— which I have threatened") and may be an insertion; LXX and other Vrs. omit.

11. *I am shaping*. The word (*yōṣēr*) is chosen because, used as a noun, it means "potter" (it is the word that occurs repeatedly with that meaning in vss. 2–6).

13. *Therefore*. An editorial transition. Cf. the thought of vss. 13–15 with ii 10–13.

14. The nation's faithless conduct is contrasted with the constancy of nature (cf. viii 7). For a slightly different treatment of this verse and the next, see now M. J. Dahood, ZAW 74 (1962), 207–9.

15. *the Fraud*. I.e., false gods, idols.

The ancient trails. On the "ancient ways" (i.e., of loyalty to Yahweh's covenant and the heritage of the past) as the "good way," cf. vi 16.

16. *A hissing*. Or, "a whistling," i.e., a sight so shocking that men whistle in awe (cf. xix 8). The verse has striking assonance: *lāśūm 'arṣām lešammāh / šerīqōt 'ōlām // kōl 'ōbēr 'ālehā yiššōm / weyānīd berō'šō*.

18. *For priestly instruction . . . will never cease*. Literally "For *tōrāh* (here 'instruction,' not 'law') will not perish from the priest, nor counsel from," etc. This sums up a prediction made by Jeremiah that all media of receiving the divine word would be withdrawn. Since from the speakers' point of view this is a lie, and one spoken in the name of Yahweh, Jeremiah deserves to be put out of the way for saying it.

let us bring charges against him. Or, "circulate slanders. . . ." Literally "let us smite him with the tongue."

let us pay no heed to anything that he says. I.e., let us pay no attention to his predictions, or: let us not listen to anything he may say in his defense. LXX, however, omits the negative: "Let us listen to all his words" (i.e., in the hope of trapping him). Both readings are possible, and attractive.

20. *That they've dug a pit to kill me*. Some omit this as a variant of

vs. 22c. LXX, on the other hand, reads differently and adds yet another colon. Cf. this verse and xv 10 f.

21. *Spill them out to the power of the sword.* I.e., hurl them down, helpless, to be slaughtered—shall we say, like fruit or vegetables dumped from a basket onto the table under the watchful eye, and the knife, of the cook.

23. *let them be hurled down before thee.* I.e., let them, like the criminals they are, be tripped and thrown sprawling before the judge. And let him (next colon) not wait for calm to prevail, but "throw the book at them" in his anger.

COMMENT

Chapters xviii through xx form an editorial unit which, though relatively brief, contains examples of all the major types of material found in the Jeremiah book: poetic oracles and confessions, prose discourses and biography. The unit falls into two parts (ch. xviii; chs. xix–xx), each of which consists of a prose passage with appended poetic sayings. The two prose passages have undoubtedly been transmitted in juxtaposition to one another because of the theme "potter–pot," which dominates both. Both, moreover, involve symbolic action.

In xviii 1–12, which is in autobiographical style, Jeremiah tells how, at Yahweh's command, he visited the potter's house and watched the potter at his work. He observed that whenever a vessel turned out poorly, no doubt because the clay was not of the right quality, the potter would reshape the clay and make of it another vessel of whatever sort seemed best to him. Then a word from Yahweh came to Jeremiah explaining to him the meaning of this (vss. 5–6): Yahweh is the potter, and he can do with Israel as the potter does with the clay. But the point is not, as some think, that Yahweh will continue to work patiently with his people and, in spite of the fact that they may temporarily thwart him, will in the end make them the "vessel" that he had intended them to be. This is to misunderstand vs. 4, the point of which is precisely that the clay *can* frustrate the potter's intention and cause him to change it: as the quality of the clay determines what the potter can do with it, so the quality of a people determines what God will do with them. This point is developed in vss. 7–10, which are not to be deleted as a mistaken expansion, as those who give the passage an optimistic interpretation are obliged to do. This, too, is the point that Jeremiah is told (vs. 11) to proclaim to the people: God's present intention is to judge them; but if they repent, they have still a chance. But this (vs. 12) they refuse to do. The incident cannot be dated; but the fact that disaster is described as still avoidable argues that it took place relatively early—probably not later than the first years of Jehoiakim's reign.

Attached to the above passage are two poetic pieces which are likewise best dated in Jehoiakim's reign—though vss. 13–17, which has (cf. the NOTES) striking similarities with parts of chapter ii, may be earlier still. The first of these (vss. 13–17) is an oracle which develops the theme of vs. 12, assailing the unnatural apostasy of the people and announcing the awful punishment that it will bring. The second piece (vss. 18–23) is another of Jeremiah's "confessions." From it one can see, though nothing further is known about it, that there has been a plot against Jeremiah's life. To this Jeremiah responds with almost indescribable bitterness. Protesting the injustice of it, he calls upon Yahweh not to forgive those who have been responsible, but to punish them without mercy. It is easy for a detached observer to be shocked at this and to find it unworthy of Jeremiah. But nothing is more perverse than to deny on that account that he uttered such words, as some scholars have done. Jeremiah was indeed a prophet of God; but he was also a human being—maybe at times an all-too-human being—not a plaster saint or, perhaps, a dictating machine. And it is only as we accept him as a human being that we can rightly hear the prophetic word that he spoke.

17. PROPHETIC SYMBOLISM AND PERSECUTION; FURTHER CONFESSIONS
(xix 1–15; xx 1–18)

The Broken Bottle; Jeremiah in the Stocks

XIX 1 Yahweh spoke *to me* thus: "Go and buy a potter's earthenware bottle *and, taking with you* some of the elders of the people and *some of the senior priests,* 2 go [out to the valley of Ben-hinnom, which is] just outside the Potsherd Gate [and there proclaim the words that I speak to you. 3 Say, 'Hear the word of Yahweh, you kings of Judah and citizens of Jerusalem! This is what Yahweh of Hosts, the God of Israel, has said: Ah, but I am going to bring a calamity on this place that will make the ears of everyone who hears of it ring— 4 because they have forsaken me, and made this an alien place by sending up sacrifices in it to other gods of whom neither they nor their fathers have known; because *the kings of Judah have filled* this place with the blood of innocent men; 5 and because they have built the high places of Baal in order to burn their sons in the fire as burnt offerings to Baal—a thing that I never commanded, never ordered, and that never even entered my mind. 6 Therefore, believe me, days are coming—Yahweh's word— when they will no longer call this place Tophet, or the valley of Ben-hinnom, but the valley of Slaughter. 7 I will cancel the plans of Judah and Jerusalem in this place. I will cause them to fall by the sword before their foes, at the hand of those who seek their life, and I will make their corpses food for the carrion birds and the wild beasts. 8 I will make this city such a horrible

a–a Added with LXX. See NOTE.
b–b Added with Syr., Tar., LXX (which does not express "with you"); though Hebrew lacks them, some such words are necessary.
c–c But LXX^BN has only "some of the priests," which may be correct.
d–d So LXX; Hebrew places "and the kings of Judah" with the preceding clause, and then begins a new clause, "and they have filled."

and shocking sight that everyone who passes near it will be appalled, and will whistle in awe at all the blows it has suffered. 9 I will make them eat the flesh of their own sons and daughters. Aye, they will eat one another's flesh under the pressure of the siege to which their enemies and those who seek their life will subject them']. 10 Then, smash the bottle in the presence of the men who have come with you, 11 and say to them, 'This is what Yahweh of Hosts has said: Just so will I smash this people and this city, like a man smashing a potter's vessel so that it can never be mended again. [And they will bury in Tophet till there is no room left.*e* 12 Thus will I do to this place—Yahweh's word —and to its inhabitants, making this city like Tophet. 13 The houses of Jerusalem, and the houses of Judah's kings—and indeed all the houses upon whose rooftops they have sent up offerings to the heavenly host, and poured out libations to other gods—will be like the place of Tophet, unclean.]' "

14 Then Jeremiah returned from Tophet, where Yahweh had sent him to prophesy, and stood in the court of Yahweh's house and said to all the people, 15 "This is what Yahweh of Hosts, the God of Israel, has said: 'Look! I am going to bring upon this city and its various towns all the evil with which I have threatened it, because they have deliberately refused to listen to what I say.' "

XX 1 Now the priest, Pashhur ben Immer, who was chief overseer in the house of Yahweh, heard Jeremiah prophesy these things. 2 So Pashhur beat Jeremiah and put him in the stocks, in the Upper Benjamin Gate of Yahweh's house. 3 But then, the next morning, when Pashhur released Jeremiah from the stocks, Jeremiah said to him, "Pashhur was not the name that Yahweh gave you, but 'Terror All Around.' 4 For this is what Yahweh has said: Believe me, I am going to make you a terror to yourself and to all your friends. They will fall by the sword of their enemies, and you are going to see it with your own eyes. And I will hand all Judah over to the king of Babylon, who will deport

e LXX omits this sentence.

them to Babylon or slay them with the sword. 5 All this city's wealth, all its possessions and valuables, together with all the treasures of Judah's kings, I will hand over to their foes, who will loot them, seize them, and carry them off to Babylon. 6 And as for you, Pashhur, and all the members of your household, you shall go into captivity. Yes, to Babylon you shall go, and there you shall die, and there be buried—you and all your friends to whom you have prophesied falsely."

Jeremiah in Tension with His Calling

7   You seduced me, Yahweh, and I let you;
       You seized and overcame me.
    I've become a daylong joke,
       They all make fun of me.

8   For whenever I speak, I cry out,
       "Outrage! Robbery!" I shout.
    Ah, the word of Yahweh has gotten for me
       Scorn and endless abuse.

9   But if I say, "I'll forget him!
       I'll speak no more in his name!"
    Then it is in my heart like a fire that burns
       Shut up in my bones;
    And I struggle to hold it in,
       But—I can't!

10   In the crowd I can hear them whisper,
       "Magor-missabib!
    Denounce him! Let's denounce him!"
       —So all my "friends,"
          Who hoped I would trip—
    "Perhaps he'll be tricked—then we'll have him,
       And can take our revenge upon him!"

11   On my side is Yahweh like a warrior dread;
       And so, those who hound me will stumble, not win.
    Dire shame will be theirs, for they cannot succeed,
       A disgrace that will ne'er be forgot'.

12 O Yahweh of Hosts, *who assayest aright,*
     Who dost see hidden motives and thoughts,
     Let me see thy vengeance upon them,
     For to thee I've committed my case.

13 Sing to Yahweh!
     Give praise to Yahweh!
     For he's saved the needy one's life
     From the clutch of the wicked.

De Profundis

14 Cursed be the day
     Whereon I was born!
     The day my mother bore me,
     Be it ever unblessed!

15 Cursed be the man who brought
     The news to my father,
     "It's a boy! You've got a son!"
     (Ah, how glad it made him!)

16 *Let him be, that man, like the cities
     Which Yahweh overthrew without pity!
     Let him hear* a shriek in the morning,
     The shout of battle at noon!

17 Because he killed me not *in the womb*;
     So had been my mother my grave,
     And pregnant forever her womb.

18 Ah, why came I forth from the womb
     To see but trouble and grief,
     And end my days in shame?

f–f MT "thou righteous assayer," or "who assayest the righteous." But perhaps it is better to read *ṣedeq* for *ṣaddīq* as in xi 20.

g–g Read *yᵉhī* and *yišmaʻ* with Vrs., for *wᵉhāyāh* and *wᵉšāmaʻ* respectively.

h–h So Vrs.; Heb. *mēreḥem* ("from the womb") is miscopied from the next verse. But if we point as *mᵉruḥḥām* ("enwombed") no emendation may be necessary (cf. M. J. Dahood, *Biblica* 44 [1963], 204 f.).

NOTES

xix 1. *to me.* Added with LXX. The original account of Jeremiah's symbolic action begins exactly as does the similar one in xiii 1–11. Some emend to read "to Jeremiah" to conform to the style of the biographical passage that follows; but xix 1–13 (even in its brief form) and xix 14–xx 6 were probably of separate origin.

bottle. Heb. *baqbuq,* a narrow-necked water decanter (cf. J. L. Kelso, "The Ceramic Vocabulary of the Old Testament," BASOR, Suppl. 5–6 [1948], 17 and fig. 20).

2–11. The original account (see COMMENT) has been expanded by the addition of an address in stereotyped language, similar to vii 31–34, etc., regarding the cult place of Tophet. Brackets indicate the approximate extent of the expansion. Note that "go . . . just outside the Potsherd Gate" leads smoothly into vs. 10 f. where, apparently, no such lengthy speech as the intervening one was made. Note too (vs. 3) that this speech addresses the kings (plural!) and people of Judah (i.e., is a public address), while (cf. vss. 1, 10) the smashing of the bottle was done before a few selected witnesses. Further, to identify the valley of Ben-hinnom by the Potsherd Gate is unnatural; this valley, which extended along the whole south side of the city needed no such identification. The words—"out to the valley of Ben-hinnom, which is"—are part of the expansion.

4. *made this an alien place.* By worshiping foreign gods they have "made this place foreign," i.e., "denationalized" it, made it unrecognizable as Israelite.

7. *I will cancel.* The verb *baqqōtī* ("empty out," i.e., make void) is chosen as a play on "bottle" (*baqbuq*), which is from the same root.

8. *horrible and shocking sight.* Literally "a horror and a hissing (whistling)"; cf. xviii 16 and NOTE.

11. *And they will bury in Tophet . . . room left.* Cf. NOTE on vii 32.

13. *unclean.* Omit article as the sense requires (predicate adjective); Heb. "the unclean ones."

14. *from Tophet.* The biographical account begins with this verse. Possibly the original reading was "from the (Potsherd) Gate," or the like, as many scholars surmise, this having been altered to conform to the inserted material above.

15. *its various towns.* Heb. "this city and all its cities" is peculiar. Apparently the "cities of Judah" are intended, but this is not the usual way of expressing it; or perhaps, "its environs, suburbs"—though again this is not the usual expression.

xx 1. *chief overseer*. Heb. *pāqīd nāgīd*. The *pāqīd* (cf. xxix 26) was apparently charged with maintaining order in the temple. It will be remembered that at his call (i 10) Jeremiah had been made "overseer" over nations. Now, ironically, the ecclesiastical "overseer" takes steps to silence God's "overseer."

2. *beat Jeremiah*. No doubt "had him beaten"; but the meaning could be that he "struck Jeremiah." Hebrew has, redundantly, "smote Jeremiah the prophet"; but LXX has simply, "smote him."

3. *'Terror All Around.'* Heb. *māgōr missābīb*, a favorite expression of Jeremiah (cf. NOTE on vs. 10). If there is any play on Pashhur's name it is not obvious (but cf. A. M. Honeyman, VT 4 [1954], 424–26). The point rather seems to be that though this priest calls himself Pashhur, that is not the name that Yahweh intends him to have; i.e., Yahweh gives him a new name symbolic of the fate he is to suffer.

4. *make you a terror to yourself and to all*. . . . Or, possibly, "I will hand you over to terror, you and all . . ."; cf. xix 13 for a similar construction.

6. *prophesied falsely*. It is apparent that this priest was also a prophet, and one who (cf. xiv 13) had declared that no harm would befall the nation. Since this was a lie uttered in Yahweh's name, he deserved to die (cf. NOTES on chs. xxvi; xxviii).

7. *You seduced me, Yahweh, and I let you*. The word "seduce" is chosen, and the familiar "you" employed, to bring out the well-nigh blasphemous tone that Jeremiah adopts; literally, "You seduced me, and I was seduced." The verb is used of seduction in Exod xxii 15[16E]; cf. Judg xvi 5.

You seized. The Qal of the verb with direct object can mean "overpower" (cf. I Kings xvi 22), the Hiphil (so Ehrl. and others read) "seize." Perhaps the sense is "you forced me," thus carrying forward the figure of seduction.

8. *Outrage! Robbery!* Cf. NOTE on vi 7. Reference is either to Jeremiah's repeated threats of ruin, or (as in vi 7) his repeated denunciations of crimes committed against the helpless. Harping on the subject has brought him derision.

9. *I'll forget him*. Or, ". . . it" (the word). Literally "I will not remember (think of) him/it."

Then it. I.e., Yahweh's word; cf. the preceding NOTE, and vs. 8b.

I struggle. Literally "I exhaust myself (trying) to. . . ."

10. *In the crowd I can hear them whisper*. Literally "I have heard the whispering of many"; but "the many" may have the sense of "the crowd" (e.g., Exod xxiii 2). Cf. this verse and Ps xxxi 14[13E].

Magor-missabib. "Terror All Around" (cf. vs. 3; vi 25; xlvi 5; xlix 29). Apparently Jeremiah had used the expression so often that it was becoming a nickname. One can imagine one man in the crowd nudging another as Jeremiah passed, and whispering, "there goes old Magor-mis-sabib."

tricked. The verb is that used in vs. 7a ("seduced").

12. The verse repeats xi 20 with variations (see NOTES there). Perhaps it has been drawn in secondarily from that context, perhaps it was simply a favorite appeal of Jeremiah, which he employed more than once.

16. *Let him be . . . Let him hear*. See textual note[g–g]. The "cities which Yahweh overthrew" are Sodom and Gomorrah and the other cities of the Plain (Gen xix 24–28).

COMMENT

Chapters xix and xx continue the editorial unit begun in chapter xviii. In xix 1–13 there is a prose account telling how Jeremiah, at Yahweh's command, went outside the Potsherd Gate of Jerusalem and there, before witnesses, smashed an earthenware bottle, announcing as he did so (vs. 11) that just so would Jerusalem be smashed beyond repair. This action of Jeremiah's was a terrifying one, and in a way difficult for us to imagine. It was a symbolic action; but by the mind of the day such an action was not understood merely as the dramatic illustration of a point, or play acting, but as the actual setting in motion of Yahweh's destroying word. It is, therefore, small wonder that it earned Jeremiah persecution, as we are told that it did. The original account of this action was very brief, and has been much expanded by the insertion (see NOTES) of a rather wordy harangue describing the awful fate of the city because of the abominable rites that had been practiced at the high place of Tophet, in the valley of Ben-hinnom, just outside its walls. In the translation the approximate extent of this expansion has been indicated by the use of brackets.

Following upon the piece just described and attached to it—undoubtedly because Jeremiah's action in smashing the bottle and his subsequent words in the temple were correctly remembered as the occasion for it—is a biographical narrative (xix 14–xx 6) telling how a certain officer of the temple, Pashhur, had Jeremiah beaten and thrown into the stocks. The date of this incident—and therefore of the symbolic action that provoked it—will be discussed further at a later place in the book (see COMMENT on Sec. 22); but apparently it occurred in the early years of Jehoiakim's reign. Although from a literary point of view the biographical account and the pre-

ceding discourse are of separate origin, they belong together factually and should be read together.

The account of Jeremiah's persecution is closely followed by another of his confessions (xx 7–13). This confession has no doubt
been transmitted here because of the catchword *māgōr-missābīb*
("Terror All Around") which is played upon both in it and in
the preceding narrative, albeit in different ways (vss. 3, 10). Here
Jeremiah addresses his God in almost blasphemous language as he
cries out at the derision and abuse that the prophetic office has
brought him, while at the same time confessing that in spite of his
desire to stop speaking in the name of Yahweh, he had found
himself unable to do so. Yet, unlike most of the others, this confession ends on a note of confident trust and praise. Following it,
however, and indicating how little Jeremiah knew of permanent
peace, is still another confession (xx 14–18), which shows us Jeremiah at the end of his resources, plunged into a well-nigh suicidal
despair. One can neither exaggerate the agony of spirit revealed
here, nor improve upon the words which Jeremiah found to express
it. There is, indeed, little in all of literature that compares with
this piece, and nothing in the Bible except perhaps the third chapter
of Job, to which it is very similar. Whether Job develops the thought
of this passage, or whether both derive from a common tradition
is a question that cannot be answered with assurance; but kinship
between the two is undeniable.

18. TO THE ROYAL HOUSE OF JUDAH
(xxi 11–14; xxii 1–30; xxiii 1–8)

The Obligation and the Failure of the Monarchy:
a Statement of Principle

XXI 11 *To the Royal House of Judah:*
Hear the word of Yahweh, 12 O house of David! This is what
Yahweh has said:
"Execute justice daily,
  Rescue the robbed from th' extortioner's clutch,
Lest my wrath break out like fire,
  And burn so that none can quench it,
  So wicked have been your*a* deeds.
13 Look! I'm against you, enthroned o'er the vale
  On the rocky plateau—Yahweh's word.
You who say, 'Who can descend upon us?
  Who can enter our lairs?'
14 I'll punish you just as your deeds deserve—Yahweh's
                              word.
  I'll kindle a fire in her forest,
  That will rage through all her environs."

XXII 1 This is what Yahweh has said: "Go down to the palace
of the king of Judah, and there speak this word. 2 Say, 'Hear
the word of Yahweh, O king of Judah, you who sit on David's
throne—you and your officials and your subjects who enter these
gates. 3 This is what Yahweh has said: Act justly and right-
eously! Rescue the one who has been robbed from the clutches
of the oppressor! Do not wrong or mistreat the resident alien,
the orphan or the widow, or shed innocent blood in this place!
4 For if you will really act to carry out this commission, then

---

a Follows Qre (Ktib: "their . . ."). See NOTE.

there will always enter the gates of this palace kings of David's line who sit on his throne and ride in chariots and on horses, *they and their officials and subjects.* 5 But if you will not heed these words, I swear by myself—Yahweh's word—that this palace will become a ruin.'"

6 For this is what Yahweh has said concerning the palace of Judah's king:

"Like Gilead are you to me,
Or Lebanon's crest;
Yet I swear that I'll make you a desert,
An abandoned town.

7   I'll commission against you wreckers,
Each with his tools;
They'll fell your splendid cedars,
Bring them down in the flames."

8 "Then many foreign peoples will pass by this city and will say to one another, 'Why did Yahweh do such a thing to this great city?' 9 And the answer will be, 'Because they forsook the covenant of Yahweh their God, and did obeisance to other gods and worshiped them.'"

Jehoahaz (Shallum)

10   Weep not for the dead, nor bemoan him;
Weep rather for him who departs,
For he'll never come back again,
Or see his native land.

11 For this is what Yahweh has said concerning Shallum ben Josiah, king of Judah, who succeeded his father Josiah on the throne: "He who has gone from this place will never come back to it again. 12 In the place to which they have deported him, he will die. He will never see this land again."

b–b Plural with LXX (Hebrew singular). The clause may be an expansion after vs. 2b.

Jehoiakim

13 "Woe to him who builds his house by unfairness,
        His upper rooms by wrong,
     Who works his neighbor for nothing,
        Nor pays him any wage.

14 *e*Who says, 'I'll build me*e* a spacious house
        With airy roof-chambers.'
     So he *d*widens its windows,
        Panels with cedar,
           And paints it bright red.*d*

15 *e*That makes you a king—
        Outdoing everyone in cedar?
     Your father—didn't he live well enough,
        *f*And enjoy himself,
     And yet do justice and right?*f*

16   He espoused the cause of the poor and the needy;
     Wasn't this what it means to know me?
        —Word of Yahweh.*e*

17 But no eyes have you, and no thought,
        Save for personal gain,
     For shedding the blood of innocents,
        And for acts of extortion and tyranny."

    18 And so, this is what Yahweh has said concerning Jehoiakim
ben Josiah, king of Judah: *g*"Woe to this man!*g*

o–o LXX reads, "You have built yourself . . . ," and begins the direct address
to the king here (cf. vs. 15)—doubtless a variant reading.
d–d Read *ḥallōnāw* for *ḥallōnāy* (haplography), and *weṣāfōn* ("paneling":
infinitive absolute) for *weṣāfūn* (passive participle). LXX reads passive
participle in each case here ("fitted with windows, paneled . . . painted . . .").
e–e The text of vss. 15 and 16 is somewhat confused (cf. LXX, which differs
from MT widely), and the translation in places conjectural.
f–f Hebrew reads *'āz ṭōb lō* at the end of vs. 15, and repeats *'āz ṭōb* after the
first colon of vs. 16. But the words are hardly original at both of the places
where MT has them. LXX omits them on the second occurrence, and perhaps
does so (though LXX is so confused it is difficult to be sure) on the first as
well, reading them instead (or, rather, similar words) before "(And . . .) do
justice and right." They do, at least, yield a good sense at that place, and
we have tentatively read them there (perhaps only *weṭōb lō*) with Duhm,
Skinner, Rudolph, and others. See further, NOTE.
g–g Added with LXX (lost by homoioteleuton?).

They'll not lament him,
  'Ah, my brother! Ah, sister!'
They'll not lament him,
  'Ah, lord! Ah, his majesty!'
19 They'll give him a donkey's funeral!
    —Hauled out and dumped
      Outside Jerusalem's gates."

Jerusalem's Doom

20 "Go up to Lebanon, and cry!
    In Bashan raise loud your voice!
  Cry out from Abarim,
    For broken are all your 'lovers.'
21 I addressed you when times were good;
    You said, 'I won't listen.'
  Such has been your way from your youth,
    Not to heed my voice.
22 All your shepherds the wind shall 'shepherd,'
    And your 'lovers' to exile shall go.
  Ah, but then you'll be shamed and disgraced
    By all your wickedness.
23 You who perch in Lebanon,
    Who nest in the cedars,
  How you'll groan when the pains come upon you,
    Pangs as of childbirth."

Jehoiachin (Coniah)

24 "As I live—Yahweh's word—even were you (Coniah ben Jehoiakim, king of Judah) the signet ring on my right hand, I would snatch you off 25 and hand you over to those who seek your life, and of whom you are afraid (that is, Nebuchadrezzar king of Babylon, and the Chaldeans).[h] 26 I will hurl you and

---

[h] The words in parentheses are possibly a (correct) gloss; LXX lacks all except "to the Chaldeans."

the mother who bore you 'into another country,' where neither
of you was born, and there you shall both die." 27 To the land
to which they will yearn desperately to return, they shall never
return.

28   Is Coniah a castoff pot,
          A utensil no one wants?
       Why, then, is he hurled, cast out
          To a land that he knows not?ʲ

29   O land, O land, O land,
          Hear the word of Yahweh!

30   ᵏ[Thus Yahweh has said:]ᵏ
       "Write down this man as childless,
          ˡ[One who'll have no success in his lifetime],ˡ
          For no offspring of his shall succeed
       In sitting on David's throne,
          Or ruling in Judah again."

Promises for the Future of Dynasty and People

XXIII 1 "Woe to the shepherds who cause the sheep of my
pasture to stray and be scattered!—Yahweh's word." 2 Therefore
this is what Yahweh, the God of Israel, has said concerning the
shepherds who shepherd my people: "You are the ones who
have scattered my flock! You have driven them away and have
not attended to them. Believe me, I am going to attend to you
for your wicked deeds—Yahweh's word. 3 I myself will gather
what is left of my flock from all the lands where I have driven
them, and will bring them back to their fold, where they will
thrive and multiply. 4 And I will place over them shepherds who
will truly shepherd them, so that they need fear no more or be
terrified; and none of them will be missing—Yahweh's word."

ⁱ⁻ⁱ Read 'ereṣ for hā'āreṣ with LXX (which omits "another"). Perhaps two
readings have been combined: "into another country," and "into a country
where you were not born."

ʲ The translation of vs. 28 follows LXX. MT has a somewhat expanded text
that obscures the meter (cf. EVV).

ᵏ⁻ᵏ The words are somewhat superfluous after vs. 29, and may be an expansion; LXX omits.

ˡ⁻ˡ These words are probably not original. See NOTE.

5 "Believe me, days are coming—Yahweh's word—
  When I'll raise a true 'Shoot' of David's line;
  As king he shall reign—and ably,
  And do justice and right in the land.
6 In his days shall Judah triumph,
  And Israel shall dwell in safety.
  And this is the name by which he'll be called,
  'Yahweh-ṣidqēnū.' "

7 "Therefore see! Days are coming—Yahweh's word—when they will no longer say, 'As Yahweh lives, who brought the Israelites up from the land of Egypt,' 8 but, 'As Yahweh lives, ᵐwho broughtᵐ ⁿthe descendants of Israelⁿ back from the north country, and from all the lands to which ᵒhe had driven them,ᵒ that they might dwell in their own land.' "

ᵐ⁻ᵐ MT has "who brought up and brought back," which combines two readings. The parallel passage, xvi 15, lacks the second.
ⁿ⁻ⁿ MT, "the seed of the house of Israel," again seems to combine readings; xvi 15 has "the sons of" for both (LXX has "the house of" there, "the seed of" here).
ᵒ⁻ᵒ So xvi 15. MT has first person here, which does not suit.

NOTES

xxi 12. *Execute justice daily*. Literally ". . . in the morning." Possibly it was the custom to adjudicate cases in morning sessions in the city gate; but the sense here is "every morning," i.e., daily, regularly— and also promptly (cf. Amos iv 4; Ps lix 17[16E], etc.).
So wicked have been your deeds. The clause is lacking in LXX and may be drawn from iv 4 (vs. 12b equals iv 4b). On the other hand, all of vss. 12–14 seems to be made up of originally separate fragments (note the shifts in person of address: second masculine plural in vs. 12; second feminine singular in vs. 13a; [second] masculine plural in vss. 13b–14a, third feminine singular in vs. 14b).
13. *enthroned o'er the vale*. Reference is to Jerusalem; but the translation (EVV) "inhabitant (feminine) of the valley" does not suit Jerusalem at all. We translate *yōšebet hā'ēmeq*, with Weiser, after the analogy of *yōšēb hakkᵉrubīm* ("enthroned on/above the cherubim": I Sam iv 4; II Sam vi 2, etc.). Jerusalem was surrounded on three sides by deep valleys. But, since the passage (see preceding NOTE) is a mosaic of fragments, conventional language originally referring to some other place may here

have been applied to Jerusalem (similar expressions are used of Moab in xlviii 8, 21, 28 f.).

On the rocky plateau. Heb. *ṣūr hammīšōr.* The translation (EVV) "rock of the plain" again does not suit Jerusalem. But *mīšōr* denotes specifically a "table land, plateau"; the expression might be rendered "[high] level rock" (cf. *'ōraḥ mīšōr,* "level path," Ps xxvii 11; *'ereṣ mīšōr,* "level ground," Ps cxliii 10). Reference is thus to the (relatively) level "rocky plateau" upon which Jerusalem stood (but see preceding NOTE).

Who can descend. The verb (*nḥt*) need not imply physical descent from a higher elevation. Note that "you" here is masculine plural, apparently the people of Jerusalem.

14. The first line is wanting in LXX and may be an addition. Yet something of the sort is needed after vs. 13b (the "you" here is also masculine plural); cf. preceding NOTE.

a fire in her forest. I.e., Jerusalem's. This is probably a reference to her great buildings of cedar, as in xxii 6–7 (see NOTE there), rather than literally to adjacent woodlands.

xxii 2. *your officials and your subjects.* Literally "your servants and your people"; "servants" (slaves) here, as regularly in this context, denotes the king's officials, courtiers, retainers.

4. *act to carry out this commission.* Literally "do this thing" (or "this word").

6. *Gilead . . . Lebanon's crest.* Both were noted for their forests. The royal palace is described in these terms no doubt because of the massive cedar pillars which, like great trees, supported "the House of the Forest of Lebanon" (I Kings vii 2–5; Isa xxii 8) and, probably, other buildings of the palace complex (cf. xxi 14).

Yet I swear that I'll make you. Literally "If I do not make you. . . ." This is the oath formula, the first part of which (normally, "May God do so to me, and more also . . . ," or the like) is omitted because God is himself the speaker.

An abandoned town. So for smoothness; Heb. plural. But perhaps the sense is: ". . . like a desert, the towns (of which) are abandoned."

7. *I'll commission.* Literally "sanctify," i.e., ritually prepare (for battle). Cf. NOTE on vi 4.

10–12. The poetic lament (vs. 10) is explained by the prose oracle (vss. 11–12). "The dead" (singular) is Josiah, slain at Megiddo in 609; the one "who departs" is his son Jehoahaz, who was deposed by Necho and deported to Egypt some three months later. Shallum was this king's personal name (cf. I Chron iii 15), Jehoahaz his throne name.

13. *works his neighbor.* Note the extreme "democracy" of the notion

of society which Israel's faith fostered: the king and the carpenter are "neighbors."

widens its windows. Or, "cuts out . . ." (EVV); but cf. the use of the verb in iv 30 ("widen [smear] the eyes"). See textual note[d–d].

15. *That makes you a king. . . .* Literally "Are you a king because you are competing (the verb is used of racing with horses in xii 5) in cedar?" The irony is biting: Does Jehoiakim think that outdoing other rulers, and his predecessors, in the luxuries with which he surrounds himself marks him as a king?

live well enough. Literally: "eat and drink." Cf. Matt xi 19 where the same words are used of Jesus in contrast to John the Baptist. The meaning is that Josiah was no ascetic, but enjoyed the good things of life and lived as befitted his station; but (see next lines of poem) he also took his obligations as king seriously.

And enjoy himself. Usually (EVV) this is given the sense: "then things went well for him." This would seem to imply that Josiah came to a sad end only after he had left off doing justly—which, while not an impossible sense, is unlikely. The sense could equally well be: "then it was pleasant for him" (i.e., he found pleasure in these things).

18. *Ah, my brother! Ah, sister!* Apparently words addressed by the mourners one to another in the course of the ritual of lament. The words, "Ah, lord! Ah, his majesty!" of course refer to the deceased king. But cf. M. J. Dahood, CBQ 23 (1961), 462–64, who, taking "lord" in the sense of "father" and reading *hōrāh* instead of *hōdōh* (a very slight change in Hebrew), translates, "Ah, father! Ah, mother!" Dahood wonders if all of these terms may not refer to the king, who was (so in Phoenician texts) supposed to be father, mother, and brother to his people.

20. *Abarim.* Mountain range in Moab of which Mount Nebo was a part. Moses is said to have viewed the Promised Land from here (Num xxvii 12; Deut xxxii 49).

your 'lovers.' Or, "friends" (cf. Hos viii 9, etc.). "Allies" are referred to, not—as some believe—Judah's own nobility, for this is a force that the expression does not have elsewhere. It is used in parallelism with Judah's rulers ("shepherds") in vs. 22, but this parallelism need not be synonymous.

22. *the wind shall 'shepherd.'* I.e., drive away. Note the wordplay; on "shepherds" and "lovers" see the preceding NOTE.

23. *Lebanon . . . cedars.* Cf. vs. 6, and NOTE there.

as of childbirth. Literally "as (those of) a woman in childbirth."

24. *even were you.* We read so arbitrarily to harmonize with the direct address that follows (cf. Giesebrecht); Heb. and Vrs. "even were Coniah." Perhaps Coniah's name was lacking in the original spoken form and, when added for clarity's sake, caused second person to be altered

to third. If third person is original, the final verb of the verse must also
be read third person (so Vulg.), and the verse assumed to have been
originally separate from what follows.

Coniah. A shortened form of Jeconiah, which was (cf. I Chron iii 16)
the personal name of Jehoiakim's son, Jehoiachin being his throne name.

30. *Write down this man as childless.* The meaning is not that Jehoiachin would have no sons. He actually had seven (I Chron iii 17 f.), the
oldest of whom had almost certainly been born when this prophecy was
uttered. The figure is that of a census list. Jehoiachin is to be entered
as childless since, as far as throne succession was concerned, he was as
good as that.

[*One who'll have no success in his lifetime*]. Literally ". . . will not
succeed in his days." It is doubtful that these words are original. They
are not appropriate as an entry in a census list, and they interrupt the
close connection between "childless" and the remainder of the verse,
which explains it. LXX, which misunderstood "childless," seems not to
have read, "who will not succeed in his days." Perhaps the colon is a
gloss by one who, knowing that Jehoiachin had sons, like LXX misunderstood the point.

xxiii 1. *the shepherds.* In this passage, as elsewhere, Judah's rulers
—but perhaps here (plural) including both the king (Zedekiah?) and
the nobles who dominated him.

2. *attended . . . attend.* A play on the verb *pqd* which on its first
occurrence has the force of "look after, care for," and on the second
that of "call to account, punish."

4. *be missing.* The play on *pqd* continues. The sheep are "looked after,"
therefore "mustered," "counted," therefore not "missing."

5–6. The prophecy has to do with the ideal king (Messiah) of the
Davidic line under whose just and victorious rule all the dynastic hopes
would be realized (cf. Pss ii; lxxii, etc.). The term "Shoot" (*ṣemaḥ*),
in most EVV "Branch," later became a technical term for this expected
king (Zech iii 8; vi 12); the figure, though not the word, is found in
Isa xi 1. The force of the prophecy, however, is disputed. The similarity
of the future Davidide's name to that of Zedekiah (see further below)
is scarcely coincidental. Very probably Jeremiah uttered these words early
in Zedekiah's reign, when dynastic hopes were being attached to that
king by certain of his courtiers (see Introduction, p. ciii); while he tacitly
accepts these hopes as in principle valid, he declares that they will not
be fulfilled in Zedekiah but in a "true Shoot" of totally different stamp.
Others, however, suggest that the prophecy was uttered at, or just prior
to, Zedekiah's accession, and that it was because of it (but not by
Jeremiah's intention) that the king was given his throne name (his per-

sonal name was Mattaniah: II Kings xxiv 17). Following MT the meter of
vss. 5–6a has been taken as 3/4, 3/4, 3/3 (or, better, 3/2/2, 3/2/2, 3/3).
But attention should be given to the suggestion of D. N. Freedman
(in a paper read before the Society of Biblical Literature; cf. JBL 72
[1953], xx) who, redividing the cola at one place, sees the meter as
3/3, 2/2, 2/2, 3/3: "Behold days are coming / When I'll raise for David
a 'Shoot' // A righteous one who will reign / A king who will prosper
// etc."

5. *a true 'Shoot' of David's line.* Literally ". . . to David [i.e., the
dynasty] a *ṣemaḥ ṣaddīq*"—which could be taken as a "righteous scion,"
or a "true scion" (as distinguished from one who falsely pretended to
that distinction).

As king he shall reign—and ably. Or, "A king shall reign. . . ." The
construction is not awkward. The "Shoot" will reign as a *king*, not a
puppet like Zedekiah. The word "ably" translates *hiśkīl*, which has the
force of "act wisely" and "have success."

6. *triumph.* Or, "be rescued, delivered, liberated."

Yahweh-ṣidqēnū. The name may be an old formula which preserves
the original verbal force of *Yahweh*: "he who brings to pass our vindication." But this was probably not understood in the sixth century B.C.,
when it would have been taken as "Yahweh is our righteousness" (i.e.,
the vindication of our right). It is almost the same as *ṣidqīyāhū* (Zedekiah): "Yahweh is my vindication."

7–8. The verses repeat xvi 14–15 with minor variations. They are out
of place there, but in place here. LXX, however, puts them at the
end of the chapter.

COMMENT

In xxi 11–xxiii 8 we find a complex of sayings, almost equally
divided between poetry and prose, and uttered over a considerable
span of time, which have been drawn together because of their
relationship to the theme stated in the heading (xxi 11): "the
Royal House of Judah." This section is of considerable interest
not only because it allows us to see something of Jeremiah's attitude toward the various kings who ruled during his adult lifetime,
every one of whom is addressed or alluded to in the course of it,
but also because it affords us our clearest insight into his view of
the institution of monarchy and its place in the divine economy.

The opening passage of the section (xxi 11–xxii 9) sets forth
what one might call a statement of principle. The principle, in a

word, is this: the Davidic monarchy has the obligation under God
of establishing justice in society, specifically of defending the rights
of the helpless as demanded in covenant law (e.g., Exod xxii 20–23
[21–24E]). If it discharges this obligation, its existence is justified
and it will endure; but since it has not done so, it is under judgment.
This passage, like others in the section, combines poetry and prose.
One gains the impression that the poetic portions (xxi 12–14; xxii
6–7) and the prose portions (xxii 1–5, 8–9) could, respectively,
be read together (note, e.g., the motif "forest," "fire" in xxi 12, 14
and in xxii 6–7), and that a poetic oracle and a prose discourse,
closely parallel in theme, have been interwoven.

Following this introductory passage are sayings concerning the
individual kings, in chronological order beginning with Jehoahaz
(there is no saying addressed to Josiah, but he is twice alluded
to in those that follow). The saying regarding Jehoahaz—or Shallum, as he is called here (see NOTE on xxii 7)—consists of a
brief lament in meter (xxii 10), followed by an explanatory oracle
in prose (vss. 11–12). Both were uttered just as that unfortunate
young king was deposed by the Pharaoh Necho and deported to
Egypt—thus in the autumn of 609. In vss. 13–19 there is an oracle
(in poetry) addressed to Jehoiakim, and doubtless uttered in the
early years of that king's reign. Possibly nothing that Jeremiah ever
said is more scathing. Jehoiakim, it appears, had so far forgotten
the welfare of his subjects as to squander his funds building himself a fine new palace, and had, moreover, used conscripted labor
for the purpose. This seemed to Jeremiah inexcusable. Pointing this
spoiled young man to his own father, Josiah, as the model he ought
to have followed, he declared him unfit to rule and predicted for
him an ignominious end. Then, after a poem lamenting the fate
of Jerusalem (vss. 20–23), apparently composed just before the
deportation of 597, chapter xxii concludes with two sayings directed
at the boy-king Jehoiachin (Coniah). The first of these (vss. 24–27,
in prose) was uttered just prior to, and the second (vss. 28–30, in
poetry) just after that king's deportation. They announce, and in a
tone of deepest pity, that Jehoiachin will never return, nor will
any of his descendants ever succeed to David's throne.

The conclusion of the section is in xxiii 1–8 and consists of three
brief oracles having to do with the future of the people, and the
future of the monarchy. The first of these (vss. 1–4), which is in
prose, may well have been uttered, as many believe, in Zedekiah's

reign—though in its present form it seems to presuppose the Exile. The last (vss. 7–8), likewise in prose and telling of Israel's restoration to her land, clearly presupposes the Exile (it appears also in xvi 14–15, where it is out of context). The second saying (vss. 5–6) is in poetry, and announces the future, ideal (Messianic) king of David's line. Although this concept otherwise plays very little part in Jeremiah's thinking, there is no convincing reason for denying this saying to him. Since it contains a play on Zedekiah's name, it must have been uttered during that king's reign (but, on the interpretation, see NOTE on xxiii 5–6).

19. TO THE PROPHETS
(xxiii 9–40)

General Moral Corruption: Involvement of the Clergy

XXIII   9 *To the Prophets*:
   My reason is staggered within me,
      My bones all give way;
   I've become like a man who is drunk,
      Like a person besotted with wine,
   Because of Yahweh—
      Because of his holy words.
10   *[Ah, because of the curse the land is in mourning,
      The steppeland pastures are sear.]
   For the land is full of adulterers,
      Whose conduct is evil,
         Whose might is not right.*
11   "Ah, prophet and priest alike are godless;
      In my very own house I've discovered their crimes
                        —Yahweh's word.
12   And so, they'll find their way to be
      A slippery trail in the dark,
         On which they'll be pushed and will fall;
   For I'll bring disaster upon them,
      The year of their doom—Yahweh's word."

The Prophets, Promoters of Godlessness

13   "In Samaria's prophets
      I saw an offensive thing:
   By Baal they prophesied,
      And led Israel, my people, astray.

a–a The text is in some confusion. See NOTE.

14   But in Jerusalem's prophets
      I've seen a shocking thing:
      Adulterers, living in falsehood,
          They so strengthen the hands of the wicked
              That none of them turns from his wickedness.
      They are all like Sodom to me,
          Its dwellers like Gomorrah."

15 Therefore this is what Yahweh of Hosts has said concerning the prophets:
      "Ah, but I'll feed them with wormwood,
          Give them poison to drink;
      For it is from Jerusalem's prophets
          That godlessness flows into all of the land."

The Marks of a False Prophet

16   This is what Yahweh of Hosts has said:
      "Hearken not to the words of the prophets!*b*
          They do but delude you.
      It's a self-induced vision they utter,
          Not one from the mouth of Yahweh—
17   Saying*c* *d*to scorners of Yahweh's word,*d*
          'All will go well with you';
      And to all those who follow their own stubborn wills,*e*
          'Misfortune will not overtake you.'"

18   But who has stood in Yahweh's council
          And seen—and heard his word?
              Who has carefully marked *f*his word?*f*
19   Look! The storm of Yahweh*g* is unleashed,
          A whirlwind blast;
      It will burst on the head of the wicked.

b Hebrew adds "who prophesy to you," which disturbs the meter. Omit with LXX.
c Heb. "saying continually" (participle and infinitive absolute). But this overloads the meter and is not reflected in LXX. Possibly the two are variant readings.
d–d Hebrew has "to those who despise me, 'Yahweh has said . . .'" (*limᵉna'ᵃṣay dibbēr*). Read *limᵉna'ᵃṣē dᵉbar* with LXX.
e Hebrew adds "they say," which is redundant and metrically disturbing. Omit with LXX (except LXX*B*).
f–f With Qre; (Ktib: "My . . ."); LXX omits "his word." See NOTE.
g Hebrew adds "wrath"; a (correct) gloss or a variant reading.

20   The wrath of Yahweh will not turn back
        Till he's finished, accomplished
            His inmost intents.
        When that day has passed
            You will see this clearly and well.

21   "I sent not these prophets,
            Yet—they ran!
        I spoke not to them,
            Yet—they prophesied!
22   But if they had stood in my council,
            They'd proclaim my words to my people,
        From their wicked way they'd turn them,
            From their evil deeds."

Dreams, and God's Word

23 ʰ"Am I a God who is near—Yahweh's word—
        And not a God far off?ʰ
24   Can anyone hide in some hole,
            And I not see him?—Yahweh's word.
        Am I not the One who fills
            Both heaven and earth?—Yahweh's word.
25 "I have heard what they have said—the prophets who
preach lies in my name, saying, 'I've had a dream! I've had a
dream!' 26 How long is this to go on? Is [my name (?)]ⁱ at all in
the minds of the prophets who preach lies, who are prophets of
their own deluded thinking, 27 whose aim it is, through their
dreams which they tell to one another, to make my people forget my name, just as their fathers forgot my name because of
Baal?
28   "The prophet who has a dream,
            Let him tell his dreamʲ;

ʰ⁻ʰ The text should not be emended. See NOTE.
ⁱ The text is in disorder here, the Heb. sentence lacking a subject. Various
conjectures have been offered: "Is my word . . . ," "Am I . . . ," "How long
shall there be lies . . ." (RSV). See the commentaries for further suggestions.
Although "my name," tentatively supplied with Rudolph, at least fits well
in context (cf. vs. 27), assurance is impossible.
ʲ So LXX; Heb. "a dream."

But he who has my word,
 Let him faithfully speak my word.
What has straw to do with wheat?
 —Word of Yahweh.

29 *k*Is not my word*k* like fire—Yahweh's word—
 Like the hammer that shatters the rock?

30 "Therefore, believe me, I am against the prophets—Yahweh's word—who keep stealing my words from one another. 31 Believe me, I am against the prophets—Yahweh's word—who, using their own speech, put forth what purports to be a prophecy. 32 Believe me, I am against *l*the prophets who preach*l* fraudulent dreams—Yahweh's word—and who, by repeating them, mislead my people with their mendacious claptrap. I never sent them or commissioned them! They are of no benefit to this people whatsoever—Yahweh's word."

The "Burden" of Yahweh

33 "And if this people—or a prophet or a priest—should ask you, 'What is the *maśśāʾ* [that is, the utterance] of Yahweh?' say to them, *m*'You are the *maśśāʾ*'*m* [that is, the burden], and I will cast you off—Yahweh's word.'

34 "As for the prophet or the priest, or whoever it may be, who says, 'The *maśśāʾ* [that is, the "burdensome utterance"] of Yahweh,' I will punish that man and his household. 35 This is what you shall say to one another, among yourselves, 'What answer did Yahweh give?' or, 'What did Yahweh say?' 36 But the expression, 'the burden of Yahweh,' you are *n*never to use again.*n* *o*Should his word, indeed, be a burden*o* to anyone that you so

k–k Heb. "Is not thus [*kōh*] my word." Some emend to *kōweh* ("burning"). But LXX, which omits "thus," seems to read an additional line at the end of vs. 28: "thus are my words"; perhaps "thus" is a relic of this.

l–l "The prophets" is added with LXX; Heb. "those who preach [prophesy]."

m–m Redividing the consonants with LXX: *ʾtm hmśśʾ*. MT has *ʾt mh mśśʾ*, "what burden?"

n–n Pointing the verb Hiphil (*tazkīrū*, "mention") with LXX; MT has Qal ("remember").

o–o Read the interrogative particle (*hᵃ*) before *maśśāʾ* instead of the article (*ha*), with Ehrl. and others. If this is not done, read "for [or: "else"] every man's word will be his own burden."

pervert the words of our God, the living God, Yahweh of Hosts?
37 This is what you shall say to the prophet, 'What answer did
Yahweh give you?' or, 'What did Yahweh say?' 38 And if you
say, 'the burden of Yahweh'—then this is what Yahweh has
said: 'Because you have used this expression, "the burden of
Yahweh," though I sent to tell you not to say, "the burden of
Yahweh," 39 believe me, ᴾI will pick you up indeed and will cast
youᴾ from my presence—you and the city which I have given to
you and your fathers. 40 And I will bring upon you an everlasting disgrace, an everlasting humiliation which will never be forgotten.' "

ᴾ⁻ᴾ MT seems to combine readings: "I will forget [wᵉnāšîtî] you and forsake
you" and "I am going to pick you up [nōśē' (?)] and cast you off" (?).
Read wᵉnāšîtî (i.e., wᵉnāśā'tî) and nāśō' (infinitive absolute). The play on
"burden" continues.

NOTES

xxiii 9. *My reason is staggered.* Literally "my heart is broken" (so
EVV). But this conveys the wrong impression; Jeremiah is not "heartbroken," but extremely disturbed in mind, upset, shocked.
10. Hebrew reads the bracketed words after, "For the land is full
of adulterers"; but this breaks the connection between these words and
the ensuing cola. LXX (which reads, "Because of these . . .": 'ēlleh for
'ālāh) begins the verse with the bracketed words, and omits, "For the
land is full of adulterers." The bracketed words may have intruded from
another context; or lines have been transposed (and perhaps words lost).
11. *In my very own house.* Yahweh is now the speaker. The clergy
have polluted the temple, apparently with pagan and immoral rites (cf.
II Kings xxiii 7; cf. xxi 4 f., 7).
12. *A slippery trail.* Literally "Like slippery places" (i.e., on a path);
cf. Ps xxxv 6.
13. The prophets of northern Israel, who are declared to have been
apostate (a statement with which Jeremiah's hearers would have agreed),
are mentioned only to point up the enormity of the conduct of Jerusalem's
prophets, who (vs. 14) are said to be even worse.
14. *Adulterers, living in falsehood.* Literally "committing adultery and
walking in the lie [lies]." Reference is probably not to apostasy and
idolatry, though both "adultery" and "the lie" can have this connotation;
were this the meaning, the contrast with Samaria's prophets would lose

its point, for this is what the latter have been charged with. Adultery is here literal immorality (cf. xxix 23), while "walking in lies" refers to the lie of unconditional divine protection to which they are committed (cf. vs. 17; xiv 14). Since the spiritual leaders did not urge repentance, and were themselves immoral, naturally no one else repented.

Its dwellers. Literally "her . . ."; the unexpressed antecedent must be Jerusalem.

16. *self-induced vision:* Literally "a vision of their (own) heart," i.e., one originating in their own minds.

18. *who has stood in Yahweh's council.* I.e., the heavenly court. The prophet was conceived of as being present there, hearing Yahweh's word and reporting it to the people (cf. Isa vi). Many scholars, taking this as a rhetorical question (which would, by its form, demand the answer, "no one"), find it in contradiction to vs. 22, where the false prophets are taxed with not having been in Yahweh's council; they therefore regard vs. 18 as a gloss in the spirit of Job xv 8, etc., asserting that no one can know Yahweh's council. Others retain the verse by adding *mēhem* and reading "Which of them (i.e., of these prophets) has stood . . ." (so RSV); the negative answer implied ("none of them has") then agrees with vs. 22. Probably, however, the question is not rhetorical at all, but has the sense: Who is it that has stood in Yahweh's council? How can you tell him? So understood, vs. 18 leads directly into vss. 19–20, where it is implied that the one who has been in Yahweh's council would know that Yahweh's word for the moment is one of judgment, not of peace.

And seen—and heard his word. Literally "that he might see (what went on there) and hear. . . ."

carefully marked his word. Literally "has paid attention to his word and heard." Emendation is unnecessary.

19–20. These verses are repeated at xxx 23–24 with small variations, and are regarded by many as an intrusion here. But they are actually out of context in chapter xxx, while they fit splendidly after vs. 18 (see above), stressing as they do the word that was really spoken in Yahweh's council, which the false prophets had not heard because they were not present.

20. *When that day has passed.* Literally "at the end of days." But this is probably not here intended in an eschatological sense, but merely with the force of "afterward," "when it is over."

23. The question is rhetorical, like the two that follow (vs. 24), and demands a negative answer. But the meaning is not that God is far away and unaware of the doings of his creatures; this would contradict both vs. 24 and the Hebrew understanding of God in general. The sense is, rather, that God is no small local deity from whom one might conceivably hide, but a God who is in heaven and therefore sees all. A

similar thought is found (cf. Rudolph) in the fourteenth-century B.C. Hymn to Aten, from Egypt: "Thou hast made the distant sky in order to rise therein, in order to see all that thou dost make" (translation of J. A. Wilson in ANET, p. 371).

24. *in some hole.* Literally: "in the secret places."

26. *who are prophets of their own deluded thinking.* Literally: ". . . of the deceit of their heart (i.e., mind)." Perhaps point *wenibbe'ē* for *ūnebī'ē*, and translate "who prophesy. . . ."

27. *my name.* I.e., my essential character, who I am (cf. vs. 26).

28. So far as we know, the classical prophets never received divine revelation through dreams (as contrasted to visionary experiences). Jeremiah clearly regarded dreams as subjective experiences having nothing to do with Yahweh's word. Here he speaks ironically: If you have a dream, tell it if you wish. But make it quite clear that it *is* a dream. Do not put it forth as Yahweh's word.

30. *stealing my words.* This is bitter irony: the prophets, having received no word, repeat what they have heard others say as if this had come to them by direct revelation from Yahweh.

31. The force of the wordplay cannot be caught without paraphrase: literally "who take [use] their [own] tongue and 'oracle an oracle' [*yin'amū ne'um*]." The *ne'um yhwh* ("utterance of Yahweh") is a characteristic formula indicating the prophetic oracle; we have consistently rendered it "Yahweh's word." The verb occurs only here, and one wonders if Jeremiah did not simply coin the verb from the noun. The sense is that the prophets' message originates with them and is couched in their words; but they deliver it in the form of prophetic address and thus convey the impression that it is an oracle from Yahweh. It is their own word, but "they word it, 'Yahweh's word.'"

32. *their mendacious claptrap.* Literally "their lies and their *paḥazūt*"— which has the force of "loose talk," "exaggerated, boastful tales," or the like.

33. The point hinges on a pun on the word *maśśā'.* This word, which derives from the root *nś'* ("to lift up"), may on the one hand have the force of a lifting up of the voice, thus of a "prophetic utterance," and on the other hand of a thing physically to be lifted up, a "burden." The *maśśā'* of Yahweh is that the people are a *maśśā'.* In vss. 34–40 the wordplay is developed in a slightly different direction. It appears that some have been using the word sarcastically, in the sense that Yahweh's utterance is a burden to them; they are therefore forbidden to use the word at all.

COMMENT

Like the preceding section, xxiii 9–40 is a complex of originally separate sayings, in poetry and in prose, which have been brought together because of their common theme. This theme, again as is the case in the preceding section, is stated in the heading (vs. 9): "To the Prophets." No one can have read this far in the Jeremiah book without having observed many unmistakable hints that, of all the classes of people in contemporary Judah, there were few with whom Jeremiah was more irreconcilably at odds than with those who, like himself, bore the title "prophet." In the biographical chapters that follow we will find him on more than one occasion in head-on collision with them. This section, however, is of especial interest in that it provides us with what is probably the classic expression of his hostility to these prophets—who, in his view, were false prophets—and also lets us see, perhaps more clearly than elsewhere, something of his reasons for it.

Actually, not all of the sayings in this collection concern the prophets directly. The poem in vss. 9–12, which consists of a brief soliloquy of Jeremiah expressing shock at the moral corruption to be observed everywhere, followed by an oracle announcing the judgment, concerns the prophets only insofar as it is indicated (vs. 11) that they, like the priests, share in this corruption. Some scholars (Volz, Rudolph) would place this piece in the very earliest period of Jeremiah's activity. The concluding piece in the collection (vss. 33–40), in prose, likewise mentions the prophets only in passing and has to do, rather, with the reception of the divine word. There is no reason to doubt the genuineness of the nucleus of this piece (in vs. 33), the point of which revolves about a pun on the word *maśśā'* (see NOTE). This nucleus has, however, been expanded (in vss. 34–40) by an extended commentary, which is rather diffuse and not altogether to the original point.

The sayings in vss. 13–32, however, do deal directly with the prophets, and are exceedingly interesting. The first of these (vss. 13–15) is a poem in oracular style. Here it is alleged that the prophets of Jerusalem have by their licentious behavior and lying words positively contributed to the breakdown of national morality and have, through this, shown themselves to be far worse than

the prophets of the defunct northern state, who were overtly apostate. The next piece (vss. 16–22), likewise in poetry (though in
vss. 16–17 the text has been expanded and the meter obscured),
begins and ends in oracular style, with a monologue of Jeremiah
between (vss. 18–20). The point of this piece, no part of which
is to be deleted as secondary (see NOTES) is: How can one tell
that these prophets who lull the people with promises of peace are
false prophets? The answer, in brief, is that Yahweh's word *for
this moment* is one of judgment, and if these fellows had really
stood in the heavenly council and heard its deliberations (as prophets were supposed to do), they would know this, and would attempt
to bring the people to repentance. The fact that they preach only
soothing words, proves that they were never sent by Yahweh at
all.

A final piece (vss. 23–32), basically in prose but with snatches
of poetry, is likewise illuminating. Here Jeremiah assails the prophets for putting forth their own words as Yahweh's word. Specifically,
he charges them with repeating at second hand what they had heard
others say, while pretending that this had come to them as a revelation from Yahweh; with concocting a message of their own and
then, by proclaiming it in the form of prophetic address, conveying
the impression that it was actually an oracle from Yahweh; and,
finally, with the bandying of dreams, and airy speculations of their
own, as the word of Yahweh, thereby leading the people into error.

None of the above sayings can be dated with precision. Since it
was, however, especially in the days of Zedekiah (cf. chs. xxvii–
xxix) that tension with the prophets reached its pitch, it may be
that most of them are best understood against the background of
that king's reign.

20. CONCLUSION OF THE FIRST BOOK OF JEREMIAH'S PROPHECIES
(xxv 1–38)

A Summarizing Discourse

XXV 1 The word that came to Jeremiah concerning the entire people of Judah in the fourth year of Jehoiakim ben Josiah, king of Judah (that is, in the first year of Nebuchadrezzar, king of Babylon), 2 which word *he then spoke* to all the people of Judah and all the citizens of Jerusalem: 3*b* "From the thirteenth year of Josiah ben Amon, king of Judah, until today—now all of twenty-three years—the word of Yahweh has come to me, and I have spoken to you incessantly and earnestly. But you have not listened. 4*c* Moreover, Yahweh sent to you, persistently and without interruption, all his servants the prophets, who, although you never listened or paid the slightest attention, 5 said, 'Turn, now, every one of you from his evil conduct and wicked deeds, and dwell in the land which Yahweh has given to you and to your fathers of old for all time to come. 6 Do not follow other gods, to worship them and do obeisance to them! Do not

---

a–a So LXX. Heb. "Jeremiah the prophet spoke," which secures what is to our taste unnecessary clarity.

b LXX omits "the word of Yahweh has come to me," and "But you have not listened." LXX takes Yahweh as the speaker ("I") through the whole of vss. 3–7.

c The verse, virtually the same as vii 25b, 26a, can be made to fit smoothly before vs. 5 only with forcing, and is, perhaps, an expansion. If one omits the last sentence of vs. 3 (so LXX), together with vss. 4, 6, and 7b (beginning with "Yahweh's word"; see textual note*e*), a consistent address by Jeremiah remains. But one cannot arrive at *ipsissima verba* in this material by such means. LXX (see textual note*b*) makes Yahweh the speaker throughout ("I sent," etc.); but the roughness is not removed.

provoke me with your manufactured gods, *a*to your own hurt!'*a*
7 But you would not listen to me—Yahweh's word.*e*

8 "Therefore, this is what Yahweh of Hosts has said: Because
you have not listened to what I said, 9 believe me, I am going to
send and get *f*all the peoples of the north*f*—*g*Yahweh's word*g*—
[that is, for Nebuchadrezzar, king of Babylon, my servant] and
I will bring them against this country and its citizens, and
against *h*all the surrounding nations*h* as well. I will devote them
to wholesale destruction. I will make them a horrible and shocking spectacle, and an everlasting reproach.*i* 10 I will banish from
among them sounds of mirth and gladness, the voice of bridegroom and bride, the sound of the hand mill, and the light of
the lamp. 11 *j*The whole land shall be an awesome waste,*j* and
*k*these nations shall serve the king of Babylon*k* for seventy years.

12 "Then, when seventy years have passed, I will punish [the
king of Babylon and] that nation [—Yahweh's word—for their
iniquity—that is, the land of the Chaldeans] and will make it
a desolation forever. 13 I will bring upon that land all the things
with which I have threatened it, that is, all that is written in
this book which Jeremiah prophesied against all the nations.
14 [Yes, many nations and great kings will make slaves of them,
for I will repay them according to their deeds, according to what
they have done]."

d–d Heb. "And I will do you no hurt" (*weˡōˀ ˀāraˁ*). But probably read *leraˁ*
(cf. LXX and following note).
e LXX omits (as frequently elsewhere) "Yahweh's word," and also (correctly)
the rest of the verse, which in Hebrew reads "in order to provoke me with
the work of your hands, to your hurt"—apparently a misplaced variant of
vs. 6b.
f–f LXX reads, "a family from the north."
g–g LXX again omits, and also the bracketed words that follow. These are
syntactically awkward, and are probably a gloss to indicate that the prophecy
was actually fulfilled by Nebuchadnezzar.
h–h So LXX. Heb. "all these. . . ."
i So with LXX (*ḥerpāh*). Hebrew reads "desolations" (*ḥārebōt*).
j–j So LXX. Heb. "This whole land shall be a desolation and an awesome
waste."
k–k LXX reads, "they shall serve among the nations."

The Divine Judgment on the Nations of the World

15 This is what Yahweh, the God of Israel, said to me: "Take from my hand ʲthis cup of the wine of wrathʲ and make all the nations to which I shall send you drink it. 16 They will drink and stagger and go out of their heads—because of the sword that I am going to send among them."

17 So I took the cup from Yahweh's hand and made all the nations to which he sent me drink it: 18 Jerusalem and the cities of Judah, together with its rulers and nobles—making them a desolation, a horrible and shocking sight, and a curse, as they now in fact are; 19 Pharaoh king of Egypt, his officials and nobles and all his people, 20 together with the whole hodgepodge of races there; ᵐall the kings of the land of Uzᵐ; all the kings of the land of the Philistines, that is, Ashkelon, Gaza, Ekron, and what remains of Ashdod; 21 Edom, Moab, and the Ammonites; 22 all the kings of Tyre and of Sidon, as well as the kings of the coastlands beyond the sea; 23 Dedan, Tema, and Buz, and all those who clip the hair of their temples, 24 [that is, all the kings of Arabia, all the kings of the mixed peoples]ⁿ who live in the desert; 25 ᵒall the kings of Zimri,ᵒ all the kings of Elam, all the kings of the Medes; 26 all the kings of the north, both far and near, one after the other—in short, all the kingdomsᵖ on the face of the earth. And the king of "Sheshak" (and you know who *that* is!) will drink last of all.

27 "Then say to them, 'This is what Yahweh of Hosts, the God of Israel, has said: Drink till you're drunk and vomit, till you fall to rise no more—because of the sword that I am going to send among you.' 28 And if, perchance, they should refuse to

ˡ⁻ˡ Heb. "this cup of wine, wrath." Read *yēn* for *hayyayin* (Syr., Vulg.). But possibly "this cup of wine / this cup of wrath" are variants.

ᵐ⁻ᵐ LXX omits. This would fit better in vs. 21 or vs. 23 f.

ⁿ The two readings in brackets are identical in an unpointed text and probably variants; LXX has only the second. But probably both are glosses on the last clause of vs. 23, to which "who live in the desert" is to be joined, as in ix 25[26E].

ᵒ⁻ᵒ LXX omits. See NOTE.

ᵖ Hebrew adds here "of the earth" (LXX omits); "kingdoms of the earth," and "kingdoms on the face of the earth" are variants.

accept the cup from your hand and drink, then say to them,
'This is what Yahweh of Hosts has said: You have to drink it!
29 For look! It is at the very city that bears my name that I begin my catastrophic work—and do you think that you will be
let off scot-free? You certainly will not be let off! For I am calling the sword against all the inhabitants of the earth—word of
Yahweh of Hosts.'

30 "As for you, you are to prophesy all these things to them.
Say to them:
> 'It's Yahweh who roars from on high,
>   From his holy abode lets his voice thunder forth;
> Loud sounds his roar 'gainst his fold,
>   Ringing out like the grape-treader's shout;
> To all the earth's dwellers the tumult resounds,
31   To the ends of the earth.
> For Yahweh has indicted the nations,
>   Is about to judge all flesh;
> The wicked he'll give to the sword—
>   Word of Yahweh.' "

32   This is what Yahweh of Hosts has said:
> "Ah look! Disaster proceeding
>   From nation to nation,
> A great tempest churning
>   From the earth's farthest bounds.

33 [Those slain by Yahweh on that day will reach from one
end of the earth to the other. They will not be lamented, or
collected, or buried, but will be like so much dung to fertilize
the soil.]

34   Howl, you shepherds! Cry!
>   Wallow, you lords of the flock!
> For the time of your slaughter has come;
>   ᵃDown you'll go like the pick of the rams.ᵃ

ᵃ⁻ᵃ The text is in some disorder. Hebrew begins the colon with an unintelligible
word (*ūtepōṣōṭīkem*), which LXX omits; possibly it conceals some form of
pṣṣ or *npṣ* (both meaning "to shatter"). "Like . . . rams" follows LXX
(*keʾēlē*); Hebrew has "like . . . a vessel" (*kikelī*). Probably "I will shatter
you (?) like a choice vessel" and "you shall fall like choice rams" are variants; but the latter fits here.

35   No flight will there be for the shepherds,
        Nor escape for the lords of the flock.
36   Hark! The cry of the shepherds,
        The howl of the lords of the flock!
     For Yahweh despoils their pasture,
37   The peaceful folds lie silent.[r]
38   Like a lion he's quitted his thicket;
        Ah, their land has become a shambles,
     [s]Before the dreadful sword,[s]
     Before his blazing anger."

[r] Hebrew has a second colon: "because of Yahweh's hot anger." This virtually duplicates the last colon of vs. 38 where (although LXX omits it there) it fits better. It is probably a dittography here.
[s–s] "Sword" follows various manuscripts and Vrs. (cf. also xlvi 16; l 16); MT "anger" is a dittography from the next colon.

NOTES

xxv 1. The words in parentheses are omitted by LXX and may be a gloss, but a correct one. Although Nebuchadnezzar's first official regnal year began in April 604 (at the New Year), he actually took the throne in September 605. The spelling "Nebuchadrezzar," though less familiar to us, represents the king's name (Nabu-kudurri-uṣur) more accurately; this spelling is usually followed in Jeremiah.

6. *with your manufactured gods*. Literally "with the work of your hands"; possibly "by what you do" (as in vs. 14), but in this context probably idols, as in i 16.

9. *all the peoples of the north*. The word *mišpᵉḥōt* ("families," "clans"), properly a subunit of a tribe, i.e., a clan, seems here, as elsewhere, to denote a political subunit. See textual note[ʲ–ʲ].

I will devote them to wholesale destruction. "I will put them to the *ḥerem*," i.e., devotion of an entire population to sacrificial destruction, as *passim* in Joshua.

11. *seventy years*. This seems to be here no more than a round number (i.e., a normal life-span). In Zech i 12 it seems to refer to the interval between the destruction of the temple in 587 and its rebuilding in 520–515. In II Chron xxxvi 20–23 it is made to refer to the period between 587 and Cyrus' edict in 538 (appreciably less than seventy years). But see NOTE on xxix 10.

12–14. On the probable expansion of the original address here, see

COMMENT. Probably only vs. 13a, "I will bring upon 'this' land all the things with which I have threatened it, that is, all that is written in this book," belongs to the original address.

15. *this cup of the wine of wrath*. See textual note*l-l*. The origin of the figure is uncertain. It may lie (Weiser) in an old sacral tradition having to do with passing judgment (Ps lxxv 8 f.[7 f.E]), perhaps in the practice of ordeal (cf. Num v 11–31), which required a person suspected of crime to drink a noxious potion, with disastrous results to him if guilty. Or is it merely a "knockout drop" given to a person marked for execution to render him incapable of struggle?

16. *because of the sword*. . . . Commentators regard this clause as an intrusion from vs. 27. To omit would be an improvement, but textual evidence is lacking.

17. *he sent*. So for smoothness. Heb. "Yahweh sent."

18. *making them*. I.e., Jerusalem and the cities of Judah. But the whole clause dangles and may be an addition (LXX omits "and a curse . . . in fact are"). Indeed, the entire verse may be an addition on the basis of vss. 1–14, since the section is directed at foreign nations, not Judah.

20. *all the kings of the land of Uz*. Uz, the home of Job (Job i 1), apparently lay somewhere along the eastern fringes of Transjordan; in Lam iv 21 it is connected with Edom. See textual note*m-m*.

what remains of Ashdod. According to Herodotus (II, 157) Ashdod was taken and destroyed by Psammetichus I (663–609) of Egypt.

22. Phoenicia (Tyre and Sidon) and its colonies overseas.

23. Cf. ix 25[26E]. These are tribes of the north-Arabian desert; cf. textual note*n*.

25. *all the kings of Zimri*. Zimri is unknown; some believe it an error for "Zimki," which could be an *Atbash* (see NOTE on vs. 26) for Elam.

26. *the king of "Sheshak."* The words in parentheses seek to convey the fact that "Sheshak" is an *Atbash* for Babylon—i.e., a cipher by which letters of one name, counted from the beginning of the alphabet, are exchanged for corresponding letters counted from the end. Thus *bbl* (Babylon) corresponds to *ššk* (Sheshak). Use of such a device points to the period prior to the fall of Babylon (in 539), for after that time no one would have troubled to refer to Babylon in so veiled a manner. LXX omits the whole sentence.

29. *begin my catastrophic work*. Literally "begin to work evil [calamity]."

30. *on high . . . holy abode*. In this context, heaven. But the expression derives from the mythical abode of the gods on a high mountain in the far north (so in the Ras Shamra texts; cf. Isa xiv 13 f., etc.). But in the very similar passages in Amos i 2; Joel iv 16[iii 16E], Yahweh roars from his abode in Zion.

the tumult resounds. The words belong with vs. 30 (cf. LXX); in Hebrew they begin vs. 31.

33. The verse is a prose expansion, interrupting the connection between vss. 32 and 34.

34. *shepherds.* Of course, the kings of the nations.

38. *Before the dreadful sword.* Literally "Before the oppressing sword." See textual note[s-s].

his blazing anger. Or, "Yahweh's . . . ," as at the end of vs. 37 in MT (cf. textual note[s-s]).

COMMENT

Chapter xxv falls into two clearly separate parts. In vss. 1–14 there is a discourse in the characteristic style of the Jeremiah prose, which is dated in the fourth year of Jehoiakim's reign (605). This was, of course, the year in which Jeremiah dictated to Baruch the scroll which was later read before the king (cf. ch. xxxvi). Although the king destroyed this scroll, it was subsequently recreated and became, apparently, the nucleus of the earliest collection of Jeremiah's prophecies. The present piece, which reaches back to and resumes certain of the themes sounded in the account of Jeremiah's call (for example, the "Foe from the North," there threatened, is here realized in Nebuchadnezzar: cf. vs. 9 and i 15 f.), seems to have been composed as the conclusion of that collection. Some scholars (e.g., Weiser) even believe that it was the conclusion of the original scroll, or perhaps a prefatory speech composed to accompany the reading of it (e.g., Volz).

As it now stands, this discourse threatens Judah with destruction at the hands of Babylon, and then declares that after seventy years Babylon will itself be judged. But the discourse has had a complicated history of transmission, and scarcely lies before us in its original form. This is evident both from the differences between MT and LXX, which are marked, and from the fact that the syntax is in places so awkward that a smooth translation can be achieved only with some forcing. Verses 12–14 are especially interesting in this connection. As was pointed out in the Introduction, LXX, which offers a considerably shorter text throughout, omits all direct mention of Nebuchadnezzar and Babylon in vs. 12—as it has in the preceding verses as well (vss. 1, 9, 11)—and ends the discourse with vs. 13a ("all that is written in this book"); it then inserts in place of vs. 14, which it omits, the whole of chapters xlvi–li (in a different order). From this it appears (cf. LXX) that vs. 13b ("[that] which Jeremiah prophesied against all the nations") was originally the heading of vss. 15–38, rather than the conclusion of the discourse described above. Nevertheless, it is most improbable that LXX is to be thought of as representing the original form of the text, although it may in general come closer to it than does MT. The original address was presumably much briefer, and concerned exclusively with warning Judah of the ruin and exile shortly to overtake her because of her failure to heed the prophetic word. Thus the nation threatened in vs. 13 was originally Judah, while "this book" was the scroll of Jeremiah's prophecies (whether in its original or recreated form) now underlying chapters i–xxv. Later the address was verbally expanded and, with the attachment to it of the prophecies against foreign nations (vss. 15–38 in MT, this plus chs. xlvi–li in LXX), so adapted as to include the promise that "after seventy years" Babylon would in turn be punished. As this was done, the country threatened in vs. 13 became Babylon, and "this book" the collection of sayings against the nations that follows in vss. 15–38 (and chs. xlvi–li in LXX).

But, although one may be confident that some such process was at work, and may even detect sentences or clauses here and there (see the NOTES) that seem clearly to be expansions, the text of the original discourse cannot be reconstructed with anything resembling assurance. What has been said regarding the nature of these prose discourses in general (cf. Introduction, "The Book of Jeremiah . . .") must be borne in mind. Though they may be assumed to rest upon the prophet's words, they do not—at least, not consistently—provide us with a *verbatim* report. Therefore, any attempt to recover from them the *ipsissima verba* by removing what one believes to be expansions is a fruitless endeavor. The translation, for this reason, seeks merely to reproduce as smoothly as possible the text of the discourse in its present form, with suggestions regarding its possible original form left for the most part to the NOTES.

The second part of the chapter (vss. 15–38) is concerned with Yahweh's judgment on the nations of the world. It consists of a piece in prose (vss. 15–29), couched in the form of an address by Yahweh to the prophet, in which the judgment is likened to a stupefying draught which the nations must drink. Following this, and editorially joined to it (vs. 30a), are two poetic pieces (vss. 30–31, 32–38) further developing and explaining the above theme. It is probable that this whole portion was attached relatively early to the preceding collection of Jeremiah's prophecies, as a sort of appendix. The relationship of the material to Jeremiah is disputed. But one should not too hastily deny it to him outright, as some are inclined to do. The very fact that he was commissioned as "a prophet to the nations" (i 5) would lead one to expect that some of his sayings —as had been the case with most of the prophets since Amos— would concern peoples other than Israel. As for the prose piece (vss. 15–29), although the list of peoples in vss. 18–26 has doubtless received expansion (but one would expect a list of some sort here!), the prophecy itself may be credited to Jeremiah. Indeed, the figure of "the cup of wrath" (cf. Ezek xxiii 32–34; Isa li 17, 21 f.) is first clearly witnessed in sayings and writings of this general period (cf. xiii 12–14; Hab ii 16; Lam iv 21) and may well have been popularized by him and his followers. The prophecy is certainly not later than ca. the mid-sixth century: Persia is not mentioned, and Babylon (vs. 26) is the ruling power of the world. As regards the poetry, some of it is composed of conventional expressions (e.g., vs. 30 f.) and may be of anonymous origin; but some of it (the poem in vss. 32, 34–38), though it cannot be proved to come from Jeremiah, is at least fully worthy of him.

II. INCIDENTS FROM THE LIFE OF JEREMIAH

21. THE "TEMPLE SERMON";
JEREMIAH NARROWLY ESCAPES DEATH
(xxvi 1–19; 24; 20–23)

XXVI 1 In the accession year of Jehoiakim ben Josiah, king of Judah, there came this word from Yahweh *to Jeremiah*: 2 "This is what Yahweh has said: Stand in the court of Yahweh's house, and speak to the people who come from all the cities of Judah to worship in Yahweh's house, saying to them everything that I have told you to say. Do not omit a word! 3 Perhaps they will listen, and will turn one and all from their wicked behavior; then I might think better of the disaster that I had planned to bring upon them because of their evil deeds. 4 Say to them, 'This is what Yahweh has said: If you will not listen to me, and conduct yourselves according to my law which I have set before you, 5 obeying the words of my servants the prophets whom with urgency and persistence I keep sending to you (a thing that you have never done!), 6 then I will make this house like Shiloh, and this city*b* a curse word to all the nations of the earth.'"

7 Now the priests, the prophets, and all the people heard Jeremiah utter these words there in Yahweh's house. 8 And as soon as Jeremiah had finished saying all that Yahweh had told him to say to all the people, the priests and the prophets*c* seized him, crying, "For this you must die! 9 Why have you prophesied in Yahweh's name, saying that this house will be destroyed just as Shiloh was, and this city left an uninhabited ruin?" And all the people thronged about Jeremiah there in the house of Yahweh.

10 But the princes of Judah heard of all this, and came up from the royal palace to Yahweh's house, and took their seats

---

a-a Not in Heb. but added for clarity with Lat., Syr. (and cf. xxvii 1).
b Hebrew repeats "I will make."
c Hebrew adds "and all the people." See NOTE.

at the entry of ^dthe New Gate of Yahweh's house.^d 11 Then the priests and the prophets said to the princes and to all the people, "A death sentence for this man! For he has prophesied against this city, as you have heard with your own ears."

12 Then Jeremiah addressed the princes^e and all the people, as follows: "It was Yahweh who sent me to prophesy against this house and this city all the things that you have heard me say. 13 Now therefore, reform your whole manner of living and heed the voice of Yahweh your God, so that Yahweh may think better of the disaster with which he has threatened you. 14 As for myself, I am of course in your power. Do to me whatever seems to you right and proper. 15 Nevertheless, make no mistake about it—if you go on and put me to death, you will be bringing innocent blood upon yourselves, upon this city, and upon its inhabitants. For Yahweh did in truth send me to you to say all these things in your hearing."

16 Then the princes and all the people said to the priests and the prophets, "There will be no death sentence for *this* man! For it is in the name of Yahweh our God that he has spoken to us." 17 Also, certain of the elders of the land stood up and addressed the whole assembled crowd, as follows: 18 "There was Micah of Moresheth who used to prophesy in the days of Hezekiah, king of Judah; and he said to all the people of Judah, 'This is what Yahweh of Hosts has said:

Zion shall become a plowed field,
    Jerusalem a heap of rubble,
        And the temple mount ^fa wooded ridge.'^f

19 Did Hezekiah, king of Judah—or, for that matter, anyone in Judah—make any move to kill him? Did they not rather fear Yahweh and seek to appease him; and did not Yahweh then think better of the calamity with which he had threatened them? Nay, we are on the point of doing ourselves a mortal injury!"

^{d–d} Heb. "the new gate of Yahweh"; "house" is restored with various manuscripts, Vrs., and xxxvi 10.
^e So LXX; Heb. "all the princes."
^{f–f} Read singular (cf. LXX, which reads "grove"); Hebrew points as plural.

24 Still, it was only the fact that Ahikam ben Shaphan lent his support to Jeremiah that prevented his being handed over to the people to be put to death.

20 There was, indeed, another man who had uttered prophecies in the name of Yahweh, Uriah ben Shemaiah, from Kiriath-jearim. He prophesied against this city and this country exactly as Jeremiah had done. 21 And when King Jehoiakim, together with all his officers and all the princes, heard what he had said, the king sought to kill him. But Uriah heard of it and, fleeing in terror, escaped to Egypt. 22 King Jehoiakim, however, sent *g*Elnathan ben Achbor*g* with a company of men to Egypt. 23 These extradited Uriah from Egypt and brought him to King Jehoiakim, who had him put to the sword and given a dishonorable burial.

g–g LXX (which has various unimportant omissions in vss. 20–23) omits these words and to the end of the verse. But both LXX and MT read just before this "[sent] men to Egypt." Perhaps this is the original reading, and the rest a correct gloss by MT; or perhaps MT has combined variants. But both readings cannot be original.

NOTES

xxvi 1. *the accession year of Jehoiakim.* The expression *rē'šīt mamlᵉkūt* does not mean vaguely "in the beginning of the reign" (EVV), but corresponds to Akk. *rēš šarrūti,* a technical term for the period between a king's accession and the following New Year, from which his first regnal year was counted: in this case between ca. September 609 and April 608.

2. *the people who come from all the cities of Judah.* Literally "all the cities of Judah which come" (cf. xi 12).

Do not omit a word. Jeremiah, who must have realized the hostility his words would arouse, and the possible consequences to himself, may well have been tempted to do this.

5. *a thing that you have never done.* Literally "but you did not listen"; the words must be taken as a parenthesis.

8. *the priests and the prophets.* Hebrew adds "and all the people." Though there is no textual evidence for omitting the words, they seem to be drawn in from vs. 7. It appears from vs. 9b that the people crowd upon Jeremiah when incited by the clergy; cf. also vs. 11. If

the words are retained, they are not to be taken literally, but in the sense of "various of the people."

For this you must die. Literally "you shall surely die." The expression (*mōt tāmūt*) recalls the formula *mōt yūmat* used in legal contexts to state the death penalty for certain offenses (e.g., *passim* in Exod xxi-xxiii), and perhaps represents the words actually used by the judge in pronouncing sentence of death. From the speakers' point of view, Jeremiah deserved such a sentence.

9. *will be destroyed just as Shiloh was.* Literally "will be like Shiloh." Shiloh was destroyed sometime after 1050 B.C. by the Philistines; cf. NOTE on vii 12.

thronged about Jeremiah. Or "crowded upon. . . ." The verb (*qhl*) usually refers to formal assembling for religious purposes, but also for war (II Sam xx 14), and even to the gathering of a crowd with hostile intent (e.g., Num xvi 3; xvii 7 [xvi 42E]). One gains the impression that Jeremiah was about to be lynched, but that the clergy wished his execution to be given the form of legality.

10. It is not clear whether the princes heard the commotion and hastened to investigate (the palace adjoined the temple), or whether someone ran to inform them. In any case, they seem to have arrived almost at once and constituted themselves as the court.

18. *Micah of Moresheth.* Cf. Mic i 1. The verse quotes Mic iii 12.
Zion shall become a plowed field. Literally ". . . shall be plowed like a field."

19. *or . . . anyone in Judah.* Literally "or all Judah."
Did they not rather fear. Reading this verb and the next plural for smoothness (so LXX). But Heb. singular takes Hezekiah as the official representative of the people.

seek to appease him. So for smoothness; Heb. ". . . appease Yahweh." The expression "seek to appease" is literally "soften (smooth) the countenance" (perhaps even more literally, "pat the cheek"). The anthropomorphism doubtless originated in Israel's pagan environment, perhaps in some ceremony involving the god's image. Here, however, the literal force has been lost.

24. *Ahikam . . . lent his support to Jeremiah.* Literally "the hand of Ahikam was with Jeremiah." Since vss. 20–23 are a parenthesis (see COMMENT), vs. 24 is to be read here. One gains the impression that but for Ahikam not even the support of the princes would have sufficed to save Jeremiah from the crowd.

20–23. Nothing further is known of Uriah. One wonders how many lesser men in Judah shared Jeremiah's feelings and spoke as he did. Not many, perhaps—but some!

21. *all his officers.* Here military officers (*gibbōrīm*).

22. *Elnathan ben Achbor.* On Elnathan, who in chapter xxxvi appears as friendly to Jeremiah, see COMMENT on Sec. 23. Incidentally, the name Achbor (ben) Ahikam has recently turned up on a seventh-century seal of unknown provenance; cf. N. Avigad, IEJ 13 (1963) 322 f. This is, of course, not the same Achbor as the one mentioned here.

23. *These extradited.* Heb. "brought out"; but they scarcely kidnaped Uriah. Since Jehoiakim was at the time the pharaoh's vassal, formal requests for extradition would have been honored routinely.

given a dishonorable burial. Literally "cast his corpse into the graves of the sons of the people"—i.e., the common burial ground (in the Kidron Valley: II Kings xxiii 6).

COMMENT

The incident described in this chapter took place in the accession year of Jehoiakim—that is to say (see NOTE on vs. 1), at some time between that king's elevation to the throne upon the deportation of his brother Jehoahaz, in the autumn (or late summer) of 609, and the following New Year (April 608), from which his first regnal year was counted. It is, therefore, chronologically the first of the accounts which Jeremiah's biographer has left us.

The chapter is for the most part straightforward narrative, with discourse held to a minimum. It opens (vss. 2–6) with the account of an address delivered by Jeremiah in the temple, in which he declared that if the people did not sincerely mend their ways the temple would be destroyed just as the ancient shrine at Shiloh had been. As is all but universally agreed, this address is the same as that already encountered in more extended form in vii 2–15, often referred to as the "Temple Sermon." The Biographer here gives the barest summary of this address, including just enough to support his narrative. He then goes on to tell how, when Jeremiah had finished, he was seized by certain of the clergy who, before a large and hostile crowd of people, demanded his execution (vss. 7–9); how certain of the princes stepped in, took charge of the situation and, having given Jeremiah a fair hearing, found him guilty of no crime (vss. 10–19); and how, finally (vs. 24), the issue apparently still hanging in the balance, it was through the intervention of Ahikam ben Shaphan—a man of the highest rank who had

been a protagonist of Josiah's reform and was perhaps the son of
that king's secretary of state (II Kings xxii 12)—that Jeremiah's
life was saved.

The account of the execution of the prophet Uriah (vss. 20–23)
is, however, a parenthesis within this narrative. It is not to be taken
as a part of the argument in Jeremiah's defense (vss. 16–19),
which it would tend to contradict, nor is it presented as an argument of his accusers. We do not, in fact, know that the execution of
Uriah had even taken place at the time of the incident described in
this chapter; since this last occurred in the very first months of
Jehoiakim's reign, in all likelihood it had not. The story of Uriah,
therefore, probably has nothing directly to do with Jeremiah's trial,
but was inserted at this place merely as an illustration of what might
well have happened to Jeremiah, had not the princes had the courage to intervene.

One must say that the conduct of these princes certainly reflects
credit upon them, and warns us against accepting Jeremiah's pessimistic evaluation of his people (e.g., v 1–5; ix 1–8) without quali-
fication. There *were* good men in Judah! At the same time, we
ought not to dismiss Jeremiah's opponents—though little good can
be said of them—merely as vicious and contemptible men who
could not bear to hear the truth. It must be remembered that Jeremiah, in speaking as he had, had contradicted a cardinal dogma of
the official state religion, namely, that Yahweh had chosen the temple
as his eternal abode and would, therefore, allow no harm to befall
it or the city in which it stood (see NOTES on vii 2–15). What is
more, Jeremiah had said what he had said in the name of Yahweh.
Since from the point of view of his opponents this was a flat lie,
Jeremiah was, as they saw it, guilty of prophesying falsely; and for
this offense the Deuteronomic law itself demanded the death penalty (Deut xviii 20). That this was the point at issue is clear from
Jeremiah's own defense of himself (vss. 12–15). He neither denied
that he had spoken as charged (he obviously had), nor contended
that his words were not out of accord with popular belief (they
obviously were); he merely insisted that Yahweh had indeed commanded him to say what he had said. The princes for their part accepted this explanation, and therefore took Jeremiah's side on the
grounds that a prophet ought not to suffer reprisals for speaking
Yahweh's word.

22. THE BROKEN BOTTLE;
JEREMIAH IN THE STOCKS
(xix 1–2; 10–11; 14–15; xx 1–6)

XIX ¹Yahweh spoke to me thus. "Go and buy a potter's earthenware bottle and, taking with you some of the elders of the people and some of the senior priests, ²go [. . .] just outside the Potsherd Gate [. . .]. ¹⁰Then, smash the bottle in the presence of the men who have come with you, ¹¹and say to them, 'This is what Yahweh of Hosts has said: Just so will I smash this people and this city, like a man smashing a potter's vessel so that it can never be mended again [. . .].'"

¹⁴Then Jeremiah returned from [the gate (?)], where Yahweh had sent him to prophesy, and stood in the court of Yahweh's house and said to all the people, ¹⁵"This is what Yahweh of Hosts, the God of Israel, has said: Look! I am going to bring upon this city and its various towns all the evil with which I have threatened it, because they have deliberately refused to listen to what I say."

XX ¹Now the priest, Pashhur ben Immer, who was chief overseer in the house of Yahweh, heard Jeremiah prophesy these things. ²So Pashhur beat Jeremiah and put him in the stocks, in the Upper Benjamin Gate of Yahweh's house. ³But then, the next morning, when Pashhur released Jeremiah from the stocks, Jeremiah said to him, "Pashhur was not the name that Yahweh gave you, but Magor-missabib ['Terror All Around']. ⁴For this is what Yahweh has said: Believe me, I am going to make you a terror to yourself and to all your friends. They will fall by the sword of their enemies, and you are going to see it with your own eyes. And I will hand all Judah over to the king of Babylon, who will deport them to Babylon or slay them with the sword. ⁵All this city's wealth, all its possessions and valuables, together with all the treasures of Judah's kings, I will hand over to their foes, who will loot them, seize them, and carry them off to Babylon. 6 And as for you, Pashhur, and all the members of your household, you shall go into captivity. Yes, to Babylon you shall go, and there you shall die, and there be buried—you and all your friends to whom you have prophesied falsely."

NOTES

xix. For textual and other notes, see Sec. 17, above.

xx. See NOTES on Sec. 17.

COMMENT

The incident described in this section has already been treated above (Sec. 17) and is repeated here merely for the sake of completeness. As was pointed out in the COMMENT there, the account of Jeremiah's symbolic action in xix 1–13, leading up to the biographical account in xix 14–xx 6, has been greatly expanded in transmission by the addition of a lengthy address from another context. In the interests of clarity xix 1–13 is here given in abbreviated form.

We have in xix 14–xx 6 the only biographical account in the book that carries no indication of date and, indeed, one of the few that are not dated precisely. That the incident took place in Jehoiakim's reign may be accepted as certain. The fact that Pashhur is here the temple overseer, while in xxix 26—which dates, as we shall see, to 594—we find another man occupying that position, would argue that Pashhur was among those deported in 597. Since the incident described in chapter xxvi took place at the very beginning of Jehoiakim's reign, it is virtually impossible that the present one could have occurred sooner. On the other hand, a date after 605/4 is, if not impossible, unlikely. For some time after that year—unfortunately we do not know for how long—Jeremiah was forced to go into hiding (cf. xxxvi 26), while at least by ca.

600/599 we find him (cf. xxxv) coming and going in the temple without hindrance. Although the present incident *might* have taken place in this interval, it is in every way more plausible to locate it between 609/8 and 605. We may suppose that the clergy, having failed in their attempt to have Jeremiah executed (ch. xxvi), then resorted to harassment in the hope of silencing him. The present incident is an example of this. It is possible that as a still further measure, and perhaps as an outgrowth of this incident, Jeremiah was forbidden to enter the temple at all. At least, this seems to have been the situation by 605/4 (cf. xxxvi 5), when Baruch was obliged to go and read the scroll in Jeremiah's place.

23. THE INCIDENT OF THE SCROLL
(xxxvi 1–32)

XXXVI 1 It was in the fourth year of Jehoiakim ben Josiah, king of Judah, that the following word came to Jeremiah from Yahweh: 2 "Get yourself a book-scroll, and write in it everything that I have said to you concerning Israel* and Judah, and all the nations, since I first spoke to you—that is, from the days of Josiah until the present. 3 Perhaps if the citizens of Judah hear of all the evil that I propose to do to them, they will turn one and all from their wicked conduct; and then I can forgive their sinful wrongdoing." 4 So Jeremiah called Baruch ben Neriah, and Baruch, at Jeremiah's dictation, wrote down in a scroll all the the words of Yahweh which Jeremiah had received.

5 Then Jeremiah instructed Baruch as follows: "I have been barred; I cannot enter the house of Yahweh. 6 So you yourself must go and, there in Yahweh's house in the hearing of the people, on a fast day, read the words of Yahweh from the scroll which you have written at my dictation. In this way you can also read them in the hearing of all the people of Judah who will be coming from their various cities. 7 Perhaps they will present their supplication before Yahweh, and will turn one and all from their wicked conduct; for great is the furious anger with which Yahweh has threatened this people." 8 And Baruch ben Neriah did exactly as Jeremiah the prophet directed him (that is, with regard to reading the words of Yahweh from the book in Yahweh's house).

9 Now it was in the ninth month of the fifth year of Jehoiakim ben Josiah, king of Judah, that all the people in Jerusalem, *together with all the people who had come to Jerusalem from the other cities of Judah,* observed a fast before Yahweh. 10 It

---

a LXX^BN read "concerning Jerusalem"; but see Note.
b–b LXX has only "and the house of Judah."

was then that Baruch read the words of Jeremiah from the book
in Yahweh's house. This he did in the hearing of all the people,
in the chamber of Gemariah, the son of Shaphan the secretary
of state, which was located in the upper court, right at the New
Gate of Yahweh's house.

11 Now Micaiah, the son of Gemariah ben Shaphan, heard
all the words of Yahweh as they were read from the book.
12 Whereupon, he went down to the royal palace, to the chamber of the secretary of state, where all the princes were at the moment in session: Elishama the secretary, Delaiah ben Shemaiah,
Elnathan ben Achbor, Gemariah ben Shaphan, Zedekiah ben
Hananiah, and the various other princes. 13 And Micaiah told
them everything that he had heard when Baruch read from the
book in the hearing of the people.

14 Then all the princes sent Yehudi ben Nethaniah ben
Shelemiah ben Cushi to Baruch with the command: "The
scroll from which you have read in the hearing of the people—
bring it with you, and come!" So Baruch ben Neriah came to
them, bringing the scroll with him. 15 And they said to him,
e"Sit down, please, and read ite to us." So Baruch read it to
them. 16 When they had heard it all, dthey were perturbed and
said to one another,d "We will certainly have to report all this
to the king." 17 And they questioned Baruch, "Tell us, now!
How did you come to write all these things?"e 18 Baruch replied,
f"Jeremiah personallyf dictated all of this to me, and I merely
wrote it down with ink in the book." 19 Then the princes said to
Baruch, "Go and hide, you and Jeremiah! Do not let anyone
know where you are!" 20 With that, they went into the court

c–c The reading of LXX, "Again, please, read it" (*šub* for *šeb*), is not to be
preferred.
d–d The text is in some confusion. Hebrew reads "They were perturbed to
one another and said to Baruch"; LXX omits "to Baruch." Transpose "to one
another" and "and said." Probably "they said to one another" and "they said
to Baruch" are variant readings.
e Hebrew adds at the end of the verse "from his mouth" (i.e., at his dictation),
which anticipates the answer in vs. 18; LXX omits *mippīw* (dittography).
But one could read *hᵃmippīw* (h lost by haplography), and translate, "Was
it at his dictation?" (so RSV).
f–f "Jeremiah" is added with LXX; Heb. "from his [own] mouth he dictated
to me."

to the king, having deposited the scroll in the chamber of Elishama the secretary of state. And they reported the whole affair to the king.

21 The king thereupon sent Yehudi to get the scroll, and he brought it from the chamber of Elishama the secretary. And Yehudi read it to the king, and to all the princes who stood about the king. 22 Now the king was seated in the winter house (it was December*g*), and there was a brazier fire*h* burning before him. 23 And whenever Yehudi would read three or four columns, the king would cut them off with a penknife and toss them into the fire in the brazier, and so on until the entire scroll was consumed. 24 Yet they were not afraid, nor did they rend their garments—neither the king nor any of his courtiers who heard all these words. 25 Elnathan, Delaiah, and Gemariah, to be sure, begged the king not to burn the scroll; but he would not listen to them. 26 On the contrary, the king ordered Prince Jerahmeel, Seraiah ben Azriel, and Shelemiah ben Abdeel to arrest Baruch the scribe and Jeremiah the prophet. But Yahweh had hidden them.

27 Now, after the king had burned the scroll containing the things that Baruch had written at Jeremiah's dictation, the word of Yahweh came to Jeremiah as follows: 28 "Get yourself another scroll, and write in it everything that was included in the original scroll, which Jehoiakim, king of Judah, burned. 29 And, as regards Jehoiakim, king of Judah, you shall say, 'This is what Yahweh has said: You have dared to burn this scroll, saying as you did so, "Why did you write here that the king of Babylon will certainly come and ravage this land, leaving alive in it neither man nor beast?" 30 Therefore, this is what Yahweh has said concerning Jehoiakim, king of Judah: "No descendant of his shall sit on David's throne! His dead body shall be flung out to the heat by day and the frost by night. 31 I will punish him and his offspring and his servants for their iniquity, bringing upon them, and upon the citizens of Jerusalem

g Heb. "in the ninth month"; LXX omits (but cf. vs. 9).
h Reading "fire" (*'ēš*) with LXX; Hebrew erroneously has the sign of the direct object (*'et*).

and the people of Judah, all the evil with which I have threatened them, but of which they refused to hear." ' "

32 So Jeremiah got another scroll and gave it to Baruch ben Neriah, the scribe, who wrote in it at Jeremiah's dictation everything that was in the book that Jehoiakim, king of Judah, had thrown into the fire. And, in addition to this, many further words of the same sort were added.

NOTES

xxxvi 1. *the fourth year of Jehoiakim*. 605 (see COMMENT).

2. *book-scroll*. The expression (*mᵉgillat sēper*) occurs only here, in vs. 4 and in Ps xl 8[7E]; Ezek ii 9. It is not certain whether it denotes a scroll of book length, or is merely the formal term for a scroll for writing purposes, commonly referred to simply as a *mᵉgillāh* (much as we refer to a newspaper as a "paper": D. N. Freedman).

concerning Israel. Most scholars prefer the reading "concerning Jerusalem" (see textual note[a]) on the grounds that while the scroll contained words of warning and judgment, Jeremiah's words concerning northern Israel do not fall in this class. But MT is probably to be preferred: the witness of LXX is not unanimous; Jeremiah's usual expression is "Judah and Jerusalem," not vice versa; reference to "the nations" indicates a broader perspective than Judah alone. Moreover, at least some of Jeremiah's words to northern Israel (e.g., iii 6–11) are intended as warnings to Judah. On this scroll generally, see Introduction, "The Book of Jeremiah . . .".

3. *the citizens of Judah*. Literally "the house of Judah" (i.e., the nation). The syntax of the verse is awkward: "Perhaps the house of Judah will hear (plural)—so that they may turn—and I may forgive."

4. *which Jeremiah had received*. Literally "which he spoke to him" —presumably "which he (Yahweh) had spoken to him (Jeremiah)"; or, less likely but possible, "which he (Jeremiah) spoke (i.e., repeated) to him (Baruch)."

5. *I have been barred*. The word (*'āṣūr*) cannot denote physical arrest (cf. vss. 19, 26) as it does in xxxiii 1; xxxix 15. The probable sense is that Jeremiah had (after the incident of xx 1–6?) been forbidden to enter the temple; or perhaps it was simply that the authorities had him under observation and would stop him if he tried to speak there.

6. *on a fast day*. As the verse explains, to take advantage of the large crowds that would be present then. Fasts were not, apparently, fixed occasions (vs. 9), but were called in times of emergency. Unfor-

tunately, we can not say how long before the fast in December 604 Baruch was given these instructions: if shortly before, the sense would be "on the fast day (which has been announced)"; otherwise, "on the next fast day."

7. *present their supplication*. Literally "their supplication will fall."

8. The words in parentheses are superfluous to the sense and anticipate the opening words of vs. 10, which they virtually repeat. Perhaps they are a gloss.

9. *the ninth month of the fifth year*. December 604 (see COMMENT).

observed a fast. Literally "proclaimed. . . ." But since the people did not themselves proclaim the fast, one must take this in a weakened sense as "observed," or understand "the people" as the object: "they (the authorities) summoned all the people (to) a fast."

10. *Gemariah, the son of Shaphan the secretary of state*. The father, Shaphan, had been Josiah's secretary of state (II Kings xxii 3, etc.); Gemariah did not himself hold that office (cf. vs. 12). Baruch certainly must have had permission to use Gemariah's chamber, which would indicate that the latter was well disposed toward Jeremiah.

12. The princes listed here were, to use modern terms, the cabinet ministers. Aside from Elnathan ben Achbor and Gemariah ben Shaphan (on whom see the COMMENT), we know nothing further of these men.

14. *Yehudi*. It is surprising that the ancestry of an otherwise unknown person is given to the third generation (even to give the second is unusual). But this probably does not entitle us to suppose, as many do, that there were two messengers: Yehudi ben Nethaniah and Shelemiah ben Cushi.

15. *Sit down, please*. Though Baruch was probably himself of noble family (see COMMENTS on Sec. 24 [xlv] and Sec. 28 [li 59]), the courtesy with which the princes treat him is further indication of their friendly attitude.

16. *We will certainly have to report all this*. The princes are not tattlers who wish to get Jeremiah and Baruch into trouble (cf. vs. 19). They are convinced of the importance of what they have heard and feel that the king must know of it.

17. The princes wish to be assured that what they have heard is actually the prophetic (i.e., Yahweh's) word, not Baruch's own.

20. Presumably they had a shrewd idea of what the king's reaction would be and wanted, if possible, to keep the scroll out of his hands.

23. *the king would cut*. Heb. "he would cut," which is ambiguous. It was, of course, the king who destroyed the scroll, not Yehudi.

the entire scroll was consumed. Hebrew then repeats "in the fire which was in the brazier," which in English (though perhaps not in Hebrew) is redundant and harsh.

24. *his courtiers*. Again, "his servants."

26. *But Yahweh had hidden them.* Hebrew makes it clear that but for divine providence Jeremiah and Baruch would have been caught; LXX has simply "But they had hidden themselves." Jehoiakim would certainly have executed Jeremiah, as he had Uriah (xxvi 20–23). How long Jeremiah remained in hiding, and what caused the king finally to drop the matter, we do not know; but Jeremiah was later able to move about freely (cf. ch. xxxv).

28. *everything that was included in the original scroll.* Literally "all the former words which were in the former scroll." LXX omits both adjectives.

29. *You have dared to burn.* Hebrew is emphatic: "You, you have burned . . . ," the translation seeks to catch this.

leaving alive in it neither man nor beast. Literally "will cause to cease from it both man and beast."

30. This verse is actually a prose parallel to xxii 18–19.

31. *but of which they refused to hear.* Literally "but they did not listen."

COMMENT

This chapter is one of the most noteworthy in the entire book. From it we learn how, in the fourth year of Jehoiakim's reign (vs. 1), Jeremiah dictated a scroll containing prophecies of his uttered since the beginning of his career, how this scroll was read publicly in the temple, then before certain members of the king's cabinet, and finally before the king himself, who destroyed it. We are then told how Jeremiah, at Yahweh's command, recreated the scroll with additions. The incident is of interest both for itself and because of the fact (cf. Introduction, "The Book of Jeremiah . . .") that the scroll here described marks, so far as we know, the first step in that process through which Jeremiah's sayings were collected and given literary fixation, and which ultimately resulted in the Jeremiah book as we have it today.

The fourth year of Jehoiakim was the year 605/4 (April to April). It will be recalled that it was in the late spring or early summer of 605 that Nebuchadnezzar crushed the Egyptian forces at Carchemish on the Euphrates and began his advance into Syria. Though we are not specifically so told, it is quite probable that this event was the occasion for the scroll's being written. How long it was in preparation, and how long it had been ready before it was

read in the temple, we have no way of saying. But as we learn
from vs. 9, its reading did not take place until the ninth month of
Jehoiakim's fifth year (December 604). It is scarcely a coincidence
that it was in this very month that the Babylonian army assaulted,
captured, and sacked the city of Ashkelon on the Philistine plain.
This turn of events placed before the kingdom of Judah, still at
least nominally a vassal-state of Egypt, a fearful decision and undoubtedly evoked the greatest consternation there; it was in all
probability the occasion for the day of national fasting upon which
the scroll was read. Apparently it was not long after this that Jehoiakim transferred his allegiance to the Babylonians.

The narrative of the chapter is straightforward and requires little
explanatory comment. In it we meet Baruch, Jeremiah's friend, dis-
ciple and amanuensis, for the first time. That Baruch was also the
Biographer who gave us this chapter and the others like it cannot,
of course, be demonstrated, although it is entirely likely that he
was. The narrative is, in any event, marked by such a wealth of
circumstantial detail that it can only have been set down by one
who was either an eye witness, or who had talked with eye witnesses. Once again, one gets a most favorable impression of certain of the nobles, including the secretary of state and others highly
placed in the national government. Not only did these men concern
themselves for the safety of Jeremiah and Baruch (vs. 19), they
acted throughout as friends and sympathizers. The more carefully
one reads the narrative, the more one is impressed with this (see
further the NOTES). One is not surprised to learn that one of them,
Gemariah, was a son of Shaphan (vss. 10, 12, 25). In all likelihood he was a brother of the Ahikam who had once saved Jeremiah's life (xxvi 24), and perhaps of the Elasah whom we find
acting as Jeremiah's agent in xxix 3; his father (vs. 10)—probably
the father of all three—was the Shaphan who had been Josiah's
secretary of state when the reform was made (II Kings xxii 3, 8,
12). These men, who had been proponents of that reform, or sons
of proponents, received Jeremiah's words with sympathy and, apparently, with a measure of sincere belief.

It is, however, somewhat surprising to read that Elnathan ben
Achbor was among them. This was the man who, it will be recalled (xxvi 20–23), had led the deputation which had been sent to
Egypt to extradite the prophet Uriah and bring him to his death,
and one would not, in view of this, expect to find him taking Jere-

miah's part. Yet Elnathan seems also (II Kings xxii 12) to have been a son of one of the reformers, Achbor ben Micaiah (that he was also the king's father-in-law [II Kings xxiv 8] is uncertain). One wonders if in the affair of Uriah he had not simply acted under orders, perhaps telling himself that the outcome was none of his business, only to be horrified when he saw what that outcome was. Or perhaps he had drifted away from his father's principles, but had subsequently had a change of heart. We do not know. In any event, when the king destroyed the scroll, Elnathan was one of the few who attempted to stop him—a tribute to his courage, to say the least.

24. BARUCH'S DESPAIR:
A REBUKE AND A PROMISE
(xlv 1–5)

XLV ¹ The word that Jeremiah the prophet spoke to Baruch ben Neriah when he wrote the above sayings in the book at Jeremiah's dictation, in the fourth year of Jehoiakim ben Josiah, king of Judah: ² "This is what Yahweh, the God of Israel, has said to you, Baruch: ³ Because*ᵃ* you have said, 'Ah me! Ah me! Yahweh has indeed added to my suffering yet further trouble. I am worn out with my sighing, but no rest do I find,'— ⁴ *ᵇ*this is what Yahweh has said: Look! What I have built I am about to tear down, and what I have planted I am about to uproot.*ᵇ* ⁵ And you—you expect great things for yourself? Expect nothing! For see! I am about to bring disaster on all flesh—Yahweh's word; and you may count yourself fortunate that I will preserve you alive wherever you may go."

ᵃ Word (*kī*) restored with LXX (lost by haplography).
ᵇ⁻ᵇ Hebrew begins the verse "Thus shall you say to him," which is superfluous and inappropriate in the immediate context. Perhaps this is a misplaced variant of vs. 2. At the end of the verse Hebrew adds "that is, the whole land," which seems to be a gloss to indicate what Yahweh is about to destroy; omit with LXX.

NOTES

xlv 1. *the above sayings.* Literally "these sayings"; of course meaning those included in the scroll described in the preceding section.

5. *and you may count yourself fortunate that I will preserve you alive.* Literally "I will give you your life as booty." This expression, which occurs several times in Jeremiah (xxi 9; xxxviii 2; xxxix 18), is a peculiar one. One suspects that it originated in the army. Victorious soldiers customarily brought home the booty they had seized; one can imagine that a soldier, returning after a defeat from which he had

barely escaped alive, might, when asked where his share of the booty was, have replied ironically that his life was all the "booty" that he could bring away. As the expression passed into general parlance, it came to mean: barely to escape with one's life (Nötscher [on xxi 9] similarly). But one cannot be sure about this.

COMMENT

If Baruch was, as we suppose, Jeremiah's biographer, it is only in this brief chapter that he reveals himself as a person. Elsewhere he is content to remain in the background, to be Jeremiah's messenger, his pen—one who tells us much of his master, nothing of himself. Here, however, he shows himself as a human being. Clearly he is in despair, and has communicated that fact to Jeremiah. We are not told what caused him to feel this way. But since the incident is dated at the time of the writing of the scroll (605/4), we should hardly be wrong in assuming that this was the occasion for it. It is quite possible that as he heard the awful words of judgment which Jeremiah dictated to him, words which in his heart he knew to be true, he became so oppressed by the horrors that the future had in store that all hope and joy died within him. No doubt, too, he realized quite well what the consequences of having to read such words would be.

Yet that is not the whole of it. It is evident from vs. 5a that Baruch had gazed at the wreckage of his own personal ambitions and hopes. What these may have been we cannot say. Perhaps it was simply that as he contemplated the future his thoughts turned, as men's thoughts will, inward upon himself: When this disaster comes, as surely it will, what will happen to me? Or perhaps he had hoped, when he had first joined Jeremiah, that the prophetic preaching would produce a change of heart among the people, perhaps even a shift in the national policy, and that this would bring him acclaim, popularity and—who knows—high position. True, this is speculation. But Baruch, being a man of the educated class, qualified as a secretary, whose brother (cf. li 59) was later an officer of high rank under Zedekiah, may well have entertained such hopes. But now he sees that the future offers him nothing but abuse and hatred and danger . . .

Whatever the reasons for Baruch's plaint (and we really do not know what they were), Jeremiah's reply must have seemed to him cold comfort. Yahweh must destroy the nation he has nurtured— and you cry because *your* hopes are dashed? Forget them! Be thankful to know that you will escape with your life. One wonders what Baruch must have felt on receiving such an answer. But one thing is clear: he accepted it—and carried on faithfully. Whatever his feelings, and regardless of his personal interests, he stayed with Jeremiah to the end.

25. JEREMIAH AND THE RECHABITES
(xxxv 1–19)

XXXV 1 The word that came to Jeremiah from Yahweh in the days of Jehoiakim ben Josiah, king of Judah: 2 "Seek out the members of the Rechabite community, speak with them, and bring them to Yahweh's house to one of the chambers there, and offer them wine to drink." 3 So I got Jaazaniah ben Jeremiah ben Habazziniah, together with his brothers and all his sons— the entire Rechabite community, in fact— 4 and brought them to Yahweh's house to the chamber of the sons of Hanan ben Yigdaliah, the man of God, which was next to the chamber of the princes, above the chamber of Maaseiah ben Shallum, the keeper of the threshold. 5 Then *I placed before the members of the Rechabite community* pitchers full of wine, and cups, and I said to them, "Have some wine!" 6 But they replied, "We do not drink wine. For our ancestor, Jonadab ben Rechab, commanded us: 'You shall drink no wine, neither you nor your sons forever. 7 Moreover, you are not to build a house, or sow seed, or plant a vineyard, or own one, but are to dwell in tents always, in order that you may long flourish on the land on which you wander as aliens.' 8 And we have obeyed the command of Jonadab ben Rechab, our ancestor, in every particular, drinking no wine as long as we live—neither we, nor our wives, nor our sons and daughters— 9 and building no houses to dwell in. We have no vineyards, no fields, and no seed, 10 but have continued to live in tents, obeying to the letter every command that our ancestor Jonadab gave us. 11 And it was only when Nebuchadrezzar, king of Babylon, invaded the land that we said, 'Come, let us go to Jerusalem, out of the way of the armies of the Chaldeans and the Arameans.' And that is why we are living in Jerusalem."

a–a LXX "I placed before them."

12 Then the word of Yahweh came to Jeremiah[b] as follows:
13 "This is what Yahweh of Hosts, the God of Israel, has said:
Go and say to the men of Judah and the citizens of Jerusalem:
Will you never accept correction and listen to what I say?
—Yahweh's word. 14 The instructions that Jonadab ben Rechab
gave to his sons, never to drink wine, have been carried out; till
this day they have drunk none, for they have been obedient to
their ancestor's command. I, on the contrary, have spoken to you
urgently and persistently, yet you have never listened to me.
15 With urgency and persistence I sent to you all my servants the
prophets to say to you, 'Turn, now, every one of you from his
wicked conduct and reform your practices! Do not follow other
gods in order to worship them, and then you shall remain in
the land which I gave to you and to your fathers before you.'
But you neither paid attention nor listened to me at all. 16 Yes,
the descendants of Jonadab ben Rechab have kept the commandment which their ancestor gave them; but this people has
never listened to me. 17 And so, this is what Yahweh, God of
Hosts, the God of Israel, has said: Believe me, I am going to
bring upon Judah and [c]upon the citizens of Jerusalem[c] all the
evil with which I have threatened them, [d]because they did not
listen when I spoke to them, or answer when I called them."[d]

18 [e]But to the Rechabite community Jeremiah said, "This
is what Yahweh of Hosts, the God of Israel, has said: Because
you have obeyed the commandment of your ancestor Jonadab,
abiding by all his instructions and doing exactly as he ordered
you to do— 19 therefore, this is what Yahweh of Hosts, the God
of Israel has said: Never for all time shall Jonadab ben Rechab
lack a descendant to stand in my service!"[e]

[b] LXX "to me," which conforms to the autobiographical style of the preceding
verses.
[c-c] So LXX; Heb. ". . . all the citizens. . . ."
[d-d] LXX omits.
[e-e] LXX abbreviates considerably, and with some changes; but the sense is
the same.

NOTES

xxxv 2. *Seek out the members of the Rechabite community.* Literally
"Go to the house of the Rechabites." But this is misleading; "house"
does not here refer to a dwelling, but to the members of a clan or, better,
a community (cf. vs. 3).

4. *the sons of Hanan ben Yigdaliah, the man of God.* In earlier times
"man of God" is a title frequently applied to prophets: to Samuel (I Sam
ix 6–10), to Elijah (II Kings i 9–13, etc.), Elisha (II Kings iv–xiii) and
others. The term occurs only here in Jeremiah, and we do not know if
by the late seventh century it had acquired a special connotation distinct
from *nābī'* (prophet). If Hanan was a prophet, or a cultic functionary of
some sort, "sons" may have the sense of "disciples." The fact that he
lent his room to Jeremiah indicates a measure of sympathy with him.

Maaseiah . . . keeper of the threshold. This was an important priestly
office (cf. lii 24). Maaseiah may have been the father of the priest
Zephaniah, mentioned in xxix 25 and elsewhere.

5. *the members of the Rechabite community.* Literally "the sons of
the house of the Rechabites" (cf. vs. 2).

7. *or own one.* Actually they are not to own any of these things (so vs.
9 explicitly), although that is not expressed here. LXX omits "plant"
and reads "you shall not own a vineyard."

wander as aliens. The Rechabites were not, of course, actually *gērīm*
(resident aliens), but native Israelites. They lived, however, as if they
had no home, as pilgrims and strangers, ready to strike their tents and
move at Yahweh's command, as Israel had done in the desert. (Whether
or not there is a reminiscence of a perpetual readiness for holy war in
this is uncertain.)

11. *And that is why we are living.* Literally "And so we live [or:
"have settled"]. . . ." The Rechabites wish it understood that the fact
that they are living in the city (presumably in houses) does not indicate
unfaithfulness to principle, but is only because of the existing emergency.

COMMENT

This chapter brings us down to the very end of Jehoiakim's reign.
Although its heading (vs. 1) gives no precise date, the situation
is clear from vs. 11, where we are told that Chaldean and Aramean
forces are ranging through the land spreading havoc everywhere.
This is the situation described in II Kings xxiv 2. It was probably

not long after the burning of the scroll (presumably sometime in 603) that Jehoiakim, who had previously ruled as a vassal of the pharaoh, transferred his allegiance to Nebuchadnezzar. According to II Kings xxiv 1, he remained Nebuchadnezzar's vassal for three years, and then rebelled. Undoubtedly he was emboldened to take such a step when the Egyptians, late in 601, met Nebuchadnezzar's army in pitched battle and inflicted such heavy casualties upon it that it was obliged to withdraw. Nebuchadnezzar was in no immediate position to take decisive action against Judah, and indeed was not until the end of 598. Pending that time, however, he dispatched against her such Babylonian troops as were available in the area, together with contingents from neighboring vassal states, no doubt with the aim of wrecking her economy and disrupting preparations for resistance. It was during this interval (presumably in 599 or 598) that the present incident took place.

The narrative itself (vss. 1–11) requires no special explanation. It tells how the Rechabites refused to drink wine in obedience to a vow laid upon them by their ancestor. Though this narrative is introduced by the Biographer, it is autobiographical in style and unquestionably derives from Jeremiah's own reminiscences, no doubt as the Biographer (Baruch?) remembered hearing him tell it. Following this are two prose oracles. The first (vss. 12–17) is addressed to the people and contrasts their disobedience to Yahweh's commands to the faithfulness with which the Rechabites have kept the command of their human ancestor; the second (vss. 18–19) is addressed to the Rechabites themselves and promises them that because of their faithfulness their family would never die out in Israel.

The Rechabite vow is in its major features clearly reminiscent of life in the desert. This is certainly true of their refusal to till the soil or live in houses, and probably of their abstinence from wine as well, viticulture doubtless being regarded by them as a symbol of the sedentary life which they rejected. The Rechabites were thus a clan who by their manner of life symbolized their renunciation of the agrarian and urban culture to which their nation had long since assimilated, and who expressed their loyalty to Yahweh and to their ancestor's wishes by clinging to the simple seminomadic life of their remote forefathers. The founder of this clan, Jonadab ben Rechab, is known from II Kings x 15–17 as one who had physically assisted Jehu in his bloody purge of the house of Ahab in the ninth century. Apparently the excesses of Ahab and Jezebel, their

importation of the worship of the Tyrian Baal, together with the
progressive urbanization of Israelite society then taking place and
the attendant disintegration of social patterns, had awakened in
many minds both revulsion and a nostalgia for the traditions and
simpler ways of the past. Some—and Jonadab was one of them
(the great prophet Elijah, in his own way, was another)—had con-
sciously returned to ancient patterns of life in protest against the
prevailing decay, both social and religious. The history of the Rechabites prior to the ninth century cannot be traced. If they were of
Kenite origin (I Chron ii 55), they stemmed from a people who
claimed kinship with Moses (Judg i 16), and who for a long time
after Israel's settlement continued their seminomadic life both in the
southern desert (I Sam xv 6), and within Israelite territory itself
(Judg iv 17; v 24). The fact that the Rechabite vow is in some
respects similar to that of the Nazirite almost certainly indicates
some connection between the two (as we learn from Num vi the
Nazirite vow forbade not only the drinking of wine, but the use of
the produce of the vine in any form, whether grapes or raisins,
grape juice or vinegar). The Nazirite vow had had a long history
in Israel, reaching back to the days of the conquest and the judges
(Samson [Judg xiii 4–7], and apparently Samuel [I Sam i 11] were
Nazirites), and may well have originally symbolized opposition to
Canaanite culture as well as ritual fitness to fight the holy wars of
Yahweh.

In any event, the Rechabites, two and a half centuries after
Jonadab's day, were still faithful to their vow. And for this Jeremiah
praises them. This does not, of course, mean that Jeremiah shared
their sentiments in every respect or regarded their way of life as a
model that all ought to follow. He himself lived in a house (he
spent most of his life in Jerusalem), presumably drank wine (as
Jesus did; it was the common daily beverage), and certainly purchased and owned land (xxxii 1–15). His point, rather, is explained
in the concluding oracles (vss. 12–19): the Rechabites, whatever
people might think of their eccentric behavior, are pleasing to Yahweh as an example of faithful obedience, and are therefore a living rebuke to a faithless and disobedient nation. We know nothing
of the subsequent history of the Rechabites, and so cannot say how
long they continued to survive as a community. But perhaps something of their spirit may be observed in certain sectarian groups in
later Judaism—and in Christianity.

26. THE GOOD FIGS AND THE BAD
(xxiv 1–10)

XXIV 1 Yahweh pointed it out to me—and there, arranged in front of the temple of Yahweh were two baskets of figs. (This was after Nebuchadrezzar, king of Babylon, had deported Jeconiah ben Jehoiakim, king of Judah, from Jerusalem, along with the princes of Judah, the artisans, and the [smiths (?)], and had taken them to Babylon.) 2 In one basket the figs were excellent, like early-ripening figs. In the other basket the figs were extremely bad, so bad, indeed, as to be inedible. 3 Then Yahweh said to me, "What do you see, Jeremiah?" I answered, "Figs! The good figs are very good, the bad figs are very bad, so bad as to be inedible."

4 Thereupon, the word of Yahweh came to me: 5 "This is what Yahweh, the God of Israel, has said: Like these good figs, so will I single out for favor the exiles of Judah whom I have sent away from this place to the land of the Chaldeans. 6 I will keep benevolent watch over them and will restore them to this land, where I will build them up, not tear them down, plant them and not uproot them. 7 And I will give them a will to know me, that I am Yahweh. They shall be my people, and I will be their God, for they shall turn to me with all their energies.

8 "But like the figs that are too rotten to eat—ah, this is what Yahweh has said—so will I treat Zedekiah, king of Judah, and his nobles, and what is left of the people of Jerusalem, both those who remain in this land and those who have settled in Egypt. 9 I will make them a sight to horrify*a* all the kingdoms

---

a Hebrew adds "for an evil" (*lerā'āh*), which appears to be a dittography; LXX omits. Perhaps, however, the word belongs at the end of vs. 8: "I will give Zedekiah . . . to disaster"; cf. *letōbāh* ("for good, favor") at the end of vs. 5.

of the earth, and an insult, a byword, a taunt, and a curse in all the places where I shall drive them. 10 And I will send upon them sword and famine and disease, until they are exterminated from the land which I gave to them and to their fathers."

NOTES

xxiv 1. *arranged*. The Hophal participle of *y'd* (*mū'ādīm*) occurs elsewhere only in Ezek xxi 21[16E] ("set, directed"); its force here is not clear. Most scholars emend to *mo'ºmādīm* ("placed") or *'ōmºdīm* ("standing"). But emendation may not be necessary.

smiths. So with EVV; but the meaning of the word (*masgēr*) is uncertain, and the translation a guess. Various other suggestions are offered, but none can be called convincing. LXX has "prisoners" (of war?), and adds "and the wealthy." In the light of the root (*sgr*) "prisoners," or even "hostages," is not impossible.

6. Note that the verbs "build up," "plant," "tear down," "uproot" are those used in i 10. They are repeatedly played upon in the prose portions of the book.

7. *a will . . . their energies*. Both words translate Heb. *lēb* ("heart"). The word "heart" has been deliberately avoided because to English-speaking readers it carries sentimental connotations which it does not have in Hebrew. The heart was regarded as the seat of the mind and will, not of the emotions (which were located in the "kidneys" or the "bowels").

8. *ah, this is what Yahweh has said*. The words fit awkwardly, and are regarded by many as an insertion, but without textual evidence.

who have settled in Egypt. This does not require us to date the passage after 587 (e.g., Hyatt) when, as we know from chs. xliii–xliv (cf. xliv 1), many Jews had settled in Egypt. Undoubtedly Jews of the pro-Egyptian party, who had favored resistance to Babylon, had fled there when Jehoiakim became Nebuchadnezzar's vassal (ca. 603), or when Nebuchadnezzar invaded Judah in 598/7.

COMMENT

With this chapter we move beyond the deportation of 597 into the reign of Zedekiah. Although the chronological notation in vs. 1 seems to have been added secondarily (it is syntactically a parenthesis), probably on the basis of II Kings xxiv 14 f., there is no reason to question its correctness. Unlike most of the chapters presently under discussion, chapter xxiv does not contain a biographical narrative, but tells in autobiographical style of an oracle that came to Jeremiah through a visionary experience. In form, it is very similar to the account of the two visions in i 11–16 (cf. also Amos vii 1–9; viii 1–3) and, like that account, may be assumed to derive —with some verbal expansion in the course of transmission—from Jeremiah's own reminiscences.

Like the two visions just mentioned, the present one probably had a physical basis. That is to say, it was probably as Jeremiah gazed at two actual baskets containing figs of contrasting quality that it came to him as a word from Yahweh that the good figs represented the exiles in Babylon, the rotten figs, Zedekiah and his nobles and the people left in Jerusalem. This estimate of the situation is reflected in various of Jeremiah's sayings from this period (cf. Introduction, "The Life and Message of Jeremiah"), and is in accord with that of his contemporary, Ezekiel. Nor was it without basis in reality. Those deported to Babylon did in fact represent the cream of the country's leadership. Moreover, those princes who had more than once (chs. xxvi; xxxvi) intervened in Jeremiah's behalf seem to have been among them, since we hear no more of them. The princes who were left to serve—and to dominate— Zedekiah were, though no doubt most of them sincere patriots, lacking in political wisdom and, so far as we know, almost without exception hostile to Jeremiah and the position that he represented. Jeremiah was to suffer cruelly at their hands, as the chapters that follow will show.

27. EVENTS OF THE YEAR 594:
THE INCIDENT OF THE OX-YOKE
(xxvii 1–22; xxviii 1–17)

Jeremiah Prophesies Wearing an Ox-Yoke

XXVII ¹[   ]*ᵃ* ² This is what Yahweh said to me: "Make yourself thongs and yoke-bars and put them on your neck. ³ Then send word*ᵇ* to the kings of Edom, of Moab, of Ammon, of Tyre, and of Sidon through *ᶜtheir ambassadorsᶜ* who have come to Jerusalem to King Zedekiah of Judah. ⁴ Give them the following charge for their masters: 'This is what Yahweh of Hosts, the God of Israel, has said, and this is what you shall tell your masters: ⁵ "It is I who by my great power and irresistible might have made the earth, together with the men and the animals who inhabit its surface, and I can give it to whomsoever I will. ⁶ And now, it is I who have delivered *ᵈall these countriesᵈ* into the power of Nebuchadnezzar, king of Babylon, my servant. Indeed, I have even given him the wild beasts to be his subjects. ⁷ All the nations shall be subject to him, and to his son and his grandson, until, in its turn, his own country's time comes, when many nations and great kings shall reduce it*ᵉ* to servitude. ⁸ As for the people or the kingdom that *ᶠwill not placeᶠ* its neck under

ᵃ MT reads "In the accession year of Jehoiakim ben Josiah, king of Judah, there came this word to Jeremiah from Yahweh," which is manifestly incorrect and apparently an erroneous recopying of xxvi 1. See Note.
ᵇ Heb. "send them." LXXᴸ omits "them"; see Note.
ᶜ⁻ᶜ So with LXX. MT has "ambassadors" (indefinite), which does not agree with the ensuing participle. But perhaps (note from D. N. Freedman) MT *mal'ākīm* simply reflects loss of intervocalic *h* in pronunciation (*mal'ākaym* or the like), so that MT and LXX actually have the same reading (*mal'ᵃkēhem*).
ᵈ⁻ᵈ LXX reads "[all] the earth." See Note.
ᵉ Hebrew ". . . him." But the threat is not to Nebuchadnezzar personally, but to his country.
ᶠ⁻ᶠ Heb. "the kingdom that will not serve him—i.e., Nebuchadnezzar king of Babylon—and that will not place. . . ." LXX omits these additional words, which may be a variant of the ensuing clause.

the yoke of the king of Babylon, by sword, by famine and plague I will harass that people—Yahweh's word—until I have delivered them into his power. 9 As for yourselves, do not listen to your prophets and diviners, your dreamers,*g* soothsayers and sorcerers, who keep telling you not to submit to the king of Babylon. 10 For it is a lie that they are preaching to you, which will only serve to remove you far from your land; for I will drive you out and you will perish. 11 But the people that brings its neck under the yoke of the king of Babylon and is subject to him, I will leave on its own land—Yahweh's word—to till it and live there.' ' "

12 *h*"To Zedekiah, king of Judah, I spoke in exactly the same terms: "Bring your neck under the yoke of the king of Babylon and be subject to him and his people, that you may live. 13 Why will you, together with your people, die by the sword, by starvation and disease, as Yahweh has threatened that any nation will that does not submit to the king of Babylon? 14 Do not listen to the talk of the prophets who keep telling you not to submit to the king of Babylon, for it is a lie that they are preaching to you.*h* 15 No, I did not send them!—Yahweh's word. But they keep prophesying falsely in my name, with the result that I will drive you out and you will perish, you and the prophets who have been prophesying to you."

16 *i*Both to the priests and to all this people I spoke as follows: "This is what Yahweh has said: Do not listen to the talk of your prophets who keep giving to you this prophecy, 'Ah, but the furnishings of Yahweh's house are going very shortly to be brought back from Babylon'; for it is a lie that they are prophesying to you.*i* 17 *j*Do not listen to them! Submit to the king of Babylon, and live! Why should this city become a ruin? 18 If

---

g So with Vrs.; Heb. "your dreams."

h–h LXX begins the quotation in vs. 12, "Bring your neck and be subject to," and then skips to "the king of Babylon" in vs. 14. But LXX is not to be preferred; the omission seems to be accidental; vs. 14a, at least, is necessary to the sense of vss. 14b–15.

i–i LXX, which has a vastly shorter text of vss. 17–22 (see textual note*j–j*), joins this discourse to the preceding by beginning: "To you and to all this people and to the priests I spoke, saying. . . ." It omits "very shortly," and adds at the end "I did not send them."

they are really prophets, if the word of Yahweh is with them at all, let them then make intercession with Yahweh of Hosts that the furnishings that are left in Yahweh's house, in the palace of the king of Judah, and elsewhere in Jerusalem, *may not also go* to Babylon. 19 For this is what Yahweh of Hosts has said concerning the pillars, the brazen sea, and the stands, and concerning the rest of the furnishings that are left in this city, 20 which Nebuchadnezzar, king of Babylon, did not take when he deported Jeconiah ben Jehoiakim, king of Judah, from Jerusalem to Babylon, together with all the nobility of Judah and Jerusalem— 21 Yes, this is what Yahweh of Hosts, the God of Israel, has said with regard to the furnishings that remain in the house of Yahweh, in the palace of the king of Judah, and in Jerusalem: 22 They shall be taken to Babylon, and there they shall remain until the day when I give attention to them— Yahweh's word. Then I will bring them back and restore them to this place."*j*

Jeremiah and Hananiah: Prophet versus Prophet

XXVIII 1 *l*In that same year, the fourth year of Zedekiah, king of Judah, in the fifth month, Hananiah ben Azzur, the prophet from Gibeon, spoke as follows to Jeremiah*m* in the house of Yahweh, in the presence of the priests and all the people: 2 "This is what Yahweh of Hosts, the God of Israel, has said: I have broken the yoke of the king of Babylon! 3 *n*Within two years' time I am going to bring back to this place all the furnish-

j–j For vss. 17–22 LXX has only: "If they are prophets, if the word of the Lord is in them, let them entreat [meet] me. For thus said the Lord: Even the rest of the furnishings, which the king of Babylon did not take when he deported Jeconiah from Jerusalem, shall be taken to Babylon, says the Lord." It is difficult to resist the conclusion that this text is more original than the much expanded form found in MT.

k–k Read either the infinitive *bō'* (transposition), or the imperfect *yābō'ū* (*y* lost by haplography); MT has the imperative *bō'ū*.

l Hebrew begins, "In that year, in the accession year of Zedekiah, king of Judah, in the fourth year. . . ." See NOTE.

m Hebrew and Vrs. read "to me." But since Jeremiah is referred to in the third person elsewhere in the chapter, "to me" (*'ly*) may represent a misunderstanding of an abbreviated writing *'ly(rmyh)* ("to Je[remiah]"), under the influence of the first person style of ch. xxvii.

ings of Yahweh's house which Nebuchadnezzar, king of Babylon, took from this place and carried to Babylon. 4 I am also going to bring back to this place Jeconiah ben Jehoiakim, king of Judah, and all the exiles of Judah who have gone to Babylon—Yahweh's word; for I will break the yoke of the king of Babylon.'"*

5 Then Prophet Jeremiah addressed Prophet Hananiah in the presence of the priests and of all the people who were standing there in Yahweh's house. 6 Prophet Jeremiah said, "Amen! May Yahweh do so! May Yahweh confirm the truth of what you have prophesied by bringing back to this place from Babylon the furnishings of Yahweh's house, and all those who have been exiled. 7 Nevertheless, please listen to what I am going to say here before you, and before all the people. 8 The prophets who were of old, before my time and yours, prophesied against many countries and great kingdoms of war, of disaster* and plague. 9 As for the prophet who prophesies of well-being—well, when that prophet's word comes to pass, then it can be acknowledged that he is the prophet whom Yahweh has really sent."

10 Then Prophet Hananiah snatched the yoke* from Prophet Jeremiah's neck, and broke it. 11 And Hananiah spoke in the presence of all the people as follows: "This is what Yahweh has said: Just so will I break the yoke of Nebuchadnezzar, king of Babylon, off the neck of all the nations—within two years' time." And, at that, Prophet Jeremiah went away.

12 But then, sometime after Prophet Hananiah had broken the yoke *from off his neck,* the word of Yahweh came to Jeremiah as follows: 13 "Go, tell Hananiah, 'This is what Yahweh has said: You have broken wooden yoke-bars, only to make iron ones in their place. 14 *For this is what Yahweh of Hosts, the

---

n–n LXX: "Within two years' time I will bring back to this place the furnishings of the Lord's house, and Jeconiah, and the exiles of Judah; for I will break the yoke of the king of Babylon." See NOTE.

o So Heb. (*lᵉrāʿāh*). But various manuscripts read "of famine" (*lᵉrāʿāb*), which is the usual word in this series. LXX may be preferable in omitting "of disaster and plague" and reading only "of war" (cf. "of peace, well-being" in vs. 9).

p Literally, "the yoke-bar." LXX reads plural (cf. vs. 13 and xxvii 2), and so in vs. 12.

q–q This follows LXX, if only to avoid the awkwardness (to our taste) of Heb. "from off the neck of Jeremiah the prophet."

God of Israel, has said: An iron yoke have I placed on the neck of all these nations, namely, to be subjects of Nebuchadnezzar, king of Babylon. And they shall be his subjects. Indeed, I have given him the wild beasts as well.' "[r] 15 So Prophet Jeremiah said to Prophet Hananiah, "Listen, Hananiah! Yahweh never sent you! And you—you have led this people to trust in a lie! 16 And so, this is what Yahweh has said: Believe me, I am going to 'send' you—right off the face of the earth! This very year you are going to die, because you have uttered rebellion against Yahweh."

17 And Hananiah the prophet did die that year, in the seventh month.

[r-r] LXX "For thus said the Lord: An iron yoke I have placed on the neck of all the nations [namely] to serve the king of Babylon."

NOTES

xxvii 1. Vs. 1, which places the events of this chapter in the accession year of Jehoiakim (see textual note[a]), is wanting in LXX and is certainly not original; without it, the chapter begins exactly as do the similar passages in chs. xiii and xix. Some evidence (three manuscripts, Syr., etc., cf. xxviii 1) supports the reading, "In the accession year of Zedekiah . . ." (and so RSV); but this is likewise inaccurate and is probably a correction of MT. In xxviii 1 the attempt is made to harmonize this (corrected) reading with the actual date of ch. xxviii (the fourth year of Zedekiah) by pointing out (correctly) that chs. xxvii and xxviii refer to the "same year."

2. *thongs and yoke-bars*. The ox-yoke consisted of a wooden bar, or bars, held about the animal's neck, or lashed to the horns, by cords or leather thongs.

3. *send word*. The Heb. "send them" would imply that Jeremiah made a yoke for each king mentioned (in addition to one for himself), put each on his neck briefly, and then gave it to the appropriate ambassador. In common with virtually all commentators (cf. RSV), this seems to me unlikely. Only one yoke seems to have been made—that worn by Jeremiah; the ambassadors are simply to report this symbolic act and its meaning. The suffix "them" (one letter in Hebrew) has probably carried over from vs. 2; omit with LXX[L].

5. *by my . . . irresistible might*. Literally "by my outstretched arm."

6. *all these countries*. LXX ("the earth") may be more original, with

MT representing an effort to make it clear that *hā'āreṣ* does not mean just "the land" (Judah), but all the countries mentioned above.

my servant. Application of this title to Nebuchadnezzar was apparently offensive in some circles. LXX omits or alters on each occurrence in the Jeremiah book (cf. xxv 5; xliii 10). Here some manuscripts of LXX omit, others read, "to serve him."

7. LXX omits this verse, and many believe it to be an expansion (cf. xxv 12, 14). But it is equally possible that it is original, and was dropped in the tradition behind LXX after Nebuchadnezzar's son was superseded (in 560) and his line ended.

8. *until I have delivered them into his power*. Heb. *'ad tummī 'ōtām* cannot be rendered "until I have consumed them," since the verb is never transitive. The best suggestion is to read *tittī* for *tummī* (so Syr., Tar.): the idiom *ntn bᵉyad* is a favorite in Jeremiah. If *tummī* is retained, a word must be assumed to have dropped out: "until I have finished ( )ing them. . . ."

10. *which will only serve to remove you*. Or, "the result of which will be to. . . ." Heb. *lᵉma'an*, properly "in order that," frequently (like Gr. *hina*) takes on the force of result—and so here, since it was hardly the intention of these prophets to destroy their respective countries.

15. *with the result that*. Cf. Note on vs. 10.

16. *the furnishings*. I really do not know the right word to translate *kᵉlī* as used in this section. "Vessels" (EVV) is rather old-fashioned and not quite accurate, for more than "vessels" are meant (vs. 19); "utensils" is better, but still does not cover the case. "Furnishings" must be understood to include movable objects of all sorts.

xxviii 1. Hebrew begins, "In that year, in the accession year of Zedekiah, king of Judah, in the fourth year. . . ." This is self-contradictory and seemingly an attempt to harmonize xxvii 1 (reading "Zedekiah" for "Jehoiakim"; see textual note[a] and Note on xxvii 1 above) with the actual date of the incident (Zedekiah's fourth year). Since xxvii 1 is not original, LXX (which omits it) may reflect the original heading, reading simply, "In the fourth year of Zedekiah. . . ." But the notation "in the same year" is factually correct, for the incident of ch. xxviii took place not long after that of ch. xxvii (Jeremiah is still wearing the yoke: vs. 10 f.).

2. *I have broken the yoke*. The figure was of course suggested to Hananiah by the sight of Jeremiah wearing the yoke (cf. vs. 10 f.).

3–4. The translation follows MT, which is grammatically unobjectionable. But the shorter text of LXX (cf. textual note[n-n]) seems more original. The expansions of MT are typical of the Jeremiah prose.

5. *Prophet Jeremiah . . . Prophet Hananiah*. Hebrew throughout

the chapter designates each of these men as "the prophet" whenever their names occur; LXX consistently omits. Though repetition of "the prophet" is to our taste redundant and awkward, it may be that the writer wished with the utmost emphasis—and irony—to point up the fact that prophet was contradicting prophet, and in the name of Yahweh.

6. Jeremiah is not speaking sarcastically. As a man and a patriot, he sincerely wishes that he could believe what Hananiah has said.

13. *only to make iron ones.* Hananiah's symbolic action, by which he supposed that Yahweh's word against Babylon was set in motion, has the exact opposite effect of making a stronger yoke. But many scholars prefer LXX, "but I will make. . . ."

14. LXX again has a shorter and, one thinks, more original text (cf. textual note[r–r]).

16. *I am going to 'send' you.* Note the wordplay: Yahweh did not "send" Hananiah to prophesy but, since he has done so anyhow, Yahweh will "send" him to death. On death as the penalty for false prophecy, cf. COMMENT.

because you have uttered rebellion against Yahweh. The clause cites Deut xiii 6[5E] and may be an expansion; LXX omits.

17. Note that he who predicted deliverance in two years (vs. 3) dies in two months (cf. "the fifth month," vs. 1).

COMMENT

Although chapters xxvii and xxviii are of different literary types and seem originally to have been transmitted separately, they belong together factually and should be read together. Both have to do with an incident, or series of incidents, that occurred in the fourth year of Zedekiah's reign (594/3), as xxviii 1 attempts to make clear (see notes on xxvii 1 and xxviii 1). It will be recalled that in that year (cf. Introduction, "The Background of Jeremiah's Career . . .") various vassal states in the western part of Nebuchadnezzar's empire, no doubt encouraged by disturbances that had erupted in Babylon the year before, began to toy with the idea of rebellion. As we see from xxvii 3, ambassadors from certain of these states had come to Jerusalem to confer with Zedekiah, presumably to enlist his support and to formulate plans. In Jerusalem, meanwhile, prophets were stirring up the populace by declaring that Yahweh would shortly overthrow Babylon and bring King Jehoiachin and the other exiles, with all the booty taken from the city, triumphantly home. It is quite plain that the country was on the verge of open revolt.

Chapter xxvii (save for the erroneous chronological notation in vs. 1) is an extended discourse, or series of discourses, in the typical style of the Jeremiah prose, with Jeremiah speaking in the first person. It begins with the account of a symbolic action similar in its intent to the smashing of the bottle in xix 1–13, or the hiding of the waistcloth in xiii 1–11. We are told that Jeremiah, at Yahweh's command, made an ox-yoke and, putting it on his neck, appeared before the ambassadors who had come to Jerusalem, and gave them a charge to convey to their respective kings (vss. 2–11): the yoke is Nebuchadnezzar's yoke, which Yahweh has in his sovereign will placed on their necks, and they must wear it or face destruction. The conviction expressed here, incidentally, goes far toward explaining Jeremiah's seemingly unpatriotic and defeatist attitude in the years that followed. Then, having delivered the above charge, Jeremiah gave the same message to his own king (vss. 12–15), and subsequently addressed the people, branding talk of a speedy return of the exiles as a lie spoken in Yahweh's name (vss. 16–22).

At few places in the book do LXX and MT differ more widely than in this chapter and, to a somewhat lesser degree, in the next. These differences, as is usually the case in the prose of Jeremiah, consist chiefly of omissions on the part of LXX. Many of these, to be sure, are trivial, and some are perhaps due to scribal error. In some cases, however (especially in xxvii 16–22, where LXX is markedly shorter), one is constrained to believe that LXX has the more original text, and that MT is a splendid illustration of the way in which the prose discourses of Jeremiah were verbally expanded in the course of transmission. Important divergencies of this sort are indicated in the textual notes.

Unlike xxvii, chapter xxviii is a biographical account: Jeremiah is referred to in the third person (but see textual note^m). The narrative itself, which tells how a prophet named Hananiah publicly contradicted Jeremiah and broke the yoke he was wearing, requires no explanation. Most instructive, however, is the light that it casts upon a problem which must have perplexed the people of the day profoundly: How could one tell a true prophet from a false one? One notes that Hananiah spoke in the form of prophetic address ("This is what Yahweh has said": cf. vss. 2, 11), just as Jeremiah did. Nor is there anything to suggest that he did not do so sincerely. Jeremiah, indeed, indicated that he wished that he could believe what Hananiah had said (vs. 6). But the result was that prophetic word flatly contradicted prophetic word—and one can imagine the puzzlement of the hearers. It is interesting that Jeremiah, when Hananiah confronted him, seemed to feel that at the moment he had no word from Yahweh to say. He therefore did not call Hananiah a liar but (vss. 6–9) merely pointed out (a) that Hananiah's words were not in the tradition of the great prophets of the past (he doubtless thought of such prophets as Isaiah and Micah), and (b) that the event would have to show who was speaking the truth (cf. Deut xviii 21 f.). Even when Hananiah snatched the yoke from his neck and broke it, Jeremiah said nothing, but meekly went away (vss. 10–11). It was only later (vss. 12–16), when a new revelation had come to him, that he denounced Hananiah in the name of Yahweh.

The denouement of the incident is likewise interesting. Hananiah (vs. 16) is sentenced to death. This accords perfectly with the thought expressed in Deut xviii 20 that to prophesy falsely in the name of Yahweh, as Hananiah had done, was to commit a capital crime. We recall that Jeremiah's enemies had tried to execute him, because they believed that *he* had prophesied falsely (see ch. xxvi and COMMENT). In this case, however, the sentence was to be executed by no human hands, but by Yahweh himself. There is no reason whatever to doubt that Hananiah, borne down—we may suppose—by this awful curse, actually did die as vs. 17 states: the incident would scarcely have been recorded otherwise.

28. THE YEAR 594:
JEREMIAH AND THE EXILES IN BABYLON
(xxix 1–15; 21–23; 16–20; 24–32; li 59–64b)

Jeremiah's Letter to the Exiles

XXIX 1 This is the text of the letter that Jeremiah the prophet sent from Jerusalem *to those who were left of the elders* of the exiles, to the priests and the prophets, and to all the people whom Nebuchadnezzar had deported from Jerusalem to Babylon. 2 (This was after King Jeconiah, the queen mother, the palace officials, the princes of Judah and Jerusalem, together with the artisans and the [smiths (?)], had gone from Jerusalem.) 3 The letter was sent through the agency of Elasah ben Shaphan and Gemariah ben Hilkiah, whom Zedekiah, king of Judah, sent to Babylon on a mission to Nebuchadnezzar, king of Babylon. It said:

4 "This is what Yahweh of Hosts, the God of Israel, has said to all the exiles whom I have deported from Jerusalem to Babylon: 5 Build houses and settle down. Plant gardens, and eat their produce. 6 Marry, and beget sons and daughters; take wives for your sons and give your daughters in marriage, that they too may have sons and daughters, in order that you may increase in number there, rather than decrease. 7 Seek the welfare of the country*b* to which I have deported you, and pray on its behalf to Yahweh, for on its welfare your own depends. 8 Yes, this is what Yahweh of Hosts, the God of Israel, has said: Do not let those prophets of yours who are in your midst, or your diviners,

a–a LXX has merely "to the elders." Although some scholars (and so RSV) prefer this, MT seems to represent the more difficult, and preferable, reading. See NOTE.
b So LXX. Hebrew has "the city." See NOTE.

deceive you. Pay no heed to *the dreams that they are always dreaming.* 9 It's a lie that they are preaching to you in my name! I did not send them—Yahweh's word.

10 "For this is what Yahweh has said: Only when Babylon's seventy years have been completed will I intervene in your behalf, and fulfill my promise to you to bring you back to this place. 11 Surely I know the plans that I have for you—Yahweh's word—plans for your welfare, not for your hurt, to give you the future you hope for. 12 *When you call on me, and come* and pray to me, I will hear you. 13 When you search for me, you will find me. Yes, when you seek me wholeheartedly, 14 *I will be found by you*—Yahweh's word. I will reverse your fortunes and will gather you out of all the nations and places to which I have driven you—Yahweh's word—and will restore you to the place from which I have deported you.

15 "Now, because you say, 'Yahweh has raised up prophets for us in Babylon,'   — 21 this is what Yahweh of Hosts, the God of Israel, has said regarding Ahab ben Kolaiah and Zedekiah ben Maaseiah, who are prophesying a lie to you in my name: Believe me, I am going to hand them over to Nebuchadrezzar, king of Babylon, who will execute them before your very eyes. 22 And a curse word will be derived from them which will be used by all the exiles of Judah in Babylon: 'May Yahweh make you like Zedekiah and Ahab, whom the king of Babylon roasted in the fire!'— 23 because they have done a scandalous thing in Israel, committing adultery with their neighbors' wives, and speaking *in my name a word* that I did not tell them to speak. But I both know this and am witness to it—Yahweh's word."

c–c This emendation, though conjectural, is adopted by many scholars; the context requires something of the sort. Hebrew is corrupt: "your dreams which you cause to be dreamed [?]"; the verb form *maḥlemīm* is a mixture, and probably is an error for *hēm ḥōlemīm*. LXX has "your dreams which you dream" (but cf. third person in vs. 9).
d–d LXX omits this; Syr. omits "and come." Possibly MT combines variants.
e–e LXX reads, "I will manifest myself to you." LXX also omits the rest of the verse, which may well be an expansion.
f–f Heb. "a word in my name, a lie. . . ." LXX omits "a lie," which is apparently a gloss.

An Inserted Saying

16 Yes, this is what Yahweh has said concerning the king who sits on David's throne, and concerning all the people who live in this city—that is, your kinsmen who did not accompany you into exile: 17 "This is what Yahweh of Hosts has said: Watch me send among them sword, starvation, and disease, and make them like putrid figs too rotten to eat. 18 I will pursue them with the sword, with starvation and disease, and make them a sight that will horrify all the kingdoms of the earth—an execration, an appalling and shocking spectacle, and a reproach among all the nations whither I have driven them— 19 because they paid no heed to what I said—Yahweh's word. When *I sent to you* my servants the prophets with such urgency and persistence, you did not listen—Yahweh's word. 20 Now, as for you, hear the word of Yahweh, all you exiles whom I have sent away from Jerusalem to Babylon. . . ."

Repercussions of the Letter

24 To Shemaiah the Nehelamite you shall say: 25 "This is what Yahweh of Hosts, the God of Israel, has said: Because you have undertaken on your own initiative to send *a letter to Zephaniah ben Maaseiah, the priest,* to this effect: 26 'Yahweh has appointed you priest in place of the priest Jehoiada, to be overseer* in Yahweh's house to put any crazy fellow who takes himself for a prophet in the stocks and collar. 27 Now then, why have you not disciplined Jeremiah of Anathoth, who takes it on himself to prophesy to you? 28 Why, he has even sent to us in Baby-

g–g So for smoothness with various manuscripts; MT ". . . to them." But the shift of persons in vs. 19 is scarcely grammatical, and cannot be cured by emendation.
h–h Heb. "send letters to all the people who are in Jerusalem, and to Zephaniah ben Maaseiah the priest, and to all the priests." But only one letter, to Zephaniah, is in question here (cf. vss. 26 ff., 29); "letters" (plural) can refer to a single communication (e.g., II Kings xix 14). Omissions follow LXX.
i So Vrs. (*pāqīd*); MT has plural, apparently in error.

lon, telling us, "It's going to be a long time! Build houses and settle down. Plant gardens, and eat their produce [. . .]." ' "

29 Zephaniah the priest, however, read this letter to Jeremiah. 30 Then the word of Yahweh came to Jeremiah as follows: 31 "Send to all the exiles and tell them, 'This is what Yahweh has said concerning Shemaiah the Nehelamite: Because Shemaiah has prophesied to you, though I did not send him, and has led you to trust in a lie— 32 this is what Yahweh has said: Ah, but I am going to punish Shemaiah the Nehelamite, and his offspring! He shall have ʲno one left among you to see the good things that I am going to do for youʲ—Yahweh's word—for he has preached rebellion against Yahweh.' "

Prophetic Symbolism: the Message of Babylon's Doom

LI 59 The commission that Jeremiah the prophet entrusted to Seraiah ben Neriah ben Mahseiah when the latter went with Zedekiah, king of Judah, to Babylon in the fourth year of that king's reign. (Seraiah was the chief quartermaster). 60 Now Jeremiah had written down on a single sheet all the evil that should overtake Babylon. 61 And Jeremiah said to Seraiah, "When you get to Babylon, see to it that you read all these words aloud, 62 and say, 'O Yahweh, it is thou who hast said that thou wouldst destroy this place so that nothing can live in it, whether man or beast, and that it would be a desolate waste forever.' 63 Then, when you have finished reading this sheet, tie a stone to it and throw it into the Euphrates, 64 and say, 'Just so shall Babylon sink to rise no more, because of the evil that I am going to bring upon it.' "ᵏ

ʲ⁻ʲ So following LXX, for smoothness' sake. Heb. is awkward: "no one living among this people, nor will he see the good that I am going to do my people." LXX also omits from this point on; the last clause of the verse (cf. xxviii 16) may be an expansion drawn from Deut xiii 6[5E].

ᵏ Hebrew adds at the end "and they shall weary themselves. Thus far the words of Jeremiah." Omit with LXX. The words belong at the end of vs. 58 ("and they shall weary themselves" ends that verse too) as the conclusion of the preceding Jeremiah collection, and were displaced when vss. 59–64 were inserted here.

NOTES

xxix 1. *to those who were left of the elders.* See textual note[a-a]. One wonders (so Duhm and others) if some of the elders had not been executed or imprisoned as a result of the unrest which the letter clearly indicates had been prevalent (perhaps during the disturbances of 595/4: cf. COMMENT).

2. The verse is a parenthetical insertion (cf. xxiv 1b), apparently based on II Kings xxiv 12–16. The connection between vss. 1 and 3 is interrupted by it; the words "The letter was sent" have been supplied at the beginning of vs. 3 to restore this connection.

the palace officials. Heb. *sārīsīm.* Usually translated "eunuchs," the word is here, as elsewhere (cf. lii 25; I Sam viii 15, etc.), a conventional title for royal officials of some sort.

smiths. The meaning of the word (*masgēr*) is uncertain; see NOTE on xxiv 1.

3. It is quite probable, though not certain, that Elasah was a brother of Ahikam ben Shaphan (xxvi 24), and of Gemariah ben Shaphan (xxxvi 10 ff.), both of whom had shown friendship to Jeremiah. Perhaps, too, Gemariah ben Hilkiah was a son of Josiah's high priest (II Kings xxii 4 ff.). The coincidence of names is, in any event, remarkable.

4. *whom I have deported.* Although the shift from third to first person is to our taste awkward, it is unwise to emend to "who have been deported" (so Syr.), as many scholars do. Such shifts are frequent in prophetic address; LXX agrees with MT.

7. *the country.* Hebrew has "the city," which might be retained if taken distributively ("whichever city"). The exiles were not all settled in one place.

on its welfare your own depends. Literally "in its welfare shall be your welfare." The appeal is frankly to self-interest (would an altruistic appeal have been heeded?), but the injunction to pray for Babylon is nonetheless remarkable (see COMMENT).

8–9. There is no compelling reason to regard these verses as an insertion, or to transpose them after vs. 15, as various scholars do. They give needed reinforcement to the preceding verses (the prophets were the ones who had told the people their stay would be short), and lead into those that follow (release will come only after "seventy years").

10. *Babylon's seventy years.* Cf. NOTE on xxv 11. The figure was no doubt originally intended as a round number (cf. xxvii 7, where Babylon's power is to last to the third generation). One cannot explain rationally why it was that Jeremiah was assured that Babylon's rule

would be so relatively brief. But there is no reason to regard the verse as a *vaticinium ex eventu;* we can only record the fact that the prediction turned out to be approximately correct (which may be why later writings made so much of it). From the fall of Nineveh (612) to the fall of Babylon (539) was seventy-three years; from Nebuchadnezzar's accession (605) to the fall of Babylon was sixty-six years.

11. *the future you hope for.* Literally "a future [latter end] and a hope"—hendiadys for "the hoped-for future" or "a future full of hope."

12. *When you call on me . . . I will hear you.* This sentence could equally well be translated, "You will call . . . and I will hear"— and the ensuing ones similarly.

13. *wholeheartedly.* Again, let it be stressed that "with all your heart" does not primarily refer to the emotions, but has the force: "with all your will, energies."

21. Verses 16–20 are an intrusion from another context; vs. 21 follows directly on vs. 15. In LXX (except Lucian which has the order vss. 14, 16–20, 15, 21–23) vss. 16–20 are missing. For the sake of clarity these verses are treated separately. Perhaps they were inserted in order to stress the fact that Yahweh, far from bringing the exiles quickly home, would finish the destruction of Judah. In vs. 21, LXX has, characteristically, a shorter text: "Thus said the Lord concerning Ahab and Zedekiah: 'Behold, I hand them over to the king of Babylon, who will. . . .' "

23. Jeremiah views the execution of these prophets as punishment for their immorality and false prophesying. Nebuchadnezzar, naturally, had them executed because their words were seditious.

I both know this and am witness. Literally "I am the one who knows and. . . ." But LXX reads only, "And I am witness."

16–20. See NOTE on vs. 21 above.

17. *putrid figs.* Or perhaps "bruised, mashed . . ." (cf. KB); the word occurs only here. The figure is that used in ch. xxiv.

18. *an appalling and shocking spectacle.* Literally "a horror and a hissing (whistling)," i.e., a sight so shocking that men whistle in awe.

20. The verse serves to restore the connection between vss. 15 and 21 (see NOTE on vs. 21) which was broken by the insertion of vss. 16–19.

24. *the Nehelamite.* Whether Shemaiah's family or place of origin is uncertain. It has recently been argued (L. Yaure, JBL 79 [1960], 297–314) that this is the Niphal participle of *ḥlm* ("to dream"): "Shemaiah the dreamer" (cf. vs. 8; xxvii 9, etc.). But there are no parallels for this usage, and the Niphal of *ḥlm* does not occur elsewhere.

26. *to be overseer.* On the function of the *pāqīd*, cf. xx 1–6. Zephaniah is also mentioned in xxi 1; xxxvii 3, and is probably the "second priest" named in lii 24.

any crazy fellow who takes himself for a prophet. Literally "any man who is crazy and prophesying," i.e., any crazy ecstatic. Prophetic ecstasy no doubt frequently fell over into wild raving (cf. I Sam xix 20–24, etc.) that had to be curbed.

29. It is not clear whether Zephaniah was sympathetic toward Jeremiah, or intended his action as a warning. In any event, Jeremiah was not disciplined.

li 59. *the latter went . . . that king's reign.* So for clarity; Heb. "he went . . . his reign."

with Zedekiah. So Hebrew, probably correctly (see COMMENT). But LXX reads "from Zedekiah" (i.e., on his orders).

chief quartermaster. Literally "officer [in charge] of the resting place" (i.e., the bivouac or billet for overnight stops en route); perhaps we would call him the king's "Headquarters Commandant." LXX, "officer of the tribute gifts" (*mᵉnāḥōt* for *mᵉnūḥāh*), is not to be preferred.

60. Hebrew ends the verse: "[i.e.] all these words that are [here] written concerning Babylon." This seems to identify the document given Seraiah, which was probably quite brief, with the oracles against Babylon in l 1–li 58; it seems to be a gloss added when these verses were (secondarily) placed in their present position.

64. See textual note[k].

COMMENT

The passages in this section relate, as do the preceding ones, to the fourth year of Zedekiah's reign (594/3). It is true that chapter xxix, the basis of which is a letter written by Jeremiah to the exiles in Babylon, bears no precise date; indeed, even the indefinite notation in vs. 2 that the events described took place after the deportation of 597 seems to be an insertion based on II Kings xxiv 12–16, as is the case in xxiv 1 (it is syntactically a parenthesis). Nevertheless, there can be little doubt that the situation is roughly the same as that of chapters xxvii and xxviii. In the midst of unrest in Jerusalem, Jeremiah had learned of similar unrest among the exiles in Babylon. He had also learned that this unrest—again as was true in Jerusalem—had been in good part provoked by prophets who were assuring the exiles that they would soon be going home. Perhaps a rebellion which had broken out in Babylon in the preceding year, and in which elements of the army seem to have been involved (cf. Introduction, "The Background of Jeremiah's Career . . ."), had helped to arouse these wild hopes. The fact that Jeremiah's letter was forwarded (vs. 3) through envoys sent by Zedekiah to Nebuchadnezzar's court fits well with a date in 594, for Zedekiah would have been obliged, after the disturbances that had taken place in Judah, to smooth matters over and assure Nebuchadnezzar of his loyalty.

After an introduction supplied by the Biographer (vss. 1, 3), the text of the letter is given. This comprises vss. 4–14, and then continues in vss. 15 and 21–23. Verses 16–20, on the other hand, are no part of the letter, but a prose saying drawn in from some other context; the verses are absent from LXX (see further, NOTES). The letter is cast in the form of a prophetic oracle, and is most instructive. In it Jeremiah charges the exiles to disregard the wild promises of their prophets and to settle down for a long stay, pursuing a normal life as peaceable subjects of Babylon, and even praying to Yahweh for that country's welfare (vss. 4–9). Although this last injunction (vs. 7) is given a practical motivation (the exiles' own welfare depends upon that of Babylon), it is nonetheless remarkable, for a command to Jews to pray for the hated heathen power is otherwise unexampled in literature of the period. One may find in it (Volz, Rudolph) a preparatory step toward that lively concern for the turning of the Gentiles to Yahweh expressed somewhat later by Second Isaiah, and the mission that he laid before Israel to be "a light to the nations" Isa xlii 6; xlix 6). Yet, in spite of the fact that he discouraged hopes of immediate return, Jeremiah did not leave the exiles comfortless. Rather, he assured them (vss. 10–14) that Yahweh would, in his own time, fulfill their hopes and lead them home and that, in the meantime, they could call on him and find him—and without temple or cult!—even in the land of their exile. The letter then closes (vss. 15, 21–23) with a specific word regarding two prophets who had been inciting unrest, and whose conduct was an open scandal. Jeremiah declared that Nebuchadnezzar would execute these prophets—which we may be sure that he did.

In vss. 24–32 the account of an incident growing out of the above letter is given. We learn that one of the exiles, a prophet named Shemaiah, took exception to what Jeremiah had said, and wrote to the ecclesiastical authorities in Jerusalem demanding that he be disciplined and silenced. This letter was read to Jeremiah, who then replied with an oracle from Yahweh denouncing Shemaiah as a false prophet and announcing that his line would die out in Israel. The text of this passage is in some confusion. After an introduction (vs. 24) in which Jeremiah is addressed by Yahweh in the second person, an oracle directed at Shemaiah is begun (vs. 25), but then interrupted and never resumed. In vs. 30 there is a new introduction, with Jeremiah now referred to in the third person, followed by an oracle concerning Shemaiah (vss. 31–32), who is also spoken of in the third person. The ancient versions differ from MT (and among themselves), but do little to alleviate the confusion. Although the general sense is clear throughout, a smooth translation can be achieved only by arbitrary emendation; the translation given follows MT, with minor changes.

The incident described in li 59–64, as its date indicates, also belongs in this context. It seems that Zedekiah himself (if MT is correct: see NOTES) was obliged to go to Babylon accompanied, we may suppose, by a considerable entourage, presumably to make his peace with Nebuchadnezzar. Jeremiah seized the opportunity to entrust to Seraiah, one of the king's officers and probably Baruch's brother, a written oracle announcing the doom of Babylon. On arrival in Babylon, Seraiah was to read this oracle aloud (though scarcely publicly) and then throw it into the river, thus symbolically indicating that Yahweh's word of judgment had been set in motion. This symbolic action is similar to that of Jeremiah in wearing the ox-yoke (ch. xxvii)—and of Hananiah in breaking it (ch. xxviii). The account of this incident has been attached to the oracles against Babylon in l 1–li 58 only secondarily (see further, textual notes); there is no reason whatever to doubt its historicity.

29. JUDAH'S LAST HOUR BEGINS: WORDS OF JEREMIAH AS THE BABYLONIAN BLOCKADE TIGHTENED
(xxi 1–10; xxxiv 1–7)

Zedekiah's Inquiry and Jeremiah's Reply

XXI ¹ The word that came to Jeremiah from Yahweh when King Zedekiah sent Pashhur ben Malkiah and Zephaniah ben Maaseiah, the priest, to him with the request: ² "Inquire, please, of Yahweh for us; for Nebuchadrezzar, king of Babylon, is attacking us. Perhaps Yahweh will perform for us one of his mighty acts and force him to withdraw."

³ But Jeremiah said to them, "Take this answer to Zedekiah: ⁴ 'This is what Yahweh, the God of Israel, has said: Believe me, I am going to repel the forces at your disposal with which, in the open field, you are resisting the king of Babylon, and the Chaldeans who are closing in upon you, and I will pull them back right into this city. ⁵ I myself will fight against you with lashing fist and mighty arm, in anger, wrath, and great fury. ⁶ I will strike down those living in this city, both men and beasts; in a great plague they shall die. ⁷ After that—Yahweh's word—I will hand over Zedekiah, king of Judah, his courtiers, *and such of the people of this city as have survived* the plague, the sword, and starvation,* to Nebuchadrezzar, king of Babylon, to their foes, and to those who seek their lives. And he will put them to the sword without pity, mercy, or compassion.'"

a–a So following LXX; Heb. "and the people, and those who survive in the city." Omit the repeated *weʾet*—dittography.
b From this point on, LXX has a different and shorter text: ". . . to their foes who seek their lives, and they will put them to the sword. I will not spare them or have compassion on them."

Jeremiah Advises Desertion

8 "To this people you shall say, 'This is what Yahweh has said: Look! I offer you a choice between the way of life and the way of death. 9 Whoever stays in this city will die by the sword, by starvation and disease. But whoever goes out and surrenders to the Chaldeans who are blockading you will live; he will at least escape with his life. 10 For I regard this city with hostility, not with favor—Yahweh's word: it will be handed over to the king of Babylon, who will put it to the torch.' "

A Further Word to Zedekiah

XXXIV 1 The word that came to Jeremiah from Yahweh while Nebuchadrezzar, king of Babylon, and his entire army, together with *ᶜall the kingdoms and peoples of the land subject to his rule,ᶜ* were attacking Jerusalem and all the cities belonging to it: 2 "This is what Yahweh, the God of Israel, has said: Go and speak to Zedekiah, king of Judah, and tell him, 'This is what Yahweh has said: Believe me, I am going to hand this city over to the king of Babylon, who ᵈwill take it andᵈ put it to the torch. 3 As for yourself, you will not escape his clutches, but will certainly be captured and handed over to him. You will be made to confront him face to face and answer to him personally; and you will go to Babylon. 4 Only heed the word of Yahweh, O Zedekiah, king of Judah! This is what Yahweh has said of you: You shall not die by the sword. 5 You shall die peacefully. And as spices were burned for your ancestors, the kings who preceded you, so shall they burn spices for you and bewail you, crying, "Ah, lord!" Truly that is a promise, and I myself have made it— Yahweh's word.' "

6 ᵉSo Jeremiah repeated all these words to King Zedekiah in Jerusalem,ᵉ 7 the forces of the king of Babylon being then

ᶜ⁻ᶜ The phrase is awkward in Hebrew and has probably suffered conflation; LXX abbreviates.

ᵈ⁻ᵈ Added with LXX.

ᵉ⁻ᵉ The reading follows LXX; Hebrew has "Jeremiah the prophet" and "Zedekiah, king of Judah," which is (to our taste, at least) redundant.

engaged in operations against Jerusalem and such of Judah's
cities as were left, that is, against Lachish and Azekah, for these
alone remained of the cities of Judah that were fortified.

NOTES

xxi 1. *Pashhur ben Malkiah.* Not to be confused with the Pashhur
ben Immer in xx 1–6. The Pashhur referred to here was among those
of the nobility who later attempted to have Jeremiah executed for treason
(xxxviii 1).

Zephaniah ben Maaseiah. The priest already encountered in xxix 24–32.
He was not, so far as we know, hostile to Jeremiah (cf. also xxxvii 3).

2. *will perform for us one of his mighty acts.* Literally "will deal
with us (point *'ittānū*) according to all his wonderful acts" (i.e., like
those of old). Doubtless they think particularly of Jerusalem's marvelous
deliverance from Sennacherib, king of Assyria, a century earlier (cf.
II Kings xviii 17–xix 37 // Isa xxxvi–xxxvii).

4. The sentence is long and clumsy in Heb.; LXX, by several omissions
which do not alter the sense (e.g., "the king of Babylon and"; "and I will
pull them back") achieves a smoother, and perhaps preferable, text.

the forces at your disposal. Literally "the weapons of war which are
in your hands"—of course a metonymy for Judah's troops.

in the open field. Literally "outside the walls." This is taken as modify-
ing "with which you are resisting." But it could as well modify "repel"
("I will turn back the forces—from the open field—into the city").

closing in upon you. Or, "blockading you, pressing you hard"; not,
however, "besieging you" (EVV), for the verse shows that the actual
siege has not yet begun.

5. *with lashing fist.* Literally "with outstretched hand," i.e., irresistible
force.

7. *his courtiers.* Literally "his servants"—which, in this context, means
"courtiers, officials," or the like.

8. *you shall say.* The verb is singular; Jeremiah is addressed by
Yahweh. Verses 8–10 are a separate saying, not part of Jeremiah's reply
to the king's messengers.

I offer you a choice between. Literally "I set before you. . . ."

9. *will at least escape with his life.* Literally "his life will be his for
booty." On the force of this idiom see NOTE on xlv 5.

xxxiv 1. *all the kingdoms and peoples . . . subject to his rule.* I.e.,
contingents from the various vassal states of the empire.

all the cities belonging to it. I.e., the outlying towns of Judah—and so LXX expressly.

3. *You will be made to confront him face to face and answer to him personally.* Literally "Your eyes will see his [so LXX; Heb. "the king of Babylon's"] eyes, and his mouth will speak with your mouth." As a rebellious vassal who had broken his oath of allegiance (cf. Ezek xvii 11–21) Zedekiah could expect no mercy.

4. One cannot understand vss. 4–5 as an outright promise; matters did not turn out so, and a prediction that did not come true would hardly have been preserved. The force is conditional: heed the word of Yahweh (and surrender), and he then promises you your life. Jeremiah continued to tell Zedekiah this to the end (xxxviii 17–18).

5. On these mourning customs cf. xxii 18; II Chron xvi 14; xxi 19, etc.

COMMENT

We know nothing of Jeremiah's activity in the years immediately following the disturbances of 594. When next we meet him, in the passages in this section and those that follow, the final siege of Jerusalem had begun. The course of events has already been sketched (Introduction, "The Background of Jeremiah's Career . . ."). It was presumably sometime in 589 that Zedekiah, pushed by his chauvinistic nobles and encouraged by promises of help from Egypt, rebelled. How quickly the Babylonians reacted, and when, is unknown—probably late in 589. At any rate, by January 588 (lii 4) their army had arrived in force and begun operations against Jerusalem. The Babylonian strategy was apparently first of all to drive Judahite forces—such as they could not destroy in the field—back upon their strong points, which they then reduced one by one, meanwhile holding Jerusalem under an ever-tighter blockade. These operations presumably went on through the winter and spring of 588 until, by the end of that time, the country was in desperate straits. The passages treated in this section all relate to this phase of the campaign (late 589 or early 588).

In xxi 1–7 we have the account of Jeremiah's reply to an inquiry on the part of Zedekiah. The king obviously wished to be assured that Yahweh would miraculously intervene and force Nebuchadnezzar to withdraw. But Jeremiah told him that nothing of the sort would happen: Yahweh was actually fighting against his people, and the city would surely be taken. This incident is very similar to the one recorded in xxxvii 3–10. But the two are not to be confused. Whereas that incident, as we shall see, took place somewhat later, while the siege had been temporarily lifted because of the approach of the Egyptians, this one clearly fell at the very beginning of the campaign, before (see NOTES on vs. 4) the siege had actually begun, and while Judahite troops were still resisting in the field. Transmitted with the piece just described is an originally separate saying (xxi 8–10) in the style of the prose discourses of the book (Yahweh addresses Jeremiah in the second person). In it Jeremiah speaks to the people and advises them to desert if they wish to save their lives. This, of course, was regarded by the nation's leaders as high treason, and very nearly cost Jeremiah his life, as we shall see (cf. xxxviii 2–4).

In xxxiv 1–7 there is a further word from Jeremiah to Zedekiah (vss. 2–5), for which the Biographer has supplied a framework describing its setting (vss. 1, 6–7). Here again Jeremiah assures his king that his cause is hopeless and urges him to surrender, promising him that if he does so his life will be spared. Judging from vs. 7, this incident must have taken place toward the end of the initial phase of the campaign, for we are told that at the time only Lachish and Azekah, of all of Judah's fortified towns, still held out. The situation is possibly illustrated from one of the Lachish Letters. These are a group of twenty-one ostraca (letters written on potsherds) discovered at Lachish (Tell ed-Duweir) in 1935 and 1938, most of which date to the year 589/8 (see W. F. Albright, ANET, p. 321 f., for a translation). In one of them (No. IV), the officer in charge of an outpost writes to the garrison commander in Lachish that he is awaiting instructions by fire signal, since he cannot see Azekah. Probably this means that Azekah also had fallen. If so, this letter was written shortly after Jeremiah spoke the words recorded in this passage.

It is scarcely surprising that the sentiments expressed in these passages caused many to regard Jeremiah as an enemy of his country. Nevertheless (see Introduction, "The Life and Message of Jeremiah"), it would be most unfair to suppose that he spoke out of cowardice or defeatism, or as one whose sympathies were pro-Babylonian. Nor, on the other hand, were his words proposed as directives to guide the policy of every nation at all times. Rather, they were specific words, for a specific nation, at a specific time.

They grew from Jeremiah's conviction, a conviction that had come to him as the word of his God, that Nebuchadnezzar's yoke had been imposed upon the nation as the divine judgment for its sins; the nation therefore had no course but to submit to it, for to rebel against Nebuchadnezzar was to rebel against Yahweh (cf. ch. xxvii) and to court certain disaster. Whatever one may think of Jeremiah's attitude, it was motivated by the desire to save his country from destruction by bringing it into conformity with the sovereign will of its God.

30. INCIDENTS DURING THE LIFTING
OF THE SIEGE
(xxxiv 8–22; xxxvii 1–10)

Perfidious Treatment of the Slaves

XXXIV ⁸ The word that came to Jeremiah from Yahweh after King Zedekiah had ᵃmade a covenant with all the people in Jerusalem to issue aᵃ proclamation of emancipation ⁹ to the effect that everyone should set free such of his slaves, both male and female, as were Hebrews, so that no one should hold his fellow Jew in bondage. ¹⁰ And all the nobles and people who had entered into the covenant to set free their male and female slaves and no longer hold them in bondage complied and, accordingly, liberated them. ¹¹ But then, later, they changed their minds, took back the slaves, male and female, whom they had set free, and forced them once more to become bondmen and bondwomen.

¹² Then it was that the word of Yahweh came ᵇto Jeremiahᵇ as follows: ¹³ "This is what Yahweh, the God of Israel, has said: I too made a covenant with your forefathers when I brought them out of the slave camp in the land of Egypt, with this stipulation: ¹⁴ 'Every seven years each of you shall set free your fellow Hebrew who has been forced to sell himself to you. He shall work for you six years, and then you must set him free from your custody.' But your fathers did not obey me or pay any attention. ¹⁵ And as for you, you had no sooner repented and done what was pleasing to me in proclaiming emancipation each to his neighbor, and made a covenant before me in the house that bears my name, ¹⁶ when you turned right around and pro-

ᵃ⁻ᵃ LXX abbreviates the sentence to read ". . . made a covenant with the people to issue a. . . ."
ᵇ⁻ᵇ Heb. "to Jeremiah from Yahweh." Omit "from Yahweh" with LXX. See NOTE.

faned my name by taking back each of you his male and female slaves, whom you had set free to go where they wished, and forcing them once more to be your bondmen and bondwomen.

17 "And so, this is what Yahweh has said: *You* have not obeyed me by proclaiming emancipation each to his brother, and each to his neighbor. So, believe me, I am going to proclaim your 'emancipation'—Yahweh's word—to the sword, to disease and starvation! And I will make you a sight to horrify all the kingdoms of the earth. 18 I will hand over the men who have transgressed my covenant, who did not keep the terms of the covenant which they made in my presence, *c*when they cut the young bull in two*c* and passed between its parts— 19 that is, the nobles of Judah and Jerusalem, the palace officials, the priests and landed gentry, who passed between the parts of the young bull— 20 I will hand them over to their enemies, to those who seek their lives. Their corpses will be food for the carrion birds and the wild beasts. 21 As for Zedekiah, king of Judah, and his nobles, I will hand them over to their enemies, to those who seek their lives, to the army of the king of Babylon which has now broken off its attack upon you. 22 Believe me, I am going to give the order—Yahweh's word—and I will bring them back to this city; and they will attack it, take it, and put it to the torch. As for the cities of Judah, I will make them a desolate, uninhabited waste."

Jeremiah Predicts the Resumption of the Siege

XXXVII 1 [Now Zedekiah ben Josiah, whom Nebuchadrezzar, king of Babylon, had made king in the land of Judah, reigned*d* in place of Coniah ben Jehoiakim. 2 But neither he nor his

c-c Hebrew is not grammatical (". . . in my presence, the young bull which they cut in two"), and some emendation is necessary. Many scholars read "I will make the men . . . like the young bull which they cut . . ." (*kā'ēgel* for *hā'ēgel*). But perhaps it is simpler to transpose "the young bull" after "they cut," as above; the main verb of the verse ("I will hand over") is then resumed by the main verb of vs. 20. See NOTE.

d Heb. "reigned as king" (*ymlk mlk*). Omit "as king" with LXX—apparently a dittography. Or perhaps read *hammelek* and translate, "And King Zedekiah . . . reigned" (cf. vs. 3).

officials nor the people of the land heeded the words of Yahweh spoken through Jeremiah the prophet.]

3 And King Zedekiah sent Jehucal ben Shelemiah and Zephaniah ben Maaseiah, the priest, to Jeremiah the prophet with the request, "Pray, now, to Yahweh our God for us." 4 Now Jeremiah still moved about freely ᵉamong the people,ᵉ for they had not yet put him in prison. 5 Meanwhile, the army of the Pharaoh had advanced from Egypt, and the Chaldeans who had been blockading Jerusalem had, on hearing the report, broken off operations and withdrawn.

6 Then the word of Yahweh came to Jeremiah the prophet as follows: 7 "This is what Yahweh, the God of Israel, has said, and this is what you shall tell the king of Judah who sent you to me to inquire of me: 'Look! Pharaoh's army which is advancing to your aid is going to return to its own country, to Egypt. 8 And the Chaldeans will come back, attack this city, take it, and put it to the torch. 9 This is what Yahweh has said: Do not deceive yourselves with the thought, "The Chaldeans are withdrawing from us permanently"—for they are not. 10 Why, even if you had defeated the entire Chaldean army that is attacking you so completely that there remained of it only severely wounded men, each of them lying in his tent, even these would get up and put this city to the torch.'"

ᵉ⁻ᵉ LXX reads, "within the city."

NOTES

xxxiv 8. *to issue a proclamation of emancipation.* Literally "to proclaim for them [i.e., for themselves; or the king issues the proclamation for them] emancipation." See textual noteᵃ⁻ᵃ.

9. *so that no one should hold his fellow Jew in bondage.* Hebrew (literally "so as not to make slaves of them, of a Jew, his brother, anyone") is awkward. But, save that *bām* ("of them") may have intruded from vs. 10, emendation helps little.

11. *But then, later.* I.e., when the siege was lifted (cf. vss. 21 f.).

12. *to Jeremiah.* Heb. "to Jeremiah from Yahweh" is redundant and harsh to our ears. But although we omit "from Yahweh," such redun-

dancy is characteristic of the prose discourses of Jeremiah, and the words
may be original.

13. *out of the slave camp in the land of Egypt.* Literally "out of the
land of Egypt, out of the house of slaves [bondage]"; the expression
occurs repeatedly in the Pentateuch.

14. *Every seven years.* Literally "at the end of seven years." But it
is actually at the end of six years, as the verse makes clear; the sense is,
"when the seventh year arrives." Nevertheless we should not emend to
"six" (so RSV following LXX), for the language of the verse is drawn
from Deut xv 1, 12, where the same expression occurs.

forced to sell himself to you. Literally "who shall have sold himself
[or, ". . . been sold"] to you"—of course, for debt.

16. *to go where they wished.* Literally ". . . to their desire" ($l^enap\check{s}\bar{a}m$);
cf. Deut xxi 14.

17. *each to his brother, and each to his neighbor.* Possibly variant
readings; LXX omits the first.

18. *when they cut the young bull in two.* See textual note^{o-o}. The
covenant ceremony of passing between the parts of the sacrificial
animal(s) may be illustrated from Gen xv 10, 17; there is also an eighth-
century parallel in the Aramaic Sūjîn (Sefîre), Stele I (cf. J. A. Fitzmyer,
JAOS 81 [1961], 181, 201). LXX alters vs. 18b, probably because the
ceremony was not understood, or was objectionable.

19. *palace officials.* The word ($s\bar{a}r\bar{\iota}s\bar{\iota}m$) is that usually translated
"eunuchs"; see NOTE on xxix 2 [Sec. 28].

who passed between the parts of the young bull. This is to our taste
needlessly repetitious; but it is unwise to omit it with LXX, since (cf.
NOTE on vs. 18) LXX may have omitted it intentionally.

xxxvii 1–2. Taking the biographical incidents in chronological order,
as we have done, these verses are superfluous, since we have for some
chapters been concerned with Zedekiah's reign. In the book's present
order they serve as a transition from ch. xxxvi (Jehoiakim's reign).
They also serve as a heading for the ensuing chapters (xxxvii–xliv), which
seem to have entered the book as a distinct unit.

2. *his officials.* Literally "his servants," as frequently in this context.

the people of the land. Frequently a technical term for the "landed
gentry" (and so in xxxiv 19), reference here seems to be to the people
generally.

3. *Zephaniah ben Maaseiah.* Cf. xxix 24–32; xxi 1. Unlike his companion Jehucal (and his companion Pashhur in xxi 1), Zephaniah is not
listed among those who (xxxviii 1) tried to have Jeremiah executed.

4. The verse leads up to vss. 13–14 (see Sec. 31), where we are told
of Jeremiah's arrest.

5. *had . . . broken off operations and withdrawn.* A paraphrase to avoid the awkward repetition of MT, "had withdrawn from Jerusalem." The verse both explains the situation and links this passage (see next section) to vss. 11 ff.

COMMENT

As we have already seen, the Babylonian army invaded Judah late in 589 and began the reduction of outlying strong points while holding Jerusalem under an ever tighter blockade. These operations presumably went on through the winter and spring of 588, until in the end most, if not all, of Judah's fortified towns had fallen. But then, just when all must have seemed lost, the beleaguered city was given respite and new hope. News arrived that an Egyptian army was approaching, and the Babylonians were obliged to lift the siege and march to meet them. This was probably in the late spring or early summer of 588. Precisely how long this respite lasted before the Egyptians were driven back and the siege resumed, we do not know. But one can readily imagine the wild joy and the profound relief that it evoked. It must have seemed to the people in Jerusalem that their God had once more, in the nick of time, intervened with his mighty acts to save them.

It was during this interval that the incidents dealt with in this section took place. The first of these is recorded in xxxiv 8–22. This passage consists of an extended prose discourse (vss. 8a, 12–22) which has been provided, no doubt by the Biographer, with a brief account (vss. 8b–11) describing the setting (note how the heading in vs. 8a is resumed in vs. 12). It seems that as the siege progressed and the situation grew more desperate, Zedekiah entered into solemn covenant with his nobles and leading citizens to free such of their slaves as were fellow Hebrews (as, no doubt, most were). One can imagine that some slaveholders agreed to this for selfish reasons: slaves had to be fed, they could no longer work in the fields—and men were needed for the defense of the city. But there was more to it than that. As vs. 14 indicates, this emancipation was carried out in compliance with the law of Deut xv 1, 12–18 (cf. Exod xxi 2–6), which required that Hebrew slaves be released after serving six years. Some scholars, to be sure, on the grounds that what took place was a general manumission rather than the normal operation of the law of seventh-year release, believe that this reference to Deuteronomy is secondary. But such a conclusion is unnecessary. As vs. 14 states, the law had been disregarded for years, which would mean that for most slaves release was long overdue. We may plausibly reconstruct the situation as follows. The people, as people at other times and places have been, were moved by their desperate plight to repentance. It being pointed out to them that they could hardly expect God's favor while disregarding important points of his law, they straightway took steps toward compliance, and then, to show the sincerity of their repentance, went on to release not only such slaves as were owed their freedom, but Hebrew slaves generally. The sequel, however, was ugly—and perhaps shows that human nature changes little. When the siege was lifted, they took their slaves back! It was, shall we say, a case of "foxhole religion," or "a death-bed repentance, with the usual sequel on recovery" (Peake). Jeremiah's reaction was scathing, as one would expect.

The incident of xxxvii 3–10 (on the editorial heading in vss. 1–2, see the NOTE) likewise belongs in this context (vs. 5). Zedekiah, hoping to be told that danger had passed, sent to Jeremiah asking him to intercede with Yahweh. But Jeremiah's reply shattered all hope: the Egyptians would be defeated, and the Babylonians would return. Indeed, said he, even if Zedekiah could defeat the Babylonians so badly that only wounded men remained in their ranks, even these casualties would get up from their beds and take the city. Words such as these, no less unpopular because proven true, tightened a noose around Jeremiah's neck, as we shall see (cf. xxxviii 3).

31. JEREMIAH IN PRISON
(xxxvii 11–21; xxxviii 1–28a; xxxix 15–18)

Arrest and Imprisonment: Interview with Zedekiah
(First Account)

XXXVII 11 Now when the Chaldean army had retired from
Jerusalem at the approach of the Pharaoh's forces, 12 Jeremiah
set out from Jerusalem to go to the land of Benjamin to attend
to a division of property among his people there. 13 But when
he got to the Benjamin Gate, the officer of the guard there, a
man named Irijah ben Shelemiah ben Hananiah, seized him,
crying, "You are deserting to the Chaldeans!" 14 Jeremiah replied, "It's a lie! I am not deserting to the Chaldeans." But
Irijah refused to listen to Jeremiah, arrested him, and brought
him to the princes. 15 And the princes, enraged at Jeremiah, had
him beaten and placed in confinement in the house of Jonathan
the secretary of state, for they had made that a prison. 16 ᵃJere-
miah was, indeed, putᵃ in one of the vaults in the cistern house
and left there for some time.

17 But then King Zedekiah sent and had him brought to him.
And the king questioned him secretly in the palace, and asked
him, "Is there any word from Yahweh?" Jeremiah replied,
"There is," and added, "You shall be handed over to the king
of Babylon." 18 Jeremiah also said to King Zedekiah, "What
sin have I committed against you or your officials or this people,
that you have put me in prison? 19 Where are your prophets who
prophesied to you that the king of Babylon ᵇwould not attack
this country?ᵇ 20 And now I beg you to hear me, my lord the
king! Let me earnestly entreat you not to send me back to the

ᵃ⁻ᵃ Heb. "Indeed [or "when"] Jeremiah went into . . ." (*kī bā'*). LXX
(*wayyābō'*), "And Jeremiah went into . . . ," may be preferable.
ᵇ⁻ᵇ So LXX; Heb. "would not attack you or this country," possibly combines
variants.

house of Jonathan the secretary, lest I die there." 21 So King
Zedekiah gave orders, and they committed Jeremiah to the court
of the guard, giving him a loaf of bread daily from the bakers'
street until all the bread in the city was gone. So Jeremiah remained in the court of the guard.

Jeremiah in Prison: Interview with Zedekiah
(Second Account)

XXXVIII 1 Now Shephatiah ben Mattan, Gedaliah ben Pashhur, Jehucal ben Shelemiah, and Pashhur ben Malkiah had
heard the things that Jeremiah had been saying to the populace,
for example: 2 "This is what Yahweh has said: Whoever stays
in this city will die by the sword, by starvation and disease. But
whoever gives himself up to the Chaldeans will live; he will at
least escape with his life, and will survive." 3 Or: "This is what
Yahweh has said: This city will certainly be handed over to the
army of the king of Babylon and be taken." 4 So these princes
said to the king, "We ask that this man be put to death, for he
is weakening the morale of the soldiers remaining in this city,
as well as that of all the people, by saying such things to them.
Indeed, the fellow does not desire the welfare of this people at
all, but rather their hurt." 5 And King Zedekiah answered, "Very
well, he is in your hands. The king can certainly do nothing to
oppose you." 6 So they took Jeremiah and cast him into the
cistern of Prince Malkiah, which was in the court of the guard,
letting him° down with ropes. And there being no water in the
cistern, but only mud, Jeremiah sank down in the mud.

7 But Ebed-melek the Ethiopian, a eunuch attached to the
royal palace, heard that they had put Jeremiah in the cistern.
So, the king being at the time seated in the Benjamin Gate,
8 Ebed-melek came from the palace and addressed the king as
follows: 9 "My lord the king, these men have committed a crime
in what they have done to Jeremiah the prophet, casting him

° So for smoothness (cf. LXX); Hebrew repeats "Jeremiah."

into the cistern and ᵈleaving him to die down there."ᵈ ¹⁰ The
king thereupon ordered Ebed-melek the Ethiopian, "Take with
you threeᵉ of these men here and get himᶠ up out of the cistern
before he dies." ¹¹ So Ebed-melek took the men with him, and
going to the palace, ᵍto the wardrobe storeroom,ᵍ got from there
some odds and ends of worn-out clothing and let them down by
ropes to Jeremiah in the cistern. ¹² And Ebed-melek the Ethiopian said to Jeremiah, "Just put these odds and ends of clothing
under your armpits as protection against the ropes." And Jeremiah did so. ¹³ Then they pulled himʰ up by the ropes and got
him out of the cistern. And Jeremiah remained in the court of
the guard.

¹⁴ Subsequently King Zedekiah sent and had Jeremiah the
prophet brought to him at the third entrance of the house of
Yahweh. And the king said to Jeremiah, "I am going to ask you
a question. Do not hide anything from me." ¹⁵ Jeremiah said to
Zedekiah, "If I were to tell you, would you not simply have me
executed? And if I were to advise you, you would not listen to
me." ¹⁶ But King Zedekiah swore to Jeremiah there in secret, "As
Yahweh lives, who is the source of our lives, I will not have you
executed, nor will I hand you over to these men who are seeking
to kill you."

¹⁷ Then Jeremiah said to Zedekiah, "This is what Yahweh,
God of Hosts, the God of Israel, has said: If you will only give
yourself up to the king of Babylon's generals, your life will be

---

ᵈ⁻ᵈ Pointing the verb wᵉyāmūt ("that he may die"), for MT wayyāmot ("and
he has died"). But MT may have the sense that Jeremiah is already as good
as dead. MT then ends the verse: "of starvation, for there is no more bread
in the city." This seems to be a mistaken gloss. No doubt the princes intended
to starve Jeremiah if he did not die of exposure, or suffocate in the mire first.
But the city's food supply was not exhausted till the eve of its fall (lii 6 f.),
and this was still some time in the future (cf. vs. 28a). Besides, if there were
no more food, how would getting Jeremiah out of the cistern save him from
starvation? The whole clause is awkward and may have intruded from another
context; the natural reading is: "And he died in his place of starvation,
for there was no food left in the city."

ᵉ So conjecturally; Heb. "thirty." See NOTE.

ᶠ So LXX; Hebrew agains repeats the noun, "get Jeremiah the prophet up."

ᵍ⁻ᵍ Reading 'el meltaḥat hā'ōṣār with Ehrl. and most commentators (cf. II
Kings x 22). Hebrew drops two letters: 'el taḥat hā'ōṣār ("to under the storeroom").

ʰ So LXX; Hebrew again repeats the noun, "pulled Jeremiah up."

spared, and this city will not be put to the torch. You yourself will live, and your household too. 18 But if you will not give yourself up,ⁱ then this city will be handed over to the Chaldeans, and they will burn it to the ground; and you yourself will not escape their clutches." 19 But King Zedekiah said to Jeremiah, "I am afraid of the Jews who have deserted to the Chaldeans, lest I be handed over to them, and they treat me roughly." 20 Jeremiah answered, "That will not happen. I beg you to heed the voice of Yahweh as regards what I am telling you, that it may be well with you, and that your life may be spared. 21 But if you refuse to surrender, this is the vision that Yahweh has let me see: 22 There! All the women who are left in the household of Judah's king being led forth to the king of Babylon's officers—and they are saying as they go:

'They misled you, overruled you,
These good "friends" of yours;
Now your feet are sunk in the bog,
They have left you and gone.'

23 All your wives, too, and your children, they will bring out to the Chaldeans; and you yourself will not escape their clutches, but will be taken prisoner by the king of Babylon. And this city ʲwill be burnedʲ to the ground."

24 Then Zedekiah said to Jeremiah, "Do not let anyone know of this conversation, if you value your life. 25 And if the princes should hear that I have spoken with you, and should come and say to you, 'Tell us, now, what you said to the king, ᵏand what the king said to you.ᵏ Do not hide it from us, or we will kill you,' 26 then say to them, 'I was but presenting my earnest plea to the king not to send me back to Jonathan's house to die there.'" 27 And, in fact, the various princes did come to Jere-

---

ⁱ Hebrew adds "to the princes [generals] of the king of Babylon." Omit for smoothness with LXX. Divergencies of this sort between LXX and MT are, as pointed out *passim*, characteristic of the Jeremiah prose. One can seldom be sure which tradition represents the more original text.

ʲ⁻ʲ Point the verb as Niphal with some manuscripts and LXX; MT reads Qal ("you will burn," i.e., you will be the cause of it).

ᵏ⁻ᵏ Hebrew reads this clause at the end of the verse; LXX does also, but repeats "what did the king say to you." Transpose with Syr., or perhaps regard the two parts as variants.

miah and question him; and he answered them exactly as the king had instructed him. So they were obliged to drop the matter, for no one had heard what had actually been said. 28a And Jeremiah stayed in the court of the guard until the day that Jerusalem was taken.

XXXIX 15 While Jeremiah was confined in the court of the guard, the word of Yahweh came to him as follows: 16 "Go, tell Ebed-melek the Ethiopian, 'This is what Yahweh of Hosts, the God of Israel, has said: Look! I am about to bring my words concerning this city to pass, for evil and not for good; ᶦon that day they will be fulfilled right before you.ᶦ 17 But I will rescue you on that day—Yahweh's word. You will not be handed over to the men of whom you are afraid, 18 for I will surely save you. You will not fall by the sword, but will come out of it alive, because you have trusted in me—Yahweh's word.' "

ᶦ⁻ᶦ See NOTE.

NOTES

xxxvii 12. *to attend to a division of property among his people there.* Literally "to divide there among the people." Though the precise force is obscure, emendation is unwise; most Vrs. read similarly, though LXX ("to make a purchase, do business") seems not quite to understand the expression. Quite probably the transaction described in xxxii 1–15 (see Sec. 32) was what Jeremiah wished to attend to.

13. *seized him.* An example of what one must frequently do in this material to secure smooth English. Hebrew often repeats the noun-antecedent where English usage demands the pronoun: "When he got to the Benjamin Gate, the officer of the guard . . . seized Jeremiah the prophet." It is not surprising that this officer supposed Jeremiah to be deserting; he had urged others to do so (xxi 9).

14. *But Irijah refused to listen to Jeremiah, arrested him.* Again one must rearrange the sentence; Heb. "But he would not listen to him, and Irijah arrested Jeremiah . . . ," is intolerable English.

15. Why the home of the royal secretary was used as a prison is not said. Perhaps other places of detention were full; or perhaps the secretary's house was a "maximum-security prison" for dangerous political offenders.

16. *one of the vaults.* Jeremiah's place of confinement was an under-ground dungeon, where he would certainly have died (vs. 20).

and left there. Literally "and he stayed there." Hebrew awkwardly repeats "Jeremiah" as the subject, which we omit with LXX for smooth-ness' sake.

18. *your officials.* As elsewhere, "your servants."

20. *Let me earnestly entreat you not to send me.* Literally "Let my supplication fall before you! Do not send me. . . ."

21. *the court of the guard.* Adjacent to the palace (xxxii 2; Neh iii 25), this was apparently used as a place of detention for prisoners who did not require strict confinement. Jeremiah enjoyed a measure of freedom there (cf. xxxii 1–15).

until all the bread in the city was gone. I.e., until the city fell, for the food supply was not exhausted till then (cf. lii 6 f. and COMMENT).

xxxviii 1. Two of the princes listed here have already been encountered as members of deputations sent to Jeremiah by the king: Jehucal (here spelled "Jucal") ben Shelemiah (xxxvii 3) and Pashhur ben Malkiah (xxi 1). LXX omits the last name, probably through error.

2. The verse cites the utterance recorded in xxi 9, which was spoken before Jeremiah's arrest. The procedure of Rudolph (and Leslie) in deleting it as a gloss is arbitrary. The princes would naturally quote statements actually made by Jeremiah.

gives himself up to. Or, "deserts to . . ."; literally "goes out to. . . ."

will at least escape with his life. Literally "his life will be his for booty." On the force of this expression, see NOTE on xlv 5.

and will survive. Possibly this (*wāḥay*) and "will live" (point *yiḥyeh* with Ktib) are doublets. The repetition is awkward and xxi 9 has only one of them; but both are represented in LXX.

3. One will find the substance of this prediction in xxxiv 2, 22; xxi 7; xxxvii 8, etc. Jeremiah had said this repeatedly.

and be taken. Literally "and it [the Babylonian army] will take it"; or, less probably, "and he [Nebuchadnezzar] will take it." The sense is, of course, the same.

4. *So these princes said.* "These" is supplied for clarity (Heb. "the princes"); the speakers are the men listed in vs. 1. Possibly (Rudolph) the consonants *h'lh* ("these") have dropped out before the ensuing ones (likewise *'lh*). LXX has simply, "and they said."

We ask that this man be put to death. Literally "Let this man, pray, be put to death."

he is weakening the morale. Literally ". . . the hands." It is interesting to note that in Lachish Letter VI (see NOTE on xxxiv 7) this very expression is used of certain of the nobles in Jerusalem. Apparently there were defeatists among them too.

5. *The king can certainly do nothing to oppose you.* Literally "Certainly [or: "for"] the king is not one who is able to do anything with you." LXX, however, reads as an explanatory parenthesis: "for the king was not able to withstand them." Nowhere does Zedekiah show himself more clearly as the weakling he was than here.

7. *Ebed-melek . . . a eunuch.* Probably in this case literally so, though the word frequently denotes a palace officer (cf. xxix 2 etc.). LXX omits "a eunuch."

seated in the Benjamin Gate. Presumably, as the custom was, to hear complaints and adjudicate cases at law. This gave Ebed-melek the chance to approach the king, as he might not readily have done in the palace.

10. *Take with you three of these men here.* I.e., of those in attendance upon the king. Heb. reads "thirty"; but that is far more men than would have been needed, and is probably an error, as commentators agree; the difference involves but one consonant in Hebrew (*šlšh* for *šlšm*).

12. *as protection against the ropes.* Literally "under the ropes," i.e., to keep them from cutting.

14. *the third entrance.* We do not know where this was, or why it was a suitable place for a clandestine interview. Perhaps it was the king's private entrance to the temple, leading directly from the palace.

a question. Literally "a thing," "a word." One could translate, "I am going to ask you for a word [from Yahweh]"; the king wanted an oracle (cf. vs. 17; xxxvii 17).

16. *who is the source of our lives.* Literally "who has made us this life" (*nepeš*).

19. Once again Zedekiah shows that fatal weakness of character which repeatedly prevented him from following the course he knew to be right (cf. vs. 5). The verse shows that not a few had deserted, whether on Jeremiah's advice (vs. 2) or otherwise; these would understandably be bitter toward the king.

20. *That will not happen.* Literally "they will not give [you into their hands]."

21. *this is the vision that Yahweh has let me see.* Literally "This is the thing that Yahweh has showed me" (in a vision). The sight that Jeremiah beheld with his inner eye is that described in the next verse.

24. *if you value your life.* Literally "that you die not."

26. *presenting my earnest plea.* Literally "letting my supplication fall"; cf. xxxvii 20.

27. *So they were obliged . . . actually been said.* Literally "So they were silent [i.e., went silently] from him, for the thing had not been [over]heard."

xxxix 16. *Go, tell Ebed-melek.* One must not take "go" literally, since Jeremiah could hardly go to Ebed-melek while in confinement. Either he sent the message, or Ebed-melek came to visit him.

they will be fulfilled. Supplying "fulfilled" for the sake of the sense; literally "they will be." LXX omits the entire clause.

17. *of whom you are afraid.* I.e., the princes mentioned in ch. xxxviii. It was very bold of a palace servant to accuse them of crime (xxxviii 9), as Ebed-melek had done.

18. *You . . . will come out of it alive.* Again, "your life shall be yours for booty"; see NOTE on xlv 5 (Sec. 24).

COMMENT

From the passages treated here we learn that shortly after Jeremiah had uttered the words recorded in the preceding section, he was arrested on charges of treason, beaten and thrown into prison, and there subjected to cruel and unusual hardships. Although he was ultimately accorded more lenient treatment, he remained in confinement until the city fell—thus for approximately a year (ca. summer 588–July 587).

As the Bible tells the story, events move through two cycles. In xxxvii 11–21 we are told that while the siege was lifted Jeremiah attempted to go to his home in Anathoth on a matter of business. But when he arrived at the city gate he was arrested on suspicion of desertion, haled before the princes, beaten and thrown into an underground dungeon beneath the home of the secretary of state, where he was left for an unspecified period of time. But then, Zedekiah sent for him and interviewed him secretly, asking for some word from Yahweh. Jeremiah used this opportunity to beg the king for milder treatment and, his request having been granted, was transferred to confinement in the court of the guard. The narrative then continues in chapter xxxviii. Here we are told that Jeremiah was again brought before the princes and, because of the things that he had said, charged with treason. The princes demanded his execution. Since Zedekiah lacked the courage to withstand them, Jeremiah was thrown into a cistern and left to die. He was, however, rescued through the good offices of one Ebed-melek, a Negro eunuch in the king's service, and returned to the court of the guard. Then, once again, Zedekiah sent for him and interviewed him secretly; and once again Jeremiah, having warned the king that his cause was hopeless, requested—and got—more lenient treatment, being left in the court of the guard until the city fell.

It is, of course, quite possible to understand this as a consecutive account of the events. Nevertheless, the reader is bound to be struck by a certain repetitiousness: everything seems to happen to Jeremiah twice! In view of this fact, serious consideration ought to be given to the suggestion, dismissed by the majority of scholars and most recently defended, so far as I know, by Skinner (pp. 258 f.), that xxxvii 11–21 and xxxviii are actually parallel accounts of the same events. The suggestion deserves all the more to be taken seriously since, in the story of Jeremiah's release in xxxviii 28b–xl 6 two separate accounts seem quite clearly to have been combined. One should not, to be sure, advance in favor of this view—as Skinner does—the argument that Jeremiah could hardly have preached sedition, as charged by the princes in xxxviii 1–4, while confined in the court of the guard, and that a new account of his arrest must therefore begin at this point. Jeremiah could quite easily have spoken seditiously in the court of the guard for, as xxxii 1–15 (see Sec. 32) indicates, he enjoyed considerable freedom there. Nevertheless, the fact remains that the princes, in preferring charges against Jeremiah, quote words that he is known to have uttered *prior to* his arrest (cf. xxxviii 2 and xxi 9; xxxviii 3 and xxxiv 2, 22; xxxvii 8). One would think that they would have confronted him with this when he was first haled before them (xxxvii 14 f.), rather than after a considerable lapse of time. Note, too, that xxxii 1–5 indicates that Jeremiah had been jailed in the first place precisely because of utterances such as these. In other words, the action of the princes in xxxviii 1–4 is best, though admittedly not necessarily, understood as taking place immediately after Jeremiah's arrest.

The similarities in outline between xxxvii 11–21 and chapter xxxviii are indeed remarkable. To be sure, the first of these accounts tells of Jeremiah's arrest, as the second does not; but in both he is brought before the princes, in both the charge is treason, and in both the place of his confinement is related to a cistern (a cistern in xxxviii 6–13; a dungeon in a cistern house in xxxvii 16). It is true that in xxxvii 15 f. this cistern house is located in the home of Jonathan, the royal secretary, while in xxxviii 6 it is called the cistern of Prince Malkiah and located in the court of the guard. But since we do not know where the secretary's house was with relation to the court of the guard (the latter was near the palace [xxxii 2], and probably the secretary's house was too), this is not in itself decisive; the cistern in connection with the secretary's house may have been popularly known as that of Prince Malkiah. In any event, both accounts know of an incarceration in the house of Jonathan the secretary (xxxvii 15, 20; xxxviii 26). It is interesting that some commentators (Volz, Rudolph, etc.), noticing this, seek to dispose of it by arbitrarily transferring xxxviii 24–28a to the end of chapter xxxvii.

Chapter xxxviii then tells of Jeremiah's rescue from the cistern, as xxxvii 11–21 does not; but both describe secret interviews with the king which subsequently took place and which, though reported in greater detail in chapter xxxviii than in xxxvii 11–21, are similar in tone. Both of these speak of Jeremiah's request not to be returned to Jonathan's house (xxxvii 20; xxxviii 26); and both end with his being placed in the court of the guard. In xxxviii 28a it is expressly stated that he remained there until the city fell. In xxxvii 21 it is merely said that he was kept there and fed a daily ration as long as the city's food supply lasted. But since we know from lii 6 f. that the food supply did not give out until the very eve of the city's fall, this verse actually says the same thing as xxxviii 28a; it implies that Jeremiah remained in the court of the guard till the city fell, and leaves no room after it for the events described in chapter xxxviii.

For these reasons it seems to me—though I am not inclined to insist upon it—that much is to be said for the view that xxxvii 11–21 and xxxviii 1–28a are slightly divergent, but complementary and not essentially disharmonious accounts of the same series of events. The brief oracle of comfort addressed to Ebed-melek in xxxix 15–18 belongs with the second of these accounts, for it is in it that Ebed-melek plays an important role. The first account clearly continues xxxvii 1–10 (cf. vss. 4 f. and vss. 11 f.). One wonders if the second account was not originally introduced by the very similar piece now found in xxi 1–10 (cf. xxxviii 2 and xxi 9). As was noted above (and see further below), there are two accounts of Jeremiah's release by the Babylonians in xxxviii 28b–xl 6, and one may regard it as probable that these, respectively, continue the two accounts just described.

32. JEREMIAH IN PRISON;
HIS PURCHASE OF LAND
(xxxii 1–16)

XXXII ¹ The word that came to Jeremiah from Yahweh in the tenth year of Zedekiah, king of Judah, which was the eighteenth year of Nebuchadrezzar, king of Babylon. ——— ² The king of Babylon's army was then besieging Jerusalem, and Jeremiah*ᵃ* was shut up in the court of the guard, in the palace of the king of Judah, ³ where Zedekiah, king of Judah, had confined him, on the complaint: "Why have you uttered such prophecies as these: 'This is what Yahweh has said: Believe me, I am going to hand this city over to the king of Babylon, and he will take it. ⁴ Zedekiah, king of Judah, will not escape the clutches of the Chaldeans, but will certainly be handed over to the king of Babylon and, confronted by him face to face, will be made to answer to him personally. ⁵ He will take Zedekiah to Babylon, and there he will remain *ᵇ*until I attend to him—Yahweh's word. If you fight the Chaldeans you will have no success'?"*ᵇ* ———

⁶ Jeremiah said, "The word of Yahweh came to me, thus: ⁷ Just wait! Hanamel, your uncle Shallum's son, is going to come to you with the request, 'Buy my field at Anathoth, for you have the kinsman's right to redeem it.' ⁸ And, just as Yahweh had said, my cousin Hanamel did come to me in the court of the guard, and say to me, 'Won't you buy my field at Anathoth,*ᶜ* *ᵈ*for the right of possession and redemption is yours. Buy it for yourself!'*ᵈ* Then I knew that this was indeed Yahweh's word.

⁹ "So I bought the field at Anathoth from Hanamel my cousin, and weighed out the money to him, seventeen silver

ᵃ So LXX; Hebrew, to our taste needlessly, reads "Jeremiah the prophet."
ᵇ⁻ᵇ LXX omits.
ᶜ Hebrew adds "in the land of Benjamin"; LXX puts this before "at Anathoth." It is probably a correct, but unnecessary, gloss.
ᵈ⁻ᵈ For the curious LXX reading, see NOTE.

shekels. [10] I put the deed in writing, sealed it, had men witness it, and weighed the money on scales. [11] Then I took the deed of purchase, the sealed copy containing the contract and the conditions, and the open copy, [12] and gave it*e* to Baruch ben Neriah ben Mahseiah in the presence of my cousin*f* Hanamel, in the presence of the witnesses who had signed the deed of purchase, and in the presence of all the Jews who happened to be in the court of the guard. [13] Then, before them all, I gave Baruch the following charge: [14]*g* 'Take these documents—that is, this deed of purchase, the sealed copy and this open one*h*—and put them in an earthenware jar, so that they may last a long time. [15] For this is what Yahweh of Hosts, the God of Israel, has said: Houses and fields and vineyards shall once again be bought in this land.'"

[16] . . .

e So with LXX for smoothness. Hebrew is not quite grammatical: "and gave the deed, the purchase." One must either read "the deed of purchase," or regard "the purchase" as an addition.

f So, correctly, LXX, Syr., and various manuscripts. MT has dropped the word "son of," making the reading "my uncle," instead of "son of my uncle"; cf. vs. 7 f.

g Hebrew begins the verse with, "This is what Yahweh of Hosts, the God of Israel, has said," which seems out of place here; it is possibly erroneously copied from the initial words of vs. 15 (so various commentators).

h Hebrew erroneously repeats "deed" (without article) with "this open," which yields an impossibly clumsy reading.

NOTES

xxxii 1. *the eighteenth year of Nebuchadrezzar, king of Babylon.* With LXX, "king of Babylon" is added. The synchronism with Zedekiah's tenth year (588/7) is correct only if Nebuchadnezzar's reign is counted from his accession in the fall of 605 (cf. xxv 1; lii 12; II Kings xxv 8); counting from his first official regnal year (604/3), as in lii 29, 588/7 was his seventeenth year.

2–5. These verses (which in the translation are set off from their context by means of dashes) are an editorial parenthesis explaining the circumstances of Jeremiah's imprisonment. Had the passage been transmitted with chs. xxxvii–xxxviii, where it belongs chronologically, they would not have been necessary. Although Jeremiah was actually arrested for trying to leave the city (xxxvii 11–14), vss. 3–5, which paraphrase xxxiv 2–3, are quite correct in finding the real reason for it in his seditious utterances (cf. xxxviii 1–4, and COMMENT on the preceding section).

4. *confronted by him . . . answer to him personally.* Literally "and his mouth will speak with his mouth, and his eyes will see his eyes"; cf. xxxiv 3.

5. *until I attend to him.* One would normally take this in a favorable sense: Zedekiah will stay in Babylon till Yahweh intervenes in his behalf. If this is correct, it argues for the early date of the prophecy, for (cf. lii 11) things did not turn out so (there is little reason to suppose, as some do, that Zedekiah has been confused with Jehoiachin: lii 31–34). But the verb (*pqd*) can have an ominous sense: until I punish him (i.e., finally, with death). LXX omits the whole second half of the verse beginning with these words.

6. The verse is not, as might appear, Jeremiah's answer to Zedekiah's complaint, but resumes the introduction of vs. 1 after the parenthesis of vss. 2–5, (see NOTE above) and introduces the first-person account that follows.

7. *for you have the kinsman's right to redeem it.* Literally "for yours is the right of redemption to buy." On the right, and duty, of the next of kin in this connection, see COMMENT.

8. *the right of possession.* Or, ". . . of inheritance." Whether or not this means that Hanamel had no living kin closer than Jeremiah is not certain (see COMMENT). For the rest of the direct quotation beginning with these words, LXX has, "for yours is the right of purchase, and you are the oldest" (one supposes, of the closest of kin).

9. *weighed out the money.* Coined money did not come into general use until the post-Exilic period; gold or silver was paid by weight. Since we know nothing of the size or quality of the field, of current land values, or the purchasing power of money, we cannot say whether seventeen shekels was much or little. Presumably, however, the symbolic nature of the act would require that a fair, normal price be paid.

10. *I put the deed in writing.* Or, perhaps (EVV), "I signed the deed." Literally "I wrote in the document" (i.e., wrote the deed out; or, wrote my name on it).

11. *the contract and the conditions.* Literally "the order and the pre-scriptions," i.e., presumably the order transferring the property and the conditions of the sale (the contract and the "fine print," one might say). LXX omits the words, possibly because they were not understood. Some scholars transfer them to the end of vs. 10 and take the meaning to be, "according to the correct legal procedure." But this is conjectural and probably unnecessary; technical legal terminology is no doubt involved. Hebrew does not make it clear whether the two copies were identical, or whether the open copy contained only a "docket" or an abstract of

the sealed one. But the former is the more likely. Examples of such documents in two copies are known from Elephantine in Egypt. The text of these documents was written in duplicate on the two halves of a single sheet of papyrus. One half of the sheet was then rolled up, tied with strips running through holes in the middle of the sheet, and sealed; the other half was then loosely rolled, but not sealed. Thus the sealed copy protected the document from fraudulent alteration, while the open copy was available for ready reference. Similar "tied deeds" have recently been found in the Judean desert; cf. Y. Yadin, IEJ 12 (1962), 236–38 and Pl. 48B, for a description. Scribes writing in cuneiform on clay tablets followed the practice of encasing the original document in an envelope, or shell, of clay bearing a copy. But this need not concern us here, since legal documents in Judah were written in ink on papyrus, or perhaps parchment.

14. *put them in an earthenware jar.* This seems to have been the usual receptacle for storing valuable documents. Those from Elephantine mentioned above (NOTE on vs. 11) were so stored, as were some of the scrolls found at Qumran (probably most, if not all, of them had originally been stored in jars).

15. *shall once again be bought.* Or, reflexively, ". . . bought and sold": i.e., normal economic activity will resume.

16. Vss. 16 ff. (properly vss. 16, 17a*ᵃ*, 24–25) continue vss. 1–15 directly. The chapter as a whole will be dealt with below, Sec. 37.

COMMENT

The passage treated in this section is of the greatest importance for the light that it casts on the hope that Jeremiah held for the future. It has, for obvious reasons, been transmitted as a part of the so-called "Book of Consolation" (chs. xxx–xxxiii), and we shall return to it in that connection below. But it must, for completeness' sake, be included here also.

According to vs. 1 f., the incident here recorded took place in the tenth year of Zedekiah's reign (588/7), while Jeremiah was confined in the court of the guard. We are told (vss. 7 f.) that Jeremiah had a presentiment, which he felt to be the word of Yahweh, that his cousin Hanamel would come to him and ask him to buy a piece of property in Anathoth to which he, Jeremiah, held the right of redemption. The legal situation is that described in the law recorded in Lev xxv 25. This law stipulates that, in the event of a man's being forced because of poverty or debt to sell all or part of his inheritance, the next of kin had both the privilege and the duty of redeeming the property in question, and thus keeping it in the family. We know too little about Jeremiah's family connection, and about the operation of property and inheritance laws at the time, to say whether in this case Jeremiah was actually the next of kin, as vs. 8 might imply, or whether these rights and privileges had devolved upon him because others closer of kin had refused to exercise them. This last sometimes occurred, as the story of Ruth (Ruth iii 9–13; iv 1–12) indicates; and one can well imagine that in disturbed times, such as Judah was undergoing in 588/7, few would be eager to invest in real estate. In any event, the cousin's visit was not unexpected. Indeed, it is probable that Jeremiah had been trying to go to Anathoth to attend to this very matter, when he was arrested (xxxvii 11–14). We must suppose that the cousin had managed to get into Jerusalem before the siege was resumed, and that he came to Jeremiah as soon thereafter as he was able. And when he came, Jeremiah knew (vs. 8) that Yahweh was in fact telling him to buy the land.

The transaction was carried out according to proper legal procedure (see NOTES), and the deed filed for safe keeping. The passage is, in fact, of peculiar interest in that it affords the clearest description that we have of the way in which transfers of property were handled in pre-Exilic Judah. As vs. 15 explains, the transaction was intended to be symbolic of Yahweh's promise—a promise which, as we shall see later (vss. 16, 24 f.), Jeremiah himself hardly dared to believe—that, beyond the impending tragedy, normal life would one day be resumed in the land. In view of this passage, the authenticity of which is unquestionable, one need not ask whether or not Jeremiah held out hope for the future. It only remains to be seen what form that hope may have taken.

33. THE FALL OF JERUSALEM; JEREMIAH'S RELEASE FROM PRISON
(xxxix 1–2; 4–10; xxxviii 28b; xxxix 3; 14; 11–13; xl 1–6)

The Fall of Jerusalem: a Summary Account

XXXIX ¹It was in the ninth year of Zedekiah, king of Judah, in the tenth month, that Nebuchadrezzar, king of Babylon, moved against Jerusalem with all his forces, and placed it under siege. ²And in the eleventh year of Zedekiah, in the fourth month, on the ninth day of the month, the city wall was breached. ⁴And when Zedekiah, king of Judah, and all his soldiers saw this,^a they fled, leaving the city by night by way of the king's garden, through the gate between the two walls, and got away in the direction of the Arabah. ⁵But the Chaldean forces pursued them, and overtook Zedekiah in the desert near Jericho and, having taken him prisoner, they brought him up to Riblah in the land of Hamath, to Nebuchadrezzar, king of Babylon, who then passed sentence upon him. ⁶The king of Babylon executed Zedekiah's sons there in Riblah before his very eyes. As for the various nobles of Judah, the king of Babylon executed them too. ⁷Then, having had Zedekiah blinded, he put him in chains to be taken to Babylon. ⁸The Chaldeans, meanwhile, burned ^bthe royal palace, the temple, and the houses of the populace^b to the ground, and tore down the walls of Jerusalem. ⁹Finally, Nebuzaradan, the commander of the royal bodyguard, carried off such of the people as were left in the city, together with those who had deserted to him, ^cand the rest of the skilled artisans,^c to exile in Babylon. ¹⁰Only some of the poorest peo-

---

^a Heb. "them." See NOTE.

^{b–b} Heb. *bēt hammelek we'et bēt hā'ām* ("the royal palace and the house of the people") has suffered loss of words. Restore (cf. lii 13) to read *bēt hammelek we'et bēt yhwh we'et bāttē hā'ām*, with Rudolph and others.

^{c–c} Read *we'et yeter hā'āmōn* (or *hā'ommān?*) as in lii 15. MT erroneously repeats "the rest of the people who were left."

ple, those who had nothing, did Nebuzaradan the commander of
the guard leave in the land of Judah, assigning to them vineyards and [fields (?)].

Jeremiah Is Released to Gedaliah: First Account

XXXVIII   28b Now when Jerusalem was taken, XXXIX   3 all
the officers of the king of Babylon came and took their seats in
the Middle Gate: *d*Nergal-sharezer, lord of Sin-magir, the Rab-
mag; Nebushazban the Rab-saris,*d* and the various other officers
of the king of Babylon.   14 And they sent and had Jeremiah brought from the court of the guard, and turned him over
to Gedaliah ben Ahikam ben Shaphan for safe conduct home.
So he remained among the people.

Jeremiah Is Released: a Second Account

11 Now Nebuchadrezzar, king of Babylon, had given Nebuzaradan, the commander of the guard, the following order with regard to Jeremiah: 12 "Find him and look after him. Do him no
harm, but accord him whatever treatment he may request." 13 So
Nebuzaradan, the commander of the guard, sent . . . .

XL   1 The word that came to Jeremiah from Yahweh after
Nebuzaradan, the commander of the guard, had set him free at
Ramah. When he found him he was in fetters in the midst of
the whole train of captives from Jerusalem and Judah who were
being deported to Babylon*e* . . . 2 The commander of the
guard had Jeremiah brought, and said to him, "It was Yahweh
your God who threatened this place with this calamity; 3 and
now Yahweh has brought it to pass, and has done just as he said
he would. It is because you sinned against Yahweh and did not
obey his voice that this thing has happened to you. 4 *f*And now,
there! I release you from the fetters that are on your hands. If it
suits you to come with me to Babylon, come, and I will look out

d–d See NOTE.
e The text has been damaged. See NOTE.

for you. But if it does not suit you to come with me to Babylon—
then don't! See! The whole land is at your disposal. Go *wherever you think it best* and most suitable to go.¹ 5 [   ].ʰ Or
go back to Gedaliah ben Ahikam ben Shaphan, whom the king
of Babylon has made governor of *the land of Judah,*ⁱ and stay
with him among the people. Or go wherever you think it best to
go." So the commander of the guard gave him provisions and a
present, and dismissed him. 6 Then Jeremiah went to Gedaliah
ben Ahikam at Mizpah, and stayed with him among the people
who were left in the land.

ⁱ⁻ⁱ MT seems clearly to have suffered conflation in this verse. LXX omits the
balance of the verse, beginning "But if it does not suit you . . ." (see also
textual noteʰ).
ᵍ⁻ᵍ Supply the article with *ṭōb*, or omit *'el ṭōb* as a variant reading.
ʰ The first words of the verse in MT (" and he was not yet going back") can
be made intelligible only by conjecture. LXX begins, "and if not, go your
way and go back to . . ."; this links well to vs. 4a (LXX omits vs. 4b; see
noteⁱ⁻ⁱ above).
ⁱ⁻ⁱ So LXX; Heb. "the cities of Judah."

Notes

xxxix 1–2. Cf. lii 4–6. At this period years were counted from the
Babylonian New Year in the spring (March/April). The siege of Jerusalem thus began in January 588 and lasted until July 587 (with a brief
interlude, probably in the summer of 588).

4. *saw this.* Heb. "saw them" (i.e., the Babylonian officers mentioned in
vs. 3 [below]) represents an adjustment of the verse to its present context.
Vs. 4 did not originally follow vs. 3 (see COMMENT). Zedekiah of course
did not wait to see the Babylonian officers seated before fleeing; he fled
(vs. 2) when the wall was breached.
and got away in the direction of the Arabah. I.e., toward the Jordan
valley (cf. vs. 5). The verb must be read as plural (cf. lii 7 and various
manuscripts and Vrs.); MT singular.
5. Nebuchadnezzar himself had not been present at the fall of Jerusalem, but had remained at his headquarters in central Syria.
9. *commander of the royal bodyguard.* The *rab ṭabbāḥīm;* literally
"the chief butcher" (or "cook"), the archaic title was retained even
though the function had changed entirely.
10. *[fields].* The word (*yᵉgēbīm*) is of uncertain meaning; "fields"

follows Syr., Tar.; Vulg. reads "cisterns" (*gēbīm*). But perhaps read the last two words as in lii 16, *lekoremīm ūleyōgebīm* ("to be vinedressers and field laborers" [?]). The verse in Hebrew ends awkwardly with "in that day," which could be taken to mean "at the same time"; but the words perhaps belong at the beginning of vs. 11 (see NOTE there).

3. *took their seats in the Middle Gate.* I.e., the Babylonian officers constituted themselves a court or, better, a military government. The names, however, are confused in Hebrew: "Nergalsharezer, Samgar-nebo, Sar-sekim the Rab-saris, Nergalsharezer the Rab-mag." We construct with the aid of vs. 13 (". . . Nebushazban the Rab-saris, Nergal-sharezer the Rab-mag") following various scholars: cf. especially J. A. Bewer, AJSL 42 (1925/6), 130; also Rudolph, p. 208. "Samgar" conceals the name Sin-magir, a district of which Nergalsharezer is known from a contemporary inscription to have been governor (read *šar simmāgir*). The two Nergalsharezers are the same person. This is almost certainly the *Nergal-šarri-uṣur* (Neriglissar) who succeeded Nebuchad-nezzar's son on the Babylonian throne in 560; here he is the Rab-mag (Bab. *rab-mūgi*), a high officer whose exact function is unknown. In "nebo Sar-sekim" there is probably a corruption of *nebūšazbān šar sārīs*, "Nebushazban the Sar-saris (a variant of Rab-saris, which follows); cf. vs. 13. The Rab-saris (not "chief eunuch!") was a high military or diplomatic official.

14. *turned him over to Gedaliah.* The name of Gedaliah is not to be removed (so Rudolph, Weiser, etc.) on the grounds that it anticipates, and contradicts, xl 1–6. These are two separate accounts (see COMMENT), and they need not be artificially harmonized.

for safe conduct home. Literally "to bring him out to home [house]." One wonders if the expression (i.e., to release to home) may not be a technical term for letting a prisoner go free. LXX omits "to home" ("and they brought him out and he sat . . .").

11. *Now Nebuchadrezzar.* Perhaps the words "in that day," which dangle at the end of vs. 10 (see NOTE), might be taken as beginning vs. 11 (reading *wayyehī bayyōm hahū'*), or possibly as an editorial link joining vss. 11–12 to the account in vss. 4–10; "that day" then refers to the occasion of Nebuzaradan's actions described in vss. 9 f.

12. *Find him and look after him.* Literally "Take him and put your eyes on him."

13. The verse ("So Nebuzaradan . . . sent, and Nebushazban the Rab-saris, and Nergalsharezer the Rab-mag"), at least after the first few words, which may be resumed in xl 2, seeks to harmonize the account

begun in vss. 11–12 with that of vss. 3, 14; "they sent" in vs. 14, the subject of which is the officers in vs. 3, now resumes the verb of vs. 13. There is a hiatus in the account begun in vss. 11–12 before its resumption in xl 2; xl 1 indicates that Jeremiah was found only after a search.

xl 1. The text has obviously been damaged here. In vs. 1a an oracle is introduced, but never given (Is there a misplaced relic of it in vss. 2–3?). Verse 2 resumes xxxix 11–13a^a, with xl 1b a parenthesis designed to explain the circumstances under which Jeremiah was found.

Ramah. Today *er-Rām*, ca. five miles north of Jerusalem.

3. LXX, characteristically, has a shorter text: "And the Lord has done it because you sinned against him and did not listen to his voice."

6. *Mizpah.* Probably the present-day *Tell en-Naṣbeh*, ca. eight miles north of Jerusalem.

COMMENT

In July 587 (cf. lii 5 f.) Jerusalem finally fell to the Babylonians. A month later (lii 12 ff.; II Kings xxv 8 ff.) Nebuzaradan, commander of Nebuchadnezzar's bodyguard, arrived at the city and, acting upon orders, systematically looted it, burned it to the ground, and then superintended the deportation of further elements of the population to Babylon, leaving only certain of the very poorest of the people to harvest the crops. Judah having been organized as a province of the empire (II Kings xxv 22 ff.), Gedaliah ben Ahikam ben Shaphan—a member of the family that had so often befriended Jeremiah, and a son of the man who had once saved his life (xxvi 24)—was appointed as its governor. The section to which we now turn tells briefly of these events, and also describes how Jeremiah was released from prison, and how he came into Gedaliah's company.

The material of the section represents an editorial interweaving of various originally separate pieces. One of these, an oracle addressed by Jeremiah to Ebed-melek (xxxix 15–18), belongs with chapter xxxviii and has already been treated in that connection. As for the rest, xxxix 1–2, 4–10 readily separates itself. These verses give a brief account of the fall of Jerusalem based upon the narrative of lii 4–16 (II Kings xxv 1–12), of which they seem to be an abridgment. It will be noted that vss. 1–2 stand as a parenthesis in their context, interrupting the connection between xxxviii 28b

and xxxix 3, which read smoothly together (cf. the transposition of
xxxviii 28b in RSV). It will also be noted (see NOTES) that vss. 4 ff.
do not follow upon vs. 3, but upon vs. 2. LXX, incidentally, omits
the whole of vss. 4–10, and also vss. 11–13, though possibly because of homoioteleuton (i.e., the scribe's eye leaping from the
ending of vs. 3 to the identical ending of vs. 13). The account
just described was no doubt inserted at this point in order to make
the situation fully clear.

The material mentioned having been subtracted, there remain
two accounts of Jeremiah's release into the custody of Gedaliah.
One suspects that these, respectively, continue the two accounts of
xxxvii 11–21 and xxxviii 1–28a, though it is impossible to be sure
which belongs with which. The first of these accounts is very brief.
It begins in xxxviii 28a, is continued in xxxix 3, and concluded in
xxxix 14 (this is even clearer in LXX which, as noted above, omits
vss. 4–13, so that vs. 14 follows vs. 3 directly). In this account,
various Babylonian officers constitute themselves, upon the city's
fall, as a military government (vs. 3). Wishing, we may suppose, to
reward those who had—they thought—been sympathetic to their
cause, they brought Jeremiah from the court of the guard (vs. 14)
and released him into the care of Gedaliah. The second account is
longer. It begins in xxxix 11–12, and informs us that Nebuzaradan
(who, it will be recalled, did not arrive until a month after the
city's fall; cf. lii 6, 12) brought with him orders from Nebuchadnezzar to show favor to Jeremiah by according to him whatever treatment he might request. We may suppose that this was actually a
general order that all friends of Babylon were to be treated well,
and that Nebuzaradan, having on his arrival made inquiry as to who
these were, found Jeremiah's name high on the list. This account,
begun in xxxix 11–12, is broken off abruptly (vs. 13, with the
possible exception of its initial words, is an editorial attempt to
harmonize the two accounts) and is resumed in xl 1–6, where the
text (see notes) is in serious disrepair. Here we are told (vs. 1)
that Nebuzaradan finally located Jeremiah among a mass of prisoners who had been assembled at Ramah for deportation. Nebuzaradan
thereupon ordered his release and, after offering him privileged
treatment if he would come to Babylon, gave him permission to go
wherever he wished. When Jeremiah elected to stay in the land, he
was courteously dismissed and allowed to join Gedaliah.

These two accounts, while not exactly harmonious, are not

necessarily contradictory. It is quite possible that Jeremiah, after
having been released from confinement by the military government
upon the city's fall, was picked up on the streets by Babylonian
soldiers as they were rounding up civilians for deportation and
herded along with the rest into the stockade at Ramah, only to be
released again on Nebuzaradan's orders. Certainly stranger things
have happened in the course of military occupation. The two
accounts, in any event, have these essentials in common: that Jeremiah was set free by the Babylonians because they thought that
he had favored their cause, and that he finally found his way into
the company of Gedaliah at Mizpah.

34. THE ASSASSINATION OF GEDALIAH
AND THE FLIGHT TO EGYPT
(xl 7–16; xli 1–13a; 14aᵝ; 13b; 14aᵃb–18; xlii 1–18;
xliii 1–3; xlii 19–22; xliii 4–7)

The Assassination of Gedaliah

XL 7 When the commanders of such troops as were still in the field, together with their men, heard that the king of Babylon had appointed Gedaliah ben Ahikam governor of the land, and had committed to him those men, women, and children of the very poorest of the people who had not been deported to Babylon, 8 they came to Gedaliah at Mizpah. These included: Ishmael ben Nethaniah, ᵃJohanan ben Kareah,ᵃ Seraiah ben Tanhumet, the sons of Ophaiᵇ the Netophathite, Jaazaniahᶜ the son of the Maacathite, as well as their men. 9 And Gedaliah ben Ahikam ben Shaphan gave his oath to them and their men, and said, ᵃ"Do not be afraid to submit to the Chaldeans.ᵃ Stay in the land and be subjects of the king of Babylon, and it will go well with you. 10 I will myself stay here in Mizpah to represent you before the Chaldeans as they come to us. As for you, you have only to bring in the wine, the summer fruit, and the olive oil, lay up a supply of provisions, and live in the towns that you have seized."

11 Meanwhile, all the Jews who were in Moab, in Ammon, in Edom, and in other countries had heard that the king of Babylon had left some survivors in Judah and had made Gedaliah ben Ahikam ben Shaphan governor over them. 12 So all these Jews

ᵃ⁻ᵃ So LXX, various manuscripts and II Kings xxv 23. Hebrew here has "Johanan and Jonathan, the sons of Kareah," which may be correct, or may be a conflation. In any case, only Johanan cuts a figure in the narrative.
ᵇ So Ktib; Qre, "Ephai."
ᶜ So in some manuscripts and II Kings xxv 23. Hebrew here spells "Jezaniah."
ᵈ⁻ᵈ So MT. But many prefer the reading of LXX and II Kings xxv 24, "Do not be afraid of the Chaldean officials."

likewise returned from the various places to which they had been scattered, and came to the land of Judah, to Gedaliah at Mizpah. And they brought in an abundant crop of wine and summer fruit.

13 Subsequently, Johanan ben Kareah and various of the commanders of troops still in the field came to Gedaliah at Mizpah, 14 and said to him, "Surely you are aware that Baalis, king of the Ammonites, has sent Ishmael ben Nethaniah to assassinate you?" But Gedaliah ben Ahikam would not believe them. 15 Then Johanan ben Kareah made a secret proposal to Gedaliah there at Mizpah: "Just let me go and kill Ishmael ben Nethaniah, and no one will be the wiser. Why should he murder you, and thus cause all the Jews who have gathered about you to be scattered, and the remnant of Judah to perish?" 16 But Gedaliah ben Ahikam said to Johanan ben Kareah, "You shall do no such thing! What you are saying about Ishmael is a lie!"

XLI 1 So it was that in the seventh month Ishmael ben Nethaniah ben Elishama, who was of royal descent,*e* came to Gedaliah ben Ahikam at Mizpah, accompanied by ten men. And, there at Mizpah, as they were eating a meal together, 2 Ishmael ben Nethaniah and the ten men who were with him leaped to their feet, and struck down Gedaliah ben Ahikam with the sword, thus killing him whom the king of Babylon had made governor of the land. 3 In addition, Ishmael struck down all the Jews who were in Gedaliah's company at Mizpah, as well as such Chaldean soldiers as happened to be there.

4 Then, the day after Gedaliah's murder, while no one as yet knew of it, 5 eighty men arrived from Shechem, from Shiloh, and from Samaria, with their heads shaved, their clothing torn, and covered with self-inflicted gashes, bringing with them cereal offerings and incense to present at the house of Yahweh. 6 Ishmael ben Nethaniah thereupon went out from Mizpah to

---

e Hebrew adds, "and the king's chief officers," which one must take as "one of the king's chief officers" (add *min*). But the words are absent from LXX and II Kings xxv 25, and are probably best omitted.

meet them, *weeping as he went.* And when he reached them, he said to them, "Welcome in the name of Gedaliah ben Ahikam!" 7 But as soon as they were well within the city, Ishmael ben Nethaniah and the men who were with him massacred them *and threw them* into the cistern. 8 There were, however, ten men among them who said to Ishmael, "Don't kill us! We have stores of wheat and barley, olive oil and honey hidden in the fields." So these he spared, and did not kill them along with their companions. 9 Now the cistern into which Ishmael threw all the corpses of the men whom he had slain *was a large one*; it was the one that King Asa built as a defense measure against Baasha, king of Israel. This Ishmael ben Nethaniah filled with the slain. 10 Then Ishmael made prisoners of all the rest of the people in Mizpah, including the king's daughters,* whom Nebuzaradan the commander of the guard had entrusted to Gedaliah ben Ahikam. These Ishmael took as prisoners, and set out with the intention of crossing into Ammonite territory.

11 Now when Johanan ben Kareah and the various military leaders who were with him heard of the dastardly thing that Ishmael ben Nethaniah had done, 12 they took all their men and marched out to engage him* in battle; and they caught up with him by the great pool at Gibeon. 13a And when all the people who were with Ishmael ——— 14aᵝ that is to say, all the people whom Ishmael had taken captive from Mizpah ——— 13b caught sight of Johanan ben Kareah and the various

---

f–f LXX (which has various unimportant omissions) reads, "they [i.e., the pilgrims] were going along weeping"—which they doubtless were. But MT seems preferable: Ishmael gains their confidence by pretending himself to be overcome with grief.

g–g Not expressed in Hebrew; but some such word (*wayyašlīkēm:* so Syr.), or perhaps "he threw their bodies" (cf. vs. 9), must be supplied. Hebrew also reads "into the midst of the cistern"; but *tōk* (LXX omits) is probably a dittography from above ("into the midst of the city").

h–h Read, following LXX, *bōr gādōl hū'*. Heb. *beyad gedalyāhū* ("by the hand /side of Gedaliah") is hardly correct. One could translate "because of Gedaliah" (so KJ, and cf. M. J. Dahood, *Biblica* 44 [1963], 302); but it seems to me that the LXX reading suits the context better.

i Hebrew then repeats, "and all the people left in Mizpah," which appears to be a variant of "all the rest of the people in Mizpah"; omit with LXX.

j So with LXX. Hebrew awkwardly repeats "Ishmael ben Nethaniah" in place of the pronoun.

military leaders who were with him, *they were overjoyed
14a*b and, turning on their heels, they hurried back to rejoin Johanan ben Kareah.* 15 Ishmael ben Nethaniah, however, with
eight of his men slipped away from Johanan and escaped into
Ammonite territory.

16 Then Johanan ben Kareah and the various military leaders
who were with him took all the rest of the people 'whom they
had rescued from Ishmael'—that is, the men,'" women, children
and eunuchs whom they brought back from Gibeon— 17 and,
setting out, they halted at Gerut-kimham, near Bethlehem,
their intention being to go on to Egypt, 18 to get away from the
Chaldeans. They were, of course, afraid of them because Ishmael
ben Nethaniah had murdered Gedaliah ben Ahikam, whom the
king of Babylon had made governor of the land.

The Flight to Egypt; Jeremiah's Warning Disregarded

XLII 1 Then all the military leaders, in particular Johanan ben
Kareah and Azariah" ben Hoshaiah, together with all the people
both small and great approached 2 Jeremiah the prophet and said
to him, "We beg you most earnestly, pray to Yahweh your God
°for us, for this whole remnant°—for we are left but a few out of
many, as you yourself can see— 3 that Yahweh your God would
tell us which way to go, and what to do." 4 Jeremiah the prophet
replied, "Very well! I will indeed pray to Yahweh your God, as
you request. And whatever answer Yahweh gives you,ᵖ I will let

k-k MT has probably suffered conflation; LXX omits "they were overjoyed"
in vs. 13, and in vs. 14 has only "and they turned back to Johanan."
l-l The reading follows LXX; Heb. "whom he had rescued from Ishmael ben
Nethaniah, from Mizpah, after he had slain Gedaliah ben Ahikam" cannot
be right. It is better to follow LXX than to emend MT, which clearly conflates the reading of LXX with "whom Ishmael ben Nethaniah had carried
away from Mizpah after he had slain Gedaliah ben Ahikam."
m Heb. adds "soldiers." But "soldiers" may be a gloss by one who mistook
gᵉbārīm ("men") for gibbōrīm ("warriors"); cf. xliii 6.
n So with xliii 2. Hebrew reads here "Jezaniah [Jaazaniah] ben Hoshaiah"
(cf. xl 8). LXX reads "Azariah" here and in xliii 2, but gives the father's
name as "Maaseiah." Possibly a third name has dropped out.
o-o This probably combines variants; LXX omits "for us," Syr. omits "for this
whole remnant."
p LXX omits "you"; some would read "your God" in its place ('ᵉlōhēkem
for 'etkem).

you know, withholding nothing from you." 5 They then assured
Jeremiah, "May Yahweh be a true and trusty witness against us,
if we do not do exactly what Yahweh your God sends you to tell
us to do. 6 Whether we like it or not, we will obey the voice of
Yahweh our God, to whom we are sending you, in order that it
may go well with us. Yes indeed, we will obey the voice of
Yahweh our God."

7 Ten days later, the word of Yahweh came to Jeremiah. 8 So
he summoned Johanan ben Kareah and the various military
leaders who were with him, together with all the people both
small and great, 9 and said to them, "This is what Yahweh, the
God of Israel, to whom you sent me to present your petition,
has said: 10 qIf you will only stayq in this land, I will build you up
and not tear you down, plant you and not uproot you; for I regard the hurt that I have inflicted upon you as sufficient. 11 There
is no need to fear the king of Babylon as you do. There is no
need to fear him—Yahweh's word—for I am with you to help
you and to rescue you from his clutches. 12 And, since I grant
you mercy, he will show you mercy, and let you return to your
land. 13 But if, unwilling to heed the voice of Yahweh your God,
you should say, 'We will not stay in this land! 14 No! We will
go to Egypt, where we will see no more of war, nor hear the
trumpet blast, nor starve for want of food, and we will stay
there,'— 15 in that case, hear the word of Yahweh, O remnant of
Judah! This is what Yahweh of Hosts, the God of Israel, has
said: If you have really made up your minds to go to Egypt, and
if you do go and settle there, 16 then the sword that you fear
will overtake you in the land of Egypt, and the famine you
dread will follow hard after you right into Egypt; and you will
die there. 17 Yes, all those who have made up their minds to go
to Egypt to settle there will die by the sword, of starvation and
disease; not a single one of them will survive, or escape the
disaster that I will bring upon them. 18 For this is what Yahweh
of Hosts, the God of Israel, has said: Just as my furious anger
was poured out upon the citizens of Jerusalem, so will my fury

q-q So LXX and other Vrs. ('im yāšōb tēšᵉbū); Heb. 'im šōb—(y lost by
scribal error) is clearly incorrect.

be poured out on you if you go to Egypt. You will become an execration, an object of horror, a curseword and a taunt. And you will never see this place again."

XLIII 1 But when Jeremiah had finished repeating to the people all the words which Yahweh their God had sent him to tell them (that is, those above), 2 Azariah ben Hoshaiah, Johanan ben Kareah, ʳand various other arrogant and self-willed fellows,ʳ said to Jeremiah, "You are lying! Yahweh did not send you ˢto tell usˢ not to go to Egypt to settle there. 3 No! Baruch ben Neriah has been inciting you against us, to get us into the clutches of the Chaldeans, so that they may kill us or deport us to Babylon."

XLII 19 Jeremiah replied, "Yahweh has told you, O remnant of Judah, not to go to Egypt. You may be quite sure of that! I warn you right now 20 that you are making a fatal mistake. For you yourselves sent me to Yahweh your God with the request: 'Pray to Yahweh our God for us! Let us know exactly what Yahweh our God says, and we will do it' 21 Yet now that I have told you, you have altogether disregarded the instructions that Yahweh your God sent me to give you. 22 So now, make no mistake about it, you shall die by the sword, of starvation and disease in the place where you wish to go and settle."

XLIII 4 But neither Johanan ben Kareah, nor any of the various military leaders, nor any of the people, would heed the voice of Yahweh and remain in the land of Judah. 5 Instead, Johanan ben Kareah and the various military leaders took the whole remnant of Judah: those who had returned to settle in the land of Judah from the various countries to which they has been scattered; 6 the men, the women and children, the princesses—in short, all those persons whom Nebuzaradan the commander of

ʳ–ʳ Hebrew, "the arrogant men, saying [said to Jeremiah]," is scarcely right. Read *hammōrīm* for *'ōmᵉrīm* with Giesebrecht and others. Or (so LXX) omit "arrogant" and read, "and all the [other] men who were speaking with Jeremiah [said . . .]."
ˢ–ˢ Literally "to us" (*'ēlēnū*) with LXX; Heb. "(Yahweh) our God" (*'ᵉlōhēnū*).

the royal bodyguard had left with Gedaliah ben Ahikam ben Shaphan, including Jeremiah the prophet and Baruch ben Neriah— 7 and, in disobedience to the voice of Yahweh, they set out for Egypt. And they arrived at Tahpanhes.

NOTES

xl 7. *such troops as were still in the field.* The wreckage of Judah's army, isolated detachments of which had escaped the Babylonian "mop-up" and still maintained themselves in out-of-the-way places.

men, women, and children of the very poorest of the people. There were others than the poor, of course (cf. xli 10; xliii 6). But "of the very poorest" is best taken as in apposition to "men, women, and children." The bulk of those left were economically underprivileged classes (xxxix 10).

9. Gedaliah seeks to pacify the land and end armed resistance. His oath to the men is not given verbatim, but presumably the substance of it is the promise in vs. 10. Though it is not said, the men may in return have formally accepted Gedaliah as governor, thus preserving a semblance of normal procedure.

10. *to represent you before the Chaldeans.* Literally "to stand before the Chaldeans"; i.e., as a mediator (cf. xv 1) between his people and the Chaldean officials, in the normal conduct of affairs.

towns that you have seized. Presumably bands of troops had occupied certain—perhaps depopulated—towns, perhaps with tacit Babylonian consent, perhaps without it, in the confusion after the withdrawal of the main Babylonian army.

11. *had left some survivors in Judah.* Literally "had given Judah a remnant."

14. *Baalis, king of the Ammonites.* We do not know what his motives were—perhaps merely to weaken Babylonian authority in any way he could. Ammon had been involved in unrest in 594 (xxvii 3), and was probably implicated in the events leading up to 587 (cf. Ezek xxi 18–32 [23–37H]). Probably Zedekiah had been trying to flee there when captured (xxxix 4 f.).

xli 1. *in the seventh month.* October. Unfortunately the year is not stated. The narrative creates the impression that it was the year of Jerusalem's fall (in the fourth month: xxxix 2), and that there had just been time to get in the summer crops when it occurred. Some feel, however, that this does not allow enough time for the events recorded in xl

7–16 (the return of Jews from foreign lands, etc.), and that Gedaliah's murder must therefore have taken place a year, or even several years, later. One cannot be sure. Later the Jews observed a fast (first mentioned in Zech vii 5; viii 19) in the seventh month in commemoration of this tragedy.

as they were eating. The dastardly nature of the crime is accentuated. By customary law the host was bound to protect his guests, and the guests were honor bound to reciprocate in good faith. Gedaliah was thus unsuspecting and, in effect, defenseless.

2. *thus killing him*. Literally "So he [i.e., Ishmael] killed him."

3. *who were in Gedaliah's company at Mizpah*. Literally "who were with him—i.e., with Gedaliah—at Mizpah"; "with Gedaliah" may be a gloss (LXX omits). Of course not all the Jews at Mizpah were killed (see vs. 10), but only those present at the meal.

such Chaldean soldiers as happened to be there. Either such as happened to be stationed at Mizpah, or such as happened to be present at the meal where Gedaliah was murdered. But Ishmael would certainly have had to dispose of all Chaldean troops in the town. Presumably the detachment was small and could be taken by surprise.

4. *while no one as yet knew of it*. No one outside Mizpah, of course.

5. These men were clearly on their way to the temple in Jerusalem. Nor were they unaware of its destruction, as their deep mourning (shaven heads, etc.) indicates. One must suppose that the temple still retained its sanctity, and that people journeyed thither on certain cultic occasions even after it had been destroyed (this was the seventh month, the time of the great autumn feast and the cultic New Year [as distinguished from the civil New Year which at this period fell in the spring, following the Babylonian Calendar]). The fact that the men came from northern Israel no doubt witnesses to the lasting effects of Josiah's reform, for they presumably continued a custom already established before Jerusalem's fall.

6. *Welcome in the name of Gedaliah*. Literally "Come in to Gedaliah," which appears to be a formula of cordial invitation, rather than a command. Why Ishmael invited these men into the city is puzzling. Unless one assumes that he was a sadist who enjoyed killing for the sake of plunder (cf. vs. 8), one must suppose that the pilgrims would have entered the city anyway to pay their respects to Gedaliah and that Ishmael, knowing this, wished to throw them off guard so that he could dispose of them before any could flee and broadcast the news of his crime. But Ishmael's motives remain unclear throughout.

8. How Ishmael proposed to lay his hands on these stores is not clear. The simplest guess is that he intended to hold the ten men as prisoners, and then communicate with their families, demanding ransom.

9. *the cistern . . . that King Asa built.* For the account of Asa's fortification of Mizpah three hundred years previously, cf. I Kings xv 22.

10. *Ishmael made prisoners.* Although Jeremiah is not mentioned, one assumes that he was among these prisoners since, after their rescue, when the party camped near Bethlehem, he was present (xlii 2 ff.).

12. *the great pool at Gibeon.* Gibeon, today ej-Jīb, is ca. six miles northwest of Jerusalem. The pool referred to (cf. II Sam ii 13) is probably the huge pit cut in the rock which archaeologists have discovered there. If Mizpah is located at Tell en-Naṣbeh, the narrative presents difficulties, since Gibeon is some three miles south-southwest of that place and not in the direction of Ammon, whither Ishmael was fleeing. Some scholars, and partly for this reason, have located Mizpah at Nebī Samwīl, south-southwest of Gibeon. But Ishmael may have followed a circuitous route to throw off pursuit, or for other reasons unknown to us.

14aβ. *that is to say, all the people . . . from Mizpah.* These words have been transposed for the sake of clarity (in Hebrew they are the subject of "they turned" ["turning"] in vs. 14). It was, of course, not Ishmael's own men, but his prisoners, who rejoiced.

16. *whom they had rescued from Ishmael.* Literally "whom he [i.e., Johanan] had rescued."

the men, women. Heb. "men, soldiers and women." See textual note[m]. It is doubtful that soldiers were among Ishmael's captives, since he seems (vs. 3) to have killed such soldiers as were at Mizpah.

whom they brought back. So for smoothness; Heb. "whom he [i.e., Johanan] brought. . . ."

xlii 2. *We beg you most earnestly.* Literally "Pray, let our supplication fall before you."

4. *Yahweh gives you.* The shift through these verses between "your God" (Jeremiah's), "your God" (the people's), and "our God," is interesting but probably not significant; there is no evidence that irony is intended. LXX, indeed, reads "our God" in this verse, and omits "your God" in vs. 5. See textual note[p].

7. Further evidence of Jeremiah's unwillingness to speak in the name of Yahweh until sure that he had in fact received Yahweh's word (cf. ch. xxviii and COMMENT on Sec. 27).

10. *If you will only stay.* Note how the verbs in this verse play on those used in the account of Jeremiah's call (i 10).

for I regard the hurt . . . as sufficient. A paraphrase to avoid misunderstanding. The literal translation, "for I repent of the evil that I have done you" (EVV), is misleading; Jeremiah does not mean that Yahweh realizes that he has made a mistake and is sorry for it. The sense of the verb is probably (cf. LXX) "I relent with regard to . . ."

(cf. Amos vii 3, 6, etc.); i.e., Yahweh is appeased by what he has
done, remits further punishment, and promises his people better things
in the future. Since the verb carries a note of regret, one might read,
"I am sorry about the hurt that I have had to inflict upon you."

12. *let you return to your land.* The words doubtless reflect the fact
that the text of Jeremiah was edited in the Exile. On the other hand,
since the fugitives had already left their homes and were on the point
of fleeing to Egypt, the sense could be: he will let you return to your
homes in peace. There is no need to emend the text. LXX reads
first person throughout: "I will show you mercy and will have mercy
on you and bring you back . . ."; but this probably represents the same
text as MT, with the forms *weriḥam* and *weḥešīb* taken as infinitive
absolute, and may be a preferable translation.

xliii 1. The transposition of xliii 1–3 will be noted in the COMMENT.
It is done merely to sharpen the force of the dialogue; xlii 19–22 indicates that Jeremiah's words have been rejected, but it is only in xliii
1–3 that this is actually done. Very probably the prose discourse of xlii
9–22 has received expansion. But it is not impossible that Jeremiah,
like many another speaker, even while he spoke knew from his hearers'
faces that he had failed to carry his point.

xlii 19. *Jeremiah replied.* Supplied, as demanded by the context; see
NOTE on xliii 1.

21. *you have altogether disregarded, . . .* Literally "you have not
heeded the voice of Yahweh your God as regards all that he sent me
to you."

xliii 7. *Tahpanhes.* See NOTE on ii 16.

COMMENT

It would be pleasant to record that, having survived the horrors of
Jerusalem's fall and the persecution to which he had himself been
subjected, Jeremiah was allowed to live out the remainder of his
days in peace. But the story has no such happy ending. Gedaliah's
career as governor soon ended in tragedy. Within but a short
while—perhaps a few months, though perhaps appreciably longer
(see NOTE on xli 1)—he was treacherously struck down by certain
die-hards who considered him a collaborationist, and the brief respite
was over. Those around Gedaliah, though themselves innocent of

complicity, quite naturally feared Babylonian reprisals, and decided to flee to Egypt. And this they did, in spite of Jeremiah's earnest warnings, taking the now aging prophet with them, never to return.

We are told of these events in a narrative unit which continues without break and, save for an extended prose discourse in xlii 9–22, with a minimum of dialogue, from xl 7 to xliii 7. The narrative itself is clear, and requires few explanatory comments beyond those given in the NOTES. It falls into two parts. The first of these (xl 7–xli 18) tells of the assassination of Gedaliah, and is remarkable in that in it Jeremiah plays no role at all. We do not know what he did in the interval of Gedaliah's governorship, what words, if any, he may have uttered (though doubtless there were some), or, indeed, how long the interval lasted. Nor do we know how he escaped the bloodbath that accompanied Gedaliah's assassination, or even if he was in Mizpah at the time—though (see NOTE on xli 10) in all likelihood he was. This silence with regard to Jeremiah need not, however, force us to the conclusion drawn by some scholars that since Jeremiah's biographer was not interested in recording events in which the prophet took no part, this portion of the narrative must come from another hand than his. Though Jeremiah was but a spectator, the murder of Gedaliah was in fact one of the tragic events of his career. It dashed forever his hope that he might end his days in the homeland where, so Yahweh had promised (xxxii 1–15), Israel would one day resume its life as a people, and it was the direct cause of his being taken to a faraway land to die, experiencing meanwhile further rejections of the prophetic word that had come to him.

The second part of the account (xlii 1–xliii 7) tells of the flight to Egypt. Here again, the narrative portions require little comment. It is not surprising that as the people debated flight, they should have asked Jeremiah for a word from Yahweh. Nor is it surprising, in view of Jeremiah's steadfast faith in Yahweh's promises of restoration, that that word, when it came, should have been to remain in the land and not flee to Egypt. But the people, still suspecting Jeremiah of pro-Babylonian sympathies, refused to listen. It is interesting, and indicative of the stature of the self-effacing Baruch, that there were some who believed (xliii 3) that he was the one who put the words in Jeremiah's mouth! The prose discourse of xlii 9–22 has probably received verbal expansion in the course of transmission. In vss. 19–22, in particular, Jeremiah assails the people for refusing to obey Yahweh's word before (cf. xliii 1–3) they had in fact done so. This is not in itself, to be sure, sufficient reason for rearranging the text. Nevertheless, and merely with the thought of sharpening the force of the dialogue, I have ventured with perhaps the majority of commentators to transpose xliii 1–3 before xlii 19–22 (see further, NOTES).

35. JEREMIAH IN EGYPT
(xliii 8–13; xliv 1–30)

Nebuchadnezzar's Invasion of Egypt Predicted

XLIII 8 In Tahpanhes, the word of Yahweh came to Jeremiah as follows: 9 "Get some large stones, and bury them in the clay flooring [?], in the terrace [?], at the entrance of Pharaoh's house in Tahpanhes, while certain of the Jews watch you. 10 Then say to them, 'This is what Yahweh of Hosts, the God of Israel, has said: See! I am going to send and bring Nebuchadrezzar, king of Babylon, my servant; and he*a* will set his throne right over these stones that you*b* have buried, and spread his canopy [?] above them. 11 He will come and smite the land of Egypt, giving those marked for the plague to the plague, those marked for deportation to deportation, and those marked for the sword to the sword. 12 He*c* will set fire to the temples of Egypt's gods, and burn the gods or carry them captive. He will pick clean the land of Egypt like a shepherd picking lice from his clothing, and then depart unmolested. 13 He will shatter the sacred pillars of Beth-shemesh—that is, the one in Egypt—and burn the temples of Egypt's gods to the ground.'"

The Last Known Words of Jeremiah

XLIV 1 The word that came to Jeremiah for all the Jews living in Egypt, that is, those in Migdol, in Tahpanhes, in Memphis, and in the land of Pathros: 2 "This is what Yahweh of Hosts, the God of Israel, has said: You yourselves have seen

---

a So with LXX; but Heb. "I will set," is not impossible.
b So LXX^BA. MT, "I have buried," does not fit well in an address where Yahweh is the speaker, although it may be that in the spoken form of the address Jeremiah identified his action as Yahweh's own.
c So with LXX and other Vrs.; Heb. "I will set fire."

what a calamity I brought upon Jerusalem and the other cities of Judah. There they lie today, in ruins and uninhabited, 3 because of the evil that they did in order to provoke me—going to offer sacrifice*d* to other gods of whom neither they, nor you, nor your fathers knew. 4 And though with urgency and persistence I sent to you all my servants the prophets, begging you, 'Oh, do not do this detestable thing that I hate!' 5 no one obeyed or paid any attention, nor did they turn from their wickedness and leave off making sacrifices to other gods. 6 So my furious anger was poured out on them, and it blazed up in the cities of Judah and in the streets of Jerusalem, leaving them the desolate and awesome waste that they are today.

7 "And now, this is what Yahweh, God of Hosts, the God of Israel, has said: Why do yourselves the fatal injury of cutting yourselves off from the midst of Judah, men and women, infants and babes, so as to leave of yourselves no remnant? 8 Why provoke me by the things that you do—making sacrifices to other gods here in the land of Egypt where you have come to seek asylum—as if it were your aim to destroy yourselves and become a curse word and a taunt among all the nations of the earth? 9 Have you forgotten the wickedness which your fathers, and the kings of Judah *e*and their wives,*e* as well as you yourselves and your wives, committed in the land of Judah and in the streets of Jerusalem? 10 To this day they have showed neither contrition nor fear, nor have they conducted themselves according to my law and my statutes, which I set before you as I had before your fathers.

11 "Therefore, this is what Yahweh of Hosts, the God of Israel, has said: Ah, but I am determined to bring evil upon you, even to the extent of destroying Judah entirely! 12 I will take those of the remnant of Judah who were determined to come to Egypt to settle, and they shall all perish. In the land of Egypt

d Heb. follows this with "to serve," which seems to be a variant; LXX, which otherwise abbreviates, omits.

e-e Heb. "and his wives." LXX reads, "the kings of Judah, and your princes, and your wives," omitting "as well as you yourselves"; but this is hardly preferable.

they shall fall by the sword *or perish through starvation*; both small and great, they shall die by the sword and of starvation, and become an execration, an object of horror, a curse word and a taunt. 13 I will punish those living in Egypt just as I punished Jerusalem—with the sword, with starvation and disease. 14 Not a single one of the remnant of Judah that has come to Egypt to settle shall escape or survive to return to the land of Judah, where they so desperately yearn to dwell once more. Indeed they shall not return—except perhaps a few fugitives."

15 Then all the men who knew that their wives were making sacrifices to other gods, together with all the women who stood by—a great crowd in all*—answered Jeremiah: 16 "As regards what you have just said to us in the name of Yahweh, we are not going to listen to you. 17 On the contrary, we will scrupulously do all that we have vowed to do, and will offer sacrifice to the Queen of Heaven and pour out libations to her, just as we and our fathers, our kings and our princes, used to do in the cities of Judah and in the streets of Jerusalem; for then we had plenty to eat, were prosperous, and experienced no misfortune. 18 But ever since we left off sacrificing to the Queen of Heaven, and pouring out libations to her, we have lacked everything, and have been destroyed by sword and famine." 19 *And the women added,* "Indeed we will go on sacrificing to the Queen of Heaven, and pouring out libations to her. Has it been without our husbands' knowledge and consent that we have made cakes depicting her, and poured out libations to her?"

20 Then Jeremiah said to all the people, the men, the women, and all those persons who had answered him in this way: 21 "The sacrifices that you and your fathers, your kings, your princes,

---

− With various manuscripts and Vrs. "or" is added. The sentence structure in this verse is extremely awkward, and one is puzzled to know how to punctuate. The text has undoubtedly suffered conflation; LXX in vss. 11–12 is scarcely half as long.

g Hebrew then adds, "and all the people living in the land of Egypt, in Pathros." This dangles, and appears not to be original; all the Jews in Egypt (including Upper Egypt) scarcely were present.

h−h Since the women are now the speakers, some such words must be understood or supplied (and so LXXL), and the ensuing participle taken as feminine.

and the populace generally, offered in the cities of Judah and
in Jerusalem's streets—do you think that Yahweh did not notice
it,[i] or that it never entered his mind? 22 No, it was because
Yahweh could no longer endure your wicked behavior, and the
detestable things which you did, that your land has become the
desolate, accursed, uninhabited waste that it is today. 23 It was
because you offered these sacrifices, because you sinned against
Yahweh, neither heeding his[j] voice nor obeying his law, his
statutes and stipulations, that the present disaster has befallen
you."

24 Jeremiah further addressed all the people, particularly the
women, as follows: "Hear the word of Yahweh![k] 25 This is what
Yahweh of Hosts, the God of Israel, has said: You women![l]
You have spoken with your mouths, and with your hands have
fulfilled your promises: 'We will scrupulously perform the vows
that we have made, to offer sacrifice to the Queen of Heaven,
and to pour out libations to her.' Very well, then, fulfill your
vows! By all means perform them![m] 26 But, in that event, hear
the word of Yahweh, all you of Judah who are living in the
land of Egypt: Ah, but I swear by my great name—Yahweh
has spoken—that never again shall my name be invoked, 'As the
Lord Yahweh lives,' by the mouth of any Jew in all of Egypt.
27 Believe me, I am watching over them for their hurt, not their
welfare. All the Jews in the land of Egypt will perish by the
sword and of starvation, until they have been annihilated; 28 such
fugitives from the sword as return to Judah from the land of
Egypt will be few indeed. Then all the remnant of Judah that
came to Egypt to settle will find out whose word stands—mine
or theirs. 29 And this shall be the sign to you—Yahweh's word—

[i] Heb. "notice them." But the grammar demands the singular (cf. the following verb); LXX omits the pronoun.
[j] So for smoothness; Hebrew awkwardly repeats "[heeding the voice] of Yahweh."
[k] Heb. adds, "all [you of] Judah who are in the land of Egypt," which is possibly an intrusion from vs. 26; omit with LXX.
[l] So with LXX (and cf. the ensuing verbs); 'attēnāh hannāšīm for MT, 'at-
tem ūnešēkem ("you and your wives").
[m] Heb. repeats "[. . . perform] your vows." Some manuscripts read "your
libations"; LXX omits the word altogether. It is probably dittography.

that I am going to punish you here in this place, so that you may know that my pronouncements of evil against you definitely stand: 30 This is what Yahweh has said, Look! I am going to hand Pharaoh Hophra, king of Egypt, over to his enemies, to those who seek his life, just as I handed Zedekiah, king of Judah, over to Nebuchadrezzar, king of Babylon, his enemy who sought his life."

NOTES

xliii 9. *in the clay flooring, in the terrace.* Both words are of uncertain meaning. The first ("in the [clay] mortar" [?]) occurs only here; the second elsewhere (II Sam xii 31; Nah iii 14) denotes a "brick-mold" or "brick-kiln," but here perhaps a "terrace of brickwork" (cf. KB). The two words are quite possibly variants, but it is difficult to choose between them. LXX, which did not understand the meaning, has only one word.

Pharaoh's house. Scarcely the royal palace, which would not have been at the frontier city of Tahpanhes. Presumably it was a government building of some sort, though perhaps used to house the pharaoh when he visited the city. The Elephantine Papyri (Cowley, No. 2) mention "the king's house" at that place, which was at the southern frontier of Egypt (cf. A. Cowley, *Aramaic Papyri of the Fifth Century B.C.* [Oxford: Clarendon Press, 1923], pp. 4–6).

10. *his canopy.* The word occurs only here and is of uncertain meaning. The context suggests a canopy or pavilion, although some have suggested a "carpet."

11. *those marked for the plague to the plague.* Of course Nebuchadnezzar could not literally do this, but the language is stereotyped; cf. xv 2.

12. *burn the gods.* Literally "burn them"; but the images of the gods are referred to.

13. *that is, the one in Egypt.* Probably a gloss to distinguish the Beth-shemesh ("House of the Sun-god") mentioned here from the place of the same name in Palestine. Heliopolis (On), near Memphis, is referred to—and so LXX explicitly (". . . the pillars of Heliopolis, which are in On").

xliv 1. The verse shows that Jewish colonies existed at an early period in various parts of Egypt. Listed here, aside from Tahpanhes, are:

Migdol (near Tahpanhes, site uncertain), Memphis (the capital city, near Cairo) and Pathros (Upper Egypt).

3. *to offer sacrifice.* It is probably best to translate so throughout the chapter, rather than "to burn incense" (so most EVV); cf. NOTE on i 16. See textual note[d].

8. *as if it were your aim to.* Literally "in order to." They behave as if their aim were self-destruction.

10. *showed neither contrition nor.* Literally "they were not crushed or . . . ," i.e., in the sense of crushed in spirit, as in Ps li 19[17E]; Isa xix 10; lvii 15. But the text is uncertain; Vrs. have various different readings.

11–12. *am determined . . . were determined.* In both cases the expression is "to set the face." The stubborn determination of the people to have their own way meets God's unyielding determination to have his way with them. In the end (vs. 28 f.) they will find out "whose word stands."

14. *except perhaps a few fugitives.* Literally "except fugitives." The sense is: a few may get back, but no number worth mentioning. The words may be, as some scholars think, a gloss to harmonize vs. 14a with vs. 28.

17. *the Queen of Heaven.* See NOTE on vii 18.

21. *the populace generally.* Literally "the people of the land." Often a technical term for the landed gentry, it may have that meaning here; but more probably the people in general are intended.

23. *offered these sacrifices.* Hebrew does not express "these"; but what is referred to are the illegitimate offerings mentioned above, not sacrifice in general.

24. *all the people, particularly the women.* Literally "all the people and all the women." Since what follows is addressed specifically to the women (cf. vs. 25), many scholars delete "all the people and."

30. *Pharaoh Hophra.* Hophra (Apries) ruled Egypt from 589 until 570, when he lost his life in a rebellion and was succeeded by Amasis (570–526). That Jeremiah lived to see this is unlikely; at least, we have no evidence that he did.

COMMENT

This section contains the last words uttered by Jeremiah of which we have knowledge. It consists of two pieces of unequal length: xliii 8–13 and xliv. The first of these follows closely upon the foregoing section and carries forward the theme of Jeremiah's words recorded there. It will be recalled that Jeremiah had bitterly

opposed the flight to Egypt as flat disobedience to Yahweh's expressed will, and had warned the people that, far from finding safety
in Egypt, disaster would overtake them even there. In xliii 8–13
we are told that, after the fugitives had arrived at Tahpanhes,
Jeremiah buried some large stones in front of the government building there, and announced to those who watched him do this that
Nebuchadnezzar would invade and ravage Egypt, and would set his
throne over the very spot where the stones were hidden. The incident
is undoubtedly authentic. Nebuchadnezzar's invasion of Egypt did
not, however, take place until that king's thirty-seventh regnal
year (568/7). From the fragmentary inscription that tells of it
(cf. ANET, p. 308), it appears that Nebuchadnezzar did not aim
at permanent conquest, but rather sought by a punitive expedition
to deter Egypt from further meddling in Asia. The pharaoh—at the
time, Amasis (570–526)—retained his throne and seems thereafter to have maintained friendly relations with Babylon.

In xliv an incident is presented in the form of a long, and rather
wordy, prose discourse. This consists of an address by Jeremiah
censuring the Jews living in Egypt for their worship of other gods,
and warning them of the consequences (vss. 2–14); the reply of the
people, telling Jeremiah that they are not going to listen to him
(vss. 15–19); and a further address by Jeremiah (in two parts:
vss. 20–23, 24–30), in which he tells the people (again, as in
xlii 9–22) of the awful fate that awaits them. As is characteristic
of the prose discourses of the book, the piece has been greatly
expanded in transmission. But there is no reason to question its
essential authenticity. Jeremiah attacks in particular the cult of the
Queen of Heaven (cf. vii 16–20), which was, it appears, especially
popular among the women. It is interesting to note how totally
Jeremiah's interpretation of the disaster that had overtaken the nation differed from that entertained by his hearers. Whereas Jeremiah
viewed the worship of pagan gods as the prime reason for the divine
judgment upon the nation, the people replied that, as they saw it,
things had gone well as long as they had propitiated the Queen of
Heaven, while disaster had set in only when they had ceased to do
so. Presumably (cf. Weiser) they were thinking of the long and
relatively peaceful reign of Manasseh, during which non-Yahwistic
cults of all sorts were freely tolerated, and of the prohibition of
these cults by Josiah in the years that followed. It appears, then,
that there were Jews who regarded Josiah's reform, not as a step

that might have saved the nation, but as one that had contributed to its downfall. After all, so they reasoned, since the nation had known nothing but calamity after the completion of that reform, must it not be that the gods whose cults had been prohibited were angry? Their "logic" is understandable. But it shows how dangerously close religious faith had come, in the minds of many, to slipping into overt polytheism.

III. THE BOOK OF CONSOLATION

36. THE RESTORATION OF ISRAEL AND JUDAH:
A COLLECTION OF SAYINGS,
FOR THE MOST PART IN POETRY
(xxx 1–24; xxxi 1–40)

Superscription of the Collection

XXX 1 The word that came to Jeremiah from Yahweh: 2 "This is what Yahweh, the God of Israel, has said: Write down everything that I have said to you in a book. 3 For look! The days are coming—Yahweh's word—when I will reverse the fortunes of my people, both Israel and Judah—Yahweh has spoken —and I will restore them to the land that I gave to their fathers, and they shall possess it."

Jacob's Distress and Deliverance

4 These are the words that Yahweh spoke concerning Israel and Judah:

5   [Yes, this is what Yahweh has said:]
    A cry of terror we hear,
      Of unrelieved dread.
6   Ask, pray, and see—
      Can a male give birth?
    Why, then, do I see every man
      Clutching his loins,*a*
    Every visage distorted
      And deathly pale?*b*
7   Ah, but that day is great

---

a Hebrew adds "like a woman in labor," which is probably a gloss. Omit with LXX.
b Hebrew begins vs. 7 with *hōi* ("alas"). LXX, however, reads this as *hāyū* (consonants transposed) and takes it with vs. 6: "they [i.e., all faces] have become pale[ness]."

Beyond all compare!
It is Jacob's time of distress—
Yet from it he'll be saved.

8 "On that day—word of Yahweh of Hosts—*I will break his
yoke from off their neck, and will snatch off their bonds*; and
foreigners shall no longer *hold them in servitude.* 9 But they
shall serve Yahweh their God, and David their king whom I
will raise up for them."

10   "So then, fear not, O Jacob my servant—Yahweh's word—
Nor be dismayed, O Israel.
For see! From that faraway place I will save you,
Your offspring from the land of their exile.
Then once more shall Jacob find rest,
Secure, with none to disturb.
11   *So then, fear not, O Jacob my servant—Yahweh's
word—*
For I'm with you to come to your rescue.
Ah, I'll make a full end of all nations
Among whom I've scattered you.
But of you I will make no full end;
Within reason I'll chasten you,
Yet by no means exempt you."

The Healing of Zion's Wounds

12   Yes, this is what Yahweh has said:
"Your hurt is mortal,
Your wound past cure,

c–c Perhaps read "the yoke" with LXX, for "his [i.e., the oppressor's] yoke."
Hebrew reads "your [singular] neck . . . your bonds," which is probably influenced by Isa x 27, which seems to be alluded to here; "their" follows LXX.
But perhaps read "his" (i.e., Jacob's); see next textual note.
d–d Heb. "hold him . . ." (i.e., Jacob, collective); LXX "and they shall no
longer serve foreigners."
e–e The first colon is lacking in MT here, and is restored after xlvi 28; "Yahweh's word" is read at the end of it as there (and in vs. 10), rather than in
the middle of the next colon, as in MT here.

13   *No salve for your sore,*
      No healing for you.
14   All your lovers have forgot* you,
      They care not how you are.
      Ah, an enemy's blow I dealt you,
      A cruel chastisement.*
15   Why cry o'er your hurt,
      Your incurable pain?
      For the mass of your guilt,
      And your countless sins,
      I did all this to you.
16   Yet* all who devour you devoured shall be,
      And your foes shall all go captive.
      Your despoilers shall be for spoil;
      All who loot you I'll give for loot.
17   Yes, cure I'll bring you,
      Of your wounds I'll heal you—Yahweh's word—
      Because they called you, 'Outcast—
      That Zion,* for whom nobody cares.'"

Restoration of the Nation and Its Institutions

18   This is what Yahweh has said:
      "Ah, I'll raise again the tents of Jacob,
      And take pity on his dwellings;

f–f Hebrew has "none who pleads your case, for [your] sore medicine." But "who pleads your case" confuses the metaphor and may be an old gloss (LXX reads it), or a variant.
g Taking "chastisement" as absolute (*mūsār*); MT, "the chastisement of a cruel one." MT then concludes the verse with, "For the greatness of your guilt, [because] your sins were many," which seems to be an erroneous repetition of vs. 15b; omit with most commentators. LXX, incidentally, omits vs. 15, save that in some recensions vs. 15b appears in the middle of vs. 16.
h Heb. "Therefore all . . ." is logically unsuitable. Perhaps (Rudolph) delete the first two letters of the verse (*lk*) as a dittography of the last two letters of vs. 15, and begin *wᵉkol*. But vss. 16–17 may originally have been uttered in another context than the present one.
i–i Hebrew, redundantly, reads "And all your foes, all of them, shall go. . . ." Perhaps variants have been combined ("all your foes" and "your foes, all of them").
j Some, following LXX, read "she is our quarry" (*ṣēdēnū hī'* for *ṣiyyōn hī'*). But MT is to be preferred. See NOTE.

The town shall be built on its mound,
  The stronghold shall stand where it should.
19 From thence shall come thanksgiving,
  And the sound of laughter.
I'll increase them—they'll not be few;
  I'll exalt them—they'll not be menials.
20 Their people shall be as of old,
  Their assembly enduring before me;
    And I'll punish all who oppress them.
21 Their prince shall be one of their own,
  Their ruler shall come from their midst;
And him I'll permit to approach me.
  For who otherwise would be so bold
    As thus to approach me?—Yahweh's word."
22 ["So you shall be my people, and I will be your God."]*k*

The Divine Judgment: a Fragment

23 Look! The storm of Yahweh*l* is unleashed,
  A whirlwind*m* blast,
It will burst on the head of the wicked.
24   Yahweh's fierce*n* anger will not turn back
Till he's finished, accomplished,
  His inmost intents.
When that day has passed
  *o*You will see this clearly and well.*o*

The Glad Restoration of Northern Israel

XXXI 1 "At that time—Yahweh's word—I will be the God of
all the clans of Israel, and they shall be my people."
  2   [This is what Yahweh has said:]

k The verse is lacking in LXX and may be an editorial addition. The covenant
formula anticipates xxxi 1 (note also the shift to the second person).
l Hebrew then adds "wrath"; omit as in xxiii 19.
m Read *miṭḥōlēl* (as in xxiii 19) for *miṭgōrēr* (meaning uncertain).
n Lacking in xxiii 20 and may be an expansion.
o–o MT here has merely "You will see [understand] this." Add *bīnāh* at the end
of the colon as in xxiii 20 (lost by haplography with *bāh*).

In the desert they've met with favor,
The people escaped from the sword.
[p]As Israel sought for rest,[p]
3 From afar Yahweh appeared to him:[q]
"With a love everlasting I love you,
So with grace I draw you to me.
4 Once again I will build you securely,
O virgin Israel!
Once again snatching up your timbrels,
You'll forth to the gladsome dance.
5 Once again you'll set out vineyards
On Samaria's hills.
Those who plant [r]will enjoy the fruit.[r]
6 For soon comes the day when the watchmen will shout
On Ephraim's hills,
'Up! Let us go to Zion,
To Yahweh our God.'"

Israel's Homecoming

7 Yes, this is what Yahweh has said:
"Sing with joy for Jacob!
Shout for the first of the nations!
Sound forth! Give praise, and say,
[s]'Yahweh has rescued his people,[s]
The remnant of Israel,'
8 Ah watch! I am going to bring them
From the northern land,
From the farthest horizons will gather them,
The blind and the lame among them,

[p–p] So following Heb. "going [infinitive absolute] to find him rest [was] Israel." But the text is uncertain, and Vrs. offer various different readings.
[q] So with LXX. Hebrew reads ". . . to me," which does not suit well, and begins the next colon with "and" (which LXX lacks). The consonants *l* and *w* should be read together as *lō*.
[r–r] LXX reads "Plant and give praise" (*hll* for *ḥll*). But MT is preferable; see NOTE.
[s–s] So with LXX and most commentators. Heb. "Save, O Yahweh, thy people," while possible, fits less smoothly.

Those pregnant, in labor, as well;
　　They'll return a mighty throng.
9　Ah see!*t* With weeping they'll come,
　　But with solace*u* I'll lead them.
By flowing brooks I'll guide them,
　　On a path too smooth for stumbling;
For I am Israel's father,
　　And Ephraim—my first-born is he."

Zion's Future Felicity

10　"Hear, O nations, the word of Yahweh!
　　On the farthest shores proclaim it! Say:
'He who scattered Israel will gather,
　　And guard as a shepherd his flock.'
11　Yes, Yahweh has ransomed Jacob,
　　Bought him back from the clutch of one stronger than
　　　　he.
12　They shall come and rejoice on Zion's height,
　　And thrill to Yahweh's bounty—
The grain, the wine, and the oil,
　　The sheep and the cattle.
They themselves shall be like a well-watered garden,
　　Never to languish again.
13　Then maidens shall dance and be gay,
　　Youths and graybeards as well*v*;
For I'll turn their mourning to mirth,
　　Give them comfort and joy for their grief.
14　I'll give the priests their fill of fat things,
　　While my people are gorged with my bounty—
　　　　Yahweh's word."

---

t In MT the word, pointed *hēnnāh* ("hither"), concludes vs. 8. But it is better
to point it as *hinnēh* and place it at the beginning of vs. 9, with most commentators.
u So with LXX (*bᵉtanḥūmīm*); Heb. "with supplications" (*bᵉtaḥᵃnūnīm*) fits
less smoothly.
v So MT, which is probably preferable to LXX, which for "as well" (*yaḥdāw*)
reads "shall be merry" (*yaḥdū*)—and so RSV.

Rachel's Lament; Ephraim's Remorse
and Yahweh's Compassion

15 [This is what Yahweh has said:]
   Hark! In Ramah a sobbing is heard,
       Weeping most bitter,
   Rachel bewailing her sons,
       For her sons refusing all comfort,
           Because they're no more.

16 This is what Yahweh has said:
   "Check your racking sobs,
       Restrain your tears!
   For there *is* a reward for your labor—Yahweh's word—
       They'll return from the enemy's land.

17 There *is* a hope for your future—Yahweh's word—
       Your sons will return to their homeland.

18 I have heard it, I have heard it—
       Ephraim's remorse:
   'For my training thou didst flog me,
       Like a fractious young bull;
   Now restore me, all repentant,
       For thou art Yahweh, my God.

19 Ah, after I'd strayed
       I repented,[w] was sorry;
   After I'd learned
       I smote on my thigh.
   I'm ashamed, yes I blush,
       For I bear the disgrace of my youth.'

20 Is Ephraim my dearest son?
       My darling child,
   That as oft as I mention his name
       I so longingly think of him still?
   I am filled with yearning for him,
       I must have pity on him—Yahweh's word.

---

[w] Supplied, following Rudolph. The meter seems to require an additional word, and *šabtī* ("I turned back, repented") may have fallen out after *šūbī* ("I strayed, turned away") through haplography.

21   "Set up your road marks,
        Plant your guideposts!
     Fix your mind on the highway,
        The road you have come.
     Come back, O virgin Israel,
        Come back to these your towns.
22   How long dillydally,
        O turnabout daughter?
     For Yahweh has created a new thing on earth:
     [A female shall compass a man (?)]."

Future Blessedness: Various Sayings

23 This is what Yahweh of Hosts, the God of Israel, has said:
"They shall once again use this expression in the land of Judah
and in its towns, when I have reversed their fortunes: 'Yahweh
bless you, O righteous abode, O holy mount!' 24 Judah and all
its people shall dwell there together, the farmers and those who
roam*a* with the flocks; 25 for I will satiate the weary ones, and
give everyone that languishes his fill." 26 At this, I awoke and
looked, for my sleep had been sweet to me.

27 "Believe me, days are coming—Yahweh's word—when I
will sow the house of Israel and the house of Judah with the
seed both of men and of beasts. 28 And, just as I kept watch
over them to uproot and tear down, to raze, destroy, and do
hurt, so I will keep watch over them to build and to plant—
Yahweh's word.
29   In those days they will no longer say,
        'The fathers ate sour grapes;
        But it's the children's teeth that rasp.'
30 No, every one shall die for his own iniquity. Whatever man
eats sour grapes, it will be his own teeth that rasp."

a Heb. "and they roam" (*wᵉnāsᵉ'ū*); supply the relative pronoun or read the
participle (*wᵉnōsᵉ'ē*).

The New Covenant

31 "Believe me, days are coming—Yahweh's word—when I will make a new covenant with the house of Israel and the house of Judah: 32 not like the covenant that I made with their fathers when I took them by the hand to bring them out of the land of Egypt, which covenant of mine *they* broke, though *I* was their Lord—Yahweh's word. 33 But this is the covenant that I will make with the house of Israel when that time comes —Yahweh's word: I will put my law within them, and on their hearts will write it; I will be their God, and they shall be my people. 34 And no longer need each man teach his neighbor, and each his brother, saying, 'Know Yahweh!' For they shall all know me, from the least of them to the greatest—Yahweh's word; for I will forgive their iniquity, and their sin I will remember no more."

"I'll Never, No Never, No Never Forsake"

35   This is what Yahweh has said—
    Who provides the sun to illumine the day,
      The moon and the stars* to illumine the night,
    Who lashes the sea so its billows resound—
      Yahweh of Hosts his name.
36   "If this fixed order should vanish
      From before me—Yahweh's word—
    Then Israel's descendants might cease
      From being a nation forever before me."
37   This is what Yahweh has said:
    "If the heavens above can be measured,
      Or earth's foundations below be explored,
    Then might *I* cast off *the descendants of Israel*
      For all that they have done—Yahweh's word."

y Heb. "The ordinances [fixed order] of the moon and stars." But the word *ḥuqqōt* overloads the meter, and is lacking in LXX. It may be a misplaced alternate reading for the synonymous word *ḥuqqīm* in the next verse.
z–z So with LXX; Heb. "all the descendants. . . ." LXX, incidentally, reads vs. 37 before vss. 35–36.

The New Jerusalem

38 "Believe me, days are coming*aa*—Yahweh's word—when Yahweh's city will be rebuilt from the Tower of Hananel to the Corner Gate. 39 And the measuring line shall reach still farther, right on to the hill Gareb, and then around to Goah. 40 And the whole valley (that is, the place where the corpses and the ashes were dumped), and all the cemeteries [?]*bb* above the brook Kidron*cc* as far as the corner of the Horse Gate to the east, shall be holy to Yahweh. It will never again be torn down or destroyed for all time to come."

aa The words "are coming" (*bā'īm*) are restored with Qre, various manuscripts and Vrs. Ktib omits (haplography).
bb The force of the word *šᵉdēmōt* (so Qre; Ktib *šᵉrēmōt* is not understandable) is disputed. See NOTE.
cc Reading *'al* ("above") for MT *'ad* ("as far as") with Volz, Rudolph; *'ad* seems to be a miscopying of the same word farther on in the verse.

NOTES

xxx 3. *reverse the fortunes*. The expression (*šūb šᵉbūt*), which occurs frequently in these chapters, and elsewhere in the Bible, is rendered in many EVV as "turn the captivity," deriving *šᵉbūt* from the root *šbh*. Though this derivation seems natural, in certain passages where the expression occurs there is no question of captivity (e.g., Job xlii 10; Ezek xvi 53), and most recent scholars connect *šᵉbūt* with the root *šūb* (i.e., "turn the turning"). But no doubt in and after the Exile "to turn the captivity" and "to reverse the fortunes" came to mean much the same thing.

4. The verse is the heading of the complex of poems in vss. 5–24.

5. *Yes, this is what Yahweh has said*. The words are editorial: Yahweh is not the speaker in vss. 5–7 (unless one reads "you hear" for "we hear" with LXX, and take "I see" in vs. 6 as referring to Yahweh). The heading introduces the whole poem, in which words of the people (or the prophet) are quoted, and then answered (in vs. 10 f.) by the divine oracle.

Of unrelieved dread. Literally "of panic and no peace," i.e., of fear unrelieved by any hope of rescue, fear that cannot be checked.

7. *that day*. I.e., the Day of Yahweh (cf. Amos v 18–20; Zeph i 14–18, etc.). The destruction of Judah by the Babylonians is here, and

elsewhere, understood as the day of Yahweh's judgment upon his people. Vs. 7b, however, promises rescue and thus leads into vss. 10 f. (vss. 8–9 are a prose insertion). One wonders if in the original form of the piece, before vss. 10–11 were appended, the last colon may not have been a question ("and will he be saved from it?").

9. *David their king.* I.e., the expected Messianic king, the "second David"; cf. Hos iii 5; Ezek xxxiv 23 f.; xxxvii 24 f., etc., for similar sentiments.

10–11. These verses occur again at xlvi 27–28. LXX omits them here, as it frequently does on the second occurrence of a doublet (which this is in the LXX order). Verse 10 resumes vs. 7.

11. Although the first line of vs. 11, like vs. 10, exhibits a style characteristic of Second Isaiah, vs. 11 also has a number of typical Jeremianic expressions: "I am with you to come to your rescue" (cf. i 8; xv 20); "make a full end" (cf. iv 27; v 10); "chasten . . . within reason" (cf. x 24.) Vss. 10–11 take the form of a priestly oracle announcing deliverance.

12. *Your hurt.* Heb. *lᵉšibrēk;* probably another instance (cf. ix 2) of "emphatic *lamed*": cf. F. Nötscher, VT 3 (1953), 380.

14. *your lovers . . . care not how you are.* Or ". . . do not inquire after you, seek you out." Judah's "lovers" are her erstwhile allies, who have deserted her.

16. *Yet all who devour you.* For the figure of Judah's foes "devouring" her, cf. ii 3; v 17; viii 16 (and x 25).

17. *cure I'll bring you.* Literally "I will bring up new flesh for you" (i.e., to cover your wound), as in viii 22.

That Zion. Scholars who believe that the poem was originally addressed to northern Israel are obliged to delete, or to read "she is our quarry." See textual note*ʲ*.

18. *I'll raise again the tents.* Literally "I will reverse (restore) the fortunes of the tents. . . ." Cf. NOTE on vs. 3 above.

on its mound. The word (Heb. *tēl*, Ar. *tell*) denotes a mound upon which stand the ruins of a destroyed and abandoned town. The reader has no doubt noticed how frequently sites excavated by archaeologists are called Tell this-or-that. Very possibly "the town" and "the stronghold" are to be understood collectively, although Jerusalem with its buildings are probably primarily in mind. For a similar thought from a somewhat later day, cf. Isa xliv 26; xlix 19; lxi 4.

19. *And the sound of laughter.* Literally "And the sound of them who laugh."

I'll increase them—they'll not be few. The verbs are those used in Jeremiah's letter to the exiles in 594 (xxix 6).

20. *Their people shall be as of old.* Literally "His [i.e., Jacob's] sons,"

and so through vss. 20 and 21a. Although there is no mention of the Messianic king of David's line, but only (vs. 21) of a native ruler, presumably the glories of the Davidic age are in mind.

Their assembly. Although the word (*'ēdāh*) is a favorite of the priestly writers, it is by no means a late word, and cannot be used to prove the lateness of the passage, as some believe. It refers to the formal assembly of the people for cultic, and also for political (e.g., I Kings xii 20), purposes.

21. *For who otherwise would be so bold.* Literally "For who is he that would give his heart in security . . . ," i.e., would gamble his life. To enter the divine presence unbidden was to risk death. The ruler here (the word "king" is avoided) discharges a sacral or priestly function, rather than one that is specifically political.

23–24. The verses repeat xxiii 19–20 with minor variations. They sit loosely in context here, and may have been inserted to place further stress upon the judgment of Israel's foes hinted at in vss. 11, 16, 20c, the "wicked" here being understood as the nations of the world generally.

24. *When that day has passed.* See NOTE on xxiii 20 (Sec. 19).

xxxi 1. Again (as in xxx 22) the formula of covenant, this time serving as a heading for the complex of poems in ch. xxxi.

2. *This is what Yahweh has said.* The oracular introduction is formal; the divine word actually begins only in vs. 3b.

In the desert they've met with favor. The expression "to find favor" (*māṣā' ḥēn*) occurs five times in the narrative of Exod xxxiii 12–17 alone. The captivity of northern Israel is here described as a new wandering in the wilderness (cf. Hos ii 16f. [ii 14 f.E]). One may see here a precursor of the "new Exodus" theme of Second Isaiah.

As Israel sought for rest. See textual note[p–p]. Although the language is not the same, one sees reminiscences of Exod xxxiii 14; Deut xxviii 65; also cf. "find rest" (the same root as here, with the verb *māṣā'*) in vi 16. Again northern Israel's captivity is described in terms suggesting the wilderness wandering.

3. *So with grace I draw you to me.* Taking "grace" (*ḥesed*) adverbially, as "love" in the preceding colon ("to me" is not expressed in Hebrew). The thought, and the construction, is similar to that of Hos xi 4; and the young Jeremiah elsewhere exhibits dependence on Hosea. But one could also translate, "So I continue *ḥesed* to you," as in Pss xxxvi 11 [10E]; cix 12. Still, in these cases the one to whom grace is extended stands as the indirect object (with *l*e), rather than as a second direct object, as here. But on this point see now M. J. Dahood, *Gregorianum* 43 (1962), 67.

4. *I will build you securely.* Literally "I will build you so that you are

built." Note the play here and in the next verse on "build" and "plant," and cf. Jeremiah's call (i 10).

snatching up your timbrels. Literally "you shall adorn yourself with timbrels."

5. *Those who plant will enjoy the fruit.* Literally "The planters who planted will profane," i.e., put the produce to ordinary use, after a period in which it was regarded as holy (cf. Lev xix 23–25; Deut xx 6). The thought is similar to that of Isa lxv 22, and opposite to that of Amos v 11; the people will be secure in the enjoyment of the fruits of their labor.

6. The verse is significant. It shows that in the days of Josiah the young Jeremiah looked forward to the cultic unification of Israel, with northern Israel coming to Zion to worship. In light of this verse (and other evidence) one can hardly believe that Jeremiah was in principle opposed to the cult or hostile to the aims of Josiah's reform.

7. *the first of the nations.* Apparently a popular, and prideful, term for Israel; cf. the almost identical expression in Amos vi 1.

8–9. These verses exhibit striking similarities in style and thought to the latter chapters of Isaiah. For the picture of Yahweh gathering his people from all parts of the earth and leading them on a "new Exodus" march, along a highway through a desert where streams gush forth, cf., for example, Isa xxxv; xl 3–5, 11; xli 18–20; xlii 16; xliii 1–7; xliv 3 f.; xlviii 20 f.; xlix 9–13.

9. *with solace.* Or "consolations."

For I am Israel's father, / And Ephraim . . . my first-born is he. The words fit well with vss. 2–6 and seem to be Jeremiah's. It is not impossible that vs. 9c, and perhaps the basis of vs. 7, originally concluded the preceding poem, which was later expanded and adapted (see NOTE on vss. 8–9) to the situation of the exiles.

10. Stylistic affinities to the latter chapters of Isaiah are again much in evidence. The word "isles" (*'iyyīm*) used in the sense of "far coastlands" is typical of Second Isaiah, as is the address to the nations of the world (e.g., Isa xli 1; xlix 1 *et passim*). Also cf. "as a shepherd his flock" and the same expression in Isa xl 11.

11. *Bought him back.* Or, "redeemed." The verb (*gā'al*) and its derivatives occur upward of twenty times in Isa xl–lxvi, but not at all in the unquestioned poetic sayings of Jeremiah (only here and l 34).

12. *And thrill.* The verb occurs elsewhere only in Isa lx 5 and Ps xxxiv 6[5E].

a well-watered garden. Cf. the same expression in Isa lviii 11.

15. *This is what Yahweh has said.* The formula, as in vs. 3, merely indicates the beginning of a new poem, one addressed by Jeremiah to northern Israel early in his career (see COMMENT). But Yahweh is not the speaker until vs. 16.

Ramah. See NOTE on xl 1 (Sec. 33). According to I Sam x 2 f. Rachel's tomb was near here. Jeremiah imagines the spirit of the mother of the Joseph tribes (Ephraim) haunting her tomb, weeping for her children who had been deported by the Assyrians one hundred years earlier (721).

16. *Check your racking sobs, / Restrain your tears.* Literally "Withhold your voice from weeping, and your eyes from tears."

18. *For my training thou didst flog me.* Literally "Thou didst chasten me, and I was chastened"; or, perhaps better with a slight change of pointing, "Thou didst chasten me that I might be chastened." Northern Israel (Ephraim), in exile, is represented as expressing bitter remorse and begging for Yahweh's mercy.

Now restore me, all repentant. Literally "Bring me back, for I would (or, 'that I may') come back."

20. *as oft as I mention his name.* Literally ". . . speak of him" (not "against him," as in many EVV). Yahweh here answers his dear "son" Ephraim; he cannot utter his name without being filled with longing for him.

21. The address now shifts to second person feminine singular ("virgin Israel"). Although the thought of the highway home from exile was given its fullest development by Second Isaiah (see NOTE on vss. 8–9), we see that it was already present in Jeremiah's mind.

22. *O turnabout daughter.* Literally "backturning" (*šōbēbāh*), i.e., apostate, backsliding (cf. iii 22, etc.).

a female shall compass a man. This is a literal translation, but the meaning is wholly obscure, and it might have been wiser to leave the colon blank. LXX reads entirely differently, but gives no help. Of the numerous emendations that have been offered, none commands confidence. Nor can one regard the colon as a gloss, since a gloss is intended to clarify, not introduce obscurity. Quite possibly we have here a proverbial saying indicating something that is surprising and difficult to believe, the force of which escapes us.

23. *O righteous abode, O holy mount.* Literally "abode of righteousness [i.e., the righteous One], mountain of holiness [i.e., the holy One]." Both titles refer to Yahweh. The temple mountain seems to be intended.

24. *Judah and all its people shall dwell there.* Literally ". . . and all its towns"; "there" ("in it") refers to the land (vs. 23) not to the temple mountain.

25. *I will satiate.* More accurately, "I will have satiated," and so the next verb also ("give . . . his fill").

26. The verse seems to be a marginal comment, but its meaning is obscure. Some see it as the ejaculation of one who, as it were, awakes refreshed from a beautiful dream; others see the dejection of one who awakes from a beautiful dream to confront the hard realities. Still others (cf. Rudolph, Weiser), translating, "For this reason (it is said), 'I awoke

. . . ,'" believe it to be a citation, perhaps of a well-known song. I confess that I am baffled.

28. Cf. the infinitives in this verse with those in i 10; cf. also "keep watch" and the key word of the vision of i 11–12.

29–30. The feeling was widespread that the nation was being punished for sins committed by previous generations (e.g., Lam v 7; Ezek xviii 1) and that Yahweh, therefore, was unjust (cf. Ezek xviii 25). Ezekiel, in particular, is concerned to refute this notion. Here it is merely said that in the future people will have no occasion to make such a complaint.

31. *and the house of Judah.* Perhaps an expansion, as many commentators think, since "the house of Israel" seems in this passage to refer to the whole people (cf. vs. 33), not just the northern state.

32. *which covenant of mine* they *broke.* One could also translate, "Because they broke my covenant."

though I *was their Lord.* One could translate, "though I was a husband [*bāʿaltī*] to them." The figure of Yahweh as the husband, Israel as the wife, had been current in prophetic speech since Hosea, and is employed elsewhere by Jeremiah (cf. ch. iii).

33. *on their hearts.* I.e., their minds and wills.

38. *Yahweh's city.* Or "the city which is Yahweh's." But the translation, "the city will be rebuilt to Yahweh" is justifiable.

the Tower of Hananel. At the northeast corner of the city (cf. Zech xiv 10; Neh iii 1; xii 39).

to the Corner Gate. Apparently at the northwest corner (cf. Zech xiv 10; II Kings xiv 13; II Chron xxvi 9).

39. The hill Gareb, and Goah, are of unknown location. But since vs. 38 is concerned with the northern limit of the city, and vs. 40 apparently with the south and east, the line to the west is presumably described here.

40. *the place where the corpses and the ashes were dumped.* Literally "the corpses and the ashes" (i.e., the fat-soaked ashes from the altar). The text seems to be corrupt, and the words may be a gloss; LXX reads quite differently. The "valley" is usually supposed to be Hinnom, south of the city, where heathen cults had been practiced (cf. ii 23; vii 31; II Kings xxiii 10, etc.), though some dispute this.

the cemeteries. The word *šᵉdēmōt* (see textual note[bb]) occurs five or six times in the Bible, and also in Ugaritic. M. R. Lehmann (VT 3 [1953], 361–71) suggests that it is a compound word *šd mt*, "field of Death," or better, "field of Mot" (the Canaanite god of death), which would correspond to Heb. *šᵉdēh māwet* (and so Symm., Vulg.); he supposes that this refers to the site where human victims, sacrificed in the valley of Hinnom, were interred. The word seems also to have taken on the broader agricultural significance of fields that had to be cultivated artificially, i.e., irrigation fields. See also more recently, J. S. Croatto and J. A. Soggin, ZAW 74 (1962), 44–50.

above the brook Kidron. The brook Kidron and the Horse Gate (Neh iii 28) were east of the city.

COMMENT

In chapters xxx–xxxiii, frequently and with good reason called "The Book of Consolation," we find collected the vast majority of Jeremiah's sayings of a hopeful nature. Chapters xxx–xxxi form a distinct unit within this "book," and must be treated together. These chapters consist of a collection—or, perhaps more properly, two collections (xxx 4–24 and xxxi)—of originally separate sayings, the greater part of them in poetry, all of which develop the theme of comfort sounded in the superscription of the section (xxx 1–3). Few portions of the book have evoked sharper disagreement among scholars, both as regards the date and interpretation of the various sayings, and as regards their relationship to Jeremiah. Chiefly because the style is at certain places remarkably similar to that of the latter chapters of Isaiah, and because much of the material seems to require a date during the period of exile, a number of scholars have argued that relatively few of these sayings are genuine utterances of the prophet. Others, on the other hand, are able by recourse to differing interpretations to defend the genuineness of the majority of them. Since the problem is a real one, a few words of explanation concerning its nature, and the position adopted here, are in order.

Now it is impossible to doubt that Jeremiah held some sort of hope for the future of his people (see especially COMMENT on xxxii 1–15, Sec. 32), and few scholars today would be inclined to do so. By the same token, the genuineness of some of the sayings in chapters xxx–xxxi is generally conceded, even by the most radical of critics. Among these, two stand out: xxxi 2–6 and xxxi 15–22. These are clearly addressed to northern Israel (Ephraim) and are, like iii 6–13, best dated (though some would dispute this) in a relatively early period of Jeremiah's career, probably while Josiah was engaged in extending his political and religious program into the territory of the erstwhile northern state. Some scholars, indeed (especially Rudolph, building on Volz), go so far as to argue that the greater part of chapters xxx–xxxi is to be understood in this way, and that the section as a whole provides us, a few non-genuine sayings having been subtracted, with words of Jeremiah addressed to northern Israel during Josiah's reign. Stylistic similarities to Second Isaiah are explained on the supposition that both prophets made use of the same conventional forms of address. This is an attractive interpretation. But it is, nevertheless, open to certain objections. It fails to explain why style of the type just mentioned is found only at a few places (especially in xxx 10; xxxi 7–14), not generally throughout these chapters or elsewhere in the book, and specifically not in the unquestionably genuine sayings addressed to northern Israel in xxxi 2–6, 15–22. It likewise ignores the fact that while in the two passages just mentioned (and in xxxi 9b) northern Israel is referred to as "Ephraim," this designation does not occur in the other sayings found in the section, some of which, at least, seem clearly to refer to Judah (cf. "Zion" in xxx 17; xxxi 12). It is interesting that scholars who hold the view just described are obliged at certain places to resort to textual emendation in order to bring the material into conformity with theory.

All in all, the safest conclusion is that chapters xxx–xxxi contain genuine sayings of Jeremiah addressed to northern Israel and uttered relatively early in his career (xxxi 2–6, 15–22), together with other words of his uttered much later, and that the material has in certain cases subsequently been expanded and supplemented in such a way as to apply Jeremiah's prophecies more directly to the situation of the exiles living in Babylon. So far as I can see, however, nothing in these chapters need date after approximately the middle of the Exilic period. Thus, although one may expect to find some adaptation of Jeremiah's thought to a later situation, any essential distortion of it is, it seems to me, highly unlikely.

In chapter xxx, after the superscription of the collection in vss. 1–3, and the heading of the complex that follows in vs. 4, we find the following units: (1) Vss. 5–11. This passage begins with a vivid poem of unquestionable genuineness (vss. 5–7) describing the terror of the people as the day of Yahweh's judgment approaches. After a prose insertion (vss. 8–9), the poem is resumed in vss. 10–11, where it is abruptly turned (as, indeed, already in vs. 7b) into a promise for the future. In vs. 10 stylistic affinities to Isa xl–lv are pronounced. Yet at the same time there are, especially in vs. 11 (see NOTE), numerous echoes of expressions found elsewhere in

Jeremiah. It is probable that a Jeremianic nucleus (vss. 5–7), perhaps uttered just prior to 587, has by means of a conventional
priestly oracle (vss. 10 f.) been made to apply to the situation
of the exiles. (2) Vss. 12–17. The beginning of this piece (vss.
12–15), which tells of Judah's incurable wound, is unquestionably
from Jeremiah. In vss. 16–17, however, the ominous tone of the
passage is suddenly reversed, and its threatening word turned into
one of hope. The transition is undeniably sharp, and has caused
many to believe that vss. 16–17 are a later addition. On the other
hand, the text (see textual note[h]) may not be entirely in order, and
the transition may not in fact be as sharp as it seems. Moreover,
vss. 16–17 exhibit none of the distinctive stylistic traits of Second
Isaiah, but are fully in keeping with Jeremiah's style as we know it
elsewhere. It is, therefore, quite possible to argue that the entire
piece was composed by the prophet toward the end of his career,
perhaps just after Jerusalem fell. (3) Vss. 18–22. As regards the
provenience of this poem, which promises the rebuilding of the city,
and describes the restoration of the people under a native ruler, it is
difficult to be sure. If Judah and Jerusalem are referred to, as seems
to me probable, the poem must date after 587. On the other
hand, there is nothing in it that necessarily requires a date long
after that time. It cannot, to be sure, be proved to have come from
Jeremiah; but there is really no compelling reason why he may not
have uttered it toward the end of his career. (4) Vss. 23–24. This
is a fragment, unquestionably Jeremianic, which repeats xxiii 19–20
with minor variations. It has been drawn into the present context,
in which it sits loosely, for reasons that are obscure (but see NOTE).

As regards the poetic portions of chapter xxxi, two passages
have already been noted: vss. 2–6 and 15–22. These are genuine
words of Jeremiah directed to northern Israel and stemming from
an early period in the prophet's career. Of the remaining poems,
those in vss. 7–9 and 10–14 are (see NOTES on vss. 8–9, 10, 11,
12) both in style and thought closely akin to certain prophecies in
the latter part of Isaiah. They seem to represent an adaptation and
application of Jeremiah's prophecies to the situation of the exiles.
It is, however, possible that the first of them contains in vs. 9b, and
perhaps in vs. 7 (see NOTE on vs. 9), a nucleus of Jeremianic
words originally addressed to northern Israel. The final poetic piece
(vss. 35–37) may originally have formed the conclusion of the
collection introduced in xxx 1–3 before the prose sayings in vss.

23–34, 38–40, which had had their own history of transmission, were added. Although one certainly cannot demonstrate that this poem comes from Jeremiah, no compelling reason for denying it to him exists.

The prose portions of chapter xxxi consist of a little saying predicting the restoration of Judah and the temple (vss. 23–26), followed by three pieces with the identical introductory formula: "Behold, the days are coming" (vss. 27–30, 31–34, 38–40). As regards the first and the last of these—the one playing upon a popular proverb also quoted by Ezekiel (Ezek xviii 2), the other describing the rebuilding of Jerusalem's walls—little can be said save that one ought not too hastily to declare that the prophet could not have expressed such sentiments. The second of these sayings (vss. 31–34) is deservedly famous. It describes the new covenant that God would one day give his people, forgiving their sins and writing his law on their hearts so that all of them know him. As regards its authenticity, one can only say that it ought never to have been questioned. Although the passage may not preserve the prophet's *ipsissima verba,* it represents what might well be considered the high point of his theology. It is certainly one of the profoundest and most moving passages in the entire Bible.

37. THE RESTORATION OF JUDAH
AND JERUSALEM: A PROSE COLLECTION
(xxxii 1–17a; 24–27; 36–44; 17b–23;
28–35; xxxiii 1–26)

Jeremiah's Purchase of Land, and Appended Sayings

XXXII ¹ The word that came to Jeremiah from Yahweh in the tenth year of Zedekiah, king of Judah, which was the eighteenth year of Nebuchadrezzar, king of Babylon. —— ² The king of Babylon's army was then besieging Jerusalem, and Jeremiah was shut up in the court of the guard, in the palace of the king of Judah, ³ where Zedekiah, king of Judah, had confined him, on the complaint: "Why have you uttered such prophecies as these: 'This is what Yahweh has said: Believe me, I am going to hand this city over to the king of Babylon, and he will take it. ⁴ Zedekiah, king of Judah, will not escape the clutches of the Chaldeans, but will certainly be handed over to the king of Babylon and, confronted by him face to face, will be made to answer to him personally. ⁵ He will take Zedekiah to Babylon, and there he will remain until I attend to him—Yahweh's word. If you fight the Chaldeans you will have no success'?" ——

⁶ Jeremiah said, "The word of Yahweh came to me thus: ⁷ Just wait! Hanamel, your uncle Shallum's son, is going to come to you with the request, 'Buy my field at Anathoth, for you have the kinsman's right to redeem it.' ⁸ And, just as Yahweh had said, my cousin Hanamel did come to me in the court of the guard, and say to me, 'Won't you buy my field at Anathoth, for the right of possession and redemption is yours. Buy it for yourself!' Then I knew that this was indeed Yahweh's word.

⁹ "So I bought the field at Anathoth from Hanamel my

cousin, and weighed out the money to him, seventeen silver shekels. 10 I put the deed in writing, sealed it, had men witness it, and weighed the money on scales. 11 Then I took the deed of purchase, the sealed copy containing the contract and the conditions, and the open copy, 12 and gave it to Baruch ben Neriah ben Mahseiah in the presence of my cousin Hanamel, in the presence of the witnesses who had signed the deed of purchase, and in the presence of all the Jews who happened to be in the court of the guard. 13 Then, before them all, I gave Baruch the following charge: 14 'Take these documents—that is, this deed of purchase, the sealed copy and this open one— and put them in an earthenware jar, so that they may last a long time. 15 For this is what Yahweh of Hosts, the God of Israel, has said: Houses and fields and vineyards shall once again be bought in this land.'

16 "Then, after I had given the deed of purchase to Baruch ben Neriah, I prayed to Yahweh as follows: 17a 'Ah, my Lord Yahweh!   24 Look! The siege ramps are already thrown up to take the city. And through sword, starvation, and disease the city is delivered to the Chaldeans who attack it. What thou didst threaten has come to pass. ªSurely thou seest it!ª 25 Yet it was thou, my Lord Yahweh, who didst tell me, "Buy the field,ᵇ pay for it, and have the transaction witnessed"—when the city is delivered up to the Chaldeans.'

26 "Then the word of Yahweh came to meª as follows: 27 Look! I am Yahweh, the God of all flesh. Is anything impossible for me?   36 Now, therefore, this is what Yahweh, the God of Israel, has said concerning this city of which ᵈyou say,ᵈ 'Through sword, starvation, and disease it is delivered up to the king of Babylon': 37 See! I am going to gather them from all the countries to which I have driven them in my furious anger

ª⁻ª LXX omits.

ᵇ From here, LXX reads, "So I wrote the deed and sealed it and got witnesses," which follows the language of vs. 10.

ª So LXX (and cf. vs. 16), which probably is preferable to MT ". . . to Jeremiah."

ᵈ⁻ᵈ LXX reads "you say" as singular, which fits best with the dialogue style of the chapter (cf. vss. 16, 24–25, and textual noteª) and is probably correct, though some regard it as a correction of MT, which reads plural.

and great indignation, and I will bring them back to this place and let them dwell here in safety. 38 They shall be my people, and I will be their God. 39 I will give them singleness of mind and of purpose to fear me always, for their own good, and for the good of their children after them. 40 And I will make with them an everlasting covenant not to turn away from them or to cease to do them good; and I will put fear of me in their hearts so that they may never turn away from me. 41 I will find joy in them and in doing them good, and will assuredly plant them in this land with all my heart and soul.

42 "Yes, this is what Yahweh has said: Just as I have brought all this great calamity upon this people, so I am going to bring upon them all the good things that I have promised them. 43 Fields shall again be bought in this land, of which *you say,* 'It's a desolate waste, empty of men and beasts, delivered into the hands of the Chaldeans.' 44 They shall buy fields and pay for them, drawing up deeds, sealing them, and having them witnessed, in the land of Benjamin, in the environs of Jerusalem and in the towns of Judah, the towns of the hill country, of the Shephelah and the Negeb; for I will restore their fortunes—Yahweh's word."

Two Insertions

17b ". . . Truly it is thou who didst by thy great power and incomparable might make the heavens and the earth. Nothing is impossible for thee— 18 thou who dost act graciously toward thousands, while paying back the iniquity of the fathers into the lap of their children after them, thou great and mighty God whose name is Yahweh of Hosts— 19 great in purpose and mighty in deed, whose eyes are open to all that mortal men do, to reward each man for his conduct, as his actions deserve; 20 who didst perform signs and wonders in the land of Egypt, and also until this day, both in Israel and among mankind generally, so gaining for thyself the renown that is thine today.

e–e Probably again to be read as singular with LXX, as in vs. 36; Hebrew has the plural.

21 Thou didst bring thy people Israel from the land of Egypt with signs and wonders, with a strong hand, with irresistible might, and with great and terrible deeds, 22 and didst give them this land, as thou didst give oath to their fathers that thou wouldst, a land flowing with milk and honey. 23 But when they entered and took possession of it, they did not heed thy voice or obey thy law. Nothing that thou didst command them to do did they do. So thou hast brought all this calamity upon them. . . ."

28 *ƒ*"Therefore this is what Yahweh has said: Believe me, I am going to hand this city over to the Chaldeans, and to Nebuchadrezzar, king of Babylon, who will take it.*ƒ* 29 The Chaldeans who are attacking this city will enter, put this city to the torch and burn it to the ground, together with the houses on whose rooftops they have made offerings to Baal, and poured out libations to other gods, to provoke me to anger. 30 Ah, the people of Israel and of Judah alike have done nothing but what is displeasing to me from the beginning of their history. *ᵍ*Indeed, the people of Israel have done nothing but provoke me by the things they have done—Yahweh's word.*ᵍ* 31 Nay, this city has so aroused my furious anger, from the day that it was built until the present, that I have resolved to remove it from my sight 32 because of all the wickedness which the people of Israel and of Judah have done in order to provoke me—they, their kings, and their princes, their priests and their prophets, the men of Judah and the citizens of Jerusalem. 33 They have showed me their back and not their face and, *ʰ*though I instructed them*ʰ* earnestly and persistently, they never listened or accepted correction. 34 Rather, they set up their detestable idols in the house which bears my name in order to defile it, 35 and built the high places of Baal in the valley of ben Hinnom in order to sacrifice their sons and their daughters to Molech—

ƒ–ƒ LXX has a shorter reading, virtually reproducing the language of vs. 3b. Hebrew has probably suffered conflation.
ᵍ–ᵍ See NOTE.
ʰ–ʰ So LXX and other Vrs. Hebrew has infinitive absolute (loss of one letter).

a thing that I did not command, nor did the doing of such an abomination ever enter my mind—in order to lead Judah into sin."

A Further Complex of Sayings

XXXIII 1 The word of Yahweh came to Jeremiah a second time, as follows, while he was still confined in the court of the guard: 2 "This is what Yahweh has said—*he who made the earth and shaped it* so as to set it firm—Yahweh is his name: 3 Call on me, and I will answer you and tell you of great and unsearchable things of which you do not know. 4 For this is what Yahweh, the God of Israel, has said concerning the houses of this city, and the houses of Judah's kings, which have been torn down [   ] 5 [   ]* in order to resist the Chaldeans, and in order to fill them with the corpses of the men whom I have slain in my furious anger, and because of all of whose wickedness I have hidden my face from this city— 6 See! I am going to bring them healing* and cure; I will heal them and reveal to them treasures [?] of peace and security. 7 I will restore the fortunes of Judah and Jerusalem,* and will build them as they were at the first. 8 I will cleanse them of all the guilt which they have incurred in sinning against me, and will forgive all their transgressions through which they have sinned and rebelled against me. 9 *And Jerusalem shall be a source of joy* and praise and pride to all the nations of the earth, who shall hear of all the good things that I do*; they shall fear and tremble at all the bountiful well-being that I provide for her.

i-i So with LXX (*'ōśēh 'ereṣ weyōṣēr 'ōtāh*). Heb. "he who made it, Yahweh who shaped it" (*'ōśāh yhwh yōṣēr 'ōtāh*) involves an erroneous recopying of "Yahweh."

j The text is corrupt. See NOTE.

k Hebrew has "it" (i.e., the city); "them" follows LXXA, Vulg., Tar. (and cf. vs. 6b).

l So with some manuscripts of LXX. Hebrew has "Judah and Israel"; but the passage seems elsewhere (vss. 10, 13) to be concerned specifically with Judah.

m-m So conjecturally with Giesebrecht, Volz, and others. Hebrew has "and she shall be to me a name of joy. . . ." Perhaps the consonants of "to me a name of," which LXX omits (*lylšm*), are a corruption of *yršlm l.*

n Hebrew adds "them" (direct object). Omit with LXX, or read "her" (*'ōtāh* or, better, *lāh*).

10 "This is what Yahweh has said: Once again shall there be heard in this place of which you say, 'It's a waste, empty of both men and beasts'—that is, in the cities of Judah and in the streets of Jerusalem, now desolate °and inhabited by neither man nor beast°— 11 sounds of mirth and gladness, the voice of bridegroom and bride, the voice of men who cry as they bring thank offerings to Yahweh's house, 'Give thanks to Yahweh of Hosts, for Yahweh is good, for his grace endures forever.' For I will restore the fortunes of the land and make it as it was at the first—Yahweh has spoken.

12 "This is what Yahweh of Hosts has said: Once again shall there be in this place, now laid waste and emptied of men and beasts, and in all of its towns, pasture for shepherds who rest their flocks. 13 In the towns of the hill country, in the towns of the Shephelah and the Negeb, in the land of Benjamin, in the environs of Jerusalem, and in the towns of Judah, flocks shall once again pass under the hands of the tally-keeper—Yahweh has spoken."

The Sure Promises of God: Further Sayings

14 "Look! The days are coming—Yahweh's word—when I will fulfill the promise that I made to the houses of Israel and Judah. 15 In those days and at that time, I will cause a true 'Shoot' of David to spring forth, who will execute justice and righteousness in the land. 16 In those days Judah will be rescued and Jerusalem will dwell in security. And this is the nameᵖ by which it will be called: 'Yahweh-ṣidqēnū.' 17 For this is what Yahweh has said: David will never lack a successor to sit on the throne of the house of Israel, 18 nor will the Levitical priests ever lack successors in my service to offer burnt offerings, to burn cereal offerings, and to make sacrifices continually."

19 The word of Yahweh came to Jeremiah as follows: 20 "This

°–° Literally "without man, without inhabitant, and without beast." LXX omits the second of these, which may be a variant of the first. But the whole clause looks like a variant of the preceding one ("in this place . . . empty of man and beast").
ᵖ Supply "the name" with Theod., Vulg.

is what Yahweh has said: If you could break my covenant with the day, and my covenant with the night, so that day and night no longer come in their proper order, 21 then might my covenant with my servant David also be broken, so that no descendant of his should sit as king on his throne—*and my covenant with my ministers, the Levitical priests,*ᵃ as well. 22 As the heavenly host is innumerable, and as the sand of the seashore is immeasurable, so will I multiply the descendants of David my servant, and the Levites ʳwho minister to me."ʳ

23 The word of Yahweh came to Jeremiah as follows: 24 "Have you not noticed what these people have been saying: 'The two families which Yahweh chose he has now rejected'—and how they so hold my people in contempt that they no longer regard them as a nation? 25 This is what Yahweh has said: If my covenant with day and with night does not stand,ˢ if I did not establish the fixed order of heaven and earth, 26 then will I also reject the offspring of Jacob, and David my servant, nevermore to select rulers from among his descendants for the offspring of Abraham, Isaac, and Jacob. Nay, I will restore their fortunes and have mercy on them."

ᵃ⁻ᵃ Hebrew does not express "my covenant" here. Hebrew also has the odd reading "the Levites, the priests" instead of the usual "the priests, the Levites." Transpose the words, or omit "the priests," as in vs. 22.
ʳ⁻ʳ For *mᵉšārᵉtē 'ōtī* it might be better, though perhaps unnecessary, to read *mᵉšārᵉtāy* ("who minister to me"), as in vs. 21.
ˢ Some such verb seems to have dropped out; Hebrew ("if not my covenant with day and night") is ungrammatical. Some, following Duhm, read *bārā'tī* for *bᵉrītī* ("If I did not create day and night.").

NOTES

xxxii 1–15. For Notes on these verses see Sec. 32.
17a. *Ah, my Lord Yahweh.* These words introduce Jeremiah's prayer and lead directly into vs. 24. The intervening material represents an expansion and will be treated below. It will be noted that vs. 17b anticipates vs. 27. Note also how *hinnēh* ("Truly") in vs. 17 is resumed by the same word in vs. 24 ("look").

24. *The siege ramps are already thrown up to take the city*. Literally "the siege ramps have come to the city to take it."

25. *Buy the field, pay for it, and have the transaction witnessed*. Literally "Buy the field for money [cf. vs. 44] and get witnesses." See textual note[b].

27. *Is anything impossible*. Literally "too marvelous," i.e., too hard.

38. Again the formula of covenant (cf. xxx 22; xxxi 1).

39. *singleness of mind and of purpose*. Literally "one heart and one way" (cf. Ezek xi 19). But LXX reads "another [i.e., a different] way and another heart"; cf. the "new heart" and "new spirit" of Ezek xviii 31; xxxvi 26 (LXX also reads "another heart" for "one heart" in Ezek xi 19). Either reading is possible; "one" (*'eḥād*) and "another" (*'aḥēr*) differ hardly at all in unpointed Hebrew, and either could have arisen from the other through scribal error. Perhaps MT should be preferred as the more difficult reading. For the rest of the verse cf. Deut iv 10; v 29, etc.

40. *an everlasting covenant*. Cf. Isa lv 3; Ezek xvi 60; xxxvii 26, and also the "new covenant" of xxxi 31. The thought of the latter part of the verse is the same as that of xxxi 33b.

or to cease to do them good. Hebrew does not express "or to cease."

41. For the thought of the verse cf. xxxi 28; Deut xxx 9; Isa lxii 5; lxv 19, etc.

44. *and pay for them*. Literally "for money"; cf. NOTE on vs. 25.

17b. *incomparable might*. Literally "outstretched arm" (so in vs. 21 also).

Nothing is impossible for thee. Literally ". . . too marvelous"; cf. vs. 27.

18. Cf. Exod xx 5 f.; Deut v 9 f. (the Decalogue).

20. *and among mankind*. But perhaps, with M. J. Dahood (*CBQ* 25 [1963], p. 123 f.), *ûbā'ādām* might better be translated "and in the steppe-land."

21. *with great and terrible deeds*. Literally "with great terror."

28–35. A saying that, following vs. 27 as in the traditional order, would be an intrusion from another context; see COMMENT. Though some would limit the intrusion to vss. 29b–35, it is probably best to see vs. 27 as continued in vs. 36. Note how "therefore" in vs. 36 resumes the same word in vs. 28.

30. *from the beginning of their history*. Literally "from their youth." The two sentences of vs. 30 are very similar; the second is lacking in

LXX and may well be a variant of the first. On the other hand the omission in LXX may be accidental; note three successive sentences (those in vs. 30 and that beginning in vs. 31) beginning with the word *kī*.

31. The Heb. syntax seems to be idiomatic, but it is intolerably clumsy to our ears: "Indeed this city has been to me upon [i.e., the occasion of (?)] my wrath and my anger from the day they built it until this day, to remove it from my sight." See further lii 3 and NOTE.

35. *in order to sacrifice.* Literally "in order to cause to pass [through the fire]", i.e., to devote. But sacrifice of sons and daughters is meant (cf. vii 31; xix 5).

xxxiii 1. Cf. xxxii 2. The verse is a link attaching the complex of sayings in xxxiii 1–13 to that in the preceding chapter.

3. *unsearchable things.* The word *bᵉṣūrōt* elsewhere means "inaccessible" or the like (i.e., of a city or fortress). Some manuscripts have *nᵉṣūrōt* ("hidden, guarded, kept in reserve"), as in the almost identical clause in Isa xlviii 6.

4–5. The text is hopelessly corrupt at the end of vs. 4 and the beginning of vs. 5. The brackets indicate words that can be translated smoothly only by forcing: ". . . torn down [to the siege ramps and to the sword] [coming] to resist. . . ." LXX reads "ramparts" for "sword" and omits "coming," but otherwise has the same text as MT. One suspects that words have fallen out and/or been transposed at one or more places. The words "and in order to fill them" (LXX "it," i.e., the city) fit poorly after the foregoing; words may have been lost here too. Reference seems to be to houses razed in order to get material for plugging gaps in the wall, raising barricades, and the like (cf. Isa xxii 10). But a coherent translation can be gained only by rewriting the text.

6. *bring them healing.* The word for "healing" is literally "new flesh" as in viii 22, etc.

treasures. The word (*'ateret*) occurs only here; a similar word (*'aṭeret*) means "diadem, crown." Perhaps read with Duhm and others *'ᵃtīdōt* ("treasures").

13. *under the hands of the tally-keeper.* I.e., the one who counted the sheep as they came into the fold at night, to see that none was missing. No doubt he literally counted by hand, particularly if it was dark.

14. *fulfill the promise.* Literally ". . . the good word." The language depends on xxix 10.

15. *a true 'Shoot.'* Or "Branch (so many EVV), i.e., a scion; cf. xxiii 5 and NOTES. But note (vs. 17) that here the promise is broadened to include not merely a single king, but the continuing dynasty.

16. *And this is the name*. On the name itself, cf. NOTE on xxiii 6; but here the name is applied to Judah and Jerusalem, rather than to the Davidic king himself.

18. *Levitical priests*. The expression is characteristic of Deuteronomy. The sense here is probably simply "legitimate priests."

20. The regular succession of day and night, established at Creation (Gen i 5; viii 22), is here described as God's "covenant" with day and night.

24. *The two families which Yahweh chose*. Here apparently the houses of Israel and Judah, rather than those of David and of Levi as in vss. 17–22; "these people" seem to be Jews who have ceased to believe in Yahweh's election of his people.

COMMENT

The second half of the "Book of Consolation" is entirely in prose, and consists of three complexes of sayings which were doubtless originally transmitted separately. The first of these comprises the whole of chapter xxxii. Here we find the account of Jeremiah's purchase of land during his confinement in the court of the guard (vss. 1–15), together with various sayings that have been appended to it. The account itself has already been dealt with in Section 32, and is repeated here merely for the sake of completeness. It will be recalled that Jeremiah's action in this regard was intended symbolically, as an earnest of Yahweh's promise that normal life would one day be resumed in the land. This theme, which is made specific in vs. 15, is developed through the remainder of the chapter, the whole of which is cast in autobiographical style (but see textual note[o] on vs. 26), and given the form of a dialogue between Jeremiah and Yahweh. Following the story of the land purchase, which is itself related in the first person, Jeremiah tells (vss. 16–25) how he prayed to Yahweh, asking why, since the situation seemed so hopeless, he had been commanded to do such a thing. It would seem from this that Jeremiah himself scarcely dared to believe the promises that he had uttered and had, in fact, uttered them simply because of the compulsion of the divine word that had come to him. But then (vss. 26–27, 36–44) Jeremiah receives his answer. Yahweh addresses him and assures him that he is a God for whom nothing is impossible and that, in spite of the apparent hopelessness of the situation, the promises will surely be fulfilled.

The chapter has received various additions in the course of transmission. In particular, Jeremiah's prayer, which in its original form was quite brief (only vs. 16, the first words of vs. 17, and vss. 24–25), has been expanded by the insertion (vss. 17aβ–23) of a whole series of clauses extolling the incomparable power of Yahweh and his gracious favor to his people. Although there is nothing in these verses that is foreign to Jeremiah's thought, they are made up entirely of conventional expressions and seem clearly to be an intrusion. In like manner, Yahweh's answer to Jeremiah's prayer is interrupted in vss. 28–35 (some would limit this to vss. 29b–35) by an oracle of threatening nature, which disturbs the progress of thought and seems to have been drawn in from another context. In the interests of clarity, these intrusions are placed at the end of the chapter in this translation.

Chapter xxxiii contains two further complexes of sayings. The first of these (vss. 1–13) is editorially linked to the foregoing chapter by the notice in vs. 1 that these words also came to Jeremiah while he was confined in the court of the guard (cf. xxxii 2). The sayings in xxxiii 1–13 (vss. 2–9, 10–11, 12–13) are similar in tone to those in chapter xxxii, and further develop the theme sounded in xxxii 15. It is probable that these two complexes entered the book together. The final complex (vss. 14–26), on the other hand, is entirely lacking in LXX and may well be a later addition to the book. It consists of three brief sayings in which Yahweh's promises to the Davidic line receive especial stress. The first of these (vss. 14–18) leans heavily on the poetic oracle in xxiii 5–6 and might be called a prose parallel to it, save that the thought is developed in a somewhat different way. The name Yahweh-ṣidqēnū, which is there applied to the Messianic king, is here transferred to Judah and Jerusalem, while the promise of the true "Shoot" of David is referred (vs. 17) to the continuing dynasty rather than to a single individual. Moreover, the promise is broadened to include a never-ending succession of Levitical priests who serve beside the king. The two final sayings (vss. 19–22, 23–26) both depend upon and develop the thought of the poem in xxxi 35–37, but with Yahweh's eternal promises to his people being here again applied specifically to the Davidic line and (in vss. 19–22) to the Levitical priests.

IV. ORACLES AGAINST FOREIGN NATIONS

38. EGYPT
(xlvi 1–28)

XLVI [1] What came as the word of Yahweh to Jeremiah the prophet concerning the nations:

Egypt's Defeat at the Euphrates

[2] About Egypt:
Concerning the army of Pharaoh Necho, king of Egypt, which was along the Euphrates River at Carchemish and which Nebuchadrezzar, king of Babylon, defeated in the fourth year of Jehoiakim ben Josiah, king of Judah.

[3]   Ready—bucklers and shields!
        Forward! Close combat!
[4]   Harness—horses!
        Riders—mount!
    Fall in—with helmets!
        Whet—lances!
        On—full armor!

[5]   But what do I see?
        Their courage gives way,
            They break and turn tail;
    Their mighty ranks shattered,
        They flee pell-mell,
        Without looking back.
    Everywhere panic
    —Word of Yahweh.

---

a–a Probably read infinitive absolute with finite verb (*nōs nāsū*) in place of the substantive (*ūmānōs nāsū*). The substantive, though perhaps grammatically possible (GK 117 q), elsewhere means "a place of refuge, escape." D. N. Freedman suggests that *ūm* represents an enclitic *m* belonging with the preceding verb, plus a dittography of its ending.

6　No flight for the swift,
　　Nor escape for the strong;
　Up north by the banks of Euphrates
　　They stagger, go down.

7　Who is this that mounts like the Nile,
　　His waters like River's in flood?
8　It's Egypt that mounts like the Nile,
　　His waters[b] like River's in flood.
　He says, "I'll mount up and cover the earth,
　　Destroying both cities and people."

9　On, you horses!
　　Roll, you chariots!
　March,[c] you soldiers!
　　Men of Cush and of Put, bearing shields,
　　　Men of Lud, [d]good shots with the bow.[d]
10　But that day is the day of Yahweh of Hosts,
　　His day of revenge, to be avenged of his foes.
　His sword[e] shall devour till it's sated,
　　Till it's gorged with their blood.
　Ah, the Lord Yahweh of Hosts holds a feast
　　In the northern land, by Euphrates' stream.

11　Go up to Gilead and bring back balm,
　　O Virgin Daughter Egypt!
　In vain do you heap up nostrums,
　　No cure have you!
12　The nations have heard your outcry,[f]

---

[b] So read as in vs. 7; Heb. "waters" (suffix lost by haplography). LXX partially omits the colon, and some critics (unnecessarily, I think) delete all of vs. 8a.
[c] The imperative (ṣeʾū) follows LXX; Hebrew reads "and let the soldiers march" (weyēṣeʾū).
[d-d] Hebrew has a word too many: tōpeśē dōrekē qešet (literally "handlers of, benders of, the bow"). Since the first of these words occurs in the preceding colon (tōpeśē māgēn), it is to be deleted here as an erroneous repetition.
[e] Hebrew has "the sword," which may be correct; but "his" (ō) may have been lost by haplography (Rudolph). LXX has "the sword of the Lord" (Yahweh).
[f] So LXX (qōlēk). Heb. qelōnēk ("your shame") does not fit the parallelism very well. D. N. Freedman suggests that qln may here be an otherwise unattested elaboration of qwl, with the same meaning. The spelling ql is attested in pre-Exilic Hebrew inscriptions and also in the Bible, while the ending in n is common; and cf. qōlān in late (and modern) Hebrew: "one making a loud noise, a shouter, crier."

Your wailing has filled the earth,
When soldier pitched against soldier,
And both went down together.

Nebuchadnezzar's Conquest of Egypt Announced

13 The word that Yahweh spoke to Jeremiah the prophet concerning the advance of Nebuchadrezzar, king of Babylon, to attack the land of Egypt:

14 *g*"Announce it in Migdol!
        Proclaim it in Memphis!*g*
    Say, 'Stand ready! Be prepared!
    For the sword has devoured all around you.'

15 *h*Why did Apis flee?*h*
        Your bull*i* not stand his ground?
    Because Yahweh did drive him

16   *j*Your multitude stumbled and fell.
    Then one man said to another,*j*
        'Up! Let us back to our people
    To the land of our birth,
        Away from the dreadful sword.'

17   *k*So give Pharaoh the nickname*k*
    'Big noise—who has missed his chance.'

g–g The reading of the first bicolon follows LXX. Hebrew has, "Announce
[it] in Egypt. Proclaim [it] in Migdol. Proclaim [it] in Memphis and Tahpanhes," which seems to represent an expansion patterned on xliv 1. See
Note there (Sec. 35) for location of the places.

h–h Hebrew reads, "Why was he swept away?" (*nišḥap*). Read as two words
following LXX (*nās ḥap*), "Why did Haf flee?" Haf is Apis (and so LXX).

i So LXX and various manuscripts; MT reads plural (plural of "majesty"?).

j–j The first two lines of the verse are unintelligible in Hebrew: "He increased
one stumbling. Also one man fell to his neighbor. And they said. . . ." For
"he increased" (*hirbāh*) LXX reads, "your multitude" (*rubbᵉkā* or the like;
or [so Giesebrecht and others] *'erbᵉkā*, "mixed multitude," as in xxv 20, which
gives a good sense. Also point as *kāšal* ("stumbled") instead of *kōšēl*
("stumbling") with LXX, and transpose "and they said" before "to one
another" (cf. LXX).

k–k So LXX (*qirᵉ'ū šēm*); MT "they cried there, 'Pharaoh is . . . ,'" (*qārᵉ'ū
šām*) has the same consonantal text. The words "king of Egypt," which follow "Pharaoh" in Hebrew, are omitted for metrical reasons.

18   "As I live—it's the word of the King,
       Whose name is Yahweh of Hosts—
    Like Tabor overtopping the mountains,
       Like Carmel rising sheer from the sea—he will come.
19   So ready your baggage for exile
       Inhabitress fair of Egypt!
    For Memphis shall be a waste,
       An uninhabited ruin."

20   A beautiful heifer is Egypt,
       ᶦAttacked by a fly from the north.ᶦ
21   The mercenaries, too, in her midst
       Were like fatted calves;
    They too turned tail and fled,
       Not a one stood his ground;
    For their day of disaster had come upon them,
       The time of their doom.
22   ᵐHear her hiss like a snakeᵐ
       When in force they approach,
    And with axes fall upon her
       Like men chopping wood.
23   They fell her forest—Yahweh's word—
       Since it is impenetrable;
    More num'rous are they than locusts,
       Beyond all count.
24   Shamed is Daughter Egypt,
       Caught in the clutch of the northern folk.

Egypt Humiliated, Israel Delivered: Two Fragments

25 Yahweh of Hosts, the God of Israel, has said, "Ah, but I am going to bring punishment on Amun of Thebes, on Phar-

---

ᶦ⁻ᶦ Hebrew reads, "A fly [precise meaning uncertain] from the north has come, has come" (*bā' bā'*). Read *bā' bāh* ("has come upon her") with various manuscripts and LXX.

ᵐ⁻ᵐ Hebrew has, "Her sound is like a snake as it goes." But "goes" (*yēlēk*) is probably a dittography from the next colon; read "hissing" (*šōrēq*) with LXX.

aoh,ⁿ and on those who trust in him. 26 I will hand them over to those who seek their life—that is, to Nebuchadrezzar, king of Babylon, and his officers—after which Egypt will dwell as in earlier times—Yahweh's word.

27 "As for you fear not, O Jacob my servant,
    Nor be dismayed, O Israel.
  For see! From that faraway place I will save you,
    Your offspring from the land of their exile.
  Then once more shall Jacob find rest,
    Secure, with none to disturb.
28 So then, fear not, O Jacob my servant—Yahweh's word—
    For I'm with you °to come to your rescue.°
  Ah, I'll make a full end of all nations
    Among whom I've scattered you.
  But of you I will make no full end;
    Within reason I'll chasten you,
      Yet by no means exempt you."

ⁿ Hebrew then adds, "on Egypt, on her gods, on her kings, and on Pharaoh," which seems to be an expansion; LXX omits. LXX also omits "Yahweh of Hosts, the God of Israel, has said."
^{o–o} The words are added with xxx 11; as it stands in MT here, the colon is rather short.

Notes

xlvi 1. This is the superscription of the entire collection (chs. 46–51). The peculiar formula also ocurs at xiv 1; xlvii 1; xlix 34.

2. The year is 605. See COMMENT (also Introduction, "The Background of Jeremiah's Career . . .").

3–4. We hear the Egyptian officers barking their commands as their troops make ready for battle. In vs. 3, ranks of infantry, their shields at the ready in a solid line in front of them, prepare to move into close combat. In vs. 4, while the charioteers mount, other soldiers scramble into their armor, or use the opportunity to sharpen their fighting tools.

5. *But what do I see*. Literally "Why do I see?" In vss. 5–6 we see that the battle is no sooner joined than the Egyptians break ranks and take to flight.

Their mighty ranks shattered. Literally "Their mighty men are crushed," i.e., their ranks are broken.

7. *His waters like River's in flood.* Literally ". . . surge like rivers" (so also in vs. 8). But the plural is probably the "plural of amplification" (GK 124 e), *nehārōt* and *ye'ōr* (Nile) both being intended as personifications of the Nile; cf. "Prince Sea-Judge River" in the mythology of Ras Shamra. Egypt's resurgence under Necho II is likened to "Sir Nile" in flood, which in turn may have suggested a breaking-out of the insurgent waters of chaos (cf. H. G. May, JBL 74 [1955], p. 16).

9. *Cush.* Ethiopia, the region along the Nile south of Egypt (roughly Nubia). *Put* is probably "Punt," along the east coast of Africa, approximately Somaliland. *Lud* ("Ludim") scarcely refers to the Lydians of Asia Minor, but to an African people (cf. Gen x 13); some would read "Lubim" (Lybians), mentioned in Nah iii 9 along with Put. Auxiliary troops of the pharaoh are of course referred to.

10. *the day of Yahweh of Hosts.* I.e., his day of judgment upon his foes. Hebrew reads ". . . of the Lord Yahweh of Hosts," which overloads the meter. The exemplar of LXX had "of Yahweh our God." Since "the Lord" (*'adōnāy*) is a surrogate for "Yahweh," and not expressed in LXX, it is best omitted.

a feast. I.e., a sacrificial feast (*zebaḥ*). For the same idea, cf. Zeph i 7; Isa xxxiv 5–7; Ezek xxxix 17–20, etc.

15. *Apis.* See textual note[h–h]. Apis was the sacred bull revered as the incarnation of the god Ptah (later of Osiris).

Your bull. Or, "your champion," Apis is again referred to.

17. One suspects that the last colon (literally "A noise who has let the appointed time pass by") contains a pun on the pharaoh's personal name or royal titles; but it is impossible to say what it may have involved.

18. The last bicolon (literally "Like Tabor among the mountains, or like Carmel by the sea, he comes") describes Babylon's irresistible might as towering over Egypt like a lofty mountain peak. Though neither Tabor (on the north of the Plain of Esdraelon) nor Carmel (by the sea, behind Haifa) are especially tall, they give that impression because of their isolated positions and sheer slopes.

19. *Inhabitress fair of Egypt.* A somewhat inexact translation in the attempt to catch the force of the expression, a poetic personification of Egypt's population; literally "Inhabitress, Daughter-Egypt." Cf. "My Daughter-My People" as a personification of Judah's citizens *passim* through the book.

23. *Since it is impenetrable.* Literally "for it cannot be searched." The figure of the woodmen attacking the snake seems to continue: since they cannot search the forest to find it, they cut the forest down.

25. *Amun of Thebes*. Thebes was the capital city in Upper Egypt, Amun its chief god.

26. LXX lacks the verse. Its last clause seems to indicate awareness that Nebuchadnezzar's invasion (in 568) did not actually result in Egypt's destruction.

after which Egypt. Literally ". . . she"; but Egypt is of course referred to.

27–28. Cf. xxx 10–11 and NOTES *ad loc* (Sec. 36).

COMMENT

Chapters xlvi–li, which consist entirely of sayings directed at foreign nations, form a distinct unit in the Jeremiah book, the superscription of which is found in xlvi 1. The fact that these chapters appear in LXX after xxv 13, and in an entirely different order (see "The Book of Jeremiah . . . ," in the Introduction), suggests that they were for some time transmitted independently of the remainder of the book, perhaps being added to it only after the textual traditions underlying MT and LXX, respectively, had diverged. The material, however, is not late. Although it includes, in addition to genuine utterances of Jeremiah, numerous sayings of anonymous origin which were cherished and handed down by those circles of the prophet's disciples to whom we owe the collection of his words, nothing in these chapters, so far as I can see, is to be dated after approximately the middle of the sixth century.

It is probable that, of all parts of the book, the oracles against foreign nations are the least frequently read. The reasons for this doubtless vary. Perhaps it is because the reader feels them to be somewhat peripheral to the distinctive theology of the prophet, perhaps because he is troubled by the seemingly vengeful and nationalistic spirit that pervades them, perhaps merely because he is puzzled by the numerous obscure allusions to places and events which they contain, and which make them at times so difficult to understand. But, whatever the reasons for this neglect may be, it is nevertheless a pity, if only because these chapters contain some of the finest poetry in the entire prophetic canon. Moreover, sayings of the type found here do represent a characteristic feature of prophetic preaching, and one that must be kept in view if a rounded picture is to be obtained.

The poems in chapter xlvi are directed against Egypt. The first of them (vss. 3–12) is dated by its heading (vs. 2) in the fourth year of Jehoiakim (605), and was undoubtedly composed either just before—or, more probably, just after—Nebuchadnezzar shattered the forces of Pharaoh Necho at Carchemish on the Euphrates in the late spring or early summer of that year (see Introduction, "The Background of Jeremiah's Career . . ."). The poem seems unquestionably to come from Jeremiah himself and is, for vividness and poetic quality, unexcelled by anything in the book. Following this poem is a further one, scarcely less vivid (vss. 14–24), depicting the terror of Egypt at Nebuchadnezzar's approach, which has its own separate heading in vs. 13. There is no reason to doubt that this poem is likewise by Jeremiah. It was probably composed somewhat later than the preceding one, perhaps as Nebuchadnezzar's army appeared in force on the Philistine Plain (in 604) and threatened Egypt with invasion (although a date in connection with the events of 587 and after has been defended). It is true (see COMMENT on Sec. 35, re xliii 8–13) that Nebuchnadnezzar did not actually invade Egypt until much later, in 568, thus almost certainly after Jeremiah's death; but the prophet seems years earlier to have regarded such an invasion as certain, and to have expected it imminently.

The chapter concludes with a brief prose commentary, probably of later date, announcing Nebuchadnezzar's conquest of Egypt, and Egypt's subsequent recovery (vss. 25–26); and a poetic fragment (vss. 27–28) bidding Israel not to fear. This last repeats xxx 10–11 with small variations (see NOTES, Sec. 36).

39. THE PHILISTINES
(xlvii 1–7)

XLVII 1 *a*What came as the word of Yahweh to Jeremiah the prophet concerning the Philistines, before Pharaoh attacked Gaza.*a*

2   This is what Yahweh has said:
   "Look! Up north the waters are rising,
     Becoming a torrent in flood.
   They'll flood the whole of the land,
     Towns with their dwellers.
   Then the people will cry, will howl,
     All who dwell in the land,
3   At the noise of the galloping hoofs of his steeds,
     The clank of his chariots, the drum of their wheels.
   Fathers wait not for their children,
     So helpless their dread
4   At the day that has come to destroy
     The Philistines all,
   Cutting off from Tyre and Sidon
     All help that remains.
   Ah, Yahweh will destroy the Philistines,
     Last leavings of Caphtor's isle.
5   Baldness has come upon Gaza,
     Struck dumb is Ashkelon.
   O you last of their strength,
     How long gash yourself?
6   Ah, sword of Yahweh,
     Will you never know rest?
   Return to your scabbard,

a–a LXX, which reads only "concerning the Philistines," probably preserves the original text; but see COMMENT. The formula of MT is that of xlvi 1.

    Desist and be still!
7 How can it^b know rest
   When Yahweh gave it orders,
Against Ashkelon and the seacoast
   Expressly did send it?"

^b So with LXX and other Vrs. (and cf. the context); MT "How can you
know rest."

NOTES

xlvii 3. *Fathers wait not. . . . So helpless their dread.* Literally "Fathers do not turn back for the children for feebleness of hands" (i.e.,
terror).

4. *Cutting off from Tyre and Sidon / All help that remains.* Literally
". . . every survivor, helper." The allusion is obscure. Presumably there
was an alliance between the Philistines and the Phoenician cities, and
Nebuchadnezzar's operations against the former were preparatory to
action against the latter. Though we know of no such alliance in the
years following 605, one may well have existed; Tyre and Sidon were
chronically in rebellion against Babylon, in 594 (cf. xxvii 3) and in
587 and after (Nebuchadnezzar besieged Tyre after the fall of Jerusalem).

Caphtor's isle: I.e., Crete and the adjacent islands, from which the
Philistines had originally come (cf. Amos ix 7).

5. *Baldness.* Shaving one's head was a sign of mourning, as was the
inflicting of gashes upon one's self (three lines below); cf. xvi 6; xli 5.

O you last of their strength. Heb. *šeʾērīt ʿimqām.* The natural
translation, "remnant of their valley," makes no sense. Perhaps *ʿmq* has
here (so also xlix 4) the force of "strength" attested in Ugaritic; cf.
Driver, *Studies in Old Testament Prophecy,* ed. H. H. Rowley, p. 61.
It is tempting both for metrical reasons, and because mention of some
city is expected, to suppose that a name, plausibly "Ashdod," has fallen
out: "O Ashdod, last of their strength" ("Ashkelon" and "Ashdod" begin
identically, and the order Gaza–Ashkelon–Ashdod is that of Zeph ii 4);
but textual evidence is lacking. LXX reads *ʿanāqīm* in place of *ʿimqām:*
"O remnant of the Anakim"—a race of giants said to have inhabited
Canaan before Israel's arrival, remnants of which were to be found,
according to Josh xi 22, in Gaza, Gath, and Ashdod. But this, while
attractive, represents an easier reading and may be a guess on the part
of LXX.

COMMENT

Chapter xlvii consists of a single poem describing the destruction
of the Philistine cities at the hands of a foe who comes from the
north. Like those in the preceding chapter, this poem is exceedingly
vivid, and no reason exists to question its genuineness. Its setting,
however, is obscure and much disputed. According to the Hebrew
text of vs. 1 it was composed "before Pharaoh attacked [smote]
Gaza." This is, of course, merely a chronological notation, for it
is clear from vs. 2 that the invader who brings destruction to the
Philistines is a people from the north, not the Egyptians themselves.
Since the notation is absent from LXX (which has only, "Concerning the Philistines," in vs. 1) many scholars regard it as an erroneous interpolation by a later editor.

In view of the reading of LXX it is quite likely that vs. 1 has
been editorially expanded. Nevertheless, it is at least possible that
the expansion is factually correct and furnishes us with the actual
occasion of the prophecy. Even so, when it comes to saying what
that occasion was, we have to admit that we do not know. Some
scholars connect the Egyptian assault upon Gaza with the supposed
activity of Necho in Philistia after his victory over Josiah in 609
and, presumably, his subsequent campaign to the Euphrates and
beyond. This reconstruction is supported by reference to the statement of Herodotus (II, 159) that Necho, after the battle at
Megiddo (Magdolon), conquered the city of Kadytis (usually identified with Gaza). If this be correct, we must suppose that even as
the Egyptians swept victoriously northward in 609, Jeremiah en-
visioned a sudden reversal of affairs and the imminent advance of
the Babylonians and their allies—for, as indicated, the invader cannot well be understood as the Egyptians themselves. Recently, A.
Malamat (IEJ 1 [1950/51], 154–59), who likewise places the fall
of Gaza to the Egyptians after the campaign of 609, has seen in
the "Foe from the North" the Umman Manda (Scythians), mentioned
in the Babylonian Chronicle, who had, he believes, swarmed across
Syria and Palestine as far as the Philistine Plain (cf. Herodotus, I,
105) after the Babylonian conquest of Harran in 610. It must be
said, however, that this movement of the Scythians remains largely
inferential (but see the remarks on the Scythian problem; Introduc-

tion, "The Book of Jeremiah . . ."), while the description of the foe in chapter xlvii (cf. vs. 3) suggests the Babylonians rather than some semi-barbarian horde. H. Tadmor (*Bulletin of the Israel Exploration Society* [Hebrew] 24 [1959], p. 29, n. 27) sees in the poem fragments of a still older prophecy relating to a rebellion of Ashkelon against the Assyrian king Esarhaddon.

Perhaps the most plausible course is to connect the chapter with the events of the years immediately after 605, as the Babylonians advanced into Palestine and reduced certain of the Philistine cities. We know from the Babylonian Chronicle that Ashkelon (vss. 5, 7) was taken and ravaged in December 604; it was probably shortly before this that the king of that city dispatched an appeal to the pharaoh for aid (cf. Introduction, "The Background of Jeremiah's Career . . ."). We also know that late in 601 Necho met Nebuchadnezzar in pitched battle and apparently defeated him badly. It may have been at this time, presumably in the attempt to re-establish his authority in Palestine, that he assaulted and took Gaza. But, once more, we must admit that we cannot be sure.

40. MOAB
(xlviii 1–47)

Moab's Devastation

XLVIII ¹ Concerning Moab:
This is what Yahweh of Hosts, the God of Israel, has said:
"Alas for Nebo! She's ravaged!
 Taken*a* is Kiriathaim,
The stronghold is humbled and shattered,
2 The glory of Moab is gone.
In Heshbon they plotted her downfall:
 'Come! As a nation we'll end her!'
You too, O Madmen, shall lie silent;
 Hard after you follows the sword.

3 "Hark! A cry from Horonaim!
  Havoc and utter disaster!
4 'Smashed is Moab!'
  Their cry can be heard clear to Zoar.*b*
5 Ah, up the hill at Luhith
  With weeping they clamber.*c*
Ah, down the slope at Horonaim
 One can hear the cry*d* of confusion.

---

a Heb. "Shamed, taken. . . ." But "shamed" (humbled) is lacking in LXX, and is probably an erroneous repetition of the same word in the next colon.
b So following LXX (*ṣō'arāh*); cf. Isa xv 5. Hebrew reads, "Her little ones (*ṣe'īrehā*) make a cry heard"; the consonantal text is the same.
c Hebrew repeats "weeping" (*bekī*) at the end of the line, which represents a dittography with the first word of the next line (*kī*). Read *bō* ("on it") with Isa xv 5, of which this verse is a variant.
d Heb. ". . . the distresses of the cry" (*ṣārē ṣa'aqat*). Omit *ṣārē* with LXX and with Isa xv 5.

6   'Flee! Run for your lives!
       ^eBe like a [   ] in the desert.'^e

7   "Yes, because of your trust in your strongholds,^f
       You too shall be taken;
       And Chemosh shall go into exile,
       His priests and his princes as well.

8   The despoiler shall fall upon every town,
       Not a one shall escape.
       And the Valley shall perish,
       The Plateau be wrecked,
       As^g Yahweh has said.

9   Provide [salt (?)] for Moab;
       She's destined for ruin.
       Her cities shall be a waste
       Where nobody dwells."

[¹⁰ Cursed be he who does Yahweh's work negligently! And cursed be he who holds back his sword from shedding blood!]

Moab's Complacency Ended

11   "Moab has never known trouble;
       He's settled upon his lees,
       Never poured from vessel to vessel,
       Never deported.
       And so he retains his flavor,
       And his scent is unchanged.

12   Therefore, believe me, days are coming—Yahweh's
              word—

^{e-e} The text of the final colon is unintelligible: "And be (feminine plural) like 'Aroer' in the desert." The verb could be taken as second masculine plural with the energic ending, misunderstood by MT (D. N. Freedman). But "Aroer" remains a mystery. In Isa xv 5 *y^e'ō'ērū* occurs in place of the verb "hear" in vs. 5 above; *'^arō'ēr* may be a corrupted marginal variant of that word which has crept into the text at the wrong place. LXX reads "like a wild ass" (*'ārōd*), which at least makes sense. Others suggest *'ar'ār* (a desert shrub of some sort, a juniper) as in xvii 6 (and so Vulg.).

^f So with LXX (*b^emā'uzzayik* or *bim^eṣudōtayik*, or the like). Heb. "in your works and in your treasures" may represent a double attempt to read an unintelligible word (Weiser).

^g But perhaps "as" (*'^ašer*) is a dittography (Rudolph).

When I'll send men to cant and decant him,
To empty his vessels,
And smash his jars."^h
[13 Then Moab will be disappointed in Chemosh, just as the house of Israel was disappointed in Bethel, the source of their confidence.]

14 "How can you say, 'Heroes are we,
Men who are valiant in battle'?
15 'Moab's destroyer has struck at his towns,
His choicest young men have gone down to the
slaughter.^i
16 Moab's disaster is close at hand,
His calamity hurries apace.
17 Bemoan him, all you his neighbors,
All you who know him by name;
Say, 'How snapped is the mighty scepter,
The glorious staff!' "

Catastrophe!

18 "Come down from glory, sit in filth [?],^j
Inhabitress fair of Dibon!
For Moab's destroyer has fallen upon you,
Has wrecked your strongholds.
19 Stand by the road and watch,
Aroer's inhabitress!
Question ^k the fugitives fleeing^k;

---

^h So following LXX; Heb. "their jars."
^i–i Hebrew "Moab is destroyed [šuddad]; and [to] her cities (we'ārehā) he has come up," cannot be correct. LXX "Moab is destroyed [with] his city." The simplest course is to point šōdēd ("destroyer") as in vs. 18, and read be'ārāw ("against his cities"); cf. bāk in vs. 18. Hebrew ends the verse with "Word of the King, Yahweh of Hosts is his name," which is metrically awkward and probably an addition; omit with LXX.
^j So (reading baṣṣō'āh) with various scholars (and cf. Syr.). Heb. ". . . in thirst" (baṣṣāmā'), or perhaps "on the parched ground" (baṣṣāmē'), as in Isa xliv 3, does not suit well. Probably baṣṣō'āh (literally "excrement") was intentionally altered by the addition of mem.
^k–k Heb. "him fleeing and her escaping." But Vrs. do not preserve this distinction.

Ask, 'What has happened?'
20   Humbled is Moab, nay shattered;
      Wail and cry!
      Tell it by Arnon,
      That Moab lies waste."

[21 Judgment has come on the tableland: On Holon, Jahzah, and Mephaath; 22 on Dibon, Nebo, and Beth-diblathaim; 23 on Kiriathaim, Beth-gamul, and Beth-meon; 24 on Kerioth, on Bozrah, and on all the cities of the land of Moab, both far and near.]
25   "Moab's horn is cut off,
      His arm is broken—Yahweh's word."¹

[26 Make him drunk, for he has defied Yahweh! So Moab shall vomit helplessly and become himself a laughingstock. 27 Was not Israel a laughingstock to you? Was he caught in the company of thieves that whenever you spoke^m of him you wagged your head in disdain?]
28   "Abandon the towns! Make your home in the cliffs,
      You who dwell in Moab!
      Be like the dove that nests
      High on the sides of the gorge."

Lament for Moab

29   We have heard of Moab's pride—
      So very proud—
      Of his swagger, his arrogant pride,
      And lofty conceit.
30   "Myself, I know of his insolence—
      ^nWord of Yahweh^n—
      False are his boasts,
      And false his deeds."
31   And so, I'll wail for Moab,
      For the whole of Moab I'll cry,
      For the men of Kir-heres I'll moan.

¹ LXX omits "Yahweh's word," and this may be preferable.
^m Point as *dabberkā*; MT *debārekā* ("your words").
^n-n Transferred from after "I know of." LXX omits.

32   O fountain of Jazer, I weep you;
           O Sibmah's vine,
       Whose tendrils reached to the sea,
           To Jazer° extended.
       On your summer fruit and your vintage,
           The spoiler has fallen.
33   Removed are gladness and joy
           ᵖFrom Moab's land.ᵖ
       Goneᑫ is the wine from the presses,
           ʳNo vintager treads,ʳ
               No glad shout [   ].ˢ

34 ᵗHeshbon and Elealeh cry outᵗ with a roar that can be
heard as far as Jahaz, from Zoar as far as Horonaim andᵘ Eglath-
shelishiyah; for even the waters of Nimrim are turned into a
wasteland. 35 "I will stop Moab—Yahweh's word—from ᵛoffer-
ing burnt offerings on the high places,ᵛ and from making sacrifices to his gods."

36 So my heart wails like a flute for Moab, yes my heart wails
like a flute for the men of Kir-heres, because all that they had
managed to accumulate is gone.

ᵒ Hebrew erroneously repeats "sea" before "Jazer" ("to the sea of Jazer").
Delete "sea" with LXX and Isa xvi 8, where the branches of Sibmah's vine
are depicted as extending from the (Dead) Sea to the desert.
ᵖ⁻ᵖ Heb. "From the fruitful land (*karmel*) and from the land of Moab," seems
clearly to combine variants; LXX has only the second, Isa xvi 10 only the
first.
ᑫ Point the verb as Hophal (Rudolph); cf. LXX at Isa xvi 10. MT, "I have
caused the wine to cease," does not suit the context.
ʳ⁻ʳ So with Isa xvi 10: "the treader [*haddōrēk*] does not tread." Hebrew
here reads *hēdād* ("a vintage shout") for "treader," an erroneous copying
from the ensuing colon.
ˢ Heb., "shout not shout," cannot possibly be correct. But LXX, though
confused, seems to have read the words. Probably some verb should be
substituted for the second "shout" ("resounds," "is raised," or the like), but
to say what it should be would be pure guesswork. But perhaps end the verse
"The glad shout has ceased" (cf. Isa xvi 10).
ᵗ⁻ᵗ So with Isa xv 4. Hebrew here is corrupt (though LXX seems to read the
same): "At the cry of Heshbon as far as Elealeh."
ᵘ With LXX, "and" added.
ᵛ⁻ᵛ Hebrew, "offering [on the] high place" (*maᵃleh bāmāh*), is hardly correct.
LXX, "going up on [the] high place" (*ʿōleh ʿal bāmāh*), is an improvement.
But perhaps (Rudolph) a haplography has occurred: *maᵃleh* [*ʿōlāh ʿal hab*]
bāmāh.

37　Ah, every head is shaved,
　　　Every beard is shorn,
　　On every hand are gashes,
　　　On every[w] waist sackcloth.

38 "Upon all the rooftops of Moab, and in all her squares, there is nothing but lamentation; for I have smashed Moab like an unwanted pot—Yahweh's word." 39 How shattered he is![x] How Moab turns his back in shame! So Moab becomes a laughingstock and a shock to all those around him.

Doom—and Final Mercy

40　Yes, this is what Yahweh has said:
　　"Look! Like an eagle he swoops,
　　　Spreading his wings over Moab.
41　The towns are taken,
　　　The strongholds seized,
　　And the courage of Moab's warriors becomes—on that
　　　　　　　　day—
　　　Like that of a woman in labor.
42　Destroyed as a people is Moab,
　　　Because he defied Yahweh.

43　"Terror and trapfall and trap
　　　Are upon you, O dweller in ·Moab—Yahweh's word.
44　Who flees from the terror
　　　Falls into the trapfall;
　　Who climbs from the trapfall
　　　Is caught in the trap.
　　[y]Ah, this I will bring upon Moab
　　　In the year[y] of their doom—Yahweh's word."

[w] Hebrew lacks "every," but it is read by LXX and various manuscripts and Vrs.
[x] Hebrew then adds "Howl!" Either supply 'ēk ("How they howl"), or delete "howl."
[y-y] Heb. "Ah, I will bring upon her ('ēlehā), upon Moab, the year of their doom." Read 'ēlleh ("these things") for 'ēlehā, and add "in" before "the year" (b lost by haplography), with LXX. But MT can be retained by regarding "upon her" and "upon Moab" as variants.

45   In the shadow of Heshbon the fugitives
          Halt, all spent;
      For a fire ascends from Heshbon,
          A flame from Sihon's town*;
      It singes Moab's forehead,
          The pate of the noisy ones.
46   Alas for you, O Moab!
          You're*ᵃ done, O people of Chemosh!
      For your sons are hauled away captive.
          Your daughters to exile.

47 "Yet, when it is all over, I will restore the fortunes of
Moab—Yahweh's word."

Thus far the judgment on Moab.

ᵍ Heb. "from between [*mibbēn*] Sihon" is impossible. Read *mibbēt* ("from the
house of . . ."); "house" here has the sense of "capital city" (cf. "House of
Omri" as a name for Samaria in Assyrian texts; cf. also *miqqiryat* in Num
xxi 28).
ᵃᵃ The second person follows Num xxi 29 and some Vrs.; MT here has third
person.

NOTES

xlviii 2. *In Heshbon they plotted.* The wordplay cannot well be caught
in translation: *beḥešbōn ḥašᵉbū.* Heshbon (*Ḥesbān*), an important city
of northern Moab, has obviously fallen to the foe; but the historical
allusion cannot be elucidated.
      You too, O Madmen, shall lie silent. Again a wordplay: *gam madmēn
tiddōmmī.* Madmen is otherwise unknown. Its name ("dung-heap"?) may
be a play on Dimon (Isa xv 9); cf. the figure in Isa xxv 10. LXX, instead
of *mdmn,* reads the infinitive absolute of the ensuing verb (*dmm*); though
this is hardly preferable, the initial *m* may be a dittography and the
text may originally have read *dīmōn.* Some believe that both "Madmen"
and "Dimon" are plays upon Dibon (*Dībān*), the city north of the Arnon
where the Moabite (Meshaʿ) Stone was found; but this is far from
certain. On the basis of Ugaritic usage, M. J. Dahood (*Gregorianum*
43 [1962], 70) would read the line "With a loud voice shall Madmen
weep" (A. Kuschke, "Verbannung und Heimkehr," *Festschrift W. Rudolph* [Tübingen: J. C. B. Mohr, 1961], p. 185, similarly).

7. *in your strongholds.* See textual note*. Moab, personified, is here addressed in the second feminine singular.

Chemosh. The patron deity of Moab.

8. *the Valley.* The lower Jordan valley, east of the river and north of the Dead Sea.

The Plateau. The Transjordanian highland from the Arnon north to Heshbon.

9. The first half of the verse is a notorious *crux.* EVV read, "Give wings to Moab, for she would fly away," or the like. But that *ṣīṣ* means "wings" is dubious, as is the translation "fly away." In the second colon forms of two verbs seem to have been combined: *nāṣōh tiṣṣeh* ("she shall surely fall in ruins"), and *yāṣō' tēṣē'* ("she shall surely come forth," i.e., surrender, as in I Sam xi 3; Isa xxxvi 16 [?]). Since LXX seems to read *ṣiyyūn* for *ṣīṣ*—a word that means a "road-mark" in xxxi 21, but a "grave-marker" in II Kings xxiii 17—some scholars read, "Set up a grave-stone for Moab, for she shall certainly be destroyed," which at least gives sense. Recently, however, W. L. Moran (*Biblica* 39 [1958], 69–71) has argued persuasively on the basis of Ugaritic evidence that *ṣīṣ* here means "salt"; he then reads, "Give salt for Moab (i.e., to sow her cities with it, as in Judg ix 45), for she shall surely surrender"; cf. also M. J. Dahood (*Sacra Pagina* 1 [1959], 274), who agrees with Moran generally, for a different understanding of the second colon. I have tentatively followed Moran on the first colon, but feel that the reading chosen in the second fits the context even better. On the whole subject of sowing cities with salt, see recently S. Gervitz, VT 13 (1963), 52–62.

10. The verse is a prose comment.

11. *Moab has never known trouble.* Literally "Secure [at ease] has Moab been from his youth." In this verse and the next Moab, which did not suffer deportation when Judah did, is likened to a fine wine that has been allowed to settle and age, thus improving its flavor. The metaphor is apt in that Moab was famed for its vineyards (cf. vs. 32 f.; Isa xvi 8–11).

12. *I'll send men to cant and decant him.* This tries to catch the word-play: "I'll send to him tilters who will tilt him"—i.e., workers in a wine cellar who decant the wine.

13. The verse is a prose insertion comparing Moab's disillusionment with the national god Chemosh with that of northern Israel with Bethel. The parallelism suggests that Bethel is here, as in the Elephantine papyri and elsewhere, a divine epithet (cf. J. P. Hyatt, JAOS 59 [1939], 81–98). No doubt it was a surrogate for Yahweh current in the official cult of northern Israel as practiced at Bethel.

18. *Inhabitress fair of Dibon.* Literally "Inhabitress, Daughter-Dibon";

cf. xlvi 19, where a similar poetic personification of Egypt's people occurs. On Dibon, see Note on vs. 2.

21–24. A prose expansion that interrupts the poem.

25. *horn . . . arm*. Both are metaphors for strength.

26–27. A further prose expansion.

26. *shall vomit helplessly*. EVV "shall wallow in his vomit." But the verb *sāpaq* always means to "clap" the hands (Num xxiv 10; Lam ii 15) or the thigh (xxxi 19)—in rage, disgust, or remorse. Literally "he shall clap on account of his vomit," which (cf. KB) may suggest one vomiting, and striking his thigh in helpless rage and disgust. Some, however, see a sense attested in Syr.: "He shall spew forth his vomit." For the divine judgment in the figure of drunkenness, cf. xxv 15–29.

28. *High on the sides of the gorge*. Literally "on the sides of the mouth of the pit (chasm)."

29. A variant of Isa xvi 6.

30. The verse expands Isa xvi 6c.

31. *I'll moan*. The context demands this; MT has third person. Verse 31 is a variant of Isa xvi 7.

32. The verse is parallel to Isa xvi 8 f.

O fountain of Jazer. Not to be read, "With more than the weeping of Jazer" (EVV); *mbk* has the meaning "fountain" in Ugaritic (and cf. Job xxviii 11, etc.), and was doubtless chosen here for the sake of word-play with *bkh* ("to weep"). Cf. G. M. Landes, BASOR 144 (1956), 30–37.

33. Cf. Isa xvi 10, of which the verse is a variant.

34–39. Save for vs. 37, these verses are prose. But similarities to Isa xv–xvi cause one to suspect that they have a metrical basis, now obscured: cf. vs. 34 and Isa xv 4–6; vs. 36 and Isa xvi 11; xv 7; vs. 37 and Isa xv 2–3; vs. 38 and Isa xv 3.

34. *with a roar that can be heard*. Literally "they give forth their voice. . . ."

38. *like an unwanted pot*. The same words are used of Jehoiachin in xxii 28.

40–41. LXX omits all of vs. 40 save the heading, and also the latter half of vs. 41. The omitted material is repeated with small variations in xlix 22, and LXX may simply be following its habit of omitting doublets on their second occurrence (which in the LXX order this is); cf. Weiser.

43. *Terror and trapfall and trap*. An attempt to catch the assonance of *pahad wāpahat wāpaḥ*. Verses 43–44 reappear with slight variations in Isa xxiv 17–18. But they need not be a secondary addition here, for Isa xxiv–xxvii, like the present chapter, is composed in good part of conventional material, some of which (cf. Isa xxv 10–12) may have been drawn from oracles originally directed at Moab (and other peoples).

45–47. LXX omits these verses. They are composed in good part of snatches of very ancient poems: cf. vs. 45b and Num xxi 28a; vs. 45c and Num xxiv 17c; vs. 46 and Num xxi 29.

45. *from Sihon's town.* Sihon was an Amorite king conquered by Israel in the days of Moses (Num xxi 21–30); his capital was Heshbon.

Moab's forehead. Perhaps more precisely "temples," the hair on the side of the head.

47. *when it is all over.* Literally "at the end of days." The verse seems to be prose.

COMMENT

This chapter consists of a long poem—or, better, a series of poems—together with numerous prose comments and expansions, all directed at Moab. Although it is only likely that words of Jeremiah are included, the material is of mixed origin and has had a complicated history of transmission. Much of it, indeed, is older than Jeremiah. This is evident from the numerous verbal similarities to various poems found elsewhere in the Bible (see NOTES), particularly to the lament over Moab in Isa xv–xvi (see especially notes on vss. 29–39). These last do not mean that the present chapter is directly dependent on Isa xv–xvi, but rather indicate that we are dealing in good part with anonymous sayings which were treasured among the followers both of Isaiah and Jeremiah, and which thus found their way, albeit in different forms, into the books of both prophets. The original setting of the poem in Isa xv–xvi (and underlying parts of this chapter) is not our present concern, although it must be said that the arguments of W. F. Albright, who connects it (JBL 61 [1942], 119) with an invasion of Arab tribes which overran Moab and adjacent lands in the middle of the seventh century, are persuasive. Even so, it is possible that the poem contains still earlier material composed on occasions of which we know nothing. In the present form of the chapter, this older, conventional material has been adapted and supplemented and made to apply to the situation that obtained contemporaneous with the last days of Judah and just after.

The precise setting of the prophecy as we now have it is difficult to determine. This is true both because the history of Moab is not well known (cf. A. H. van Zyl, *The Moabites* [Leiden: E. J. Brill, 1960] for a summary of the evidence), and because much of the material, having been reapplied to a situation other than that for which it was originally composed, yields few usable indices of date. Presumably Moab, like Judah, had submitted to the Babylonians when the latter advanced into Palestine after their victory at Carchemish in 605 (cf. ch. xlvi, in Sec. 38). But when Jehoiakim rebelled in 600–598 Moab remained loyal and even assisted the Babylonians in bringing Judah to her knees (II Kings xxiv 2). This undoubtedly caused hatred between the two peoples, always latent, to blaze to a new intensity. Although Moab was party to the rebellion that was being planned in 594 (xxvii 3), she seems to have stood aloof when Judah struck for independence in 589, and doubtless rejoiced over the fall of her rival. Nevertheless, Moab did not long survive. If Josephus (Antiquities X. ix. 7) is to be believed, Nebuchadnezzar, presumably because of rebellion, marched against Moab and Ammon in 582—and apparently against Judah too, for this was the year of the third deportation mentioned in lii 30—defeated and subdued them. Soon thereafter Moab, like Edom, fell victim to a new invasion of Arab tribes from the desert and ceased to exist as a nation. Although the present chapter may have been subjected to later editorial expansion and rearrangement, it is unlikely that any significant portion of its material was composed after approximately the end of the first quarter of the sixth century.

The chapter is noteworthy for the extraordinary number of place names which it contains, and which make it an invaluable source of knowledge for Moabite geography. To attempt to identify all these places, many of them of unknown or uncertain location, would be out of place in a book of this sort. The interested reader should consult a reliable atlas such as G. Ernest Wright and Floyd V. Filson, *The Westminster Historical Atlas to the Bible* (Philadelphia: Westminster Press, rev. ed., 1956) or L. H. Grollenberg, *Atlas of the Bible,* tr. and ed. by Joyce M. H. Reid and H. H. Rowley (London: Thos. Nelson & Sons, 1956); cf. also Rudolph, pp. 245–47. On vss. 1–8, see also A. Kuschke, "Verbannung und Heimkehr," *Festschrift W. Rudolph,* pp. 181–96.

41. AMMON
(xlix 1–6)

XLIX   1 Concerning the Ammonites:
This is what Yahweh has said:
"Has Israel no sons?
   No heir at all?
Why, then, does Milcom*a* take possession of Gad,
   And his people inhabit its towns?
2 And so, believe me, days are coming—
   Word of Yahweh—
When I'll make Rabbath-ammon to hear
   The shout of battle.
She'll become a desolate mound,
   Her villages burned to the ground;
Then shall Israel evict his evictors—
   Yahweh has spoken.
3 Howl, O Heshbon! *b*For [Ai (?)] is laid waste.*b*
   Cry, you daughters of Rabbah!
Gird you with sackcloth! Lament!
   Rush to and fro [   ].*c*
For Milcom is going to exile,
   His priests and princes too.
4 Why boast of your strength, your ebbing strength,
   O faithless daughter—
Who trusts in her treasures, and says,*d*

---

a The pointing follows LXX and other Vrs. (so also in vs. 3); MT *malkām* ("their king").

b–b So Hebrew and Vrs. For other suggestions, see NOTE.

c The missing word, "among the sheep pens" (*baggedērōt*), is difficult to understand; LXX omits. Some suggest *bigedudōt*, "[covered] with gashes" (i.e., in mourning; cf. xlviii 37), which at least suits the context and involves a very slight change in the consonantal text.

d Supplied with Vrs.

'Who can attack me?'

5   Believe me, I'll bring upon you
      Terror*e* from every direction;
    You'll be driven in headlong flight,
      With no one to rally the fugitives.

6 But afterward, I will restore the fortunes of the Ammonites
—Yahweh's word."

e Hebrew then reads, "Word of the Lord Yahweh of Hosts," which must be either deleted for metrical reasons or moved to the end of the line. LXX has only, "Word of Yahweh."

NOTES

xlix 1. *Milcom.* Milcom (Molech) was the appellation of the patron deity of Ammon. He is depicted here as appropriating the territory of the neighboring tribe of Gad and adding it to his land.

2. *Rabbath-ammon.* The Ammonite capital (Rabbah in vs. 3), today 'Ammān, the capital of the Kingdom of Jordan.

a desolate mound. "A desolate *tell*"; cf. NOTE on xxx 18 (Sec. 36).

Her villages. Literally "her daughters," i.e., the towns of her realm, dependent upon her.

3. *Howl, O Heshbon! For [Ai (?)] is laid waste.* Heshbon was a Moabite city (cf. xlviii 2), but one must suppose that it was at the time in Ammonite control (it lay near the frontier). Ai, however, presents difficulties, since no place of that name in Ammon is known. For "Ai is laid waste" (*šudd°dāh 'ay*), some read "the city (*hā'îr*) is laid waste," others "the destroyer has come up" (*šōdēd 'ālāh*), as in xlviii 18. Assurance is impossible.

4. *Why boast of your strength, your ebbing strength.* Literally "Why boast of strength, your strength ebbs away?" The reading follows M. J. Dahood (*Biblica* 40 [1959], 166 f.), who argues that *'mq* here, as in xlvii 5, has the meaning "strength, might" as in Ugaritic. The apparent plural ending of *ba'°māqīm* is to be taken as an enclitic *mem*. The translation of EVV, "Why boast in the valleys, flowing is your valley," makes no sense.

5. *in headlong flight.* Literally "each man before him," i.e., *sauve qui peut!*

6. A prose comment; cf. xlviii 47. LXX omits the verse.

COMMENT

Chapter xlix contains a number of shorter sayings directed at various peoples which, as the entirely different order in which they appear in LXX indicates, were originally transmitted separately. The first of these concerns Ammon, and seems to reflect the same general situation as do the oracles against Moab in the preceding chapter.

Intermittent friction had existed between Ammon and Israel since the period of the Judges, the Ammonites thrusting into Israelite territory as opportunity offered, and the Israelites retaliating when they had the strength to do so. The deportation of a part of the Israelite population of Transjordan by Tiglath-pileser III in 733 (II Kings xv 29), and the subsequent collapse of the northern state, created a vacuum into which the Ammonites apparently moved, annexing portions of the territory of Gad (vs. 1). Through most of the seventh century Ammon enjoyed a considerable prosperity as a semi-autonomous kingdom nominally subject to Assyria (see G. M. Landes, BA 24 [1961], 66–86, for a convenient summary of Ammonite history and culture). Though doubtless hurt by the Arab invasions that crippled Moab in the mid-seventh century (see the preceding chapter), she undoubtedly regained her independence as Assyria collapsed. To what degree, if at all, her territory was restricted by Josiah's vigorous policy is uncertain.

In the late seventh and early sixth centuries Ammon's history closely parallels that of Moab. Presumably she submitted to Nebuchadnezzar when the latter's forces advanced into Palestine in 605/4, for when Judah rebelled in 600–597 Ammonite troops, along with those of Moab, assisted in the pacification of that land (II Kings xxiv 2). Again like Moab, Ammon was implicated in the projected rebellion of 594 (xxvii 3). Although she seems to have been disloyal to Babylon in 589/87 (cf. Ezek xxi 18–32[23–37H], she was not, so far as we know, able to offer Judah tangible assistance; subsequently, as we have seen (cf. xl 13–xli 15), her king was a party to the plot that led to Gedaliah's assassination. It was presumably because of these disloyal actions that Nebuchadnezzar visited reprisals upon Ammon, along with Moab and Judah, in 582 (see COMMENT on preceding chapter). Soon after this Ammon fell victim to the Arab invasions that destroyed Moab (and Edom) and, before the middle of the sixth century, ceased to exist as a people. Though the precise occasion of the present prophecy is unknown, a date prior to the fall of Judah—and of Ammon—is indicated.

42. EDOM
(xlix 7–22)

XLIX   7 Concerning Edom:
This is what Yahweh of Hosts has said:
"Is wisdom no longer in Teman?
    Has counsel departed the shrewd,
        Or their wisdom gone stale?
8   Flee! Turn tail!
    Hide yourselves well,
        You who dwell in Dedan!
    For Esau's disaster I bring upon him,
        The time of his doom.
9   If vintagers came to you,
    Would they not leave gleanings?
    If thieves in the night,
        They'd but loot what they wanted.
10   But I, I have stripped Esau,
    Uncovered his lairs,
        So he cannot hide.
    Destroyed are his offspring,
        His kinsmen and neighbors;
         And there's no one to say,
11   'Leave your orphans, I will support them;
    Your widows may count upon me.'"

12 Yes, this is what Yahweh has said: "Look! If those who did not deserve to drink the cup nevertheless have to drink it, should you be the one to get off scot-free? You will not get off, but will assuredly have to drink. 13 Nay, I have sworn by my-

a–a Reading *we'ēn 'ōmēr* with Symm., LXX^L, and various commentators for MT *we'ēnennū* ("and he is no more"). The direct discourse of the next verse requires some such introduction.

self—Yahweh's word—that Bozrah shall become a horror, a taunt,[b] and a curse word, and that all her cities shall be desolate wastes forever."

14 I have heard a report from Yahweh;
       An envoy's been sent to the nations:
    "Assemble, and march to attack her!
       Up! To the battle!
15 Ah, but I'll make you the least of the nations,
       Despised among men.
16 Your 'horror' has deceived you,
       Your arrogant pride—
    You who dwell in the clefts of the rock,
       Who cling to the lofty height.
    Though you nest as high as the eagle,
       Down I will bring you—Yahweh's word.

17 Edom shall become a shocking sight. Everyone who passes by her will be shocked, and will whistle in awe at all the blows she has suffered. 18 Just as was the case when Sodom and Gomorrah and their neighbor cities were overthrown—Yahweh has spoken—

       No more shall any man live there.
       Nor human being settle there.

19 "Look! Like a lion ascending
       From the thicket of Jordan to pasture perennial,
    So[c] I'll pounce and chase them[d] from her,
       [e]Singling out her choicest rams [?].[e]
    For who is like me? Who can challenge me?
       What shepherd is there that can stand before me?"

[b] Heb. "a taunt, a desolation, and a curse word"; but l[e]ḥōreb may be a dittography of l[e]ḥor[e]bōt ("desolate wastes") in the next clause; LXX omits.
[c] Reading kēn with Duhm and others for MT kī ("for" or "surely"). Literally "So I will suddenly chase them . . ." (the first verb has adverbial force).
[d] The pronominal suffix "them" follows LXX and other Vrs., and 1 44 (Qre); MT here has "him [it]."
[e-e] Reading ūmibḥar 'ēlehā for ūmī bāḥūr 'ēlehā ("And who is chosen? Over her [I will place]"): a conjectural emendation with Rudolph and others, following Cornill, which at least yields good sense and leaves the consonantal text unchanged.

20 Therefore, hear the plan that Yahweh has planned against Edom, the schemes that he has schemed against the inhabitants of Teman:

"Ah, away they shall drag them, the least of the flock;
Ah, their fold shall be shocked at their fate.
21   The earth is rocked by the crash of their fall;
The cry can be heard to the Sea of Reeds.*f*
22   "Look! Like an eagle *g*he mounts, he swoops,*g*
Spreading his wings over Bozrah,
And the courage of Edom's warriors becomes—on that
day—
Like that of a woman in labor."

f Hebrew adds "its sound" at the end of the colon, which is either a gloss, or a variant of "the cry"; omit with LXX and 1 46.
g–g LXX and xlviii 40 omit the first of these verbs; the two may be variants.

NOTES

xlix 7. *Teman.* A district in Edom, here as elsewhere (cf. vs. 20) a poetic appellation for the entire land.

8. *Dedan.* Southeast of Edom, in the Hedjaz; probably the oasis of el-ʿUlā and the surrounding area (cf. W. F. Albright, "Geschichte und Altes Testament," *Festschrift A. Alt* [Tübingen: J. C. B. Mohr, 1953], pp. 1–12).

Esau. Brother of the patriarch Jacob (Israel), and ancestor of Edom (Gen xxxvi).

The time of his doom. More literally, as pointed by MT, "the time when I doom him."

9. *If vintagers came . . . Would they not leave gleanings.* Unless the verse is to be regarded as a secondary addition, the sentence must be taken as a question, as in Obad 5 (vss. 9–10a parallel Obad 5–6). The sense is: Whereas vintagers would leave gleanings, and thieves would not take everything, Yahweh (vs. 10) has stripped Edom bare.

12. This verse resembles xxv 28–29. In this prose insertion (vss. 12–13) the figure of the cup of Yahweh's wrath developed in xxv 15–29 is applied specifically to Edom.

13. *Bozrah.* The chief city of Edom, today el-Buṣeirah.

14–16. These verses closely parallel Obad 1–4.

16. *Your 'horror.'* The word *tipleṣet* occurs only here (it is not in Obad) and is of uncertain meaning; EVV translate, "your terribleness,"

or the like. One wonders if it does not have the same sense as *mipleṣet* (I Kings xv 13), "your horrible idol," i.e., a contemptuous epithet for Edom's god. Does the fact that the noun (feminine) is followed by a masculine verb indicate that the name of the god originally stood here?

17. This verse, which is in prose, is almost identical with xix 8. The whole of vss. 17–22, in fact, is a patchwork of material found elsewhere in the book (see the ensuing NOTES).

18. The verse is repeated with minor variations at l 40; the poetic snatch at the end reappears at vs. 33b.

19–21. These verses are repeated at l 44–46, where they are applied to Babylon.

19. *the thicket of Jordan.* Cf. xii 5. Yahweh is likened to a lion in search of food coming up from his lair in the tangled bush of the Jordan trench to nearby pastures where sheep are grazed.

chase them from her. I.e., chase the sheep (Edom's people) from her.

Who can challenge me. Literally ". . . summon me, set me a time," probably with the sense of "call me out," i.e., challenge me (cf. Job ix 19).

20. *Ah, away they shall drag them.* Both this colon and the next are cast in the oath formula, i.e., "I swear that . . ." (literally ". . . if they do not").

their fold shall be shocked at their fate. Literally ". . . on account of them." The fold, here personified, is appalled at the fate of the lambs. But one could take it that the fold is "desolate" (i.e., empty) because of what has happened to the sheep.

21. *the Sea of Reeds.* The Reed Sea (*yam sūf*)—not the "Red Sea," as in EVV!—was the place of the Exodus deliverance (location uncertain, but probably near the northeast frontier of Egypt).

22. The verse is parallel to xlviii 40–41.

COMMENT

The prophecy concerning Edom is similar to that directed against Moab in chapter xlviii both in that its metrical form is interrupted by various prose comments and expansions, and in that so much of its material is to be found in substantially identical form elsewhere in the Bible. Parallels with the little book of Obadiah, as well as with other oracles in this same part (IV) of the Jeremiah book, are striking, and are pointed out in the NOTES. We must, therefore, assume that the present prophecy, though doubtless containing words uttered by Jeremiah himself, consists in good part of anonymous sayings which were treasured and repeated in prophetic circles, and which were in the course of time applied to various different situations.

Although some of its material may well have been composed on earlier occasions (see the remarks in the COMMENT on Sec. 40 above on the original setting of the poem in Isa xv–xvi which is paralleled in parts of chapter xlviii), the prophecy in its present form reflects the bitter hatred which Jews felt toward the Edomites as a result of the perfidious behavior of the latter during and after the calamity of 587. It also gives a hint of the awful fate that overtook Edom in the years that followed. Although we have no direct information on the point, the Edomites had presumably submitted to Nebuchadnezzar along with the other states of Syria and Palestine in or just after 605, for we find them (xxvii 3), together with Moab and Ammon, among those who were plotting rebellion in 594. But when Judah struck for independence in 589/87, Edom not only gave no assistance but, as various passages indicate (e.g., Ezek xxv 12–14; Ps cxxxvii 7; Obad), actively participated on the side of the Babylonians. Subsequently, forced from their homeland by mounting Arab pressure, Edomites moved into Palestine and occupied southern Judea to a point north of Hebron (the later Idumea). By approximately the end of the sixth century Edom had been entirely taken over by Arab tribes, and sedentary occupation there had ended. The prophecy as we now have it seems to reflect an early phase in this series of events, later stages of which may be seen in Obadiah and in Mal i 2–4 (cf. Isa xxxiv).

43. DAMASCUS, ARAB TRIBES, ELAM
(xlix 23–39)

Damascus

XLIX   23 Concerning Damascus:
> Dismayed are Hamath and Arpad,
> > For disastrous news they have heard.
> *a*Their heart dissolves with worry [?],*a*
> > It cannot be still.

24   Faint is Damascus,
> > She turns to flee;
> Panic has seized her,
> > *b*Anguish has gripped her,
> > > Pangs as of childbirth.*b*

25   How deserted she is,*c*
> > The city renowned,
> > > The joyous town!*d*

26   "And so, her youths shall fall in her squares,
> > And all her soldiers lie lifeless
> > > In that day—Word of Yahweh of Hosts—
27   And I'll kindle a fire at the wall of Damascus
> > That will burn Ben-hadad's strongholds."

a–a A very conjectural reading (*nāmōg libbām midde'āgāh*) following Volz and others, which at least gives good sense and involves a minimum of change in the consonantal text. MT, "They melt; in the sea is anxiety" (*nāmōgū bayyām de'āgāh*), cannot be right; LXX reads two verbs for the clause.

b–b See NOTE.

c Heb. "How is she *not* deserted!" But such an idiom, possible in English, is not attested in Hebrew. Though the negative is clearly wrong, its presence is difficult to explain. See the commentaries for various suggestions. Perhaps the simplest expedient is to regard *lō'* as an error for the emphatic *lamed* (*le*): "How utterly forsaken she is" (suggested to me by D. N. Freedman; but see already F. Nötscher, VT 3 [1953], 374).

d Heb. "my joyous town." Omit "my" with most Vrs. (or regard *ī* as the archaic genitive ending).

Arab Tribes

28 Concerning Kedar and the chieftains of Hazor whom
Nebuchadnezzar, king of Babylon, defeated:
This is what Yahweh has said:
"Up! Advance on Kedar!
Despoil the Eastern People!—
29 Seizing their tents and their flocks,
Their tent-cloths and all their effects,
Taking their camels from them,
Shouting against them, 'Terror surrounds you!'

30 "Flee! Take to your heels!
Hide yourselves well,
You who dwell in Hazor—Yahweh's word—
For Nebuchadrezzar, Babylon's king,
Has laid a plan against you,
Has schemed against you a scheme.
31 'Up! Advance on a nation at ease,
That lives secure,*
That has neither gates nor bars,
That dwells all alone.
32 Their camels shall be for booty,
Their countless herds for spoil.'
To the winds I will scatter these clipped-templed men,
From every direction their doom I will bring—
Yahweh's word.
33 And Hazor shall be a jackal's lair,
A howling waste forever.
No more shall any man live there,
Nor human being settle there."

* Hebrew adds "Yahweh's word." Omit with LXX; Nebuchadnezzar is the
speaker.

Elam

34 What came as the word of Yahweh to Jeremiah the prophet concerning Elam, in the accession year of Zedekiah, king of Judah:

35   This is what Yahweh of Hosts has said:
   "Look! I'll break the bow of Elam,
      Mainstay of their might.
36   And I'll bring upon Elam four winds,
      From the heaven's four quarters.
[I will scatter them to all these winds, so that there shall not be a nation to which Elamite fugitives do not go.]
37   I'll terrify them*f* before their foes,
      Before those who seek their life;
   I'll bring disaster upon them,
      My furious anger—Yahweh's word.
   I'll send the sword to chase them,
      Until I've consumed them.
38   And I'll place my throne in Elam,
      Removing from thence both king and princes—
                  Yahweh's word.
39 But when it is all over, I will restore the fortunes of Elam—Yahweh's word."

f So LXX, which is smoother if not more original; Heb. "I'll terrify Elam."

NOTES

xlix 24. *Anguish has gripped her, / Pangs as of childbirth.* The cola are rendered metrically by the transposition of two words; Heb. "Anguish and pangs has (sic!) gripped her as of one in childbirth." But LXX omits both cola; they may be secondary.

26–27. The verses seem to have been appended to supply a conclusion to the foregoing. But vs. 26 ("therefore," "and so") does not really continue the preceding verse, and is only doubtfully metrical. Verse 26 is repeated at l 30; vs. 27 resembles Amos i 4, 14.

27. *Ben-hadad.* The name of the dynasty that ruled Damascus in the ninth–eighth centuries, and also of individual kings.

28. *Kedar and the chieftains of Hazor*. Kedar was the name of an Arab tribe of the Syrian desert east of Palestine (cf. ii 10). Hazor, of course, is not the well-known city in Palestine of that name, but likewise refers to the eastern desert. Whether it is the name of a specific place (as vss. 30, 33 seem to indicate), or merely a designation for the unwalled villages (*ḥᵃṣērīm*) in which certain Arab tribes had settled (cf. vs. 31, and "the villages that Kedar inhabits" in Isa xlii 11) is uncertain. Perhaps the locality in which these *ḥᵃṣērīm* were concentrated was known as *ḥāṣōr*. Heb. *mamlᵉkōt ḥāṣōr* is probably not to be taken as "kingdoms of Hazor" (EVV), but as "chiefs (kings) of Hazor" or, perhaps better, "village chieftains"; cf. NOTE on i 15.

the Eastern People. The *bᵉnē qedem*, a well-known tribe of the Syrian desert since earliest times (e.g., Gen xxix 1; Judg vi 3, 33; Job i 3).

29. *Terror surrounds you*. Heb. *māgōr-missābīb*, a favorite Jeremianic expression (e.g., vi 25; xx 3 f., 10), here made to represent the shout of raiders as they pounce on their victims ("You're surrounded!" or the like).

30. *For Nebuchadrezzar, Babylon's king, / Has laid a plan*. This can be rendered metrically only with forcing. To omit "Nebuchadrezzar" (so LXX) or "the king of Babylon" (Rudolph) does not help much. Possibly both are a gloss, the original reading being simply, "He has laid a plan." Perhaps this gloss, and the prose heading in vs. 28a, serve to adapt an older poem to Nebuchadnezzar's campaign.

31. The verse resembles Ezek xxxviii 11, but there is no reason to suppose that either is directly dependent on the other.

32. *these clipped-templed men*. The *qᵉṣūṣē pē'āh;* Arabs of the desert (cf. ix 25[26E]; xxv 23).

33. The language is conventional. The first part of the verse resembles ix 10[11E]; x 22. The latter part is identical with vs. 18b.

34. For the introductory formula, cf. xlvi 1; xlvii 1.

the accession year of Zedekiah. On this technical term see NOTE on xxvi 1. One supposes that it refers to the single month between the surrender of Jerusalem on 2 Adar 597 (so Babylonian Chronicle) and the New Year on 1 Nisan.

35. *the bow of Elam*. The Elamites were evidently famous archers (cf. Isa xxii 6).

36. The latter part of the verse seems to be a prose expansion.

37. *I'll send the sword to chase them*. This colon and the next repeat ix 15b[16bE]—conventional language.

39. A prose comment: cf. xlviii 47; xlix 6.

COMMENT

Chapter xlix concludes with three short prophecies which, although originally unrelated to one another, may for the sake of convenience be treated together. The first of these (vss. 23–27) is directed against Damascus with passing mention of Hamath and Arpad, two petty states in central and northern Syria, respectively, which figure prominently in texts of the eighth century and before. Although it may be in good part because of the incompleteness of our knowledge, it is impossible to relate this prophecy to any known event during Jeremiah's lifetime. All three of the places just mentioned fell before the Assyrian king Tiglath-pileser III in the course of his various campaigns in the west—Arpad and Hamath (cf. Isa x 9; xxxvi 19; xxxvii 13) before 738, Damascus (II Kings xvi 9) in 732 (a further rebellion in Hamath was crushed by Sargon II in 720)—and thereafter lost independent existence. Presumably the Aramean peoples of Syria, having regained their freedom when Assyria collapsed, had subsequently undergone a period of nominal subjection to Egypt (after 609), and then had submitted to Nebuchadnezzar after his victory over Necho in 605. But save for the mention in the Babylonian Chronicle of a further victory of Nebuchadnezzar over the Egyptians in the neighborhood of Hamath, none of the above-mentioned places plays any role in texts relating to events of Jeremiah's lifetime. And the Bible, aside from the notice in II Kings xxiv 2 that Aramean troops assisted in the pacification of Judah in 600–597, gives us no information. In view of the mention of Hamath and Arpad, as well as the fact that the conclusion of the prophecy in vss. 26–27 is made up of conventional material found elsewhere in the Bible (see the NOTES), it is possible that we are dealing with an anonymous saying much older than Jeremiah, perhaps of eighth-century date, which has been reapplied to Damascus perhaps in connection with one of Nebuchadnezzar's campaigns, or other events of which we know nothing.

The next prophecy (vss. 28–33) is concerned with a campaign of Nebuchadnezzar against certain Arab tribes of the eastern desert (see further, NOTES). Assyrian kings had on more than one occasion been forced to take action against these people. It will be recalled (see COMMENT on ch. xlviii [Sec. 40]) that in the mid-seventh century a particularly serious Arab invasion of lands in Transjordan and southern Syria along the fringe of the desert had provoked Asshurbanapal to vigorous punitive measures. Presumably the Arabs had given Nebuchadnezzar trouble too, for the Babylonian Chronicle tells of a campaign against them in 599/8. This may have been the occasion of the present prophecy (so Wiseman, pp. 31 f.)—although it is again not impossible (see further, NOTES) that an earlier prophecy has been adapted and reapplied for the purpose.

The final prophecy (vss. 34–39) concerns Elam, and is dated in the accession year of Zedekiah (597). What may have provoked it we do not know. Elam, an important state to the east of Babylonia in southwest Iran, had, after a long history of conflict with Assyria, been conquered by Asshurbanapal ca. 640. Thereafter, until the rise of the Persian Empire, the history of Elam is obscure. It seems to have regained its independence ca. 626/5 as Assyria weakened (cf. Wiseman, pp. 8–10, 51), and in 540/39 it played a role in the overthrow of Babylon. But, unless certain damaged lines in the Babylonian Chronicle (cf. Wiseman, p. 73; cf. pp. 36, 48) tell of an engagement between Nebuchadnezzar and the Elamites in 596/5, we have no tangible information regarding their fortunes during this interval. We know of no way in which their activity may have impinged upon affairs in Judah. Whether they played some role in connection with Jehoiakim's rebellion, or whether they were behind subsequent unrest in Babylon in which Jews were involved (ch. xxix [Sec. 28]), we cannot say. But there is no reason to question the accuracy of the date—although, once again, it is not impossible that older material (relating to Asshurbanapal's campaigns?) has been reused.

44. BABYLON
(l 1–46; li 1–58; 64c)

L 1 *The word that Yahweh spoke concerning Babylon, concerning the land of the Chaldeans, by Jeremiah the prophet*:

Babylon's Fall and Israel's Release: Various Sayings

2 "Make it known to the nations! Proclaim it!*
    Openly say it:
'Babylon's taken,
    Bel disgraced,
        Marduk dismayed;
    Her idol's disgraced,
        Her "godlets" dismayed.'
3 For a nation has come from the north to attack her,
    That will leave her land a shambles
With no one living there,
    Both man and beast *having fled, having gone.*

4 "In those days and at that time—Yahweh's word—
    The people of Israel shall come,
        And the people of Judah too,
And, weeping as they go,
    Shall seek Yahweh their God.
5 They shall ask the way to Zion,
    Toward which their faces are turned:

a-a LXX is abbreviated, "The word of Yahweh, which he spoke concerning Babylon."
b Hebrew adds, "Raise the signal! Proclaim it!"—which seems to be a variant of the preceding colon; omit with LXX.
c-c So in ix 9[10E], which the latter part of the verse resembles. But the two verbs may be variants of one another (LXX omits both).

'Come! *Let us cleave* to Yahweh
In a covenant eternal that won't be forgot.'

6 "Lost sheep were my people,
    Led astray by their shepherds.
Turned out on the mountains,
    They ranged from mountain to hill,
       Their fold forgot'.

7 Whoever encountered them ate them;
    Said their foes, 'We do no wrong,
For they've sinned against Yahweh,
    Their pasture true, their fathers' hope.'

8 "Ho!*e* Flee from Babylon's midst,
    From Chaldean land!
Out, and be like bellwethers
    Leading the flock!

9 For see! I'm going to rouse
    And bring against Babylon
A horde of mighty nations
    From the northern land.
They'll take position against her;
    By them she'll be taken.
Their arrows are like a trained soldier
    Who never returns empty-handed.

10 So Chaldea shall be for spoil;
    Her spoilers shall all have their fill—Yahweh's word.

11 "Ah, rejoice! Ah, exult,
    You who plundered my property!
Yes, frisk *ᶠlike calves at pasture,ᶠ*
    And neigh like stallions!

12 Deeply shamed your mother shall be,

---

a–a Read *wᵉnillāweh;* MT *wᵉnilᵉwū,* "and they shall cleave." If MT is retained, read *ūbāʾū* ("they shall come") for *bōʾū* with LXX.
e Hebrew at the end of vs. 7 adds "Yahweh," which is redundant; omit with LXX. The consonants *yhwh* may be corruption of *hōy (hwy),* which should be read at the begining of vs. 8 (Volz, etc.), or perhaps even better of *hōy hōy,* as in Zech ii 10, which the first line of vs. 8 somewhat resembles.
f–f Read *kᵉʿeglē* (or *kᵉʿēgel) baddeše'* with LXX. MT *kᵉʿeglāh dāšāh* ("like a heifer threshing") does not give good sense.

Disgraced she who bore you.
Look! The lowest of nations,
A desert, dry and barren!

13 Through the wrath of Yahweh uninhabited,
Wholly a waste shall she be;
All who pass by Babylon shall whistle,
Appalled at all her wounds.

14 "Take stations surrounding Babylon,
You archers all!
Let fly at her! Spare not the arrows!*g*

15 Shout the attack from all sides!
She signals surrender!
Her bulwarks [?] are fallen,
Her walls battered down.
Ah, this is Yahweh's vengeance—
Take vengeance upon her!
Do to her as she has done!

16 Cut off from Babylon the sower,
Him who wields the sickle at harvest time.
For fear of the dreadful sword
Everyone turns toward his people,
Everyone flees to his homeland.

17 "A scattered flock is Israel,
Chased by lions.
First the king of Assyria devoured him, and now lately Nebuchadrezzar, king of Babylon, has gnawed his bones. 18 Therefore, this is what Yahweh of Hosts, the God of Israel, has said: See! I am going to punish the king of Babylon and his country, just as I punished the king of Assyria. 19 And I will bring Israel back to his pasture; and he shall feed on Carmel and in Bashan, and on the hills of Ephraim and Gilead shall eat his fill.

20 In those days and at that time—Yahweh's word—
Israel's guilt shall be sought for—in vain;
And Judah's sin—it's not to be found;
For I'll pardon the remnant I spare."

g Hebrew adds "For she has sinned against Yahweh." Omit with LXX.

The Divine Judgment on Babylon: Continued

21 *"March against the land of Merathaim!*
   March to attack her,
      And the people of Pekod!
   Slay and devote to destruction—Yahweh's word—
      Do just as I have commanded you!"

22 *The din of battle,
      A mighty crash
   In the land of Chaldea!*

23 How broken it is and shattered,
      The whole earth's hammer!
   How Babylon has become
      A horror to the nations!

24 You set you a snare and were trapped,
      O Babylon, ere you knew it;
   You were caught and held fast,
      For you dared to challenge Yahweh.

25 Yahweh has opened his armory,
      Brought forth his weapons of wrath;
   For the Lord Yahweh has work
      In the land of Chaldea.

26 Come on her from every side!
      Open her granaries!

h-h MT begins the verse "Against the land, Merathaim." A haplography seems to have occurred, as various commentators surmise; for *'al hā'āreṣ* read *'alēh ('al) 'ereṣ*.

i-i The text of the colon is difficult. The first verb (*ḥrb*), which usually means "be dry," here (and in vs. 27) seems to be a denominative of *ḥereb* ("sword"), i.e., "put to the sword." After the second verb Hebrew reads "after them" (*'aḥᵃrēhem*), which must be deleted with LXX (unless one reads *'aḥᵃrītām*, "the last of them," as some scholars do). One wonders if the text does not conflate readings, and if the original may not have had infinitive absolute with imperative of *ḥḥrm* ("devote them to utter destruction," or the like).

j-j The reading follows LXX. Heb. "The din of battle in the land, and a mighty crash."

k-k Heb. "For this is a work of the Lord Yahweh of Hosts." Omit *hī'* ("this [is]") and "of Hosts" with LXX, for metrical reasons.

Pile her in heaps, destroy her!
   Leave her no remnant!
27 Slay all her bulls,
   Let them go to the slaughter!
Woe to them! Their day has come,
   The time of their doom.
28 Hark! Fugitives and refugees come from the land of Babylon to tell in Zion of the vengeance of Yahweh our God,
vengeance for his temple.

29 "Call out against Babylon archers,[l]
   All who can draw the bow!
Invest her on every side,
   Let no one escape!
Repay her as she deserves,
   Do to her as she has done!
For she's proudly defied Yahweh,
   Israel's Holy One.
30 And so her youths shall fall in her squares,
   And all her soldiers lie lifeless[m]—Yahweh's word.
31 Look! I'm against you, 'Sir Pride'—
   Word of the Lord Yahweh of Hosts!
Ah, your day has come,
   The time [n]of your doom![n]
32 'Sir Pride' shall stumble and fall,
   And no one shall lift him.
I'll kindle a fire in his towns
   That will rage through all his environs."

Judgment on Babylon: Further Sayings

33 This is what Yahweh of Hosts has said:
"Oppressed are the people of Israel,
   And the people of Judah too;

[l] Pointing as *rōbīm* with most commentators (cf. Gen xxi 20). MT has *rabbīm* ("a host"), which is less suitable.
[m] Hebrew then has "in that day"; omit with LXX for metrical reasons. But
cf. xlix 26, with which this verse is almost identical.
[n–n] So Vrs.; MT, with a different pointing, "The time when I doom you."

Their captors all hold them fast,
They won't let them go.
34   Their Redeemer is strong—
Yahweh of Hosts his name.
He will surely espouse their cause,
And so bring rest to the earth—
But unrest to Babylon's dwellers.

35   "A sword on the Chaldeans—
Word of Yahweh—
On Babylon's citizens,
Her princes and sages!
36   A sword on her 'boasters'°—they rave!
A sword on her warriors—they panic!
37   ᵖA sword on the hirelings within herᵖ—
They turn into women!
A sword on her treasures—they're looted!
38   A swordᑫ on her waters—they're dry!
Ah, it's a land of idols—
Made fools byʳ their 'frights!'
39   And so—goblins and ghouls shall live there,
And ostriches inhabit her;
She shall never again be peopled,
Nor lived in for all generations.
40 As was the case when God overthrew Sodom and Gomorrah and their neighbor cities—Yahweh's word—
No more shall any man live there,
Nor human being settle there."

41   Look! A people coming from the north
A mighty nation
And many kings astir
From the earth's farthest bounds.

° MT "the boasters" (*habbaddīm*); but "her boasters" (*baddehā*) would be smoother (Rudolph); see NOTE.
ᵖ⁻ᵖ MT has suffered expansion: "A sword on his horses and on his chariots and on all the mixed peoples in her midst." Delete "on his horses and on his chariots" (note the change of pronoun); also omit "all" with LXX. See NOTE.
ᑫ MT "A drought on her waters." See NOTE.
ʳ Vrs. read "they boast in . . ." (same consonants); but this is not preferable.

42   Armed with bow and blade,
         Cruel are they and ruthless.
      On they come with a roaring like the sea,
         Mounted on chargers,
      Drawn up in battle array—
         Against you, Daughter Babylon!
43   Babylon's king has heard the news,
         His hands hang limp;
      Anguish has gripped him,
         Pangs as of childbirth.

44   "Look! Like a lion ascending
         From the thicket of Jordan to pasture perennial,
      So I'll pounce and chase them from her,
         Singling out her choicest rams.
      For who is like me? Who can challenge me?
         What shepherd is there that can stand before me?
      45 So, hear the plan that Yahweh has planned against Bab-
ylon, the schemes that he has schemed against the land of the
Chaldeans:
         Ah, away they shall drag them, the least of the flock!
         Ah, their fold shall be shocked at their fate!
46   At the shout, 'Babylon's taken!'
         The earth is rocked.
         The cry is heard 'mongst the nations."

Again—the Judgment on Babylon

LI   1 This is what Yahweh has said:
      "Look! I rouse against Babylon,
         And the dwellers in 'Leb-kamai,'
         A destroying wind.
2   I'll send to Babylon winnowers⁸
         To winnow and empty her land.
      ᵗAh, they'll attack herᵗ from every side

---

⁸ Pointing *zōrīm* (so Aq., Symm., Vulg., and most commentators); MT *zārīm*
("strangers").
ᵗ⁻ᵗ MT "Truly, they have been [*kī hāyū*] against her." Emend to *kī yaḥᵃnū*
following Volz or, perhaps more simply, *kī yihyū* (haplography).

On the day of disaster.

3 ^u[Let the bowman draw his bow against her (?),]
  [Against her rise up in full armor (?)]^u
Spare not her youths!
Destroy her whole army!

4 Slain shall they fall in Chaldea's land,
Thrust through in her streets."

5 Truly Israel and Judah have not been "widowed"
Of their God, Yahweh of Hosts,
Though their land was filled with guilt
  Against Israel's Holy One.

6 Flee from Babylon's midst!
  Every man for himself!
    Perish not for her guilt!
For it's Yahweh's time of vengeance;
He'll repay her as she deserves.

7 A golden cup was Babylon
  In Yahweh's hand,
    To make all the earth drunk.
Of its wine the nations drank,
  ^vThereupon went mad.^v

8 Suddenly Babylon fell and was broken;
  Wail over her!
Get ointment for her hurt—
  Perhaps it's curable.

9 Though we treated her, Babylon mends not;
  Give her up! Let us go every one to his land,
For her judgment reaches to heaven,
  Ascends to the skies.

---

^{u–u} The first bicolon is unintelligible in Hebrew: "Unto (against) let bend
let bend the bowman his bow; unto (against) let him rise up in his mail." It
would be simple to read the negative 'al for the preposition 'el ("unto") in
both cases, and to omit the repeated "let bend" with Qre (and so RSV). The
sense is then that the Babylonians are not to be given time to offer resistance.
But since this fits poorly in the context, it would be better to omit 'el altogether with LXX, or, still better, to read 'ēlehā ("against her") with LXX^L
(and so AJV). This reading at least yields good sense, but it is quite conjectural.
^{v–v} Heb. "thereupon the nations went mad"; omit "the nations" with Vrs.

10   Yahweh has produced our vindication.
         Come! Let us tell in Zion
            Of the deed of Yahweh our God.

11   Sharpen the arrows!
         Ready the shields [?]!
[Yahweh has stirred up the spirit of the kings[w] of the Medes,
for his purpose concerning Babylon is to destroy it.
         Ah, Yahweh's revenge is this,
            Revenge for his temple.]
12   Signal attack upon Babylon's walls!
         Strengthen the watch!
Set up the road blocks!
         Place men in ambush!
For Yahweh has both planned and done
         What he spoke against Babylon's citizens.
13   You who dwell by many waters,
         Rich in treasure,
Your end has come,
         Your life's thread is cut.
14   Yahweh of Hosts has sworn by himself:
"Ah, I'll fill you with men as with locusts,
         And they'll shout their triumph over you."

15   . . . He who made the earth by his power,
         Established the world by his wisdom,
            By his skill stretched out the heavens.
16   At the sound of [his thunderous voice (?)]
            [   ]
A roaring of waters in heaven.
         He brings up the clouds from the farthest horizons,
The rainstorm with lightning provides,
         And sends forth the wind from his storehouse.
17   All mortals stand stupid and witless,
         Every smith is ashamed of his idol;
For a fraud are his images, lifeless things;

w LXX, "the king of the Medes," may be preferable.

18   Nonentities they, a ridiculous joke;
         At the time of their doom they will perish.
19   Not like these is the Portion of Jacob;
         Nay, framer of all is he;
         And Israel his very own tribe—
         Yahweh of Hosts his name.

The Hammer, and the Mountain

20   "My mace are you,
         My weapon of war;
         With you I shatter nations,
         With you lay kingdoms low.
21   With you I shatter horse and rider,
         With you I shatter chariot and driver,[a]
22   With you I shatter man and woman,
         With you I shatter graybeard and boy,
         With you I shatter youth and maiden,
23   With you I shatter shepherd and flock,
         With you I shatter farmer and team,
         With you I shatter governors and prefects.
24 But I will repay Babylon and the inhabitants of Chaldea
before your very eyes for all the evil that they did in Zion—
Yahweh's word.
25   Look! I defy you, O mountain of raiders,
         Who raid the whole earth.
       I'll stretch out my hand and seize you,
         Roll you down from the crags,
         And make you a burnt-out mountain.
26   Nevermore shall they quarry a cornerstone from you,
         Or stone for foundations.
       Nay, a waste forever you'll be—
         Word of Yahweh."

[a] MT "chariot and rider"; point *we̱rakkābō* ("and charioteer") for *we̱rōke̱bō*.

The Nations against Babylon: Her Fall

27 "Raise the signal in the land!
      Sound the trumpet 'mongst the nations!
    Consecrate nations against her,
      Call out against her kingdoms—
        Ararat, Minni, and Ashkenaz—
    Appoint against her marshals [?];
      Bring up the horses like bristly [?] locusts."
    [28 Consecrate nations against her: the king*y* of the Medes,
his*y* governors and all his*y* prefects, and all the land of his
domain]
29   Then the land did tremble, did writhe,
        For Yahweh's plans against Babylon stand,
      To make the land of Babylon
        An uninhabited waste.
30   Babylon's warriors have ceased to fight,
        They skulk in the strongholds;
      Their courage exhausted,
        They act like women.
      Her houses are burning,
        Her bars broken down.
31   Runner after runner comes running,
        Courier after courier,
      To tell the king of Babylon
        That his city is taken, entire,
32   That the fords are seized,
        The marshes set on fire,
        And the soldiers gripped with panic.
33   For this is what Yahweh of Hosts, the God of Israel, has
                                                said:

y The singular follows LXX. MT has "kings" and "her" (i.e., Media's) governors and prefects (but cf. "his domain").

"Daughter Babylon's a threshing floor
When time comes to tamp it;
Soon, very soon,
Her harvest will come."

Babylon's Crime against Jerusalem; Yahweh's Requital

34 He devoured me,*aa* consumed [?] me,
Did Nebuchadrezzar, Babylon's king,
Set me down an empty dish.
Like a monster he swallowed me,
Filled his maw with my titbits*bb*
And rinsed me *cc*[(?)].*cc*

35 "On Babylon be my broken flesh,"
Let Zion's inhabitress say;
"And my blood on Chaldea's inhabitants,"
Let Jerusalem say.

36 Therefore, this is what Yahweh has said:
"Look! I'll espouse your cause
And get you requital;
I'll drain her sea,
Dry up her fount.

37 Then Babylon shall be a ruinheap,
A jackal's lair,
An appalling waste
Where nobody dwells.

38 "Like lions they roar in chorus,
Like lions' cubs they growl.

---

z–z Heb. "the time of her harvest. . . ." Perhaps *'ēt* is repeated from the preceding line; LXX omits (if omitted, read *ūbā'* for *ūbā'āh*).
aa Read all pronominal objects in vs. 34 "me" with Qre; Ktib "us."
bb Point *ma'adannāy;* MT *mē'adānāy* ("from my delights"). Some commentators, redividing the cola, read "He filled his belly; from my delights he thrust me out" (see textual note*cc–cc*). But this is anticlimactic.
cc–cc With a slight change of pointing (*hiddīḥānī* for *hedīḥānī*) one could read, "he thrust me out," "expelled me" (cf. LXX). But the colon is short, and a word seems to have been lost; one wonders if an indelicate expression has not been suppressed (see further, NOTE on vs. 35).

39   While they fret, I'll ready their banquet,
         I'll besot them and make them tipsy[dd];
      Then they'll sleep a perpetual sleep,
      And never awake—word of Yahweh—
40   I'll haul them like lambs to the slaughter,
         Like so many rams and goats."

Various Other Sayings regarding Babylon's Doom

41   How she[ee] is taken, yes captured,
         The whole earth's praise!
      How Babylon has become
      A horror to the nations!
42   The sea has surged over Babylon;
         By its boisterous waves she is covered.
43   Her towns are awesome wastes,
         A dry and desert land;
      [ff]Not a soul is living in them,
         Nor does any human visit them.

44   "I'll punish Bel in Babylon,
         And make him disgorge what he's swallowed.
      No more shall the nations stream to him;
      Aye, down comes Babylon's wall!
45   Out from her midst, my people!
         Let everyone run for his life,
            From Yahweh's hot anger.
46 Now, lest your hearts grow faint, and you fear because of
the rumors heard in the land—for one year there comes a rumor,
and then, the year after, there comes another rumor, rumors of
violence in the land and of ruler fighting ruler—
47   Therefore, believe me, days are coming,
         When I'll punish the idols of Babylon;

[dd] Literally "in order that they may rejoice" (ya'alōzū)—perhaps with the
sense of "be merry," i.e., tipsy. But perhaps the reading of LXX (ye'ullāpū),
"that they may be stupefied" (i.e., "pass out"), is to be preferred.
[ee] Heb. "How 'Sheshak' is taken." See Note.
[ff] Hebrew erroneously repeats "a land" at the beginning of the colon. Omit
with LXX (cf. "in them," i.e., the towns).

All her land shall be humbled,
And her slain shall all lie in her midst.

48 Heaven and earth shall exult over Babylon,
They and all that is in them,
When there come from the north upon her
The destroyers—Yahweh's word.

49 "Yes, Babylon must fall for*gg* Israel's slain,
As for Babylon have fallen the whole earth's slain.

50 You escaped *hh*from the sword,
Go!*hh* Do not wait!
Remember Yahweh from afar,
Let Jerusalem come to your mind."

51 We've been shamed, for we've suffered abuse;
Confusion has covered our face,
For aliens have entered *ii*our shrine,
The house of Yahweh.*ii*

52 "Therefore, believe me, days are coming—
Word of Yahweh—
When I'll punish her idols,
And throughout her land the wounded shall groan.

53 Were Babylon to scale the heavens,
And seal off her lofty keep,
Yet despoilers from me would reach her—
Word of Yahweh."

54 Hark! A cry from Babylon!
A mighty crash from Chaldea's land!

55 Ah, Yahweh is wrecking Babylon,
Bringing to silence her clamorous din.
Their billows roar like mighty waters,
Loud their crash resounds.

---

gg Supply "for," which is lacking in Hebrew (haplography).

hh–hh MT offers an abnormal form of the imperative "go." Perhaps redivide the words and for *mēḥereb hilkū* read *mēḥarbāh lᵉkū* ("you escaped from her sword, go").

ii–ii Heb. ". . . have entered the sanctuaries of Yahweh's house," which is unusual, since *miqdāš* normally refers to the entire shrine. Read *miqdᵉšēnū* for *miqdᵉšē* with LXX. Perhaps, however, the consonants *mqdšy* actually stand for *miqdaš y(hwh)*, of which *bēt yhwh* is a doublet.

56   *Ah, ruin has come upon Babylon*;
         Her soldiers are captured,
         Their bows are broken.
      Ah, Yahweh is a God who requites,
         Who surely repays!

57   "I'll besot her princes and sages,
         Her governors, prefects, and soldiers;
      They'll sleep a perpetual sleep
         And never awake—word of the King,
         Yahweh of Hosts his name."

58   This is what Yahweh of Hosts has said:
      "Babylon's walls so broad
         Shall be razed to the ground;
      And her gates so tall
         Shall be put to the torch.
      Thus, 'peoples toil for nought,
         And nations drudge*kk*—for the flames.'"

64c   Thus far the words of Jeremiah.

jj–jj Reading *šōd* ("destruction") in place of *šōdēd* ("a destroyer"); cf. LXX.
The sense is the same. Hebrew reads, "upon her, upon Babylon," which combines variants. Omit the first with LXX.
kk Or, "wear themselves out." Read the verb as *yī'āpū* as in Hab ii 13, of
which the last two cola are a quotation (or both quote a common source),
with slight variations. MT here has *weyā'ēpū* (perfect tense, with conjunction).

NOTES

l 1. The superscription of the prophecy.
2. *Bel . . . Marduk.* Marduk was the chief god of Babylon, Bel an
appellation of Marduk ("lord").
   Her "godlets." Her *gillūlīm*, an indelicate word ("balls of excrement,"
or the like) frequently applied to foreign gods, and an especial favorite
of Ezekiel (nearly forty times). It may have been Isaiah who first called
foreign gods *'elīlīm* ("nothings," or the like: a pun on *'ēlīm*, *'elōhīm*);
gillūlīm no doubt represents a further, and cruder, extension of the pun.
Similar puns are frequent in Jeremiah (cf. ii 5, 8, 11, etc.).
   5. *a covenant eternal.* Cf. xxxii 40.

7. The verse echoes ii 3, where it is said that all who "eat" Israel are "held guilty" (the verb is the same as that used here: "do . . . wrong").

9. *By them she'll be taken.* Literally "From there . . . ," i.e., by the foe coming from the north.

Their arrows are like a trained soldier. But *maśkīl* (so point), here translated "trained," could have the force of "successful" (i.e., victorious). Just as a soldier who knows his trade never returns from battle without booty, so their arrows never miss.

11. The verbs are to be taken as second masculine plural with Qre. Verse 11 is the protasis of vs. 12; *kī* is concessive, literally "though you rejoice—yet deeply shamed."

12. *your mother . . . she who bore you.* I.e., "mother Babylon," the nation personified.

13. The verse resembles xlix 17 and xix 8; the language is conventional.

15. *She signals surrender.* Literally "She has given her hand," i.e., as a sign of submission (cf. I Chron xxix 24; II Chron xxx 8).

Her bulwarks. The word occurs only here and the meaning is uncertain.

16. Cf. xlvi 16. The last part of the verse is nearly the same as Isa xiii 14b. Foreigners who had been attracted, or forcibly brought, to Babylon flee to their homelands as the invader approaches.

17. *A scattered flock.* Literally ". . . sheep," but probably intended collectively (or, a sheep driven away and separated from the flock). Verses 17b–19 are a prose commentary developing the theme of vs. 17a.

21. *March against the land of Merathaim . . . the people of Pekod.* Merathaim is probably the district of *marratim* at the head of the Persian Gulf; Pekod is *puqudu,* a people in East Babylonia. The names were chosen for the sake of wordplay: Merathaim on the root *mrh,* "to rebel" (Land of Double Rebellion), Pekod on the root *pqd,* "to punish" (Land of Doom).

Slay and devote to destruction. I.e., put under the ban (*ḥerem*), as frequently in the stories of Joshua.

23. *The whole earth's hammer.* Babylon is like a hammer that has pounded the whole earth into submission.

24. *You set you a snare.* The verb *yāqōštī* is to be taken as second feminine (cf. ii 20) rather than as first (EVV); cf. "Yahweh" referred to in the third person below.

26. *from every side.* The sense of *miqqēṣ* is uncertain, but probably "from end [to end]," i.e., from all sides (cf. *miqqāṣeh* in li 31; Gen xix 4, etc.).

destroy her. Put her to the *ḥerem* (cf. vs. 21).

27. *Slay all her bulls.* Figurative for Babylon's soldiers. On the verb (*ḥrb*) cf. vs. 21.

28. The verse is a prose comment. The words "vengeance for his temple" are lacking in LXX and may be secondary (but cf. li 11).

31. 'Sir Pride.' EVV "O proud one." But the word (zādōn) is a noun; Babylon is apostrophized as "insolence" personified.

32. The last part of the verse is almost the same as xxi 14b, save that there Jerusalem is referred to; xxi 14 has "her forest" in place of "his towns" (and so LXX here). The language is conventional.

36. her 'boasters.' The word (baddīm) is probably meant as a pun on *bārīm (the bāru priests, priests who practiced divination by hepatoscopy and the like, a class well known in Babylon); cf. Isa xliv 25.

37. the hirelings. Literally, the "mixed peoples" ('ereb; cf. xxv 20) apparently are auxiliary troops and mercenaries from various lands who were serving in the Babylonian army.

38. A sword on her waters. MT "a drought. . . ." But "drought" and "sword" have the same consonants (ḥrb), and the latter is preferable; when war comes, the canals upon which the country's life depends are neglected and dry up.

their 'frights.' A contemptuous term for their gods ('ēmīm), "hoodoos" or "bogies," as we might say.

39. goblins and ghouls. An effort to catch the alliteration: ṣiyyīm, 'iyyīm. These are probably not animals but uncanny beings of some sort (cf. KB; also C. C. Torrey, The Second Isaiah [New York: Chas. Scribner's Sons, 1928], pp. 289 f., on Isa xxxiv 13 f.). Verses 39–40 resemble Isa xiii 19–22; vs. 39b is nearly the same as Isa xiii 20a.

40. Cf. xlix 18, 33b, and also Isa xiii 19b.

41–43. These verses repeat vi 22–24 with minor changes (see NOTES there). The words are Jeremiah's; but whereas they were originally addressed to Judah, they are here applied to Babylon.

44–46. The verses repeat xlix 19–21 (where they are addressed to Edom) with a few changes; see NOTES there.

li 1. 'Leb-kamai.' Literally "the heart of those who rise up against me." The name is an atbash (see xxv 26 and NOTE) for Chaldea (so LXX reads), the consonants kśdym being exchanged for lbqmy. Ciphers of this sort may have developed as clever marginal glosses (cf. NOTE on vs. 41, where "Sheshak" appears to be a gloss), perhaps designed to serve magical purposes, perhaps for reasons that escape us. But it is entirely possible that they began to be developed in the Exilic period as a means of protecting the writers. At least, such subterfuges make historical sense in the context of the Exile, but scarcely in a later period when the Babylonian empire had vanished.

A destroying wind. So understood by LXX and some EVV (cf. the figure of winnowing in vs. 2). But one could translate, "the spirt of a destroyer" (and cf. vs. 11).

3. *Destroy.* Again, "put to the *ḥerem*" (cf. 1 21).

5. The sense of the verse is disputed, and one feels that it is intrusive. Read as it stands, "their land" would seem to be Israel's, and the second half of the verse must be taken as concessive. If, however, "their land" refers to Babylon, as many scholars think, it would be best for the sake of clarity to transpose the two halves of the verse (note the paraphrase to which RSV feels obliged to resort).

6. *for her guilt.* Or, "in her punishment"; the word *'āwōn* can have either force.

11. *Ready the shields.* The force both of verb and of noun is uncertain. The latter seems to denote a shield of some sort (cf. II Sam viii 7; II Kings xi 10; though Y. Yadin, *The Scroll of the War of the Sons of Light against the Sons of Darkness,* p. 134, has recently argued that it is a kind of dart), but the former (*ml'*) normally means "to fill." Perhaps it has here a technical sense (cf. II Sam xxiii 7; Zech ix 13) of "to arm one's self with, take up," or the like. LXX, "fill the quivers," looks like a guess.

Verse 11b seems to be an explanatory comment; vs. 11a leads into vs. 12.

12. *Set up the road blocks.* Or, "station watchmen." But the sense is probably not to post sentries (for security), but to station men to block possible sorties, and also ("place men in ambush") to take advantage of any sortie to rush the city gate.

13. *many waters.* The source of the allusion is mythological; the *mayim rabbīm* denote the great underground ocean, source of the streams that fertilize the earth (cf. H. G. May, JBL 74 [1955], 9–21). Here, of course, reference is to the Euphrates and the various canals that watered the Babylonian plain.

Your life's thread is cut. Literally "the cubit [at which] you are cut off." The metaphor is taken from the weaving industry; the cutting of the web from the loom is a figure for death (cf. Isa xxxviii 12).

14. *Ah, I'll fill you with men as with locusts.* On the syntax of *kī 'im millē'tīk 'ādām,* cf. II Kings v 20. The enemy will swarm into Babylon like a cloud of human locusts. Some scholars, however, with a slight change (*kī 'im mālē't kᵉādām*) read "Even if you were filled with people as with locusts [i.e., in number], yet. . . ."

15–19. These verses repeat x 12–16; see NOTES there.

20–23. The power that is addressed as Yahweh's battle-hammer is not identified, but in the context it is clearly Babylon (cf. "the whole earth's hammer," 1 23). Babylon has served as Yahweh's agent of judgment, but soon (vss. 24–26) will herself be judged. The thought is fully in accord with prophetic theology; cf. Isaiah's view of the place of Assyria in the divine purpose (e.g., Isa x 5–19; xxxvii 22–29), and Jeremiah's view of Nebuchadnezzar as Yahweh's "servant" (xxvii 4–11).

24. The verse is a prose transition linking the poem of vss. 20–23 to that of vss. 25–26 in such a way that the latter is made the conclusion of the former.

25. *mountain of raiders*. The force of the expression *har hammašḥīt* (EVV "destroying mountain") is obscure. Since *mašḥīt* at times denotes a detachment of troops engaged in pillage, i.e., raiders (I Sam xiii 17; xiv 15), the picture may be of a mountain from which robber bands descend to loot and plunder (cf. the verb *šḥt* in vs. 20). But the expression may be a conventional one with overtones that escape us (in II Kings xxiii 13 it is apparently a pun on the Mount of Olives, *har hammišḥāh*), perhaps of a mythological nature (cf. J. Morgenstern, JBL 80 [1961], 70, who suggests that *hammašḥīt*, "the Destroyer," refers to the god of death and the underworld).

a burnt-out mountain. Literally "a mountain of burning." Yahweh burns the mountain to a cinder so that (vs. 26) even its stones are useless. Once again, one sees the ambiguity of the figure: Babylon both *is* the mountain, and is seized and rolled down from it.

27. *Consecrate nations against her*. I.e., ritually, for combat; cf. vi 4; xxii 7, etc.

Ararat, Minni, and Ashkenaz. All were roughly in present-day Armenia and are known from cuneiform texts: Urartu, Mannai, Ashguzai (probably the Scythians). At the time this poem was composed all were subject to the Medes (cf. vs. 28).

marshals. The word (*tipsār*) is Akkadian (*tupšarru*, "tablet writer") and apparently denotes a high military officer (cf. Nah iii 17, where it likewise occurs in connection with locusts).

like bristly [?] *locusts*. I.e., like locusts in number (cf. vs. 14). The word translated "bristly" (*sāmār*) is of uncertain meaning.

28. The verse is prose and seems to be a gloss on "consecrate nations against her" in vs. 27. One wonders if the material of the poem is not earlier than the Exilic period, with this verse added to apply it to the contemporary situation when the Median empire controlled the territory north and east of Mesopotamia.

31. *entire*. Literally "from end," i.e., from end to end (cf. 1 26).

32. *The marshes*. Emendation seems unnecessary. The word *'agammīm* probably does not mean "pools" (which, of course, could not be set on fire), but "reedy swamps" (cf. *'agmōn*, "swamp grass, reeds"). The marsh grass is fired both to cut off escape and to burn out fugitives who might have sought refuge there.

33. *to tamp it*. Literally "to tread it." In preparation for the harvest the threshing floor was pounded hard and smooth by stamping upon it.

34. *consumed* [?] *me*. The precise sense of the verb (*hmm*) is uncertain. Normally it means "to confuse, throw into commotion"; LXX, "he divided me" (i.e., cut me up, chewed me?).

And rinsed me. So MT, which fits tolerably with the figure of the empty dish. See textual note^{cc–cc}.

35. *On Babylon be my broken flesh.* The translation seems to be *ad sensum,* even though the text is difficult. Cf. Driver on the syntax: literally "my violence (i.e., that done me; cf. Gen xvi 5) and my flesh be on Babylon"—i.e., my violated flesh. In any event, "my flesh" is not to be deleted or emended, since it is needed to parallel "my blood" in the next line. One might be inclined to transfer "my violence" to the preceding verse (see textual note^{cc–oo}) and see in it a relic of the word that seems to be missing there ("he violently thrust me out," or the like), save for the fact that textual evidence for this is lacking (LXX, though confused, reads two nouns here).

36. *her sea . . . her fount.* See NOTE on vs. 13. Babylon's life depended on her rivers and canals, and this surface water was thought to come from the underground ocean.

37. *An appalling waste.* Literally "a horror and a whistling" (i.e., something at which men whistle in awe); cf. ix 10[11E], which this verse resembles (also x 22).

38. *roar in chorus.* Literally ". . . together." The Babylonians are like lion cubs growling in anticipation of devouring the prey.

39. *While they fret.* Literally ". . . are heated"; i.e., their appetites inflamed, they are greedy, eager for their food.

41. *How she is taken.* Heb. "How 'Sheshak' is taken." "Sheshak" is an *atbash* for Babylon (cf. xxv 26 and NOTE) and is probably a gloss here (LXX omits); without it the structure of the verse is exactly parallel to that of l 23.

42. *The sea has surged over Babylon.* Not literally, of course. Babylon's foes surge over her like the chaotic waters of the primeval ocean.

44. *Bel.* See NOTE on l 2.

46. The verse is a prose transition leading from the exhortation in vs. 45 to the oracle in vs. 47 f. It does not necessarily indicate an abandonment of the historical perspective of the rest of the prophecy (in which the fall of Babylon is expected imminently) for one that is purely eschatological. The numerous upheavals and throne changes that plagued Babylon after Nebuchadnezzar's death (in 562) doubtless awakened fear, while at the same time arousing premature hopes of release only to dash them.

55. *Their billows roar.* I.e., the invading army, likened to the sea rolling over Babylon (as in vs. 42). But some scholars emend to "her billows" and take vs. 55b as further describing the din of Babylon that is silenced (cf. LXX).

57. The verse is only doubtfully poetry; it repeats the theme of vs. 39.

64c. *Thus far the words of Jeremiah.* This belongs at the end of vs.
58, from which position it was displaced by the insertion of vss. 59–64
(on this incident, see above, Sec. 28).

COMMENT

The final prophecy in the collection concerns Babylon. That it is
by far the longest of them all occasions no surprise when one thinks
of the destruction of Jerusalem, the ending of Judah's national existence, the deportation of the population to Babylon, the physical
suffering that all this involved, and, above all, when one considers
the humiliation, the indescribable emotional and spiritual shock that
these events occasioned. In a word, no power in ancient times affected the fortunes of Israel in a more catastrophic way than did
Babylon. It is, therefore, not to be wondered at that many a Jew
came to look upon Babylon as the very arch-foe of the people of
God, and that the prophecy directed against that nation should ex-
ceed all the others both in volume and in the emotional intensity
that informs it.

The section consists of a series of shorter poems, with a few prose
expansions, which have been drawn together in such a way that it
is frequently difficult to tell where one poem leaves off and another
begins. Although the material has been broken down in the translation by the use of subheadings in the hope that the reader will
not find himself too confused, it must be admitted that the analysis
adopted is largely one of convenience; others just as satisfactory
could doubtless be proposed. Actually, all of these poems are
dominated by a single theme: the imminent overthrow of Babylon
and the restoration of the Jews to their homeland. The section
therefore lacks any semblance of thematic progress, and this fact
alone necessarily renders any analysis of it somewhat artificial.

Jeremiah clearly expected the ultimate overthrow of Babylon
(e.g., xxvii 7; xxix 10), and on one occasion (cf. the incident of li
59–64, the authenticity of which there is really no reason to question) even caused Yahweh's destroying word to be, as it were, symbolically set in motion against that city. Nevertheless, the majority
of the poems in this section are probably anonymous, and represent
the sort of oracles that were uttered in prophetic circles during the
Exilic period. Some of them are composed of traditional material

which we find repeated elsewhere (see NOTES), while in some cases words spoken by Jeremiah himself, but on other occasions, have been adapted and applied to Babylon (e.g., 1 41–43: see NOTE). Still, it must be emphasized that this is not late material. All of it was clearly composed prior to the fall of Babylon to the Persians in 539, as is evident from the fact that Babylon's overthrow is an event that lies still in the future and is eagerly expected. Moreover, it is to be noted that the actual fate of Babylon at the hands of Cyrus could scarcely have been more unlike the awful picture of slaughter and destruction that we see in these poems. Cyrus actually entered Babylon without a fight, refrained from harming it in any way, and treated its citizens with the utmost consideration. In view of this fact, it is unthinkable that a prophecy such as the present one could have been composed after the event. Indeed, it is probable that it was composed not only before the event, but considerably before (say, around 550), with much of its material even earlier. This may be argued from the fact that in the entire prophecy (as in Isa xiii–xiv, which it in some ways resembles) there is no mention of the Persians at all; the destruction of Babylon is expected at the hands of the Medes and other peoples of the north (e.g., li 11, 27 f.; cf. Isa xiii 17). One might suppose from this that these poems reflect, at least in good part, the period prior to Cyrus' overthrow of the Median king Astyages (550), and the beginning of his spectacular career of conquest.

APPENDIX

45. THE FALL OF JERUSALEM
(lii 1–34)

LII 1 Zedekiah was twenty-one years old when he became king, and he reigned eleven years in Jerusalem. His mother's name was Hamutal, the daughter of Jeremiah of Libnah. 2 He acted in a manner displeasing to Yahweh, just as Jehoiakim had done. 3 Indeed, the situation in Jerusalem and Judah so provoked Yahweh's anger that he cast them from his sight.

Zedekiah rebelled against the king of Babylon. 4 It was in the ninth year of his reign, in the tenth month, on the tenth day of the month, that Nebuchadrezzar, king of Babylon, with his entire army moved against Jerusalem and invested it, erecting siegeworks against it on all sides. 5 And the city was under siege until King Zedekiah's eleventh year. 6 On the ninth day of the fourth month of that year, when famine had gripped the city and the populace had nothing left to eat, 7 the city's defenses were breached. ^aWhen the king and all the soldiers saw this, they fled,^a leaving the city by night by way of the gate between the two walls, near the king's garden (the Chaldeans were all around the city); and they went off in the direction of the Arabah. 8 But the Chaldean forces ^bpursued the king and overtook him^b in the plains of Jericho, all his troops having been scattered. 9 They captured the king, and brought him up to Riblah in the land of Hamath, to the king of Babylon, who then passed sentence upon him. 10 The king of Babylon executed

^{a–a} The text is restored, with most commentators, after xxxix 4: *wayyᵉhī kaʾăšer rāʾāh hammelek . . . wayyibrᵉḥū*, or the like. Hebrew both here and in Kings, and LXX have lost words (Hebrew here reads "and all the soldiers flee" [sic!]).
^{b–b} So with LXX and II Kings xxv 5. In xxxix 5 the reading is, "pursued them and overtook Zedekiah." Here Hebrew seems awkwardly to combine the two: "pursued the king and overtook Zedekiah."

Zedekiah's sons before his very eyes and, in addition, executed various of the princes of Judah who had been brought to Riblah. 11 As for Zedekiah, the king of Babylon had him blinded, thrown into chains, and taken to Babylon, where he held him in prison until the day of his death.

12 Then, in the fifth month, on the tenth day of the month (that is, of the nineteenth year of the reign of Nebuchadrezzar, king of Babylon), Nebuzaradan, the commander of the royal bodyguard and °a member of the king of Babylon's personal entourage,° arrived at Jerusalem 13 and set fire to the house of Yahweh, the royal palace and, indeed, every house in Jerusalem (that is, he set fire to the house of every important person). 14 Moreover, the Chaldean troops who were with the commander of the guard demolished the entire city wall of Jerusalem on all sides. 15 Finally, Nebuzaradan the commander of the guard deported*d* such of the people as were left in the city, together with those who had deserted to the king of Babylon, and the rest of the *e*skilled artisans*e*; 16 only some of the poorest of the populace did the commander of the guard leave as vinedressers and field laborers [?].

17 As for the bronze pillars that pertained to Yahweh's house, the wheeled stands, and the bronze sea that was in Yahweh's house, the Chaldeans broke them up and transported all the bronze to Babylon. 18 They also took away the pots, the shovels, the snuffers, the basins, the incense bowls—indeed, all the bronze utensils used in the temple service. 19 In addition, the commander of the guard took the small bowls, the firepans, the basins, the pots, the lampstands, the incense bowls, the libation bowls—both the ones that were of gold and the ones that were of silver. 20 As for the two pillars, the one sea, the twelve bronze

c–c Literally "one who stood [point *'ōmēd* with LXX; MT "he stood"] before the king. . . ." II Kings xxv 8 has "the servant of the king . . . ," which means the same thing.
d Hebrew inserts "some of the poorest of the people," which seems to be an intrusion from the next verse; omit with xxxix 9 and II Kings xxv 11.
e–e The pointing should probably be *hā'ommān* (Akk. *ummānu*) rather than *hā'āmōn*. The reading of II Kings xxv 11, *hehāmōn* ("the crowd") is not to be preferred; xxxix 9 is also corrupt (*hā'ām*, "the people").

bulls that were under the sea[f] and the ten [?][g] wheeled stands
which King Solomon had made for the house of Yahweh—there
was no weighing the bronze that was in all these things. 21 As
for the pillars, the height of each pillar was eighteen cubits, its
circumference twelve cubits, and its thickness four fingers (it
was hollow). 22 Upon it was a bronze capital five cubits high;
and all around the capital there was a grillwork with pomegranates, all of bronze. And the second pillar was just like it. And
pomegranates [   ][h]; 23 and there were ninety-six pomegranates evenly spaced [?].[i] In all, there were one hundred pomegranates around the grillwork.

24 In addition, the commander of the guard took Seraiah the
chief priest, Zephaniah the second priest, and the three keepers
of the threshold, 25 while from the city he took a certain official
who had been commissioner over the troops, seven men of the
king's personal entourage who happened to be in the city, the
adjutant of the commanding general who mustered the populace for military service, together with sixty men from among
the ordinary people who happened to be in the city. 26 These
Nebuzaradan the commander of the guard seized and conveyed
to the king of Babylon at Riblah. 27 And at Riblah, in the land
of Hamath, the king of Babylon had them put to the sword and
killed.

So Judah was deported from its land. 28 [j]This is the count of
the people whom Nebuchadrezzar deported: in the seventh
year of his reign, three thousand and twenty-three men of Judah;
29 in Nebuchadrezzar's eighteenth year, eight hundred and
thirty-two persons from Jerusalem; 30 in Nebuchadrezzar's

[f] Hebrew lacks "the sea"; it is restored with LXX (cf. I Kings vii 25).
[g] The numeral "ten" is lacking in Hebrew and is supplied conjecturally (so
Driver, Rudolph, etc.). There were ten stands (I Kings vii 27) and "ten"
('eśer) could easily have dropped out before "which" ('aśer).
[h] Words have obviously been lost. II Kings xxv 17 begins the sentence with
"On the grillwork," and then breaks off just as abruptly (and omits vs. 23
altogether). Perhaps (cf. Rudolph) something about the four pomegranates
not described in vs. 23 originally stood here—and perhaps more. LXX reads
"eight pomegranates to the cubit for the twelve cubits."
[i] MT rūḥāh ("windwards" [?]) is unintelligible. One wonders if a form of the
verb rwḥ, with the force of "spaced," "at intervals," should not be read; cf.
the noun rewaḥ ("space, interval") in Gen xxxii 17[16E].

twenty-third year, Nebuzaradan the commander of the guard deported men of Judah to the number of seven hundred and forty-five persons—all told, four thousand and six hundred persons.[j]

31 In the thirty-seventh year of the exile of King Jehoiachin of Judah, in the twelfth month, on the twenty-fifth day of the month Evil-merodach, king of Babylon, in his accession year, showed favor to Jehoiachin, king of Judah, releasing him from prison, 32 addressing him cordially, and giving him a more honorable position than that of the other kings who were about him in Babylon. 33 So Jehoiachin was allowed to put off his prison clothes and eat regularly in the king's company as long as he lived. 34 And, for his support, a regular allowance was given him by the king of Babylon, on a daily basis, until the day of his death.[k]

[j–j] Verses 28–30 are lacking in LXX (as is vs. 27b), and in II Kings xxv.
[k] Hebrew adds "as long as he lived," which is a tautology. Probably variants have been combined; LXX has only the first, II Kings xxv 30 only the second. The second may have intruded from the preceding verse.

NOTES

lii 3. The syntax seems to be idiomatic, but it is intolerably awkward to our taste: literally "Indeed, upon the anger of Yahweh it was in Jerusalem and Judah until he cast them from his sight." EVV "Indeed, because of the anger of Yahweh it was so in Jerusalem . . . that he cast them . . ." (or the like), is hardly right. It is unlikely (cf. Rudolph) that the historian meant to say that the situation in Judah was *occasioned* by the divine anger. The syntax is the same as that of xxxii 31; see NOTE.

4. *the ninth year.* I.e., 589/8, the years being counted from the Babylonian New Year in March/April. The siege thus began (tenth month, tenth day) approximately at the beginning of January 588. In all likelihood, however, Nebuchadnezzar had begun operations against Judah some months earlier.

5–6. *eleventh year . . . fourth month.* July 587. The month is not given in LXX or in II Kings xxv 3; Syr. reads "fifth month" (cf. vs. 12). The month, then, may have been August.

7. *When the king and all the soldiers saw this, they fled.* See textual

note*ᵃ⁻ᵃ*. MT omits mention of the king, but that the king also fled is clear from what follows.

8. *his troops having been scattered*. Literally ". . . scattered from him." Presumably in the pell-mell flight in the dark the company did not keep together, so that the king found himself alone. But the meaning may be that his troops scattered and ran as the Chaldeans approached.

10. *executed various of the princes of Judah who had been brought to Riblah*. A slight paraphrase but *ad sensum*. Heb. "executed all the princes of Judah at Riblah"; but of course he executed only those who were held prisoner there. II Kings xxv does not mention this; but cf. xxxix 6. Since these prisoners must have been brought from Jerusalem, the execution presumably took place some weeks after that city's fall.

12. *the fifth month*. August. For "the tenth day," II Kings xxv 8 has "the seventh day." One cannot say which is correct. Nebuzaradan seems in any event to have arrived at Jerusalem a month after that city's fall (cf. vs. 6).

nineteenth year . . . of Nebuchadnezzar. The year 587, counting from his actual accession to power in 605, as the author of Kings (from which this account is taken) seems to have done. But cf. vss. 28–30 and NOTES.

the commander of the royal bodyguard. The *rab ṭabbaḥīm* (see NOTE on xxxix 9).

arrived at Jerusalem. Cf. II Kings xxv 8. The text could be rendered, "entered Jerusalem," which, of course, Nebuzaradan did. But the implication is that he had just arrived there with orders from Nebuchadnezzar.

13. *that is, he set fire to the house of every important person*. Or (so II Kings xxv 9), ". . . every great house." The words look like a gloss qualifying "every house in Jerusalem." But one can appreciate that even if the Chaldeans intentionally set fire only to important buildings, the flames would quickly have spread to the whole city.

15. *skilled artisans*. This is the most likely meaning. See textual note *ᵉ⁻ᵉ* and cf. Song of Sol vii 2[1E].

16. *field laborers*. Both the spelling and the meaning of the word are uncertain; cf. xxxix 10 and NOTE (Sec. 33).

17–23. Discussion of these various items of the temple's furnishings and equipment is out of the question here. Most of them are mentioned, and some are described in detail, in I Kings vii. The precise nature of some is uncertain. For further information consult G. E. Wright, *Biblical Archaeology* (Philadelphia: Westminster Press, 1957), pp. 136–45; also J. L. Kelso, *The Ceramic Vocabulary of the Old Testament* (BASOR, Suppl. Studies 5–6 [1948]).

19. *both the ones that were of gold and the ones that were of silver*.

Literally "which were gold—gold, and which were silver—silver." This is to be taken as distributive and applying to each of the items in vs. 19. Almost all of them are mentioned in I Kings vii 49 ff. and/or Exod xxv 29 ff. as being of gold.

20. *the twelve bronze bulls that were under the sea.* The whole phrase is lacking in II Kings xxv 16, and some scholars delete it since, according to II Kings xvi 17, the bronze bulls had been removed and sent as tribute to Assyria a century and a half earlier. This may be correct —though, for all we know, the bulls could have been replaced in the meantime.

21. *height . . . eighteen cubits.* So Hebrew correctly (cf. I Kings vii 15). LXX, like II Chron iii 15, has "thirty-five cubits." The origin of this alternate tradition is obscure, but it can scarcely be correct since the temple itself was only thirty cubits high (I Kings vi 2), i.e., about forty-five ft. (a cubit is approximately eighteen inches).

its circumference twelve cubits. Literally "a line of twelve cubits would go around it."

23. *one hundred pomegranates.* In I Kings vii 20, 42, each capital has two hundred pomegranates, in two rows.

24. *Seraiah the chief priest.* According to I Chron v 39–41 (vi 13– 15E) Seraiah was the grandson of Hilkiah, Josiah's high priest, and the father of Jehozadak who (cf. Ezra v 2; Hag i 1, etc.) was in turn the father of Joshua, who was high priest when the temple was rebuilt after the Exile.

Zephaniah the second priest. Perhaps the man mentioned in xxix 24– 32; xxxvii 3.

keepers of the threshold. Apparently high-ranking clergy, perhaps custodians of the temple.

25. *a certain official who had been commissioner over the troops.* Literally "a certain eunuch who had been *pāqīd* (overseer) over the soldiers." The word "eunuch" here, as elsewhere, denotes an official. What his precise function was we do not know; he seems to have been a civilian official rather than a military commander. Perhaps he was the equivalent of an "inspector general," or perhaps he was minister of defense or the like.

seven men of the king's personal entourage. Literally ". . . of those who saw the king's face," i.e., had access to his person, were in his confidence. II Kings xxv 19 reads "five"; we cannot say which is right.

the adjutant of the commanding general who mustered the populace. Literally "the secretary of the commander of the army. . . ." We would see in him the equivalent of the Adjutant General in charge of personnel or, perhaps, the head of "selective service."

sixty men from among the ordinary people. This involves an interpretation; literally "sixty men from the *'am hā'āreṣ* ("the people of the land"). Since this expression has just been used of "the populace" who were mustered for military service, it probably means that sixty men were singled out from the ranks of the conscripted soldiers for representative punishment as a warning to the rest. But, except for the fact that 'am hā'āreṣ denotes the populace generally in the immediate context, one would be tempted to translate, "sixty men from the landed gentry," a force that the expression frequently has.

27. *had them put to the sword.* Literally "smote them," which can mean "struck them down," or (Rudolph) in view of the next verb (which LXX lacks), "flogged them." Doubtless they were beaten before being put to death.

28. *in the seventh year.* I.e., 598/7 according to Babylonian reckoning, which seems to be followed here, and which counted Nebuchadnezzar's reign from the New Year in the spring of 604 rather than from his accession in the fall of 605 (as is done in Kings; cf. vs. 12 above). There is no reason to emend the text, as some scholars do; Nebuchadnezzar captured Jerusalem in 597 and deported elements of the population (II Kings xxiv).

three thousand and twenty-three men of Judah. I.e., from the entire kingdom. The total does not agree with those given in II Kings xxiv 14, 16 (ten thousand, eight thousand). But the latter figures are probably round numbers including all the people deported, while 3023 may be an exact count of adult males.

29. *eighteenth year.* According to Babylonian reckoning 587/6. According to that followed in Kings (cf. vs. 12) it was his nineteenth year.

30. *twenty-third year.* I.e., 582/1. On this deportation see Introduction, "The Background of Jeremiah's Career . . .".

31. *the thirty-seventh year of the exile of King Jehoiachin.* I.e., 561. For "the twenty-fifth day" LXX reads "the twenty-fourth," II Kings xxv 27 "the twenty-seventh." Who can say which is right?

Evil-merodach. Nebuchadnezzar's son, who ruled 561–560. His name was actually Awel (Amel)-marduk ("man of Marduk"). The Heb. spelling may be an intentional corruption; 'ewīl means "a stupid person."

releasing him from prison. When, and why, he was jailed is unknown, but he was not in prison at least as late as 592 (see Introduction, "The Background of Jeremiah's Career . . .").

32. *kings who were about him.* I.e., about Evil-merodach: other kings who, like Jehoiachin, were detained in Babylon.

33. *So Jehoiachin . . . in the king's company.* So to avoid ambiguity; Hebrew has the pronoun in both places ("so he . . . in his company").

COMMENT

As the concluding words of chapter li indicate, chapter lii forms
an appendix to the Jeremiah book. The account of the fall of Jerusalem which it contains is identical, minor textual variations ex-
cepted, with that of II Kings xxiv 18-xxv 30, save that it omits the
brief description of the assassination of Gedaliah found in II Kings
xxv 22–26 (itself a summary of the narrative of chs. xl–xli), and
adds (vss. 28–30) a register, drawn from a separate source and not
found in Kings, of the totals of those deported to Babylon.

Why this account should have been appended here (it has already been encountered in abridged form in ch. xxxix) is not certain. One recalls, of course, that the collection of Isaiah's prophecies
found in Isa i–xxxix likewise concludes with a historical appendix
drawn from the book of Kings, or one of its sources (Isa xxxvi–
xxxix//II Kings xviii–xx). But whereas these chapters contain various authentic words of Isaiah, and describe events in which that
prophet played an important role, in the present chapter Jeremiah
is not even mentioned. Perhaps the editor felt that an account of
the fall of Jerusalem, the event that brought vindication to Jeremiah's lifelong announcement of the divine judgment, would furnish
a fitting conclusion to the book because it would allow history itself
to give its silent witness to the truth of the prophetic word. Perhaps, too, he saw in the account of the release of Jehoiachin from
prison with which the chapter closes (vss. 31–34) some hint, some
foreshadowing of the hoped-for future which Jeremiah, at the bidding of his God, had promised beyond the tragedy. In its present
context the chapter seems to say: the divine word both has been
fulfilled—and will be fulfilled!

KEY TO THE TEXT

Chapter	Verse	§	Chapter	Verse	§
	4–7	34		7–22	42
	8–13	35		23–39	43
xliv	1–30	35	l	1–46	44
xlv	1–5	24	li	1–58	44
xlvi	1–28	38		59–64b	28
xlvii	1–7	39		64c	44
xlviii	1–47	40	lii	1–34	45
xlix	1–6	41